The Writer's Handbook

The Writer's Handbook

EDITOR
Barry Turner

M

MACMILLAN
REFERENCE
BOOKS

First published 1987 by
THE MACMILLAN PRESS LTD
London and Basingstoke

This edition published 1988

Associated companies in Auckland, Delhi,
Dublin, Gabarone, Hamburg, Harare, Hong
Kong, Johannesburg, Kuala Lumpur, Lagos,
Manzini, Melbourne, Mexico City, Nairobi,
New York, Singapore, Tokyo

British Library Cataloguing in Publication
Data

The Writer's handbook.
  1. Authorship
  I. Turner, Barry
  808'.02   PN145

  ISBN 0–333–47657–3
  ISBN 0–333–47658–1 Pbk

Typeset by August Filmsetting, Haydock,
St Helens
Printed by Richard Clay Ltd, Suffolk

Contents

Introduction

This second edition of *The Writer's Handbook* is indebted to the network of informants spirited up by the first edition. My thanks goes to all those who have offered advice and information; in particular, dare I say, to the bearers of publishing horror stories, of which there seems to be a limitless source. May the correspondence long continue.

This year the onerous task of collating responses to some five thousand questionnaires has fallen to Jill Fenner – who deserves a holiday. Jill's respect for detail and her determination to get at the facts put her in the same league as the professional sleuth. Her assistance has been invaluable.

Josephine Pullein-Thompson of PEN, Mark le Fanu of **The Society of Authors** and Walter Jeffrey of the **Writers' Guild** have given generously of their time and talents. It is thanks to their wholly constructive criticism that the scope of *The Writer's Handbook* has increased so substantially for this edition.

Under the heading of specialist knowledge, a debt of gratitude attaches to Peter Finch for the poetry section and to A.P. Kernon for his conducted tour through the maze of tax legislation.

For any errors or omissions that might be spotted, the Editor alone takes responsibility.

Publishing in Turmoil – The Latest Changes

It has been a traumatic year for publishers and a perplexing year for authors. The frenetic buying and selling of famous lists which gave 1986/87 its distinctive mark continued unabated into 1988. Who was next for takeover remained a favourite guessing game amongst book people. Writers, who value consistency in their publishers as a counterbalance to their own erratic lives, were made nervous by their editors switching jobs whenever the music stopped.

But the latest signs are of a deceleration in the pace of change. While further amalgamations can be expected to add a few names to the top league, publishing strategy for the 1990s will be determined by the transatlantic conglomerates, of which, currently, there are six.

Bertelsmann

With profits from its book clubs (16 million members world-wide) this thriving German company started buying into American publishing in the late 1970s. It now owns **Bantam Books Inc** and **Doubleday** (including the Literary Guild and the Doubleday book clubs) and, in the UK, has a controlling interest in Book Club Associates and Leisure Circle.

Gulf & Western

From its American power base, Gulf & Western controls **Prentice Hall**, **Simon & Schuster** and a host of smaller publishers. Having lost out to International Thomson in its bid for Associated Book Publishers it is on the look-out for other UK prospects.

News Corporation

Entered book publishing four years ago when Rupert Murdoch acquired 41.7% of **Collins**. This encouraged him to buy **Harper & Row** for $300 million – a big deal in book-publishing terms but dwarfed by the company's investment in newspapers, film and television. He also has a substantial holding in the Pearson group.

Newhouse

In 1982 bought **Random House**, which in turn acquired **Chatto, Bodley Head, Cape**. Also owns the book interests of the *New York Times*, **Alfred A. Knopf**, paperback firm, **Ballantine/Del Rey/Fawcett Books**, the *New Yorker* and the magazine publishers Condé-Nast.

Pearson

Owns **Penguin, Longman, Pitman, Frederick Warne, Hamish Hamilton, Michael Joseph** and **Sphere**. In America, Pearson controls **Viking, New American Library (NAL)** and **Addison-Wesley**, now to be linked with **Longmans** which itself has made a series of minor US acquisitions to acquire a firm stake in the schools and college market. Wider interests include the *Financial Times* and 50% of *The Economist*.

International Thomson

Having sold its British general publishing interests in 1985, the Canadian-based travel and energy group specialises in educational and information publishing. After buying Associated Book Publishers, the general side (**Methuen London**, **Methuen Children's**, **Eyre & Spottiswoode** and **Pitkin Pictorials**) was sold on to Octopus. Famous names trading under the Thomson hammer include **Routledge**, Methuen (academic books), Tavistock, Croom Helm, **Chapman & Hall**, and **Sweet & Maxwell**.

Among those who are chasing close behind the leaders are Reed International, recent purchaser of **Octopus** (including Bookwise, **Hamlyn**, **Heinemann** and **Mitchell Beazley**) and Maxwell Communications, still smarting from the rejection of an audacious $2 billion bid for **Harcourt Brace Jovanovich**. Both are keeping a close eye on the market along with some continental publishers who are harbouring global ambitions. Hachette's successful bid for Grolier, the US encyclopaedia company, makes that company a front runner.

How will authors fare under the rule of the giants? To answer this we need to know what is feeding the amalgamative urge.

In part, the strategy is dictated by a wish to survive. Having outgrown their home markets the publishing moguls must extend their interests overseas or risk losing out to those of stronger commercial muscle. But the pursuit of fame and fortune is the more important motive. By rising to the global challenge, the publishers hope to exploit new markets while at the same time achieving huge economies of scale. Imagine the return on a standard college text which can be printed in hundreds of thousands and sold in every campus, or on a steamy romance which can be printed in millions and sold in every supermarket and petrol station.

Then there are the rewards from publishers' overlap into other sectors of communications – film, television, newspapers and magazines. The possibilities have yet to be fully explored, though Rupert Murdoch for one is excited by the potential. His buy into **Collins** in 1984 was inspired by the prospect of securing a self-generating source of new material for his film and broadcasting interests.

All this must be good news for authors with famous names or with marketable subjects to offer. The income generated by a potential best-seller, i.e. before it has sold a single copy, can be awe-inspiring. When Michael Holroyd accepted a £625,000 advance on his biography of George Bernard Shaw, the news appeal of the story was hoisted, once by the revelation that **Chatto & Windus (Random House)** had bought UK rights *only*, and again when Holroyd admitted he had turned down at least one publisher who had put in a higher bid.

Yet the author's return on a multi-volume life of Shaw (which Michael Holroyd hastens to point out will occupy many years of writing) is small beer compared to the sums on offer to the top American names in popular fiction. The likes of Stephen King and Danielle Steel can rely on making at least four million dollars on paperback rights alone. In this country, publishers have taken to poaching authors on a prodigious scale – wooing them with champagne lunches and impressive marketing plans. It cost **Collins** £800,000 to bring Susan Howatch from **Hamish Hamilton**, and £450,000 to attract Fay Weldon from **Hodder**.

Admittedly, the risks of blockbuster publishing are great. *Whirlwind*, the James Clavell latest bought by **Morrow** for five million dollars, flopped in the States with nearly half the 900,000 hardback print-run returned from the shops. But the conglomerates can afford the occasional lapse of judgement. Even if, at the top of their lists, the market is volatile, they are cushioned by the steady and highly profitable sale of school and college texts, and by healthy backlists with titles which will be in print until kingdom come.

That all the conglomerates are pushing hard for a bigger share of the education market suggests that it is not only the glamour authors who will benefit from large-scale publishing. Among the **Longman** authors who are no doubt happy with the transatlantic connection are the writers of Latin texts who now find their books adopted by schools in the mid-West. Hitherto the American school market has been reserved exclusively for domestic product. But where Latin has taken a lead, other fruits of British education are sure to follow. In the case of **Longman**, the **Addison-Wesley** connection will see to that.

Where then, is the bad news? (Authors are possessed of an innate cynicism. There is always a catch.) The bad news starts with the role of the accountant, the numerate barbarians who can calculate to the last penny how to maximise profit by holding back on royalty cheques (computerised banking allows a company to make money by investing its surplus overnight) or minimising loss by delaying publication or cancelling a contract to suit the commercial mood of the moment.

To deal with a big publisher is to accept management by bureaucracy – with all its limitations. Too many meetings are held at which nothing is decided; and when decisions are made, too often they go awry because their interpretation depends on ill-phrased or ill-digested memoranda. Except for the lucky few who create lead titles, contact with an editor will be rare and perfunctory. Gone are the days when a writer could automatically look to an editor as a sympathetic friend, ever ready with sensitive and constructive criticism.

There are those, like Simon Master, UK's Chief Executive of **Random House**, who declare their intention of preserving the one-to-one relationship between authors and editors. More typical, however, is the view of Ian Irvine, Chief Executive of **Octopus** who, as reported in a recent edition of *The Author*, lectured his staff on the need to keep writers and books away from the vicinity of staff 'work stations'. It will be interesting to see how long the one-to-one author/editor relationship lasts in that environment.

But the biggest worry provoked by the rise of the conglomerates concerns authors as yet unpublished. Who, in the age of mega publishing, will devote time and effort to nurturing new writing talent? **The Society of Authors** fears that 'increasing obsession with profitability and quick sales . . . is discouraging the commissioning of books that are unusual, difficult or challenging'. Really?

Just before his retirement as literary editor of *The Daily Telegraph*, David Holloway speculated that with all the take-overs even James Joyce could not get published in England today. This brought a few guffaws from those who recalled that Joyce could not get published in England first time round. He had to go to Paris to get the chance to put *Ulysses* into print.

Those who made their fortunes in what are now seen as the good old days of pre-war publishing were not exactly imbued with the spirit of adventure. Even the revered Allen Lane, founder of the **Penguin** empire, made his money reprinting the safe bets plucked from the lists of the hardback houses. The risk-takers were and remain the independents. Fortunately for publishing and for first-time writers there are still plenty of these around.

In the month of the last **Booker Prize** awards, *The Sunday Times* had the interesting idea of looking ahead to the next generation of Booker prospects with a profile of nine emergent writers of great promise. Of these, three were published by the smaller independents – Martin Millar by **Fourth Estate**, Jeanette Winterson by **Pandora Press** and **Bloomsbury** and Candia McWilliam by **Bloomsbury**, four by well-known publishers who are outside the range of the conglomerates – Caryl Phillips and Kazugo Ishiguro by **Faber**, Iain Banks by **Macmillan**, and Patrick Gale by **Century Hutchinson**, and only two by imprints from the top seven – Carlo Gebler by **Hamish Hamilton** of the Pearson dynasty and Richard Burns by **Cape** (Newhouse).

Moreover, of these publishers two – **Bloomsbury** and **Fourth Estate** – are of recent creation, clear evidence that the urge towards empire-building has done nothing to dampen literary enterprise on the lower reaches of publishing. It is the same in the States where small houses flourish even in the best-seller lists. Last year, **Farrar, Straus & Giroux**, who publish about a hundred books a year, mostly literary novels and poetry, brought out Tom Wolfe's *The Bonfire of the Vanities*, surely destined to be a modern classic and Scott Turow's *Presumed Innocent*, said to be among the most popular first novels to be published in the last fifty years.

Making it Easier for Newcomers

That publishing is a business which thrives on diversity is a thought that should encourage the first-time writer. If his work has any value at all, somewhere out there is a commissioning editor who will recognise its worth. Finding him is the problem. A study of *The Writer's Handbook* list of publishers will point out the likeliest prospects. There is no virtue in sending a children's book to **Kogan Page** who specialise in business and management, or a novel to **William Kimber** who are strongest on military history. Yet it is staggering how many writers aim at totally unsuitable publishers, relying presumably on pot luck. Or maybe they think it wiser to steer away from publishers who bring out a lot of titles which sound curiously like their own. Isn't this where the competition is toughest? But publishers who do well in one area, are usually keen to exploit their editorial and marketing expertise. They want more of the same.

For the author who is just starting out there is much to be said for mixing with other writers – in clubs, societies or unions. Drawing on the fund of common experience can save time and spare the pain of frustration.

First on the list of friendly tips is to resist bludgeoning a publisher with an 80,000-word manuscript. A synopsis and a sample chapter are all that is needed to elicit a response which, if favourable, may bring some useful thoughts on the best way to develop the project. The author who can afford to reject the advice of a friendly publisher is a rarity. Similarly, the unsolicited manuscript which is accepted without radical amendments is so unusual as to assume news value. When, early in the year, *Chekago*, a first novel by Natalya Lowndes was contracted by **Hodder**, publisher Ion Trewin declared he could not remember the last occasion when 'the slush pile' had yielded a marketable book. Words of wisdom from Heather Godwin, who reads unsolicited manuscripts for **Heinemann**, are worth framing:

'The most irritating are the computer-produced manuscripts from men who tend to work in large companies. They must have read an article on Jeffrey Archer and decided to get rich too . . . You are shocked by the impertinence of it. There's an assumption there that writing is easy; that talent, skill, technique, practice and experience, even ideas, are irrelevant. It's like me glancing at a chair, liking it and deciding to make one tomorrow.'

That said, publishers should not be seen as the final arbiters. Their judgements are as frail and fallible as anyone else's; it is just that they have the commercial clout to make them count. Jerzy Kozinski, the Polish–American writer, once sent a typescript of one of his best-selling novels to several New York publishers under another name. All of them rejected it.

As an insurance against prejudice, lazy reading or sheer incompetence ('Letter? What letter? It must have been lost in the post.'), it is as well to try several publishers at the same time. If any one of them is at all interested sooner or later (usually later) he will suggest a meeting. Don't be impatient. Writers are often sinned against but they can be unreasonable in their assumption of a quick decision on what, after all, is a risky investment.

If, after three or four weeks, nothing is heard, a telephone call is justified. But a polite inquiry is more likely to get results than a demand to know 'what the hell is going on'. It helps to have sent material to a named editor. That way you avoid the risk of being sucked into the whirlpool of internal company communications.

If the outcome of the first meeting is encouraging, the next discussion should focus on the size of the advance. Any author who wants to make a living by writing must establish early on that his publisher is prepared to make a downpayment on account of royalties. The bigger the advance the more likely the publisher will be to put his back into the marketing effort. Even if he winds up hating the book, he will want his money back.

Usually, an advance is split three ways, part on signature of contract, part on delivery of the script, and part on publication. *Except in the case of a best-selling author, it is difficult to secure an advance much above the equivalent of 60% of the royalties likely to be payable on the first edition.*

The advance may be on account of royalties on the publishers' own editions or on account of all income, including subsidiary rights. The former arrangement is preferable, but where the advance is substantial, it may be reasonable for the publisher to recoup his outlay from, say, the proceeds of a US or paperback deal. In either case the advance should be non-returnable, except when the author fails to deliver a manuscript.

And so to the contract

Contracts vary significantly from one company to another and since they are all hideously complicated the differences do not always show up to the unpractised eye.

This is where an agent can be invaluable. But the writer who handles his own affairs is not entirely alone. Having campaigned vigorously for ten years or more, the writers' unions have hammered out a minimum terms agreement (MTA) which has met with the approval of several leading publishers.

A copy of the MTA, which can be obtained from either *The Society of Authors* or the *Writers' Guild* (free of charge to members who send a stamped addressed envelope), is a useful standard against which to judge the virtue of a publisher's offer. When it comes to signing on the bottom line, you may feel you have had to give way on a few points, but if the general principles of the MTA are followed the chances of securing a reasonable deal are much enhanced.

Probably the most important break from tradition contained in the MTA is the clause allowing for the length of licence granted by the author to the publisher to be negotiable. The custom is for the licence to run for the duration of copyright (i.e. the author's lifetime plus 50 years). Originally the writers' unions pressed for a maximum of 20 years but have since compromised on a review procedure which permits the contract to be revised every ten years. This gives the author the opportunity to claim, for example, improved royalties if the book has been a success.

Other basic principles covered by the MTA include:

- *Reversion of Rights* As well as the author being able to recover rights after a book goes out-of-print (which is defined in more detail than in most contracts), the author may also terminate the contract if sales fall below certain figures. This gives the author the opportunity to leave a publisher if he feels that the book is not being properly marketed or that the publishers are simply clinging on to rights unnecessarily.
- *Accounting* The publishers will pay over to the author income from sub-licences straight away, once the advance has been earned.
- *Indexing* The cost of indexing, if not done by the author, is shared equally with the publishers.
- *Free Copies* The author will receive twelve free copies of a hardback and twenty free copies of a paperback.
- *Print-run* The author will be informed of the size of print-runs.

Author Involvement

The MTA confirms the extent to which authors should be involved in the publication of their books. For example:

- There will be full discussion prior to signing the contract of illustrations, quotations etc., the costs thereof, and the party responsible for paying them. Normally, the publishers will pay some or all of the costs involved.
- There will be full consultation on all the illustrations, the jacket, blurb and publication date.
- The author will be invited to make suggestions for publicity and will be shown the proposed distribution list for review copies.
- The author will be fully consulted before any major sub-licences are granted by the publishers (e.g. paperback, American, film, television and merchandising deals).

Royalties

On the touchy question of royalties:

- The basic hardback scale is 10% to 2500 copies, $12\frac{1}{2}\%$ on the next 2500 copies and 15% thereafter – on the published price (home sales) or the publisher's receipts (exports). On certain small reprints the royalty may revert to 10%.
- On home (mass-market) paperback sales the minimum royalty is $7\frac{1}{2}\%$ of the published price, rising to 10% after 50,000 copies. On exports the minimum royalty is 6% of the published price. If paperback rights are sub-licensed, the author receives at least 60% of the income, rising to 70% at a point to be agreed.
- The author receives 85% of the income from the sale of American rights and 80% from translations.
- The author receives 90% from first serial rights, TV and radio dramatisations, film and dramatic rights, etc. Other percentages to the author include: anthology and quotation rights, 60%; TV and radio readings, 75%; merchandising, 80%.

But bear in mind that the royalty percentages do not necessarily apply to all books. For example, heavily illustrated books are excluded and there are certain exceptional circumstances in which publishers may pay lower royalties (for example, long works of fiction published in short print-runs for libraries).

As a spot check on the acceptability of a contract confirm four essential points before adding your signature:

First, there should be a firm and unconditional commitment to publish the book within a specified time, say twelve months from delivery of the typescript or, if the typescript is already with the publisher, from signature of the agreement. It is also as well for the approximate published price to be specified.

The obligation to publish should not be subject to approval or acceptance of the manuscript. Otherwise what looks like a firm contract may be little more than an unenforceable declaration of intent to publish. It is equally important to watch that the words 'approval' or 'acceptance' do not appear in the clause relating to the advance payment. For example, if the advance, or part of it, is payable 'on delivery and approval' of the script, this might qualify the publishers' obligation to publish the work.

This point about the publishers' commitment to publishing a book is of vital importance, particularly since publishers' editors change jobs with increasing frequency. An author who has started a book with enthusiastic support from his editor may, when he delivers it, find he is in the hands of someone with quite different tastes and ideas. The publishers should satisfy themselves at the outset that the author is capable of writing the required book – if necessary by seeing and approving a full synopsis and sample chapter. Provided the book, when delivered, follows the length and outline agreed, the publishers should be under a contractual obligation to publish it (subject possibly to being entitled to ask the author to make reasonable and specified changes to the typescript before publication).

However, even when the contract contains a firm undertaking to publish, the publishers cannot be compelled to publish the book. But should they fail, the author is legally entitled to compensation for breach of contract.

Secondly, there should be a proper termination clause. This should operate when the publishers fail to fulfil or comply with any of the provisions of the contract or if, after all editions of the work are out-of-print or off the market, the publishers have not within six months of a written request issued a new edition or impression of at least 1500 copies.

When, in any of these circumstances, rights revert to the author, this should be done without prejudice to any claims you may have for monies due. Occasionally termination clauses state that if the publishers fail to reprint a new edition after due notice from the author, the agreement shall terminate provided the author refunds any unearned balance of the advance and buys back blocks, stereo-plates etc., at a proportion of their original cost. You should insist on the deletion of such a proviso.

Thirdly, there should not be an option clause that imposes unreasonable restrictions on future work. The best advice is to strike out the option clause but if this proves impossible, an option should be limited to one book on terms to be mutually agreed (not 'on the same terms'). The publishers should be required to make a decision within, say, six weeks of delivery of the complete work in the case of fiction, or of submission of a synopsis and specimen chapter in the case of non-fiction. (An option clause which provides for publication 'on the same terms', or which states that the author shall grant 'the same rights and territories' as in the original agreement, can be most disadvantageous to the author and should certainly be altered or deleted.)

It is as well to specify the type of work covered by the option, for example, your next work of fiction, non-fiction or children's books, since you may want to publish different types of book with different publishers. Another wise precaution is to exclude works you may be invited to write for a series published by another firm. Very occasionally, in the case of a new author, the publishers may try to obtain a two-book option. If you accede, it is important to provide that, if the publishers reject the first option book, they should automatically lose their option on the second.

Finally, the author should not be expected to contribute towards the cost of publication of his book. Every writers' organisation warns against subsidised or vanity publishing. It is expensive (some vanity publishers charge up to £6000 for a modest print-run), the quality of production is inferior to that offered by conventional publishers, and the promises of vigorous marketing and impressive sales are rarely born out by experience.

A pile of rejection slips may be a sad sight but it is not half as depressing as a garage full of unsold books.

UK Publishers

AA Publishing
The Automobile Association, Fanum House,
Basingstoke, Hants RG21 2EA
☎0256 492929
Telex 858538 AABAS G   Fax 0256 493389

Managing Director *D.R. Thomas*
Approx Annual Turnover £10 million

Publishes maps, atlases and guidebooks, motoring and leisure. 90 titles in 1987.

Editorial Director *M. Buttler* Unsolicited mss not welcome.

Author's Rating Mass-market weighty reference books conceived in-house and commissioned from a team of regulars. Few opportunities for outsiders.

AB Academic Publishers
PO Box 97, Berkhamsted, Herts HP4 2PX
☎04427 74150

Managing Director *E. Adam*

Mainly a publisher of journals, with only a few books. *Publishes* learned journals and books in the fields of materials science and metallurgy, mathematics, agriculture, forestry, nutrition, medicine, education, economics and related subject areas. New journals for 1988 include *Biorecovery* an international journal of biotechnology applied to materials recovery and handling; *International Journal of Catering and Health* hygiene and nutrition in food service; *Bioacoustics* international journal of animal sound and its recording (in asociation with the British Library National Sound Archive). Unsolicited synopses and ideas for books are welcome provided they are of a high academic level.
Royalties paid annually.

Abacus
See **Sphere Books Ltd**

Abacus Kent Ltd
Abacus House, Tunbridge Wells,
Kent TN4 0HU
☎0892 510646   Telex 957137 Abacus G

Chairman & Managing Director
N.A. Jayasekera
Approx Annual Turnover £1.15 million

The company was established in 1970. Its first titles were translations of advanced scientific technical material from Eastern Europe. Since the late 1970s the emphasis has switched to British, American and European authors, mainly academic/high level titles. *Publishes* computer science, information technology, systems science, energy and engineering science, natural science and maths. Future plans include publishing books for a much wider readership, branching out into social science, management, business and current affairs. 12 titles in 1987.

ABACUS PRESS
Unsolicited mss, synopses/ideas for books welcome. *Royalties* paid annually. *Overseas associates* Abacus Press, Cambridge, Mass., USA.

Abelard-Schuman Ltd
See **Blackie & Son Ltd**

Aberdeen University Press

Farmers Hall, Aberdeen AB9 2XT

☎0224 630724

Telex 739477   Fax 0224 643286

Managing Director *Colin Maclean*

FOUNDED 1840, the company was restricted to printing until 1979. Owned by Pergamon Holdings. *Publishes* academic and general, principally Scottish with particular interest in dictionaries, Scottish history and Scottish literature. 33 titles in 1987.

Editorial Head *Colin Maclean*   TITLES *Concise Scots Dictionary; A Linguistic Atlas of Late Mediaeval English; The History of Scottish Literature; The Waterfalls of Scotland; The Scottish Cat.* Unsolicited mss will be considered if they fall within AUP's categories of interest. Synopses and ideas for books welcome.
Royalties paid annually. *Overseas associates* Distribution overseas, as in the UK, by Pergamon.

Harry N. Abrams Inc.

43 High Street, Tunbridge Wells,
Kent TN1 1XL

☎0892 45355

Telex 957565   Fax 0892 34905

Publishes architecture and design; cinema and video; cookery; wines and spirits; fine art, art history; photography. 63 titles in 1987.

Editorial office in America. See **US Publishers**.

Absolute Press

14 Widcombe Crescent, Bath,
Avon BA2 6AH

☎0225 316013

Telex 449212 LANTEL G   Fax 0225 69845

Managing Director *J.M. Croft*

FOUNDED 1980, the company brings out up to 10 titles a year. *Publishes* food- and wine-related subjects.

Editorial Director *J.M. Croft* Unsolicited

mss not welcome, though synopses and ideas for books are.
Royalties paid twice yearly.

Abson Books

Abson, Wick, Bristol, Avon BS15 5TT

☎027582 2446

Partners *A. Bickerton, P. McCormack*

FOUNDED 1970, Abson publishes original paperbacks, but no fiction. National and European representation. 4 titles in 1987. *Publishes* English language glossaries, literary puzzle books, West Country, general information.

Editorial Head *A. Bickerton*   TITLES *American English; Cockney Rhyming Slang; Jane Austen Quiz and Puzzle Book; Get Squash Straight; Job Hunters' Work Book; Correct Way to Speak Bristol; Resolving Rubik's Magic Cube.* Unsolicited mss welcome if with return postage.
Royalties either once or twice yearly.

Academic Press Inc. (London) Ltd

24–8 Oval Road, London NW1 7DX

☎01–267 4466

Telex 25775 Acpres G   Fax 01–482 2293

Managing Director *J. Fujimoto*

Part of **Harcourt Brace Jovanovich, USA.** Now also own **Holt Rhinehart & Winston; W.B. Saunders Co. Ballière Tindall.** *Publishes* academic, agriculture, animal care, archaeology, biology, chemistry, economics, educational, engineering, geography, geology, mathematics and statistics, medical, physics, psychology, reference books, scientific, technical, sociology, veterinary. Over 150 titles in 1987.

Editorial Director *Dr Conrad Guettler*

DIVISIONS

Academic Press, Medical Books Mss synopses and ideas welcome.
Royalties paid annually for Academic Press titles, twice yearly for **Holt Saunders** titles.

Authors' Rating A good, solid list closely tied to the university market. A natural for academics who put reputation before earnings.

Academy Editions

7 Holland Street, London W8 4NA
☎01–937 6996
Telex 896928 Academ G   Fax 01–723 9540

Managing Director
Dr Andreas C. Papadakis

FOUNDED 1967. Belongs to the Academy Group Ltd. *Publishes* books and magazines on art and architecture: *Architectural Design Magazine, Art & Design Magazine* and *The UIA Journal.* 25 titles in 1987. Owns The London Art Bookshop in Holland Street, London W8, and the Art Shop at the Royal College of Art (selling art objects and materials).

Editorial Director *Dr Andreas C. Papadakis* TITLES *Architecture Today* Charles Jencks; *Architectural Composition* Rob Krier; *Alphonse Mucha* Jim Mucha; *Post-Modern Design* Andreas Papadakis and Michael Collins; *Leonidov* Dr Catherine Cooke. No unsolicited mss but welcome unsolicited synopses and ideas.
Royalties paid annually.

Authors' Rating Beautiful books for modest up-market sales.

Acair Ltd

Unit 8a, 7 James Street, Stornaway,
Isle of Lewis, Scotland
☎0851 3020

Manager/Editorial Director *Agnes Rennie*

Publishes academic, biography and autobiography, children's, educational and text books, history/antiquarian, military, music, poetry, reference books and dictionaries, religious, sports and games, transport, Gaelic adults' and children's books, titles on Scottish culture. Unsolicited mss welcome.
Royalties paid twice yearly.

Addison–Wesley Publishers Ltd

Finchampstead Road, Wokingham,
Berks RG11 2NZ
☎0734 794000
Telex 836136 ADIWES G   Fax 0734 794035

Vice-President International
Peter Hoenigsberg
Chairman *Don Hammonds*
Director & General Manager
Roderick Bristow

Together with its parent company, A–W Publishers Inc., Massachusetts, USA, was bought by Pearson Longman in 1988 to make it part of one of the half dozen biggest book publishers in the western world. *Publishes* scientific, technical, academic and senior school books, and is one of the leading computer science publishers. Several series covering computer science, microelectronics and international business, for the international market. 300 titles in 1987.

Head of Acquisitions *Sarah Mallen* Unsolicited mss, synopses and ideas for books welcome.
Royalties paid twice yearly, in April and October.

Authors' Rating Under new ownership, exciting prospects for education writers to break into the American market.

Adlard–Coles Ltd

See Grafton Books Ltd

Airlife Publishing Ltd

7 St John's Hill, Shrewsbury,
Shropshire SY1 1JE
☎0743 235651
Telex 35161 HOGROB G   Fax 0743 232944

Chairman/Managing Director
A.D.R. Simpson
Approx Annual Turnover £1 million +

Established to publish specialist aviation titles, Airlife is gradually broadening its list. *Publishes* technical and general aviation, military and maritime, travel and adventure, country pursuits and local interest. 24 titles in 1987.

Editorial Head *A.D.R. Simpson* TITLES *Open Season; Flying the Big Jets; Whittle – The*

True Story; *The Trees of Shropshire*. Unsolicited mss, synopses and ideas for books welcome.

Royalties paid annually, twice by arrangement.

Albyn Press

See Charles Skilton Publishing Group

Alison Press

See Secker & Warburg Ltd

Ian Allan Ltd

Coombelands House, Addlestone,
Weybridge KT15 1HY
☎0932 585511   Telex 929806

Chairman/Managing Director *David Allan*

Publishes atlases and maps, aviation, auto/biography, hobbies, guide books, defence and militaria, nautical, reference books and dictionaries, transport, travel and topography. 100 titles in 1987.

Editorial Director *Michael Harris* Unsolicited mss considered.

Philip Allan Publishers

Market Place, Deddington, Oxford OX5 4SE
☎0869 38652

Managing Director *Philip Allan*
Approx Annual Turnover £850,000

FOUNDED 1973. Specialist publishers of books in economics, politics, finance, accounting and business studies. In 1983 launched a teaching magazine, the *Economic Review* (5 issues per year, circulation 32,000). This was followed in 1985 by the *Social Studies Review* (circulation 9000), and in 1987 by the *Geography Review* (circulation 19,000). Also launched in 1987 a British politics journal, the *Contemporary Record*. 24 titles in 1988.

DIVISIONS

Business *Philip Allan* TITLES *Current Issues in Accounting* Bryan Carsberg and Tony Hope. **Economics** *Philip Allan* TITLES *Modern Economics* David Heathfield. **Finance** *Philip Allan* TITLES *Multinational Finance* Adrian Buckley. **Politics** *Philip Cross* TITLES *British Party Politics* Gillian Peele. Almost all titles are commissioned; do not welcome unsolicited mss. Unsolicited synopses and ideas for books are welcome.

Royalties paid annually.

Allardyce, Barnett, Publishers

14 Mount Street, Lewes,
East Sussex BN7 1HL
☎0273 479393

Publisher *Fiona Allardyce*
Managing Editor *Anthony Barnett*

FOUNDED 1981. *Publishes* literature, art and music with emphasis on substantial collections by current English language poets. 2 titles in 1987.

Editorial Director *Anthony Barnett* TITLES *Poems* J.H. Prynne; *All Is Where Each Is* Andrew Crozier; *Kind* Douglas Oliver; *The Resting Bell* Anthony Barnett.

IMPRINT
Agneau 2
Unsolicited mss or synopses not encouraged.

J.A. Allen & Co. Ltd

1 Lower Grosvenor Place, Buckingham Palace Road, London SW1W 0EL
☎01–831 5606 (3 lines)/834 0090/828 8855
Telex 28905/3810 Fax 01–831 9489 Ref 3810

Chairman/Managing Director
Joseph A. Allen
Approx Annual Turnover £600,000

Inaugurated in 1926 as part of J.A. Allen & Co. (The Horseman's Bookshop) Ltd. A separate independent company since 1960. *Publishes* equine and equestrian non-fiction. Presented with the British Horse Society's Award of Merit in 1980. 12 titles in 1987.

Editor *Mrs Caroline Burt* TITLES *Side Saddle Riding* Mrs Houblon; *Cavalletti* Klime; *Dressage Riding* Watjen; *Horsemanship in Europe* Kidd; *Baily's Hunting Directory*; *Introduction to Polo* Mountbatten. Unsolicited mss, synopses and ideas for books welcome.

Royalties paid twice yearly.

W.H. Allen & Co. plc

44 Hill Street, London W1X 8LB
☎01–493 6777 Telex 28117

Chairman *Bob Tanner*
Managing Director *Tim Hailstone*
Approx Annual Turnover £7 million

ESTABLISHED early 1800s. Recently acquired **Virgin** and **Allison & Busby**. *Publishes* art, ballet, biography and memoirs, current affairs, educational, fiction, films, general history, humour, practical handbooks, reference, sociology, television, theatre, travel.

DIVISIONS
W.H. Allen *Mike Bailey* General hardbacks **Comet** *Bill Massey* General, biography, paperbacks **Crescent** *Chelsey Fox* Large print hardbacks and paperbacks. **Mercury** *Robert Postema* Business books **Planet** *Pat Hornsey* Illustrated books **Star** *Chelsey Fox* Paperbacks **Target** *Jo Thurm* Children's, TV and film tie-ins, *Dr Who* **Virgin** *Cat Ledger* **Allison & Busby** *Clive Allison*. Unsolicited mss, synopses and ideas for books welcome. *Royalties* paid twice yearly.

Authors' Rating Once the home of fast-formula show-business biographies, W.H. Allen is struggling for a more upmarket identity. An injection of Richard Branson money will help, not to mention the **Virgin** and **Allison & Busby** lists. A varied output allows plenty of room for new ideas.

Allison & Busby

See **W.H. Allen & Co. plc**

Alphabooks

Alpha House, South Street, Sherborne, Dorset DT9 3LU
☎0935 814944 Telex 46534 Alphab G

Managing Director *Tony Birks-Hay*
Editorial Director *Leslie Birks-Hay*

Taken over by **A. & C. Black** in March 1987 but continues to operate from Sherborne. *Publishes* illustrated books on architecture, beekeeping, ceramics, genealogy, and horticulture.
Royalties paid twice yearly.

Amber Lane Press

9 Middle Way, Summertown, Oxford OX2 7LH
☎0865 510545

Chairman *Brian Clark*
Managing Director *Judith Scott*

FOUNDED 1979 to publish modern play texts. *Publishes* plays and books on the theatre. 12 titles in 1987.

Editorial Head *Judith Scott* TITLES *Children of a Lesser God*; *Whose Life is it Anyway*; *Another Country*; *J.J. Farr*; *The Best of Friends*; *The Dresser* (play texts); *Playwrights' Progress*, *Patterns of Postwar British Drama* Colin Chambers and Mike Prior; *Sir Donald Wolfit* Ronald Harwood. No unsolicited mss. Synopses and ideas welcome.
Royalties paid twice yearly.

Amsco

See **Omnibus Press**

Andersen Press Ltd

62–5 Chandos Place, Covent Garden, London WC2N 4NW
☎01–240 8162
Telex 261212 Litldn G Fax 01–240 8636

Managing Director/Publisher
Klaus Flugge

FOUNDED 1976 by Klaus Flugge and named after Hans Christian Andersen. *Publishes* children's hardcover fiction. Sixty per cent of their books are sold as co-productions abroad. 40 titles in 1987.

Editorial Director *Audrey Adams* Best selling titles include *Not Now Bernard* David McKee; *A Dark, Dark Tale* Ruth Brown; *I Want my Potty* Tony Ross; *Badger's Parting Gift* Susan Varley. AUTHORS Christine Nostlinger, Michael Foreman, Hazel Townson, Satoshi Kitmura, Philip Curtis, Ursula Moray-Williams, Louis Baum, Jean Willis. Unsolicited mss are welcome, providing they are for picture books or young readers (up to 12).
Royalties paid twice yearly.

Angus & Robertson Ltd

16 Golden Square, London W1R 4BN
☎01–437 9602   Telex 897284

Managing Director *Barry Winkleman*

Bought by Bay Books in 1981. Part of **Times Books**. FOUNDED over 100 years ago in Australia. *Publishes* biography and autobiography, children's books, cinema and video, cookery, wines and spirits, fiction, humour, illustrated and fine editions, natural history, photography, sports and games, theatre and drama, travel and topography. 100 titles in 1987.

Senior Editor *Valerie Hudson* TITLES Cinema & Theatre: *Slapstick!* Tony Staveacre; *Golden Turkey Awards* Medved Brothers; Humour: *The World's Best Jokes Series*; *Kenny Everett's Ultimate Loo Book*. General nonfiction: *Eye on Australia* Michael Ruetz; *Little Books of Hugs* Kathleen Keating. Design: *The Designer's Guide to Colour Series*. Adult Fiction: *Fatal Moments* Bruce Hanna.

Children's non-fiction: *Activity Books Series*: *Fold Your Own Dinosaurs*; *Hand Shadows*; *More Tricks and Games with Paper*. Health & Self Help: *Dr Claire Weekes' Self-Help series*. Wine: *Halliday's Australian Wine Compendium* and annual *Wine Guides*. Welcome unsolicited mss, synopses and ideas for books. *Royalties* paid twice yearly.

Authors' Rating Mostly light entertainment books which sell as strongly in newsagents as in bookshops. Close links with Australian market.

Antique Collectors' Club

5 Church Street, Woodbridge,
Suffolk IP12 1DS
☎03943 5501   Telex 987271 Antbok G

Joint Managing Directors *John Steel, Diana Steel*

FOUNDED 1966. Has a five-figure membership spread throughout the world. It was in response to the demand for information on 'what to pay' that the price guide series was introduced in 1968 with the first edition of *The Price Guide to Antique Furniture*. Club membership costs £14.95 per annum. Members buy the Club's publications at concessional rates. *Publishes* specialist books on antiques and collecting. Subject areas include furniture, silver/jewellery, metalwork, glass, textiles, art reference, ceramics, horology. Also books on architecture and gardening.

Editorial Head *John Steel*   TITLES *The English Garden in Our Time* Jane Brown; *The Book of Wine Antiques* R. Butler and G. Walking; *The Price Guide to Antique Furniture* John Andrews; *English Country Houses* (3 vols) C. Hussey; *Popular 19th Century European Painting* Hook and Politmore; *The Dictionary of British Watercolour Artists* (2 vols) H. Mallalieu. Unsolicited mss, synopses and ideas for books welcome.
Royalties paid quarterly as a rule, but can vary.

Anvil Press Poetry

69 King George Street, London SE10 8PX
☎01–858 2946

Managing Director *Peter Jay*

FOUNDED 1968 to promote contemporary English and foreign poetry (in translation). English list includes Peter Levi and Carol Ann Duffy, and has now developed to the point at which most of Anvil's new titles are new volumes by their regulars. Only one or two first collections by new writers a year.

Editorial Director *Peter Jay* Welcome unsolicited mss.

Apple

See Quarto Publishing plc (UK Packagers listing)

Appletree Press Ltd

7 James Street South, Belfast, Co. Antrim, Northern Ireland BT2 8DL
☎0232 243074/246756
Telex 42904 Books G

Managing Director *John Murphy*

FOUNDED 1974. Currently have about 100 books in print. *Publishes* Irish interest non-fiction.

Senior Editor *Douglas Marshall* TITLES *Irish Touring Guide; Faces of Ireland; Caught In the Crossfire – Children and the Northern Ireland Conflict.* Welcome unsolicited mss and synopses.
Royalties paid twice yearly.

Aquarian Press Ltd
See **Thorsons Publishing Group Ltd**

Aquila Publishing (UK) Ltd
PO Box 418, Leek, Staffs ST13 8UX
☎0538 387368

Chairman & Managing Director
J.C.R. Green

FOUNDED 1968 in Glasgow by J.C.R. Green. Became part of the Johnston Green group in the later half of the 1970s. James and Anne Green 'bought out' the company from Johnston Green in 1986 and moved to Staffordshire where Aquila now operates as a wholly independent concern. *Publishes* biography, critical studies, essays, fiction, poetry. Particularly well known for its list of translation titles. Also publishes the literary quarterly, *Prospice*. 50 titles in 1987.

IMPRINTS
Aquila Books; Aquila Critical Studies; Aquila Fiction; Aquila Guides; Aquila Pamphlets; Aquila Pamphlet Poetry; Aquila Poetry; Iolaire Selection. Enquiries preferred to unsolicited mss. Unsolicited synopses and ideas for books welcome. 'We often commission books from ideas, and indeed from essays submitted to our magazine, *Prospice*, but we do need to know that a writer has a track record and the ability to follow through a commission.' (J.C.R. Green) *Royalties* paid twice yearly. *Overseas associates* Aquila Publishing (Ireland) Ltd, Dublin; Aquila America Inc., Washington State, USA; Black Moss Press, Ontario, Canada.

Arcady Books Ltd
2 Woodlands Road, Ashurst, Southampton, Hants SO4 2AD
☎042 129 2601

Managing Director *Michael Edwards*
Approx Annual Turnover (small)

FOUNDED 1981. *Publishes* second editions, general non-fiction, literature, the outdoors, and books about the New Forest. Has published 9 books. 1 new title in 1987 *The Family Outdoors;* second edition of *In the Steps of Jane Austen.*

Editorial Director *Anne Edwards* TITLES *The New Forest Companion* Anne Edwards. Unsolicited mss and synopses welcome. *Royalties* paid twice yearly.

The Architectural Press
9 Queen Anne's Gate, London SW1H 9BY
☎01–222 4333   Telex 9853505

Managing Director *Leslie Fairweather*

The Architectural Press book titles have been taken over by **Butterworth & Co. Ltd**, and publications now consist of four magazines: *The Architects' Journal, The Architectural Review, Designers' Journal* and *A.J. Focus.*

Arena
See **Century Hutchinson Publishing Group Ltd**

Argus Books Ltd
Wolsey House, Wolsey Road, Hemel Hempstead, Herts HP2 4SS
☎0442 41221

Managing Director *Peter Welham*
Publisher *Rab Macwilliam*
Approx Annual Turnover £600,000

The book-publishing division of Argus Specialist Publications, magazine publisher. *Publishes* modelling, woodwork, crafts, field sports, new technology, wine and beer making, leisure and hobbies in general. 35 titles in 1987. Prefer to see synopses rather than complete mss.
Royalties paid twice yearly.

Aris & Phillips Ltd

Teddington House, Warminster,
Wiltshire BA12 8PQ
☎0985 213409

Managing & Editorial Director
Adrian Phillips

FOUNDED 1972, publishing books on Egyptology. A family firm which has remained independent. *Publishes* academic, classical, oriental and hispanic classics. 21 titles in 1986.

Classics Editor *Philip Mudd* **Hispanic Classics Editor** *Lucinda Phillips* With such a highly specialised list, unsolicited mss and synopses are not particularly welcome, although synopses will be looked at.
Royalties paid twice yearly.

Arlington Books, Publishers, Ltd

15–17 King Street, St James's,
London SW1Y 6QU
☎01–930 0097   Telex 896616 SENDIT G

Chairman *Desmond Elliott*

FOUNDED 1960 by Desmond Elliott. Has remained independent. *Publishes* biography and autobiography, general fiction and crime, cookery, wines and spirits, health and beauty, humour, illustrated and fine editions. 18 titles in 1987.

Editor *Peter Dankwerts* TITLES *The Closet Hanging* Tony Fennelly; *The Nightmare Candidate* Ramona Stewart; *The Ice* Stephen J. Pyne; *Mastering Pain* Dr Richard Sternback; *Vitamins & Minerals for a Healthy Pregnancy*; *A Victorian Christmas* Evelyn Dix and Jean Smith; *Pocket Guide to Stress* Dr Dick Thompson; *Where Do I Come From?* Claire Rayner; *The Traveller's Guide to the Great Art Treasures of Europe* David L. Morton. Can no longer receive unsolicited mss but welcome preliminary phone calls from authors or their agents.
Royalties paid twice yearly.

Armada

See **Collins Publishers**

Arms & Armour Press Ltd

Artillery House, Artillery Row,
London SW1P 1RT
☎01–222 7676
Telex 9413701 Caspub G   Fax 01–799 1514

Chairman/Managing Director
Philip Sturrock

Part of **Cassell plc**. *Publishes* aviation, crafts and hobbies, military and war, nautical, politics and world affairs, transport. 50 titles in 1987.

Editorial Director *Rod Dymott* TITLES *Top Gun – The U.S. Navy's Fighter Weapons School* George Hall; *Weapons and Equipment of Counter-Terrorism* Michael Dewar; *Britain's First War Planes* Jack Bruce; *Argentine Air Forces in the Falkland's Conflict* S.M. Huertas and J.R. Briasco. Unsolicited mss and synopses welcome.
Royalties paid annually.

E.J. Arnold Publishing

Lockwood Distribution Centre, Parkside Lane, Dewsbury Road, Leeds LS11 5TD
☎0532 772112   Telex 556347

Managing Director *Chris Bundy* (Group)

Owned by the Pergamon Group. *Publishes* atlases and maps, biology and zoology, chemistry, computer science, computer software (educational), economics, educational and textbooks, geography and geology, history and antiquarian, languages and linguistics, mathematics and statistics, music and physics. 125 titles in 1987.

Publishing Director *Stan Sharp* Unsolicited mss considered.
Royalties paid annually.

Edward Arnold (Publishers) Ltd

See **Hodder & Stoughton Ltd**

Arrow Books Ltd

See **Century Hutchinson Publishing Group Ltd**

Artech House

28 Eaton Row, London SW1 0JA
☎01–235 8121   Telex 885744 MICSOL G

Managing Director (in USA) *William Bazzy*

FOUNDED 1970. The European office of Artech House Inc., Boston. *Publishes* electronic engineering. 35 titles in 1987.

Editorial Head *Daniel Brown* Will consider unsolicited mss and synopses.
Royalties paid twice yearly.

Artist's House

See **Mitchell Beazley Ltd**

Ashford Press Publishing

1 Church Road, Shedfield,
Hampshire SO3 2HW
☎0329 834265
Telex 859783   Fax 04862 27430

Chairman *Clive Martin*
Managing Director *Jane F. Tatam*
Approx Annual Turnover £750,000

FOUNDED 1984 and taken over by Martins Printing Group in 1987. Now publishes about 60 books a year. Successful 1987 titles included *Groc's Candid Guides to Greece*, *How to be a Wine Know* and *Take a Buttock of Beefe*. Specialises in non-fiction, nautical, field sports, sports, travel, education, business titles.

Editorial Head *Jane F. Tatam* Unsolicited mss welcome if return postage included. Synopses and ideas for books considered.
Royalties paid twice yearly.

Authors' Rating An exciting young company with a strong sense of marketing and promotion.

Ashgrove Press Ltd

19 Circus Place, Bath, Avon BA1 2PW
☎0225 25539

Chairman & Managing Director
Robin Campbell

FOUNDED 1980. Originally published local history but moved more into 'alternative' lifestyles. *Publishes* health, healing and diet, psychology, metaphysics, countryside, regional and local subjects. 8 titles in 1987. Unsolicited mss welcome, preferably after initial letter. Synopses and ideas for books welcome.
Royalties paid twice in the first year; thereafter annually.

Athlone Press

44 Bedford Row, London WC1R 4LY
☎01–405 9836   Telex 261507 ref 1334

Managing Director *Brian Southam*

ESTABLISHED 1950 as the publishing house of the University of London. Now wholly independent, but preserves links with the University via an academic advisory board. Anticipated developments in the near future: more emphasis on women's/feminist studies and environmental/'green' issues, including medicine. *Publishes* archaeology, architecture, art, economics, history, medical, music, Japan, oriental, philosophy, politics, religion, science, sociology, zoology, women's/feminist issues. 35 titles in 1987.

Editorial Head *Brian Southam* Unsolicited mss welcome. Synopses/ideas for books considered.
Royalties paid annually/twice yearly by arrangement. *Overseas associates* The Athlone Press, Atlantic, New Jersey, USA.

Atlantic Large Print

See **Chivers Press (Publishers)**

Attic Books

The Folly, Rhosgoch, Painscastle,
Builth Wells, Powys LD2 3JY
☎04975 205

Managing Director *Jack Bowyer*

FOUNDED 1984 by its architect owners. *Publishes* books on building crafts, architecture and engineering. Technical books for the industry mainly dealing with restoration and conservation. 2 titles in 1987 (both dealing with stonemasonry).

Editorial Head *Jack Bowyer*

IMPRINT
Orion Books TITLES *A History of Buildings* Jago V. Swillerton and Toomer. Unsolicited mss, synopses and ideas for books welcome. *Royalties* paid annually.

Aurum Press Ltd

33 Museum Street, London WC1A 1LD
☎01–631 4596
Telex 299557 AURUM G   Fax 01–631 4596

Managing Director *Timothy J.M. Chadwick*

FOUNDED 1977. A member of The Really Useful Group plc. Committed to producing high quality illustrated non-fiction books, biographies, travel and health. 25 titles in 1987.

Publishing Directors *Michael Alcock* (adult books), *Sue Tarsky* (children's books) TITLES *Maxwell – The Outsider*, Tom Bower; *Glasshouses*, May Woods and Arete Schwarz-Warren; *Alexander and the Dragon*, Helen Craig and Katharine Holabird; *Miss Poppy and the Honey Cake*, Elizabeth Macdonald and Claire Smith.

IMPRINT
Aurum Books for Children launched Autumn 1988, specialising in picture books for the under fives and classic story books.

Must see synopsis before considering completed mss.
Royalties paid twice yearly.

Authors' Rating After a period of uncertainty, Aurum has been given a welcome injection of capital and confidence by Andrew Lloyd Webber. First signal of a more aggressive spirit was the Tom Bower unauthorised biography of Robert Maxwell.

Auto Books

See **A. & C. Black (Publishers) Ltd**

Avebury

See **Gower Publishing Group Ltd**

Badger Books Ltd

Lenches Press, Hill Barn Orchard, Church Lane, Evesham, Worcs WR11 4UB
☎0386 871035

Managing Director *Marlene Badger*

FOUNDED 1980. *Publishes* children's books, humour.

Editorial Director *Marlene Badger* TITLES *Matt and the Mermaid* Chris Skelton and Ron Smith. Do not welcome unsolicited mss but will consider synopses.
Royalties paid annually.

Samuel Bagster & Sons Ltd

See **Marshall Pickering Holdings Ltd**

Bailey Bros & Swinfen Ltd

Warner House, Bowles Well Gardens, Folkestone, Kent CT19 6PH
☎0303 850501
Telex 96328 Bailey G   Fax 0303 850162

Chairman and Managing Director
J.R. Bailey
Approx Annual Turnover £5 million +

FOUNDED 1929. In 1967, to accommodate the expanding business in educational and trade publishing, they moved from London to Folkestone. Now cover distribution for book publishers, subscription processing for journal publishers, and a mailing and publicity service. Part of Bailey & Swinfen Holdings. *Publishes* general, children's and reference. 6 titles in 1987.

Editorial Director *J.R. Bailey* TITLES *The Data Book for Pipe Fitters and Pipe Welders* E.H. Williamson; *The Basic Gurkhali Dictionary*; *White Tie Tales* John Morecroft; *Act Imaginatively* Stanley Blow; *Raise the Herald* Fred Vandenbussche. Do not welcome unsolicited mss but will consider unsolicited synopses and ideas.
Overseas offices in Australia and New Zealand.

Howard Baker Press Ltd

27a Arterberry Road, Wimbledon,
London SW20 8AF
☎01−947 5482

Chairman/Managing Director
W. Howard Baker

FOUNDED 1968 in Bloomsbury and moved to Wimbledon in 1971. *Publishes* general non-fiction, political science, autobiography, de-luxe editions, biography, maps, reference books, specialist facsimile editions in volume form of pre-war magazines such as *Magnet*, *Gem*, etc.

IMPRINTS
Howard Baker, Greyfriars Press, Greyfriars Book Club No unsolicited mss. Synopses welcome if accompanied by s.a.e. *Royalties* paid twice yearly.

John Baker Publishers Ltd

See A. & C. Black (Publishers) Ltd

Bantam

See Transworld Publishers Ltd

Arthur Barker Ltd

See Weidenfeld & Nicolson Ltd

Barny Books

The Cottage, Hough on the Hill, nr
Grantham, Lincs NG32 2BB
☎040050 246

Managing Director *Molly Burkett*
Approx Annual Turnover £10,000

Founded with the aim of encouraging new writers and illustrators. *Publishes* children's books.

Editorial Head *Molly Burkett* Too small a concern to have the staff/resources to deal with unsolicited mss. Writers with strong ideas should approach Molly Burkett by letter in the first instance.
Royalties Division of profits 50/50.

Barracuda Books Ltd (Quotes Ltd)

Meadows House, Well Street, Buckingham,
Bucks MK18 1EW
☎0280 814441/2

Managing Directors *Clive Birch*
(Barracuda), *Carolyn Birch* **(Quotes Ltd)**

Barracuda was formed in 1974, and its sister company Quotes in 1985. The **Sporting and Leisure Press** imprint was launched in 1976, and **Saga** in 1987. Now moving into co-publishing ventures in the general interest field with particular emphasis on heritage-based books. *Publishes* local and natural history, country and sporting life, military and genealogical histories. 41 titles in 1987.

DIVISIONS
Barracuda Books *Clive Birch* TITLES *Nature of Nottinghamshire; Yesterday's Town: Colchester; The Book of Darlington.* **Quotes Ltd** *Carolyn Birch* TITLES *Hemel Hempstead in Camera; Sussex Buses in Camera.* **Saga** TITLES *Jubilee; Goings on at Pimple Pond.* Unsolicited mss, synopses and ideas for books welcome.
Royalties paid annually.

Barrie & Jenkins Ltd

289 Westbourne Grove, London W11 2QA
☎01−727 9636
Telex 267009   Fax 01−229 4571

Managing Director *Julian Shuckburgh*

Part of **Century Hutchinson**. *Publishes* general non-fiction, including antiques, history, art, gardening. Planning to publish fiction in the near future.

Editorial Director *Anne Furniss* TITLES *Italian Food* Elizabeth David; *Letters from Egypt* Florence Nightingale. Will consider unsolicited mss but prefer initial introductory letter.
Royalties paid twice yearly.

Authors' Rating A welcome revival of a publishing name which dates back to Florence Nightingale (one of Barrie & Jenkins' first authors). Substance is provided by a merger with packager Shuckburgh Reynolds with Julian Shuckburgh as MD of the new company. His change of hat, from packager to publisher, could start a trend.

John Bartholomew & Son Ltd

12 Duncan Street, Edinburgh EH9 1TA
☎031–667 9341
Telex 728134   Fax 031–662 4282

Chairman *George Barber*
Managing Director *David Ross Stewart*
Approx Annual Turnover £7 million

Established over 150 years ago. Produces everything from town plans to world atlases including the cartography for the *Times Atlas of the World* (**Times Books** is now its sister company). Family owned until nine years ago, when it was sold to Reader's Digest. Bought by News International in 1985. 60 titles in 1987.

DIVISIONS
Bartholomew *Colin Kirkwood* TITLES *Road Atlas Britain; Walk the South Downs; Walk the Dales; Children's World Atlas; 1:100,000 Leisure Maps; Scottish Clan and Family Names.*

IMPRINTS
Geographia *Colin Kirkwood* Street maps and atlases TITLES *Greater London Street Atlas; 30 Miles Around London.* **J & B Maps** *Colin Kirkwood* TITLES *Touring Map of Scotland; Irish Family Names Map.* **Clyde/Bartholomew** Joint publications of leisure/tourist maps of overseas countries and island groups. No unsolicited mss. Letter essential in the first instance.
Royalties paid twice yearly.

B.T. Batsford Ltd

4 Fitzhardinge Street, London W1H 0AH
☎01–486 8484
Telex 943763 CROCOM G   Fax 01–487 4296

Managing Director *P.A.J. Kemmis Betty*
Approx Annual Turnover £4 million

FOUNDED 1843, as a bookseller; started publishing in 1874. An independent company which has become the world leader in books on chess and lacecraft. Acquired the **Dryad Press** in 1983. *Publishes* non-fiction: academic and scholarly, archaeology, architecture and design, cinema, crafts/hobbies, educational/textbooks, fashion and costume, history and antiquarian, literary criticism and linguistics, sports and games, theatre and drama, transport, travel and topography, vocational training/careers. 147 titles in 1987. Generally, they publish 150 non-fiction titles a year, with a backlist of 1200. Dryad publishes 40 titles a year.

DIVISIONS
Academic/Educational *Peter Kemmis Betty* TITLES *Mitchell's Building Construction; Batsford Chess Openings; Living Through Nazi Germany; Understanding Archaeological Excavation.* **Trade** *Tim Auger* TITLES *Inspiration for Embroidery; The Lilies of China; The Illustrated Dictionary of Film Stars; The Encyclopaedia of World Costume.*

IMPRINTS
Dryad Press *Bill Waller* TITLES *Complete Book of Tatting; Acid Rain.* **Mitchell Publishing Company** *Tony Seward* TITLES *Maintaining Building Services; Auditoria.* This imprint specialises in building and architecture. Welcomes unsolicited mss and synopses/ideas for books.
Royalties paid twice in first year, annually thereafter.

Authors' Rating A quietly thriving independent company which does well by sticking to what it knows best – mainly hobbies and intellectual games. Chess list may suffer from editor Paul Lamford's departure to **Pergamon**.

BBC Books

80 Wood Lane, London W12 0TT
☎01–576 0202
Telex 265781   Fax 01–749 0538

Head of Book Publishing
Nicholas Chapman
Senior Commissioning Editors
Sheila Ableman, Suzanne Webber

BBC Books, a division of BBC Enterprises, is expanding its list to the extent that it now publishes books which, though linked with BBC television or radio, may not simply be the 'book of the series'. An example of this is the publishing of cookery books by past television cooks who no longer have series running. 110 titles in 1987.

TITLES *Latin Americans* Hugh O'Shaughnessy; *The Crimewatch Guide to Home Security* Sue Cook; *Scottish Islands* Ian Grimble; *Go Birding!* Tony Soper; *Food and Drink Quizbook* Jeremy Mills; *Having a Baby* Nancy Kohner; *Batty Adventures* Chris Allen; *The Animals Roadshow* Dr Desmond Morris; *Tales from the Edge of the the World* Martin Riley. Books with no BBC link are of no interest, and unsolicited mss (which come in at the rate of 15 weekly) are rarely even read. If books are not commissioned, they are packaged and devised in consultation with known writers, or through known agents. Having said that, strong ideas well expressed will always be considered, and promising letters stand a chance of further scrutiny.
Royalties paid twice yearly.

Authors' Rating After a long period of hibernation, BBC Books is shaping up to be a first-rank publisher. Home of natural bestsellers like *Yes, Prime Minister* which for the second volume had an initial print run of 250,000. Plans to go into children's books in a big way.

Beaver
See **Century Hutchinson Publishing Group Ltd**

Bedford Square Press
26 Bedford Square, London WC1B 3HW
☎01–636 4066

Managing Director *Jonathan Croall*
Approx Annual Turnover £100,000

FOUNDED 1968. Publishing imprint of The National Council for Voluntary Organisations. Established to reflect the concerns of the NCVO in relation to the voluntary sector. In 1987 new policy led to wider brief to publish books on social issues for a wider audience, and representation by Hutchinson Education. *Publishes* information, ideas and campaigning books on a range of social issues. 15 titles in 1987.

Editorial Head *Jonathan Croall* TITLES *Voluntary Agencies Directory; Love and Pain: A Survival Handbook for Women; Opening the Town Hall Door: An Introduction to Local Government.* Unsolicited mss welcome, though most books commissioned.
Royalties paid twice yearly.

Bellew Publishing Co. Ltd
Nightingale Centre, 8 Balham Hill,
London SW12 9EA
☎01–673 5611
Telex 8951182 GECOMS G Fax 01–675 3542

Chairman/Managing Director *Ib Bellew*
Approx Annual Turnover £250,000

FOUNDED 1983 as a publisher/packager. *Publishes* illustrated non-fiction, craft books, general interest. 10 titles in 1987. Welcomes unsolicited mss and synopses.
Royalties paid annually.

Ernest Benn
See **A. & C. Black (Publishers) Ltd**

Berg Publishers Ltd
77 Morrell Avenue, Oxford OX4 1NQ
☎0865 245104   Telex 312440 PBSSPA G

Chairman/Managing Director
Marion Berghahn
Approx Annual Turnover £250,000

Publishes scholarly books in the fields of history, economics and other social sciences. Scholarly and general titles in literature and the arts, biography and current affairs published under the recently acquired imprint **Oswald Wolff**. Specialises in translations into English. 39 titles in 1987.

Editorial Head *Janet Godden* TITLES *Schopenhauer: Manuscript Remains* in 4 volumes; *Women of Theresienstadt* R. Schwertfeger.

IMPRINTS

Oswald Wolff Books *Ilse Wolff* TITLES *Leonard Bernstein* Gradenwitz; *Heinrich Böll* J.H. Reid. No unsolicited mss. Unsolicited synopses and ideas for books welcome. *Royalties* paid annually.

BFI Publishing

British Film Institute, 21 Stephen Street, London W1P 1PL
☎01–255 1444
Telex 27624   Fax 01–436 7950

Head of Publishing *Geoffrey Nowell-Smith*
Approx Annual Turnover £100,000

FOUNDED 1982. Part of the British Film Institute. *Publishes* film- or television-related academic books. 5 titles in 1987.

Editorial Head *Geoffrey Nowell-Smith* TITLES *The Cinema of Andrei Tarkovsky* Mark Le Fanu; *Eisenstein Writings Volume 1: 1922–34* Richard Taylor; *Home is Where the Heart is: Studies in Melodrama and the Woman's Film* Christine Gledhill; *The Last Picture Show: Britain's Changing Film Audience* David Docherty; *The Logic of the Absurd: On Film and Television Comedy* Jerry Palmer; *Ozu* David Bordwell; *Public Secrets, EastEnders and its Audience* David Buckingham. Prefer unsolicited synopses/ideas rather than complete mss.
Royalties paid annually.

Bishopsgate Press Ltd

37 Union Street, London SE1 1SE
☎01–403 6544

Chairman & Managing Director *Ian F.L. Straker*

FOUNDED 1800. Since then has been mainly producing financial books for the City but for the last five years has developed into general publishing. *Publishes* general books, biography, non-fiction, crafts, arts and crafts, religious books, poetry, children's books.

Publishing Director *Austen Smith* TITLES *Small Hand Big Ideas* Tony Hart; *Old Garden Flowers* Brian Halliwell; *Just Like You and Me* Johnny Morris; *New Foods for Healthy Eating* Liz Brand; *Hyperactive Children: A Parent's Guide* Shirley Flack. Softcover series *Practical Guides* series. Unsolicited mss and synopses welcome.
Royalties paid twice yearly.

A. & C. Black (Publishers) Ltd

35 Bedford Row, London WC1R 4JH
☎01–242 0946   Telex 32524 Acblac

Chairman *Charles Black*
Joint Managing Directors *Charles Black and David Gadsby*
Approx Annual Turnover £4.8 million

Publishes academic, agriculture, antiques and collecting, archaeology, architecture and design, aviation, children's books, crafts and hobbies, educational and textbooks, fashion and costume, fine art and art history, geography and geology, guide books, history and antiquarian, medical, music, nautical, reference books, dictionaries, sports and games, theatre and drama, travel and topography, veterinary. 150 titles in 1987. TITLES *Writers' & Artists' Yearbook*; *The Blue Guides* Travel series.

IMPRINTS

Alphabooks, Autobooks, John Baker Publishers Ltd, Ernest Benn, Adam & Charles Black, E.P. Publishing, Lepus, F. Lewis (Publishers) Ltd, Nautical Publishing Company. Welcome unsolicited mss and synopses/ideas for books.
Royalty payments vary according to each contract.

Authors' Rating With *Who's Who* on the list, how can a publisher go wrong? Recent acquisitions suggest a revival of energy and a more assertive style of publishing. Well regarded in education and children's books.

Black Spring Press Ltd

46 Rodwell Road, East Dulwich,
London SE22 9LE
☎01–299 1514

Managing Director *Simon Pettifar*

FOUNDED 1986. *Publishes* fiction, literary criticism, theatre and cinema studies, popular music. 1 title in 1986.

Editor *Simon Pettifar* TITLES *The Paris Olympia Press: An Annotated Bibliography* Patrick J. Kearney; *D.H. Lawrence, An Unprofessional Study* Anais Nin. Prefer to see a proposal rather than completed ms.
Royalties paid twice yearly.

Black Swan

See **Transworld Publishers Ltd**

Blackie & Son Ltd

Wester Cleddens Road, Bishopbriggs,
Glasgow G64 2NZ
☎041–772 2311
Telex 777283 BLACKI G   Fax 041–762 0897
Chairman & Managing Director
R. Michael Miller

FOUNDED 1809. Still independently owned. Educational and Academic divisions based in Glasgow. Children's division in London (see below). *Publishes* educational textbooks (*Modern Maths for Schools*), children's books (*Flower Fairies*), academic and professional. 150 titles in 1987.

DIVISIONS

Academic *Dr A.G. Mackintosh* **Children's** *A.D. Mitchell* located at 7 Leicester Place, London WC2H 7BP **Educational** *A. Rosemary Wands* TITLES **Academic and Professional** animal behaviour, plant biology and agriculture, aquatic biology, biochemistry, developmental biology and genetics, environmental biology/ecology, microbiology, neurobiology, physiology and immunology,

instrumental analysis, food science and technology. **Children's** picture books for the very young/older children: *Topsy and Tim*; *Flower Fairies*; general fiction; fairy tales, folk tales and anthologies; non-fiction. Unsolicited mss, ideas and synopses welcome. Subsidiary company **Abelard–Schuman Ltd** (children's books).

Authors' Rating Mostly publish formula texts for the core curriculum and children's whimsy. Not exactly riveting but steady and reliable.

Blackstaff Press Ltd

3 Galway Park, Dundonald,
Belfast BT16 0AN
☎02138 7161/2

Directors *Michael Burns and Anne Tannahill*

FOUNDED 1971 by Jim and Diane Gracey and bought by Michael Burns and Ann Tannahill in 1980. *Publishes* mainly but not exclusively Irish interest books, fiction, poetry, history, politics, natural history, and folklore. 18 titles in 1987.

Editorial Head *Michael Burns* Unsolicited mss, synopses and ideas welcome.
Royalties paid twice yearly.

Authors' Rating One of the best of the small publishers.

Basil Blackwell Ltd

108 Cowley Road, Oxford OX4 1JF
☎0865 791100   Telex 837022
Chairman *Nigel Blackwell*
Managing Director *David Martin*

Part of the the Blackwell Group, 50 Broad Street, Oxford. FOUNDED 1922 as an academic and educational publishing house; the early list included fiction, poetry and (curiously) Enid Blyton. Expanded into journals and now owns more than 50. Rapid growth in the 1970s and 1980s included the establishment of a wholly-owned distribution company and the takeover of Martin Robertson. *Publishes* academic, humanities, social sciences, primary and secondary schoolbooks, books for teachers, general books. 300 titles in 1987.

DIVISIONS
Academic & General *John Davey*
Schools *James Nash*

IMPRINTS
Shakespeare Head Press *David Martin*
Raintree Press *James Nash* Unsolicited mss welcome, but prefer synopses with specimen chapter and table of contents.
Royalties paid annually. *Overseas associates* Basil Rockwell Inc., New York.

Authors' Rating Family-owned which at least guarantees shelf space in a certain leading bookseller. Comfortable relationships with authors. Strong in school publishing.

Blackwell Scientific Publications Ltd

Osney Mead, Oxford OX2 0EL
☎0865 240201
Telex 83355 Medbok G   Fax 0865 721205

Chairman *Per Saugman*
Managing Director *Robert Campbell*
Approx Annual Turnover £15–20 million

FOUNDED 1939. Part of the **Blackwell Group**. Growth in the 1960s led to a move to Oxford. In 1987 the company broadened its base by buying **Collins'** professional list. *Publishes* medical, professional and science. 230 titles in 1987.

Editorial Director *Per Saugman* TITLES *Textbook of Dermatology* edited by Rook *et al; Essential Immunology* Roitt; *Lecture Notes in Clinical Medicine* Rubenstein. Unsolicited mss and synopses welcomed.
Royalties paid annually. *Overseas associates* Blackwell Scientific Publications Inc., USA; Blackwell Scientific Publications Pty Ltd, Australia.

Authors' Rating A tightly organised, highly competent publisher. Rewards may not be madly generous but they do pay on time.

Blackwood Pillans & Wilson

61 North Castle Street, Edinburgh EH2 3LJ
☎031–225 8282

Chairman/Managing Director
Graham Wilson

Did not publish any books in 1986 and are now concentrating on printing rather than publishing. Do not welcome unsolicited material.

Blandford Publishing Ltd

Artillery House, Artillery Row,
London SW1P 1RT
☎01–222 7676
Telex 9413701 CASPUB G   Fax 01–799 1514

Chairman/Managing Director
Philip Sturrock

FOUNDED 1919, the company took its name from the location of its first office in London's West End. Taken over ten years ago by Link House and four years ago by United Newspapers. Acquired by **Cassell plc** who plan a rapid programme of expansion. *Publishes* animal care and breeding, art and graphics, aviation, aviculture, bodybuilding and sport, crafts and hobbies, do-it-yourself, fashion and costume, gardening, humour, magic and the occult, military and war, natural history, photography, popular music, sports and games, theatre and drama, transport, woodworking. 190 titles in 1987.

Editorial Director *Clare Howell*

DIVISIONS
Art & Graphics TITLE *Watercolour Painting* Ron Ranson. **Aviculture** TITLE *Parrots, Their Care and Breeding* Rosemary Low. **Bodybuilding** TITLE *Hardcore Bodybuilding* Robert Kennedy. **Crafts** TITLE *China & Porcelain Painting Projects* Sheila Southwell. **Gardening** TITLE *Fuchsias in Colour* Brian and Valerie Proudley. **Military** TITLE *War at Sea 1939–1945* John Hamilton. **Music** TITLE *New Rock Record* Terry Housome. **Natural History** TITLE *Wildest Britain* Roland Smith. Unsolicited mss and synopses/ideas for books are welcome.

IMPRINTS
Javelin: Editorial Director *Jonathan Grimwood* Mass-market paperback imprint covering wide-ranging subjects.
Royalties paid twice yearly.

Bloodaxe Books Ltd

PO Box 1SN,
Newcastle upon Tyne NE99 1SN
☎ 091–232 5988

Chairman *Simon Thirsk*
Managing Director *Neil Astley*

Publishes poetry, literature and criticism, photography, literary fiction, theatre and drama, women's studies. 25 titles in 1987. Ninety per cent of their list is poetry.

Editorial Director *Neil Astley* Unsolicited poetry mss welcome. Authors of other material should write first with details of their work.
Royalties paid annually.

Authors' Rating One of the best of the small publishers – enterprising and imaginative.

Bloomsbury Publishing Ltd

2 Soho Square, London W1V 5DE
☎ 01–494 2111
Telex 21323 Blooms   Fax 01–434 0151

Chairman/Managing Director
Nigel Newton

One of the three major new imprints set up in 1986, Bloomsbury was launched in a glare of publicity which made much of its radical manifesto: the attempt to bring authors into far greater involvement with the machinery of publishing, and the setting aside of a share of the company's equity for division among its authors. Bloomsbury was founded by Nigel Newton (ex-**Sidgwick & Jackson**) together with David Reynolds (ex-Shuckburgh Reynolds), who then headhunted Alan Wherry from **Penguin** (marketing) and Liz Calder from **Cape** (editorial). How many authors would leave Cape with Liz Calder became a common topic of trade gossip in early

1987; 3 of the 25 titles launched between April and July were by novelists who did. In only 10 months Bloomsbury had put 6 books onto *The Sunday Times* Bestseller list.

Publishing Directors *David Reynolds, Liz Calder* **Editorial Directors** *Kathy Rooney, Mike Petty* TITLES *Trust* Mary Flanagan; *Anywhere but Here* Mona Simpson; *Temporary Shelter* Mary Gordon; *Look Homeward: A Life of Thomas Wolfe* David Donald; *Natural Parenting* Peter and Fiona Walker; *Marilyn Among Friends* Shaw and Rosten; *Presumed Innocent* Scott Turow; *A Case of Knives* Candia McWilliam; *Elvis World* Jane and Michael Stern; *Inside Left* Derek Hatton; *The Bloomsbury Dictionary of Quotations*; *Esther's Mission* Paul Bailey; *Story of My Life* Jay McInerney; *A Prayer for Owen Meannie* John Irving. Welcome unsolicited mss and synopses.
Royalties paid twice yearly (April and October).

Authors' Rating Backed by blue chip venture capital, Bloomsbury is aiming for the big time. Brave support for first novels but so far non-fiction has made the running in sales. Latest expansion is into reference books. Early in the year, Bloomsbury became the eighth publisher to sign the Minimum Terms Agreement.

Bobcat

See **Omnibus Press**

The Bodley Head

32 Bedford Square, London WC1B 3EL
☎ 01–631 4434   Telex 299080 CVBCSE G

Publishing Director *Chris Holifield*

Taken over by **Random House Inc.**, New York. Formerly part of the Chatto, Virago, Bodley Head and Jonathan Cape group. FOUNDED 1887, and run by John Lane for the first 31 years, The Bodley Head remains editorially inviolate. Its early list included H.G. Wells, Arnold Bennett, Saki and later Agatha Christie. Allen Lane, John Lane's nephew, left the company to found **Penguin**. Max Reinhardt acquired the firm in 1957; authors who subsequently joined the list include Graham Greene, Alistair Cooke, Georgette Heyer, Solzhenitsyn, Muriel Spark and William Trevor. A strong children's list was developed, with writers such as Maurice Sendak, Pat Hutchins and Shirley Hughes. *Publishes* general non-fiction (biography, history, travel, current affairs); fiction; children's (fiction, non-fiction, picture). 98 titles in 1987. Max Reinhardt left the company in 1987.

DIVISIONS
Editorial Directors (Adult List) *Chris Holifield, Caroline Upcher* TITLES General: *London Guide* Louise Nicholson; *Queen Mary's Doll's House* Mary Stewart-Wilson; *Ganzl's Complete Book of the Musical Theatre* Kurt Ganzl; *The English and their Horses* Libby Purves, Paul Heiney and Kit Houghton; *Byron* Stephen Coote. Fiction: *The Silence in the Garden* William Trevor; *Night Soldiers* Alan Furst; *The Grotto* Coral Lansbury. **Editorial Director** (Children's List) *Rona Selby* TITLES *Catch That Hat!* Emma Chichester Clark; *The Big Alfie and Annie Rose Storybook* Shirley Hughes; *The Burning Questions of Bingo Brown* Betsy Byars; *Enough is Too Much Already* Jan Mark. Unsolicited mss welcome if they include return postage. Synopses and ideas for books welcome. *Royalties* paid twice yearly.

Authors' Rating Still in the process of resetting after the departure of Max Reinhardt with Graham Greene, Maurice Sendak and Alistair Cooke. To rub salt in the wound, **Constable** managed to win over Muriel Spark. For the moment, anyway, the main strength of the company is in its children's list which is blessed with imagination and originality. Some complaints of late royalty payments.

The Book Guild Ltd
Temple House, 25–6 High Street, Lewes, East Sussex BN7 2LU
☎0273 472534
Telex NOSLIP VIA 987562 COCHAS

Chairman *Gerald Konyn*
Managing Director *Carol Biss*
Approx Annual Turnover £500,000

FOUNDED 1982. *Publishes* fiction, general, juvenile, sport. 60 titles in 1987.

DIVISIONS
Biography *Carol Biss* TITLES *Harry Lauder in the Limelight* William Wallace; *Royal Brides: Queens of the Middle Ages* E.L. Black; *Brangwen: Letters from John Masefield* John Gregory; *Interior with Figure: The Life and Paintings of Charles McCall* Mitzi McCall. **Fiction** *Carol Biss* TITLES *Tar and Cement* Martyn Goff; *Angel Assignment* Rene Ray; *The Pasha* Marlin Sorsbie. **Religion & Philosophy** *Carol Biss* TITLES *God and Human Chance* Bishop Paul Burrough; *Everyman Revisited* Drusilla Scott; *Tentative Answers to Ten Questions* Norman Dockeray CBE; *Christianity for Today* Robert Douglas Richardson. **Sport** TITLE *Athletic World Records of the 20th Century*, L. Blackman.

IMPRINTS
Temple House Books *Carol Biss* Paperback TITLES *Breaking The Ice* Ian Crichton; *Selling: How to Succeed in the Sales Arena* David Baldwin; *Holiday Retreats for Cats and Dogs* Scarlett Tipping; *Weathervanes of Sussex* Brigid Chapman. No unsolicited mss. Ideas and synopses welcome
Royalties paid twice yearly.

Authors' Rating An efficient and competently run small publisher but with a tendency to drift over into vanity publishing. In all cases of vanity publishing, would-be authors should take independent advice before committing their own money.

Bookmarks Publication
265 Seven Sisters Road, Finsbury Park, London N4 2DE
☎01-802 6145

Managing Director *Peter Marsden*
Approx Annual Turnover £75,000

FOUNDED 1979 to project the international socialist movement. Linked with the Socialist

Workers Party and its internationally related organisations. 'Our aim is to build a list of socialist books and pamphlets which reaches across the spectrum of political issues.' *Publishes* politics, economics, labour history, trade unionism, international affairs. 13 titles in 1987.

DIVISIONS

General Publishing *Peter Marsden* TITLES *The Revolutionary Ideas of Karl Marx* Alex Callinicos. **Revolutionary Classics** *Charles Hore* TITLES *Labour in Irish History* James Connolly. Unsolicited synopses and ideas welcome as long as they are compatible with existing policy. No unsolicited mss.
Royalties paid annually. *Overseas associates* Chicago, USA; Melbourne, Australia.

Bounty Books

Michelin House, 81 Fulham Road,
London SW3 6RB
☎01–581 9393
Telex 920191   Fax 01–589 8419

Managing Director *Jonathan Goodman*

Part of **Paul Hamlyn Publishing** which is itself a part of the **Octopus Publishing Group**. FOUNDED 1981 as the Bargain Reprint Division of **Octopus**. *Publishes* out-of-print titles only; antiques, children's, cookery, facsimiles, fiction, gardening, general interest, humour, militaria, natural history, sport. No unsolicited mss, synopses or ideas for books.

Bowker–Saur Ltd

Borough Green, Sevenoaks, Kent TN15 8PJ
☎0732 884567
Telex 95678   Fax 0732 884079

General Manager *Phillip Woods*

Part of **Butterworths**. *Publishes* biography and library service; biography and autobiography, politics and world affairs.

Editorial Director *Shane O'Neill.* Unsolicited mss considered.
Royalties paid twice yearly.

Boxtree

36 Tavistock Street, London WC2E 7PB
☎01–240 7419   Fax 01–349 0049

Chairman *Hugh Campbell*
Managing Director *Sarah Mahaffy*

FOUNDED APRIL 1987 to publish books related to television programmes primarily in the areas of current affairs, children's, leisure and general interest. No fiction. TVS (Television South) is the major shareholder in the company. Around twenty titles by the end of 1987. 25 titles in 1988.

Editor *Cheryl Brown* Unsolicited mss not welcome; because the company publishes tie-ins with television, close consultation with writers well in advance of the writing of mss is essential. However, synopses and ideas welcome.
Royalties paid twice yearly.

Authors' Rating One of the few hopeful signs of intelligent and constructive co-operation between publishing and commercial television.

Marion Boyars Publishers Ltd

24 Lacy Road, London SW15 1NL
☎01–788 9522

Managing Director *Marion Boyars*

FOUNDED 1975. Formerly Calder and Boyars. *Publishes* academic and scholarly, architecture and design, biography and autobiography, business and industry, economics, fiction, health and beauty, law, literature and criticism, medical, music, philosophy, poetry, politics and world affairs, psychology, religion and theology, sociology and anthropology, theatre and drama, travel, women's studies. 25 titles in 1987.

Editorial Director *Arthur Boyars* **Editor-in-Chief** *Marion Boyars* **Non-fiction Editor** *Ken Hollings* **Iris Series Editor** *Stephanie Lewis* TITLES *Taking It All In* Pauline Kael; *State of the Art* Pauline Kael; *Potboilers* Charles Marowitz; *Memory Gardens* Robert Creeley; *X: Writings '79–'82* John Cage; *The Flood* John Broderick; *Marat/Sade* Peter Weiss; *Selected*

Letters Federico Garcia Lorca; *Cathy Come Home* Jeremy Sandford. Unsolicited mss welcome for fiction. Unsolicited synopses and ideas welcome for non-fiction.
Royalties paid annually. *Overseas associates* Marion Boyars Publishers Inc., 26 East 33rd Street, New York, NY 10016, USA.

Authors' Rating A publisher with an eye for originality. A refuge for talent which others have failed to appreciate.

Boydell & Brewer Ltd
PO Box 9, Woodbridge, Suffolk IP12 3DF
☎0394 411320

Publishes non-fiction only. All books commissioned. Most definitely do not welcome unsolicited material.

Authors' Rating A self-contained publisher best left to make their own decisions unhindered by authors or agents. Reports of confusing royalty statements.

Brentham Press
40 Oswald Road, St Albans, Herts AL1 3AQ
☎0727 35731

Director *Margaret Tims*

FOUNDED 1974 by three people with professional publishing experience. Now run mostly by editorial director. The aim is to publish material of literary merit and social value which falls outside the commercial mass market. 'Such a press is not economically viable and cannot be run as a source of income!'

TITLES Criticism *Lawrence and Murry* F.A. Lea; *D.H. Lawrence: A Living Poet* Charles Davey; *The Relevance of Ruskin* Roy Shaw. Poetry *Poet's England 8: Staffordshire* ed. A.V. Simcock; *Feathers Cut Stone* Peter Williamson; *The Dance of the Blessed Spirits* John Adlard. Education *Making for Peace: Patterns in Education* Anthony Weaver.

Brimax Books Ltd
4–5 Studlands Park Industrial Estate,
Exning Road, Newmarket, Suffolk CB8 7AU
☎0638 664611
Telex 817625 BRIMAX G   Fax 0638 665220

Managing Director *Patricia Gillette*

Old established publisher specialising in children's books. Some educational; reading books for young children up to the age of 13; board books for very young children. All fully coloured and illustrated. Now part of **Octopus**. Over 90 hardback titles in 1988. Unsolicited mss will be considered but would prefer to see synopses.
Royalties paid twice yearly.

Bristol Classical Press
226 North Street, Bristol BS3 1JD
☎0272 664093

Managing Director *T.A.G. Foss*
Approx Annual Turnover £180,000

Offshoot of Chapter & Verse Bookshops Ltd. FOUNDED 1977 to attempt to revive the study of classics in schools and colleges by producing cheap texts. *Publishes* academic and scholarly, archaeology, educational and textbooks, English literature, languages and linguistics, literature and criticism, philosophy, classics textbooks. 29 titles in 1988.

General Editor *John H. Betts* Unsolicited mss and synopses welcome.
Royalties paid annually.

The British Academy
20–21 Cornwall Terrace, London NW1 4QP
☎01–487 5966

Publications Officer *J.M.H. Rivington*
Approx Annual Turnover £90,000

FOUNDED 1901. The primary body for promoting scholarship in the humanities, the Academy publishes 10–15 titles a year, mostly in series of source material stemming from its own longstanding research projects. Main subjects include history, art and archaeology.

Series include *Auctores Britannici Medii Aevi; Early English Church Music; Oriental Documents; Records of Social and Economic His-*

tory. Unsolicited proposals are forwarded to the relevant project committees. 'The British Academy does not publish for profit; royalties are paid only when titles have covered their costs.'

Brown, Son, Ferguson Ltd
4–10 Darnley Street, Glasgow G41 2SP
☎041–429 1234

Chairman/Managing Director
T. Nigel Brown

FOUNDED 1850. First publication, March 1832. Specialises in nautical text books, both technical and non-technical. Also *publishes* Boy Scout and Girl Guide books, and Scottish one-act and three-act plays.

Unsolicited mss, synopses and ideas for books welcome.
Royalties paid annually.

Brown Watson (Leicester) Ltd
55A London Road, Leicester LE2 0PE
☎0533 545008
Telex 342678 BWL G   Fax 0533 555782

Managing Director *Michael B. McDonald*

FOUNDED 1982. Part of **Peter Haddock Ltd.** *Publishes* children's books. 80 'series' in 1986. Most books are commissioned and therefore unsolicited mss and synopses are not welcome.

Authors' Rating Children's books for the cheaper end of the market. Authors must work fast to make money.

Buchan & Enright Publishers Ltd
53 Fleet Street, London EC4Y 1BE
☎01–353 4401

Chairman *R.V. Rhodes James*
Joint Managing Directors *J.W. Buchan, Dominique Enright*

FOUNDED 1982 in a spare bedroom by two ex-**Cassell** editors. Planning to expand operations in the near future though not intending to be a big publishing house. *Publishes* biography, country pursuits, history and antiquarian, humour, military and war, sports and games. 7 titles in 1987.

Editors *J.W. Buchan and Dominique Enright.*
TITLES *Shooting From Scratch* Michael Paulet; *Mutiny* Lawrence James; *Never Such Innocence* ed. Martin Stephens; *Land Fit for Heroes?* Christopher Grayling; *These for Remembrance* John Buchan. Prefer to see synopses and ideas rather than unsolicited mss.
Royalties paid twice yearly.

Authors' Rating One of the recent outcrop of small publishers who have secured a good, strong foothold in the market.

Burke Publishing Co. Ltd
Pegasus House, 116–20 Golden Lane, London EC1Y 0TL
☎01–253 2145   Telex 975573 Burke G

Chairman *Harold K. Starke*
Managing Director *Naomi Galinski*

FOUNDED 1935 to publish general books and children's fiction and non-fiction. Reconstituted in 1960 to concentrate on education. *Publishes* children's books, educational and textbooks (all levels), medical, reference books and dictionaries, the latter under the imprint of a wholly-owned subsidiary, **Harold Starke Limited.** 30 titles in 1987.

Editorial Director *Naomi Galinski* TITLES *Headstart Books; Read for Fun; Sparklers; Animals and their Environment; Encyclopaedia of Psychoactive Drugs; World Leaders; Young Specialist; Wake Up to the World of Science.* Welcome unsolicited mss and

synopses/ideas but require return postage or s.a.e.
Royalties paid annually.

Authors' Rating Modest payer but open to ideas.

Graham Burn

28D High Street, Leighton Buzzard,
Beds LU7 7EA
☎0525 377963/376390
Telex 825562 Chacom G Burnpub
Fax 0525 382498

Publishes mainly for the overseas market. Current emphasis on total production services for other publishers.

Burns & Oates

See **Search Press Ltd**

Business Education Publishers

Leighton House, 17 Vine Place,
Sunderland, Tyne & Wear SR1 3NA
☎091–567 4963

Joint Managing Directors *P.M. Callaghan and T. Harrison*
Approx Annual Turnover £150,000

FOUNDED 1981. Currently expanding into further and higher education, computing and books for the Health Service. *Publishes* business education, economics, law. 3 titles in 1987.

TITLES *BTEC National Course Studies* Paul Callaghan, Tom Harrison and John Ellison; *Law for Housing Managers* Tom Harrison; *The Abbotsfield File* Paul Callaghan and John Ellison; *Computer Studies* (for BTEC National) Knott, Waites, Callaghan and Ellison; *Information Processing* (for BTEC National Information Processing Option Module) Knott and Waites; *Business Law* (for BTEC National Business Law Option Module) Ellison and

Bedingfield. Unsolicited mss and synopses welcome.
Royalties paid annually.

Businessmate

See **Richard Drew Ltd**

Butterworth & Co. Ltd

Borough Green,
nr Sevenoaks, Kent TN15 8PH
☎0732 884567
Telex 95678
Fax 0732 882108

Chairman *W. Gordon Graham*
Chief Executive *G.R.N. Cusworth*
Approx Annual Turnover £90 million

FOUNDED 1818 by Henry Butterworth. Now part of Reed International. By the turn of the century Butterworth was publishing many of the legal titles familiar today. The Bond family bought the company at that time, and added to its list such classics as *Halsbury's Laws of England* and *Encyclopaedia of Forms and Precedents*. Recent acquisitions include K.G. Saur, the Munich-based publisher, **John Wright** and Professional Books. *Publishes* legal, medical, scientific, technical, bibliographic books and journals. 267 titles in the UK in 1987.

DIVISIONS
British and Irish Legal *D.L. Summers* Located at 88 Kingsway, London WC2B 6AB Tel 01–405 6900. TITLES *All England Law Reports; Stones Justices Manual; Simon's Taxes;* plus full legal, tax, banking textbook lists. **Butterworth Scientific** *E.J. Newman and G. Burn* Located at Westbury House, Bury Street, Guildford, Surrey GU2 5AW Tel 0483 31261. TITLES *Operative Surgery; A History of British Architecture; General Anaesthesia.* **Focal Press** TITLES *Techniques of TV Production; Basic Photography.* **Bowker–Saur** *K.G. Saur, P.W. Woods and S. O'Neill* TITLES *Books in Print: Ulrich's International Periodicals Directory; British Library Catalogue; German Books in Print.* Also

recently bought the book titles of **Architectural Press**. Unsolicited mss welcome, but preliminary letter preferred. Synopses and ideas for books should be addressed to the relevant publishing director.

Royalties paid twice yearly. *Overseas associates* in Australia, Ireland, Malaysia, New Zealand, Singapore, Canada, USA.

Authors' Rating Shares with **Sweet & Maxwell** the highly profitable market for law books. But while classics like *Halsbury's Laws of England* ensure a sound base income, the scientific and medical lists are coming up fast and further expansion can be expected.

Byway Books

Unit 2, Tweedbank Craft Centre,
Haining Drive, Tweedbank,
Selkirkshire TD1 3RJ
☎0896 57869

Managing Director *W.F. Laughlan*

FOUNDED 1981. Small publishing house now concentrating on children's books. *Publishes* children's picture books in paperback series: *Byway Bairns*

TITLES *A Fury of Fairy Wind*; *Hi Johnnie*; *The Brownie*; *The Enchanted Boy* – all by Mollie Hunter. Prefer synopses to unsolicited mss. *Royalties* paid twice yearly.

Cadogan Books Ltd

16 Lower Marsh,
Waterloo, London SE1 7RJ
☎01–633 0525
Telex 917706   Fax 01–928 6539

Chairman *Tom Hempenstall*
Managing Director *Paula Levey*
Approx Annual Turnover £320,000

Part of Metal Bulletin plc. The company was once called Gentry Books, and published motor titles, anthologies and guide books. In 1985 they decided to concentrate solely on guide books. 15 titles in 1988.

Editorial Director *Rachel Fielding* TITLES *Cadogan Guides* Unsolicited mss not welcome; introductory letter and synopsis

essential. Unsolicited synopses/ideas for books welcome.
Royalties paid twice yearly.

John Calder (Publishers) Ltd

18 Brewer Street, London W1R 4AS
☎01–734 3786

Chairman and Managing Director
John Calder

A publishing company which has grown around the tastes and contacts of its proprietor/manager/editorial director John Calder, the iconoclast of the literary establishment. *Publishes* autobiography, biography, drama, fiction (literary), literary criticism, music, opera, poetry, politics, playscripts, sociology.

Editorial Head *John Calder*   TITLES include all Beckett's prose and poetry. AUTHORS William Burroughs; Marguerite Duras; P.J. Kavanagh; Alain Robbe-Grillet; Nathalie Sarraute; Claude Simon; Howard Barker (plays); ENO and ROH opera guides. No unsolicited mss. Synopses and ideas for books welcome. *Royalties* paid annually. *Overseas associates* Riverrun Press, New York.

Authors' Rating A brave publisher who has often ventured where others fear to tread. But the operation is of modest size and sometimes (as with late payments) gives the impression of being run on a shoestring.

University of California Press

15A Epsom Road, Guildford,
Surrey GU1 3JT
☎0483 68364   Fax 0483 301625

Director (in the USA) *James Clark*

Became part of The University Presses of Columbia and Princeton in June 1987. *Publishes* academic, art, Asian studies, scholarly. 210 titles in 1987. Editorial work carried out in the USA. It is very rare for unsolicited work to be published since most of the list is derived from the University of California.

Cambridge University Press

The Edinburgh Building, Shaftesbury Road, Cambridge CB2 2RU

☎0223 312393

Telex 817256   Fax 0223 315052

Chief Executive *Geoffrey A. Cass*
Managing Director (Publishing Division) *A.K. Wilson*
Approx Annual Turnover £50 million

The oldest press in the world, and part of Cambridge University. Recently the Press has diversified into reference publishing, ELT and software and expanded its activities in Australia and the USA. 1988 sees the establishment of a joint publishing imprint for reference titles with **W. & R. Chambers**. *Publishes* academic and educational for international English-language markets, at all levels from primary school to post-graduate. Also publishes bibles and academic journals. 900 titles in 1987.

DEPARTMENTS
Bibles *R. Coleman* **ELT** *A. du Plessis*
Humanities/Social Science *R.J. Mynott*
Journals *D. Forbes* **Schoolbooks** *R. Davidson* **Science** *S. Mitton*

Authors' Rating Smaller than its younger Oxford counterpart (no children's list, for example) but probably the best managed of all the academic presses.

Canongate Publishing Ltd

17 Jeffrey Street, Edinburgh EH1 1DR

☎031–557 5888

Telex 72165 Canpub   Fax 031–557 5665

Managing Director *Stephanie Wolfe Murray*
Approx Annual Turnover £200,000

FOUNDED 1973. Bought in 1987 by Musterlin Group plc, owners of **Phaidon Press**. 36 titles in 1987.

TITLES *The Quarry Wood* Nan Shepherd; *Imagined Corners* Willa Muir; *Consider the Lilies* Iain Crichton Smith; *The Story of My Boyhood and Youth* John Muir; *Island Landfall* Robert Louis Stevenson; *Land of Leal*

James Barte. Prefer to consider synopses rather than unsolicited mss.
Royalties paid twice yearly.

Authors' Rating One of the best of the small publishers. Especially good on children's books and Scottish literature. Marketing arm strengthened by link with Musterlin.

Jonathan Cape Ltd

32 Bedford Square, London WC1B 3EL

☎01–636 3344

Telex 299080 Cvbcse G   Fax 01–255 1620

Chairman *Tom Maschler*
Managing Director *Bing Taylor*

Taken over by **Random House** in May 1987, along with its partners **Bodley Head** and **Chatto**. *Publishes* academic and scholarly, archaeology, architecture and design, children's books, economics, fiction, fine art and art history, history and antiquarian, humour, illustrated and fine editions, literature and criticism, natural history, philosophy, poetry, politics and world affairs, psychology, reference books and dictionaries, sociology and anthropology, travel and topography. 100 titles in 1987.

Editorial Director *Frances Coady* TITLES Children's *Cyril of the Apes* Jonathan Gathorne-Hardy; *Kelpie* William Mayne; *Fred* Posy Simmonds; *Mathilda* Roald Dahl. Fiction *Love and Shadows* Isabel Allende; *Einstein's Monsters* Martin Amis; *Bluebeard's Egg* Margaret Atwood; *The Songlines* Bruce Chatwin; *A Sport of Nature* Nadine Gordimer; *The Counterlife* Philip Roth; *The Bonfire of the Vanities* Tom Wolfe; *Love in the Time of Cholera* Gabriel Garcia Marquez; *The Fifth Child* Doris Lessing. Non-fiction *Land of the Snow Lion* Elaine Brooke; *Greetings From the Fast Lane – 32 postcards for the Post-Modern World Chix Pix; Bob Dylan Lyrics 1962–1985; The Secrets of Service* Anthony Glees; *The Life of R.A. Butler* Anthony Howard; *Whale Nation* Heathcote Williams; *The Traveller's Guide to Malta and Gozo*. Will consider unsolicited mss for fiction and synopsis with sample chapters for non-fiction.
Royalties paid twice yearly.

Authors' Rating Trying hard to re-establish its identity as leading fiction publisher after the recent vicissitudes of ownership and control and the loss of key personnel. An encouraging initiative is the promotion of emerging talent as 'Gilt Edged New Writers'.

Carcanet Press Ltd
208 Corn Exchange Buildings,
Manchester M4 3BQ
☎061–834 8730

Chairman *Robert Gavron* (proprietor)
Managing Director *Michael Schmidt*

Carcanet has grown in 15 years from an undergraduate hobby into a substantial venture. Anglo-European in orientation, they are Manchester-based. Robert Gavron bought the company in 1983. *Publishes* academic, biography, educational and textbooks, fiction, memoirs, translations but mostly poetry. Success has led to tie-ins with **Grafton**. Some Carcanet titles now appear in Paladin editions, and **Grafton** has launched its own poetry list in association with Carcanet. 45 titles in 1987 (and 6 issues of P.N. Review).

Editorial Director *Michael Schmidt* **Fiction Editor** *Michael Freeman* AUTHORS John Ashbery, Edwin Morgan, Elizabeth Jennings, Iain Crichton Smith, Natalia Ginzburg, Stuart Hood, Leonardo Sciascia, Christine Brooke-Rose, Pier Paolo Pasolini.

Authors' Rating A small publisher of high repute. Strong on poetry. Described by *The Times* as the 'last serious publisher in this country to pay more attention to its books than its balance sheet'. The cosmopolitan touch comes from Michael Schmidt whose family emigrated from Saxony to Mexico; hence his claim to be the only Mexican in UK publishing.

Cardinal
See **Sphere Books Ltd**

Cargate Press
25 Marylebone Road, London NW1 5JR
☎01–935 2541

Part of the Methodist Church, Overseas Division. No longer publish books, but leaflets for use internally by the Methodist Church. Do not welcome unsolicited material.

Frank Cass
Gainsborough House,
11 Gainsborough Road, London E11 1RS
London E11 1RS
☎01–530 4226
Telex 987719   Fax 01–530 7795

Managing Director *Frank Cass*

Publishes Africa, development/strategic studies, education, history and antiquarian, literature, Middle East, politics and world affairs.

Editorial Head (books) *Margaret Goodare* TITLES *Dilemmas of Nuclear Strategy* ed. Roman Kolkowicz; *Looking Back on India* Hubert Evans; *From Fair Sex to Feminism* ed. Mangan and Park; *Studies in Public Enterprise* V. Ramanadham; *Wilfred Owen – Anthem for a Doomed Youth* Simcox; *The Best of Enemies – Israel and Trans-Jordan in the War of 1948* Uri R.B. Joseph; *Strategic and Operational Deception in the Second World War* ed. Michael I. Handel; *Media Diplomacy – The Foreign Office in the Mass Communication Age* Yoel Cohen; *An African Victorian Feminist: The Life and Times of Adelaide Smith Casely Hayford* Adelaide M. Cromwell. Although unsolicited mss will be considered, a synopsis with covering letter is preferred.

IMPRINT
Woburn Press *Margaret Goodare. Publishes* educational TITLES *The Study of Education* ed. Peter Gorden; *Educational Policy in England in the Twentieth Century* Peter Gorden, Richard Aldrich and Dennis Dean; *Special Needs in Ordinary Schools – A Teacher's Guide* Neville Jones; *Dictionary of British Educationist* ed. Richard Aldrich and Peter Gorden.
Royalties paid annually.

Cassell plc

Artillery House, Artillery Row,
London SW1P 1RT
☎01–222 7676
Telex 9413701 CASPUB G   Fax 01–799 1514

Chairman/Managing Director
Philip Sturrock
Approx Annual Turnover £10 million

FOUNDED 1848 by John Cassell; bought by
Collier Macmillan the same year, sold to CBS
Publishing Europe in 1982, and finally
achieved independence in 1986, as Cassell
plc. In its first year of operations, Cassell
acquired the book publishing division of
Tycooly Publishing Ltd and Link House
Books, which has been renamed as
Blandford Publishing Ltd. Part of Link
dealing with railway books sold to **Haynes** in
1987. Other imprints include **Arms &
Armour Press, Javelin, Geoffrey Chapman** and New Orchard Editions. *Publishes*
business, education, English language teaching, general non-fiction, primary and secondary school books, religious. 150 titles in
1987.

DIVISIONS
Blandford *John Newth*   TITLES *Animal Folk-
lore, Myth & Legend*. **Cassell Business and
Accounting** *Stephen Butcher*   TITLES *Man-
agerial Finance*. **Cassell Education** *Juliet
Wight-Boycott*   TITLE *Psychology and the
Teacher*. **Cassell ELT** *Simon Nugent*   TITLE
Exploring English. **Cassell Trade** *Barry
Holmes* TITLE *Brewer's Dictionary of Phrase
and Fable*. **Cassell Tycooly** *Francis
O'Kelly* TITLE *Industrial Water Use and
Treatment*. **Geoffrey Chapman** *Robert B.
Kelly* TITLE *Pope John XXIII*. **Wisley Hand-
books** *Barry Holmes*   TITLE *Plans for Small
Gardens*. Unsolicited mss welcome. Non-
fiction only. Synopses/ideas for books also
welcome.
Royalties payment depends on the title.

Authors' Rating A mixed bag of publishers
being given a new lease of life by strong management. Still to develop clear identity but
those who remember Cassell as a fiction pub-

lisher should be under no illusions. It is now
non-fiction all the way.

Godfrey Cave Associates Ltd

42 Bloomsbury Street, London WC1B 3QT
☎01–636 9177   Telex 266945

Managing Director *John Maxwell*
Deputy Managing Director
Geoffrey Howard

No new books. The list consists entirely of
reprints of illustrated books where rights
have reverted and the re-issue of out-of-print
titles. Fourteen of these were published in
1986. 50 titles in 1988.

Centaur Press Ltd

Fontwell, Arundel, Sussex BN18 0TA
☎024–368 3302

Chairman & Editorial Head
Jon Wynne-Tyson

FOUNDED 1954. A one-man outfit which adds
only 1–3 new titles a year to its list of biography, education, environment, literature,
philosophy, reference. No unsolicited mss.
Centaur is not currently seeking new books.

IMPRINT
Linden Press

Central Books Ltd

14 The Leathermarket, London SE1 3ER
☎01–407 5447

Managing Director *William Norris*
Approx Annual Turnover £1 million

FOUNDED 1939 principally as book distributors. Imports from Eastern Europe, USA and
West Germany, as well as distributing books
from small presses and originate some titles.
Publishes children's books, economics, history, politics, scientific and technical. 200
titles (mostly imported) in 1987.

Editorial Director *William Norris* As
(mainly) book importers they do not welcome unsolicited mss, but will consider
synopses and ideas.
Royalties paid annually.

Century Hutchinson Publishing Group Ltd

Brookmount House, 62–5 Chandos Place,
London WC2N 4NW
☎01–240 3411
Telex 261212 Litldn G   Fax 01–836 1409

Chairman *Anthony Cheetham*
Managing Director *Peter Roche*
Managing Director (Hardcover Division)
Piet Snyman

Publishes antiques and collecting, aviation, biography/autobiography, business and industry, children's books, cinema and video, computer software (business/entertainment), cookery, crime, crafts and hobbies, DIY, fashion and costume, fiction, fine art and art history, gardening, guide books, health and beauty, humour, illustrated and fine editions, magic and the occult, military and war, natural history, photography, poetry, politics and world affairs, reference books and dictionaries, sports and games, theatre and drama, travel and topography, wines and spirits. Bought Muller, Blond & White in 1987. 500 titles in 1987.

DIVISIONS
Arrow Books *Jane Wood* **Children's** *Caroline Roberts* **Fiction** *Rosemary Cheetham* **Hutchinson** *Richard Cohen* **Non-fiction** *Gail Rebuck* **Stanley Paul** *Roddy Bloomfield* **Reference** *Simon Littlewood* *Publishes* **Fiction** crime, general, horror and the occult, science fiction and fantasy, thriller/suspense, war, women's. **Non-fiction** astrology, biography/autobiography, general, health/self help, humour, poetry and anthologies, travel, true crime, war. **Children's books** 250 titles in 1987. **Frederick Muller** imprint recently revived to publish fiction, biography, humour, and general interest. **Barrie & Jenkins** (see separate entry).

IMPRINTS (Arrow Books)
Arena *Peter Lavery* *Publishes* international contemporary fiction. **Beaver** *Alison Berry* *Publishes* activities, children's paperbacks, humour, picture books.

Century Hutchinson welcome unsolicited mss and synopses/ideas for books.
Royalties paid twice yearly. *Overseas associates* Century Hutchinson Australia/New Zealand/South Africa.

Authors' Rating First prize for marketing. Best-sellers sell even better with Century Hutchinson. Some of those who remember the cosiness of an independent Hutchinson sigh for the good old days but most authors appreciate greater efficiency and stronger sales. **Arrow** paperbacks have moved down market; closer to **Star** or **Futura** than to **Penguin** or **Pan**. Generous on advances – for the right books – and prompt on royalty payments.

Ceolfrith Press

Northern Centre for Contemporary Art,
17 Grange Terrace, Sunderland,
Tyne & Wear SR2 7DF
☎091–514 1214

Sunderland Arts Centre was founded by Chris Carrell whose original connection with the arts was a second-hand-bookshop. Premises were obtained at Grange Terrace and development has led to a concentration on visual arts and crafts exhibitions. *Publishes* criticism, design, general, visual arts, visual poetry. 4 titles in 1987.

Editorial Director *Tony Knipe* Not particularly keen to receive unsolicited mss but will consider synopses.
Royalties paid twice yearly.

Chadwyck-Healey Ltd

Cambridge Place, Cambridge CB2 1NR
☎0223 311479   Telex 265871 MONREF G

Chairman *Sir Charles Chadwyck-Healey*
Approx Annual Turnover £1½ million

FOUNDED 1973. Chadwyck-Healey Inc., Washington DC followed the next year, and Chadwyck-Healey France in 1985. *Publishes* mainly on microform with a few reference works and guides for microform collections. Occasionally publishes monographs on fine t and architecture. Winner of a 1987 Queen's Award for Exports. 50 titles in 1987.

Editorial Head *Alison Moss* TITLES *The English Satirical Print; Theatre in Focus; Index of Manuscripts in The British Library; Government Documents; Bibliographies.* No unsolicited mss. Synopses and ideas for books welcome.
Royalties paid annually.

W & R Chambers

43–5 Annandale Street,
Edinburgh EH7 4AZ
☎031–557 4571
Telex 727967   Fax 031–557 2936

Chairman *A.S. Chambers*
Managing Director *W.G. Henderson*

The company was established in the early 1800s to publish self-education books, but soon diversified into dictionaries and other reference works. *Publishes* reference, school and college text books, Scottish non-fiction, self-help guides in medical, social, language subjects. 38 titles in 1987. Now commencing co-publication of major reference books in association with **Cambridge University Press.** Prefer synopsis accompanied by letter to unsolicited finished mss.

Editorial Director *R.S.R. Mair*
Royalties paid annually. *Overseas representation* by Cambridge University Press, among other agents/publishers.

Authors' Rating After a long period of sleep walking, Chambers is reviving under a new management team. The link up with **CUP** bodes well.

Chapman & Hall Limited

11 New Fetter Lane, London EC4P 4EE
☎01–583 9855
Telex 263398 ABPLDN G   Fax 01–583 0701

Managing Director *Paul Gardner*

FOUNDED 1830. Formerly part of Associated Book Publishers, now owned by International Thomson plc. Chapman & Hall embraces the old ABP companies, Chapman & Hall and **E. & F.N. Spon,** and has now been joined by **Van Nostrand Reinhold International.** *Publishes* scientific, technical and medical books. 200 titles in 1987.

Publishing Director *Phillip Read* Unsolicited mss and synopses in science, technology and medicine welcomed.
Royalties paid twice yearly.

Paul Chapman Publishing Ltd

144 Liverpool Road, London N1 1LA
☎01–609 5315

Managing Director *Paul R. Chapman*

FOUNDED October 1987 when Paul Chapman, formerly managing director of **Harper & Row Ltd** acquired their geography, business and management, educational and accountancy titles. Welcome unsolicited mss and synopses.
Royalties paid twice yearly.

Chappell Plays Ltd (formerly English Theatre Guild)

129 Park Street, London W1Y 3FA
☎01–629 7600
Telex 268403   Fax 01–499 9718

Managing Director *Jonathan Simon*

Part of the Chappell group which includes the literary agency of the same name (see *Agents*). *Publishes* theatre playscripts in paperback form

Editorial Head *Michael Callahan* TITLES *Crown Matrimonial* Royce Ryton; *Arsenic and Old Lace* Joseph Kesselring; *Not Now Darling* Ray Cooney and John Chapman; *Bouncers* John Godber; *Mumbo Jumbo* Robin Glendinning (winner of the Mobil Playwriting Competition); *The Light of Day* Graham Swannell; *Scales of Justice* Peter Saunders. Preliminary letter essential.
Royalties paid twice yearly.

Chatto & Windus Ltd/The Hogarth Press Ltd

30 Bedford Square, London WC1B 3RP
☎01–631 4434
Telex 299080 CVBCSE G   Fax 01–255 1620

Chairman *John Charlton*
Managing Director *Carmen Callil*

Taken over by **Random House Inc.**, New York in May 1987. Formerly part of the Chatto, Virago, Bodley Head and Jonathan Cape group. The original Chatto was founded in 1855, and took over The Hogarth Press, which had been founded by Leonard and Virginia Woolf, in 1946. The Hogarth Press was relaunched as a paperback imprint in 1984. *Publishes* academic and scholarly, archaeology, architecture and design, autobiography, business and industry, cookery, crime, fiction, fine art and art history, gardening, health and beauty, history and antiquarian, humour, illustrated and fine editions, literature and criticism, music, natural history, philosophy, photography, poetry, politics and world affairs, psychology, science fiction, sociology and anthropology, theatre and drama, travel and topography, women's studies. 104 titles in 1987.

IMPRINTS
Chatto & Windus Editorial Director *Robert Lancaster* **Consultant Director** *Andrew Motion* AUTHORS include Iris Murdoch; A.S. Byatt; Angela Carter; Timothy Mo; Blake Morrison; Michael Holroyd; Alan Hollinghurst; Marina Warner; Anthony Sher. **The Hogarth Press Ltd Editorial Director** *Rupert Lancaster* (Hardbacks) TITLES include works by Virginia Woolf, Sigmund Freud and others in the *International Psycho-Analytic Library*. **Editorial Director** *Christine Carswell* (paperbacks) Fiction, lives and letters, crime, travel, poetry, critics. Unsolicited mss, synopses and ideas for books welcome if sent with return postage.
Royalties paid twice yearly. *Overseas associates* Australasian Publishing Co., Sydney; Book Reps Ltd, New Zealand.

Authors' Rating Carmen Callil divides her time between Chatto, **Virago** (where she led a management buy-out) and **Channel Four**. An energetic lady who has been described as 'the hand grenade of British publishing', she made the publishing news story of the year with her £625,000 bid for Michael Holroyd's biography of G.B. Shaw. Her rivals suspect she may not get her money back but the investment will boost the Chatto reputation with other lead authors. Tuning in to a growing market the Chatto theatre list has been revamped to appeal to a general readership.

Chatto, Bodley Head, Cape (CBC)

32 Bedford Square, London WC1B 3EL
☎01–631 4434   Telex 299080 CVBCSE G

Parent organisation for three publishers who, together with their then other partner, **Virago**, came into a spot of trouble last year when their joint administration was publicly criticised by leading author Graham Greene. The crisis was resolved by **Random House** who came up with an attractive takeover bid while **Virago** staged a management buy-out. Simon Master, formerly managing director of **Pan**, was chosen to head the company. (See separate entries for **Chatto & Windus, The Bodley Head, Jonathan Cape.**)

Cherrytree Children's Books

See **Chivers Press (Publishers)**

University of Chicago Press Ltd

126 Buckingham Palace Road, London SW1W 9SA
☎01–730 9208
Telex 23933   Fax 01–730 8728

Chairman *N.C. Gosling*
Approximate Annual Turnover £2 million

The European office of the American-based company, **University of Chicago Press**, which acts as a distribution and marketing office, servicing not only the UK, but Europe, the Middle East, Africa and Asia. All the editorial decision-making machinery is in the USA. If a potential title does not have a significant market in the States it has little chance of even being considered. *Publishes* scholarly books in architecture, the arts, engineering and computers (MIT), humanities and sciences (Chicago/Harvard) and social sciences. 550 titles in 1987.

DIVISIONS
Chicago Press *Mrs P. Kaiserlian* (Chicago office) Chicago Press, 5801 Ellis Avenue, Chicago, Illinois 60637, USA. All enquiries to **Harvard University**, Cambridge, MA 02138, USA. **MIT Press** All enquiries to the Editorial Division of MIT Press, 55 Hayward Street, Cambs. MA 02142, USA. **The Brookings Institution**, a represented list as from January 1988, specialising in economics and foreign policy.

Chivers Press (Publishers)
Windsor Bridge Road, Bath, Avon BA2 3AX
☎0225 335336
Telex 444633   Fax 0225 310771

Chairman *G.M. Nutbrown*
Managing Director *Roger H. Lewis*

Part of The Gieves Group. Originally part of Cedric Chivers; known as Chivers Press since 1979. *Publishes* mainly reprints for libraries – biography and autobiography; children's books; crime; fiction; large-print editions, complete and unabridged; spoken word cassettes. Launching a new children's information book imprint in 1988. **Cherrytree Children's Books**. 750 titles in 1987.

IMPRINTS
Atlantic Large Print, Firecrest Books, Gunsmoke Westerns, Lythway Children's Large Print, Lythway Large Print, New Portway Facsimile Reprints, New Portway Large Print, Swift Children's Books, Cherrytree Children's Books, Windsor Large Print Cassette Imprints: **Chivers Audio Books, Chivers Children's Audio, Cavalcade Story Cassettes, Moonlight Romance** Do not consider mss or synopses as are con-

centrating on reprinting for the time being. *Royalties* paid twice yearly.

Churchill Livingstone
Robert Stevenson House, 1–3 Baxter's Place, Leith Walk, Edinburgh EH1 3AF
☎031–556 2424
Telex 727511   Fax 031–558 1278

Managing Director *Andrew Stevenson*

Part of the **Longman Group**. Founded in early 1970s from two originally private companies, E. & S. Livingstone and J. & A. Churchill, which had earlier become separate parts of **Longman**. *Publishes* medical and nursing books, medical journals. 147 titles in 1987.

Publishing Managers (books) *Timothy Horne, Mary Law, Peter Richardson*; (journals) *Sally Morris* Do not welcome unsolicited mss. Welcome synopses/ideas.
Royalties paid annually. *Overseas associate* Churchill Livingstone Inc., New York.

Authors' Rating The best of the medical publishers.

Churchman Publishing Ltd
117 Broomfield Avenue, Worthing, West Sussex BN14 7SF
☎0903 692430

Chairman and Managing Director
E. Peter Smith

Publishes religion and theology (ecumenical), travel, psychology, biography, history, social science and education.

IMPRINTS
The Lantern Press *E.P. Smith* **Landmark Books** *E.P. Smith* Unsolicited mss and synopses welcome in all non-fiction subjects. No fiction. Very little poetry.
Royalties paid annually. *Overseas associates* in Canada, Australia and New Zealand.

Authors' Rating A publisher dedicated to 'small is beautiful'. Mainly religious list but has been known to offer vanity deals. The usual warnings apply. Authors who are thinking of contributing to the cost of publication should take independent advice before signing up.

John Clare Books
106 Cheyne Walk, London SW1O 0JR
☎01–352 7521/7333

Proprietor *Bryan Breed*

FOUNDED 1979. Started with a wide general list and became increasingly specialised. Parent Company Interpress Features *Publishes* non-fiction with an educational bias, social education.

TITLES *Music Therapy* Juliet Alving; *Social Drama* Bert Amies. Prefer synopses and ideas for books within their specialist field.
Royalties paid twice yearly.

Clarendon Press
See Oxford University Press

T. & T. Clark Ltd
59 George Street, Edinburgh EH2 2LQ
☎031–225 4703
Telex 728134   Fax 031–662 4282

Chairman *David Ross Stewart*
Managing Director *Geoffrey Green*
Approx Annual Turnover £500,000

FOUNDED 1821. Acquired by **John Bartholomew & Son Ltd** in 1984. *Publishes* religion, theology, law, philosophy (all academic). 24 titles in 1987.

Editorial Head *Geoffrey Green* TITLES *Church Dogmatics* Karl Barth; *A Textbook of Christian Ethics* ed. Robin Gill; *Sources of Law, Legal Change and Ambiguity* Alan Watson. Unsolicited mss, synopses and ideas for books welcome.
Royalties paid annually.

Clematis Press Ltd
18 Old Church Street, Chelsea,
London SW3 5DQ
☎01–352 8755

Chairman & Managing Director
Clara Waters

Clematis Press act as distributors of imported books and have no editorial facilities. No unsolicited mss.

The Cleveland Press
1 Russell Chambers, Covent Garden,
London WC2E 8AA
☎01–240 9849

Managing Director *A.R. Powell*
Approx Annual Turnover £150,000

FOUNDED 1984. *Publishes* mostly railway histories. Also travel, historical, political.

TITLES *Down the Line* series; *Metro* series; *Settle to Carlisle, A Tribute* Welcome unsolicited mss and synopses.
Royalties paid annually.

Clio Press Ltd
55 St Thomas' Street, Oxford OX1 1JG
☎0865 250333
Telex 83103 CLIO G   Fax 0865 790358

Chairman and Managing Director
John Durrant
Approx Annual Turnover £2 million

Part of ABC-Clio Inc., Santa Barbara, California. FOUNDED 1971 in Oxford to publish academic reference works. Now also publishes art reference and large print titles for both children and the elderly, and unabridged talking books for a wide audience. *Publishes* social sciences and humanities; general fiction and non-fiction in large print. 87 titles in 1987.

DIVISIONS
Isis Large Print *V. Babington Smith* TITLES *Know Your Medicine; Charles and Diana.* **Windrush Large Print** *V. Babington*

Smith   TITLES *Charlie and the Chocolate Factory*. **Clio Press** *R.G. Neville*   TITLES *World Bibliographical Series*. **Art Bibliographies** *A.J. Sloggett* TITLES *Artbibliographies Modern* **Isis Audio Books** *John Durrant*   TITLES *Moontiger*.
Royalties paid twice yearly.

Clyde/Bartholomew

See **John Bartholomew & Son Ltd**

Frank Coleman Publishing

Maulden Road, Flitwick, Beds MK45 5BW
☎0525 712261
Telex 825115   Fax 0525 718205

Managing Director *Neil Goldman*
Approx Annual Turnover under £100,000

Publishes children's books. 6 titles in 1987. Set to double output in 1988. Unsolicited mss welcome. Synopses and ideas for books considered.
Royalties paid annually.

Colley-Moore International Publishers

14 Lyon Square, Tilehurst, Reading, Berks RG3 4DD
☎0734 417748/420329

Managing Director *Steve Colley-Moore*

A new lively company committed to the promotion of multi-culturalist ideals and the elimination of racist and sexist stereotypes in literature. *Publishes* children and young adults, educational, fiction, non-fiction, poetry, and plays (screen/TV/radio/stage). Particularly keen on new and first-time writers; Afro-Caribbean; women. Aims to publish 6 books annually.

Editor *Pauline Colley-Moore* TITLES *No Tears in Paradise*; *Consequences*; *The Great Moment*; *A Dejected Tomboy*. Unsolicited mss welcome. Also synopses and ideas for books; s.a.e. required.

Collins Publishers

8 Grafton Street, London W1X 3LA
☎01−493 7070
Telex 25611 Colins G   Fax 01−493 3061
PO Box, Glasgow G4 0NB
☎041−772 3200

Chairman *Ian Chapman*

Group Managing Director (Publishing)
J.C. Clement
Approx Annual Turnover £144 million

Collins' remarkable growth of the past six years continues in spectacular style. In 1987 the company grew by 12.6%. Publishing turnover was up 12.9% at £76.6 million with children's publishing now incorporated in a Children's Division, making the greatest advances. Hatchards, Collins' retail book chain, opened five new outlets and increased its sales by over 25% to £19.5 million. 1217 titles in 1987.

DIVISIONS
Collins General Division incorporating **Collins** (general hardbacks) **Collins Harvill** (see below) **Crime Club Fontana Paperbacks** (IMPRINTS **Fontana, Flamingo, Fontana Press**) *M. Chapman, C.O. O'Brien, Michael Fishwick* TITLES recent non-fiction *The Mountbatten Diaries, Vol. 1* Philip Ziegler; *Perestroika* Mikhail Gorbachev; *The Life of My Choice* Wilfred Thesiger; *The Profligate Duke* Mary Soames; *Travel Diaries of a Naturalist, Vol. 3* Sir Peter Scott. Recent fiction *Winter Hawk* Craig Thomas; *Cold New Dawn* Ian St James; *Weaveworld* Clive Barker; *Glittering Images* Susan Howatch; *Heaven and Hell* John Jakes. 427 titles in 1987.

Collins Children's Division *L. Davis, R. Sandberg* TITLES fiction *Little Grey Rabbit books; Paddington Bear*. Classics: *Narnia* stories; Noel Streatfeild novels. Non-fiction *Beginner* Books, nature, history, prehistoric world, hobbies, dictionaries and language; *Help Your Child* series. 433 titles in 1987.

IMPRINTS
Armada, Dinosaur Publications and **Dragon Books**

Collins Reference *A. Macfarlane* located at the Glasgow office   TITLES *Collins Dictionary & Thesaurus in One Volume; Collins Concise English Dictionary; Collins Reference Dictionaries* (Art & Artists; Biology; Computing; Classical Mythology; Economics; Electronics; Mathematics; Music; Quotations; Statistics); **Natural History** *Crispin Fishe* 433 titles in 1987.
Adlard Press sailing books only. **Bibles** *A. Watson* ELT *R. Thomas* **Collins Grafton** (see Grafton) **Collins Harvill** *Mark Crean* **Maps & Atlases** *D. Thompson* **Religion** *Ron Chopping* **Collins Special Interest Division** *J. Clibbon* 84 titles in 1987.

Authors' Rating Who can believe that just a few years ago, Collins was struggling to hold its balance? Now it delivers punches, from a position of great strength. The transformation has much to do with Ian Chapman's aggressive style of leadership but credit must also go to Rupert Murdoch who put the frighteners on the entire book publishing industry when he bought a substantial minority interest in Collins. Murdoch went on to buy **Harper & Row**, recruited Ian Chapman and friends to revive the sleepy giant and then sold half the company to Collins. This progression together with the success of the Collins-owned American publishing of the *Day in the Life of . . .* series (1.5 million copies sold so far) raises the prospect of rapid expansion on both sides of the Atlantic.

Columbia University Press

15A Epsom Road, Guildford,
Surrey GU1 3JT
☎0483 68364   Fax 0483 301625

Director (in the USA) *John Moore*

Distributor for New York University Press. Wide range of academic books, with slight emphasis on social sciences. 250 titles in 1987. Editorial department in the USA.

Columbus Books Ltd

19–23 Ludgate Hill, London EC4M 7PD
☎01–248 6444   Telex 28673 CONSOL G

Chairman *Eric Dobby*
Managing Director *Medwyn Hughes*
Approx Annual Turnover £3 million

FOUNDED 1980 as a subsidiary of Transatlantic Books Service Ltd. Taken over in 1985 by Stancroft Trust, the majority shareholder is **Harrap Ltd.** *Publishes* biography and autobiography, cinema and video, cookery, crafts and hobbies, guide books, health and beauty, photography, travel and topography, vocational training and careers, women's studies. 100 titles in 1987.

DIVISIONS
Columbus Books *Gill Rowley* TITLES *A Nice Girl Like Me* Gloria Lovatt; *Unholy Matrimony* Liz Hodgkinson; *A Leaf in the Wind* Peter Hudson; *Beauty Bound* Rita Freedman. **Harrap Columbus** *Medwyn Hughes* Welcome unsolicited mss and synopses/ideas for books.
Royalties paid twice yearly.

Comet

See **W.H. Allen & Co. plc**

Condor

See **Souvenir Press Ltd**

Constable & Co Ltd

10 Orange Street, London WC2H 7EG
☎01–930 0801   Telex 27950

Chairman & Managing Director *Benjamin Glazebrook*

In 1890 Archibald Constable founded the publishing company of Archibald Constable which then became Constable & Co. in 1909. Controlling interest bought by Benjamin Glazebrook in 1967 with a minority interest owned by **Hutchinson**. *Publishes* archaeology, architecture and design, biography and autobiography, cookery, fiction, guide books, history and antiquarian, natural history, psychology, sociology and anthropology, travel and topography, wines and spirits. 69 titles in 1987.

Editorial Director *Robin Baird Smith*
TITLES *A Far Cry From Kensington* Muriel
Spark; *Dublin, A Travellers' Companion* Thomas and Valerie Pakenham; *The Pursuit of Happiness* Peter Quennell; *A History of Parliament* Ronald Butt. Unsolicited mss and synopses/ideas for books welcome.
Royalties paid twice yearly.

Authors' Rating A major coup in attracting Muriel Spark from **Bodley Head**. Other eminent writers may soon be attracted by the personal style of management which emphasises the relationship between author and editor. Distinguished by paying to authors at least two thirds of income from the sale of paperback rights. The average is closer to 60%.

Contemporary Christian Studies
See **Marshall Pickering Holdings Ltd**

Corgi
See **Transworld Publishers Ltd**

Cornwall Books
See **Golden Cockerel Press Ltd**

Coronet
See **Hodder & Stoughton Ltd**

Costello
43 High Street, Tunbridge Wells,
Kent TN1 1XL
☎0892 45355   Fax 0892 34905

Chairman *Rosemary Costello*
Managing Director *David Costello*
Approx Annual Turnover £0.7 million

FOUNDED 1972 as agent for major US publishers. Began educational publishing in 1978 and general publishing in 1985. Commissions history, militaria, arts and crafts. 16 titles in 1987.

Arts and Crafts *Rosemary Costello* **History and Education** *Anne Cree* Unsolicited synopses and ideas for books welcome. 'We always reply quickly.'
Royalties more likely to be paid than fees.

Countryside Books
3 Catherine Road, Newbury,
Berks RG14 7NA
☎0635 43816

Publisher *Nicholas Battle*

FOUNDED 1978. *Publishes* mainly paperbacks on regional subjects, generally by county. Pictorial and local history and leisure. 27 new titles in 1987. Welcome unsolicited mss and synopses.
Royalties paid twice yearly.

Crescent Books
See **W.H. Allen & Co. plc**

Cressrelles Publishing Co. Ltd
311 Worcester Road, Malvern,
Worcs WR14 1AN
☎06845 65045

Managing Director *Leslie Smith*

Publishes general children's books. Own **Kenyon-Deane** who publish theatre and drama.

The Crowood Press
Crowood House, Ramsbury,
Marlborough, Wilts SN8 2EG
☎0672 20320
Telex 449703   Fax 0672 20134

Chairman/Managing Director *John Dennis*
Approx Annual Turnover £1 million

FOUNDED 1982 by John Dennis as a one-man concern, The Crowood Press has grown steadily to employ more than twenty people. *Publishes* sport and leisure including animal and land husbandry, climbing and mountaineering, country sports, equestrian, fishing and shooting. Branching out into cookery, gardening and health in 1988. 43 titles in 1987; 65 titles in 1988.

Editorial Head *Ken Hathaway* Preliminary letter preferred in all cases. Synopses and ideas for books welcome.
Royalties paid twice yearly for initial year, annually thereafter.

Crucible
See **Thorsons Publishing Group Ltd**

Curzon Press Ltd
42 Gray's Inn Road, London WC1
☎01–242 8310

Managing Director *John F. Standish*

Scholarly and specialised publishing house with imprints on Asian and African studies. *Publishes* academic and scholarly, archaeology, history and antiquarian, languages and linguistics, Oriental and African studies, philosophy, religion and theology, sociology and anthropology. 16 titles in 1987. Unsolicited mss considered.
Royalties according to contract.

Dalesman Publishing Co. Ltd
Clapham, Lancaster LA2 8EB
☎04685 225

Managing Director *Dennis Bullock*

Also publishers of the famous country magazine of the same name. *Publishes* crafts and hobbies, geography and geology, guide books, history and antiquarian, humour, transport, travel and topography. 24 titles in 1987.

Editorial Director *David Joy* Unsolicited mss considered in all subjects.
Royalties paid twice yearly.

Darf Publishers Ltd
50 Hans Crescent, London SW1X 0NA
☎01–581 1805

Chairman *M.Fergiani*
Managing Director *M.B. Fergiani*
Approx Annual Turnover £500,000

Formed in 1982 to publish and republish books on the Middle East, theology and travel. Strong emphasis on students' books. *Publishes* geography, history, language, literature, oriental, politics, theology, travel. 50 titles in 1986.

Editorial Head *M. Fergiani*   TITLES *The Historical Geography of Arabia, vols. 1 & 2; Let's Learn Arabic; Spoken Arabic: Self Taught; The Life of Mahomet; Carthage and her Remains.* Unsolicited mss, synopses and ideas for books welcome.
Royalties paid twice yearly. *Overseas associates* Dar Al-Fergiani, Cairo and Tripoli.

Darton, Longman & Todd Ltd
89 Lillie Road, London SW6 1UD
☎01–385 2341

Chairman *Derek Stevens* (non-executive)
Managing Director *Christopher Ward*
Approx Annual Turnover £750,000

Founded by Michael Longman, who broke away from Longman Green in 1959 when that publisher decided to stop its religious list. First major publication was the *Jerusalem Bible*. The company is in the process of becoming a common ownership business. *Publishes* Christian books of all types. 40 titles in 1987.

Editorial Director *Miss L.J. Riddle*   BEST SELLING TITLES *Jerusalem Bible; New Jerusalem Bible; God of Surprises.* Unsolicited mss, synopses and ideas for books welcome.
Royalties paid twice yearly.

David & Charles Ltd
Brunel House, Forde Road, Newton Abbott, Devon TQ12 4PU
☎0626 61121
Telex 42904 BOOKS G   Fax 0626 64463

Chairman *David St John Thomas*
Approx Annual Turnover £10.4 million

FOUNDED 1960 as a specialist company. Still family controlled. Major subsidiary the Readers' Union Book Clubs for Enthusiasts. *Publishes* practical: crafts, gardening, military, hobbies, travel, wide-ranging non-fiction. No fiction, poetry, memoirs or children's. 150 titles in 1987.

Editorial Head *Michael de Luca* TITLES *Knitting in Vogue; Sunday Times Travel Book; Great Days of the Country Railway; Complete Book of Microwave Cookery; Passion for Cats; Cool's Out; Jean Greenhowe's Bazaar Bestsellers.* Unsolicited mss, synopses and ideas welcome. *Authors' Guide* available on receipt of a first class stamp.
Royalties paid annually; twice yearly in first two years on request.

Authors' Rating No longer the high flyer but strong in leisure and hobby books. Can be tough on payments. Run like a cottage industry – but on a large scale. Readers' Union is among the leading non-fiction book clubs.

Christopher Davies Publishers Limited

PO Box 403, Sketty,
Swansea, West Glamorgan SA2 9BE
☎0792 48825

Managing Director *Christopher T. Davies*
Approx Annual Turnover £100,000

FOUNDED 1949 to increase the output of Welsh language publications. By the 1970s this had reached the level of over 50 titles a year. The drop in Welsh sales in that decade led to the establishment of a small English list, which has continued. The company now publishes around 6 Welsh language titles and 12 English titles annually. *Publishes* biography, cookery, fiction, general sport, history and literature. 4 Welsh language and 7 English titles in 1987.

Editorial Head *Christopher Davies* TITLES *English/Welsh Dictionaries; Wild Mushrooms;*

Minutes of Time; Rugby Wales '88; Castles of the Welsh Princes Paul R. Davies; *John Morgan's Wales.* Unsolicited mss welcome only if relevant to their field. Synopses and ideas for books welcome.
Royalties paid twice yearly.

Authors' Rating A favourite for Celtic readers. Plans are in hand to beef up marketing and promotion.

Debrett's Peerage Ltd

73–7 Britannia Road, London SW6 2JR
☎01–736 6524/6   Fax 01–731 7768

Chairman *Ian McCorquodale*
Managing Director *Geoffrey Fox*

FOUNDED 1769. Main publication *Debrett's Peerage* every five years and *Debrett's Distinguished People of Today* annually. *Publishes* books on sporting subjects, etiquette, modern manners and correct form, royalty. 5 titles in 1987.

Publishing Manager *Kitty Hunter* Welcome unsolicited mss and synopses.
Royalties paid twice yearly.

Dennys Publications Ltd

2 Carthusian Street, London EC1M 6ED
☎01–253 5421

Chairman *P.P. Maher*

FOUNDED 1976. Part of the Dennys Group. *Publishes* academic books.

Editorial Director *A. Maher* TITLES *The Handbook of Mathematical Formulae For Scientists and Engineers* Welcome unsolicited mss and synopses.
Royalty payments vary from contract to contract.

Dent Children's Books
See Weidenfeld & Nicolson Ltd

Dent General & Everyman
See Weidenfeld & Nicolson Ltd

André Deutsch Ltd

105–6 Great Russell Street,
London WC1B 3LJ
☎01–580 2746
Telex 261026 Adlib G   Fax 01–631 3253

Joint Chairman *André Deutsch*
**Joint Chairman & Sole Managing
Director** *T.G. Rosenthal*

FOUNDED 1950 by André Deutsch, the original list included *Books are Essential, To Live In Mankind* and *Jewish Cookery*. A major fiction list followed, with writers like V.S. Naipaul, Philip Roth and Norman Mailer. *Publishes* adult fiction, art illustrated, children's picture books, fiction and non-fiction, general books (particularly biography, current affairs, history, politics), photographic. 120 titles in 1987.

DIVISIONS
Adult books (and submissions) *Esther Whitby* AUTHORS John Updike, Paul Erdman, Penelope Lively, Carlos Fuentes, William Gaddis, Gore Vidal, Dan Jacobson, Gerald Priestland, Malcolm Bradbury, Dale Spender, Julian Critchley. **Children's books** (and submissions) *Pam Royds* TITLES *Postman Pat; You're Thinking about Doughnuts; Different Friends; The Tooth Ball; The Story of a High Street; House Inside Out*. Unsolicited mss, synopses and ideas for books welcome. *Royalties* paid twice yearly.

Authors' Rating One of the last of the distinguished independents to resist takeover. Supported for years on André Deutsch's favourite maxims – low overheads and minimum borrowing – the company was given a new lease of life when Tom Rosenthal came over from **Heinemann**. Celebrated writers one and all. A fine children's list.

Dinosaur Publications

See Collins Publishers

Dobson Books Ltd

Brancepeth Castle, Durham DH7 8DF
☎0385 780628

Managing Director *Margaret Dobson*

Stopped publishing books two or three years ago and at present have no plans to recommence publishing.

Dolphin Book Co. Ltd

Tredwr, Llangrannog, Llandysul,
Dyfed SA44 6BA
☎023978 404

Managing Director *Martin L. Gili*
Approx Annual Turnover £5000

FOUNDED 1957. A small publishing house specialising in Spanish and South American academic books. No publications in 1987, 2 titles forecast for 1988.   TITLE *Mediaeval and Renaissance Studies in Honour of Robert Brian Tate* Ian Michael and Richard A. Cardwell. Unsolicited mss not welcome. First approach by letter.
Royalties paid annually.

John Donald Publishers Ltd

138 St Stephen Street, Edinburgh EH3 5AA
☎031–225 1146

Managing Director *Donald Morrison*

Publishes academic and scholarly, agriculture, archaeology, architecture and design, business and industry, economics, educational and textbooks, guide books, history and antiquarian, languages and linguistics, military, music, religious, sociology and anthropology, sports and games, transport. 30 titles in 1987.

Editorial Director *John Tuckwell* Unsolicited mss considered.
Royalties paid annually.

Dorling Kindersley Ltd

9 Henrietta Street, London WC2E 8PS
☎01–240 5151   Telex 8954527 Deekay G

Chairman *Peter Kindersley*
Deputy Chairman *Peter Davis*

FOUNDED 1974. Packagers for the international market and publishers in the UK.

Publishes illustrated non-fiction on subjects such as cookery, gardening, health. Average 50 titles annually.

Editorial Director *Alan Buckingham* TITLES *Baby Care* and *Pregnancy and Birth Book*, both by Miriam Stoppard; *The Complete Book of Dried Flowers* Malcolm Hillier and Colin Hilton. Welcome unsolicited synopses and ideas for books.

Dragon Books
See Collins Publishers

Richard Drew Ltd
6 Clairmont Gardens, Glasgow G3 7LW
☎041–333 9341   Telex 777308

Managing Director *Richard Drew*

Publishes fiction, general non-fiction, travel, children's books, Scottish books. Approximately 30 titles in 1987.

Editorial Head *Richard Drew*

IMPRINTS (Paperback & Hardback) **Businessmate** French and German **The Scottish Collection** TITLES *The Lost Glen* Neil Gunn; *The Bull Calves* Naomi Mitchison. **Swallows** TITLES *The Flute in Mayferry Street* Eileen Dunlop; *The White Nights of St Petersburg* Geoffrey Trease. **Travelmate** French and Italian. Welcome unsolicited mss and synopses/ideas for books.
Royalties paid twice yearly.

Dryad Press
See B.T. Batsford Ltd

Gerald Duckworth & Co. Ltd
The Old Piano Factory,
43 Gloucester Crescent,
London NW1 7DY
☎01–485 3484

Managing Director *Colin Haycraft*

FOUNDED 1898. Authors on their early list included Hilaire Belloc, August Strindberg,

Henry James and John Galsworthy. *Publishes* mainly academic with some fiction. Approximately 60 titles in 1987.

Editorial Head *Colin Haycraft* TITLES *Wittgenstein, A Life* Brian McGuinness; *East End 1888* W.J. Fishman; *Language Logic and Experience* Michael Luntley; *Matters, Space and Motion* Richard Sorabji; *Moving Pictures* Judy Carver; *Archaeology Explained* Keith Brannigan.

PAPERBACK IMPRINT
Paperduck Welcome unsolicited mss and synopses/ideas for books.
Royalties paid twice yearly.

Authors' Rating Colin Haycraft believes in a business relationship with authors which excludes third parties. As he puts it, 'If you can't cope with life, write about it; if you can't write, publish; if you can't get a job in publishing, become a literary agent; if you are a failed literary agent – God help you'.

The Dunrod Press
8 Brown's Road, Newtonabbey,
Co. Antrim BT36 8RN
☎02313 2362

Managing Director *Ken Lindsay*

FOUNDED 1979. *Publishes* children's books, politics and world affairs. 4 titles in 1987.

Editorial Head *Ken Lindsay* Preliminary letter essential. Synopses and ideas for books welcome.
Royalties paid annually. *Overseas associates* The Dunrod Press, Irish Republic.

E.P. Publishing
See A. & C. Black (Publishers) Ltd

Ebury Press
Coloquhoun House, 27–37 Broadwick Street, London W1V 1FR
☎01–439 7144
Telex 263879 NATMAG G Fax 01–439 0062

Publishing Director *Charles Merullo*
Approx Annual Turnover £4.5 million

The book-publishing division of National Magazine Company, publishers of *Harpers & Queen, Cosmopolitan, She, Country Living, Company* and other leading magazines. Ebury is a part of the Hearst Corporation and as such is associated with **William Morrow Co.** and **Avon** in the United States. *Publishes* illustrated reference books in subject areas ranging from biography to cookery, crafts, homecraft, humour and photography. 60 titles in 1987.

Editorial Director *Yvonne McFarlan* Unsolicited mss, synopses and ideas for books welcome.
Royalties paid twice yearly.

Economist Publications Ltd
40 Duke Street, London W1M 5DG
📞01–493 6711
Telex 266353   Fax 01–499 9767

Managing Director *Hugo Meynell*
Approx Annual Turnover £560,000

Owned by *The Economist*. *Publishes* business and finance, economics, educational and textbooks, guide books, politics and world affairs, reference books. 12 titles in 1987.

Editorial Director *Sarah Child* Unsolicited mss considered.
Royalties paid twice yearly.

Authors' Rating Powerful marketing via *The Economist* distribution network. Strong on direct sales.

Edinburgh University Press
22 George Square, Edinburgh EH8 9LT
📞031–667 1011
Telex 727442 Unived   Fax 031–667 7938

Publishes academic and scholarly, biology and zoology, computer science, history, Islamic studies, law, linguistics, literary criticism, philosophy, physics, social sciences. 20 titles in 1987. Would prefer to be approached

with a letter or synopsis rather than unsolicited mss.
Royalties paid annually.

Authors' Rating One of the smaller university publishers drawing mainly on local talent.

Element Books Ltd
The Old School House, The Courtyard, Bell Street, Shaftesbury, Dorset SP7 8BP
📞0747 51448   Fax 0747 51394

Chairman/Managing Director
Michael Mann
Approx Annual Turnover £2 million

FOUNDED 1978 by John Moore and Michael Mann. Publish 40 of their own titles annually, and in addition represent and distribute for over 60 publishers from the UK, USA, Australia and Europe, bringing the present list to over 700 titles. An increase of new titles to around 60 per year is anticipated. 15 titles in 1987. *Publishes* art, astrology, complementary medicine and therapies, esoteric traditions, mysticism, philosophy, psychology and religion.

DIVISIONS
Broadcast Books Ltd *Laura Sanderson*
Element Books Ltd *Michael Mann*

Senior Commissioning Editor
Simon Franklin
Royalties paid twice yearly.

Elliot Right Way Books
Kingswood Buildings, Lower Kingswood, Tadworth, Surrey KT20 6TD
📞0737 832202

Joint Managing Directors *Clive Elliot, Malcolm G. Elliot*

FOUNDED 1946 by Andrew G. Elliot. All the early books were entitled *The Right Way to ...*, but this format became too restrictive. However, most books are still *How to* titles, instruction books illustrated with line drawings, published in **Paperfronts**. *Publishes*

How to books on car repairs, cooking, DIY, family financial and legal matters, family health and fitness, fishing, looking after pets and horses, motoring, popular education, puzzles and jokes, quizzes. 13 titles in 1987.

IMPRINT
Paperfronts *Clive Elliot* Unsolicited mss, synopses and ideas for books welcome.
Royalties paid annually.

Aidan Ellis Publishing Ltd
Cobb House, Nuffield, Henley-on-Thames, Oxon RG9 5RT
☎0491 641496

Chairman *Lucinda Ellis*
Managing Director *Aidan Ellis*
Approx Annual Turnover £250,000

Publishes fiction and general trade books. 14 titles in 1987.

Editorial Heads *Aidan Ellis, Lucinda Ellis*
Unsolicited mss, synopses and ideas for books welcome.
Royalties paid twice yearly.

Elm Tree Books
See **Hamish Hamilton Ltd**

Elsevier Applied Science Publishers
Crown House, Linton Road, Barking, Essex IG11 8JU
☎01–594 7272   Fax 01–594 5942

Managing Director *Hans Gieskes*
Parent company *Elsevier Science Publishers, Amsterdam*

Robert Maxwell (BPCC) bought minority stake in 1987. *Publishes* scientific and technical books. 117 titles in 1987.

DIVISIONS
Applied Biosciences *Norman Paskin*
Applied Sciences *Robert Lomax* Welcome unsolicited mss and synopses/ideas for books.
Royalties paid annually.

Authors' Rating An offshoot of the second largest Dutch publisher. Refreshingly open with authors in the tradition of northern European publishers – early news on print-runs and sales and royalties paid promptly.

Elvendon Press
The Old Surgery, High Street, Goring on Thames, Reading RG8 9AW
☎0491 873003
Telex 849021   Fax 0491 32468

FOUNDED 1978. *Publishes* cookery, drink, food and nutrition, but is branching out into other areas and will consider all general subjects except fiction. Also expanding its packaging operation. 10 titles in 1986.

Editorial Head *Mr R. Hurst* No unsolicited mss. Preliminary letter essential. Synopses and ideas for books welcome.

Enitharmon Press
22 Huntingdon Road, East Finchley, London N2 9DU
☎01–883 8764

Chairman/Managing Director *Alan Clodd*

A one-man publishing house, FOUNDED 1969. *Publishes* poetry and literature.

TITLES *Selected Poems* Frances Bellerby; *Selected Stories* Frances Bellerby.
Do not welcome unsolicited mss or synopses.
Royalty payments vary according to contract.

Epworth Press
Room 195, 1 Central Buildings, Westminster, London SW1H 9NR
☎01–222 8010 ext. 234

Chairman *John Stacey*

Publishes humour, philosophy, religion and theology. 12 titles in 1987.

Editorial Director *John Stacey* TITLES *A History of the Methodist Church in Great*

Britain Ruper Davies, A. Raymond, George and Gordon Rupp; *What Methodists Believe* Rupert Davies; *Charles Wesley's Verse* Frank Baker. Unsolicited mss considered.
Royalties paid annually.

Evans Brothers Ltd
2a Portman Mansions, Chiltern Street,
London W1M 1LE
☎01–935 7160
Telex 8811713 EVBOOK G   Fax 01–487 5034

Managing Director *Stephen Pawley*
Approx Annual Turnover £2 million

FOUNDED 1908 by Robert and Edward Evans. Originally published educational journals, books for primary schools and teacher education. But after rapid expansion into popular fiction and drama, both lists were sacrificed to a major programme of educational books for schools in East and West Africa. A new UK programme launched in 1986. *Publishes* UK children's and educational books, adult travel, educational books for Africa, Caribbean and Far East. 25 titles in 1986.

DIVISIONS
Overseas *F.J. Austin* TITLES *Effective English for Junior/Secondary Schools.* **UK Publishing** *F.J. Austin* TITLES *Ready Steady Go; Foundations of Geography; Kenya – A Visitor's Guide.* Unsolicited mss, synopses and ideas for books welcome.
Royalties paid annually. *Overseas associates* Kenya, Cameroon, Sierra Leone, Hong Kong & Pacific, Evans Bros (Nigeria Publishers) Ltd.

Authors' Rating A company which has suffered more than most from the vagaries of African currencies. From being one of the leaders in educational publishing in the 1960s, Evans all but disappeared in the late 1970s. Now well on its way on the long haul back to prosperity but publishing mostly for overseas education.

University of Exeter Publications
Publications Office, Reed Hall,
Streatham Drive, Exeter EX4 4QR
☎0392 263061   Telex 42894

Publications Officer *Mrs B.V. Mennell*

FORMED 1956 as a publisher of scholarly books for members of staff and research students. *Publishes* academic books. 17 titles in 1987. Do not welcome unsolicited mss as the University only publishes works by members of staff and present or former research students.
No royalties paid.

Exley Publications
16 Chalk Hill, Watford, Herts WD1 4BN
☎0923 48328/50505

Managing Director *Richard Exley*

FOUNDED 1976. *Publishes* general non-fiction, gift books, humour. Has a very substantial children's non-fiction list. 14 titles in 1987.

Editorial Director *Helen Exley* Do not welcome unsolicited mss but will consider synopses if accompanied by s.a.e.

Eyre & Spottiswoode (Publishers) Ltd
North Way, Andover, Hants SP10 5BE
☎0264 332424

Managing Director *A. Holder*

Part of the **Octopus Group Ltd** *Publishes* bibles, prayer books and religious books. No unsolicited mss. Will consider synopses and ideas for books.
Royalties paid twice yearly.

Faber & Faber Ltd
3 Queen Street, London WC1N 3AU
☎01–278 6881   Telex 299633 Faber G

Chairman & Managing Director
Matthew Evans

Geoffrey Faber and Richard de la Mare founded the company in the 1920s, with T.S. Eliot as an early recruit to the board. The original list was based on contemporary poetry and plays (the distinguished backlist includes

Eliot, Auden and MacNeice). *Publishes*, in addition to poetry and drama, art books, a children's list, fiction, nursing and medical, music, specialist cookery, and a growing number of miscellaneous one-offs. The new blood of recent years including Pete Townshend (of *The Who* fame) has led to Faber looking to new areas, though it remains in most respects deeply conservative, with hotspots of street-credibility.

Art *Giles de la Mare* **Children's** *Phyllis Hunt* AUTHORS Gene Kemp, Helen Cresswell, Errol le Cain. **Cookery** *Rosemary Goad* Specialist titles only: *The Vegan Cookbook*; *The Student Cookbook*. **Fiction** *Robert McCrum* AUTHORS P.D. James, Lawrence Durrell, William Golding, Milan Kundera, Mario Vargas Llosa, Caryl Phillips, Rachel Ingalls. **Music** *Patrick Carnegy* **Nursing & Medical** *Paddy Downie* Specialist titles and popular books, e.g. physiotherapy, general health. **Plays** *Frank Pike* AUTHORS Samuel Beckett, David Hare, Sam Shepard, Tom Stoppard. **Poetry** *Craig Raine, Chris Reid* AUTHORS Seamus Heaney, Douglas Dunn, Tom Paulin. TITLES include the *Hard Lines* anthology of street poetry. **Others** *Will Silkin* TITLES *Tooth and Claw – Inside Spitting Image*; *The Hip-Hipsters, Jazz and the Beat Generation*; *Sex, Drink, and Fast Cars*. Unsolicited mss will be considered; synopses and ideas for books welcome. *Royalties* paid twice yearly. *Overseas offices*: Boston.

Authors' Rating Applause for one of the original signatories of the Minimum Terms Agreement (MTA). Heavily dependent on its dealings with the literary establishment, Faber is trying to liven up its image with bright, distinctive book jackets and a new logo. But new ideas are still thin on the list. Poetry accounts for one sixth of total turnover.

Falling Wall Press Ltd
75 West Street, Old Market,
Bristol, Avon BS2 0BX
☎0272 559230

Managing Director *Jeremy Mulford*

FOUNDED 1971. *Publishes* autobiography, biography, history, non-fiction, politics.

Editorial Director *Jeremy Mulford* TITLES *The Disinherited Family* Eleanor Rathbone (with introductory essay by Suzie Fleming); *Wonderful Adventures of Mrs. Seacole in Many Lands*; *Black Women and the Peace Movement* Wilmette Brown; *Ask Any Woman – A London Enquiry into Rape and Sexual Assault*.

IMPRINT
Loxwood Stoneleigh *Publishes* high quality new fiction and poetry. Prefer to see synopses and ideas for books, plus s.a.e. *Royalties* paid twice yearly for the first year and then annually.

Falmer Press
Rankine Road, Basingstoke,
Hants RG24 0PR
☎0256 840366   Telex 858540

Managing Director *Malcolm Clarkson*

Publishes educational: books about education, educational materials for all levels. Largely commissioned.

Editorial Director *Malcolm Clarkson* Unsolicited mss considered. *Royalties* paid annually.

Firecrest Books
See **Chivers Press (Publishers)**

Floris Books
21 Napier Road, Edinburgh EH10 5AZ
☎031–337 2372

Managing Director *Christian Maclean*
Approx Annual Turnover £150,000

Trading since 1977, Floris Books publishes books related to the Steiner movement including arts & crafts, children's, the Christian Community, history, religious, science, social questions. 20 titles in 1987.

Editorial Head *Michael Jones*

IMPRINT
Floris Classics *Michael Jones* No unsolicited mss. Unsolicited synopses and ideas for books welcome.
Royalties paid annually.

Fontana
See **Collins Publishers**

G.T. Foulis & Co Ltd
See **Haynes Publishing Group**

Fountain Press Ltd
45 The Broadway, Tolworth,
Surrey KT6 7DW
☎ 01–390 7768   Telex 4107

Managing Director *Mr H.M. Ricketts*
Approx Annual Turnover £1 million

FOUNDED 1923 when it was part of the Rowntree Trust Group. Owned by the British Electric Traction Group until four years ago when it was bought out by the present Managing Director. *Publishes* architecture and design, British history, children's books, crafts and hobbies, do-it-yourself, medical, photography, veterinary.

TITLE *Photography Year Book*. Unsolicited mss and synopses are welcome.
Royalties paid twice yearly.

Fourth Estate Ltd
Classic House, 113 Westbourne Grove,
London W2 4UP
☎ 01–727 8993   Fax 01–727 9840

Chairman/Managing Director
Victoria Barnsley
Approx Annual Turnover £200,000

FOUNDED 1984. Independent publishers with strong emphasis on literary fiction and well-designed upmarket non-fiction. Emphasis on high media profile books and design. Winner of 1987 **David Higham Prize** for The Best First Novel with the first novel they published – Adam Zameenzad's *The 13th House*. *Publishes* current affairs, design, fiction, gardening, humanities, humour, popular culture, reference (hardback and trade paperback). 17 titles in 1987. Plan to be publishing approximately 30 titles a year by 1989.

DIVISIONS
Fiction *Giles O'Bryen* TITLES *The 13th House* Adam Zameenzad; *Milk Sulphate and Alby Starvation* Martin Millar. **Non-fiction** *Victoria Barnsley* TITLES *Waugh on Wine* Auberon Waugh; *Talking Horses* Jeffrey Bernard; *Shakespeare's Lost Play* Eric Sams. Unsolicited mss, synopses and ideas for books welcome.
Royalties paid twice yearly.

Author's Rating Awarded *The Sunday Times* accolade of 'best small publisher of 1987', the judges praised Fourth Estate for its 'freshness and originality'. Greatest coup has been to extract a book from Jeffrey Bernard. 'All we did was sit an editor next to him on a bar stool with a recorder and let him work his way through three months of vodka and tonics.'

W.H. Freeman & Co. Ltd
20 Beaumont Street, Oxford OX1 2NQ
☎ 0865 726975   Telex 83677

President *Linda Chaput* (New York Office)
Managing Director *Graham Voaden*
(Oxford)

Part of W.H. Freeman & Co., USA. *Publishes* academic, agriculture, animal care and breeding, archaeology, artificial intelligence, biochemistry, biology and zoology, chemistry, computer science, economics, educational and textbooks, engineering, geography and geology, mathematics and statistics, medical, natural history, neuroscience, paleontology, physics, politics and world affairs, psychology, *Scientific American Library*, sociology and anthropology, veterinary. 50 titles in 1987 (both UK and USA).

Editorial office in New York (Oxford is a sales and marketing office only), but unsolicited mss can go through *Graham Voaden*, who filters out the obviously unsuitable and passes the rest on to America.
Royalties paid annually.

Freeway
See **Transworld Publishers Ltd**

Samuel French Ltd
52 Fitzroy Street, London W1P 6JR
☎01–387 9373

Chairman *M.A. Van Nostrand*
Managing Director *John L. Hughes*

FOUNDED 1830 with the object of acquiring acting rights and publishing plays. Part of Samuel French Inc., New York. *Publishes* plays only. 50 titles in 1987.
Unsolicited mss welcome and should be addressed to The Performing Rights Department. No synopses or ideas.
Royalties paid twice yearly.

Authors' Rating Unlike some drama publishers who limit themselves to critically approved plays, Samuel French takes a more liberal view of what makes a publishable text. A boon to playwrights and amateur dramatic societies alike.

Futura Publications
See **Macdonald & Co. Ltd**

Geographia
See **John Bartholomew & Son Ltd**

Ginn & Company Ltd
Prebendal House, Parson's Fee,
Aylesbury, Bucks HP20 2QZ
☎0296 88411
Telex 83535 GINN G   Fax 0296 25487

Chairman *Nicholas Thompson*
Managing Director *William Shepherd*

Part of the Educational and Professional Division of **Octopus Publishing Group**. Though started in Boston, USA, in 1867, Ginn now has no US connections. *Publishes* educational books for primary school and home use. 800 titles in 1987.

Editorial Director *Olga Norris* Almost all titles are commissioned and unsolicited mss are generally not considered. Synopses and ideas for books are welcome largely as a means of introduction to potential authors.
Royalties paid annually. *Overseas* various agency and representative arrangements.

Authors' Rating With the decline of the *Janet and John* readers, Ginn was a sad little company when it was bought by **Heinemann**. It is now busily trying to re-establish its credentials in the educational market.

Mary Glasgow Publications Ltd
Avenue House, 131–3 Holland Park
Avenue, London W11 4UT
☎01–603 4688   Fax 01–602 5197

Managing Director *Alfred Waller*

Part of the Wolters Kluwer Group. Mary Glasgow founded Mary Glasgow & Baker Ltd in 1956 with the publication of her first French magazine, *Bonjour*. Her objective was to provide a service for teachers and learners of languages, aiming to make their work more effective and more enjoyable. The company changed its name in January 1970 to Mary Glasgow Publications Ltd. Apart from a regular output of magazines, there is a steadily growing list of main course, text and audio-visual materials not only in the area of foreign languages but also English, social studies, religious education and media studies. *Publishes* mainly language magazines, books and audio material.

DIVISIONS
Books *Nick Hutchins* TITLES *Arc-en-ciel*; *Bibliobus*. **Magazines** *Neil Durham* TITLES

Bonjour; Hoy Dia; Das Rad; Catch. No unsolicited mss. Will consider synopses/ideas for books.

GMP (Gay Men's Press) Ltd

PO Box 247, London N15 6RW
☎01–800 5861   Telex 94013925 GMPP G

Managing Director *Aubrey Walter*

Publishes primarily books by gay authors about gay-related issues; art – painting and drawing, poetry, biography and autobiography, fiction – literary and popular (historical romance to crime and science fiction). Works submitted must be on author's disc.

Editors *Richard Dipple* (fiction and rights), *Aubrey Walter* (art and photography), *David Fernbach* (non-fiction). One-off payments rather than royalties. Terms open to negotiation.

Golden Cockerel Press Ltd

25 Sicilian Avenue, London WC1A 2QH
☎01–405 7979   Telex 23565

Chairman/Managing Director
Thomas Yoseloff

Set up in London in 1980 to distribute the books published by its overseas associate company, Associated University Presses Inc., New Jersey, Golden Cockerel Press now acts as a full publishing house, with its own editorial function. *Publishes* art, collecting, film, history, Judaica, literary criticism, music, philosophy, sociology, special interest. 80–100 titles in 1987.

Editorial Head *Michael Wright*

IMPRINTS
AUP member presses include **Bucknell, Delaware, Fairleigh Dickinson, Folger Shakespeare Library.** *Publishes* scholarly, academic. **Cornwall books** *Publishes* trade hardbacks **Lehigh University Press, Susquehanna University Press.** Unsolicited mss, synopses and ideas for books welcome. *Royalties* paid annually.

Victor Gollancz Ltd

14 Henrietta Street, London WC2E 8QJ
☎01–836 2006
Telex 265003   Fax 01–379 0934

Chairman *Livia Gollancz*
Managing Director *Stephen Bray*

FOUNDED 1928 by Victor Gollancz as a general publishing company and famous for its political books during the 1930s and 1940s (*Left Book Club*), it has continued as an independent company every since. *Publishes* biography and memoirs, bridge, children's, cookery, current affairs, detective stories and thrillers, general fiction, history, mountaineering, music, science fiction, travel, vernacular architecture. Wholly owned subsidiary: **H.F. & G. Witherby Ltd** which publishes angling, natural history, ornithology, travel, wine.

Editors *Chris Kloet*, (Children's) *Joanna Goldsworthy* (Fiction and general nonfiction), *Livia Gollancz* (Music and Mountaineering), *Julia Wisdom* (Paperbacks), *Peter Crawley* (Vernacular architecture and bridge), *David Burnett* (H.F. & G. Witherby). Prefer typescripts to be preceded by descriptive letter. Unsolicited synopses and ideas for books welcome. *Royalties* paid twice yearly.

Authors' Rating Until recently, thought to be too closely tied to the eccentric ideals of their founder. But the old-fashioned image is fast disappearing. Prompt and, in some ways, generous payers. For example, Gollancz offers a standard 15% on overseas sales, a third higher than most publishers.

Gordon & Breach Science Publishers

1 Bedford Street, London WC2E 9PP
☎01–836 5125
Telex 23258 SCIPUB G   Fax 01–379 0800

Managing Director *Alan Davies*

FOUNDED 1961. *Publishes* books and journals across a range of disciplines including dance, engineering, history, mathematics and computing, music, political science, science, sociology. 200+ titles in 1987.

IMPRINT
Harwood Academic Publishers *Publishes* biomedical, medical and science books and journals. Unsolicited mss and synopses welcome.
Royalties paid annually. *Overseas office* Gordon & Breach Publishers Inc., New York.

Gowan Publishing Ltd
24 Fremount Drive, Beechdale,
Nottingham NG8 3GL
☎0602 292995

Managing Director *Joan Wallace*

FOUNDED 1983, initially to help and encourage new writers. *Publishes* fiction. Particularly interested in showbiz books, both fiction and non-fiction. Published 3 books since 1983.

Editorial Head *Joan Wallace* TITLES *Two of Clubs* Joan Wallace, and, forthcoming, *Independent Street at War* Joan Wallace. Welcome synopses and ideas for books.
Royalties 'not applicable'.

Gower Medical Publishing
See Harper & Row Ltd

Gower Publishing Group
Gower House, Croft Road, Aldershot,
Hants GU11 3HR
☎0252 331551   Telex 858001

Chairman/Managing Director
Nigel Farrow

FOUNDED 1967. *Publishes* professional and academic books in business, the humanities, the professions, social sciences, and technology. 300 titles in 1987.

DIVISIONS
Avebury *John Irwin* Research monographs on the social sciences. **Gower** *Malcolm Stern*

Business, professional and academic books and journals. **Scolar** *James Price* Quality-produced hardbacks on art, architecture, biography, books and illustration, cinema/photography, history, literature, medieval studies, music. **Technical Press** *Jill Pearce* Books on applied technology and industrial process, especially in the areas of construction and building technology, project management and quality management. **Wildwood House** *John Irwin* The paperback imprint of the group. Unsolicited mss welcome. Unsolicited synopses and ideas for books considered.
Royalties paid as per contract. *Overseas associates* USA, Australia, Hong Kong, Singapore.

Authors' Rating Growing fast in the area of quality non-fiction for the general reader. The purchase of its US distributor, Brookfield Publishing of Vermont, could well be the preliminary to expansion in the States. Some complaints of confused royalty statements and slow payments.

Grafton Books Ltd
8 Grafton Street, London W1X 3LA
☎01-493 7070
Telex 25611   Fax 01-493 7070 ext. 4517

Chairman *F.I. Chapman*
Managing Director *Jonathan Lloyd*

Part of **Collins**. Formerly known as Granada Publishing, the company was sold by The Granada Group in 1983. Name changed to **Grafton Books** in 1985. *Publishes* general trade hardbacks, fiction, non-fiction, paperbacks, sailing books. 370 titles in 1987.

DIVISIONS
Adlard Coles *Janet Murphy Publishes* sailing books on technical, instructional, building and design, travel subjects. **Grafton Hardbacks** *John W. Boothe* TITLES *Non-fiction: The Misfits* Colin Wilson; *Guts and Glory: The Oliver North Story* Ben Bradlee Jnr; *Coastal Walks in England and Wales* Christopher Somerville; *Musical Events 1980–1983* Andrew Porter; *Korea* Simon Winchester;

The Faces of Hemingway Denis Brian;
Waldheim: The Missing Years Robert E.
Herzstein; *John Lennon: My Brother* Julia
Baird; *Bodyguard* Tony Geraghty; *Spectator
Book of Travel* ed. Philip Marsden Smedley;
Pick of Punch; *Venice* Christopher Hibbert;
Journey Back From Hell Anton Gill. FICTION:
The Icarus Agenda Robert Ludlum; *To Be the
Best* Barbara Taylor Bradford; *Treasure* Clive
Cussler; *Zero* Eric Van Lustbader; *The Para-
dise Eater* John Ralston Saul; *Freedom* Wil-
liam Safire; *Paper Chase* William Garner;
Women in Love D.H. Lawrence; *Faerie* Ray-
mond E. Feist. **Grafton Paperbacks** *Nick
Austin* TITLES *Death is a Lonely Business*
Ray Bradbury; *Day of Creation* J.G. Ballard;
An Academic Question Barbara Pym; *Winter*
Len Deighton; *The Last Romantics* Caroline
Seebohm; *Stamp Album* Terence Stamp;
Flight of the Old Dog Dale Brown; *Empire of
the Sun* J.G. Ballard (film tie-in); also books
by Arthur C. Clarke, William Goldman, Isaac
Asimov. **Paladin** *Nick Austin* Accepts
unsolicited mss. Welcomes synopses and
ideas for books.
Royalties paid twice yearly. *Overseas asso-
ciates* see **Collins**.

Authors' Rating Still trying to establish a
clear identity after abandoning the Granada
label three years ago. A tightly-organised,
commercially sharp company, aiming fair
and square at the mass market.

Graham & Trotman Ltd

Sterling House, 66 Wilton Road,
London SW1V 1DE
☎01–821 1123
Telex 298878 GRAMCO G   Fax 01–630 5229

Chairman *Dr F.W.B. van Eysinga*
Managing Director *Alastair M.W. Graham*

FOUNDED 1974. Part of the Kluwer UK Group
from 1986. *Publishes* books, directories,
journals and looseleaf in the fields of earth
sciences and environmental sciences, finance, international business and law. There
are plans to increase output. 56 titles in 1987.

DIVISIONS
Business *A.M.W. Graham* **Law** *A.M.W.
Graham* **Technical** *H. van Dorssen*. Unsolicited mss, synopses and ideas for books
welcome.
Royalties paid twice yearly. *Overseas sister
company* Kluwer Inc., Boston.

Graham-Cameron Publishing

10 Church Street, Willingham,
Cambridge CB4 5HT
☎0954 60444

Editorial Director *Mike Graham-Cameron*
Art Director *Helen Graham-Cameron*

FOUNDED 1984 mainly as a packaging operation. *Publishes* illustrated books for children
and for institutional and business customers.
Also publishes biography, educational materials and social history. 10 titles in
1987. TITLES *Up From the Country* (children's); *Anglo-Saxon Households* (educational); *In All Directions* (biography).
Synopses and ideas for picture books of professional standard welcome. Enclose s.a.e.
Royalties paid annually.

Granville Publishing

102 Islington High Street, London N1 8EG
☎01–226 2904

Managing Director *John Murray-Brown*
Approx Annual Turnover 'very small'

FOUNDED 1983. Part of a bookshop. *Publishes*
literature reprints.

TITLES *The Future in America* H.G. Wells; *The
American Scene* Henry James. Do not welcome unsolicited material.

Green Books

Ford House, Hartland, Bideford,
Devon EX39 6EE
☎023 74 621

Chairman *Satish Kumar*
Approx Annual Turnover £30,000

FOUNDED 1986 and supported by the Schuma-
cher Society, Friends of the Earth, the Council

for the Protection of Rural England, the Dartington Hall Trust, *Resurgence* magazine and other environmental organisations. Established to meet the increased interest in and demand for environmental literature. *Publishes* environmental books covering a wide range of topics from a green philosophy. 6 titles in 1987 and an anticipated 10 titles in 1988.

Managing Editor *Elizabeth Saxby* TITLES *Schools of Tomorrow, Education as if People Matter* Richard North; *The Countryside We Want* editors, Charlie Pye-Smith and Chris Hall. Welcome unsolicited mss but prefer introductory letter and outline in the first instance. Welcome unsolicited synopsis and ideas.
Royalties paid twice yearly.

Greenprint
See **Marshall Pickering Holdings Ltd**

Gresham Books
PO Box 61, Henley-on-Thames,
Oxon RG9 3LQ
☎073522 3789

Managing Director *Mary V. Green*
Approx Annual Turnover £80,000

Bought by Mary Green in 1980 from Martins Publishing Group. A small specialist one-woman publishing house. *Publishes* hymn and service books for schools; *The Headmasters' Conference Hymnbook*. No unsolicited material or ideas. Only deals with schools and music publishers.

Grevatt & Grevatt
9 Rectory Drive,
Newcastle-upon-Tyne NE3 1XT

Chairman *Dr S.Y. Killingley*

Part-time business started in 1981 as an alternative publisher of works not normally commercially viable. Authors waive royalties on the first 500 copies. Three books have appeared with financial backing from professional bodies. *Publishes* academic books, especially on language, linguistics and religious studies. Some poetry. Typical of the 1987 list is *Prosodic Phonology: The Theory and its Application to Language Acquisition and Speech Processing* and *Views of Durham Cathedral*, the latter compiled by Dr Killingley.

Editorial Head *Dr S.Y. Killingley* No unsolicited mss. Synopses and ideas should be accompanied by an s.a.e.
Royalties annually after the initial 500 copies.

Authors' Rating Since print-runs are invariably low, the prospect of receiving royalties are limited.

Grosvenor Books
54 Lyford Road,
Wandsworth, London SW18 3JJ
☎01–870 2124

Managing Director *J.H.V. Nowell*

FOUNDED 1967. Part of The Good Road Ltd. Publishers for Moral Rearmament. *Publishes* biographies, children's books, contemporary issues, educational and religious. 4 titles in 1987.

TITLES *Listen for a Change*; *Making Marriage Work* Annejet Campbell; *For the Love of Tomorrow* Jacqueline Piguet; *A Different Accent* Michael Henderson; *The Return of the Indian Spirit* Phyllis Johnson. Do not welcome unsolicited mss but will consider synopses.
Royalties paid twice yearly. *Overseas associates* in Australia, New Zealand, USA, Canada.

Grotius Publications
PO Box 115, Cambridge CB3 9BP
☎0223 323410   Fax 0223 313545

Managing Director *C.J. Daly*

FOUNDED 1979 for the publication of the *International Law Reports* and other related titles in the international law sphere. 20 titles in 1987.

Editorial Director *S.R. Pirrie* TITLES *International Law Reports* E. Lauterpacht QC (ed.); *International Law* Dr M.N. Shaw; *International Wildlife Law* Simon Lyster; *Chernobyl: Law and Communication* P.J. Sands (ed.); *War, Aggression and Self-Defence* Professor Yoram Dinstein. Welcome unsolicited mss and synopses/ideas for books if within specialist framework.
Royalties paid annually.

Guinness Superlatives Ltd
33 London Road, Enfield, Middx EN2 6DJ
☎01–367 4567
Telex 23573　　　　　　Fax 01–367 5912

Chairman *Shaun C. Dowling*
Managing Director *David F. Hoy*
Approx Annual Turnover £6 million

FOUNDED 1954 to publish *The Guinness Book of Records*, now the highest-selling copyright book in the world, published in 26 languages. In the later 1960s, the company set about expanding its list with a wider range of titles mostly linked to records and record-breaking. 34 titles in 1988.

Editorial Director *Donald F. Sommerville* TITLES *The Guinness Book of Records*; *British Hit Singles*; *Guinness Book of Answers*. Welcome ideas and synopses for books if they come within their field of sport, human achievement, travel, and family reference.

Authors' Rating Any idea must seem inferior to the first book – in itself a record breaker. However the company does want to broaden its base and it has the resources to achieve its aim.

Peter Haddock Ltd
Pinfold Lane, Bridlington,
E. Yorks YO9 5BT
☎0262 678121
Telex 52180　　　　　　Fax 0262 400043

Managing Director *Peter Haddock*

FOUNDED 1952. *Publishes* children's picture story books, activity books. Published 120 series in 1987. Welcomes ideas for picture books.
Royalty payments vary according to contract.

Authors' Rating Cheap end of the market. Writers need to work fast to make a living.

Robert Hale Ltd
Clerkenwell House, 45–7 Clerkenwell Green, London EC1R 0HT
☎01–251 2661
Telex 23353 NURBKS G　　　Fax 01–251 0584

Chairman and Managing Director
John Hale

FOUNDED 1936, and still a family company. *Publishes* most types of adult fiction; every kind of adult non-fiction, excluding specialist areas (such as educational/legal/medical and scientific). 398 titles in 1987.

Commissioning Editor *Robin Frampton* TITLES Fiction: *A Demon Close Behind* Leslie Halliwell; *Nothing Larger Than Life* David Holbrook; *Never Laugh at Love* Barbara Cartland; *Personal Relations* Pamela Street. Non-fiction: *Elvis in Private* Peter Haining; *The People in Britain* Roy Kerridge; *Psychic Animals* Dennis Bardens. Unsolicited mss, synopses and ideas for books welcome.
Royalties paid twice yearly.

Authors' Rating Takes good care of authors but can be tough on advances. Favours the popular end of the fiction market.

The Hambledon Press
102 Gloucester Avenue, London NW1 8HX
☎01–586 0817

Chairman/Managing Director
Martin Sheppard
Approx Annual Turnover £120,000

FOUNDED 1980 when cricket books were top of the list. These have now been dropped. *Publishes* academic history, some academic literature, history – English and European, post-classical to modern. 10–15 titles annually.

Editorial Head *Martin Sheppard* TITLES *Studies in Medieval Thought from Abelard to Wyclif* Beryl Smalley; *Godly People: Essays on English Protestantism and Puritanism* Patrick Collinson. No unsolicited mss. Preliminary letter. Synopses and ideas for books welcome.
Royalties paid annually. *Overseas associates* The Hambledon Press (USA), West Virginia.

Hamish Hamilton Ltd

27 Wright's Lane, London W8 5TZ
☎01–938 3388   Telex 917181
Fax 01–937 8704 (general)
01–937 8783 (production)

Managing Director
Christopher Sinclair-Stevenson
Approx Annual Turnover £6.5 million

FOUNDED 1931, subsequently bought by the Thomson Organisation and taken over by **Penguin** in 1985. *Publishes* Africana and natural history, biography, children's books, current affairs, fiction, history, language and literature, politics, travel. 253 titles in 1986.

DIVISIONS
Elm Tree *Penny Hoare* AUTHORS Philip Norman, Les Dawson, Val Doonican, Roger Phillips. **Hamish Hamilton** *Penny Hoare* AUTHORS Peter Ackroyd, William Boyd, Paul Theroux, Brigid Brophy, Jennifer Johnston, Ed McBain. **Hamish Hamilton Children's** *Jane Nissen* AUTHORS Raymond Briggs, Eric Carle, Joan Lingard, Mollie Hunter.

IMPRINTS
Hamish Hamilton Trade Paperbacks *Penny Hoare* AUTHORS Harold Acton, Nancy Mitford, Kenneth Clark, Sir Peter Hall, Marina Warner. Unsolicited mss and synopses/ideas for books welcome.
Royalties paid twice yearly. *Overseas associates* see **Penguin**.

Authors' Rating One of the best of the general publishers and they know it. With many highly marketable names among its authors, editors can afford to pick and choose from the newcomers. Do not expect a quick response to correspondence. Exciting children's list. Only major publisher to issue hand-written royalty statements – old fashioned but at least they can be understood.

Paul Hamlyn Publishing

Michelin House, 81 Fulham Road,
London SW3 6RB
☎01–581 9393
Telex 920191   Fax 01–589 8419

Managing Director *David Blunt*
Publishing Director *Paul Richardson*

FORMED 1987 out of Octopus Books Ltd and the Hamlyn Publishing Group. It is a major international illustrated popular reference and information publisher with a world-wide reputation for quality and value. *Publishes* atlases, aviation, children's, cookery, fashion, gardening, general interest, lifestyle, natural history, reference, and sport. It is the main supplier of own-brand books to Marks & Spencer, Tesco and Sainsbury.

DIVISIONS
Adult *Jonathan Goodman* TITLES *Larrouse Gastronomique; Michelin Road Atlas of Europe; The Hollywood Story; Beatles Recording Session.* **Children's** *Theresa Carlson* TITLES *Wizzpax; Pink Flamingoes; The Parent and Child Programme; Colour Fax.* **New Editions** *Terence Cross* TITLES *Bounty Bargain Books; Filofiction; Hamlyn Books on Tape.* Prefer to see synopses and ideas for books.
Royalties paid twice yearly.

Harcourt Brace Jovanovich Ltd

24–8 Oval Road, London NW1 7DX
☎01–267 4466

Managing Director *Joan Fujimoto*

Harcourt Brace Jovanovich Inc., New York, owns **Academic Press** (see separate listing). *Publishes* academic, accountancy and taxation, archaeology, biology/zoology, business and industry, chemistry, children's, cinema and video, computer science and business software, economics, educational and textbooks, EFL, fiction, fine art, geography and geology, history, antiquarian, languages and linguistics, law, literature and criticism, mathematics and statistics, medical, music, philosophy, physics, poetry, politics, psychology, religious, sociology and anthropology, theatre and drama, training and careers, women's studies.

Editorial Director *Peter Brown* Unsolicited mss welcome.
Royalties paid twice yearly.

Harper & Row Ltd
Middlesex House, 34–42 Cleveland Street, London W1P 5FB
☎01–636 8300
Telex 21736   Fax 01–631 3594

Managing Director *David Inglis*

Offshoot of the American company now jointly owned by **Collins** and News International. The new chief executive is George Craig, formerly vice chairman of **Collins**. *Publishes* academic, non-fiction, professional medical and nursing, trade books. Unsolicited mss welcome.

IMPRINT
Gower Medical Publishing
Royalties paid twice yearly.

Harrap Columbus
See Columbus Books

Harrap Ltd
19–23 Ludgate Hill, London EC4M 7PD
☎01–248 6444   Telex 28673 CONSOL G

Chairman *N.W. Berry*
Managing Director *Eric R. Dobby*

Part of the Harrap Group. *Publishes* biography and autobiography, cinema and video, costume, some crime, fine art and art history, guide books, history, humour, illustrated and fine editions, magic and the occult, military and war, photography, political and world affairs, reference and dictionaries, sports and games, theatre and drama, travel and topography. 145 titles in 1987.

DIVISIONS
Columbus Books *Gill Rowley* (see separate entry) **Dictionaries and Reference** *Jean-Luc Barbanneau* TITLE *Harrap's Paperback French–English Dictionary*. **Harrap General Books** *Derek Johns* TITLES Astronomy: *TV Astronomer* Patrick Moore. Biography and Memoirs: *Rosa Luxemburg* Elzbieta Ettinger. General: *Backstage* Judith Cook. The Occult: *The Encyclopedia of Unsolved Mysteries* Colin Wilson. Photography: *Perspectives* Don McCullin. **Impact Books** *Jean-Luc Barbanneau* TITLES *Wiltshire Village* Heather and Robin Tanner; *College on a Shoestring* Eve Luddington; *It's Never Too Late . . .* Joan Perkin. **Self Study** *David Skinner* **Threshold Books Ltd** *Barbara Cooper* TITLES *Priceless* Virginia Leng; *Long Distance Riding* Marion Eason; *Pick Your Own Cookbook* Ann Nicol. Unsolicited mss and synopses welcome.
Royalties paid twice yearly.

Authors' Rating Solid foundation of reference books with a list of middle-of-the-road non-fiction, dramatically enlivened last year with the appearance of the John Stalker biography.

Harvester Wheatsheaf
16 Ship Street, Brighton, East Sussex BN1 1AD
☎0273 723031   Telex 877101 OLSHIP

Managing Director *Robert Bolick*

Owned by **Simon & Schuster**, New York. The majority of their titles are co-published with American publishers. Current major projects include *Key Women Writers* series. *Publishes* cognitive psychology, defence and strategic studies, economics, literature, philosophy, psychology, Soviet studies, women's studies, and reference books on these subjects. 90 titles in 1987.

TITLES *Court and Country* Rowse; *Radical Tragedy* Dollimore; *Christopher Hill's Collected Essays; Collected Papers* Plumb; *Great Economists Before Keynes* Blaug; *Great Economists Since Keynes* Blaug; *International Economic Border* Kindleberger. Unsolicited mss will be considered if return postage included; letters of enquiry with synopses are preferred. *Royalties* paid annually.

Authors' Rating Harvester is the extraordinary achievement of John Spiers who set up in the early 1970s to produce esoteric reprints for the university libraries. Now he has sold this thriving academic list to **Simon & Schuster** and set off on his own once more to establish **John Spiers Publishing Ltd** (see separate entry).

Haynes Publishing Group

Sparkford, nr Yeovil, Somerset BA22 7JJ
☎0963 40635   Telex 46212 HAYNES G

Chairman *John H. Haynes*
Managing Director *Jim Scott*
Approx Annual Turnover £8.5 million

FOUNDED 1960 by John H. Haynes. In the mid-sixties produced the first *Owners' Workshop Manual,* now the mainstay of the programme. A family-run business which does its own typesetting and printing on the premises. *Publishes* DIY workshop manuals for cars and motorbikes. Now branching out into wider areas but keeping a strong bias towards motoring and transport.

IMPRINTS
G.T. Foulis & Co. Ltd *R. Grainger* Cars and motoring-related books. **J.H. Haynes & Co. Ltd** *J.R. Clew and P. Ward* **Oxford Illustrated Press** *Jane Marshall* General titles: photography; sports and games; gardening; travel and guide books. **Oxford Publishing Co.** *R. Grainger* Railway titles. Welcome unsolicited mss if they come within the subject areas covered.
Royalties paid annually. *Overseas associates* Haynes Publications Inc., California, USA.

Authors' Rating Making a strong impact in its specialist market. A good year encouraged the purchase of the *Oxford Publishing Co.* (railway books) from **Cassell**.

Headline Book Publishing plc

Headline House, 79 Great Titchfield Street, London W1P 7FN
☎01-631 1687
Telex 268326 HEADLN G   Fax 01-631 1958

Managing Director *Tim Hely-Hutchinson*

ESTABLISHED 1986 with substantial City funding, Headline specialises in commercial fiction, both hardback and paperback, and also publishes non-fiction, particularly in the areas of biography, cinema, design and film, food and wine, and TV tie-ins. The company is a signatory of a Minimum Terms Agreement with the **Society of Authors** and **The Writers' Guild of Great Britain.** 200 titles planned for 1989.

Editorial Director *Sue Fletcher*   TITLES *The Confession of Brother Haluin* Ellis Peters; *Lightning* Dean R. Koontz; *The Cat's Whiskers* Beryl Reid; *Conner Street's War* Harry Bowling; *Food & Wine Adventures* Jancis Robinson; *Shark* Jeremy Stafford-Deitsch; *Dicken's London* Peter Ackroyd; *I Am the Only Running Footman* Martha Grimes; *Encounters* Isaac Asimov; *City of Nets* Otto Friedrich; *Professional Illustration & Design* Simon Jennings; *The Rose & The Vine* Unity Hall; *Talent* Nigel Rees; *Scandals* Una-Mary Parker; *It's Only a Movie* Ingrid Alexander Walker. Welcome unsolicited mss and synopses.
Royalties paid twice yearly.

Authors' Rating A newcomer to publishing with a young management team set on rapid expansion. Looking to double turnover to £10 million within five years. A strong second year, especially with paperbacks, suggests Headline is on target. Open to ideas for commercial fiction and popular non-fiction.

Heinemann Educational Books Ltd

Halley Court, Jordan Hill, Oxford OX2 8EJ
☎0865 311366
Telex 837292　　　　　Fax 0865 310043

Chairman *Nicholas Thomson*
Managing Director *David Fothergill*

Parent Company **Octopus Publishing Group**. *Publishes* textbooks, readers, drama and other educational resources for primary and secondary education and for English language teaching; textbooks and literature for overseas markets, principally in Africa and the Caribbean.

DIVISIONS
International Publishing *Mike Esplen* (**African & Caribbean Publishing Director** *Vicky Unwin*) TITLES *African & Caribbean Writers Series; Heinemann Guided Readers; New Generation; Snap.* **Schools Publishing** *Bob Osborne* (**Humanities Publishing Director** *Kay Symons*, **Science and Maths** *Stephen Ashton*) TITLES *The New Windmill Series; Hereford Plays; Scottish Primary Maths; Sunshine.* Unsolicited mss and synopses/ideas for books welcome.
Royalties paid twice yearly. *Offices* in Oxford, London, Edinburgh, Melbourne, Sydney, Auckland, Singapore, Madrid, Athens, Ibadan, Nairobi, Gaborone, Harare, Kingston, Portsmouth NH.

Authors' Rating Though part of the all-embracing Octopus, Heinemann Educational has managed to keep a distinct identity, an achievement endorsed by an office move to the Oxford Business Park. Strong on African and Caribbean books.

Heinemann Kingswood

See William Heinemann Ltd

William Heinemann Ltd

Michelin House, 81 Fulham Road, London SW3 6RB
☎01–581 9393
Telex 920191　　　　　Fax 01–589 8419

Publisher *Helen Fraser*

FOUNDED 1890 by William Heinemann, whose policy of publishing a broad range of literary and popular fiction, non-fiction, children's illustrated and information books has, despite many changes and the development of specialised divisions of the list, remained the characteristic publishing style. In 1985 the Heinemann Group became part of the **Octopus Publishing Group**. *Publishes* adult fiction and general non-fiction, sport and leisure, popular psychology, inspirational.

Editorial Directors *Dan Franklin, Amanda Conquy* **Fiction & General** TITLES *Rage* Wilbur Smith; *Wolf Winter* Clare Francis; *Dick Gentley's Holistic Detective Agency* Douglas Adams; *Anthills of the Savannah* Chinua Achebe; *Behind the Wall* Colin Thubron.

IMPRINTS
Heinemann Kingswood Sport and leisure
Heinemann Young Books TITLES *The Jolly Postman; Thomas the Tank Engine; Where's Spot?; The Velveteen Rabbit.* Unsolicited mss, if preceded by a preliminary enquiry, and synopses/ideas for books welcome.
Royalties paid twice yearly. *Overseas associates* Heinemann Books Australia (Pty), 85 Abinger Street, Richmond 3121, Victoria, Australia; Heinemann Publishers (NZ) Ltd, PO Box 36064, Auckland 9, New Zealand; Heinemann Publishers South Africa (Pty), PO Box 61581, Marshalltown 2107, Johannesburg, RSA.

Authors' Rating Has come through a period of traumatic change, unsettling for many authors but necessary if Heinemann's general publishing was to survive as an economic entity. Now needs a little time to settle.

Heinemann Young Books

See William Heinemann Ltd

The Herbert Press Ltd

46 Northchurch Road, London N1 4EJ
☎01–254 4379　　　　　Telex 8952022

Managing Director *David Herbert*

Publishes archaeology, architecture and design, biography and autobiography, crafts and hobbies, fashion and costume, fine art and art history, natural history, photography, travel and topography. 10 titles in 1988.

Editorial Director *David Herbert* Unsolicited mss welcome.
Royalties paid twice yearly.

Heretic Books
PO Box 247, London N15 6RW

Managing Director *David Fernbach*

Publishes books relevant to the growing Green movements: animal liberation, deepecology, Green politics and philosophy, how-to, vegetarianism. Work submitted for publication must be on author's disc.

Editorial Directors *David Fernbach, Aubrey Walter*. One-off payments rather than royalties. Terms open to negotiation.

Hippo Children's Paperbacks
See Scholastic Publications Ltd

Hippopotamus Press
PO Box 120, Sutton, Surrey SM2 5WG
☎01–643 1470

Approx Annual Turnover £20,000

FOUNDED 1974 as a poetry press. In 1986 took over the UK's oldest, independent poetry magazine, *Outposts Poetry Quarterly*. Receives financial assistance from the Arts Council. *Publishes* poetry. 5 titles in 1987.

TITLES *Images of Summer* Roy Bennett; *The Hollow Landscapes* William Bedford. Welcome unsolicited mss.
Royalties paid quarterly.

Hobsons Publishing plc
Bateman Street, Cambridge CB2 1LZ
☎0223 354551   Telex 81546 HOBCAM

Managing Director *Adrian A. Bridgewater*
Approx Annual Turnover £4.7 million

FOUNDED 1973 by Adrian Bridgewater, went public in 1987. *Publishes* textbooks, career guides, computer software; particularly successful in the directories market, with comprehensive listings and advertisements giving job and product information. Consultancy publishing work for employers and government departments. Bought Johansen Publications Ltd in 1987, publishers of *Recommended Hostels in UK*. 360 titles in 1988.

Editorial Head *Julie Horne*

Authors' Rating Formula publishing based on a close and shrewd analysis of the education and business markets.

Hodder & Stoughton Ltd
47 Bedford Square, London WC1B 3DP
(editorial office)
☎01–636 9851   Telex 885887

Chairman/Managing Director
Philip Attenborough
Approx Annual Turnover £55 million

FOUNDED 1868. An independent company which engages in a diverse range of publishing. *Publishes* academic, children's books, fiction, medical, non-fiction, religious. Also paperbacks – see imprints list below. 800 titles in 1987.

Publishing Director *Michael Attenborough*

DIVISIONS
Children's *David Grant* AUTHORS R. Goscinny/A. Uderzo (*Asterix*), Eric Carle. **Educational** Now fully merged with **Edward Arnold** – see below. **General** *Eric Major/Ion Trewin* AUTHORS John le Carré, Jeffrey Archer, James Clavell, Thomas Keneally, Gavin Lyall, Mary Stewart. **New English Library** *Clare Bristow* AUTHORS Stephen King, Rosamunde Pilcher, James Herbert. **Religious** *David Wavre* AUTHORS Catherine Marshall, John Wimber, Michael Green (also publish the *NIV Bible*).

IMPRINTS
Edward Arnold *Richard Morris* (Managing Director). *Brian Steven* (Managing Director – school books), *Richard Stileman* (Managing Director – tertiary publishing).
Publishes secondary education, further education, *Teach Yourself* series, colleges of education books, academic, scientific, medical, ELT. Paperbacks: **Coronet Books** and **Sceptre Books** *Adrian Bourne* (Managing Director), *Amanda Stewart* (Editorial Director); **Knight Books** *Elizabeth Roy* AUTHORS as for **General/New English Library** and **Children's** lists. Hodder & Stoughton actively discourage the submission of unsolicited mss, though 'the company is very willing to assess synopses and sample chapters'.
Royalties paid twice yearly. *Overseas associates* Australia, New Zealand and a widespread network of other overseas companies and agencies.

Authors' rating A paternalistic reputation but renowned for loyalty to authors. By far the best for prompt royalty payments and informative statements. There is a heartening story of Philip Attenborough's shocked surprise and angry rejection of a suggestion by a fellow publisher that if booksellers are late in paying, authors should wait for their royalties.

The Hogarth Press Ltd
See **Chatto & Windus Ltd**

Holmes McDougall Ltd
Allander House, 137–41 Leith Walk, Edinburgh EH6 8NS
☎031–554 9444   Telex 727508 Holmes G

Managing Director *F.J. Baillie*
Approx Annual Turnover £1.5 million

FOUNDED 1962. *Publishes* educational and textbooks (primary and secondary). 50 titles in 1987.

Editorial Director *E. Ketley*   TITLES *Schools Council History; Link-Up Reading Scheme; Pri-*
mary English; Science and Creative Technology. Welcome unsolicited manuscripts and synopses.
Royalties paid twice yearly.

Holt Rinehart & Winston
24–8 Oval Road, London NW1 7DX
☎01–267 4466

Owned by CBS Inc., USA, until bought by **Academic Press** in 1987. *Publishes* academic, accountancy and taxation, biology and zoology, business and industry, chemistry, computer science, computer software (business and educational), economic, educational and textbooks, engineering, languages and linguistics, mathematics and statistics, physics, reference books and dictionaries, scientific and technical, sociology and anthropology.

Holt Saunders Ltd
See **Academic Press Inc.**

Human Horizons
See **Souvenir Press Ltd**

C. Hurst & Co.
38 King Street, London WC2E 8JT
☎01–240 2666

Chairman/Managing Director
Christopher Hurst

FOUNDED 1967. Independent, and active in the **Publishers' Association**. Aims to cultivate a small publisher's concern for literacy, detail and the visual aspects of the product. *Publishes* autobiography, contemporary history, political science, religion. 12 titles published in 1987.

Editorial Head *Christopher Hurst* with *Michael Dwyer*   TITLES *German Imperialism in Africa; Muslims in the Soviet Empire; The Spanish Economy; Venezuela: A Century of Change; Political Parties and Elections in West Germany* (also in paper). No unsolicited mss but unsolicited synopses and ideas for books welcome.

Royalties paid twice yearly twice after publication and annually thereafter.

Hutchinson
See **Century Hutchinson Publishing Group Ltd**

J & B Maps
See **John Bartholomew & Son Ltd**

Arthur James Ltd
1 Cranbourne Road, London N10 2BT
☎01–883 1831/8307 and 883 2201 (24 hrs)

Managing Director *Denis Duncan*
Approx Annual Turnover £80,000

FOUNDED 1944 by A.J. Russell, a Fleet Street journalist. *Publishes* day books, devotional, psychological, religious, social work, New Testament translation.   TITLES *God Calling* (2 million sales); *God at Eventide* (1 million sales). **Editorial Head** *Jillian Tallon* No unsolicited mss.
Royalties paid annually. *Overseas associates* Dodd Mead, New York; Buchanan, Australia.

Jane's Publishing Company Limited
238 City Road, London EC1V 2PU
☎01–251 9281
Telex 894689   Fax 01–251 8900

Managing Director *Michael Goldsmith*
Approx Annual Turnover £25 million

FOUNDED 1898 by Fred T. Jane with publication of *All The World's Fighting Ships*. Since then the company has grown to produce, in 1987, 15 yearbooks; the leading weekly defence magazine, *Jane's Defence Weekly*. In 1985, Jane's acquired DMS Inc. of the USA, a market research company, and in 1987 purchased Interavia Publishing Group of Switzerland. Jane's is a subsidiary of Thomson Information Services Limited and is part of the International Thomson Organisation. *Publishes* defence, aerospace and transport topics, including yearbooks which give de-

tails of equipment and systems, directories and strategic studies. Planning publication of a number of new yearbooks including *Jane's Military Logistics*, *Jane's Air-Launched Weapons*, and *Jane's Counter-Insurgency Equipment*.

DIVISIONS
Jane's Defence Weekly *Peter Howard* **DMS Inc.** *Jay Gast* TITLES *World Armoured Vehicle Forecast*. **Interavia Publishing Group** *Pierre Condom* TITLES *Interavia Aerospace Review*; *Interavia Data*. **Jane's Publishing Company Limited** *Bob Hutchinson* TITLES *Jane's Fighting Ships*; *US Maritime Strategy*; *International Defence Directory*. **Jane's Transport Press Limited** *Ken Harris* TITLES *Jane's World Railways*. Welcome unsolicited mss, synopses and ideas for books.
Royalties paid twice yearly. *Overseas associates* Jane's Publishing Inc., USA; DMS Inc., USA; Interavia Publishing Group SA, Switzerland.

Javelin
See **Blandford Publishing Ltd**

Michael Joseph Ltd
27 Wright's Lane, London W8 5TZ
☎01–937 7255
Telex 917181/2   Fax 01–937 8704

Managing Director *Alan Brooke*
Editorial Director *Susan Watt*

FOUNDED 1936. Parent company **Penguin Books Ltd**. *Publishes* belles-lettres, biography and memoirs, current affairs, fiction, general, history, humour. 120 titles in 1987.

IMPRINT
Mermaid Books Paperback *Publishes* non-fiction colour illustrated. Unsolicited manuscripts welcome.
Royalties paid twice yearly. *Overseas associates* Penguin Overseas.

Authors' Rating Open to ideas for popular non-fiction. Great improvement of late in their relationship with authors, not least in the information provided of print-runs and sales.

The Journeyman Press Ltd

97 Ferme Park Road, Crouch End,
London N8 9SA
☎01–348 9261   Telex 265871 MONREF G

Chairman R. Weinstein
Managing Director P. Sinclair
Approx Annual Turnover Less than £100,000

FOUNDED 1974 to publish fiction and historical reprints. 15–20 titles are scheduled for 1988, with the emphasis on fiction, art and history. Journeyman is a literary political publisher with a feminist/socialist identity. *Publishes* art and graphics, feminist and socialist fiction, general, politics, social history.

No unsolicited mss. Synopses and ideas for books welcome.
Royalties paid twice yearly.

Kahn & Averill

9 Harrington Road, London SW7
☎01–743 3278

Managing Director M. Kahn

FOUNDED 1967. Originally published juvenile titles but gradually changed to music titles. A small independent publishing house. *Publishes* mainly music titles with some general non-fiction. 6 titles in 1986. Do not welcome unsolicited mss but will consider synopses and ideas for books.
Royalties paid twice yearly.

The Kensal Press

Riverview, Headington Hill,
Oxford OX3 0BT
☎0865 750302   Telex 849462 Telfac G

Managing Director Mrs Betty Millan

FOUNDED 1982. *Publishes* historical biographies. 10 titles in 1987.

General Manager Miss Georgina Shomroni
TITLES *The Musical Peacemaker, The Life and*
Music of Sir Edward German Brian Rees; *My Brother Benjamin* Beth Britten; *The Harlot and the Statesman, The Story of Elizabeth Armitstead and Charles James Fox* I.M. Davis. Prefer to see a synopsis rather than completed mss.
Royalties paid twice yearly for the first year and annually thereafter.

Kenyon-Deane

See **Cressrelles Publishing Co. Ltd**

William Kimber Ltd

Denington Estate, Wellingborough,
Northants NN8 2RQ
☎0933 440033
Telex 311072 THOPUB G/312511 TPGBKS
                         Fax 09333 440512

Chairman/Managing Director
William Kimber

FOUNDED 1950. Bought by **Thorsons** in 1988. *Publishes* biography and memoirs, current affairs, fiction (including historical romance), general history, military and aviation, naval, sport, travel. 45 titles in 1987.

TITLES *Nigel Mansell, The Makings of a Champion* Christopher Hilton; *Colditz Last Stop* Major Jack Pringle; *Stratagem: A Novel of the Secret Service* Harman Grisewood; *One Man's SAS* Lofty Large; *Stormy Heritage* Mary Williams; *Countdown to War* Geoffrey Cox; *Tales from the Hidden World* R. Chetwynd-Hayes; *U-Boat Aces* Geoffrey P. Jones. Prefer preliminary letter and synopsis.
Royalties paid twice yearly. *Overseas associates* in Australia, Canada, Ireland, Isle of Man, New Zealand, Scandinavia and Western Europe, South Africa.

Kingfisher Books

Elsley House, 24–30 Great Titchfield Street,
London W1P 7AD
☎01–631 0878
Telex 27725 Gridem G   Fax 01–323 4694

Managing Director Daniel Grisewood

The publishing imprint of Grisewood and Dempsey Ltd. *Publishes* children's books (poetry and fiction, history, general reference, paperbacks, young readers, picture books), dictionaries, natural history and reference books. 75 titles in 1988.

Editorial Head *Jane Olliver* TITLES Children's Reference: *Picture Encyclopedia of Our World*; *Astronomy Today*; *The Age of Dinosaurs*; *Kingpin Superbooks/Factbooks*. Science & Nature: *Exploring the Countryside*; *Dictionary of Animals*; *National Trust Book of the Armada*. Poetry/Fiction: *A Spider Bought a Bicycle*; *The Odyssey*. ADULT TITLES *Coastline: Britain's Threatened Heritage*; *Historical Atlas of Britain*; Guides to *Birds/Mushrooms/Herbs*; Field Guides to *Wild Flowers/Wildlife/Plantlife/Birds of Britain and Europe*. Welcome unsolicited mss.
Royalties paid twice yearly.

Kluwer Academic Publishers (bv)

1 Harlequin Avenue, Great West Road, Brentford, Middx TW8 9EW
☎01–568 6441
Telex 917490 ELEKTR G   Fax 01–847 2610

Managing Director *Colin B. Ancliffe*

FOUNDED 1900. Kluwer Academic Publishers is a specialist academic publishing house incorporating Martinus Nijhoff Publishers, D. Reidel Publishing Company, Dr W. Junk Publishers and **MTP Press**. The head office is in Dordrecht, the Netherlands with additional editorial/marketing centres in Boston, USA, and Lancaster in the UK. *Publishes* books for the professional and business markets, science and technology, legal and fiscal, educational, literary and reference works. See also **MTP Press**.

DIVISIONS
Law *Elizabeth A.O. Bramwell* **Professional** *Colin B. Ancliffe* 99% of the work is commissioned and therefore synopses and outlines are preferred to complete mss.
Royalties paid twice yearly.

Authors' Rating Third-biggest Dutch publisher in which Robert Maxwell has a stake. Recently fought off takeover bid from

Elsevier. Strong on scholarly books, many of which are published in English.

Knight Books

See **Hodder & Stoughton Ltd**

Kogan Page Ltd

120 Pentonville Road, London N1 9JN
☎01–278 0433
Telex 263088 KOGAN G   Fax 01–837 3768

Managing Director *Philip Kogan*
Approx Annual Turnover £3 million

ESTABLISHED 1967 by Philip Kogan, the company originally published one title only: *The Industrial Training Yearbook*. Now *Publishes* business and management, education and careers, marketing, personal finance, personnel, science and technology, small business, training and industrial relations, transport, plus journals. Continuing to expand, particularly in the professional and technical areas. 150 titles in 1987.

DIVISIONS
Kogan Page *Piers Burnett, Pauline Goodwin, June Lines* TITLES *New Technology Modular* series; *New Generation Computing* series; *Working for Yourself* series; BIM books; *Professional* paperbacks; *Careers* series; *Stoy Hayward Business Tax Guide*. **North Oxford Academic Publishers** *Piers Burnett* TITLES *World Yearbook of New Generation Computing*. *Publishes* computer science. Unsolicited mss, synopses and ideas for books welcome.
Royalties paid twice yearly.

Authors' Rating An object lesson on how to succeed in publishing by carving out a section of the market. Publishing decisions based on a close knowledge of the industrial and commercial scene.

Ladybird Books Ltd

Beeches Road, Loughborough,
Leics LE11 2NQ
☎0509 268021
Telex 341347   Fax 0509 234672

Chairman *T.J. Rix*
Managing Director *M.P. Kelley*
Approx Annual Turnover £12 million

FOUNDED 1860s. Part of the **Longman Group**. The Ladybird name and format was established as a result of the development of a children's list during World War 1. In the early 1960s the print side of the operation was abandoned in favour of publishing and in 1971 the company was bought by the Pearson Longman Group. *Publishes* children's trade titles only. 80 titles in 1987.

Editorial Head *M.H. Gabb* TITLES *Well Loved Tales; Puddle Lane series; Activity Books and Packs; Learning to Read; Read it Yourself; Thomas the Tank Engine; Transformers; Rupert; Action Force; Disney; Beatrix Potter; Barbie; Classics; Friezes; Nursery Rhymes; Fairy Tales; Information Books.* Very rarely able to make use of unsolicited mss as material is generally commissioned once publication programme has been determined.
Overseas Associates Ladybird Books, Auburn, Maine, USA.

Authors' Rating Good, simple stuff for kiddies of a sentimental turn of mind. Criticised for perpetuating the image of female subservience. But popular in the bookshops. One of the few imprints everybody has heard of.

Lakeland Paperbacks
See **Marshall Pickering Holdings Ltd**

Allen Lane The Penguin Press
See **Viking**

Lawrence & Wishart Ltd
39 Museum Street, London WC1A 1LQ
☎01–405 0103

Chairman *R. Simon*
Managing Director *Sally Davison*

ESTABLISHED 1936 in its present form. *Publishes* cultural politics, economics, history, politics, and sociology. 13–20 titles a year.

Editorial Head *Stephen Hayward* TITLES *Liverpool – Gateway of Empire; War Without End; Solidarity Forever; The IWW, an Oral History of the Wobblies; We Refuse to Starve in Silence; Banking on Sickness.* Unsolicited mss welcome if in keeping with the character of the list. Synopses preferred to complete mss. Ideas welcome.
Royalties paid annually, unless by arrangement.

Authors' Rating One of the few genuine left-wing publishers. Authors should expect to surrender profit to principles.

Leicester University Press
Fielding Johnson Building,
University of Leicester, University Road,
Leicester LE1 7RH
☎0533 523333
Telex 341198   Fax 0533 522200

Secretary to the Press *P.L. Boulton*

Part of the University of Leicester. *Publishes* academic books in archaeology, defence studies, history, literature, politics and international relations. 13 titles in 1987.

Unsolicited mss considered if on appropriate subjects. Synopses and ideas for books welcome.
Royalties paid annually.

Authors' Rating Strong but small academic list does not allow for many opportunities for outsiders.

Lennard Publishing
Lennard House, 92 Hastings Street, Luton,
Beds LU1 5BH
☎0582 404333   Fax 0582 27748

Chairman *A.K.L. Stephenson*
Managing Director *Adrian Stephenson*
Approx Annual Turnover £800,000

A division of the book-packaging company, Lennard Books. FOUNDED 1986 by Adrian Stephenson. First publishing list appeared in 1987 with titles such as *The World's Worst Golf Club* Bill Tidy; *Monty: The Man Behind the Legend* Nigel Hamilton, and *Entertainment USA.* 11 titles in 1987. 20 titles in 1988.

Editorial Head *Roderick Brown*   TITLES *In Search of English Gardens* ed. Priscilla Boniface; *Unexplored London* Paul Barkshire. Unsolicited mss, synopses and ideas for books welcome.
Royalties paid twice yearly.

Lepus

See A. & C. Black (Publishers) Ltd

F. Lewis (Publishers) Ltd

See A. & C. Black (Publishers) Ltd

Lewis Brooks Ltd

2 Blagdon Road, New Malden,
Surrey KT3 4AD
☎01–949 4699   Telex 24667 Impemp G

Chairman *John M. Verge*

Publishes academic and scholarly, architecture & design, engineering, reference books and dictionaries, scientific and technical.

Editorial Director *John M. Verge*

Line One Publishing

Unit 2, Mead Park, Mead Road,
Cheltenham, Glos GL53 7EF
☎0242 584407

Managing & Editorial Director
Malcolm Cook

Publishes aviation, biography and autobiography, military and war, nautical, transport.

Unsolicited mss not welcome.
Royalties paid twice yearly.

Lion Publishing plc

Icknield Way, Tring, Herts HP23 4LE
☎0442 82 5151
Telex 825850 LION G   Fax 044282 7251

Approx Annual Turnover £5.5 million

FOUNDED 1971; went public 1975. A Christian book publisher strong on illustrated books for a popular readership. International mar-ket, with rights sold in 41 languages worldwide. Set up US subsidiary in 1984. *Publishes* diverse list with Christian viewpoint the common denominator. All ages, from board books for children to multi-contributor adult reference. Children's fiction and non-fiction, educational, paperbacks, and colour co-edition. 60 titles in 1987.

Contacts Unsolicited adult mss: *Mrs Pat Alexander* (Editorial Director); unsolicited children's mss: *Ms Su Box*. Unsolicited mss welcome providing they have a positive Christian viewpoint intended for a wide general and international readership. No books on academic theology, or books intended expressly for the Church. Unsolicited synopses and ideas for books also welcome.
Royalties paid twice yearly. *Overseas associates* Lion Publishing Corp., USA.

Liverpool University Press

PO Box 147, Liverpool L69 3BX
☎051–709 6022   Telex 627095

Managing Director *Robin Bloxsidge* (Acting)

FOUNDED 1899 as the publishing arm of the university, LUP has made its mark in the social sciences and humanities. Recently, the list has expanded to take in medicine and veterinary science. *Publishes* academic and scholarly, hardback and paperback books in the fields of: archaeology, architecture, business studies, commerce, economics, education, geography, ancient and modern history, English literature, philosophy, politics, psychology, sociology, town planning, veterinary science and medicine. 14 titles in 1987.

Acting Publisher/Editorial Head *Robin Bloxsidge*   TITLES *Greek, Etruscan and Roman Vases in the Lady Lever Art Gallery, Port Sunlight; Byron and the Limits of Fiction; The Chester Mystery Cycle – A New Staging Text; En Marge du Classicisme – Essays on the French Theatre from the Renaissance to the Enlightenment; Ida Rubinstein (1885–1960) – A*

Theatrical Life; Aspects of Hypoxia; A Handbook of Pig Diseases. Unsolicited mss, synopses and ideas for books welcome.
Royalties paid annually.

Livewire
See The Women's Press

Longman Group UK Limited
Longman House, Burnt Mill, Harlow, Essex CM20 2JE
☎0279 26721
Telex 81259   Fax 0279 31059

Chairman *Tim Rix*
Approx Annual Turnover £71 million

FOUNDED 1724 by Thomas Longman. Now the largest educational publishing house in the English-speaking world (outside the United States). Part of Pearson plc. *Publishes* educational, medical books and journals, professional and reference. Over 1000 titles in 1987 (excluding **Pitman** and **Ladybird**).

DIVISIONS
Academic Scientific & Medical *Robert Duncan* **Business & Professional** *Patrick Munday* **International** *Paula Kahn* **UK Schools** *Roger Watson*

MAIN IMPRINTS
Churchill Livingstone, Longman, Longman Professional, Longman Scientific & Technical, Olive & Boyd, Pitman.
All unsolicited mss should be addressed to Mr David Lea, **Contracts & Copyright Manager.**
Royalties paid annually. *Overseas associates* in 23 countries around the world.

Authors' Rating Spearhead for the Pearson assault on the American education market. The recent purchase of **Addison-Wesley** was a big advance on this front. One area of uncertainty is Rupert Murdoch's 14% interest in Pearson. Could this presage a link with **Collins/Harper & Row**? Possibly, conclude the boardroom pundits, but not before the Monopolies Commission has had its say.

Longman is responsible for much formula publishing for the education market. Not especially exciting but always profitable. The best way in is to get to know one of the series editors.

Loxwood Stoneleigh
See Falling Wall Press

Lund Humphries Publishers Ltd
16 Pembridge Road, London W11 3HL
☎01–229 1825   Telex 8950511 Lundhump

Chairman *Lionel Leventhal*
Managing Director *Clive Bingley*

Part of Book Publishing Development plc (same address). Founded to publish fine art books, the first Lund Humphries titles appeared in 1895. The company became Percy, Lund Humphries in the 1930s, and achieved its present identity in 1969. *Publishes* graphics, design, art and architecture, plus language guides. 20 titles in 1986. Plans are in progress to expand the graphic arts and design list in the years to come. Unsolicited mss welcome, although an advance letter is preferred. Synopses and ideas for books considered.
Royalties paid twice yearly.

Lutterworth Press
PO Box 60, Cambridge CB1 2NT
☎0223 350865   Fax 0223 66951

Managing Director *Adrian Brink*

Lutterworth Press dates back to the eighteenth century when it was founded by the Religious Tract Society. In the nineteenth century it was best known for its children's books, both religious and secular, including *The Boys' Own Paper.* Bought by the Cambridge publishing house, James Clarke & Co. Ltd in 1984 and absorbed Patrick Hardy Books. *Publishes* general non-fiction: antiques and collecting, architecture and design, children's books, crafts and hobbies, educational and textbooks, fine art and art history, gardening, natural history, religion and theology, sports and games, theatre and drama. 23 titles in 1987.

Senior Editor *Linda Yeatman* TITLES *Forbidden Knowledge: The Paranormal Paradox* Bob Couttie; *The Quest for Olwen* Gwyn Thomas and Kevin Crossley-Holland; *Anthony Salvin: Pioneer of Gothic Revival Architecture* Jill Allibone; *Terry Bond's Book of Birds* Terry Bond; *A Small Pinch of Weather* Joan Aiken. Unsolicited mss and synopses are welcome. *Royalties* paid both quarterly and bi-annually.

Authors' Rating The list is expanding but it still has its anchor in evangelical publishing. Imaginative children's list.

Lythway Large Print
See **Chivers Press (Publishers)**

Macdonald & Co. Ltd
3rd Floor, Greater London House,
Hampstead Road, London NW1 7QX
☎01–377 4600   Telex 885233

Managing Director *James Mann*
Approx Annual Turnover in excess of £30 million

FOUNDED 1930s. Part of BPCC since the 1960s Now part of Maxwell Communications. *Publishes* architecture and design, auto/biography, children's books, cinema, cookery, crafts and hobbies, DIY, educational/textbooks, fiction, gardening, geography/geology, guide books, history, humour, illustrated editions, medical, natural history, nautical, photography, poetry, reference, sports/games, theatre and drama, travel and topography, wines and spirits. 801 titles in 1986.

DIVISIONS
Children's *Mary Tappissier* Many titles, from board books for the very young to the **Junior Fiction** Series. **Fiction** TITLES *A Long Road Winding* Margaret P. Kirk; *Shadows on the Snow* Madge Swindells; *The Eyes of the Dragon* Stephen King; *Patience of a*

Saint Andrew M. Greeley. **Non-Fiction** TITLES *World War I in Photographs*; *Travelling With Children*; *The Psychology of Cancer*; *Francoise Bernard's French Cooking*; *Les Routiers Guide to France 1987*; *How To Draw and Sketch/Paint Nature, etc.*; *Creative Knitting*.

IMPRINTS
Futura *Alan Samson* TITLES *Eavesdropper* John Francombe and James MacGregor; *Down Our Street* Lena Kennedy; *Children First and Always* Derek and Gillian Mercer; *Joyful Voices* Doris Stokes. **Orbis** *Sarah Snape* Illustrated books. **Optima** *Phillipa Stewart* Alternative publishing. **Queen Anne Press** *Alan Samson* TITLES *Joan Sutherland* Norma Major; *The Complete British Motorist* Lord Montagu of Beaulieu; *You'll Never Walk Alone* Stephen Kelly; *Middle Stump* Graham Thompson; *Playfair Racing Annual*; *The Good Golf Guide*; *Glassfibre Boat Manual*. Welcome unsolicited mss.
Royalties paid twice yearly.

Authors' Rating A company in some confusion after the sudden departure of Christopher Falkus. He was Chief Executive for just two months. His problems may well have arisen with the fuss over the Maxwell biographies.

McGraw-Hill Book Co. (UK) Ltd
McGraw-Hill House, Shoppenhangers Road,
Maidenhead, Berks SL6 2QL
☎0628 23432
Telex 848484   Fax 0628 35895

Parent Company *McGraw-Hill Inc.*, New York
Managing Director *Stephen White*

FOUNDED 1899 in London and moved to Maidenhead in 1963. The British publishing programme started in 1965. *Publishers* high-level textbooks, academic books in the fields of sciences and chemistry, educational and reference books for the professions and management. 60 titles in 1987.

DIVISIONS
Education *Stephen White* **Professional** *Roland Elgey* Unsolicited mss, synopses and ideas for books welcome.
Royalties paid twice yearly.

Authors' Rating Nowadays, tends to keep a low profile, but works on a solid foundation of academic and high-level textbooks. No wayout ideas. No to be confused with the aggressive American parent company.

Macmillan Children's Books Ltd
4 Little Essex Street, London WC2R 3LF
☎01–836 6633   Telex 262024

Publishing Director *Michael Wace*

Publishes children's fiction and non-fiction. Mss and synopses welcome.
Royalties paid twice yearly.

Authors' Rating A popular list overseen by one of the pioneers of imaginative children's publishing.

Macmillan Education Ltd
Houndmills, Basingstoke, Hants RG21 2XS
☎0256 29242   Telex 858493

Chairman *A. Soar*
Managing Director *J.E. Jackman*

Publishes biology and zoology, business and industry, computer science, computer software (educational), economics, educational and textbooks, engineering, geography and geology, history and antiquarian, languages and linguistics, law, literature and criticism, mathematics and statistics, medical, music, natural history, philosophy, physics, politics and world affairs, psychology, reference books and dictionaries, religion and theology, scientific and technical, sociology and anthropology, theatre and drama, vocational training and careers, women's studies.

Publishing Director (primary and secondary) *R.S. Balkwill* **Publishing Director** (college) *P.I. Murby* TITLES *New Way Reading Scheme; Macmillan Master Series; Macmillan*

Work Out Study Aids. Unsolicited mss welcome.
Royalties paid annually.

Authors' Rating After a rocky few years when school budgets were tight, the company is now restored as a major force in the market. Some authors' complaints of insensitive handling but efforts have been made to improve communications.

Macmillan London Ltd
4 Little Essex Street, London WC2R 3LF
☎01–836 6633   Telex 262024

Chairman *Nicholas Byam Shaw*
Managing Director *Philippa Harrison*

Publishes biography and autobiography, cookery, crime, fashion and costume, fiction, fine art and art history, gardening, guide books, health and beauty, history and antiquarian, humour, literature and criticism, music, natural history, photography, poetry, politics and world affairs, psychology, sports and games, theatre and drama, wines and spirits.

DIVISIONS
Crime *Hilary Hale* AUTHORS Colin Dexter, Paula Gosling, Julian Symons, Loren D. Estleman **Fiction** *James Hale* AUTHORS Nina Bawden, Anne Schlee, Derek Robinson, Iain Banks, Mary Wesley, E.V. Thomson **Non-Fiction** *Adam Sisman* AUTHORS Elizabeth Taylor, Alistair Horne, Anton Mosiman, Hugo Young **Papermac** *Kyle Cathie* AUTHORS Victoria Glendinning, Anthony Howard, Marcella Hazan, Rob Buckman. Unsolicited mss and synopses welcome.
Royalties paid twice yearly.

Authors' Rating After years of jogging along on limited resources, Macmillan London is beginning to go after the big titles. This could be good news for emerging talents who need a push from an ambitious publisher.

The Macmillan Press Ltd
4 Little Essex Street, London WC2R 3LF
☎01–836 6633   Telex 262024

Chairman *A. Soar*
Managing Director *C.J. Paterson*

Publishes academic and scholarly, accountancy and taxation, agriculture, animal care and breeding, archaeology, architecture and design, bibliography and library service, biography and autobiography, biology and zoology, business and industry, chemistry, cinema and video, computer science, economics, engineering, art history, geography and geology, guide books, history and antiquarian, languages and linguistics, law, literature and criticism, mathematics and statistics, medical, military and war, music, natural history, philosophy, physics, politics and world affairs, psychology, dictionaries, religion and theology, scientific and technical, sociology and anthropology, theatre and drama, transport, travel and topography, business reference and directories, biotechnical reference, telecommunications, vocational training and careers, women's studies. 500 titles in 1987.

DIVISIONS
Medical & Scientific Books & Journals *H. Holt* **Postgraduate & Scholarly** *T.M. Farmiloe* **Reference & Professional & Music** *J.F.K. Ashby* Unsolicited mss welcome. *Royalties* paid annually.

Authors' Rating A strong list of academic and reference books, with the *New Palgrave* creeping up on *Grove's Dictionary of Music* as the lead moneyspinner. Some risk of confusing modest sellers (mainly to academic libraries) with the titles which should have a more general appeal.

Macmillan Publishers Ltd
4 Little Essex Street, London WC2R 3LF
☎01–836 6633   Telex 262024

Chairman *Earl of Stockton*
Managing Director *N.G. Byam Shaw*
Approx Annual Turnover £160 million

DIVISIONS
Parent Company of **BASW Macmillan, Ltd Macmillan Children's Books Ltd, Macmillan Education Ltd, Macmillan Intek Ltd, Macmillan London Ltd, Macmillan Magazines Ltd, The Macmillan Press Ltd, Pan Books Ltd, Sidgwick & Jackson Ltd**

Overseas associates Gill & Macmillan (Eire), Macmillan India Ltd, The Macmillan Co. of Australia Ltd, Macmillan Shuppan KK Ltd (Japan), Macmillan South-East Asia Pty Ltd, Macmillan Publishers (Overseas) Ltd, Macmillan Publishers (China) Ltd, Macmillan Kenya (Publishers) Ltd, The Macmillan Co. of New Zealand Ltd, Macmillan Boleswa Publishers Ltd, Macmillan Nigeria Publishers Ltd, **St Martin's Press Inc.** (New York), The College Press Ltd (Zimbabwe), Editorial Macmillan de Mexico SA de CV, Macmillan Publishers (Malaysia), Grove's Dictionary of Music Inc. (New York), Stockton Press Inc. (New York), Nature America Inc. (New York), Nature Japan KK, The Macmillan Language House Ltd, Japan, Bookmark Associates Ltd (Hong Kong).

Authors' Rating Still a family company (the chairman is the second Earl of Stockton), Macmillan has self-financed its way to the top. Very much a loner in the publishing business (the company has just left the **Publishers' Association**) its future is not easy to predict. But the recent acquisition of Pan shows the group on the expansion trail.

Julia MacRae Books
87 Vauxhall Walk, London SE11 5HJ
☎01–793 0909
Telex 8955572   Fax 01–587 1123

Managing Director *Julia MacRae*

FOUNDED 1979 by Julia MacRae (previously with **Hamish Hamilton**). A division of **Walker Books**. *Publishes* children's books, mostly fiction with some non-fiction. Some general books. Approx. 45 titles in 1987.

TITLES *Gorilla* Anthony Brown; *Through the Doll's House Door* Jane Gardam; *Nature of the Beast* Janni Howker; *Running Scared* Bernard Ashley. Welcome unsolicited mss, synopses and ideas for books.
Royalties paid twice yearly.

Magnet
See Methuen Children's Books

Mainstream Publishing Co. (Edinburgh) Ltd
7 Albany Street, Edinburgh EH1 3UG
☎031–557 2959
Telex 265871 Ref MNU 377

Directors *Peter MacKenzie, Bill Campbell*

Publishes alternative medicine, autobiography, biography, current affairs, fiction, history, illustrated and fine editions, literature and criticism, military and war, politics and world affairs, popular paperbacks. 40 titles in 1987.

Editorial Director *Bill Campbell* Unsolicited mss welcome.
Royalties paid twice yearly.

Manchester University Press
Oxford Road, Manchester M13 9PL
☎061–273 5539
Telex 668932 MCHRUL   Fax 061–274 3346

Chief Executive *Francis Brooke*
Approx Annual Turnover £1 million

A department of Manchester University founded early this century. The list remained largely history-based until after the war, when it took up anthropology with great success. It is now Britain's third-largest university press. *Publishes* academic and educational books in the areas of anthropology, biomedical science and non-linear dynamics, history, law (especially international), literature, modern languages, politics, sociology. 90 titles in 1987. It also publishes 5 journals.

DIVISIONS
Humanities *John Banks* **Science** *Alec McAulay* Unsolicited mss welcome.
Royalties paid annually.

George Mann Books
PO Box 22, Maidstone, Kent ME14 1AH
☎0622 595591

Chairman & Managing Director *John Arne*
Approx Annual Turnover £50,000–£75,000

FOUNDED 1972 originally as library reprint publishers but with the collapse of the library market moved on to other things. *Publishes* selected reprints with some original non-fiction: autobiography, militaria, the occult and prophecy. No new fiction. Must have synopsis with preliminary letter.
Royalties paid twice yearly.

Marshall Pickering Holdings Ltd
3 Beggarwood Lane, Basingstoke,
Hants RG23 7LP
☎0256 59211   Telex 858669

Managing Director *John T. Hunt*

Part of Zondervan Corporation, USA. One of the biggest Christian paperback publishers. *Publishes* academic and scholarly, biography and autobiography, children's, fiction, music, poetry, reference books and dictionaries, religion and theology. 107 titles in 1987.

Editorial Director *Deborah Thorpe*

IMPRINTS
Samuel Bagster & Sons Ltd, Contemporary Christian Studies, Lakeland Paperbacks, Marshall's Paperbacks, Marshall Pickering Marshall's Theological Library, New Century Bible Commentaries, Oliphants Unsolicited mss welcome.

SUBSIDIARIES
Greenprint Professional and **Business Information Ltd**
Royalties paid twice yearly.

Mercury
See W.H. Allen & Co. plc

Merlin Press Ltd
3 Manchester Road, London E14 9BD
☎01–987 7959

Managing Directors *Martin Eve, Norman Franklin*
Approx Annual Turnover £100,000

FOUNDED 1956 by Martin Eve. *Publishes* economics, history, philosophy, left wing politics. 10 titles in 1987.
AUTHORS Georg Lukacs, Ernest Mandel, Istvan Meszaros, Ralph Miliband, E.P. Thompson. No unsolicited mss; letter essential before sending either finished mss or synopses.
Royalties paid twice yearly.

Authors' Rating A more varied output expected now that Norman Franklin, former chairman of **Routledge**, has joined the executive team.

Mermaid
See **Michael Joseph Ltd**

Merrill Publishing Company
Holywell House, Osney Mead,
Oxford OX2 0PS
☎0865 791497   Fax 0865 727830

Manager *Michael Brightmore*

Part of Bell & Howell Inc., USA. *Publishes* academic and scholarly, business and industry, computer science, educational and textbooks, engineering, geography and geology, psychology, scientific and technical. 120 titles in 1987. Editorial office is in America (sales and marketing function only in UK) but all mss and queries should go through Michael Brightmore in Oxford. Unsolicited mss will be passed on to **Merrill Publishing Co.**, 1300 Alum Creek Road, Columbus, Ohio 43216, USA.

Methuen Children's Books
Michelin House, 81 Fulham Road,
London SW3 6RB
☎01–581 9393
Telex 290191   Fax 01–589 8419

Publisher *Rosemary Carter*

A division of **Octopus**. *Publishes* children's books (picture, fiction, non-fiction for young children to early teens). Children's paperbacks under the **Magnet** imprint. 250 titles in 1987. Welcomes unsolicited mss, synopses and ideas for books.
Royalties paid twice yearly.

Methuen London
Michelin House, 81 Fulham Road,
London SW3 6RB
☎01–581 9393
Telex 290191   Fax 01–589 8419

Publishing Director *Geoffrey Strachan*

A division of **Octopus**. *Publishes* general (adult fiction and non-fiction). 200 titles in 1987. Welcome unsolicited mss, synopses and ideas for books.
Royalties paid twice yearly.

Authors' Rating Still shell-shocked from recent changes of ownership – from Associated Book Publishers to Thomson International to **Octopus** – not to mention a move across London, Methuen will have to fight hard to retain its identity. A full and varied list is distinguished by a new drama imprint, putting Methuen ahead in this area of publishing.

Milestone Publications
62 Murray Road, Horndean, Hants PO8 9JL
☎0705 597440   Fax 0705 591975

Managing and Editorial Director
Nicholas J. Pine

Publishes antiques and collecting, business, economics, guide books, local history, military and war, reference books, sport, theatre, transport. 15 titles in 1986. Unsolicited mss not welcome. Approach in writing in first instance.
Royalties paid twice yearly.

Miller's Publishing
See **Mitchell Beazley Ltd**

Mills & Boon Ltd

Eton House, 18–24 Paradise Road,
Richmond, Surrey TW9 1SR
☎01–948 0444
Telex 24420 Milbon G   Fax 01–940 5899

Chairman *John T. Boon*
Managing Director *R.J. Williams*

FOUNDED 1908. *Publishes* fiction only. Over 500 titles in 1987.

Editorial Director *Frances Whitehead*

IMPRINTS
Doctor Nurse & Masquerade *Judith Murdoch* Established in the 1950s, and still going. *Doctor Nurse* romances are love stories set in a realistic medical world. *Masquerade* are historical romances, slightly longer than usual. **Gold Eagle Action Adventure** Fast-paced books, for action adventure fans, in which danger, suspense and split-second timing are essential. **Gold Eagle Novels** An exciting author-led range of thrillers, and powerful espionage and suspense novels. **Harlequin** *Linda Fildew* Longer than **Masquerade**, and aim to be 'sophisticated, unpredictable and well-written'. **Harlequin Love Affair** aim to be very contemporary in feel and are set in the USA. **Mills & Boon Romances** The traditional formula, with happy endings assured. **Mills & Boon Temptation** *Linda Fildew* Modern storylines aimed at younger and more affluent readers; temptation and choices with satisfying resolutions. **Silhouette** *Linda Fildew* Stories where 'there is more to love than mere romance'. **Silhouette Desire** are provocative and highly sensual. Unsolicited mss very welcome.
Royalties paid twice yearly.

Authors' Rating Not so much a company, more a national institution. So overwhelmed are they by writers dreaming of becoming romantic novelists (2000 unsolicited mss arrive over a year), Mills & Boon have produced a forty minute cassette tape, *And Then He Kissed Her*, which gives advice on how to construct a novel for this highly specialist market. (£2.99 from PO Box 236, Croydon, Surrey) Last year they came up with the

brightest marketing wheeze. Surplus stock was sold to a frozen food company who gave away books with fish fingers. Writing for Mills & Boon is nowhere near as easy as it looks but for those who can work the formula, the rewards are great.

The MIT Press Ltd

126 Buckingham Palace Road,
London SW1W 9SD
☎01–730 9208   Telex 23993

Chairman *F. Urbanowski*
Managing Director *N.C. Gosling*

Part of **MIT Press**, USA. *Publishes* academic, architecture and design, bibliography, biography and autobiography, biology and zoology, business and industry, chemistry, cinema and video, computer science, economics, educational and textbooks, engineering, fine art and art history, geography and geology, history and antiquarian, languages and linguistics, law, mathematics and statistics, medical, music, natural history, philosophy, photography, physics, politics and world affairs, psychology, reference, scientific and technical, sociology and anthropology, transport, travel and topography. All mss should go to the American office: 55 Hayward Street, Cambridge, Mass. 02142.

Mitchell Beazley Ltd

Artists' House, 14–15 Manette Street,
London W1V 5LB
☎01–439 7211
Telex 24892 Mbbook G   Fax 01–734 0389

Chairman *Ian Irvine*
Managing Director *Duncan Baird*
Approx Annual Turnover *£8 million*

FOUNDED 1969 by James Mitchell and John Beazley. Bought by **Octopus**, May 1987 for £4.85 million. *Publishes* illustrated non-fiction only, in general and leisure subjects: antiques, archaeology, cinema, cookery, crafts, fine art, gardening, geography/geology, guide books, health/beauty, history, humour, medical, music, natural history, photography, reference books/ dictionaries, religion/theology, travel and topography, wines. 35 titles in 1986.

DIVISIONS

Gardening Bob Saxton TITLES R.H.S. Gardening Guides **General Reference** James Hughes TITLES World Atlas of Archaeology; Atlas of the Universe **House & Interiors** Bob Saxton TITLES The House Book **Mitchell Beazley Encyclopaedias** Frank Wallis TITLES The Joy of Knowledge **Photography** Bob Saxton TITLES Kodak Encyclopaedia of Creative Photography **Travel** Chris Foulkes TITLES American Express Travel Series **Wine** Chris Foulkes TITLES World Atlas of Wine

IMPRINTS

Artist's House Kelly Flynn TITLES Men of the Stars Patrick Moore. **Emblem** Trade paperbacks. **Miller's Publishing** Judith Miller TITLES Miller's Antiques Price Guide Yearbook Welcome unsolicited mss, synopses and ideas for books within their subject areas listed.
Royalties paid twice yearly.

Moorland Publishing Co. Ltd

Moorfarm Road, Airfield Estate, Ashbourne, Derbyshire DE6 1HD
☎0335 44486
Telex 377106 Chacom G MPC

Managing Director Mr L. Porter
Approx Annual Turnover £500,000

FOUNDED 1971. Represented by **David & Charles** since 1986. Publishes travel guides, history of transport, collecting, and countryside guides. 16 titles in 1986.

Editorial Head Dr J. Robey Unsolicited mss will be considered, but synopses accompanied by letters of introduction preferred. Royalties paid annually.

A.R. Mowbray

Saint Thomas House, Becket Street, Oxford OX1 1SJ
☎0865 242507

Chief Executive Dennis Edwards
Managing Director (Publishing Division) Kenneth Baker
Approx Annual Turnover £400,000

FOUNDED 1858. Member of the **Publishers' Association** since 1899, Mowbray has retail shops in London, Cambridge and Birmingham. Publishes theology, Christian paperbacks, handbooks for clergy and laity. 36 titles in 1987.

Editorial Head Robert Williams Unsolicited mss welcome if accompanied by postage. Synopses and ideas for books considered.
Royalties paid twice yearly (unless under £10 is due).

MTP Press Ltd

Falcon House, Queen Square, Lancaster LA1 1RN
☎0524 68765/6/7
Telex 65212   Fax 0524 63232

Managing Director Dr F.W.B. van Eysinga
Approx Annual Turnover £1.5 million

MTP Press specialises in medical and scientific publishing at the postgraduate level. Publishes research monographs, postgraduate textbooks, colour atlases and texts for family physicians. Particular areas of specialisation include cardiology, nephrology, radiology, oncology, pathology, neurosciences and immunology. 55 titles in 1987.

TITLES AIDS (second edition) Dr V. Daniels; The Inner Consultation Dr R. Neighbour; Current Histopathology Series A Gresham (series ed.); Immunology and Medicine G. Reeves (series ed.); Developments in Cardiology Series; Replacement of Renal Function by Renal Dialysis (third edition) Maher; Peritoneal Dialysis Nolph. Imprint to be gradually phased out in favour of **Kluwer**.

Frederick Muller

See **Century Hutchinson Publishing Group Ltd**

John Murray (Publishers) Ltd

50 Albemarle Street, London W1X 4BD
☎01–493 4361
Telex 21312 Murray G   Fax 01–499 1792

Chairman *John R. Murray*
Managing Director *Nicholas Perren*

FOUNDED 1768 and continuously independent since then with its own distribution operation. Original publishers of Lord Byron, Jane Austen, Charles Darwin, Sir Arthur Conan Doyle, Freya Stark, Kenneth Clark and John Betjeman. *Publishes* general trade books, educational (secondary school and college textbooks), success studybooks. 64 titles in 1987.

DIVISIONS
General Books *Grant McIntyre* **Educational Books** *Keith Nettle* **Success Studybooks** *Bob Davenport* Welcome unsolicited mss or synopses.
Royalties paid twice yearly.

Authors' Rating One of the old school of publishers. High quality non-fiction for the erudite reader. Sensitive to authors and reliable on payments.

Nautical Publishing Co. Ltd

See A. & C. Black (Publishers) Ltd

Thomas Nelson & Sons Ltd

Nelson House, Mayfield Road,
Walton-on-Thames, Surrey KT12 5PL
☎0932 246133
Telex 929365 Nelson G   Fax 0932 246109

Managing Director *Michael Thompson*
Approx Annual Turnover £10 million

FOUNDED 1798. Part of the International Thomson Organisation. *Publishes* educational (infant, primary, secondary); school atlases and dictionaries, English language teaching world-wide, educational books for Africa, Caribbean and SE Asia.

Editorial Director *Graham Taylor* TITLES *Breakaway; Deutsche Heute; Peak Maths; Action!; ¡Vaya!; Nelson Handwriting; Counter-*

point. Unsolicited mss and synopses are welcome.
Royalties paid twice yearly.

Authors' Rating Coming back to life after a long period in the doldrums. Open to ideas for books on the practical side of education.

New Century Bible Commentaries

See **Marshall Pickering Holdings Ltd**

New English Library

See **Hodder & Stoughton Ltd**

New Portway Large Print

See **Chivers Press (Publishers)**

NFER–Nelson Publishing Co. Ltd

Darville House, 2 Oxford Road East,
Windsor, Berks SL4 1DF
☎0753 858961
Telex 937400   Fax 0753 856830

Managing Director *Michael Jackson*

FOUNDED 1981. Jointly owned by **Thomas Nelson** and the National Foundation for Educational Research. *Publishes* educational and psychological tests, educational books and journals. 45 titles in 1987.

Editorial Head *Tim Cornford* Some books and tests are commissioned, but unsolicited material is welcomed.
Royalties payments vary according to contract.

Nonesuch Press

See **Reinhardt Books Ltd**

North Oxford Academic Publishers

See **Kogan Page Ltd**

Northcote House Publishers Ltd

Harper & Row House, Estover Road,
Plymouth PL6 7PZ
☎0752 705251
Telex 45635   Fax 0752 777603

Managing Director *Roger Ferneyhough*
(Editorial)

FOUNDED 1985 by Roger Ferneyhough and
Brian Hulme following the purchase of 100
titles from **Longman** and **Mitchell Beazley**.
Distributed by **Harper & Row**, it was formed to develop trade paperbacks, business,
student and other titles designed to meet the
needs of a young and forward-looking
readership. *Publishes* self-help paperbacks,
textbooks and revision aids for students,
business, professional and reference, and
travel books. 19 titles in 1987.

Editorial Director *Roger Ferneyhough* 'Well-
thought out proposals with marketing arguments welcome.'
Royalties paid annually.

Oak
See **Omnibus Press**

Octopus Publishing Group
Michelin House, 81 Fulham Road,
London SW3 6RB
☎01–581 9393
Telex 920191   Fax 01–589 8419

Chairman *Paul Hamlyn*
Chief Executive *Ian Irvine*
Director of Publishing Development *Paul*
Richardson

FORMED 1971. Launched its first list in 1972
with 55 titles. Went public in 1983. The
Octopus Group acquired Bookwise Service
Ltd in 1984, and the Heinemann Group merged with Octopus in September 1985. Acquired Hamlyn Publishing Group in March
1986 and half of the Collins share of **Pan**
Books in September 1986. **Pan** interest sold
to **Macmillan** in 1987. Bought **Methuen**
London, Methuen Children's Books, Eyre
and Spottiswoode and **Pitkin Pictorials**
December 1987. Acquired **Mitchell Beazley**
in May 1987. Now owned by Reed International.

DIVISIONS
Conran Octopus Paul Hamlyn Publishing
comprising   **William   Heinemann,**

Heinemann Young Books, Leo Cooper,
Methuen London, Methuen Children's
Books, Eyre and Spottiswoode, Pitkin Pic-
torial, Octopus Books, Hamlyn Books,
Spring Books, Bounty Books. Hamlyn
Publishing Group (see **Paul Hamlyn Pub-**
lishing) **Heinemann Educational** and **Pro-**
fessional comprising **Heinemann**
Educational Books, Ginn & Co.,
Heinemann Professional Publishing,
Mitchell Beazley, Octopus Books Ltd (see
Paul Hamlyn Publishing).

Authors' Rating Paul Hamlyn is one of the
great publishing buccaneers who seems to
gain energy with the years. Having sold his
group to Reed International for £540 million,
he remains the man in charge, resisting all
unsolicited invitations to move on to a
quieter life. The move to Michelin House has
been complicated by the arrival of **Methuen**
from Thomson International. Lines of demar-
cation between imprints are, at the time of
writing, somewhat blurred.

Oliphants
See **Marshall Pickering Holdings Ltd**

Omnibus Press
8–9 Frith Street, London W1V 5TZ
☎01–434 0066
Telex 21892   Fax 01–439 2848

Managing Director *Robert Wise*

FOUNDED 1971 by Robert Wise and remains
independent. Produces books, song sheets,
songbooks, educational tutors, cassettes,
videos and software. *Publishes* music books
and rock and pop biographies. 45 titles in
1986.

Editorial Head *Chris Charlesworth*

IMPRINTS
Amsco, Bobcat, Oak, Omnibus, Proteus,
Wise. Welcome unsolicited mss and
synopses/ideas for books.
Royalties paid twice yearly. *Overseas assoc-*
iates Music Sales Corporation, New York;
Music Sales Pty, Sydney.

Open Books Publishing Ltd

Beaumont House, Wells, Somerset BA5 2LD
☎0749 77276

Managing Director *Patrick Taylor*

FOUNDED 1974. *Publishes* academic and
general. 6 titles in 1986. All books are commissioned and therefore do not welcome unsolicited mss and synopses.
Royalties paid twice yearly. *Overseas associates* Cambridge University Press Australia,
Century Hutchinson, South Africa.

Optima

See Macdonald & Co. Ltd

Orbis

See Macdonald & Co. Ltd

Orchard Books

10 Golden Square, LondonW1R 3AF
☎01–734 8738
Telex 262655 GROLOK G   Fax 01–439 1440

Managing Director *Judith Elliott*

FOUNDED 1985. Part of **Franklin Watts Ltd**.
Publishes children's hardbacks. 38 titles in
1987. Unsolicited mss, synopses and ideas for
books welcome.
Royalties paid twice yearly. *Overseas associates* Franklin Watts, Australia.

Oriel Press Ltd

See Chapman & Hall Limited

Orion Books

See Attic Books

Osprey

See George Philip & Son Ltd

Peter Owen Ltd

73 Kenway Road, London SW5 0RE
☎01–373 5628/370 6093

Chairman *Peter Owen*
Senior Editor *Michael Levien*

ESTABLISHED 1951. Known for its fiction, both
English and translated. Authors include Shu-
sako Endo, Paul Bowles, Anaïs Nin, Jane
Bowles, Anna Kavan, Peter Vansittart. *Publishes* biography, general books, literary fiction, sociology. No romance, thrillers, or
children's books. 30 titles in 1988. Unsolicited synopses welcome; mss should be preceded by a descriptive letter with s.a.e.
Royalties paid annually. *Overseas associates*
'Represented throughout the world'.

Authors' Rating Publishes very good books
which are not strong sellers. One of the few
publishers willing to risk new fiction. Good
on translations. Sometimes slow on payments.

Oxford Illustrated Press

See **Haynes Publishing Group**

Oxford Publishing Co.

See **Haynes Publishing Group**

Oxford University Press

Walton Street, Oxford OX2 6DP
☎0865 56767   Telex 837330

Chief Executive *Professor Sir Roger Elliot*
Approx Annual Turnover £100 million

A department of the university for several
hundred years, the company grew out of the
university's printing works and developed
into a major publishing business in the nineteenth century, concentrating on bibles and
education. *Publishes* academic books in all
categories, student texts, scholarly journals,
schoolbooks, ELT material, dictionaries, reference books, music, bibles, imported titles
from the USA and beyond, as well as paperbacks, general non-fiction and children's
books. Approximately 1000 titles per year.

DIVISIONS
Academic *R.D.P. Charkin* TITLES include
the *Concise Oxford Dictionary*. **Education**

P.R. Mothersole GCSE titles. **ELT** *G.P. Lewis* Streamline ELT course.

IMPRINTS
Clarendon Press *R.D.P. Charkin* Monographs in sciences, humanities, and social sciences. OUP welcomes first-class academic material in the form of proposals or accepted theses.
Royalties paid once/twice yearly. *Overseas subsidiaries* branches in Australia, India, Canada, Singapore, Hong Kong, Japan, East Africa, South Africa, New Zealand, plus sister company in New York.

Authors' Rating Inhibited for many years by its ties with the university and by the fanciful notion that academics know all there is to know about publishing, OUP has lately streamlined its administration and editorial services for a belated leap into the second half of the twentieth century. Can safely claim one of the finest academic lists in the world. Publishing policy allows for the acceptance of some unremunerative but worthy titles. Authors who still complain of production delays and unanswered correspondence agree that OUP are at least good payers.

Pagoda Books
79 Great Titchfield Street,
London W1P 7FN
☎ 01-637 0890
Telex 23539 VISION G   Fax 01-631 0043

Managing Director *David Alexander*

FOUNDED 1983. *Publishes* astrology, highly illustrated fiction, illustrated non-fiction, fine art, health, humour, juvenile, music, parenting. 9 titles in 1987.

Editorial Head *Susan Pinkus* TITLES *The Bible in Twentieth Century Art*; *Series of Illustrated Opera Libretti*; *The Dream – A Rebus*; *Gottle O' Geer* Ray Alan; *Ming Shu – The Art and Practice of Chinese Astrology* Derek Walters. Welcome unsolicited mss, synopses and ideas for books.
Royalties paid twice yearly.

Pan Books Ltd
18–21 Cavaye Place, London SW10 9PG
☎ 01-373 6070
Telex 917466   Fax 01-370 0746

Managing Director *Alan Gordon Walker*
Publishing Director *Ian S. Chapman*
Approx Annual Turnover £30 million

Mass-market paperback house. FOUNDED 1944. Published its first list in 1947. In 1961 had its first million-selling title, *The Dam Busters*. In 1961 published *Dr No* which went on to sell over 2 million copies. In 1964 instituted the Golden Pan Award for authors whose titles sold a million. The first winner was Alan Sillitoe for *Saturday Night, Sunday Morning*. **Piccolo**, the children's imprint, was set up in 1971. **Picador**, international modern fiction and non-fiction, started in 1972. The first Pan bookshop opened in the Fulham Road in 1975. **Pavanne** set up in 1984. **Macmillan** took over warehousing and distribution in 1981. Jointly owned by **Macmillan** and **Octopus** until 1987 when **Macmillan** bought out its co-owner. (The third founding partner, **Collins**, sold out to **Macmillan** and **Octopus** in 1986.) *Publishes* archaeology, architecture and design, atlases and maps, biography and autobiography, business and industry, children's, cinema and video, cookery, crafts and hobbies, economics, fiction, gardening, guide books history and antiquarian, humour, languages and linguistics, literature and criticism, medical, military and war, natural history, philosophy, photography, politics and world affairs, psychology, reference books and dictionaries, sports and games, theatre and drama, travel and topography, wines and spirits. Approximately 300 titles in 1987.

IMPRINTS
Pan *Ian S. Chapman* (Fiction) AUTHORS Douglas Adams, Jackie Collins, Daphne du Maurier, Colin Forbes, Dick Francis, Arthur Hailey, Georgette Heyer, Jack Higgins, Susan Howatch, John Le Carré, Somerset Maugham, Jean Plaidy, Tom Sharpe, Sidney Sheldon, Nevil Shute, Wilbur Smith, John Steinbeck. *Hilary Davies* (Non-fiction)

AUTHORS Gordon Burn, Heather Couper, Arthur Eperon, Frances Edmunds, Keith Floyd, Linda Goodman, Max Hastings, James Herriot, Madhur Jaffrey, Jack Nicklaus, Christopher Nolan, Roger Phillips. **Pavanne** *Suzanne Baboneau* AUTHORS Renata Adler, Hilary Bailey, Joan Didion, Gail Godwin, Alice Hoffman, Sara Maitland, Bel Mooney, Joyce Carol Oates, Lisa St Aubin de Teran, Susan Fromberg Schaeffer, Jill Tweedie, Fay Weldon **Picador** *Geoffrey Mulligan* AUTHORS Julian Barnes, Samuel Beckett, William Burroughs, Italo Calvino, Angela Carter, Bruce Chatwin, Umberto Eco, Germaine Greer, Gabriel Garcia-Marquez, Knut Hamsum, Russell Hoban, Clive James, Ken Kesey, Doris Lessing, Ian McEwan, Mario Vargas Llosa, Vladimir Nabokov, Thomas Pynchon, Jonathan Raban, Salman Rushdie, Edmund White, Tom Wolfe **Piccolo** (children's non-fiction) **Piper** (children's fiction – launched January 1988) *Marion Lloyd* AUTHORS Enid Bagnold, Judy Blume, Enid Blyton, Stephen Bowkett, Paula Danziger, Rudyard Kipling, Thomas Rockwell, Robert Westall, David Henry Wilson, Aliki and Franz Brandenburg, Michael Bond. Welcome unsolicited mss and synopses/ideas for books
Royalties paid twice yearly. *Overseas associates* Pan Books Australia (Pty) Ltd.

Authors' Rating Now entirely owned by **Macmillan**, this leading paperback house needs a chance to adjust to the departure of Sonny Mehta, the much admired chief editor of **Picador**, and managing director Simon Master, both of whom went to **Random House**. But it seems not all links are broken. Simon Master, who now heads up the **Chatto**, **Bodley Head**, **Cape** group, has agreed a co-publishing deal with Pan for new and backlist titles. This should keep up the supply of highly marketable titles at a time when paperback houses are in fierce competition. A huge range of titles benefits from skilful presentation and sales but there is a worry that the quality end of the market may be under pressure.

Pandora Press
See **Unwin Hyman Ltd**

Paperduck
See **Gerald Duckworth & Co. Ltd**

Paperfronts
See **Elliot Right Way Books**

Papermac
See **Macmillan London Ltd**

Partridge Press
See **Transworld Publishers Ltd**

Stanley Paul
See **Century Hutchinson Publishing Group Ltd**

Pavanne
See **Pan Books Ltd**

Pavilion Books Ltd
196 Shaftesbury Avenue,
London WC2H 8HL
☎01–836 1306
Telex 268369   Fax 01–240 7684

Joint Chairmen *Tim Rice,*
Michael Parkinson
Managing Director *Colin Webb*

Publishes biography, some children's, cinema and video, cookery, gardening, humour, knitting, popular art, sport, travel. 54 titles in 1987.

Editorial Director *Vivien Bowler* TITLES *Madhur Jaffrey's Cookbook*; *The Country House Garden, A Grand Tour* Gervase Jackson-Stops; *My East End* Anita Dobson; *The Complete Phantom of the Opera* George Perry; *The Lord's Cricket Companion* Benny Green; *Classic Country Pubs* Neil Hanson. Unsolicited mss not welcome. Synopses and ideas considered.
Royalties paid twice yearly.

PBI Publications
Britannica House, High Street,
Waltham Cross, Herts EN8 7DY
☎0992 23691
Telex 23957   Fax 0992 26452

Chairman & Managing Director *Dr D.G. Hessayon*

Part of the Tennant Group. Paperback publisher of gardening and agriculture books by Dr D.G. Hessayon.

TITLES *The Armchair Book of the Garden; The Garden Expert; The House Plant Expert; The Rose Expert; The Lawn Expert; The Flower Expert; The Tree & Shrub Expert; The Vegetable Expert; The Indoor Plant Spotter; The Home Expert* D.G. Hessayon. Do not consider unsolicited material.

Pelham Books

27 Wright's Lane, London W8 5TZ
☎01–937 7255   Telex 917181/2

Publisher *Roger Houghton*

FOUNDED 1960 specifically to publish *Pears Cyclopaedia* when the rights were bought from Lever Bros. The general imprint of **Michael Joseph**; parent company, **Penguin Books Ltd**. *Publishes* crafts, cookery, DIY, handbooks, sports biographies, sport and some leisure. 50 titles in 1987.

Senior Editor *John Beaton* TITLES *Pears Cyclopaedia; Benson & Hedges Cricket Year; Benson & Hedges Snooker Year; Born Lucky* John Francome; *Cross Country Riding* Lucinda Green. Welcome unsolicited mss, synopses and ideas for books.
Royalties paid twice yearly. *Overseas associates* Penguin Overseas.

Pelican

See **Penguin Books Ltd**

Penguin Books Ltd

27 Wright's Lane, London W8 5TZ
☎01–938 2200
Telex 917181/2   Fax 01–938 8704

Chairman *Peter Mayer*
Managing Director *Trevor Glover*
Approx Annual Turnover £225 million (1987)

Owned by Pearson. *Publishes* general and academic books of all kinds; atlases and maps, (auto)biography, business, children's, classics, crime, ELT, fiction, guide books, health, literature and criticism, poetry, reference books and dictionaries, sports, travel, women's studies. (See also **Michael Joseph, Hamish Hamilton, Sphere**.)

Publishing Director *Peter Carson*
Responsible for Penguin's adult publishing.

IMPRINTS
Pelican High-quality paperback non-fiction largely in the fields of the humanities and social sciences. **Peregrine** Academic paperbacks of lasting cultural or intellectual significance. **Puffin** *Elizabeth Attenborough* The leading children's paperback list in the UK, publishing in virtually all general fields, fiction, non-fiction, picture books, poetry. **Viking** (see separate listing) **Viking Kestrel** (see **Viking** entry) **Frederick Warne** (see separate listing). Unsolicited mss generally welcome. (Preliminary letter essential in the case of **Frederick Warne**.)
Royalties paid twice yearly. *Overseas associates* in Australia, New Zealand, and USA. Associate companies throughout the world including **New American Library**, Dutton and Dial.

Authors' Rating One of the great names of publishing which nearly disappeared under a surfeit of self satisfaction. Recovery began with the appointment of Peter Mayer who managed to inject American enterprise without destroying the character of an essentially British institution. 75% of Penguin's sales come from the backlist, a uniquely high figure in paperback publishing. Links with **New American Library** have improved chances of British writers crossing the water.

Pergamon Press plc

Headington Hill Hall, Oxford OX3 OBW
☎0865 64881
Telex 83177 Pergap G   Fax 0865 60285

Managing Director *G.F. Richards*

FOUNDED 1948. Owned by Maxwell Communications Corporation. *Publishes* academic and professional text and reference books and journals in agriculture, bibliography and library service, biology and zoology, business and industry, chemistry, computer science, economics, education, engineering, geography and geology, languages and linguistics, mathematics and statistics, medical, open learning, philosophy, physics, politics and world affairs, psychology, sociology and anthropology, vocational training and careers, women's studies. 300 titles in 1987. Also publishes *Chess* magazine and chess books.

Chief Executive *Kevin Maxwell* **Associate Publisher** (for Books) *Alan J. Steel* **Associate Publisher** (for Journals) *Dr Ivan Klimes* **Editorial Directors** *Barbara Barrett* (Social & Life Sciences), *Dr Colin Drayton* (Major Reference Works), *Jim Gilgunn-Jones* (Physical Sciences & Engineering). Welcome unsolicited mss if within specialist range.
Royalties paid annually. *Overseas associates* in USA, Australia, Japan, China, Germany and France.

Authors' Rating Factory publishing true to the ideals of Robert Maxwell. Impersonal but efficient as long as the author is prepared to do his own editing.

Phaidon Press Ltd
Littlegate House, St Ebbe's Street, Oxford OX1 1SQ
☎0865 246681
Telex 83308   Fax 0865 251959

Chairman *George J. Riches*
Managing Director *Geoff Cowen*

Publishes antiques and collecting, archaeology, architecture and design, crafts and hobbies, fine art and art history, guide books, photography, theatre and drama. 60 titles in 1988.

Editorial Head *Roger Sears* TITLES *Art Expo '88; Turner's Birds; Contemporary Women Artists; Women Expressionists; Altarpiece in Renaissance Italy; Hugh Casson's Oxford; Simone Martinie; Art Deco Sourcebook; Creative Typography; Phaidon Theatre Manuals; Phaidon Cultural Guides;*

The Tower of London; Vuillard; Dame Laura Knight; Elizabeth Blackadder; Atkinson Grimshaw. Welcome unsolicited mss although 'only approximately one per cent of unsolicited material gets published'.
Royalties paid quarterly.

Authors' Rating One of the two leading art publishers (the other is **Thames and Hudson**). Beautiful books on esoteric subjects.

George Philip & Son Ltd
27A Floral Street, London WC2E 9DP
☎01–836 1321
Telex 21667   Fax 01–240 3806

Managing Director *M.A. Bovill*
Approx Annual Turnover £10 million

Taken over by **Octopus** in April 1988. 150 years of atlas publishing with a relatively young list of specialist aviation and motoring books (**Osprey** imprint) which is a thriving growth area. *Publishes* aerospace, astronomy, atlases, automotive, maps, military, road atlases, sailing, travel.

DIVISIONS
Osprey *John Gaisford* TITLES *Men at Arms; Car Restoration; Air Combat* **George Philip** *John Gaisford* TITLES *Great World Atlas; RAC Road Atlases of Britain & Europe* **Stanford Maritime** *John Gaisford* TITLES *New Coastal Navigation; Sailing By the Stars.* Welcome unsolicited mss, synopses and ideas for books.
Royalties paid twice yearly.

Piatkus Books
5 Windmill Street, London W1P 1HF
☎01–631 0710
Telex 266082 PIATKS G   Fax 01–436 7137

Managing Director *Judy Piatkus*
Approx Annual Turnover £2 million

FOUNDED 1979. *Publishes* business, cookery, fiction, gift, health, practical, women's interests. Developing a new list of popular, inexpensive books. 80 titles in 1987.

Fiction *Judy Piatkus* TITLES *The Tiger's Heart* Lewis Orde; **Non-fiction** *Gill Cormode* TITLES *Colour Me Beautiful Make Up Book.* Welcome unsolicited mss, synopses and ideas for books.
Royalties paid twice yearly.

Authors' Rating Piatkus Books has grown from a one-room band to a thriving independent list. The company claims to give commitment to each book they take on and to treat every non-fiction title as a lead.

Picador
See **Pan Books Ltd**

Piccadilly Press
5 Canfield Place, London NW6 3BT
☎01–625 9582
Telex 295441   Fax 01–328 8256

Managing Director *Brenda Gardner*
Approx Annual Turnover £400,000

FOUNDED 1983 by Brenda Gardner. First titles published February 1984. Piccadilly plans to stay small, publishing between 20 and 25 titles per year. A total staff of 3. *Publishes* children's hardbacks, picture and story books, some teenage non-fiction. Just moving into teenage fiction. Unsolicited synopses and ideas for books welcome with s.a.e.
Royalties paid twice yearly.

Authors' Rating Inspired by the former children's editor of **W.H. Allen**, the company is gaining a reputation for quality and originality.

Piccolo
See **Pan Books Ltd**

Pitkin Pictorials Ltd
See **Octopus Publishing Group**

Pitman Publishing
128 Long Acre, London WC2E 9AN
☎01–379 7383
Telex 261367 Pitman G   Fax 01–240 5771

Chairman *Robert Duncan*
Managing Director *Ian Pringle*
Approx Annual Turnover £6.5 million

Part of the **Longman Group.** FOUNDED 1837 as the publisher of the Pitman Shorthand System ('150 years of innovation in business education.') Pitman has now joined **Longman** as its specialist Business Education and Information Technology publishing house. *Publishes* textbooks, reference and dictionaries in business education, including secretarial, business studies, management and professional studies. Professional and textbook publishers in all areas of information technology, including computers, microelectronics and telecommunications. 120 titles in 1987.

DIVISIONS
Business Education *K.C. Roberts* TITLES *Business A/Cs 1 & 2* Frank Wood **Business Management** *Simon Lake* TITLES *English Law; Accounting Theory and Practice* **Information Technology** *John Cushion* TITLES *Research Notes in Artificial Intelligence; Systems Design with Advanced Microprocessors* **Professional Studies** *Pat Bond* TITLES *M & E Handbooks* **Secretarial Studies** *Margaret Berriman* TITLE *Universal typing*

IMPRINTS
M & E *Pat Bond* TITLES *M & E Handbooks* **Pitman** *Ian Pringle* **Polytech Publishers** *Ian Pringle* TITLE *Finance* Frank Wood. Unsolicited mss, synopses and ideas for books welcome.
Royalties paid annually.

Authors' Rating Formerly a medical publisher of note, some authors were unhappy when they were hived off to other parts of the **Longman** empire. But Pitman are reasserting themselves with a growing reputation for good quality business books.

Planet
See **W.H. Allen & Co. plc**

Plenum Publishing Ltd
88–90 Middlesex Street, London E1 7EZ
☎01–377 0686

Chairman *Martin E. Tash* (USA)
Managing Director *Dr Ken Derham*

FOUNDED 1940. Part of **Plenum Publishing** New York. The London office is the editorial and marketing base for the UK and Europe. *Publishes* postgraduate, professional and research level scientific, technical and medical monographs, conference proceedings, reference books. Approximately 325 new titles (world-wide) per year.

Editorial Head *Dr Ken Derham* (UK and Europe)

IMPRINTS
Consultants Bureau, IFI Plenum Data Company, Plenum Medical Company, Plenum Press Synopses preferred to finished mss.
Royalties paid annually.

Plexus Publishing Ltd
30 Craven Street, London WC2N 5NT
☎01–839 1315/6   Telex 947157

Chairman *T.C. Porter*
Managing Director *S.M. Wake*

FOUNDED 1973. *Publishes* high quality illustrated books, specialising in international co-editions with an emphasis on art and cinema, biography, popular culture, popular music, rock'n'roll. 7 titles in 1987. Lead titles in 1988 *Bertolucci by Bertolucci*, *Hollywood Lolita* and *Hemingway Rediscovered*.

Senior Editor *Sandra Wake* Unsolicited mss, synopses and ideas welcome.
Royalties paid twice yearly.

Pluto Press Ltd
11–21 Northdown Street, London N1 9BN
☎01–837 3322

Bought by Zwan Publishers in 1987. *Publishes* academic and scholary books: cultural studies, general theory and ideology, politics and world affairs, social sciences, socialist and Marxist books, socialist reprints. 50 titles planned in 1988.

Authors' Rating Zwan takeover led to a radical editorial rethink. Now less cultural (no more theatre, cinema, literary criticism), much more political.

Polity Press
Dales Brewery, Gwydir Street,
Cambridge CB1 2LJ
☎0223 324315   Fax 0223 461385

FOUNDED 1984. All books are published in association with **Basil Blackwell Ltd,** Oxford. Archaeology and anthropology, criminology, economics, feminism, general interest, history, human geography, literature, media and cultural studies, medicine and society, philosophy, politics, psychology, religion and theology, social and political theory, sociology. 45 titles in 1987. Welcome unsolicited mss, synopses and ideas for books.
Royalties paid annually.

Polygon
48 The Pleasance, Edinburgh EH8 9TJ
☎031–558 1117/8

General Manager *Bob Sinclair*
Approx Annual Turnover £60,000

Owned by Edinburgh University Students Association and work with a group of Edinburgh University students. Took on the name of Polygon in 1980 since when there has been a steady increase in the number of titles published. *Publish* contemporary fiction, culture, general books, history, politics and Scottish literature. 14 titles in 1987.

Editorial Director *Pam Smith* Welcome unsolicited mss.
Royalties paid twice yearly.

Princeton University Press
15A Epsom Road, Guildford,
Surrey GU1 3JT
☎0483 68364   Fax 0483 301625

Director *Walter Lippincott* (in the USA)

Wide range of academic books, especially on biology, history and literature. 156 titles in 1987. Editorial department in the USA.

Prism Press Book Publishers Ltd

2 South Street, Bridport, Dorset DT6 3NQ
☎0308 27022   Fax 0308 27376
Telex 265871 MONREF G 84 MNU 247

Managing Director *Julian King*
Approx Annual Turnover £250,000

FOUNDED 1974 by Julian King and Colin Spooner. *Publishes* alternative medicine, architecture, building, conservation, environment, farming, feminism, health, law, mysticism, occult, philosophy, politics and wholefood cookery. 15 titles in 1987.

TITLES *Our Drowning World* Antony Milne; *Feminism & Censorship*; *Self Help Osteopathy* Robert Bowden; *Index Hortensis* Piers Trehane; *Reincarnation* David Christie-Murray. Unsolicited mss and synopses/ideas welcome.
Royalties paid twice yearly. *Overseas associates* Prism Press, USA.

Proteus

See Omnibus Press

Puffin

See Penguin Books Ltd

Quartet Books

27–9 Goodge Street, London W1P 1FD
☎01–636 3992
Telex 919034   Fax 01–439 6489

Chairman *Naim Attallah*
Approx Annual Turnover £1·4 million

FOUNDED 1972 by four ex-Granada employees, the company was acquired by Naim Attallah in 1976. Part of the Namara Group which includes **The Women's Press** (1977) and Robin Clark Ltd, (bought in 1980, now an imprint of Quartet Books). *Publishes* classical music books, fiction, jazz, literary biography, literature in translation (including French, Spanish, Russian, German, Swedish and Arabic), photographic, politics, popular non-fiction. 75 titles in 1987.

Editorial Director *Stephen Pickles*

DIVISIONS
Anthony Blond, Robin Clark, Quartet Crime, Quartet Encounters (a series of European literature in translantion, prose only)
TITLES *Hard Luck* James Maw; *Promise* Hugo Barnacle; *Cutting Timber* Thomas Bernhard; *The Dream of Heroes* Adolfo Bioy Casares; *A Dream of Something* Pier Paolo Pasolini; *The Temptation to Exist* E.M. Cioran; *Russian Novel* Edward Kuznetsov; *The Star Chernobyl* Julia Voznesenskaya; *Diary* Witold Gombrowicz; *Portraits* Helmut Newton; *A Woman in Your Own Right*, *The Mirror Within* Anne Dickson; *Judith Gautier* Joanna Richardson. Welcomes unsolicited mss and synopses/ideas for books.
Royalties paid twice yearly.

Authors' Rating A high-profile company riding on the flamboyant reputation of its owner, Naim Attallah, a wealthy Palestinian-born entrepreneur whose other publishing interests include the best of the book journals, *The Literary Review*. Owns Pipeline, one of the most efficient of the paperback wholesalers. Writers are encouraged to think big but payments can be erratic.

Queen Anne Press

See Macdonald & Co. Ltd

Quiller Press

46 Lillie Road, London SW6 1DN
☎01–499 6529   Telex 21120

Managing Director *Jeremy Greenwood*

Quiller specialise in sponsored books and publications sold through non-book trade channels as well as bookshops through **Century Hutchinson**. But not vanity publishing. *Publishes* architecture, biography, business and industry, children's, cookery, crafts and hobbies, DIY, gardening, guide books, humour, reference, sports, travel, wine and spirits. 15 titles in 1987.

Editorial Director *Jeremy Greenwood* Unsolicited mss not welcome, as ideas nearly always originate in-house.
Royalties paid twice yearly.

Raintree Press
See Basil Blackwell Ltd

The Ramsay Head Press
15 Gloucester Place, Edinburgh EH3 6EE
☎031–225 5646

Joint Managing Directors
Mrs Christine Wilson and *Conrad Wilson*

A small independent family publisher. FOUNDED 1968 by Norman Wilson OBE. *Publishes* biographies, cookery, Scottish fiction and non-fiction. Approximately 6 titles in 1986.

TITLES *White Stone Country; Reminiscences of Growing Up in Buchan* David Ogston; *Murder, Murder, Polis* Maureen Sinclair; *A Handy Guide to Scots* William Graham; *The Autobiography of a Poet* Duncan Glen; *Shadows from the Greater Hill* Tessa Ransford. Welcome synopses and ideas for books if they come within their range (Scottish).
Royalties paid twice yearly.

Reinhardt Books Ltd
27 Wright's Lane, London W8 5TZ
☎01–938 1253

Chairman/Managing Director
Max Reinhardt

FOUNDED 1987 by Max Reinhardt after resigning from the **Chatto, Bodley Head, Cape** group. 'A team of friends and colleagues publishing for pleasure.' With authors Graham Greene, Alistair Cooke and Maurice Sendak under their wing, plan to publish biography, children's books and fiction. First publication in September 1988 – Graham Greene's new novel, *The Captain and the Enemy*. Own

Nonesuch Press, publishers of famous classics and limited editions.

Editorial Consultant *Judy Taylor* Will consider unsolicited mss for fiction and synopses for non-fiction.

Authors' Rating The grand old man of publishing sets out on his own – with a little help from Graham Greene and other devotees. Max Reinhardt believes there is a niche for publishers 'who are small, personal and more attentive to their authors'. He is right. But he admits the need for accommodation and a distribution service – provided by big brother **Penguin**.

Robinson Publishing
11 Shepherd House, Shepherd Street, London W1Y 7LD
☎01–493 1064   Telex 28905 Ref 778

Managing Director *Nick Robinson*

FOUNDED 1983. *Publishes* general fiction and non-fiction trade paperbacks, some hardbacks. Specialist areas include cookery, crime, fantasy and science fiction. 20 titles in 1987.

Editorial Head *Nick Robinson* No unsolicited mss. Synopses and ideas for books welcome.
Royalties paid twice yearly.

Robson Books Ltd
Bolsover House, 5–6 Clipstone Street, London W1P 7EP
☎01–323 1223   Fax 01–636 0798

Managing Director *Jeremy Robson*

FOUNDED 1973 by Jeremy Robson. *Publishes* mainly general non-fiction including biography and autobiography, cinema, cookery, gardening, guide books, health and beauty, humour, science fiction, sports and games, theatre and drama, travel and topography, wine and spirits. 60 titles in 1987.

Editorial Head *Anthea Matthison* Unsolicited mss (accompanied by s.a.e.), synopses and ideas for books welcome.
Royalties paid twice yearly.

Authors' Rating Sensitive to authors but decisions take time to filter through.

Routledge

11 New Fetter Lane, London EC4P 4EE
☎01–583 9855
Telex 263398 ABPLDN G   Fax 01–583 0701

Managing Director *David Croom*
Approx Annual Turnover £10 million

A division of **Routledge, Chapman & Hall Ltd.** George Routledge set up business as a bookseller in 1836 and published his first book in that year. In 1911 Routledge took over the management of Kegan Paul, Trench, Trübner, a soundly-based academic company. It became Routledge & Kegan Paul in 1977. At the beginning of the war it published a mixture of trade books, political books and an increasing academic list. In 1979 they published their first best-seller since *Uncle Tom's Cabin*, Stephen Pile's *Book of Heroic Failures*. Bought by Associated Book Publishers in 1985 and now owned by International Thomson plc. *Publishes* archaeology, anthropology, art, business and management, criminology, dictionaries, economics, education, geography, history, literary criticism, philosophy, political economy, psychiatry, psychology, reference, social administration, sociology, women's studies. 700 titles in 1987.

DIVISIONS
Business *Peter Sowden* **Humanities** *Janice Price* **Reference** *Wendy Morris* **Social & Behavioral Science** *Gill Davies* Prefer to see synopses and ideas rather than complete mss.

Routledge, Chapman & Hall Ltd

11 New Fetter Lane, London EC4P 4EE
☎01–583 9855
Telex 263398 ABPLDN G   Fax 01–583 0701

The new trading company since takeover by International Thomson in 1987 for **Routledge** and **Chapman & Hall Ltd.** Since this major reorganisation the following companies have ceased publishing: Croom Helm, Methuen and Co., Routledge and Kegan Paul, and Tavistock Publications. All of these have been incorporated in the new **Routledge.** (see separate entry). **Chapman & Hall** embraces the old ABP companies, Chapman & Hall and **E & F.N. Spon,** together with **Van Nostrand Reinhold International** (see separate entry for **Chapman & Hall**).

Authors' Rating A formidable combination of talents in academic publishing who needed to come together and rationalise to survive. Improvements in marketing are expected to achieve more satisfactory sales figures and, hopefully, less confusing royalty statements.

Sackville Books Ltd

2 ABC, Hales Barn, Stradbroke, nr Eye, Suffolk IP21 5JG
☎0379 848213
Telex 97177 SACK G   Fax 0379 84797

Managing Director *Al Rockall*

FOUNDED 1986. Part of the Sackville Design Group, the successful packaging operation. *Publishes* illustrated cookery, home, leisure and sports titles.

Editorial Director *Heather Thomas* TITLES *Salad Days*; *The Pregnancy Beauty Book*; *No-Cook Cookery*. Prefer synopses and ideas for books.
Royalties usually twice yearly but can vary according to contract.

Sage Publications Ltd

28 Banner Street, London EC1Y 8QE
☎01–253 1516   Telex 296207 SAGE

Managing Director *David Brooks*

FOUNDED 1967 in California. The London office has been going for eleven years. *Publishes* academic and scholarly.

Editorial Director *David Hill* TITLES *Robert Colquhoun* Raymond Arron. Welcome unsolicited mss and synopses.
Royalties paid quarterly.

Salamander Books Ltd

52 Bedford Row, London WC1R 4LR
🐷01–242 6693
Telex 261113 Salama G   Fax 01–404 4926

Managing Director *Malcolm H. Little*

FOUNDED 1973. Independent publishing house. *Publishes* collecting, cookery and wine, knitting and craft, military and aviation, pet care, sport, technical books. 55 titles in 1987.

Editorial Directors *Ray Bond, Philip de Ste Croix* TITLES *Creative Cookery Series; Creative Craft Series; Fishkeepers' Guides; The Intelligence War.* Welcome unsolicited synopses and ideas for books.
Royalties Pay an outright fee instead of royalties.

Sangam Books Ltd

57 Fruit Exchange, Brushfield Street, London E1 6EP
🐷01–377 6399

Executive-In-Charge *Anthony de Souza*

Traditionally educational publishers at school and college levels but also publishes books on art, India, medicine, science and technology, and social sciences. Some fiction in paperback list. Unsolicited mss and synopses welcome.

W.B. Saunders Co.

See Academic Press Inc. (London) Ltd

Sceptre Books

See Hodder & Stoughton Ltd

Scholastic Publications Ltd

Marlborough House, Holly Walk, Leamington Spa, Warwickshire CV32 4LS
🐷0926 813910
Telex 312138 SPLS G   Fax 0926 883331

Chairman *M.R. Robinson*
Managing Director *John Cox*
Approx Annual Turnover £8.5 million

FOUNDED 1964 as a subsidiary of **Scholastic Inc.** of New York, Scholastic is the largest school-based book club operator in the UK, publishing teachers' magazines including *Child Education*, as well as general children's titles. The **Hippo** children's paperback imprint was launched in 1980, and educational books were added to the list in 1984. A major expansion of the educational book publishing programme is planned for the near future. *Publishes* children's paperbacks, professional reference books for primary school teachers, primary school pupil materials, plus magazines for primary school teachers. 100 titles in 1987.

DIVISIONS
Hippo Children's paperbacks *Anne Finnis* TITLES *Postman Pat; Cheerleaders; 101 Dalmations* and other Disney Classics; *Conrad's War.* **Scholastic Educational Books** *Peter Osborn, Priscilla Chambers* TITLES *Bright Ideas* series *Teacher Handbooks; Management Series.* Unsolicited mss, synopses and ideas for books welcome.
Royalties paid twice yearly.

Authors' Rating Has been described as the Heineken of the book trade – reaching parts other publishers cannot reach. Books on offer come from a variety of sources with about a quarter of all titles from the Scholastic imprint, **Hippo**. A skilful and fast-growing marketing operation bringing welcome rewards to education writers.

SCM Press Ltd

26–30 Tottenham Road, London N1 4BZ
🐷 01–249 7262/5
Telex 295068 THEOLO G   Fax 01–249 3776

Managing Director *Rev. Dr John Bowden*

Publishes mainly religion and theology with some ethics and philosophy. 50 titles in 1987. Will consider unsolicited mss and synopses, with s.a.e.
Royalties paid annually.

Authors' Rating Leading publisher of religious ideas with well-deserved reputation for fresh thinking.

Scolar

See **Gower Publishing Group**

Scorpion Publishing Ltd

Victoria House, Victoria Road, Buckhurst Hill, Essex IG9 5ES
☎01–506 0606   Telex 896988 SCOOPS G

Managing Director *Leonard Harrow*

FOUNDED 1976. Part of the Scorpion Group. *Publishes* Islamic art, history and culture plus a socialist list.

Editorial Director *Leonard Harrow* Welcome unsolicited mss and synopses if they come within their subject areas.
Royalty payments vary according to contract.

Scottish Academic Press

33 Montgomery Street, Edinburgh EH7 5JX
☎031–556 2796

Managing Director *Dr Douglas Grant*

FOUNDED 1969. *Publishes* academic (architecture, education, geology, history, journals, literature, social sciences, theology). Work in conjunction with Handsel Press (theology). Distribute titles for **Sussex University Press**. 30 titles in 1987.

TITLES *Longer Scottish Poems, Volumes 1 & 2; In a Distant Isle – The Orkney Background of Edwin Muir*. Most of the books are commissioned but will consider unsolicited mss and synopses.
Royalties paid annually.

Search Press Ltd/Burns & Oates

Wellwood, North Farm Road, Tunbridge Wells, Kent TN2 3DR
☎0892 510850   Telex 957258

Managing Director *Countess de la Bedoyère*

Burns & Oates were founded in 1847 and were publishers to the Holy See. Search Press publishes full colour arts and craft books and cookery books *Publishes* art, biography, cookery, craft, educational, needlecrafts, philosophy, reference, social sciences, theology, literary criticism, history, spirituality, educational and Third World. 24 titles in 1987.

Academic *John Bright-Holmes* **Craft etc** *Pam Dawson (***Search Press***)* Unsolicited mss, synopses and ideas for books welcome.
Royalties paid annually.

Secker & Warburg Ltd

Michelin House, 81 Fulham Road, London SW3 6RB
☎01–581 9393
Telex 920191   Fax 01–589 8419

Publisher *David Godwin*

Part of the **Octopus Publishing Group**. FOUNDED 1936 by Fred Warburg when he bought out Martin Secker. *Publishes* academic and scholarly, architecture and design, autobiography and biography, cinema, crime, fiction, fine art and art history, history, humour, illustrated and fine editions, literature and criticism, photography, poetry, politics and world affairs, theatre and drama. 120 titles in 1987.

TITLES *Porterhouse Blue* Tom Sharpe; *Alaska* James A. Michener; *The Collected Stories* of *Angus Wilson; The Modern World* Malcolm Bradbury; *Small World* David Lodge; *Inflagrante* Chris Killit.

IMPRINT

Alison Press *Barley Alison* (Publisher) TITLE *More Die of Hearbreak* Saul Bellow. Welcome Unsolicited mss and synopses.
Royalties paid twice yearly.

Authors' Rating The odd-man-out of the Octopus group. Quality books appealing to the literary establishment.

Serpent's Tail

27 Montpelier Grove, London NW5 2XD
☎01–267 1956   Fax 01–404 5049

Approx Annual Turnover £70,000

FOUNDED 1986. 'Serpent's Tail has introduced to British audiences a number of major internationally-known writers who have been otherwise neglected by UK publishers.' A strong emphasis on design – including flaps on paperback covers in the continental style – and an eye for the unusual. *Publishes* contemporary fiction, including works in translation; related fields, including autobiography. 11 titles in 1987.

IMPRINTS

Masks *Peter Ayrton/Marsha Rowe* TITLES *Landscapes After the Battle* Juan Goytisolo; *Who Was That Man?* Neil Bartlett. **Serpent's Tail** *Peter Ayrton/Marsha Rowe* TITLES *Forties' Child* Tom Wakefield Unsolicited synopses and ideas for books welcome. *Royalties* normally paid twice yearly.

Severn House Publishers

2nd Floor, 40–2 William IV Street, London WC2N 4DF
☎01–240 9683
Telex 295041 SEVERN G   Fax 01–379 6489

Chairman *Edwin Buckhalter*

FOUNDED 1974, a leader in library fiction publishing. Several bestsellers both in the UK and overseas. *Publishes* mainly hardcover fiction, with a growing paperback non-fiction list plus some mass-market titles. 135 titles in 1987.

DIVISIONS

Fiction *Stephanie Townsend* **Non-Fiction** *Julie Briscoe* NB All unsolicited mss should be sent to *Hilary Gibb*. Welcome unsolicited mss. Synopses/proposals only through bona fide literary agents.
Royalties paid twice yearly. *Overseas associates* Severn House Publishers Inc. New York.

Shakespeare Head Press

See **Basil Blackwell Ltd**

Shepheard-Walwyn (Publishers) Ltd

Suite 34, 26 Charing Cross Road, London WC2H 0DH
☎01–240 5992

Managing Director *Anthony Werner*
Approx Annual Turnover £100,000–150,000

FOUNDED 1972 and has published on average 4–6 titles a year. 'We are more interested in original ideas than re-hashes of previous books, unless in the form of a good anthology'. *Publishes* general non-fiction in three main areas: Scottish interest, books handwritten by calligraphers, and history, political economy, philosophy/religion. 4 titles in 1987. Welcome synopses and ideas for books. *Royalties* paid twice yearly.

Shire Publications Ltd

Cromwell House, Church Street, Princes Risborough, Aylesbury, Bucks HP17 9AJ

Managing Director *John Rotheroe*

FOUNDED 1967. *Publishes* original non-fiction paperbacks. 90 titles in 1987. No unsolicited material. Prefer introductory letter with detailed outline of idea.
Royalties paid annually.

Sidgwick & Jackson Ltd

1 Tavistock Chambers, Bloomsbury Way, London WC1A 3AA
☎01–242 6081
Telex 8952953 SIDJAK G   Fax 01–831 0874

Chairman *Sir William Rees-Mogg*
Managing Director *William Armstrong*
Approx Annual Turnover £3.75 million

FOUNDED 1908, the company was controlled by Lord Forte from the early 1960s until its sale to **Macmillan** in 1986. Sir William Rees-Mogg took over from Lord Longford as

Chairman in 1986. *Publishes* astronomy, autobiography, biography, cinema and theatre, cookery, craft, current affairs, humour, illustrated classics, illustrated gift books, management and business, military history, pop/rock, popular fiction, religion, sport. 100 titles in 1986.

Editorial Director *Robert Smith* **Deputy Editoral Director** *Susan Hill* **Fiction Editor** *Oliver Johnson* **Editor** *Carey Smith.* Bestselling titles have included *Superwoman; Lace and Savages* Shirley Conran; *The Third World War* General Sir John Hackett; Lee Iacocca's autobiography; *Is That It?* Bob Geldof. Unsolicited mss are always welcome but rarely published. Prefer to see a synopsis and sample chapter. Most of the titles published are as a result of commissioned ideas (such as the Geldof autobiography), submissions from agents, or from staff contacts.
Royalties paid twice yearly.

Authors' Rating Once renowned for stealing a march on bigger publishers by its imaginative promotion of best-selling titles, the company has got more cautious of late with its range of middle-brow culture. The new fiction list promises well.

Simon & Schuster Ltd
West Garden Place, Kendal Street, London W2 2AQ
☎01–724 7577
Telex 21702   Fax 01–402 0639

Chairman and Managing Director *Clyde Hunter*

FOUNDED 1986. Offshoot of the leading American publisher. *Publishes* general books (no academic or technical), specialising in trade books – children's fiction, sport, and travel. 50 titles in 1987.

Children's Books Editor *Denise Johnstone-Burt* **Fiction Editor** *Robyn Sisman* **Non-fiction Editor** *Nicholas Brearley* TITLES *The Spy in Question* Tim Sebastian; *Jericho Falls* Christopher Hyde; *Yamani, The Inside Story* Jeffrey Robinson; *Gershwin* Edward Jablonski; *Power Golf* Ben Hogan; *Webster's*

Wine Tours; Frommer's Dollarwise Guides; The Ogre and the Frog King Grégoire Solotareff; *Edward Loses His Teddy* Michaela Morgan and Sue Porter. Welcome unsolicited mss and synopses.
Royalties paid twice yearly.

Authors' Rating A breath of fresh air on the UK publishing scene. Exciting new fiction including first-time authors. Eager for product and open to ideas with the necessary resources to back their judgement.

Charles Skilton Publishing Group
2 Caversham Street, London SW3
☎01–351 4995

Chairman & Managing Director *Charles Skilton*

FOUNDED 1945. Independent publisher with offices in London and Scotland. *Publishes* general books including poetry and fiction, art, architecture, memoirs, plus all Scottish subjects. 35 titles in 1987.

DIVISIONS
Charles Skilton Ltd *Leonard Holdsworth* TITLE *Collected Poems of Randle Manwaring.* **Charles Skilton – Albyn Press** *Leonard Holdsworth* TITLES *Historic South Edinburgh* Vol 4; *Essex Mills* Vols 1–5; *My War, My Mules & Me.*
Unsolicited mss, synopses and ideas for books welcome.
Royalties paid twice yearly.

Authors' Rating A tendency towards vanity publishing. The usual warnings apply.

Society for Promoting Christian Knowledge (SPCK)
Holy Trinity Church, Marylebone Road, London NW1 4DU
☎01–387 5282

Chairman *Rt Rev. David Young, Bishop of Ripon*
Gen. Secretary *Mr P.N.G. Gilbert*
Approx Annual Turnover £1.5 million

FOUNDED 1698, **SPCK** is the oldest religious publisher in England. *Publishes* theological works and self-help of a serious-minded pastoral nature. 80 titles in 1987.

DIVISIONS
SPCK *Judith Longman* TITLES *Dictionary of Pastoral Care; The Study of Spirituality.*

IMPRINTS
Sheldon Press *Darley Anderson* TITLES *Overcoming Common Problems; Body Language; Curing Arthritis – The Drug-Free Way.* **Triangle** (paperback) *Myrtle Powley* TITLES *Living by the Book; Praying with St Augustine* Unsolicited synopses/ideas for books welcome.
Royalties paid annually.

Authors' Rating Religion with a strong social edge.

Souvenir Press Ltd
43 Great Russell Street, London WC1B 3PA
☎ 01–580 9307/8 & 637 5711/2/3
Telex 24710 SOUVNR G

Chairman/Managing Director
Ernest Hecht

Publishes academic and scholarly, animal care/breeding, antiques and collecting, archaeology, auto/biography, business and industry, children's, cookery, crime, crafts and hobbies, educational, fiction, gardening, health and beauty, history/antiquarian, humour, illustrated and fine editions, magic and the occult, medical, military, music, natural history, philosophy, psychology, religious, sociology, sports, theatre, veterinary, and women's studies. 46 titles in 1987.

Senior Editor *Tessa Harrow* TITLES *Trooping the Colour* Michael Gow; *Seeds of Liberty* John Miller; *Kafka's Milena* Jana Černá; *The Krone Experiment* J. Craig Wheeler; *Late Harvest* Barbara Masterton; *Searle's Cats* Ronald Searle.

IMPRINTS
Condor, Human Horizons (books for the disabled and those who care for them), **Souvenir Press Ltd** Unsolicited mss welcome.
Royalties paid twice yearly.

Authors' Rating One of the best independent publishers in London. Ernest Hecht takes all important decisions which can make life difficult if he happens to be away. But he does have a wonderful ability for judging public taste two years in advance. Authors feel comfortable with him.

Spellmount Ltd
12 Dene Way, Speldhurst, nr Tunbridge Wells, Kent TN3 0NX
☎ 089 286 2860

Managing Director *Ian Morley-Clarke*
Approx Annual Turnover £200,000

FOUNDED 1983. Jointly owned by Ian and Kathleen Morley-Clarke and Vale Packaging Ltd, of Tonbridge. *Publishes* non-fiction hardback titles; biographies of composers, popular musicians, jazz, cricketers, county anthologies, militaria, companion guides to music and the arts. 14 titles in 1987.

DIVISIONS
Composers' biographies and Militaria *Kathleen Morley-Clarke* **Cricket biographies** *John Bright-Holmes* **Jazz biographies** *Alyn Shipton* **London Guides** *Robert Hardcastle* No unsolicited mss. Synopses/ideas for books in Spellmount's specialist fields only.
Royalties paid annually.

Sphere Books Ltd
27 Wright's Lane, London W8 5TZ
☎ 01–937 8070
Telex 917182   Fax 01–937 8704

Managing Director *Nicholas Webb*
Approx Annual Turnover £10.5 million

FOUNDED 1967. A medium-sized paperback house, formerly belonging to International Thomson, now part of **Penguin**. Remaining chiefly mass market, it has also successfully diversified into Management and Reference publishing. The trade paperback imprints, **Abacus** and **Cardinal**, are covered by the Sphere umbrella. *Publishes* paperback fiction and non-fiction of all kinds, except children's books. Particularly strong on literary/popular fiction, reference and management titles. 230 titles in 1987.

DIVISIONS

Abacus *Julian Evans* TITLES *The Periodic Table* Primo Levi **Cardinal** *Chris Potter* TITLES *Byron* Frederic Raphael **Sphere** Barbara Boote TITLES *The Lady of Hay* Barbara Erskine **Sphere Reference** James Tindall TITLES *Manager's Handbook* Unsolicited mss are tolerated, 'despite being time-consuming and rarely bringing to light a commercially appealing book'. A qualified welcome for synopses. These should be accompanied by a sample chapter: 'execution is all'. Similarly, authors of ideas must show some evidence of their ability to deliver a publishable finished book. Buys on a volume-rights basis with **Hamish Hamilton** and **Michael Joseph**.
Royalties paid twice yearly.

Authors' Rating Rumours of sale (why should the **Penguin** group want two paperback imprints?) now firmly discounted though **Octopus** and **Random House** continue to show interest. Several key authors have been lost – Craig Thomas and Clive Barker to **Collins**, Danielle Steel to **Transworld** – but Sphere still has P.D. James and Paul Erdman and new best-selling authors are promised. With the company back in profit after several years of losses, Sphere is well placed to take advantage of its family links with **Michael Joseph**.

John Spiers Publishing Ltd

16 & 17 Ship Street, Brighton, East Sussex BN1 1AD
☎0273 26611
Telex 878380 HILTON G   Fax 0273 23983

Chairman/Managing Director *John Spiers*
Approx Annual Turnover £200,000

FOUNDED 1988 by John Spiers after he sold his interests in three other international companies, successfully developed by him over 20 years: The Harvester Press Ltd, and Wheatsheaf Books Ltd (both sold to **Simon & Schuster**) and Harvester Press Microform

Publications Ltd, subsequently sold to International Thomson Organisation. Specialises in scholarly and trade books in Soviet studies, defence studies, strategic studies, intelligence, disinformation and terrorism. Expecting to publish 10–12 titles in first year.

TITLES *The Soviet Propaganda Network: A Directory of Organisations Serving Soviet Foreign Policy* Sir Clive Rose; *Key Facts in Soviet History: A Directory and Chronology of Major Events Since 1971* Stephen de Mowbray; *The KGB In Britain* Peter Shipley; *Gorbachev: The New Russian Revolution?* T.P. McNeill; *The Soviet Approach to Arms Control* James Sherr; *On Soviet War: Force, Ideology and Communism* J.N. de W. Lash. Prefer initial letter with outline in the first instance. Welcome synopses and ideas for books if they come within their specialist subjects. In the market for ideas and authors.
Royalties paid twice yearly.

E. & F.N. Spon
See **Chapman & Hall Limited**

Spring Books
See **Octopus Publishing Group**

Springwood Books Ltd
Springwood House, The Avenue, Ascot, Berks SL5 7LY
☎0990 24053   Telex 8813271 GECOMS G

Chairman & Managing Director
Christopher K. Foster

FOUNDED 1977. *Publishes* general non-fiction: astrology, autobiographies, children's books, company histories, sports. No unsolicited mss. Will consider synopses and ideas for books.
Royalties vary from contract to contract.

Squirrel Publications Ltd
210 Carlton Road, Romford, Essex RM2 5BA
☎0708 20343

Managing Director *L.W.H. Pepall*

FOUNDED 1984. First title was *The Book of Arguments*. A very young company still finding their feet but hoping to branch out into wider fields in due course. *Publishes* children's books, fiction, humour.

Editorial Head *L.W.H. Pepall* TITLES *The Wags* series (4 titles); *The Lolobal Book*. Do not welcome unsolicited mss. Prefer to see synopsis or outline first.
Royalties paid annually.

Stainer & Bell Ltd
PO Box 110, 82 High Road,
London N2 9PW
☎01–444 9135

Chairman *Allen Dain Percival*
Managing Directors *Carol Y. Wakefield and Keith M. Wakefield*
Approx Annual Turnover £437,000

FOUNDED 1907 to publish sheet music. Now *publishes* music and religious subjects, mainly related to hymnody. 2 titles in 1987.

Editorial Director *A.D. Percival* Mss welcome only if preceded by letter enclosing brief précis. Unsolicited synopses/ideas for books welcome.
Royalties paid annually.

Star
See **W.H. Allen & Co. plc**

Patrick Stephens
See **Thorsons Publishing Group Ltd**

Studio Publications (Ipswich) Ltd
The Drift, Nacton Road,
Ipswich, Suffolk IP3 9QR
☎0473 270880
Telex 98551 STUDIO G   Fax 0473 270113

Chairman *Mr M. Kelley*
Managing Director *Mr B.J. Henderson*
Approx Annual Turnover £1 million+

FOUNDED 1973. Part of **Ladybird Books** (which is part of the **Longman Group**).

Initially published sports books, but soon branched out into children's titles. Acquired by **Ladybird** in 1986. Studio Publications intend to broaden their range of titles to cater for older children, but will remain mass-market publishers. *Publishes* picture story books, board books, early educational, novelty and activity books; age range 0–10 years. Also television character series and short stories. 50 titles in 1987.

Editorial Head *H.V. Jones*

IMPRINTS
Badger Books TITLES *Wacky Races* series; *Playskool* (pre-school range); *Stick-a-Tale* (sticker story books); *Balloon Heads* (3-D novelty story books). **Bunny Books** TITLES *Cobweb* series. Unsolicited mss welcome if illustrated; otherwise submit synopses/ideas only.
Royalties paid twice yearly.

Surrey University Press
Bishopbriggs, Glasgow G64 2NZ
☎041–772 2311
Telex 777283 BLACKI G   Fax 041–762 0897

Chairman & Managing Director
R. Michael Miller

An imprint of **Blackie & Son Ltd**. *Publishes* academic, scientific and technical, and professional books.

Editorial Head *A. Graeme Mackintosh* Prefer synopses rather than complete mss.
Royalties paid annually and twice yearly.

Sussex University Press
No longer publishes. Distribution by **Scottish Academic Press Ltd**

Alan Sutton Publishing Ltd
30 Brunswick Road, Gloucester GL1 1JJ
☎0452 419575
Telex 43690   Fax 0452 302791

Managing Director *Alan Sutton*

FOUNDED 1979. *Publishes* academic, archaeology, biography, countryside, history, local history, pocket classics – lesser known novels by classic authors, topography. 130 titles in 1987.

Director *Peter Clifford* Prefer to see synopses rather than complete mss.
Royalties paid twice yearly.

Swallows
See Richard Drew Ltd

Sweet & Maxwell Ltd
11 New Fetter Lane, London EC4P 4EE
☎01–583 9855   Telex 263398

Managing Director A. *Prideaux*

Part of **Thomson Information Services Ltd**. Publishes law books. 120 titles in 1987.

Editorial Directors *Robert McKay, Jane Belford, Hugh Jones* TITLES (for the practitioner) *Company Accounts; Encyclopedia of Professional Partnerships; Planning Decisions Digest.* (For the student) *Litigation for the Law Society Finals; Administrative Law; ILEX: Introduction to Law.* Although mss will be considered it is unlikely they will be published due to the highly specialised nature of the list. Synopses and outlines welcome.
Royalties payments vary according to contract.

Swift Children's Books
See Chivers Press (Publishers)

Target
See W.H. Allen & Co. plc

Technical Press
See Gower Publishing Group

Temple House Books
See The Book Guild Ltd

Thames and Hudson Ltd
30–4 Bloomsbury Street,
London WC1B 3QP
☎01–636 5488
Telex 25992   Fax 01–636 4799

Managing Director *Thomas Neurath*

Publishes art books. Also archaeology, architecture and design, crafts, fashion, history and antiquarian, illustrated and fine editions, mythology, music, photography, psychology, sociology and anthropology, theatre and drama, travel and topography. 120 titles in 1987.

Editorial Head *Jamie Camplin* TITLES *World of Art series; The International Design Yearbook; David Hockney: A Retrospective; Design After Modernism; Fashion Illustration Today; Henri Cartier-Bresson in India; Exploring the World of the Pharaohs; Akhenaten: King of Egypt; Thames and Hudson Literary Lives; 1791 – Mozart's Last Year; How to Identify Prints; Beauty in History; The English Country Town; Russian and Soviet Theatre.* Preliminary letter and outline before mss.
Royalties paid twice yearly.

Authors' Rating One of the two leading art publishers (the other is **Phaidon Press Ltd**). High-quality books which make you proud to be an author.

Stanley Thornes (Publishers) Ltd
Old Station Drive, Leckhampton,
Cheltenham, Glos GL53 0DN
☎0242 584429
Telex 43592   Fax 0242 221914

Managing Director *Roy Kendall*
Approx Annual Turnover £5.2 million

FOUNDED 1972 by Stanley Thornes. Merger with Kluwer NV of the Netherlands in 1976. Original aims were to publish in maths/science for GCE O- and A-Level, and CSE and Technician education. Now publishes across the whole secondary and NAFE curriculum and, with the acquisition of Hulton Educational, list covers complete school range from age five upwards. Merger of Kluwer with Wolters Samson in 1987. 110 titles in 1987.

Publishing Director *Mike Rigby* TITLES *A Complete GCSE Maths* Greer; *A Practical Guide to Child Development* Reynolds; *British Economic and Social History* Sauvain; *Office*

Skills Foster; *Bookshelf* – Primary reading scheme. Welcome unsolicited mss, synopses and ideas for books if appropriate to specialised list.
Royalties paid annually.

Thornhill Press

24 Moorend Road, Cheltenham,
Glos GL53 0EU
☎0242 519137

Managing Director *Desmond Badham-Thornhill*
Approx Annual Turnover £50,000

FOUNDED 1972. *Publishes* mainly walking and touring guides, sport, plus some general titles (no fiction or poetry). 5 titles in 1986.

Editorial Head *Desmond Badham-Thornhill*
Unsolicited mss, synopses and ideas for books welcome.
Royalties paid quarterly.

Thorsons Publishing Group Ltd

Denington Estate, Wellingborough,
Northants NN8 2RQ
☎0933 440033　　　　Fax 0933 440512
Telex 311072 THOPUB G/312511 TPG BKS

Managing Director *David Young*
Approx Annual Turnover £10 million

FOUNDED 1930, acquired the **Aquarian Press** in 1955, and added **Patrick Stephens** to the group in 1984. The **Crucible** imprint was launched in 1986, and the **Equation** imprint in March 1988. 257 titles in 1987.

IMPRINTS
Thorsons *Annie Smith* alternative medical, business, cookery, crafts and hobbies, health, medical, parenting, pets, self-improvement and women's non-fiction. TITLES *Better Health Through Natural Healing; The Food For Thought Cookbook; Soft Tissue Manipulation; Hypnothink; Pregnancy & Childbirth; Beyond the Bars; Fit to Manage; The Changing Image of Women.*
Aquarian *Eileen Campbell* astrology, divination, freemasonry, healing/yoga, occultism, paranormal, self-development, tarot.

TITLES *Highways of the Mind; The Alternative I Ching; Yeats' Golden Dawn; You and Your Aura; Practical Celtic Magic.* **Crucible** *Eileen Campbell* History of ideas, history of religion. TITLES *The Templars; Immaculate and Powerful; Handbook of Christian Mysticism.* **Patrick Stephens Ltd** *Darryl Reach* Aviation, the countryside, health and fitness, maritime, military and wargaming, model making and model engineering, motor cycling, motoring, railways and railway modelling. TITLES *The Berlin Airlift; Stirling Moss; Great Locomotives of the Southern Railway; Famous Ocean Liners; Fully Fit Through Walking; Classic Competition Motorcycles; Hitler's Teutonic Knights.*

Authors' Rating Market leader in health books. Other areas of popular non-fiction developing rapidly. Plan to increase turnover from £10 million to £17 million by 1991. Open to ideas and ready to back them with imaginative sales promotion.

Times Books Ltd

16 Golden Square, London W1R 4BN
☎01–434 3767
Telex 897284 ARPUB G　　　Fax 01–434 2080

Managing Director *Barry Winkleman*

Part of News International. *Publishes* mainly atlases with some reference and non-fiction. 8 titles in 1987.

Editorial Head *Paul Middleton* Unsolicited mss should be preceded by letter with outline.
Royalties paid twice yearly.

Titan Books

58 St Giles High Street, London WC2H 8LW
☎01–836 4056

Managing Director *Nick Landau*

FORMED 1981 by Nick Landau and has grown 'incredibly' in the last seven years to become the largest publisher of graphic novels and graphic albums in the UK. Moving into mass-market paperbacks with a range of *Star Trek* novels. *Publishes* film and television fantasy, comic strip. 25 titles in 1986.

Managing Director *Bernie Jaye* TITLES *Batman, Dark Night Returns* Frank Miller; *The Ballad of Halo Jones* Alan Moore; *Judge Dread, No. 12* Wagner Grant and R. Smith. Although they do not originate a lot of new material unsolicited ideas will be considered. *Royalties* paid twice yearly.

Transworld Publishers Ltd
61–3 Uxbridge Road, London W5 5SA
☎01–579 2652
Telex 267974   Fax 01–579 5479

Managing Director *Paul Scherer*

FOUNDED 1950. A subsidiary of **Bantam Books**, New York, which, in the early 1980s was taken over by Bertelsmann, the West German publishers, which also owns **Doubleday**. *Publishes* children's books, general fiction and non-fiction, sports and leisure.

IMPRINTS

Bantam *Anthony Mott* AUTHORS Pat Conroy, Erica Jong, Bill Cosby, Louis L'Amour. Young Adult series: *Sweet Dreams*; *Sweet Valley High*; *All That Glitters*. **Bantam Press** *Mark Barty-King* AUTHORS Catherine Cookson, Frederick Forsyth, Sally Beauman, Jilly Cooper, Judith Krantz. Also in 1987 *One Day For Life – Search 88*. **Black Swan** *Patrick Janson-Smith* AUTHORS Joseph Heller, John Irving, Mary Wesley, Isabel Allende, James Baldwin. **Corgi** *Patrick Janson-Smith* AUTHORS Catherine Cookson, Frederick Forsyth, James Michener, Jilly Cooper, William Styron. **Freeway** *Philippa Dickinson* AUTHORS Jean Ure, Robert Leeson, Judith Saxton, Barbara Jacobs. **Partridge Press** *Debbie Beckerman*   TITLES *Sport in Focus*; *Hedgerow*; *Rally*; *Embury* biography. **Picture Corgi** *Philippa Dickinson* AUTHORS/ARTISTS Shirley Hughes, Frank Muir, Frank Asch, Emilie Boon. **Young Corgi** *Philippa Dickinson* AUTHORS Bernard Ashley, Terrance Dicks, Catherine Sefton, Helen Cresswell, Nicholas

Fisk. Unsolicited mss welcome only if preceded by preliminary letter.
Royalties paid twice yearly. *Overseas associates* Transworld Australia/New Zealand; Trans-South Africa Book Distributors.

Authors' Rating Paying out big money to create a list of bestsellers. Recent recruits include Frederick Forsyth from Hutchinson, Catherine Cookson from Heinemann and Danielle Steel from Sphere. Pulping the Thompson and Delano unauthorised biography of Robert Maxwell must have hurt – but not for long. A **Doubleday** imprint will be launched next year. Transworld pays well and on time.

Travelmate
See **Richard Drew Ltd**

Unwin Hyman Ltd
15–17 Broadwick Street, London W1V 1FP
☎01–439 3126
Telex 886245   Fax 01–734 3884

Managing Director *Robin Hyman*
Approx Annual Turnover £13.5 million

Allen & Unwin and Bell & Hyman merged in 1986, and in their first full year published over 70 trade hardbacks and over 100 paperbacks. The combined lists of the two companies amount to over 3000 titles, with Tolkien and Pepys the most prominent names on the reprint list. To the company Hyman brought a strong craft and leisure markets list, and Unwin brought academic titles. Sport, science fiction/fantasy and general interest non-fiction are also important elements of the new look set-up. Imprints have been phased out and quality titles for the serious reader have been introduced.

Publishing Director *Mary Butler* **Senior Commissioning Editor** *Michael Pountney* TITLES *The Rise and Fall of Great Powers* Paul Kennedy; *A View From a Window* Heather Angel; *Wind In the Ash Tree* Jeanine McMullen; *Food Adulteration* The London Food Commission. Acquired **Pandora Press**

in March 1988 **Publishing Director** *Philippa Brewster*

DIVISIONS

Academic *Nigel Britten* **Educational** *Christopher Kington* Welcome unsolicited mss, synopses and ideas for books.
Royalty payments vary according to contract.

Authors' Rating Rationalisation is beginning to prove its value with a successful mix of academic and general non-fiction. Editorial tensions created by the merger seem to have diminished.

Usborne Publishing Ltd

20 Garrick Street, London WC2E 9BJ
☎01–379 3535
Telex 8953598 USPUB G   Fax 01–836 0705

Managing Director *T. Peter Usborne*
Approx Annual Turnover £7.5 million

FOUNDED 1975. *Publishes* primarily non-fiction books for children, young adults and parents. 50–60 titles in 1988.

Editorial Directors *Heather Amery, Jenny Tyler* About 500 titles on geography, history, science, sports and pre-school subjects.

DIVISIONS

Usborne Books at Home Davies House, Oasis Park, Eynsham, Oxford OX8 1TP. Books are written in-house to a specific format and therefore do not welcome unsolicited mss. Will consider ideas which may then be developed in-house. Always very keen to hear from new illustrators and designers.
Royalties paid twice yearly.

Authors' Rating One of the best publishers of information books for children. Potential authors must believe that knowledge can be fun.

Van Nostrand Reinhold International

Molly Millars Lane, Wokingham,
Berks RG11 2PY
☎0734 789456   Telex 848268 VNR UK G

Managing Director *Mr P.A. Gardner*

VNR has been owned by the International Thomson Organisation since 1981. *Publishes* academic, professional and reference titles, and is responsible for the distribution of all Thomson books into the UK, Europe, the Middle East and Africa. It has worldwide agreements/agencies, mainly in the States, Canada, Australia and the Far East. 40 titles in 1987.

Publishing Director *Dr D. Recaldin*

DIVISIONS

Professional & Reference *D. Smith* **University & College** *S. Wellings* **Vocational & Technical** *A. Taylor*.

IMPRINTS

Brooks Cole *R. Taylor* **Boyd & Fraser** *R. Taylor* **Gee** *Dr D. Recaldin* **Delmar** *A. Taylor* **Jones & Bartlett** *R. Taylor* **PWS Kent** *R. Taylor* **VNR (US)** *J. Anthony* **Wadsworth** *R. Taylor*. Unsolicited mss welcome in Van Nostrand's subject areas. Unsolicited synopses and ideas for books considered.
Royalties paid twice yearly.

Viking

27 Wright's Lane, London W8 5TZ
☎01–938 2200
Telex 917181/2   Fax 01–937 8704

Approx Annual Turnover £5 million

FOUNDED 1983 as the 'hardback imprint' of **Penguin Books, Viking** has developed a distinct identity in the course of those five years. AUTHORS include John Mortimer, V.S. Naipaul, Dirk Bogarde, Barbara Vine (Ruth Rendell), Graham Swift, Robertson Davies, Joseph Brodsky, Christopher Hibbert. *Publishes* biography, gardening, highly illustrated art books, history, literary and commercial fiction, poetry, thrillers, and all kinds of general non-fiction.

Editorial Director *Tony Lacey*

IMPRINTS

Allen Lane The Penguin Press A new imprint (or rather a revival of an old), launched in April 1988, to publish a small range of significant academic books. Early titles include *Modern Ireland 1660–1972* Roy Foster, and a political biography of Bertrand Russell by Alan Ryan. **Viking Kestrel** The children's hardcover imprint of **Penguin**, mirroring much of **Puffin**'s range, with a particular emphasis on quality children's fiction. **Editorial Director** *Elizabeth Attenborough*

Authors' Rating' Impressive names head an exciting list. Great successes with Stephen King's *Misery* and Garrison Keillor's *Leaving Home* (both over 800,000 copies) plus, of course, the infamous *Spycatcher*, now chasing the one-million sale. Recently captured Salman Rushdie against strong competition. The **Allen Lane** imprint will embrace 'works of outstanding cultural and academic importance'.

Virago Press Ltd

20–3 Mandela Street, Camden Town, London NW1 0HQ
☎01–383 5150   Telex 927560

Chairman *Carmen Callil*
Joint Managing Directors *Ursula Owen and Harriet Spicer*
Approx Annual Turnover £2.5 million

Escaped from the Cape, Virago, Bodley Head and Chatto group just before the latter was taken over by **Random House**. FOUNDED 1973 by Carmen Callil, with the aim of publishing a wide range of books – education, fiction, health, history and literature – which illuminate and celebrate all aspects of women's lives. Nearly all titles are published in paperback; a distinguished reprint list makes up two thirds of these, with one third original titles commissioned across a wide area of interest. These areas currently include: biography, educational, fiction, health, history, non-fiction, philosophy, poetry, politics, reference, women's studies, young adults. 100 titles in 1988.

Editorial Director *Ursula Owen*   TITLES Fiction: *Union Street* Pat Barker; *The Men's Room*

Ann Oakley; *Death in the Faculty* Amanda Cross; *Sweet Desserts* Lucy Ellmann; Politics: *Wigan Pier Revisited* Beatrix Campbell; *Is the Future Female?* Lynn Segal; *Insiders: Women's Experience of Prison* Prue Stevenson and Una Padel; *Let it Be Told Essays by Black Women Writers in Britain* edited by Lauretta Ngcobo; Psychology: *The Drama of Being a Child* Alice Miller; *A Life of One's Own* Marion Milner. Unsolicited mss welcome. Prefer to see a synopsis and a few sample chapters in the first instance in the case of non-fiction; for fiction prefer to see whole mss.
Royalties paid twice yearly. *Overseas associates* Australasian Publishing Company, Australia Book Reps., New Zealand, Random House Canada.

Authors' Rating Broadening out from strictly feminist literature towards illustrated books, and titles on international and Third World subjects. At present the reprint list tends to dominate. Scored blooper of the year when a Brighton vicar persuaded Virago to publish him as an Asian woman author.

Virgin

See **W.H. Allen & Co. plc**

University of Wales Press

6 Gwennyth Street, Cathays, Cardiff CF2 4YD
☎0223 31919   Fax 0222 396040

Director *John Rhys*
Approx Annual Turnover £250,000

Set up as an extension of the university in 1922. *Publishes* academic and scholarly books, mainly within the humanities and social sciences. Also works of Celtic scholarship. Occasionally publishes on behalf of learned bodies, such as the National Museum of Wales. 29 titles in 1987.

DIVISIONS
GPC Books *John Rhys* **Gwasg Prifysgol Cymru** *John Rhys* **University of Wales Press** *John Rhys* TITLES *David Jones: A*

Commentary on Some Poetic Fragments Christine Pagnoulle; *Eamon de Valera* Owen Dudley Edwards; *Gwaith Iolo Goch* D.R. Johnston. Unsolicited mss considered.
Royalties paid annually; more frequently by negotiation.

Walker Books Limited

87 Vauxhall Walk, London SE11 5HJ
☎01–793 0909
Telex 8955572   Fax 01–587 1123

Managing Director *Neal Porter*

FOUNDED 1979. *Publishes* illustrated children's books and teenage fiction. 200 titles in 1987.

Editor *Wendy Boase* TITLES *Pop Goes the Weasel!* Robert Crowther; *Where's Wally?* Martin Handford; *Vampire Master* Virginia Ironside; *All in One Piece* Jill Murphy; *There's an Awful Lot of Weirdos in our Neighbourhood.* Welcome unsolicited mss and synopses.
Royalties paid twice yearly.

Authors' Rating An extraordinary success story based on sound marketing. Output of titles doubled in 1987 alone! Walker Books publish more original children's books than any other British firm. One third of total sales goes through Sainsbury's supermarkets. Good terms for authors who can achieve the necessary standard.

Ward Lock Ltd

8 Clifford Street, Mayfair,
London W1X 1RB
☎01–439 3100
Telex 262364 WARLOK G   Fax 01–439 1582

Chairman *Robin H.D. Wood*
Managing Director *Chris Weller*
Approx Annual Turnover £3 million

FOUNDED 1854. Part of Egmont UK Ltd. The original list consisted of popular information and general education, supplemented by Mrs Beeton. A magazine interest was also developed late last century. The now defunct list was founded on Conan Doyle, Edgar Wallace and Leslie Charteris, with children's information books, most notably the *Wonder Books*, coming later. *Publishes* general non-fiction, including crafts, cookery, decorating and design, and gardening. 70 titles in 1987.

Editorial Head *David Holmes*

IMPRINTS
Ward Lock *David Holmes* TITLES *Shorter Mrs Beeton*; *The Complete Man*; *Pergolas, Arbour, Gazebos and Follies.* **Warwick Press** *David Holmes* TITLES *Bible Stories*; *Creative Cooking.* Unsolicited mss, ideas and synopses welcome.
Royalties paid twice yearly.

Ward Lock Educational Co. Ltd

47 Marylebone Lane, London W1M 6AX
☎01–486 3271
Telex 266231 Wleco G   Fax 01–487 2655

Managing Director *Stanley B. Malcolm*

FOUNDED 1952. Owned by Ling Kee, Hong Kong. Formerly part of **Ward Lock Ltd** but now completely independent. *Publishes* educational books (primary, middle, some secondary, teaching manuals). 25 titles in 1987.

TITLES *Now!* projects; *KMP Maths Scheme*; *Reading Workshops*; Unsolicited mss welcome.
Royalties paid twice yearly.

Frederick Warne

27 Wright's Lane, London W8 5TZ
☎01–938 2200
Telex 917181/2   Fax 01–938 8704

Approx Annual Turnover £7 million (1987)

See **Penguin**. *Publishes* children's books including Beatrix Potter – children's list is dominated by classics and reprints; also Beatrix Potter non-fiction books for adults; general books, including walking guides and the *Observer* series (transport, hobbies, natural history, pets). Around 45 titles in 1987.

Editorial Director *Sally Floyer* No unsolicited mss. Letter essential – many books are commissioned.
Royalties paid twice yearly.

Authors' Rating An astute takeover by Penguin has led to intensive exploitation of Beatrix Potter books. Not too much room for other titles.

Warwick Press
See Ward Lock Ltd

The Watts Group
12A Golden Square, London W1R 4BA
☎01–437 0713   Telex 262655 GROLUK G

Part of the Franklin Watts Group, New York. *Publishes* general non-fiction, information and fiction books for children. 180 titles in 1986.

DIVISIONS
Franklin Watts *Chester Fisher* TITLES *Making Pencils* Ruth Thomson **Orchard Books** *Judith Elliott* TITLES *Little Monsters* Jan Piénkowski. Unsolicited mss, synopses and ideas for books welcome.
Royalties paid twice yearly. *Overseas associates* in India, Caribbean, Scandinavia, Germany, France, Japan, South Korea, N. Ireland, Eire, S. Africa, Australia and New Zealand, US and Canada.

Wayland (Publishers) Ltd
61 Western Road,
Hove, East Sussex BN3 1JD
☎0273 722561
Telex 878170 Waylan G   Fax 0273 29314

Managing Director *John Lewis*
Approx Annual Turnover £5 million

Part of the Wolters Samson Group, Zwolle. FOUNDED 1969. Specialised in history in those days. Now publish a broad range of subjects – in approximately 23 subject areas – illustrated almost entirely in colour. *Publishes* illustrated non-fiction for children of 7 years and upwards. 200 titles in 1986.

Editorial Director *Paul Humphrey* Do not welcome unsolicited mss or synopses as all books are commissioned.
Royalties paid annually. *Overseas associates* Bookright Press Inc., USA.

Webb & Bower (Publishers) Ltd
9 Colleton Crescent,
Exeter, Devon EX2 4BY
☎0392 35362
Telex WEBBOW 42544   Fax 0392 211652

Managing Director *Richard Webb*

Publishes general interest illustrated books for the UK, US and international markets. 25 titles in 1987.

Editorial Head *Delian Bower* TITLES *AA Visitors' Guide; Country Diary Crafts; V & A Colour Books; Countryside Commission; National Parks series.* Unsolicited mss, synopses and ideas for books welcome so long as they conform to type.
Royalties paid twice yearly.

Authors' Rating Small publisher noted for high standard of book production.

Weidenfeld & Nicolson Ltd
91 Clapham High Street, London SW4 7TA
☎01–622 9933   Telex 918066

Chairman *Lord Weidenfeld*
Deputy Chairman *Mark Collins*
Joint Managing Directors *Alan Miles and Richard Hussey*
Editorial Director *Christopher Falkus*
Approx Annual Turnover £11 million

FOUNDED 1949 by George W. and Nigel N., the original list revolved around biography, history, memoirs, politics and quality fiction. Ten years later the sports/leisure publishers **Arthur Barker** was acquired; art and illustrated books followed, and the company developed the *Great* series – houses, gardens, rivers and so on. Today the reputation of the company rests in part on superbly produced and illustrated volumes on art, architecture, history and nature. Also publishes academic, archaeology, atlases and maps, auto/biography, business, cinema, health and beauty, humour, law, literature and criticism, philosophy, politics and sports. The publishing side of J.M. Dent was acquired in 1987 enlarging the company activities with Everyman and children's lists. 208 titles in 1987.

DIVISIONS
Academic *Juliet Gardiner* TITLES *Introduction to Positive Economics; Law in Context; Voltaire; Social History of Rural England; Beginning Psychology; Global Economy; Market Economy.* **Art/Illustrated** *Michael Dover* TITLES *Royal Academy Catalogues; National Trust* titles: *Westminster Abbey; Gardens; Britain/London/Italy/Holy Land From the Air; Stills by Snowdon; Laura Ashley* titles. **Fiction** *Juliet Gardiner* TITLES *Jemima Shore* stories, Antonia Fraser; *The Radiant Way* Margaret Drabble; *Illusions* Charlotte Vale Allen; Claire Rayner titles; *Levant Trilogy* Olivia Manning. **General Non-fiction** *Juliet Gardiner* TITLES *Under the Eye of the Clock; Life of Kenneth Tynan; Vivien Leigh; Harold Wilson Memoirs; Kissinger Memoirs; Olivier Memoirs; Marcus Sieff Memoirs.* **Humour/Sport/Business** *David Roberts* TITLES *Bunbury Series; Brookside/The Archers Companions; Geoff Boycott; Ali Ross on Skiing; Steve Davis; Alan Border; Lloyd's; Saatchi & Saatchi Story.* Unsolicited mss welcome if legible; 'most publications come from selected authors' however. Synopses and ideas for books welcome.

NEW IMPRINTS
Arthur Barker & Weidenfeld Special Books Dent Children's Books *Vanessa Hamilton* **Dent General & Everyman** Malcolm Gerratt.
Royalties paid twice yearly for first two years, annually thereafter. *Overseas associates* Weidenfeld & Nicolson, New York.

Authors' Rating After a few dodgy years, made secure by Getty money. A publishing house dominated by a single, charismatic personality who enjoys the extravagant gesture. Big-name authors do well. Growth potential boosted by recent purchase of J.M. Dent. Sometimes slow on royalty statements and payments.

Wildwood House
See Gower Publishing Group

John Wiley & Sons Ltd
Baffins Lane, Chichester, Sussex PO19 1UD
☎0243 770234
Telex 86290   Fax 0243 775878

Chairman *Mr W. Bradford Wiley* (USA)
Managing Director *Michael Foyle*

Part of John Wiley & Sons, New York, which dates from 1807. The London Office was opened in 1960. *Publishes* medical, professional, reference and textbooks, scientific, technical. 280 titles in 1987 (UK).

Editorial Director *Dr John Jarvis*

DIVISIONS
Behavioral Sciences and Management *Michael Coombs* **Chemistry and Earth Sciences** *Dr Ernest Kirkwood* **Life Sciences** *Dr Michael Dixon* **Maths, Computing and Engineering** *Ian McIntosh* **Medicine** *Nicholas Dunton.* Unsolicited mss welcome, as are synopses and ideas for books. *Royalties* paid annually.

Authors' Rating A strong publisher in medicine and the sciences with good overseas marketing.

Windsor Large Print
See Chivers Press (Publishers)

Wise
See Omnibus Press

Wisley Handbooks
See Cassell plc

Woburn Press
See **Frank Cass**

Wolfe Publishing Ltd

Brook House, 2–16 Torrington Place,
London WC1E 7LT
☎01–636 4622   Telex 8814230

Chairman *John F. Dill*
Managing Director *Michael Manson*
Approx Annual Turnover £5 million

Part of Time Mirror Group, USA. FOUNDED
1962 by Peter Wolfe. Sold to Year Book Medical Publishers of Chicago in 1985. *Publishes*
dental, medical, scientific, technical and veterinary. 35 titles in 1987.

Editorial Director *Patrick Daley*   TITLES *A
Colour Atlas of Head and Neck Surgery* Jatin
P. Shah; *Diagnostic Picture Tests in Rheumatology* V. Wright; *A Colour Atlas of Removable Partial Dentures* J.C. Davenport *et al.* No
unsolicited mss. Welcome synopses and ideas
for books.
Royalties paid twice yearly.

Oswald Wolff Books

See **Berg Publishers Ltd**

The Women's Press

34 Great Sutton Street, London EC1V 0DX
☎01–251 3007
Telex 919034 NAMARA G

Managing Director *Ros De Lanerolle*
Approx Annual Turnover £1 million

Part of the Namara Group (who also own
Quartet). First titles appeared in 1978;
expanded to 60 titles in 1987. The Women's
Press also publish a Women Artists Diary
annually and feminist postcards. *Publishes*
feminist fiction and non-fiction. Fiction usually has a female protagonist and a woman-centred theme. International writers and
subject matter encouraged; some novels
appear in translation and considerable
emphasis is placed on the work of Third
World and black women. Non-fiction:
general subjects of interest to feminists, both
practical and theoretical, and to women generally; art books, feminist theory, health and
psychology, literary criticism. 60 titles in
1987.

DIVISIONS
Women's Press Crime *Jen Green* **Women's
Press Science Fiction** *Sarah Lefanu/Jen
Green*.

IMPRINTS
Livewire *Carole Spedding/Christina Dunhill*
Fiction and non-fiction for the teenage
market. Unsolicited mss, synopses and ideas
for books welcome.
Royalties paid twice yearly, in September
and March.

Authors' Rating Energetic devotion to the
feminist cause. Budgets are tight and payments are sometimes slow.

John Wright

See **Butterworth & Co. Ltd**

Yale University Press (London)

13 Bedford Square, London WC1B 3JF
☎01–580 2693
Telex 896075 YUPLDN G   Fax 01–631 3913

Managing Director *John Nicoll*

The UK company of **Yale University Press**,
New Haven, Connecticut, USA. FOUNDED
1961. *Publishes* academic and humanities.
160 titles (jointly with the US company) in
1987.

Editorial Director *John Nicoll*   TITLES *Gustave Caillebotte* Kish Varnedoe; *The People's
Armies* Richard Cobb. Unsolicited mss and
synopses welcome if within specialised subject areas.
Royalties paid annually.

Zomba Books

165–7 High Road, London NW10 2SG
☎01–459 8899
Telex 919884   Fax 01–451 3900

Managing Director *Ralph Simon*

A division of Zomba Group of Companies
specialising in the music and entertainment
industry. *Publishes* fashion, film, music,
paperback originals. 8 titles in 1987. Welcome unsolicited material only if relevant to
their specialised subject matters. All correspondence to *Miss Dede Millar*.
Royalties paid twice yearly.

The Author in the Marketplace

Time was that when a publisher wanted to give an author a warm feeling of being needed, he would invite him to lunch. Nowadays, he calls him in for a marketing meeting.

The elevation of leading publishers to international, multi-billion pound businesses has simultaneously lifted the status of sales and marketing. No longer is it thought to be in slightly bad taste to talk of a book as 'a product' or bookshops as the 'marketplace'. In the brave new world of book retailing, competiton for shelf space can be as tough as in any supermarket. Ambitious writers have quickly attuned themselves to economic realities. Even those who are jealous of their literary reputations are rarely averse to promotional gimmicks, however bizarre. Justification can always be found in a rising sales curve.

A strong candidate for the bestseller list makes its first appearance in the publisher's marketing plan well before the manuscript is completed (or, in some cases, even started). The author and his agent are presented with a detailed breakdown of a publicity budget with ideas for attracting retailer and reader interest ranging from advertising to in-store displays. Always the pressure is on the publisher to spend more on promotion while he, in turn, exhorts the writer to use his skills as a performer, on radio and television, at sales conferences and on the lecture circuit. The author must justify his book before all-comers, including those who will never get beyond reading the blurb on the dust jacket.

The climax to all this activity comes with publication, the signal for a punishing succession of book signings and interviews with Melvyn Bragg look-alikes. ('Tell me Mr Smith, what does it *feel* like to be a famous author?') At the end of two weeks, three weeks at most, the excitement dies, the computer clocks up the sales score and the author is left wondering if it was all worthwhile. If the critics are nasty and sales are poor, he might think of the rival attractions of running a whelk stall. The publisher, however, has no time for these philosophical considerations. He is already off on another hype.

If there were awards for book promotion (and there should be) a first prize would undoubtedly go to **Century Hutchinson**, a company led by a marketing wizard. Anthony Cheetham, declares one of his authors, has his 'spiritual home somewhere in rug bazaars of Samarkand'. In 1987 he made *Sarüm*, a novel virtually ignored by the critics, a top seller by giving it six different jackets. The bookshop displays alone were worth the price of commissioning the half dozen leading illustrators. The total promotion budget for *Sarum* was in excess of £50,000.

The same figure was attached to the marketing of the **Arrow** paperback edition of *Communion: Encounters with the Unknown*. The advertisement which appeared on bus shelters round the country showed a weird, ethereal creature staring out over a telephone number – nothing else. Anyone ringing the number heard a tingly message about the book. 13,000 calls were taken. The book went straight into the bestseller list at number three.

The latest **Century Hutchinson** blockbuster – *Gondar* by Nicholas Luard – was test-marketed by circulating a special advance edition of 500 copies round the trade.

The warm response helped to determine the first print run and to boost the promotion budget to accommodate a clever video 'telling the book's story in a kaleidoscope of images, voices and sounds'. Another first.

But at **Century Hutchinson**, as at all publishers, there is a huge gap between the star treatment and the resources allocated to run of the mill books. With a yearly national output of over fifty thousand titles, how could it be otherwise? The sales director of one large publisher calculates that if he were to give equal time to all the books on his list each author could expect allocation of just two hours – barely long enough to reserve an ad in *The Bookseller* and to send out the review copies.

Whether publishers should devote more effort to marketing entire lists is a moot question. Many books have a strictly limited sale no matter how much money is spent on them. A first novel, say, or an academic treatise may peak at between 1500 and 2000 copies. If the first 1500 can be secured by routine promotion (a catalogue entry, selected mailing and a brief appearance on the back shelves of friendly bookshops) it takes a brave sales manager to advocate a supreme effort to win the extra five hundred. Or a stupid one. The cost of bringing in the marginal sales will almost certainly be out of all proportion to the cost.

If the sales manager wants to increase profit ratio – for his publisher and author – he will do better to raise the price of the book. This is to act on the reasonable assumption that most of his base sale consists of readers who are committed enough not to worry about paying an extra pound or two. That the formula works is proven by the fact that in recent years when book prices have risen well above the rate of inflation, publishers' turnover and profits have increased while volume sales have remained virtually static.

But the argument thus far fails to take any consideration of the middle range of books – those that sell five to ten thousand copies – and assumes that all possible is being done to promote the best sellers. Yet the difference between these two categories can be narrow. It is quite possible to get into the bestseller lists with a sale of fifteen thousand copies. Could not more be done to make the good sellers, bestsellers and the bestsellers, supersellers?

Over the years there has been much talk of the potential benefits of co-operative promotion – the publishers and/or the booksellers getting together to proclaim the virtue of the written word. But the ideas seldom get beyond the talking stage. In the book trade the co-operatists are no match for the loners. The publishers have their Book Marketing Council but after a promising start, it has seemed to lose its spark of originality. Lately the booksellers have endorsed the creation of a Book Promotion House, naively assuming that the publishers will rush forward to finance the project by imposing a small levy on cover prices. Some hope!

The successful marketing ploys which have extended beyond a single publisher or bookseller can be counted on one hand. Book Tokens is the obvious example. **The Booker Prize** is another.

Television advertising is regarded as too expensive though the ITV companies are forever coming up with schemes to try to make screen promotion more economical for publishers. The value of TV tie-ins for book sales indicates a potential for marketing that, so far, has been woefully underexploited.

A long time ago, a marketing director who was faced with the challenge of shifting a multi-volume European history came to a deal with *The Observer* on a full page pre-publication offer in the colour magazine. The healthy contribution to turnover might reasonably have been expected to encourage other experiments. Yet book advertising (as opposed to book club advertising) in the colour supplements is still virtually unknown.

Part of the problem is the sensitivity of the bookshops who instinctively react against special offers in the form of discounts or premiums. These offend the terms of the net book agreement (NBA), a restrictive practice legitimised by case law and tradition whereby publishers are allowed to fix the price at which fiction and general non-fiction books are sold. The Booksellers' Association supports the net book agreement because it protects small bookshops against the potentially devastating competition of the discounters – the powerful retail chains who would cut prices on popular books to achieve mass sales.

The risks of discounting to the general health of the book trade is highlighted by experience in America where the market is dominated by two chains – Barnes & Noble and Waldenbooks – who together account for nearly half of all books sold over the counter. With price cutting established as common practice, many small booksellers have gone to the wall. Those that remain show less and less interest in middle range titles including literary novels, which hang about on the shelves taking up valuable space which could more profitably be occupied by fast moving bestsellers. Book sales (as well as turnover) are booming in the States but the expansion is nearly all at the top end of the market.

Could it happen here? Even with the net book agreement, the squeeze on small booksellers is beginning to hurt. A 1987 survey suggests that up to 300 independents will go out of business in the next decade. Already, W.H. Smith handles one in every five books sold over the counter. But the evidence from other sectors – Hatchards, Pentos Blackwells, Hammicks and, most notably, Waterstones – suggests that the market for literary novels, poetry, new fiction and biography may be stronger in Britain than in the States. Whether it would remain so if the net book agreement was abandoned is an open question much debated in the book trade.

We may not have to wait too long for an answer.

The NBA was designed for a simpler age. In these days of convoluted wheeler-dealing, it is frequently evaded, by exclusive deals between publisher and retailer, for example (**Paul Hamlyn** with Marks and Spencer, **Walker Books** with Sainsburys) or by the frequent recourse to book sales for which substantial discounts are permitted.

But it is the advance of the big retail chains (Hammicks alone is forecasting a six-fold increase of turnover to £100 million by 1990) and the Anglo-American heavyweight publishers with their phalanx of mighty bestsellers which will eventually do away with price fixing. To renounce the freedom to shift prices in line with market variations is to blunt competitiveness. The emerging generation of aggressive entrepreneurs can see no sense in that.

Meanwhile, the middle range publishers of middle range titles are unwilling to risk offending the book trade by selling direct to the public or by dreaming up sales campaigns which flout the NBA. They fear that in the short run they would lose more business than they would gain. This is why we see so much tame promotion urging the potential buyer to pop into his nearest bookshop (maybe miles away) to ask for an advertised volume which may, or more probably may not, be in stock.

With the best will in the world, the average bookseller cannot hope to display more than a small selection of the annual output of titles. What he can do, if he is conscientious, is to accept an order which, given the general slackness of the publishers' distribution system, will take weeks, if not months, to fulfil. It's a strange way to run a business.

PLR and the Libraries

It seems, after all, that Public Lending Right, the system by which authors are paid for library borrowings, is here to stay.

After a shaky start early in the decade when funding was set at a mere £2 million, there was a recurring fear that PLR would eventually suffocate on government meanness. Just one increase, in 1984, brought the total for distribution to £2.75 million where it stayed until 1987. With more authors registering each year, the handout per loan fell to 1.12p, far less than the figure suggested by the first campaigners for PLR thirty years ago. But then Arts Minister, Richard Luce took everyone by surprise by increasing the PLR fund to £3.5 million. In itself, the figure is not greatly impressive – allowing for inflation it does not even make up the loss in real terms since the PLR Act was passed in 1979. And yet, the very fact of an increase at a time when budget restrictions are biting at every sector of the arts, has to be seen as a gesture of commitment. No writer will get rich on PLR alone but there is at least the assurance that the principle of rewarding authors for their contribution to the library service will not be allowed to wither away.

An aspect of PLR which must impress the government and make claims for higher funding more acceptable is the sheer efficiency of the administration. Authors owe a note of thanks to John Sumsion, PLR Registrar, and his team who keep the show on the road at a cost of only £350,000 a year. The rules for participation are refreshingly simple and form filling is reduced to a minimum. Would that such clear thinking prevailed at the Passport Office or the Inland Revenue.

To qualify for PLR an author must be resident in the United Kingdom or West Germany (the latter as part of a reciprocal deal). For a book to be eligible it must be printed, bound and put on sale. It must not be mistaken for a newspaper or periodical, have more than three writers or illustrators named on the title page or be a musical score. Crown copyright is excluded, also books where authorship is attributed to a company or association. But – and this is where mistakes often occur – the author does *not* have to own copyright to be eligible for PLR. Anyone who has disclaimed copyright as part of a flat fee commission, for instance, will still have a claim if his name is on the title page.

Under PLR, the sole writer of a book may not be its sole author. Others named on the title page, such as illustrators, translators, compilers, editors and revisers, may have a claim to authorship. Where there are joint authors, two writers say, or a writer and illustrator, they can strike their own bargain on how their entitlement is to be split. But translators may apply, without reference to other authors, for a 30% fixed share (to be divided equally between joint translators). Similarly, an editor or compiler may register a 20% share provided he has written 10% of the book or at least 10 pages of text. Joint editors or compilers must divide the 20% share equally.

Authors and books can be registered for PLR only when application is made during the author's lifetime. However, once an author is registered, the PLR on his books continues for 50 years after his death. If he wishes, he can assign PLR to other people and bequeath it by will.

If a co-author is dead or untraceable, the remaining co-author can still register for a share of PLR so long as he provides supporting evidence as to why he alone is making application. The PLR office keeps a file of missing authors (mostly illustrators) and help is available from publishers, the writers' organisations and the Association of Illustrators, 1 Colville Place, London W1P 1HN

The calculation of PLR is deceptively simple. It is based on all loans from a representative sample of public libraries (about 1% of the national total). These figures are then multiplied in proportion to total library lending to produce, for each book, an estimate of its annual total loans throughout the country. To counteract possible errors, libraries in the sample change every two to four years.

A recent survey by the PLR Office shows remarkably few critics of the sampling procedure though some individual responses make interesting and provocative reading. 'The secret of PLR is to write lots of short books', argues one author. 'Write *War and Peace*, you're in dead trouble; it takes the average Englishman six months to read.' A more persuasive variation on this complaint comes from an education writer.

'My books tend to be taken out on student's loans. This means that, like many educational text books, they are kept for six weeks before renewal. As they are only recorded for PLR purposes when first borrowed from public libraries, this has the effect of under-recording the time they spend in the borrowers' hands.'

There was evidently some relief at the PLR Office that 'the anticipated chorus asking for academic and reference books to be included did not materialise' in the survey. But many of the authors and editors who feel strongly on this point do not bother to register and thus were not asked for an opinion. Without question, there is some resentment that the PLR sample covers only public libraries (no academic, private or commercial ones) and only loans made over the counter (not consultations of books on library premises).

On the other hand, to widen the scope of PLR is to bring about a fall in the value of the scheme to existing participants. Already the return on PLR for most authors is pitifully small. A clear majority fail to break the £100 barrier and close to 90% make less than £500. Even with the increase of the PLR fund by nearly a third, these ratios are likely to endure since new authors signing on – 1671 in 1986/87 alone – are nearly all in the lowest category of payout.

As one of the writers who regularly scores on the £5000 top limit of PLR, Jeffrey Archer takes the charitable view that he and his bestseller colleagues should be cancelled out of the scheme to allow for more cash to go to young writers and first-time authors. The idea has its obvious attractions but it diverts the PLR from its declared purpose – to pay authors in proportion to the use made of their books by the public libraries. There is certainly a good case for encouraging young talent but prevailing public opinion is against PLR as an agency for distributing subsidies. The argument is put succinctly by Brigid Brophy, a pioneer campaigner for PLR who also happens to be quite a modest beneficiary. 'I may not like the judgement of the public', she says, 'but it is not for me to say that it is wrong.' John Sumsion agrees; 'You should not confuse books with literature.'

Not that books of quality are entirely excluded from PLR. Conscious that popular attention veers without pause between the top and the bottom earners, John Sumsion is at pains to point out that 'serious novelists of high literary standing' are well represented in the list of those getting £1000 or more from PLR. Last year, Anita Brookner's *Hotel du Lac*, a Booker prize winner but by no means an easy read, featured in the top one hundred most frequent borrowings.

Another plus for PLR is in bringing financial recognition to those authors whose main sale is to the libraries. Many of these are now making as much or more from PLR as from royalties. A respondent to the 1987 survey picked up on this feature when he called for more publicity of the stars of the library circuit. 'After all, we have bestseller lists; why not best borrowed lists?'

To judge the future of PLR is to make assumptions about the future of the entire library service. Everybody knows that the public lending libraries are in a bad way. The cause of their travail is said by loyalists to be a simple shortage of funds. If the government came across with an extra few millions all would be well. But there has to be more to the problem. Why is it that while library spending has, just about, kept up with inflation the number of titles lent out is stagnant and the number of borrowings is dropping by about six million per year?

One possible explanation is that many libraries, particularly in the cities, are dull and uninspiring places where staff seem to be more concerned with politics than with their profession. My own choice library experience of the year was when my local branch was peremptorily closed for the day. The reason offered by a straight-faced security man, was that the staff were attending a protest meeting – against library closures!

But if libraries that don't care are clearly bad news for authors, those that do care are not much better – if they happen to care about the wrong things. When there is common agreement on the need for a prudent allocation of resources, it is surely outrageous that so many libraries should go in for the free lending of records, cassettes, videos; even computer games and pictures. What next? Free film shows? Free rock concerts? No wonder that books are hard to come by.

A way forward has been chartered by the Arts Minister, Richard Luce, who thinks that the library service could benefit from a touch of privatisation. While committing the government to a basic free book lending service, he has raised the prospect of charging for non-print services such as information stored on electronic databases. Library users might have to pay for research facilities or for borrowing more than a certain number of books. Other services could be put out to tender – the delivery of books to old people's homes, for instance, or even the running of branch libraries.

All this is open to consultation and discussion but the **Library Association** has already come out strongly against any attempt to restrict the free access to information – whether books, records or videos. This is to ignore the fact that some libraries already make money by selling advertising space and that the charge for reserving books or obtaining them from other libraries, though too low to be economic, is long-established.

The more adventurous, noting that Mr Luce estimates raising £50 million if his proposals go ahead, are urging him towards bolder and more profitable action. Sir Roy Strong advocates book sales in libraries.

'A public library with a commercial concern could be the pattern of the future, following that already pioneered within museums and galleries, where it is possible to purchase, for example, contemporary craft and art books.'

Others have dared to challenge the sanctity of the free loan. John Banham, former head of the Audit Commission, has pointed out that a charge of 20p for each book borrowed would raise enough to treble the £60 million spent annually on new books. The Adam Smith Institute, a right-wing research body, wants a borrowing charge of 30p plus an annual subscription of £4 and a daily fee of £1 for reference facilities. Allow for reduced rates for the young, elderly, students and unemployed, these charges could bring in about £350 million, effectively doubling the present library income from rates and taxes.

The counter-argument warns of a collapse in demand for books if library members are forced to pay for their reading pleasure. But this is by no means certain. Well-heeled patrons of the system who, in most parts of the country, are in a clear majority are not likely to turn away at the prospect of a modest contribution towards their library upkeep.

Looked at from the point of view of authors – who, of all the workers in the library service, have most cause for complaint – the prerequisite for any major change in the financing of the system should be a clear promise to allocate a decent share of extra revenue to PLR.

PLR application forms and details can be obtained from:
The Registrar, PLR Office, Bayheath House, Prince Regent Street, Stockton-on-Tees, Cleveland TS18 1DF Tel 0642 604699
Authors' Reaction to Public Lending Right, a 1987 Questionnaire Survey, is available from the same address, price £2.95, post free.

What Chance for Poetry?
— Peter Finch

For a time now publishing poetry has been considered a growth industry. Certainly more poetry has been sold in the last few years than at any time since the 1960s but compared to most other types of writing it is really small beer. There are exceptions, of course, but an off-the-cuff comparison would give a paperbacked novelist sales in the region of 25,000 with the new poet notching up only 5 or 600. Hardly worth bothering you might think. Yet the march of new and emerging poets goes on and on.

The situation is really one of inverted supply and demand. The number of readers available for new poetry is actually very small. Despite relatively good sales from market leaders such as Ted Hughes and doyen of the greeting card versifiers Helen Steiner Rice poetry in general fairs pretty badly. Check the shelves of your local library for proof. You will find a lot of biography but little verse. Yet there are so many new writers around seeking publication that presses and periodicals have been forced to emerge specifically to service them. For the first time in history we apparently have more writers of poetry practising than we have readers. It is an amazing situation. The Victorians kept diaries; we write poetry. Nearly all of the present day population is literate so in our spare time it's either creativity or graffiti. Judge for yourself which is coming in first.

The Traditional Outlets

There exists a small, traditional market for new verse – *The TLS*, *The Listener*, the quality Sunday papers, *London Magazine*, *The Spectator*, the occasional poem in magazines like *The Lady*, *Encounter* and *The Countryman*. All paying outlets, which sounds quite reassuring. But the truth is that were poetry to cease to exist overnight then these periodicals would continue to publish without a flicker. Who, other than the poets, would notice? Book publishers like **Faber**, **Chatto**, **Hutchinson**, **OUP** and **Secker** all have small but healthy poetry lists yet these are hardly central to their business operations. A little decoration for their catalogues perhaps? Poetry implies quality – unless it's Roger McGough it hardly means money.

The Specialists

The real growth has been among the specialist presses – **Anvil, Bloodaxe, Carcanet, Poetry Wales Press**. Begun as small operations, often the burning interest of one individual, these apparently non-commercial literary ventures have by now acquired staff, offices and even national distribution. They stay distinct from their trade cohorts, however, by continuing to put art before cash. They remain open to new writers and to new ideas. They are not afraid to experiment. Their titles are well designed and stand comparison with anything else the booktrade has to offer. They are able to continue publishing mainly with the support of public money channelled via

Arts Council or arts association. They are models of what poetry publishing should be – active, alert, exciting. The problem is that they are too few.

The Small Press and the Little Magazine

Most poetry in this country actually sees the light of day through the small presses and little magazines. These have been the backbone of literary publishing here since the Second World War. The advance of printing technology – the advent of cheap duplicating, desk-top litho, photocopying and now home wordprocessing has brought the once arcane art of publishing within the reach of all. Small presses, usually one person activities run from back bedrooms, have flourished. Little magazines published on a shoe string by enthusiasts have sprung up everywhere from Cardiff to Caithness. Don't expect printing perfection. Many of these spare time operations produce home stapled pamphlets set on typewriters and magazines with covers coloured by hand. But standards are rising. From the **Atlas Press** to **Writers Forum** and from **Aquarius** to **Westwords** magazine text is being typeset and pages are being professionally bound. Gone are the spirit duplicated, wastepaper swatches of yesteryear. Today it is colour, texture and quality. Small presses may not yet be the mirror image of their commercial rivals but they are a respectable alternative. For the new writer they are the obvious place to begin. Indeed some writers see little point in publishing anywhere else. This is where literature has its cutting edge.

Cash

A lot of writers new to the business are surprised to learn that their poetry will not make them much money. Being a poet is not really much of an occupation. You get better wages delivering papers. There will be the odd pound from the better heeled magazine, perhaps even as much as £20 or so from those periodicals lucky enough to be in receipt of a grant but generally it will be free copies of the issues concerned, thank you letters and little more. Those with collections published by a subsidised, specialist publisher can expect £100 or so as an advance on royalties. Those using the small presses can look forward to a few dozen complimentary copies. The truth is that poetry itself is undervalued. You can earn money writing about it, reviewing it, lecturing on it or giving public recitations of it. In fact most things in the poetry business will earn better money than the verse itself. Expect to spend a lot on stamps and a fair bit on sample copies. Most of the time all you will get in return is used envelopes.

Competitions

Competitions have been very much in vogue recently with the most unlikely organisations sponsoring them. The notion here is that anonymity ensures fairness. Entries are made under pseudonyms so that if your name does happen to be Seamus Heaney then this won't help you much. Results seem to bear this out too. The big competitions such as the one run by the **Arvon Foundation** or the **Poetry Society's** *National* attract an enormous entry and usually throw up quite a number of complete unknowns among the winners. It might be worth questioning though why people bother. The money prizes can be large – thousands of pounds – but it costs at least a pound a poem to enter in the first place. If it is cash you want then horses are a better bet. And there has been a recent trend for winners to come from places like Cape Girardeau, Missouri and Tibooburra, Australia. The odds are getting longer. Who won the 1986 **Arvon**? I don't remember. But if you do fancy a try then it is a pretty innocent activity. You tie up a poem for a few months and you spend a couple of pounds. Watch the small magazines for details, write to your local arts association.

Where to start

Probably the best place for the new poet to start will be locally. Find out through the library or the nearest arts association which writers groups meet in your area and attend a few. There you will meet others of a like mind, encounter whatever locally produced magazines there might be and get a little direct feedback on your work. 'How am I doing' is a big question for the emerging poet and although criticism is not all that hard to come by do not expect it from all sources. Magazine editors, for example, will rarely have the time to offer advice. It is also reasonable to be suspicious of that offered by friends and relations – they will no doubt be only trying to please. Writers groups present the best chance for poets to engage in honest mutual criticism. But if you'd prefer a more detailed, written analysis of your efforts and are willing to pay a small sum then you could apply to the service operated nationally by the **Poetry Society** (21 Earls Court Sq., London SW5) or to one of those run on an area basis by your local arts association.

If you made the decision to publish your work, and I don't suppose you'd be reading this if you hadn't, then the first thing to do is a little market research. I've already indicated how overstocked the business is with periodicals and publications yet surprisingly you will not find many of these in your local W.H. Smith. Most poetry still reaches its public via the specialist. Begin, though, by reading a few newly published mainstream books. Ask at your bookshop for their recommendations. Enquire at the library. Try selecting a recent anthology of *contemporary* verse. Progress to the literary magazine. Write off to a number of the addresses which follow this article and ask for sample copies. Enquire about subscriptions. Expect to pay a little but inevitably not a lot. It is important that poets read not only to familiarise themselves with what is currently fashionable and to increase their own facility for self-criticism but to help support the activity in which they wish to participate. Buy, read, and then, if appropriate, think about sending in.

How to do it

Increase your chances of acceptance by following simple, standard procedure:

- Type, single side of the paper, A4 size, single-spacing with double between stanzas *exactly* as you'd wish your poem to appear when printed.
- Give the poem a title, clip multi-page works together, include your name and address at the foot of the final sheet.
- Keep a copy, make a record of what you send where and when, leave a space to note reaction.

- Send in small batches, six is a good number, include a brief covering letter saying who you are. Leave justification, apology and explanation for the writers circle.
- Include a self addressed, stamped envelope of sufficient size for reply and/or return of your work.
- Be prepared to wait some weeks for a response. Don't pester. Be patient. Most magazines will reply in the end.
- Never send the same poem to two places at the same time.
- Send your best. Work which fails to fully satisfy even the author is unlikely to impress anyone else.

Where?

Try the list which follows, sending for samples as I've suggested. The total market is vast – 200 or so addresses here – more than 800 in *Small Presses and Little Magazines of the UK and Ireland* (**Oriel**, 53 Charles Street, Cardiff – £1.80), literally thousands and thousands worldwide in Judson Jerome's *Poet's Market* (Writer's Digest Books) and Len Fulton's *Directory of Poetry Publishers* (Dustbooks) – the two main American directories.

The Next Step

Once you have placed a few poems you may like to consider publishing a booklet. There are as many small presses around as there are magazines. Start with the upmarket professionals by all means – **Secker, OUP, Chatto, Hutchinson, Faber, Virago** – but be prepared for compromise. The specialists and the small presses are swifter, more open to new work. If all else fails you could do it yourself. Blake did, so did Ezra Pound. Modern technology puts the process within the reach of us all.

These lists are not exhaustive. Publishers come and go with amazing frequency. There will always be a new press on the look out for talent and the project magazine desperate for contributions. Keep your ear to the ground.

Commercial Publishers with poetry on their lists

(Those with a substantial interest are preceded by *)
Aberdeen University Press
Allison & Busby (see **W.H. Allen**)
Angus & Robertson Ltd
The Bodley Head Ltd
Marion Boyars Ltd
John Calder Ltd
Cambridge University Press
Canongate Publishing Ltd
Jonathan Cape Ltd
Cassell
*****Century Hutchinson**, including **Arena**
W & R Chambers
*****Chatto & Windus Ltd/The Hogarth Press**
Collins, including **Grafton/Paladin**

J.M. Dent & Sons Ltd see **Weidenfeld & Nicolson Ltd**
André Deutsch Ltd
Gerald Duckworth
***Faber & Faber Ltd**
GMP Ltd (Gay Men's Press)
Robert Hale Ltd
Hamish Hamilton Ltd
Hodder & Stoughton Ltd
Macdonald & Co Ltd
Macmillan Publishers Ltd
Methuen London
***Oxford University Press**
***Penguin Books**
Quartet Books
Routledge
Scottish Academic Press
***Secker & Warburg Ltd**
Sidgwick & Jackson Ltd
Souvenir Press Ltd
Viking
Virago Press Ltd
Weidenfeld & Nicolson Ltd
The Women's Press

The Specialists

Anvil Press Poetry (press/magazine) *Peter Jay* see **UK Publishers** section

Blackstaff Press (press) *Michael Burns* see **UK Publishers** section

Bloodaxe Books (press) *Neil Astley* see **UK Publishers** section

Carcanet Press (press/magazine) *Michael Schmidt* see **UK Publishers** section

Poetry Wales Press (press/magazine) *Cary Archard*, Andmor House, Trewsfield Industrial Estate, Tondu Road, Bridgend CF3 4LJ

Small Presses

Actual Size Press *Paul Brown*, 40 Elm Grove, Peckham, London SE15 5DE

The ADA Press *Andrew Hale*, 31 Ada Road, Canterbury, Kent CT1 3TS

Agenda & Editions Charitable Trust (press/magazine) *William Cookson*, 5 Cranbourne Court, Albert Bridge Road, London SW11 4PE

Akira Press *Desmond Johnson*, Box 409, London E2

All in Wallstickers *Nina Steane*, 27 Harpes Road, Oxford

Allardyce, Barnett, Publishers *Anthony Barnett*, see **UK Publishers** section

Alun Books *Sally Jones*, 3 Crown Street, Port Talbot, West Glamorgan

Arlen House, The Women's Press *Catherine Rose*, 69 Jones Road, Dublin 3

Atlas Press *Alastair Brotchie*, 10 Park Street, London SE1 9AB

BB Books (press/magazine) *Dave Cunliffe*, 1 Springbank, Longsight Road, Salebury, Blackburn, Lancashire BB1 9EU

Bedlam Press *David Moody*, Church Green House, Old Church Lane, Pateley Bridge, Harrogate HG3 5LZ

Big Little Poem Books *Robert Richardson*, 42 Peaksfield Avenue, Grimsby, South Humberside DN32 9QF

Blind Serpent Press 65 Magdalen Yard Road, Dundee DD2 1AL

Blue Bridge Press *David Tipton*, 24 Aireville Road, Frizinhall, Bradford BD9 4HH

Brentham Press *Margaret Tims* see **UK Publishers** section

Dangaroo Books PO Box 186, Coventry CV4 7HG

Christopher Davies Publishers Ltd *Christopher Davies* see **UK Publishers** section

Dedalus Poetry Press *John F. Deane*, 46 Seabury, Sydney Parade Avenue, Dublin 4

Dollar of Soul/Chicken Sigh Press *Owen Davis*, 15 Argyle Road, Swanage, Dorset BH19 1HZ

Downlander Publishing *Derek Bourne-Jones*, 88 Oxenden Gardens, Lower Willingdon, Eastbourne, East Sussex BN22 0RS

Echo Room Press (press/magazine) *Brendan Cleary*, 45 Bewick Court, Princess Street, Newcastle upon Tyne NE1 8EG

Enitharmon Press *Stephen Stuart-Smith* see **UK Publishers** section

Equofinality (press/magazine) *Red Mengham*, 147 Selly Oak Road, Bournville, Birmingham B30 1HN

Ferry Press Bridges Farmhouse, Laughton, Lewes, East Sussex

Five Seasons Press The Butts, Shenmore, Madley, Herefordshire HR2 9NZ

Fleeting Monolith Enterprises 35 Dresden Road, London N19 3BE

Forest Books *Brenda Walker*, 20 Forest View, Chingford, London E4 7AY

Four Eyes Press (press/magazine) 510 Wilmslow Road, Withington, Manchester M20 9BT

Gallery Press *Peter Fallon*, 19 Oakdown Road, Dublin 14

Galloping Dog Press *Peter Hodgkiss*, 45 Salisbury Gardens, Newcastle upon Tyne NE2 1HP

Genera Editions/Shadowcat *Colin Simms*, Temperance Farm, Halton-lea-Gate, Carlisle, Cumbria CA6 7LB

Gomer Press *John Lewis*, Llandysul, Dyfed SA44 4BQ

Hangman Books *Billy Childish*, 2 May Road, Rochester, Kent

Hard Pressed Poetry *Billy Mills*, 1 New Ireland Road, Rialto, Dublin 8

Hearing Eye *John Rety*, Box 1, 99 Torriano Avenue, London NW5

Hippopotamus Press (press/magazine) *Roland John* see **UK Publishers** section

Honno *Ailsa Craig*, Heol Y Cawl, Dinas Powys, South Glamorgan

International Concrete Poetry Archive *Paula Claire*, 11 Dale Close, Thames Street, Oxford OX1 1TU

Iron Press (press/magazine) *Peter Mortimer*, 5 Marden Terrace, Cullercoats, North Shields, Tyne and Wear NE30 4PD

Jackson's Arm (press/magazine) *Michael Blackburn*, 62 Juniper House, Pomeroy Street, New Cross, London SE14 5BY

Johnson Green Publishing (UK) Ltd/Aquila (press/magazine) *J.C.R. Green*, PO Box 418, Leek, Staffordshire, ST13 8UX

Keepsake Press *Roy Lewis*, 2 Park House Gardens, East Twickenham TW1 2DE

KQBX *James Sale*, 30 Fitzroy Avenue, Luton LU3 1RS

Littlewood Press *John Killick*, 5 Slater Bank, Hebden Bridge, West Yorkshire HX7 7DY

Lobby Press (press/magazine) *Richard Tabor*, 1 Dairy Cottages, Compton Road, Yeovil, Somerset BA22 7EW

Lokamaya (Press) Bookpublishing *Bahauddeen Latif*, 8 Batoum Gardens, London W6 7QD

Lucas Publications 85 Brasenose Road, Liverpool L20 8QA

Magenta Press *Maggie O'Sullivan*, 40 Maldon Road, Acton, London W3 6SZ

Mammon Press (press/magazine) *Fred Beake*, 12 Dartmouth Avenue, Bath, Avon

Manderville Press *Peter Scupham*, 2 Taylor's Hill, Hitchin, Hertfordshire

The Many Press (press/magazine) *John Welch*, 15 Northcott Road, London N16 7BJ

Mariscat Press *Hamish Whyte*, 3 Mariscat Road, Glasgow G41 4ND

Merseyside Poetry Circuit (press/magazine) *Dave Ward*, 38 Canning Street, Liverpool L8 7NP

Microbrigade *Ulli Freer*, 107 Woodside Lodge, Finchley Park, London N12 9JJ

Midnag Publications Northumberland Technical College, College Road, Ashington, Northumberland NE63 9RG

The Milvus-Milvus Press (press/magazine) *Chris Broadribb*, 153 Lake Road West, Cardiff CF2 5PJ

New Beacon Books 76 Stroud Green Road, London N7 5EN

New Broom Private Press *Toni Savage*, 78 Cambridge Street, Leicester LE3 0JP

North and South *Frances Presley*, 23 Egerton Road, Twickenham, Middlesex TW2 7SL

Northern House 19 Haldane Terrace, Newcastle upon Tyne NE2 3AN

Northern Lights 66 Belsize Park, London NW3 4NE

Oasis Books *Ian Robinson*, 12 Stevenage Road, London SW6 6ES

Oleander Press *Philip Ward*, 17 Stansgate Avenue, Cambridge CB2 2QZ

Open Township (press/magazine) *Michael Haslam*, 14 Foster Clough, Heights Road, Hebden Bridge, West Yorkshire HX7 5QZ

Oscars Press BM Oscars, London WC1N 3XX

Overdue Books *Jan Maloney*, 37 Melbourne Street, Hebden Bridge, West Yorkshire HX7 6AS

Peterloo Poets (press/magazine) *Harry Chambers*, 2 Kelly Gardens, Calstock, Cornwall PL18 9SA

Pig Press (press/magazine) *Ric Caddel*, 7 Cross View Terrace, Neville's Cross, Durham DH1 4JY

Poetical Histories 27 Sturton Street, Cambridge

Polygon (press/magazine) *Peter Kravitz* see **UK Publishers** section

Prest Roofs 34 Alpine Court, Kenilworth CV8 2GP

Raven Arts *Dermot Bolger*, PO Box 1430, Finglas, Dublin 11

Red Sharks Press (press/magazine) *Chris Mills*, 122 Clive Street, Grangetown, Cardiff CF1 7JE

Redbeck Press (press/magazine) *David Tipton*, 24 Aireville Road, Frizinghall, Bradford BD9 4HH

Rivelin Grapheme Press *Snowdon Barnett*, The Annex, Kennet House, 19 High Street, Hungerford, Berkshire RG17 0NL

Sea Dream Music *Simon Law*, 236 Sebert Road, Forest Gate, London E7 0NP

Shearsman Books *Tony Fraser*, 47 Dayton Close, Plymouth PL6 5DX

Ship of Fools *Robert Sheppard*, 15 Oakapple Road, Southwick, Sussex

Slow Dancer Press (press/magazine) *John Harvey*, Flat 4, 1 Park Valley, Nottingham NG7 1BS

Smith/Doorstop (press/magazine) *Peter Sansom*, 51 Byram Arcade, Westgate, Huddersfield HD1 1ND

Spanner (press/magazine) *Allen Fisher*, 64 Lanercost Road, London SW2 3DN

Spectacular Diseases (press/magazine) *Paul Green*, 83b London Road, Peterborough PE2 9BS

Spectrum *Chris Bendon*, 14 Maes y Deri, Lampeter, Dyfed SA48 7EP

Stone Lantern Press *Phil Maillard*, 10 Severn Road, Canton, Cardiff CF1 9EB

Stride Publications (press/magazine) *Rupert Loydell*, 37 Portland Street, Newtown, Exeter, Devon EX1 2EG

Sub-Voicive 21 Cecile Park, London N8

Swan Books and Educational Services *E.O. Evans*, 13 Henrietta Street, Swansea

Taurus Press of Willow Dene *Paul Peter Piech*, 11 Limetree Way, Danygraig, Porthcawl, Mid Glamorgan CF36 5AU

Tiger Bay Press *Olly Rees*, 84 Drakefield Road, London SW17

Toad's Damp Press *Patricia Farrell*, 4 Balham New Road, London SW12

Tuba Press (press/magazine) *Peter Ellison*, 23 Kinfauns Avenue, Eastbourne, East Sussex BN22 8SS

Turret Books *Bernard Stone*, 42 Lamb's Conduit Street, London WC1N 3LJ

Ver Poets *May Badman*, Haycroft, 61/63 Chiswell Green Lane, St Albans, Hertfordshire AL2 3AG

Virgil Publications *John Howard*, 94 Howeth Road, Bournemouth, Dorset BH10 5ED

Wellsweep Press/Nodding Donkey (press/magazine) *John Cayley*, 26 Teesdale Road, Leytonstone, London E11 1NQ

The Wide Skirt Press (press/magazine) *Geoff Hattersley*, 93 Blackhouse Road, Fartown, Huddersfield, West Yorkshire HD2 1AP

Womenwrite Press *Luana Dee*, PO Box 77, Cardiff CF2 4XX

Word and Action (Dorset) Ltd (press/magazine) 43 Avenue Road, Wimbourne, Dorset BH21 1BS

Words Press Hod House, Child Okeford, Dorset DT11 8EH

Writers Forum (press/magazine) *Bob Cobbing*, 89a Petherton Road, London N5 2QT

Yew Tree Books *Mollie Rallings*, Skipton Office Services, 2 Otley Street, Skipton BD23 3NT

Little Magazines

Acumen (press/magazine) *Patricia Oxley*, 6 The Mount, Furzeham, Brixham, South Devon TQ5 8QY

Agenda (press/magazine) *William Cookson*, 5 Cranbourne Court, Albert Bridge Road, London SW11 4PE

Agog *Ed Jewasinski*, 116 Eswyn Road, Tooting, London SW17 8JN

Ambit (press/magazine) *Martin Bax*, 17 Priory Gardens, London N6 5QY

Angel Exhaust (press/magazine) *Adrian Clarke*, 2 Lovelace Gardens, Southend SS2 4NV

Anthem (press/magazine) *Martin Tatham*, 57 Cyril Avenue, Bobbers' Mill, Derbyshire

Aquarius *Eddie S. Linden*, Flat 3, 116 Sutherland Avenue, London W9

Argo Museum of Modern Art, 30 Pembroke Street, Oxford OX1 1BP

The Bad Seed Review (press/magazine) *Martin Myers*, 2 Ashleigh Grove, West Jesmond, Newcastle upon Tyne NE2 3DL

Bête Noire *John Osborne*, Dept of American Studies, The University of Hull, Cottingham Road, Hull HU6 7RX

Bogg *George Cairncross*, 31 Belle Vue Street, Filey, Yorkshire YO14 9HU

Borderlines *Andrew Morrison*, Anglo-Welsh Poetry Society, The Flat, Cronkhill, Crosshouses, Shrewsbury SY5 6JP

Bradford Poetry Quarterly *Clare Chapman*, 9 Woovale Road, Bradford BD7 2SJ

Briggistane *Shetland Arts Trust*, 22–24 North Road, Lerwick, Shetland

Celtic Dawn PO Box 271, Oxford OX2 6DU

Chapman (press/magazine) *Joy M. Hendry*, 80 Moray Street, Blackford, Perthshire PH4 1QF

Core *Mevlut Ceylan*, 37b Packingham Square, Islington, London N1 7UJ

Corpus *Paul Habberjam*, 13 Colwyn Road, Leeds LS11 6QZ

Dada Dance *Dee Rimbaud*, 12 Blairhall Avenue, Glasgow G41 3BA

Distaff *Isabel Gillard*, St Lawrence Cottage, Sellman Street, Gnosall, Stafford ST20 0ED

A Doctor's Dilemma *Peter Godfrey*, Flat 3, 32 Brunswick Terrace, Hove, East Sussex BN3 1JH

The Echo Room (press/magazine) *Brendan Cleary*, 45 Bewick Court, Princess Street, Newcastle upon Tyne NE1 8EG

Ecutorial *Will Rowe*, Dept of Spanish, Kings College, Strand, London WC2

Edinburgh Review (press/magazine) *Peter Kravitz*, 48 Pleasance, Edinburgh EH8 9TJ

Envoi (press/magazine) *Anne Lewis Smith*, Penffordd, Newport, Dyfed SA42 0QT

Exe-Calibre *Ken Taylor*, Flat 1, 33 Knowle Road, Totterdown, Bristol BS4 2EB

Figs (press/magazine) *Tony Baker*, Mews Cottage, Winster, Derbyshire DE4 2DJ

First Offence *Tim Fletcher*, Syringa, The Street, Stodmarsh, Canterbury, Kent CT3 4BA

First Time (press/magazine) *Josephine Austin*, 80 St Helens Road, Hastings TN34 2LN

Folded Sheets 14 Foster Clough, Heights Road, Hebden Bridge, West Yorkshire HX7 5QZ

Footnotes (press/magazine) *James Sale*, Schools' Poetry Assoc., 30 Fitzroy Avenue, Luton, Bedfordshire

The Frogmore Papers *Jeremy Page*, 28 Welta House, Hazellville Road, Highgate, London N19 3LZ

Gallery Valerie Sinason, 3 Honeybourne Road, London NW6 1HH

Giant Steps (press/magazine) *Maggie Mort*, The Beeches, Riverside, Clapham via Lancaster LA2 8DT

Global Tapestry Journal (press/magazine) *Dave Cunliffe*, 1 Springbank, Longsight Road, Salebury, Blackburn, Lancashire BB1 9EU

The Green Book (press/magazine) *Keith Spencer*, 72 Walcot Street, Bath BA1 1XN

Grosseteste Review (press/magazine) *Tim Longville*, Robertswood, Farley Hill, Matlock, Derbyshire

Groundworks Fen Poetry Centre, The Fish, Sutton Gault, nr Ely, Cambridgeshire CB6 2BE

Harry's Hand (press/magazine) *Michael Blackburn*, 115 Westcott Street, Holderness Road, Hull HU8 8LZ

Hat *Ian Hogg*, 1a Church Lane, Croft, nr Skegness, Lincolnshire

The Honest Ulsterman *Frank Ormsby*, 70 Eglantine Avenue, Belfast BT9 6DY

Impressions 84 Colwyn Road, Northampton NN1 3PX

Inkshed *Anthony Smith*, Flat 4, 387 Beverly Road, Hull HU5 1LF

Iota *David Holliday*, 67 Hady Crescent, Chesterfield, Derbyshire SH1 0EB

Iron (press/magazine) *Peter Mortimer*, 5 Marden Terrace, Cullercoats, North Shields, Tyne and Wear NE30 4PD

Issue One (press/magazine) *Ian Brocklebank*, 2 Tewkesbury Drive, Grimsby, South Humberside, DN34 4TL

Jennings Magazine *Philip Sydney Jennings*, 336 Westbourne Park Road, London W11 1EQ

Joe Soap's Canoe (press/magazine) *Martin Stannard*, 90 Ranelagh Road, Felixstowe, Suffolk IP11 7HY

Kite (press/magazine) *Chris Broadribb*, 153 Lake Road West, Cardiff CF2 5PJ

Label *Paul Beasley*, 57 Effingham Road, Lee Green, London SE12 8NT

Litmus *Laurie Smith*, The City Lit, Stukeley Street, Drury Lane, London WC2B 5ZJ

London Magazine (press/magazine) *Alan Ross*, 30 Thurloe Place, London SW7 2HQ

Magazing *Chris Mitchell*, 6 Athole Gardens, Glasgow G12 9AY

Margin 20 Brook Green, London W6 7BL

Momentum *Christine Stace*, 31 Alexandra Road, Wrexham, Clwyd LL13 7SL

Network of Women Writers *Melissa Mitcheson-Lee*, 8 The Broadway, Woking, Surrey GU21 5AP

New Departures (press/magazine) *Mike Horovitz*, Piedmont, Bisley, Stroud, Gloucestershire GL6 7BU

New Hope International *Gerald England*, 23 Gambrel Bank Road, Ashton under Lyme OL6 8TW

New Welsh Review *Belinda Humfrey*, Dept of English, St David's University College, Lampeter SA48 7ED

Ninth Decade (press/magazine) *Robert Vas Dias*, 52 Cascade Avenue, London N10

The North (press/magazine) *Peter Sansom*, 51 Byram Arcade, Westgate, Huddersfield HD1 1ND

Numbers *John Alexander*, 6 Kingston Street, Cambridge CB1 2NU

Orbis *Mike Shields*, 199 The Long Shoot, Nuneaton, Warwickshire CV11 6JQ

Ore *Eric Ratcliffe*, 7 The Towers, Stevenage, Hertfordshire SG1 1HE

Other Poetry *Evangeline Paterson*, 2 Stoneygate Avenue, Leicester

Outposts (press/magazine) *Roland John*, 2b Cedar Road, Sutton, Surrey SM2 5DA

Oxford Poetry Magdalen College, Oxford OX1 4AU

Pages (press/magazine) *Robert Sheppard*, 15 Oakapple Road, Southwick, Sussex BN4 4YL

Paraphernalia *Harvey Doctors*, 41 Maynard Road, Walthamstow, London E17 9JE

Pennine Ink *J. McEvoy*, c/o MPAA, The Gallery Downstairs, Yorke Street, Burnley, Lancashire

Pennine Platform *Brian Merrikin Hill*, Ingmanthorpe Hall Farm Cottage, Wetherby, West Yorkshire LS22 5EQ

Planet *Ned Thomas*, PO Box 44, Aberystwyth, Dyfed

PN Review (press/magazine) *Michael Schmidt*, 208–12 Corn Exchange Buildings, Manchester M4 3BQ

Poetry and Audience *Jonathan Ward*, School of English, University of Leeds, Leeds, West Yorkshire LS2 9JT

Poetry Durham *Michael O'Neill*, Dept of English, University of Durham, Elvet Riverside, New Elvet, Durham DH1 3JT

Poetry Express *David Orme*, Schools Poetry Association, 27 Pennington Close, Golden Common, nr Winchester, Hampshire SO21 1UR

Poetry Ireland Review 44 Upper Mount Street, Dublin 2

Poetry Nottingham *Howard Atkinson*, 21 Duncombe Close, Nottingham NG3 3PH

Poetry Review *Peter Forbes*, The Poetry Society, 21 Earls Court Square, London SW5 9DE

Poetry Voice *George Robinson*, 32 Ridgemere Road, Pensby, Wirral L61 8RL

Poetry Wales (press/magazine) *Mike Jenkins*, 26 Andrew's Close, Heolgerrig, Mid-Glamorgan CF48 1SS

Poets Voice (press/magazine) *Fred Beake*, 12 Dartmouth Avenue, Bath, Avon BA2 1AT

Prospice (press/magazine) *J.C.R. Green*, PO Box 418, Leek, Staffordshire ST13 8UX

Reality Studios (press/magazine) *Ken Edwards*, 85 Balfour Street, London SE17 1PB

The Rialto *John Wakeman*, 32 Grosvenor Road, Norwich NR2 2PZ

RSVP 29 Calversyke Street, Keighley, BD21 1PA

Scribble *Graham Kendall*, 28 Westwood Avenue, Timperley, Altrincham, Cheshire WA15 6QF

Slow Dancer (press/magazine) *John Harvey*, Flat 4, 1 Park Valley, Nottingham NG7 1BS

Smoke (press/magazine) *Dave Ward*, 38 Canning Street, Liverpool L8 7NP

Soot (press/magazine) *Paul Green*, 83b London Road, Peterborough, Cambridge PE2 9BS

Spokes *Julius Smit*, 15 The Ridgeway, Flitwick, Bedfordshire MK45 1DM

Stand (press/magazine) *Jon Silkin*, 19 Haldane Terrace, Newcastle upon Tyne NE2 3AN

Staple Magazine *Don Measham*, c/o School of Humanities, Derbyshire College of Further Education, Matlock, Derbyshire DE4 3FW

Start *Paul Smith*, Burslem Leisure Centre, 24a Market Place, Burslem, Stoke on Trent

Strength Beyond Bingo *Jeremy Tattersall*, 112 Sandock Road, Lewisham, London SE13

Stride (press/magazine) *Rupert Loydell*, 37 Portland Street, Newtown, Exeter, Devon EX1 2EG

Success *Kate Dean*, 17 Andrew's Crescent, Peterborough PE1 6XL

Talus *Hanne Bramness*, c/o Dept of English, Kings College, The Strand, London WC2R 2LS

Tears in the Fence *David Caddy*, 38 Hod View, Stourpaine, nr Blandford Forum, Dorset DT11 8TN

Thursdays (press/magazine) *John Denny*, 70 Poplar Road, Bearwood, Warley, West Midlands B66 4AN

Tops The Old Police Station, 80 Lark Lane, Toxteth Park, Liverpool L17 8XH

Tremenos *Kathleen Raine*, 47 Paultons Square, London SW3 5DT

Verse St Hugh's College, Oxford OX2 6LE

Verse Dept of English Literature, University of Glasgow G12 8QQ

Vision *Louis Foley*, 32 Gilchrist Avenue, Corby, Northamptonshire NN17 1BA

Westwords *Dave Woolley*, 15 Trelawney Road, Peverell, Plymouth, Devon PL3 4JS

Weyfarers *Margaret Pain*, 9 Whiterose Lane, Woking, Surrey GU22 7JA

The Whiterose Literary Magazine *Nancy Whybrow*, 14 Browning Road, Temple Hill, Dartford, Kent DA1 5ET

The Wide Skirt (press/magazine) *Geoff Hattersley*, 93 Blackhouse Road, Fartown, Huddersfield, West Yorkshire HD2 1AP

Words International *Jean Shelley*, Bird-in-Eye, Uckfield, East Sussex TN22 5HA

Writers' Own Magazine (press/magazine) *Eileen M. Pickering*, 121 Highbury Grove, Clapham, Bedford MK41 6DU

Writing *Barbara Horsfall*, 87 Brookhouse Road, Farnborough, Hampshire GU14 0BU

Writing Women 10 Mistletoe Road, Newcastle upon Tyne NE2 2DX

Z *Victoria Hurst*, 6a Switzerland Terrace, Douglas, Isle of Man

ZLR *Neil Cross*, 23 Netherfield Road, Sandiacre, Nottingham NG10 5LP

The Economics of Packaging

Book packaging is the no-nonsense end of publishing. Everybody works to a set plan, including the writer, who should not get any fancy notions about his place in the production hierarchy. In book packaging, the words must fit the design, not the other way around.

The process starts with an idea for a big seller, typically a highly illustrated work of general reference such as made the fortune of **Dorling Kindersley** – *The Photographer's Handbook* and *Baby and Child* – before they became publishers in their own right. More recent examples are *Dictionary of World Stamps* (**Autumn Publishing**), *Animals in the Wild* (**Belitha Press**), *The Atlas of British Birds* (**Curtis Garratt**) and the *Macmillan Encyclopedia* (**Market House Books**).

Having settled on an idea, the packager commissions a designer to show him how his book might look on a display shelf. Will it attract the roving eye of a bookshop browser? Is it the sort of present Aunt Hilda might want for Christmas? If yes, what about other Aunt Hildas or their equivalent round the world? Their reaction is critical because to achieve its bestseller status, the book must appeal across linguistic and cultural boundaries.

At this stage, the question of who will write the book is the least of the packager's worries. Like the newspaper or magazine editor, he knows that if the subject is strong enough he will have no trouble in finding a suitable wordsmith. But for credibility's sake, he may want to sound out a likely frontman – a well-known expert (preferably a TV personality) who might be persuaded to lend his name as editor – for a sizeable fee, of course.

Having invested a few hundred, or maybe a few thousand pounds on a visual presentation, the packager must hurry on to his Armageddon, the Frankfurt Book Fair, where he will do battle with other packagers for the favours of the big publishers. He needs at least one of them to add commercial muscle to his scheme: some money in advance, at least enough to keep the printer happy, and a commitment to buy a minimum number of copies for selling on to the trade. It is only when the deal is struck between packager and publisher that the editorial head-hunting begins and writers are hired.

Warnings against packagers are loud and frequent. Financial insecurity, it is said, is endemic to businesses which operate on such narrow margins. A succession of bankruptcies a few years ago seems to confirm the arguments. But while it is undeniable that most packagers have fewer resources than publishers – why else would they be packagers? – there is no reason why they should not be run profitably. It is all a question of managing a tightly organised team of equals.

What the writer must decide, once he has established that he is dealing with a packager of good repute, is whether he can work to order, suppressing individuality (normally the writer's strongest suit) to the needs of a genuinely cooperative venture.

'Our books tend to be practical', says Bruce Marshall, Chairman of the Book Packagers' Association. 'The style of writing is most notable for the absence of style. We want a hard, factual beginning that picks off the most important point, a middle that proves it and an ending that explains why it matters so much. We want that done perhaps 150 times in a book, to support independent unit headings that will appear on every left hand page.'

Since deadlines are sacrosanct – if the packager cannot supply copies to the publisher by the contract date he is in deep financial trouble – the writer must be able to deliver copy as and when requested. Eight hundred words next Wednesday means just that. Seven hundred and fifty words on Friday will not do.

It helps to have an eye for detail. Bruce Marshall again: 'We are addressing intelligent people who are assumed to have little or no knowledge of the subject in hand. They want to know why a roast beef should rest for ten minutes before being carved. The gardening cliché "water frequently" gives little help to the new gardener; tell me, pray, *how* frequently? I don't want the hazy word "special" substituted for a precise qualifier; I won't accept "a large number" when an exact figure could be found.'

But the writer is no mere lackey. The packager who cares about the quality of his product will involve the writer in every stage of the creative process. This can mean attending a lot of meetings where illustrations are chosen and layout discussed. 'The writer's membership of the team', argues Bruce Marshall, 'gives him as much influence over the other creative partners as they have over him.'

The rewards for the job are variable but average out at about £100 a thousand words. Much less than this suggests that the packager is being screwed too tightly by his publisher client, or that he is trying it on.

Where packagers are often misjudged is on their preference for paying a flat fee or a combination of fee and a small royalty. A flat fee agreement makes sense when there are several contributors to a book. It may seem to offer less than a royalty deal with a conventional publisher but the comparison is not really a fair one. For a start, a publisher's royalty is a percentage of shop price, whereas the packager's royalty is based on the price per copy he gets from the publisher, a quarter or less of the retail price.

Another factor worth considering is the speed of payment. Fees are settled soon after delivery of copy; with royalties a writer may have to wait up to two years before receiving his due. This point takes on added significance when the writer has to work intensively to produce a substantial number of words. A fee payment of several thousand pounds is a great consolation for a hard slog.

The only proviso is that copyright should not be surrendered. In other words, a flat fee should be related to the sale of a certain number of copies of the book. Otherwise, years later, the writer can feel a sense of injustice when his words, modified and updated perhaps but still *his* words, are bringing in income for packager and publisher but not for him. Contributors to the partwork magazines of the sixties and seventies, most of which continue to sell in packaged book form, are among those who lament their disregard for subsidiary rights.

At the same time, the advantages of flat fees, properly negotiated, are coming to be recognised in other areas of publishing, notably where advances are modest. Education writers in particular see the virtue of short cutting their invariably lengthy journey from completed manuscript to publication to first royalty cheque. The author who can persuade a publisher to put up a large sum of money just for his signature on a contract may be more favourably inclined towards royalties. But he is still a rarity.

UK Packagers

The Albion Press Ltd

P.O. Box 52, Princes Risborough,
Aylesbury, Bucks HP17 9PR
☎08444 4018   Telex 83138 TELKAY G

Chairman/Managing Director
Emma Bradford

FOUNDED 1984 to produce high quality illustrated titles. Client publishers in the UK include **William Collins**, **Bloomsbury Publishing**, **Cassell**, **Macdonald**, **Michael Joseph**, **Heinemann**. Commissions illustrated trade titles, particularly English literature, social history, art, cookery, children's. 14 titles in 1987.

TITLES *The Grasmere Journal*, Dorothy Wordsworth; *The Illustrated Queen Victoria*, Lytton Strachey; *Step by Step series*, Diane Wilmer and Nicola Smee. Unsolicited synopses and ideas for books not generally welcome.
Royalties paid and fees paid for introductions and partial contributions.

Amanuensis Books Ltd

12 Station Road, Didcot, Oxon OX11 7LW
☎0235 811066   Fax 0235 510134

Chairman *Kit Maunsell*
Managing Director *Loraine Fergusson*
Approx Annual Turnover £100,000

FOUNDED 1986. Commissions children's, crafts, medicine for the layperson, sport, travel. 4 titles in 1987. 18 planned for 1988. Co-editions sold in the US, Finland, and Holland.

Editorial Head *Lynne Gregory* TITLES *Sports Injuries Handbook*; *Freestyle Knitting*; *China Journey*; *Childhood Illnesses Handbook*.

Unsolicited synopses and ideas for books welcome
Royalties paid twice yearly. Fees also paid on occasions, depending on contract.

AS Publishing

89 Woodstock Avenue, London NW11 9RH
☎01–458 3552

Managing Director *Angela Sheehan*

FOUNDED 1987. Commissions children's illustrated non-fiction. Do not welcome unsolicited synopses and ideas for books. Fees paid.

Autumn Publishing Ltd

10 Eastgate Square,
Chichester, West Sussex PO19 1JH
☎0243 783587   Fax 0243 774433

Managing Director *Campbell Goldsmith*

FOUNDED 1976. Highly illustrated non-fiction: mainly children's, some cookery and books with a sporting slant. 10 titles in 1987.

Editorial Director *Ingrid Goldsmith* TITLES *Journey Into Space*; *Children's First Dictionary*; *Dictionary of World Stamps*. Unsolicited synopses and ideas for books welcome if they come within relevant subject areas.
Usually pay a flat fee.

Beanstalk Books Ltd

89 Park Hill, London SW4 9NX
☎01–720 9109
Telex 8950459 ASPAC G   Fax 01–633 0427

Directors *Shona McKellar, Penny Kitchanham*

FOUNDED 1983. Beanstalk Books work in three main areas: for publishers, for own brand retailers and for commercial firms who want a book geared up to their own company and marketing. Commissions adult highly illustrated non-fiction and children's illustrated fiction and non-fiction. 10 titles in 1987. Welcome unsolicited synopses and ideas for books, particularly adult fine arts and travel. Also children's picture books, novelties, poetry and very interested in seeing writers and artists from ethnic minorities and third world countries.

Royalties paid twice yearly and/or fees.

Belitha Press Ltd

31 Newington Green, London N16 9PU
☎01–241 5566

Chairman/Managing Director *Martin Pick*
Approx Annual Turnover £620,000

FOUNDED 1980. Books packaged for **Franklin Watts, Methuen, Macdonald, Deutsch** and **Collins.** Belitha have a joint venture with Collins which now has 48 books in its backlist. Planning to undertake more publishing with their own educational selling operation. Commissions mostly children's books with occasional general books. 23 titles in 1987.

TITLES *People of the Bible* (24 titles); *Great Tales from Long Ago* (25 titles); *Animals in the Wild* (16 titles); *Animal Habits* (16 titles); *Let's Read Together* (8 titles).

IMPRINT
Belitha/Collins. TITLES *Now I Can Write/Spell/Count; Getting on with Writing/Spelling/Counting; Let's Draw; Match Them.* No unsolicited mss. Welcome unsolicited synopses and ideas for books from experienced children's writers.

Bison Books Ltd

176 Old Brompton Road, London SW5 0BA
☎01–370 3097
Telex 888014   Fax 01–244 7139

Chairman *S. L. Mayer*

Part of **Bison Group,** Connecticut, USA; 'the world's largest book packager'. *Publishes* large format, illustrated books on history, transport, travel, cookery, militaria, and art.

67 new titles and about 200 reprint and foreign editions.

Editorial Head *Jane Laslett* TITLES History: *Rise & Fall of the Third Reich,* William L. Shirer; Transport: *Encyclopaedia of Sports Cars;* Art: *Masterpieces of American Painting,* Leonard Everett Fisher. Unsolicited mss not welcome. The vast majority of titles originate by commission but synopses/ideas are considered.

Royalties by arrangement.

BLA Publishing Ltd

T.R. House, 1 Christopher Road,
East Grinstead, West Sussex RH19 3BT
☎0342 313844
Telex 94011210 BLAP G   Fax 0342 410471

Owner *Ling Kee, Hong Kong*
Editorial Director/Chief Operating Officer *Martin F. Marix Evans*

Commissions multi-volume encyclopedias for younger readers; information book series on various topics including science and natural history for primary school children. 40–50 titles annually.

TITLE *Into Science* (**Oxford University Press**)

DIVISION
Thames Head Illustrated general non-fiction. TITLES *The Frampton Flora; War at Sea.* Will consider unsolicited synopses and ideas for books if they have good translation potential.

Payment varies according to contract (reference books tend to be flat fees; royalties for single author or illustrator).

The Bowerdean Press

85 Battersea Business Centre,
103–109 Lavender Hill, London SW11 5QF
☎01–223 7870

Managing Director *Mr R. H. Dudley*

FOUNDED 1986 as a packager of illustrated non-fiction. Interested in books on royalty, architecture, gardening, wine, sport, humour.

Editorial Director *R. H. Dudley* Unsolicited mss and synopses are welcome. *Royalties* 'does not apply'.

Breslich & Foss

Golden House, 28–31 Great Pulteney Street, London W1R 3DD
☎01–734 0706   Telex 264188 Bresl G

Director *Paula Breslich*
Approx Annual Turnover £500,000

Started with a reprint list but now mainly packagers of a wide variety of non-fiction subjects including art, children's, gardening, crafts, sport and health. Unsolicited mss welcome although synopses preferred. Always include s.a.e. with submissions.
Royalties paid twice yearly.

Brown Wells and Jacobs Ltd

2 Vermont Road, London SE19 3SR
☎01–653 7670
Telex 21685 FOTOGR   Fax 01–653 7670

Managing Director *Graham Brown*

FOUNDED 1979. Commissions non-fiction, novelty, pre-school, natural history, science, first readers, character license. 48 titles in 1987. Unsolicited synopses and ideas for books welcome.
Fees paid.

John Calmann & King

71 Great Russell Street, London WC1B 3BN
☎01–831 6351   Telex 29846 OLKG

Chairman *Marianne Calmann*
Managing Director *Laurence King*
Approx Annual Turnover £2 million

FOUNDED 1976. Commissions books on design, art and nature. 16 titles in 1987. Unsolicited synopses and ideas for books welcome.
Royalties paid annually.

Cameron Books (Production) Ltd

2A Roman Way, London N7 8XG
☎01–609 4019

Directors *Ian A. Cameron, Jill Hollis*
Approx Annual Turnover £250,000

Commissions natural history, social history, decorative arts, collectors' reference, gardening, cookery, conservation, film, design. 6 titles in 1987. Welcomes unsolicited synopses and ideas for books, but 'we are sometimes slow in responding'.
Payment varies with each contract. 'Sometimes royalties; sometimes percentage of receipts from publishers'.

Chancerel Publishers

40 Tavistock Street, London WC2E 7PB
☎01–240 2811
Telex SJJ130 16288   Fax 01–836 4186

Managing Director *W. D. B. Prowse*

FOUNDED 1976. Commissions educational books. 10 titles in 1987. Welcomes unsolicited synopses and ideas for books.
Payment generally by flat fee but royalties sometimes.

Creative Comics

80 Silverdale, Sydenham, London SE26 4SJ
☎01–699 7725

Proprietor *Denis Gifford*

Specialises in children's comic strips and produce custom-made single strips or complete comics, cartoon booklets, paperbacks, etc., especially promotional and giveaway comics. Past projects include a weekly comic supplement in *Reville* and a full colour comic for National Savings. No unsolicited material. Have 100 freelance cartoonists on their books.

Curtis Garratt Ltd

The Old Vicarage, Horton cum Studley, Oxon OX9 1BT
☎086735 536   Fax 086735 844

Directors *Neil Curtis* (Editorial), *Richard Garratt* (Design)

FOUNDED 1983. General illustrated non-fiction trade books. 9 titles in 1987.

TITLES   *The Atlas of British Birds* (**Countryside Books**); *The Gardener's Labyrinth* (**Oxford University Press**). Will consider synopses/ideas for books though most of the work stems from their own ideas or from publishers.
Pay both royalties and fees.

Diagram Visual Information Ltd

195 Kentish Town Road, London NW5 8SY
☎01–482 3633   Telex 21120 Ref 2978

Managing Director *Bruce Robertson*

FOUNDED 1967. Library, school, academic and trade reference books. 20 titles in 1987. Welcomes unsolicited synopses and ideas for books without obligation to pay for sample material.
Fees paid.

Eddison Sadd Editions

St Chad's Court, 146B Kings Cross Road, London WC1X 9DH
☎01–837 1968
Telex 929879   Fax 01–837 2025

Managing Director *Nick Eddison*
Approx Annual Turnover £1 million

FOUNDED 1982 in the back bedroom of a Harrow-on-the-Hill flat. Now own premises in WC1 with a wide range of international publishing contacts. Commissions popular illustrated non-fiction in all general trade areas with particular interest in travel, natural history, divination, astrology, humour, sex. All must be of international interest. 8 titles in 1987.

Editorial Director *Ian Jackson*   TITLES *The New Dinosaurs*, Dougal Dixon; *Earth Mysteries*, Paul Devereux & Nigel Pennick; *The Art of Sensual Loving*, Drs Penny and Andrew Stanway; *Astrology and your Cat*; *The Celtic Ogham Tree Cards*, Colin & Liz Murray; *Marion Foale's Classic Knitwear*; *The Way of the Warrior*, Howard Reid & Michael Croucher. *Royalties* paid twice yearly. Flat fee agreements also negotiated.

Equinox (Oxford) Ltd

Littlegate House, St Ebbe's Street, Oxford OX1 1SQ
☎0865 251499
Telex 83308   Fax 0865 251959

Chairman *G. J. Riches*
Managing Director *B. T. Lenthall*
Approx Annual Turnover £3.5 million

FOUNDED 1981. Sister company to **Phaidon Press**. Part of **Musterlin Group plc**. Commissions international illustrated reference single volumes and series. 10 titles in 1987.

Editor *Lawrence Clarke*   TITLES *Health and the Human Body*; *The Great Scientists*. **Editor** *Dr Graham Bateman*   TITLES *Encyclopedia of Mammals*; *Encyclopedia of Geography*. **Editor** *Dr Graham Speake*   TITLES *Cultural Atlas of China*; *Atlas of Ancient Egypt*. **Editor** *Peter Furtado*   TITLES *Encyclopedia of the 20th Century*. Welcomes unsolicited synopses and ideas for books provided they 'come within our narrow expertise'. Recommend letter in the first instance.
Royalties paid annually. Fees paid in addition to or instead of royalties.

Facer Publishing Ltd

7/9 Colleton Crescent, Exeter, Devon EX2 4DG
☎0392 50188
Telex 42603 CHAMCO G   Fax 0392 211652

Chairman *Nick Facer*

FOUNDED 1983 by Nick Facer as a Book Production Consultancy. Began packaging in 1986 with *Judo* for **Guinness Books**, followed by *Modern Gym Fitness*. In 1987 was awarded contract to publish annually *The Official Football League Yearbook*. *The European Football Yearbook* planned for 1988 and further books on football. General leisure interest and sport. 3 titles in 1987.

Editorial Director *Rob Kendrew* TITLES *Flywheel; Self Defence*. Unsolicited synopses and ideas for books welcome.
Royalties paid twice yearly. Fees paid in addition to royalties.

Gaia Books Ltd

12 Trundle Street, London SE1 1QT
☎01–407 9003
Telex 914074   Fax 01–378 0258

Managing Director *Joss Pearson*

FOUNDED 1983. Natural living, health and environmental books. 4 titles in 1987.

Editorial Director *Lucy Lidell*   TITLES *Book of Massage; The Gaia Atlas of Planet Management*. No unsolicited material. Most projects conceived in-house.
Royalties paid.

Hamilton House

17 Staveley Way, Brixworth Industrial Estate, Northampton NN6 9EL
☎0604 881889   Fax 0604 880735

Chairman and Managing Director
Tony Attwood
Approx Annual Turnover £400,000

FOUNDED 1979. Often works in collaboration with inexperienced authors, repackaging material, clearing copyright, etc., before selling the infant product on. *Publishes* business, employment, careers. Also book packagers for educational (secondary school), TV and radio tie-ins, directory and diary titles. 10 titles in 1987. Letter first. Mss should enclose s.a.e. Synopses and ideas for books also considered if accompanied by s.a.e.
Royalties paid annually.

Holland & Clark Ltd

53 Calton Avenue, Dulwich,
London SE21 7BL
☎01–693 3204
Telex 8813433 MARINE G Fax 01–737 7881

Managing Director *Philip Clark*

A founder member of the Book Packager's Association, Holland & Clark's first packaged book was *The Industrial Heritage of Britain*, published by **Ebury Press**. Since then the company has produced heavily illustrated books on a variety of subjects for nearly thirty publishers in the UK and overseas. Due to planned reorganisation and expansion the company may be changing its name in the near future. 8 titles in 1987. Unsolicited synopses and ideas for books welcome.
Fees paid.

Ilex Publishers Ltd

29–31 George Street, Oxford OX1 2AJ
☎0865 723148
Telex 837709 ILEX G   Fax 0865 791267

Managing Director *Peter Sackett*

FOUNDED 1986. Highly illustrated colour information books for children and adults covering the whole information spectrum. 20 titles in 1987.

TITLES *Children's Animal Atlas* (**Macmillan**); *Daily Telegraph Atlas of the World Today*. No unsolicited material. All ideas are generated in-house.
Payment Outright fee or fee plus 10% royalty against profit.

Johnson Editions Ltd

15 Grafton Square, London SW4 0DQ
☎01–622 1720
Telex 265871 G Ref REX 029

Managing Director *Lorraine Johnson*
Approx Annual Turnover £350,000

Commissions practical and art-related books on fashion, gardening, interior design, architecture, cookery. 2 titles in 1987, 6 in 1988.

Knitwear *Louisa McDonnell*; **Interior Design** *Gabrielle Townsend*; **Gardening** *Georgina Harding*.   TITLES *A Table in Tuscany; A Table in Provence*. Unsolicited synopses and ideas for books welcome.
Royalties paid 'as agreed'. Fees paid in addition to or instead of royalties.

Justin Knowles Publishing Group

9 Colleton Crescent, Exeter,
Devon EX2 4BY
☎0392 55467
Telex 42833 JKPUB G   Fax 0392 211652

Managing Director *Justin Knowles*
Approx Annual Turnover £1 million +

Part of **Black Pig Editions Ltd**. Commissions highly illustrated non-fiction, including Disney books, gardening, knitting, collectibles. 20 titles in 1987. Unsolicited synopses and ideas for books welcome.
Royalties paid twice yearly. Fees paid according to authors' choice.

Lexus Ltd

181 Pitt Street, Glasgow G2 4DR
☎041 221 5266
Telex 777308   Fax 041–226 3139

Managing Director *P. M. Terrell*

FOUNDED 1980. Language reference, bi-lingual books. 10 titles in 1987.

Editorial Director *P. M. Terrell*. TITLES *Collins Italian Concise Dictionary; Harrap Study Aids; Hugo's Phrase Books*. No unsolicited material. All books commissioned in-house.
Flat fee paid.

Frances Lincoln Ltd

Apollo Works, 5 Charlton Kings Road,
London NW5 2SB
☎01–482 3302
Telex 21376   Fax 01–485 0490

Managing Director *Frances Lincoln*

FOUNDED 1977. Commissions highly illustrated books on gardening, craft, interiors, health. 6 titles in 1987.

TITLES *Fabric Magic; The All Seasons Garden*, John Kelly.
Will consider synopses and ideas for books.
Royalties paid twice yearly.

Lionheart Books

10 Chelmsford Square, London NW10 3AR
☎01–459 0453

Senior Partner *Lionel Bender*
Approx Annual Turnover £100,000

A design/editorial packaging team that has been in successful operation for three years. Clients include all the major children's books publishers. 'Packages' include titles conceived by the partnership and commissioned work from publishers. Highly illustrated non-fiction for children aged 8–14, mostly natural history and general science. 12 titles in 1987. Welcomes unsolicited synopses and ideas only if conceived as illustrated works within special subject areas.
Royalties paid, and fees paid in addition to and instead of royalties.

Market House Books Ltd

2 Market House, Market Square,
Aylesbury, Bucks HP20 1TN
☎0296 84911   Fax 0296 436895

Managing Director *Dr Alan Isaacs*

FOUNDED 1981. Dictionaries, encyclopedias and reference. 15 titles in 1987.

Editorial Director *Dr John Daintith*   TITLES *The Collins English Dictionary; The Macmillan Encyclopedia*. Unsolicited material not welcome as most books compiled in-house.
Fees paid.

Marshall Editions Ltd

170 Piccadilly, London W1V 9DD
☎01–629 0079
Telex 22847   Fax 01–834 9785

Managing Director *Bruce Marshall*

FOUNDED 1978. Non-fiction subjects including gardening, needlework, war. 9 titles in 1987.

Managing Editor *Ruth Binney*   TITLES *The Atlas of Mysterious Places; The 35mm Photographer's Handbook; Great Battles of World War II*.

Merehurst Limited

5 Great James Street, London WC1N 3DA
☎01–242 5969
Telex 296616   Fax 01–405 1129

Chairman *Robert Kiernan*
Managing Director *Carole Saunders*

Commissions books on cake decorating, cookery, travel, crafts & hobbies, pet care & aviculture, horses & equitation, natural history, horticulture. Unsolicited synopses and ideas for books welcome.
Fees paid to authors in addition to royalties which are paid twice yearly.

MM Productions Ltd

86 East Street, Ware, Herts SG12 9HJ
☎0920 66003
Telex 818369 WORDS G   Fax 0920 2267

Chairman/Managing Director
Mike Moran
Approx Annual Turnover £1.5 million

Started as a packager for publishers six years ago, now also in mainstream publishing. Fiction, educational, technical & scientific, medical, naval & military, dictionaries, art & architecture, children's, sports, games, pastimes, travel & adventure, directories & guide books. 10 titles in 1987. Unsolicited synopses and ideas for books welcome.
Fees paid to authors in addition to royalties which are paid twice yearly.

Neil Morris & Ting

27 Riverview Grove, London W4 3QL
☎01–994 1874

Partners *Neil Morris, Ting Morris*

FOUNDED 1979. Mainly children's fiction and non-fiction. 20 titles in 1987. No unsolicited mss but sometimes interested in seeing examples of illustrators' work.
Royalties usually paid.

Phoebe Phillips Editions

6 Berners Mews, London W1P 3DG
☎01–637 1673/7933   Fax 01–436 4819
Telex 912881 Telex G (Attn PPE)

Managing Director *Phoebe Phillips*
Approx Annual Turnover £900,000

FOUNDED 1982. Commissions medieval history, gardening, cookery, crafts, decorative arts, illustrated poetry. Publishers include **Weidenfeld & Nicolson, Collins, Thames & Hudson, Bantam Press, Century Hutchinson, Boydell & Brewer**. Planning to expand operations by 1989. 10 titles in 1987. Welcomes unsolicited synopses and ideas for books.
Payment Both fees and royalties paid (by arrangement).

Playne Books

New Inn Lane, Avening, Tetbury,
Glos GL8 8NB
☎045 383 5155
Telex 94011175 PLAY G   Fax 045 383 5590

Chairman *David Playne*

FOUNDED 1987 as a sister company to Playne Design and Playne Photographic to look after the book packaging and commercial book side of the business. Commissions highly illustrated books on any subject and practical books. 1 title in 1987.

TITLE   *Battlefields of Northern France and the Low Countries*. Welcomes unsolicited synopses and ideas for books.
Royalties paid 'on payment from publishers'. Fees sometimes paid instead of royalties.

Pluto Projects

Torriano Mews, London NW5 2RZ
☎01–482 2820

Directors *Anne Benewick, Nina Kidron*

Originally part of **Pluto Press Ltd** but now an independent packager concentrating on one book a year. Commissions general adult current affairs information books.

TITLES   *The State of the World Atlas; The Book of Business, Money and Power*. Welcomes unsolicited synopses and ideas for books.
Royalties paid twice yearly.

Matthew Price Limited

Old Rectory House, Marston Magna,
Yeovil, Somerset BA22 8DT
☎0935 851158
Telex 46720 MPRICE G   Fax 0935 851285

Chairman/Managing Director
Matthew Price
Approx Annual Turnover £5 million

Commissions high quality, full colour picture books, fiction for young children, novelty books and non-fiction. 11 titles in 1987. Unsolicited synopses and ideas for books welcome.
Fees sometimes paid in addition to royalties.

Quarto Publishing plc

The Old Brewery, 6 Blundell Street,
London N7 9BH
☎01-609 2222
Telex 298844   Fax 01-700 4191

Chairman *Laurence Orbach*
Approx Annual Turnover £12 million

FOUNDED 1975 and now Britain's largest book packaging company. Since 1986, Quarto has also published under the **Apple** imprint. USM flotation in 1986. Also magazine publishers since 1987. Illustrated non-fiction, including painting, graphic design, visual arts, history, cookery, gardening, crafts. 70 titles in 1987 published under the Apple imprint and packaged for other publishers. Unsolicited synopses and ideas for books welcome.
Payment Flat fees paid.

Roxby Press Ltd

126 Victoria Rise, London SW4 0NW
☎01-720 8872
Telex 2918929 TLXG   Fax 01-622 9528

Chairman/Managing Director *Hugh Elwes*
Approx Annual Turnover £1 million

FOUNDED 1974. Part of Roxby & Lindsey Holdings Ltd. Commissions illustrated non-fiction titles for international co-edition market. 6 titles in 1987. Unsolicited synopses and ideas for books welcome, 'provided the author is prepared to work with the editors to prepare any material submitted for the international markets'.
Royalties paid annually. Fees paid only for books with many different contributors.

Sackville Design Group Ltd

Hales Barn, Stradbroke, Suffolk
☎0379 848213   Fax 0379 84797

Managing Director *Al Rockall*

FOUNDED 1973. Highly illustrated books in the field of home, leisure and sports. 20 titles in 1987.

Editorial Director *Heather Thomas*   TITLES *Improve Your Sports series* for **Collins**. No unsolicited mss. Will consider synopses and ideas for books if they come within their subject area.
Fees usually paid rather than royalties.

Sadie Fields Productions Ltd

8 Pembridge Studios, 27A Pembridge Villas,
London W11 3EP
☎01-221 3355
Telex 262284 Ref 1255   Fax 01-229 9651

Directors *David Fielder, Sheri Safran*
Approx Annual Turnover £1 million

FOUNDED 1981. Quality children's books. Conceive, design and produce pop-ups, three-dimensional, novelty, picture and board books. Several books have won awards in the UK and USA. Concentrate on books with international co-edition potential. 20 titles in 1987. Approach with preliminary letter and sample material in the first instance.
Royalties based on a per copy sold rate and paid in stages.

Savitri Books Ltd

71 Great Russell Street, London WC1B 3BN
☎01-242 2875   Telex 298246 OWLS

Managing Director *Mrinalini S. Srivastava*
Approx Annual Turnover £200,000 +

FOUNDED 1983. Consider it important to work 'very closely with authors/illustrators and try to establish long-term relationships with them and doing more books with the same team of people'. Commissions books on nature, natural history and craft. Any subject which comes under the heading of 'high quality illustrated non-fiction'. 4 titles in 1987. Unsolicited synopses and ideas for books 'very welcome'.

Royalties between 10–15% of the total price paid by the publisher. 'Rarely work on a flat fee basis except in the case of some books for which the text would be compiled in-house and an illustrator was commissioned a series of pictures. In such a case, and should the illustrator's contribution to the book have been of great importance, a small royalty may be paid on subsequent editions'.

Sceptre Books Ltd

Time and Life Building, New Bond Street, London W1Y 0AA
☎01–499 4080   Telex 22557

Managing Director *David Owen*

FOUNDED 1976. Wholly owned by Time-Life. High quality illustrated books.

TITLES   *The Family Book of Games; National Parks*. No unsolicited mss. Will consider synopses and ideas for books.
Royalties or fees paid, according to contract.

Sheldrake Press Ltd

188 Cavendish Road, London SW12 0DA
☎01–675 1767   Fax 01–675 7736

Managing Director *Simon Rigge*
Approx Annual Turnover £400,000

Controlling company is Sheldrake Publishing. Commissions illustrated non-fiction: cookery, travel, style, and history of technology. 3 titles in 1987. Unsolicited synopses and ideas for books welcome.
Fees paid.

Swallow Books

11–21 Northdown Street, London N1 9BN
☎01–837 3322
Telex 265628   Fax 01–278 1677

Managing Director *Michael Edwards*
Approx Annual Turnover £1 million

Part of Swallow Publishing Ltd. Started trading in 1981. Steady growth since then as packagers of international co-editions. Commissions illustrated non-fiction. 14 titles in 1987.

Editorial Head *Stephen Adamson*   TITLES
Cuisine Sante; Japanese Design; The RHS Encyclopedia of House Plants; Natural History of the USSR. Unsolicited synopses and ideas for books welcome.
Royalties paid annually. Fees paid in addition to royalties.

Earning His 10 Per Cent – The Role of the Literary Agent

With so many publishers subscribing to the big is beautiful school of management, authors can be forgiven if they feel a growing sense of isolation. Authors do what they do because they like to work independently. They are easily daunted by massed ranks of bureaucrats, and their accountant minders.

This is where an agent comes in. If he is any good at his job he will know his way around the publishing jungle. He must be able to spot talent, to identify editors who are hungry for product, to anticipate where problems (mostly financial) are likely to arise, and be ready to perform as advocate for his clients' ambitions and as a doughty champion of their interests.

According to Ed Victor, 'The agent has become the fixed star in an ever-shifting firmament – a sort of friend, career counsellor, literary adviser and shaman that editors used to be.'

If an agent lives up to his promise, at 10 per cent he is cheap at the price.

Most publishers are happy for agents to act as a clearing house for unwanted manuscripts. An agent will put forward a synopsis or manuscript only when he is convinced that it has a good chance of publication – and of securing a decent return on sales. He will make mistakes – how could it be otherwise? – but if his judgement is consistently at fault he will soon be out of a job.

There are those who resent the intrusion into what they see as a purely personal relationship between writer and publisher. 'A good agent is a contradiction in terms', declares Colin Haycraft, Chairman of **Duckworth**. 'Anyway, I don't like three in a bed'. But he speaks for a tiny minority. That over 90 per cent of popular fiction and non-fiction books are said to come via literary agents, gives an idea of how strongly the tide is running in their favour.

The best approach to an agent is to send an example of work in hand with a background letter and samples of published material. As with any business correspondence which calls for a personal response, it is bad practice to send out a duplicated letter to all and sundry. It is a strict rule of the agency business that round robins plummet straight into the waste bin.

When submitting a completed manuscript, state openly if any publishers have already turned it down. Make sure you direct your sales pitch at an agent who covers your area of interest. Some agencies do not deal directly with plays or television scripts, for example, though they may well have outside associates who handle this side of the business.

Most agents do not charge reading fees but a writer who sends a stamped addressed envelope with his material will be off to a good start. It has been argued, by writers as well as agents, that a reading fee is a guarantee of serious intent; that if an agent is paid to assess the value of a manuscript, he is bound to give it professional attention. Sadly, this is not necessarily the case. While there are respectable agents who deserve a reading fee they are outnumbered by the charlatans who take the money and run.

Do not be disappointed if an agent, or even several agents, turn you down. All writing is in the realm of value judgement. Where one agent fails to see talent, another may be more perceptive. The best advice is to keep trying.

When you do strike lucky, the first priority is to arrive at a clear understanding as to the scope of your mutual commitment. Do you want your agent to handle all freelance work including, for example, journalism, personal appearances on radio and television, and lecturing – or just plays and scripts – or just books? Are you prepared to let the agent take a percentage of all earnings including those he does not negotiate? This is a touchy subject. Some writers think of their agency as an employment exchange. Any work they find themselves should not be subject to commission. But this is to assume a clear dividing line between what the agent does and what the writer achieves on his own account. In reality the distinction is not always apparent.

Understanding the market, what subjects are needed, by whom, in what form and in which media is all part of an agent's job. Once he knows what you can do, he is able to promote your talents to the people most likely to want to buy. Eventually, when your reputation is established, offers will come out of the blue – an invitation to write for a newspaper, say, or an editing job or a chance to present a television programme. It is at this point that the writer is tempted to bypass his agent. 'Why should I pay him, he didn't get me the work?' But the chances are he did, by making you into a saleable property in the first place.

An agent negotiates contracts, often a fiddly and worrying business if handled without professional advice, and secures the best possible financial terms. Writers are generally inhibited when it comes to arguing money. It is a brave man who can say 'This is the figure I want because this is what I believe I am worth'. But an agent who has the full range of market rates at his fingertips, can more easily assert the incomparable talents of his client and press for a reward that is commensurate with his ability. Moreover, when it is time for money to be paid to the writer, the agent is usually in the best position to put the squeeze on recalcitrant bookkeepers.

A growth area of agents' responsibility is the sale of subsidiary rights. These can include paperback and serial rights; TV, film and radio adaptations; US and other overseas rights outside the publisher's declared market and translation rights. A book does not have to be a bestseller to earn advances and royalties in several countries, languages and formats, sums which in themselves may be quite small but which can add up to a healthy income. A writer acting on his own behalf is unlikely to realise all the possibilities.

If a writer is persuaded that his agent is no good, or no good for him, he should look elsewhere. Actors do it all the time but writers seem curiously reluctant to jump from one agency to another. The distinction may have less to do with degrees of apathy or generosity of spirit than with the competitive nature of the agency business. Theatrical agents are by and large a tougher breed. They have to be because there are so many of them chasing a limited amount of business. Literary agents are altogether a more gentlemanly crowd. Since they rarely go in for poaching each other's clients, there is little incentive for authors to switch allegiance. But times are changing. With the rise of the trans-Atlantic publisher, American agents are showing a greater interest in writers whose appeal extends beyond the domestic market. Their eagerness to compete for top-flight clients is already having an impact with certain high profile authors making it known that they would not be averse to a move.

A writer who has yet to make his reputation and is thus unlikely to be head-hunted needs to think carefully before dumping his agent. It is one thing if the agent is incompetent (and in a profession without qualification or necessary training there are bound to be duds) but quite another if the writer is expecting too much, too quickly.

Think of it in economic terms. Giles Gordon, from **Anthony Sheil Associates**, calculates that it costs an average, adequately staffed agency from £1000 to £2000 a year in overheads to have an author on its books. These overheads include, but are not limited to, rent, rates, salaries, secretarial expenses, postage, telephone, printing, stationery, photocopying, entertaining publishers and, just as frequently, entertaining clients. This means that on standard terms, a writer must earn between £10,000 and £20,000 a year before his agent even begins to see a profit.

Most writers are not in this league, though quite a few more might get there and well beyond, with the right sort of help. They are the clients an agent is looking for, the ones who show promise of literary achievement and of a decent return on his investment of time and effort.

For his part, an agent can only serve the best interests of his client when he is a good salesman. But, curiously, he is unlikely to admit to this. If asked to provide his own job definition, he would probably call himself a professional adviser. (Not, he would hasten to add, a teacher. An agent does not expect to tell anyone *how* to write.)

Yet another way of defining an agent is to think of him as a partner. The relationship between writer and agent, assuming they get on well together, invariably lasts longer than any connection with individual editors, publishers, producers or directors.

To a confused world, the agent brings a welcome note of stability.

UK Agents

A. & B. Personal Management Ltd
5th Floor, Plaza Suite, 114 Jermyn Street, London SW1Y 6HJ
☎01–839 4433   Telex 21901 JWPPLG

Contact *Bill Ellis*

FOUNDED 1982. Interested in anything that has the potential to become a film or play. TV/radio and theatre scripts. No unsolicited mss. Prefer preliminary letter with synopsis, with s.a.e. Reading fee: £25 including VAT for full mss.
Commission Home 12½%; US 15%; Translation either 12½% or 15%.

Aitken & Stone Ltd
29 Fernshaw Road, London SW10 0TG
☎01–351 7561   Telex 298391

Contact *Gillon Aitken, Brian Stone, Antony Harwood*

Gillon Aitken joined with **Hughes Massie** in 1986. Fiction and non-fiction. No plays or scripts unless by existing clients. Require a preliminary letter, synopsis and return postage in the first instance. No reading fee. CLIENTS include Germaine Greer, Paul Theroux, Agatha Christie, V. S. Naipaul, Bruce Chatwin, Salman Rushdie (a recent coup), Piers Paul Read.
Commission Home 10%; US 15%; Translation 20%. *Overseas office* **Wylie, Aitken & Stone Inc.**, 250 West 57th Street, New York, NY 10107, USA.

Jacintha Alexander Associates
47 Emperor's Gate, London SW7 4HJ
☎01–373 9258

Contact *Jacintha Alexander, Julian Alexander*

FOUNDED 1981. Jacintha Alexander previously with **A. M. Heath**. Fiction and non-fiction of all kinds. Scripts handled for established clients only. No romantic fiction, science fiction, academic books. Mss should be preceded by a letter. No reading fee.
Commission Home 15% US 20%; Translation 20%.

AZA Artists Ltd
652 Finchley Road, London NW11 7NT
☎01–458 7288

Contact *Morris Aza*

FOUNDED 1972. Television scripts, sketches, comedy material and film scripts only. No books. No reading fee.

Badcock & Rozycki
12 Flitcroft Street, London WC2H 8DJ
☎01–836 0782   Telex 923995

Contact *June Badcock, Barbara Rozycki*

Not literary agents in the usual sense. Badcock & Rozycki are scouts representing ten international publishers. They seek out suitable books for translation, and deal with other agents and publishers only. Do not send mss of any kind to them direct.

Blake Friedmann Literary Agency Ltd
37–41 Gower Street, London WC1E 6HH
☎01–631 4331
Telex 27950   Ref 3820   Fax 01–323 1274

Contact *Carole Blake* (books), *Julian Fried-mann* (film/TV), *Conrad Williams* (radio), *Marisa Lesser* (short stories/journalism)

FOUNDED 1977. All kinds of fiction, from genre to literary; a varied range of specialised and general non-fiction; some juvenile titles, plus scripts. No poetry. *Special interests* thrillers, commercial women's fiction. Un-solicited mss welcome, but preferably pre-ceded by a letter with a synopsis and the first two chapters. Letters should contain as much information as possible on previous writing experience, aims for the future, etc. No read-ing fee. CLIENTS include Ted Allbeury, John Trenhaile, Barbara Erskine, Pamela Vandyke Price.

Commission Home 15%; US 20%; Transla-tion 20% (books); Radio/TV/film 15%. Journalism/short stories 25%. *Overseas as-sociates* throughout Europe and USA.

David Bolt Associates

12 Heath Drive, Send, Surrey GU23 7EP
☎04862 21118

Contact *David Bolt*

FOUNDED 1983. Ex-**David Higham**. Fiction, general non-fiction. No books for small chil-dren, or verse (except in special circum-stances). No scripts. *Special interests* fiction, military, history, theology, African writers, biography. Preliminary letter with s.a.e. es-sential. £25 reading fee except for published writers. CLIENTS include Colin Wilson, Pro-fessor Arthur Jacobs, Ellis Dillon, Chinua Achebe.

Commission Home 10%; US 19%; Transla-tion 19%.

Curtis Brown Ltd

162–168 Regent Street, London W1R 5TB
☎01–437 9700
Telex 261536 BRNSPK G   Fax 01–437 0226

Contact No one person. Material should be addressed to the company. It is then dealt with by the appropriate agent.

Long established literary agency. First sales were made in 1899. Wide range of subjects including fiction, general non-fiction, chil-dren's, academic, professional and specialist, scripts for TV/radio and television. 'Being a large agency we will consider anything.' Pre-fer to see a synopsis with covering letter and c.v. rather than complete mss. No reading fee.

Commission Home 10%; US 15%; Transla-tion 20%. *Overseas offices* Curtis Brown (Australia) Pty Ltd; Curtis Brown Associates Ltd, New York; Curtis Brown, Toronto, Canada.

Peter Bryant

51 Allerton Road, London N16 5UF
☎01–802 0798

Contact *Peter Bryant* (writers)

FOUNDED 1980. Mostly fiction, but also hand-les scripts of all kinds, with drama the agen-cy's special interest. Unsolicited mss welcome, and no one should write unless they also send 'something to read'. No read-ing fee. CLIENTS include Gerald Frow, Owen Holder, Gwen Cherrell.

Commission Home 10%; US 10%. *Overseas associates* James Brookes & Associates, New South Wales, Australia.

Diane Burston Literary Agency

46 Cromwell Avenue, Highgate,
London N6 5HL
☎01–340 6130

Contact *Diane Burston*

FOUNDED 1984. Fiction, non-fiction and short stories. No scripts. Particularly interested in short stories suitable for women's magazines, middle of the road fiction, and adventure non-fiction. Unsolicited mss usually con-sidered, but preliminary letter or phone call preferred. S.a.e. essential.

Commission Home 10%; US 15%; Transla-tion 20%.

Campbell Thomson & McLaughlin Limited

31 Newington Green, London N16 9PU
☎01–249 2971

Contact *John McLaughlin, John Richard Parker, Charlotte Bruton*

FOUNDED 1972. All mss except plays, film scripts, articles or poetry. Short stories from existing clients only. No reading fee.
Overseas associates Fox Chase Agency (Philadelphia) and **Raines & Raines** (New York).

Carnell Literary Agency
Danes Croft, Goose Lane, Little Hallingbury, Herts CM22 7RG
☎0279 723626

Contact *Pamela Buckmaster*

FOUNDED 1951. Fiction and general non-fiction but mainly specialises in science fiction and fantasy books. No poetry and no scripts unless by published authors. No unsolicited mss. S.a.e. and preliminary letter essential. No reading fee. Works in conjunction with agencies worldwide.
Commission Home 10%; US and Translation 19%.

Chappell Plays Ltd (formerly English Theatre Guild)
129 Park Street, London W1Y 3FA
☎01–629 7600
Telex 268403   Fax 01–499 9718

Contact *Michael Callahan*

Chappell are both agents and publishers of scripts for the theatre. No unsolicited mss – introductory letter essential. No reading fee. CLIENTS include Arthur Miller, John Steinbeck, Ray Cooney.
Commission Home 10%; US 20%. *Overseas* represented in USA, Canada, Australia, New Zealand, India, South Africa and Zimbabwe.

Serafina Clarke
98 Tunis Road, London W12 7EY
☎01–749 6979

Contact *Serafina Clarke, Jan Ward* (children's)

FOUNDED 1980. Fiction: romance, horror, thrillers, literary. Non-fiction: travel, hum-

our, cookery, gardening, biography. No science fiction. Only deal in scripts by authors already on the books. *Special interests* gardening, history, country pursuits. Unsolicited mss welcome, though introductory letter with synopsis (and return postage) preferred. No reading fee. CLIENTS include Elizabeth Walker, Christopher Fowler, Peter Hudson, Deborah Kellaway, Leonid Borodin. *Commission* Home 10%; US 20%; Translation 20%.
Represents Permanent Press (USA), Second Chance Press (USA), James Fox Associates (USA), Possev Verlag (Germany).

Jonathan Clowes Ltd
22 Prince Albert Road, London NW1 7ST
☎01–722 7674
Telex 23973   Fax 01–722 7677

Contact *Jonathan Clowes, Ann Evans, Brie Burkeman*

FOUNDED 1960. Pronounced Clewes. Now one of the biggest fish in the pond, and not really for the untried unless they are true high-flyers. Fiction and non-fiction, plus scripts. No textbooks or children's. *Special interests* situation comedy, film and television rights. No unsolicited mss; authors come by recommendation or by successful follow-ups to preliminary letters. CLIENTS include Doris Lessing, Kingsley Amis, Len Deighton, David Bellamy, Carla Lane.
Commission Home 10%; US 15%; Translation 19%. *Overseas associates* **Andrew Nurnberg Associates**; Lennart Sane Agency, Sweden; Tuttle Mori Agency, Japan; Agenzia Letteraria Internazionale, Italy.

Elspeth Cochrane Agency
11–13 Orlando Road, London SW4 0LE
☎01–622 0314

Contact *Elspeth Cochrane, Donald Baker*

FOUNDED 1960. Fiction, biography and autobiography, children's books, picture books. Books are usually a spin-off from show business deals, books on Lord Olivier, Leonard

Rossiter, Sir Ralph Richardson, Shakespeare, Sir John Gielgud, Dame Peggy Ashcroft. Also handles scripts for all media. *Special interest* drama. No unsolicited mss. Preliminary letter with a description of the work, a brief outline, plus s.a.e. No reading fee.   CLIENTS include David Pinner, Michael Dibdin, John Charters, Robert Tanitch.
Commission Home 10%; US 10%; Translation 10% ('but this can change – the % is negotiable, as is the sum paid to the writer').

Dianne Coles Literary Agent

The Old Malthouse, St John's Road,
Banbury, Oxon. OX16 8HX
☎0295 50731   Telex 838967 BB MOAT G

Contact *Jim Reynolds* (Managing Director)

FOUNDED 1980. Dianne Coles was trained as a librarian and for many years owned and managed a successful bookshop. She is proprietor of Special Libraries Book Service. Jim Reynolds was a top executive in London publishing houses for 25 years. *Special interests* biography, history (social, political and military), investigative journalism, and quality fiction. No unsolicited mss. Send outline of plot or non-fiction project with 15–20 pages of text. No category fiction (i.e. romances, detective stories, science fiction), no plays, film scripts, children's books, articles or short stories. No reading fee but return postage essential. Preliminary letter advisable.
Commission 10% of amount received. *Overseas associates* in USA, Germany, Italy, France, Spain, Japan, Scandinavia, Holland.

Rosica Colin Ltd

1 Clareville Grove Mews, London SW7 5AH
☎01–370 1080

Contact *Joanna Marston*

FOUNDED 1949. All full length mss handled, plus theatre, film, television and sound broadcasting. Preliminary letter with return postage essential; writers should outline where their mss have previously been sub-

mitted. Takes 3 to 4 months to consider full mss; would prefer to see synopsis. No reading fee.
Commission Home 10%; US 15%; Translation 20%.

Colley-Moore Literary Agency

14 Lyon Square, Tilehurst,
Reading, Berks RG3 4DD
☎0734 417748/420329

Contact *Steve Colley-Moore*
(Managing Director),
Pauline Colley-Moore (Editor)

Fiction, non-fiction, children & young adults, educational, plays (Screen/TV/radio & stage), poetry. All unsolicited mss must be accompanied by s.a.e. No reading fee.

Vernon Conway Ltd

19 London Street, Paddington,
London W2 1HL
☎01–262 5506/7

Contact *Vernon Conway*

FOUNDED 1977. *Special interests* novels, biographies, plays. No textbooks or academic. Welcomes unsolicited mss, preceded by an introductory letter, plus return postage. No reading fee.   CLIENTS include Ian Grimble, Elspeth Sandys, Clive Barker, Monty Haltrecht, David Halliwell, Elizabeth Morgan.
Commission 10% on all sales.

Jane Conway-Gordon

213 Westbourne Grove, London W11 2SE
☎01–229 4451

Contact *Jane Conway-Gordon*

FOUNDED 1982. Fiction and self help books; e.g. *Conversations with Lord Byron* (Cape), *Talleyman* (Gollancz), *The Working Mother's Survival Guide* (Simon & Schuster), *Women Who Love Too Much* (Arrow). Occasionally handle scripts for TV/radio/theatre. No poetry or science fiction. Unsolicited mss welcome; preliminary letter and return postage preferred. No reading fee.   CLIENTS in-

clude Amanda Prantera, John James, Dr Brian Roet, Juliet Dymoke.
Commission Home 10%; US 20% Translation 20%. *Overseas associates* **McIntosh & Otis Inc.**, New York; plus agencies throughout Europe and Japan.

Rupert Crew Ltd

King's Mews, London WC1N 2JA
☎01–242 8586   Fax 01–831 7914

Contact *Mrs D. Montgomery, Miss S. Russell*

FOUNDED 1927. Fiction and non-fiction. No plays, scripts or poetry. No unsolicited mss. Preliminary letter essential. No reading fee. *Commission* 10–20% by arrangement.

Cruickshank Cazenove Ltd

97 Old South Lambeth Road,
London SW8 1XU
☎01–735 2933   Fax 01–735 2934

Contact *Harriet Cruickshank*

FOUNDED 1983. Fiction, general non-fiction, scripts for TV/radio/film. No unsolicited mss. Preliminary letter with synopsis and s.a.e. essential. Works with foreign agents abroad. *Commission* Home 10%; US and Translation varies according to contract.

Judy Daish Associates Ltd

83 Eastbourne Mews, London W2 6LG
☎01–262 1101
Telex 916824 DAISH G   Fax 01–706 1027

Contact *Judy Daish, Louise Cooper, Sara Stroud*

FOUNDED 1978. Theatrical literary agent only. Scripts for film/TV/theatre/radio. No books. Preliminary letter essential. No unsolicited mss. *Commission* negotiable.

Reg Davis-Poynter

118 St Pancras, Chichester,
West Sussex PO19 4LH and
11 Bolt Court, Fleet Street, London EC4A 3DU
☎0243 779047/01–353 9365

Contact *R. G. Davis-Poynter*

Books and scripts (TV, radio, theatre, film). *Special interests* sociology, politics, history, biography, autobiography, theatre. No children's or religious. Unsolicited mss welcome if accompanied by letter, synopsis, sample chapter and return postage. Prefer that writers approach with preliminary letter and return postage, then send complete mss. No reading fee.
Commission Home 15%; US 20%; Translation 15%; Theatre, films, television and radio 10%. *Overseas associates* in Germany, Scandinavia, Japan, Italy, France and USA.

Felix de Wolfe

Manfield House, 376/378 The Strand,
London WC2R 0LR
☎01–379 5767   Telex 931770 A/B WIBU G

Contact *Felix de Wolfe*

FOUNDED 1938. Handle quality fiction and scripts only. No non-fiction or children's. No unsolicited mss; approach by letter in the first instance. No reading fee. CLIENTS include S. Campbell-Jones, Brian Glover, Jennifer Johnston, John Kershaw, Bill MacIlwraith, Charles Savage, Alan Sievewright, and Julian Slade.
Commission Home 10%; US 20%.

John Dorman

7 Waterside, Stratford-upon-Avon,
Warwickshire CV37 6BA
☎0789 293801   Telex 418253

Contact *John Dorman*

FOUNDED 1983. Sport — autobiography and instructional, and sports-related subjects, leisure activities. Autobiographies of John Francome, Geoff Boycott, Graham Dilley. No scripts, no fiction, no children's. *Special interests* cricket, horse racing, rugby union, soccer. No unsolicited mss — initial letter and typed synopses essential. No reading fee. CLIENTS include Alan Lee (*Times* cricket correspondent), Matthew Engel (former *Guardian* cricket correspondent), Peter Scu-

damore (National Hunt jockey), Clive Norling (rugby referee), Graham Gooch, Pat Eddery, John Emburey.
Commission Home 10%; US 15%; Translation 15%.

John Farquharson

162–168 Regent Street, London W1R 5TB
☎01–437 9700
Telex 261536　　　　　　Fax 01–437 0226

Contact *Vivienne Schuster, Vanessa Holt, Andrew Lownie*

FOUNDED 1919. Sister company to **Curtis Brown**. 'We pride ourselves on being a general agency'. Commercial and literary fiction, and general non-fiction. *Special interests* bestseller fiction, top crime novels. No academic, no technical, no scripts. Detailed brochure available giving full guidelines and listing clients. Unsolicited mss welcome.
Commission Home 10%; US 20%; Translation 20%.

Film Link Literary Agency

31 Oakdene Drive,
Tolworth, Surrey KT5 9NH
☎01–330 3182

Contact *Yvonne Heather*

FOUNDED 1979. Fiction, general non-fiction and TV scripts. No poetry, short stories. No unsolicited mss. Send synopsis, sample pages and introductory letter, together with s.a.e. No reading fee. CLIENTS include Peter May and Michael Elder (writers for *Take The High Road*).
Commission Home 10%; 15–20% Overseas.

Film Rights Ltd

4 New Burlington Place, Regent Street, London W1X 2AS
☎01–437 7151

Contact *Laurence Fitch*

FOUNDED 1932. Only handle stage/radio/TV/film scripts. Do not consider unsolicited mss or synopses. Preliminary letter giving full de-

tails, including c.v. of the writer, essential. No reading fee.
Commission Home and Abroad 10%.

Laurence Fitch Ltd

4 New Burlington Place, Regent Street, London W1X 2AS
☎01–437 7151

Contact *Laurence Fitch, Judy Quinn*

FOUNDED 1954. Scripts only, for all media. Particularly interested in plays for the stage, especially comedies. Ambivalent about unsolicited scripts; writers should send a preliminary letter. Can take up to 6 months to consider mss. CLIENTS include Dodie Smith, John Chapman and Ray Cooney.
Commission Home 10%; US 15%; Translation 20% 'sometimes'.

Jill Foster Ltd

19a Queen's Gate Terrace, London SW7 5PR
☎01–581 0084

Contact *Jill Foster, Alison Finch, Ann Foster*

FOUNDED 1976. Non-fiction and scripts only (mainly TV, drama and comedy). No fiction, short stories or poetry. No unsolicited mss; approach by letter in the first instance. No reading fee. CLIENTS include Colin Bostock-Smith, Julia Jones, Chris Ralling, Paul Hines, Susan Wilkins.
Commission Home 10%; US 15%; Translation 15%.

Fraser & Dunlop Scripts Ltd

91 Regent Street, London W1R 8RU
☎01–734 7311　　　　　　Telex 28965

Contact *Kenneth Ewing* (theatre), *Tim Corrie* (film), *Richard Wakeley* (television), *Mark Lucas* (books)

FOUNDED 1959. Major re-organisation likely following merger with **A.D. Peters & Co.** Scripts of all kinds, but also fiction, non-fiction (especially humorous) books. Vastly experienced as a show business agency, and good for radio and television writing. Book

side coming on with Mark Lucas (ex **Futura**). No unsolicited mss; synopsis/treatment (sample chapter optional) with accompanying letter essential. No reading fee. CLIENTS include Tom Stoppard, Charles Wood, David Butler, Gerald Scarfe, Jane Asher and Bernice Rubens.
Commission Home 10%; US 20%; Translation 20%. *Overseas offices* New York and Los Angeles.

French's

26 Binney Street, London W1
☎01–629 4159

Contact *John French*

FOUNDED 1973. Novels and factual material; also scripts for all media. No religious or medical books. No unsolicited mss. 'For unpublished authors we offer a reading service at £70 per ms, inclusive of VAT and postage'. Interested authors should write a letter in the first instance. CLIENTS include Barry Heath, James Duke, Hal Middleton, Shaun Prendergast.
Commission Home 10%.

Pamela Gillis Management

46 Sheldon Avenue, London N6 4JR
☎01–340 7868

Contact *Pamela Gillis*

FOUNDED 1975. TV scripts and radio material. No books. Prefer preliminary letter of introduction. No reading fee.
Commission 10% Home and Abroad.

Eric Glass Ltd

28 Berkeley Square, London W1X 6HD
☎01–629 7162   Telex 296759 KALLIN G

Contact *Eric Glass, Janet Crowley*

FOUNDED 1934. Fiction and non-fiction; e.g. *Gioconda* (Wolf Mankowitz); *The Prime Ministers* (ed. William Douglas-Home); *Somerset And All The Maughams* (Robin Maugham); *The Unforgiving Minute* (Beverley Nichols). No poetry. Handle scripts both for publication and production in all media. Resumés and sample chapters in the first instance (complete mss by request) with return postage. No reading fee. CLIENTS include Philip King, estates of Jean Cocteau and Jean-Paul Sartre, Wolf Mankowitz, William Douglas-Home.
Commission Home 10%; US 15%; Translation 20% (minimum rates). *Overseas associates* in USA, Germany, Scandinavia, France, Italy, Spain, Czechoslovakia, Holland, Greece, Poland, Australia, South Africa, Japan.

Goodwin Associates

12 Rabbit Row, Kensington Church Street, London W8 4DX
☎01–229 8805

Contact *Ms Phil Kelvin*

FOUNDED 1977. Scripts for film/TV/theatre/radio only. No prose or poetry. Welcome unsolicited mss with return postage. No reading fee. CLIENTS include Susan Boyd, Jim Hill, Stephen Lowe, Louise Page, Christina Reid, Fay Weldon.
Commission 10% on all sales.

Christine Green (Authors' Agent) Ltd

8 Albany Mews, Albany Road, London SE5 0DQ
☎01–703 9285

Contact *Christine Green*

FOUNDED 1984. Fiction – general and literary; general non-fiction. No scripts, poetry, or children's. Unsolicited mss welcome if return postage included. Initial letter and synopsis preferred. No reading fee.
Commission Home 10%; US 15%; Translation 20%.

Elaine Greene Ltd

31 Newington Green, Islington, London N16 9PU
☎01–249 2971

Contact *Elaine Greene, Ilsa Yardley*

A small, choosy agency that likes really to involve itself with its authors. Novels and quality non-fiction, journalists' books. No academic, no original scripts for theatre, film or television. *Special interests* crime writing. No unsolicited mss without preliminary letter. CLIENTS include P. D. James, Colin Forbes, William Shawcross, Conor Cruise O'Brien.
Commission Home 10%; US 15%; Translation 20%.

Gregory & Radice Author's Agents

4 Westwick Gardens, London W14 0BU
☎01–603 5168
Telex 268141   Fax 01–602 8520

Contact *Jane Gregory, Lisanne Radice*

FOUNDED 1986. Crime and thrillers only; a single-minded approach makes them specialists in the field. No scripts. No unsolicited mss; preliminary letter with synopsis and couple of sample chapters (plus return postage) essential. No reading fee.
Commission Home 10%; US 20%; Translation 20%.

The Jane Gregory Agency

4 Westwick Gardens, London W14 0BU
☎01–603 9998/1669   Telex 268141

Contact *Jane Gregory, Felicia Dykstra*

FOUNDED 1982. Fiction and non-fiction. No plays, poetry, academic or children's. No unsolicited mss; preliminary letter essential. No reading fee. Represent three American companies, including **Simon & Schuster**.
Commission Home 10%; US 20%; Translation 20%.

David Grossman Literary Agency Ltd

110–114 Clerkenwell Road,
London EC1M 5SA
☎01–251 5046   Telex 263404 BK BIZ G

Contact *David Grossman*

FOUNDED 1976. Full-length fiction and general non-fiction. No verse or technical books for students. No original screenplays or teleplays but sell performance rights in works existing in volume form. *Special interests* suspense and thriller writers, historical novelists, sagas, biographies, political affairs, health, contemporary history, travel, film, anything controversial; good writing of all kinds. Prefer a preliminary letter giving full description of the work. No unsolicited mss. No reading fee.
Commission rates vary for different markets.
Overseas associates throughout Europe, Japan, Brazil and USA.

June Hall Literary Agency

19 College Cross, London N1 1PT
☎01–609 5991   Fax 01–607 0682

Contact *June Hall, Clare Loeffler, Shân Morley-Jones*

FOUNDED 1979. Fiction and general non-fiction. No scripts. No unsolicited material. Preliminary letter and s.a.e. essential. No reading fee. Nov 1981 – sponsored 'Woman of the '80's' book award with Hodder & Stoughton.
Commission on application.
Overseas associates Brazil, France, German-speaking countries, Greece, Hong Kong, Israel, Italy, Japan, Netherlands, Scandinavia, Spanish-speaking countries, Turkey.

Roger Hancock Ltd

8 Waterloo Place, Pall Mall,
London SW1Y 4AW
☎01–839 6753

Contact *'The company'*

FOUNDED 1961 *Special interest* drama and light entertainment. Scripts only. No books. Unsolicited mss not welcome. Initial phone call required. No reading fee.
Commission 10% throughout.

Sally Harrison Management
100 Albert Palace Mansions,
Lurline Gardens, London SW11 3DH
☎01—720 9203

Contact *Sally Harrison*

FOUNDED 1979. Film/TV/theatre/radio scripts.
No books. Preliminary letter preferred. No
reading fee.
Commission Home and Abroad 10%.

Hatton & Baker Ltd
18 Jermyn Street, London SW1Y 6HN
☎01—439 2971   Fax 01—439 7633

Contact *Terence Baker, Richard Hatton*

FOUNDED 1980. Scripts and screenplays only.
No books. No reading fee.
Commission Home 10%; US 15%; Transla-
tion 15%. *Overseas associates* worldwide.

Headline Enterprises Ltd
19a Queen's Gate Terrace, London SW7 5PR
☎01—584 8568

Contact *Malcolm Hamer, Jill Foster,*
Alison Finch

FOUNDED 1971. Non-fiction only especially
sporting/leisure, show business autobiography, guide books, food and wine. No fiction
or poetry. No unsolicited mss; writers should
send a letter in the first instance. No reading
fee.   CLIENTS include Gareth Edwards, Cliff
Temple, David Lemmon, Tony Pawson,
Simon Reed, Ray French, Chris Dodd, Bill
Breckon.
Commission Home 10/15%; US 20%.

A. M. Heath & Co. Ltd
79 St Martin's Lane, London WC2N 4AA
☎01—836 4271   Telex 27370

Contact *Mark Hamilton, William Hamilton,*
Michael Thomas, Sara Fisher

FOUNDED 1919. Fiction and general non-
fiction. No scripts or poetry. Preliminary
letter and synopsis essential. No reading

fee.   CLIENTS include Anita Brookner, Saul
Bellow and Jean Plaidy.
Commission Home 10%; US 15%; Translation 20%; Film & TV 15%. *Overseas associates* in USA.

Duncan Heath Associates Ltd
Paramount House, 162—170 Wardour Street,
London W1V 3AT
☎01—439 1471/2111   Fax 01—439 7274

Contact *Ian Amos*

FOUNDED 1973. Film/TV/theatre scripts. No
books. No unsolicited mss. Preliminary letter
essential. No reading fee.
Commission 10% throughout. *Overseas associates* ICM New York and Los Angeles.

David Higham Associates Ltd
5—8 Lower John Street, Golden Square,
London W1R 4HA
☎01—437 7888   Telex 28910 HIGHAM G

Contact *Anthony Croft*; scripts *John Rush,*
Elizabeth Cree

FOUNDED 1935. Ex-**Laurence Pollinger**. Fiction, general non-fiction; biography, history,
current affairs, art, music etc. Also scripts.
No educational, highly specialised books or
children's story books. Unsolicited mss welcome, provided they are preceded by introductory letter and accompanied by return
postage. No reading fee.   CLIENTS include Richard Adams, James Herriot, Russell Hoban
and James Herbert.
Commission Home 10%; US 15%; Translation 19%.

Valerie Hoskins (in association with Jeremy Conway Ltd)
Eagle House, 109 Jermyn Street,
London SW1Y 6HB
☎01—839 2121

Contact *Valerie Hoskins*

FOUNDED 1983. Script agent dealing in film,
theatre, television and radio. *Special interests*
feature films. No unsolicited scripts; pre-

liminary letter of introduction essential. No reading fee. CLIENTS include Tony Craze, Robin Miller, Gillian Richmond, Peter Berry, Jeremy Newson, Kit Hesketh-Harvey. *Commission* Home 10%; US 20% (maximum).

Teresa Howard Associates
298 South Lambeth Road, London SW8 1UJ
☎01–720 6858

Contact *Teresa Howard*

FOUNDED 1985. Specialises in plays for stage, TV, radio and film. Send preliminary letter and s.a.e. Dramatic associate for **Laurence Pollinger Limited**. AUTHORS include H.E. Bates, Dorothy Parker, D.H. Lawrence, William Saroyan.
Commission 10%.

Tanja Howarth
19 New Row, London WC2N 4LA
☎01–240 5553   Telex 27370

Contact *Tanja Howarth*

FOUNDED 1970. Specialise in translations from the German, e.g. *Perfume – The Story of a Murder* (Patrick Suskind); also interested in taking on both fiction and non-fiction English writers. Tanja Howarth is also 'constantly on the look-out for suitable plays for Germany', as she represents the theatre department of S. Fischer, Frankfurt. Reputation for smooth efficiency. No children's books. All subjects other than this considered, providing the treatment is intelligent. Unsolicited mss welcome, preliminary letter preferred. No reading fee.
Commission Home 10%; Translation 15%.

Hughes Massie Ltd
(now **Aiken & Stone Ltd**)

Michael Imison Playwrights Ltd
28 Almeida Street, Islington, London N1 1TD
☎01–354 3174
Telex 934999 TX Link G   Fax 01–359 6273

Contact *Michael Imison, Alan Brodie*

FOUNDED 1944. Michael Imison is the brother of Richard Imison, deputy head of BBC radio drama. Plays, plus books based on scripts, e.g. *Yes Minister*. TV, radio and theatre. Specialise in theatre writing. No fiction or general books. *Specially interested in* writers who are primarily motivated by writing for the theatre; translators, particularly from the Russian and Italian. Unsolicited mss not welcome. Initial letter with recommendation from a known theatre professional essential. S.a.e. No reading fee. CLIENTS include David Edgar, Dario Fo, John Godber, Doug Lucie, the Noel Coward estate.
Commission Home 10%; US 12.5%; Translation 12.5%. *Overseas associates* Judy Ferris at Stagewise, Sydney, Australia; Abbe Levin, New York.

International Copyright Bureau Ltd
Suite 8, 26 Charing Cross Road,
London WC2H 0DG
☎01–836 5912

Contact *Joy Westendarp*

FOUNDED 1905. Handles exclusively scripts for TV/theatre/film/radio. No books. Preliminary letter essential. Agents in New York and most foreign countries.
Commission Home 10%; US 19%; Translation 19%.

International Scripts
1 Norland Square, Holland Park,
London W11 4PX
☎01–229 0736

Contact *Bob Tanner, Mrs J. Lawson, Veronica Brown*

FOUNDED 1980. Bob Tanner is managing director of the publishers **W. H. Allen**. All types of books handled, as well as scripts for all media. No poetry. Unsolicited mss welcome, though preliminary letter preferred. No reading fee. CLIENTS include Robert A. Heinlein, Peter Haining, Richard Laymon, Shaun Hutson.
Commission Home 10–15%; US 20%; Translation 20%. *Overseas associates* **Ralph Vicinanza**, **Spectrum**, New York.

John Johnson Ltd

Clerkenwell House,
45–47 Clerkenwell Green,
London EC1R 0HT
☎01–251 0125

Contact *Andrew Hewson, Margaret Hewson, Elizabeth Fairbairn*

FOUNDED 1956. Very conscientious and sympathetic to new writers. Full length and short mss; dramatic works for radio and television. No unsolicited mss; preliminary letter with synopsis and s.a.e. essential. No reading fee. *Commission* Home 10%; US 10% (20% with sub-agent); Translation 20%. *Overseas associates* Works in conjunction with agents in the US and many European countries.

L'Epine Smith & Carney Associates

10 Wyndham Place, London W1H 1AS
☎01–724 0739

Contact *Eric L'Epine Smith*

FOUNDED 1957. Interested in good material of all categories: fiction, general non-fiction, scripts. Welcome unsolicited mss preceded by introductory letter or phone call. CLIENTS include Barry Bliss, Terence Dudley, Stuart Cameron, Michael Sawyer. *Commission* Home 10% (no US or translation work at present).

Lemon & Durbridge Ltd

24–32 Pottery Lane, London W11 4LZ
☎01–727 1346
Telex 27618 Author G   Fax 01–727 9037

Contact *Rowena Skelton-Wallace*

Theatrical literary agency (see also **Unna & Durbridge Ltd**, same address) which came out of the merging of Stephen Durbridge Ltd with Sheila Lemon Ltd in February 1986. Theatre, TV, film and radio scripts. No books. No unsolicited mss; preliminary letter and outline essential. No reading fee.
Commission Home 10%; US and Translation varies. *Overseas associates* worldwide.

Christopher Little

49 Queen Victoria Street, London EC4N 4SA
☎01–236 5881
Telex 883968   Fax 01–236 2789

Contact *C. J. Little, P. R. Overnell, B. Godfrey*

FOUNDED 1979. Full length fiction, non-fiction, film scripts, TV scripts. *Special interests* crime, thrillers, historical fiction. Unsolicited mss welcome., No reading fee. CLIENTS include Erin Pizzey, A. J. Quinnell, Carolyn Terry and W. Wright (alias David Graham). *Commission* Home 20%; US 20%; Translation 20%.

Lloyd-George & Coward

12 Fairfax Place, Dartmouth, Devon TQ6 9AE
☎08043 2448

Contact *Bruce Coward*

FOUNDED 1959. Biography, travel, natural history, general fiction and nautical. No drama scripts, poetry, educational, academic or translations. *Special interests* Nautical. No unsolicited mss; send introductory letter with synopsis and s.a.e. No reading fee. CLIENTS include Jane Gillespie, Tom Jaine, Jeremy Purseglove, Wallace Breem. *Commission* Home 10%; US 15%. *Overseas associates* Lyle Steele & Co., New York.

London Independent Books Ltd

1a Montague Mews North, London W1H 1AJ
☎01–935 8090

Contact *Mrs C. Whitaker*

FOUNDED 1971. A self-styled 'small and idiosyncratic' agency, which handles fiction and non-fiction reflecting the tastes of the proprietors. All subjects considered (except computer books) providing the treatment is strong and saleable. Scripts handled only if by a writer already a client. *Special interests* boats, travel, travelogues, commercial fiction. No unsolicited mss – letter, synopsis and first two chapters with return postage

the best approach. No reading fee.   CLIENTS
'none are household names, yet!'
Commission Home 15%; US 20%; Translation 20%.

London Management

235–241 Regent Street, London W1A 2JT
☎01–493 1610
Telex 27498   Fax 01–408 0065

Contact *Heather Jeeves, Tony Peake* (general),
Marc Berlin (TV/film/theatre)

FOUNDED 1959. Part of the Grade organisation,
the biggest show-biz agency in the country.
Recent build up on the book side. Sympathetic to new talent. Full length fiction and
general non-fiction, including illustrated
books, craft, health, music, theatre, film, the
arts, graphic design, humour/cartoon, military. No science fiction/fantasy, educational,
short stories, category romance or children's.
Special interests South African fiction and
non-fiction. Writers should approach by
telephone in the first instance, followed by
letter with synopsis/sample chapters, and
s.a.e. No unsolicited mss. No reading fee.
Commission Home 10%; US 19%; Translation 19%. *Overseas associates* **The Lantz
Office**, New York, plus full coverage by
foreign rights agents.

Bill McLean Personal Management

23b Deodar Road, Putney,
London SW15 2NP
☎01–789 8191

Contact *Bill McLean*

FOUNDED 1972. Scripts only, for all media. No
books, no unsolicited mss. Phone call or
introductory letter essential. No reading
fee.   CLIENTS Jeffrey Segal, Bill Lyons, Peter
Batt, John Maynard, Dwynwen Berry, Frank
Vickery, Mark Wheatley.
Commission Home 10%.

Maclean Dubois (Writers & Agents)

10 Rutland Square, Edinburgh EH1 2AS
☎031–229 6185   Fax 031–228 1319

Contact *Charles Maclean, Piers Schreiber,
Geraldine Coates* (UK), *Patrick Deedes-Vincke*
(Paris)

FOUNDED 1977. General fiction and non-
fiction, children's, biography, history, photography. No poetry or plays (unless, occasionally, for own authors). *Special interests*
literary fiction, Scottish history and topography, food and wine, historical fiction. Unsolicited mss welcome. Reading fee for
supply of detailed report on mss offered.
Writers should approach the agency by
phone or in writing for explanation of
terms. CLIENTS include Colin Mackay
(literary fiction), Ken Begg (thrillers), David
Williams (photos), Helen Mackenzie (children's) Seamus Carney (Scottish history).
Commission Home 10%; US 20%; Translation varies. *Overseas associates* Patrick
Deedes-Vincke, 38 bis Rue de Rivoli, 75004
Paris.

Andrew Mann Ltd

1 Old Compton Street, London W1V 5PH
☎01–734 4751

Contact *Anne Dewe, Tina Betts*

FOUNDED 1975. Fiction and general non-
fiction. Film/TV/theatre/radio scripts. No
unsolicited mss. Preliminary letter, synopsis
and s.a.e. essential. No reading fee. Associate
agencies overseas.
Commission Home 10%; US 15%; Translation 20%.

Marjacq Scripts Ltd

32 Cumberland Mansions, Nutford Place,
London W1H 5ZB
☎01–724 0565

Contact *Jacqui Lyons*

FOUNDED 1974. Fiction and non-fiction, plus
radio and television scripts. No children's or
religious. Unsolicited mss welcome with
s.a.e. but telephone conversation first preferred. No reading fee.
Commission Home 10%; US 10%; Translation 20%.

Marlu Literary Agency

26 Stratford Road, London W8 6QD
☎01–937 5161   Telex 268141

Contact *Mary Hall Mayer*

All subjects except children's and poetry.
Special interests general fiction, non-fiction,
computer and visual books.
Commission Home 10%; US 20%.

Marsh & Sheil Ltd

43 Doughty Street, London WC1A 2LF
☎01–405 7473
Telex 94013093 MARS G   Fax 01–831 2127

Contact *Paul Marsh, Susanna Nicklin*

FOUNDED 1985. Marsh & Sheil deals in transla-
tion rights only, on behalf of selected British
and American agents. CLIENTS include
**Anthony Sheil Associates, Wallace & Sheil
Agency, Don Congdon Associates, Barrie
& Jenkins Ltd.** No unsolicited mss, ideas or
synopses.
Commission Translation 10%.

Blanche Marvin

21a St John's Wood High Street,
London NW8 7NG
☎01–722 2313

Contact *Blanche Marvin*

FOUNDED 1968. Fiction, general non-fiction
and film, radio, TV and play scripts. No
poetry. Welcomes synopses if accompanied
by introductory letter, giving author's c.v.
and outline of the work. No reading fee.
Commission 12½% throughout.

MBA Literary Agents Ltd

45 Fitzroy Street, London W1P 5HR
☎01–387 2076/4785

Contact *Diana Tyler, John Richard Parker,
Meg Davis*

FOUNDED 1971. Full length fiction and non-
fiction. Particularly interested in science
fiction/fantasy. Scripts for all media a
speciality. No poetry or short stories (unless

by established authors). No reading fee but
preliminary letter with s.a.e. essential.
Commission Home 10%; US 20%; Translation 20%; Theatre, TV, Radio 10%; Film
10–15%.

Richard Milne Ltd

28 Makepeace Avenue, London N6 6EJ
☎01–340 7007

Contact *R. M. Sharples, K. N. Sharples*

FOUNDED 1956. Specialises in drama and
comedy scripts for radio and television, but
are not presently in the market for new
clients – they are 'fully committed in handling work by authors we already represent'.
No unsolicited mss.
Commission Home 10%; US 15%; Translation 25%.

William Morris Agency UK Ltd

31/32 Soho Square, London W1V 5DG
☎01–434 2191
Telex 27928   Fax 01–437 4427

Contact *Lavinia Trevor*

FOUNDED 1967. Fiction and general non-
fiction. No scripts, academic, technical,
poetry, children's. Welcome unsolicited mss
but must be preceded by a preliminary letter
with s.a.e.
Commission Home 10%; US 20%; Translation 20%.

Michael Motley Ltd

78 Gloucester Terrace, London W2 3HH
☎01–723 2973

Contact *Michael Motley*

FOUNDED 1973. All subjects except short mss
(e.g. freelance journalism), poetry, original
dramatic material. No scripts. *Special
interests* crime novels and thrillers. Unsolicited mss will be considered but must be preceded by a preliminary letter. No reading
fee. CLIENTS include Simon Brett, K. M. Pey-
ton, Barry Turner, Doug Nye.

Commission Home 10%; US 15%; Translation 20%. *Overseas associates* in all publishing centres.

Jolie Mulvany Literary Agency

85c Linden Gardens, London W2 4EU
☎01–229 8042
Telex 291829 TLX G Attn: IBIS

Contact *Jolie Mulvany*

FOUNDED 1979. Literary fiction: *The Dolls Room* Lorenzo Villalonga; Thrillers: *Tuareg* A. Vasquez-Figueroa; Non-fiction: *The Snake House Test* Mark R. F. Hanau, *You and Your Handwriting* Peter West. Also Cookery and Health (*The Wholefood Cookbook*); Crime; Art/Art History; Auto/biography; Humour; Feminist titles, both fiction and non-fiction. No category romances, science fiction, poetry, history, medical or academic. *Special interests* cookery, astrology and related subjects. No unsolicited mss. Preliminary letter (with s.a.e.) giving information about the author, previous credits, and with synopsis. No reading fee. However, not taking on any new clients at present. CLIENTS include Peter West, Loren D. Estleman, Miguel de Unamuno, Dorothy Bart, Dung Tran Van. *Commission* Home 10%; US 20%; Translation 20%.

The Maggie Noach Literary Agency

21 Redan Street, London W14 0AB
☎01–602 2451

Contact *Maggie Noach*

FOUNDED 1982. (Pronounced no-ack). Ex-A. P. Watt. Handles a wide range of books, including literary fiction, general non-fiction, and some children's. Film/TV rights handled in association with **Linda Seifert Associates** (see entry). No scientific, academic or specialist non-fiction, romantic fiction, poetry, or books for the very young. Recommended for promising young writers but few new clients taken on as it is considered vital to give individual attention to each author's work. Unsolicited mss not welcome. Approach by letter giving a brief description of the book and enclosing a few sample pages. Return postage essential. No reading fee. *Commission* Home 10%; US 20%; Translation 20%.

Andrew Nurnberg Associates Ltd

Clerkenwell House,
45–47 Clerkenwell Green,
London EC1R 0HT
☎01–251 0321
Telex 23353   Fax 01–251 0584

Directors *Andrew Nurnberg, Klaasje Mul and Sarah Nundy*

FOUNDED mid-1970s. *Specialises* in foreign rights, representing leading authors and agents.

Deborah Owen Ltd

78 Narrow Street,
Limehouse, London E14 8BP
☎01–987 5119/5441
Telex 918214 DOWEN

Contact *Deborah Owen, Judith Dooling*

FOUNDED 1971. Wife of a well-known politician. 'Not for old ladies who write knitting books'. Very high-powered. International fiction and non-fiction (books which can be translated into a number of languages). No scripts, poetry, science fiction, children's books, short stories. No unsolicited mss. Not taking on new authors ('haven't done so for some time'). CLIENTS include Jeffrey Archer, Delia Smith, Ellis Peters, Wendy Savage. *Commission* Home 10%; US 15%; Translation 15%.

Mark Paterson & Associates

10 Brook Street, Wivenhoe,
Colchester, Essex CO7 9DS
☎0206 225433/4   Telex 988805 PATEM G

Contact *Mark Paterson*

FOUNDED 1961. *Specialises* in psychiatric books, psychoanalytical, psychotherapy. No song or play scripts. No articles. No unsoli-

cited mss. Prefer preliminary letter. May possibly charge reading fee. CLIENTS include Peter Moss, Hugh Brogan, Hugh Schonfield, Vivian Cook, Dorothy Richardson, Sir Arthur Evans, D. W. Winnicott. Represents the estate of Sigmund Freud.
Commission 20% throughout (including subagent's commission).

John Pawsey
Hollybrae, Hill Brow Road,
Liss, Hants. GU33 7PS
☎0730 893065

Contact *John Pawsey*

FOUNDED 1981. Non-fiction and fiction, e.g. show business (Dudley Moore biography), gardening (*Illustrated Encyclopedia of Trees and Shrubs*), DIY, travel, sport (Brian Clough biography), cookery, humour (*How to Survive School*), crafts. Also thrillers, crime, historical, war, women's and fantasy fiction. Experience in the publishing business has helped to attract some top names and although the agency is a long way from any centre of publishing, John Pawsey does come in to town twice a week to see authors and publishers. No scripts, poetry, science fiction, academic and educational. *Special interests* sport, political, current affairs, and popular fiction. Preliminary letter with s.a.e. essential. No reading fee.
Commission Home 10%; US 19%; Translation 19%.

Norman Payne TV Scripts (Abemarle Scripts)
109 Ullswater Crescent, London SW15 3RE
☎01–546 9747

Contact *Norman Payne*

FOUNDED 1947. Television and radio scripts, but mostly television. Particularly interested in comedy sitcom and sketch material. Prospective writers should write a letter in the first instance. No reading fee.
Overseas associates West Germany (Cologne).

Penman Literary Agency
175 Pall Mall, Leigh-on-Sea, Essex SS9 1RE
☎0702 74438

Contact *Leonard G. Stubbs* FRSA

FOUNDED 1950. Mainly fiction. Small amount of non-fiction (biography and autobiography). Occasional scripts. No Westerns. No unsolicited mss. Prefer preliminary letter with synopsis. No reading fee.
Commission Home 10%; Overseas 15%.

Peterborough Literary Agency
181 Marsh Wall, London E14 9SR
☎01–538 5000 Ext. 6271/6272

Contact *Ewan MacNaughton*

FOUNDED 1973. General non-fiction only. No unsolicited mss. Preliminary letter essential. No reading fee.
Commission Home 10%; US 20%; Translation 20%.

A. D. Peters & Co. Ltd
10 Buckingham Street, London WC2N 6BU
☎01–839 2556   Fax 01–925 2262

Contact *Michael Sissons* (books), *Anthony Jones* (Film/TV), *Pat Kavanagh* (books and serials), *Norman North* (TV drama/fiction), *Caroline Dawnay* (books), *Charles Walker* (TV documentary/books), *Araminta Whitley* (books).

FOUNDED 1924. Major re-organisation likely following merger with **Fraser & Dunlop**. All sorts of books, plus scripts. No third-rate DIY. *Special interests* 'Building careers for writers of talent'. Michael Sissons, Pat Kavanagh (married to Julian Barnes) and Anthony Jones are one of the most high-powered teams in London. Agency handles Evelyn Waugh estate. No unsolicited mss. Prospective clients should write 'a full and honest letter, with a clear account of what he/she has done and wants to do'. No reading fee. CLIENTS include John Mortimer, Mar-

garet Drabble, Ruth Rendell, Sally Beauman, Anthony Sampson, Douglas Reeman, Clive James, Robert McCrum.
Commission Home 10%; US 20%; Translation 20%.

Laurence Pollinger Limited

18 Maddox Street, Mayfair,
London W1R 0EU
☎01–629 9761

Contact *Gerald J. Pollinger, Margaret Pepper, Romany van Bosch, Juliet Burton* (Negotiating Editor), *Lesley Hadcroft* (children's books)

FOUNDED 1958. A division of **Pearn, Pollinger & Higham**. All types of books handled, except pure science, academic, technological. Scripts occasionally. Authors include Graham Greene and the literary estates of H. E. Bates, Scott Fitzgerald, D. H. Lawrence and other notables. Good for romantic fiction. Unsolicited mss welcome if preceded by letter (not phone). Charge £5 contribution towards editorial costs.
Commission Home 15%; US 15%; Translation 20%.

Murray Pollinger

4 Garrick Street, London WC2E 9BH
☎01–836 6781

Contact *Murray Pollinger, Gina Pollinger*

FOUNDED 1969. Part of the Pollinger dynasty (Murray is the younger brother of Gerald) with a particularly strong name for new writers. Securely based on Roald Dahl and one or two big selling literary novelists. All types of general fiction and non-fiction, except poetry, plays and travel. No scripts of any kind. No unsolicited mss; writers should send a letter with synopsis and names of other agents and publishers previously approached. CLIENTS include Roald Dahl, Lyall Watson, Molly Keane, J. M. Coetzee, Penelope Lively, John Gribbin.
Commission Home 10%; Foreign 20%. *Overseas associates* in all major cultural countries.

Shelley Power Literary Agency Ltd

48 Kings Road, Long Ditton, Surrey KT6 5JF
(Postal address) PO Box 149a,
Surbiton Surrey KT6 5JH
☎01–398 7723/8723
Telex 265 871 Mon Ref (Quote ref 87: SQQ256)

Contact *Shelley Power*

FOUNDED 1976. General commercial fiction, quality fiction, business books, self-help, film and entertainment, investigative exposés, writers from South Africa. No scripts, short stories, children's, poetry. Preliminary letter essential describing briefly the project offered, and enclosing s.a.e. No reading fee. CLIENTS include Madge Swindells, Lewis Nkosi, Peter Lambley, Stephen Gray and Terence Pettigrew.
Commission Home 10%; US 15–19%; Translation 19%.

PVA Management Ltd

Alpha Tower, Paradise Circus,
Birmingham B1 1TT
☎021–643 4011

Contact *Ruth Scriven*

FOUNDED 1978. Mainly non-fiction with some fiction. Scripts. Prefer preliminary letter with synopsis and return postage.
Commission 15% Home and Abroad. *Overseas associates* **Paul Vaughan Associates**. Los Angeles.

Radala & Associates

17 Avenue Mansions, Finchley Road,
London NW3 7AX
☎01–794 4495   Telex 295441

Contact *Richard Gollner, István Siklôs* (East European expert), *Prince Radala* (East European)
The philosophy of the agency is oriented towards representing authors rather than specialising in particular areas of publishing. Radala 'invented' the popular computing book, and handled over 1000 titles in the

early 1980s. Now targeting itself towards the audio tapes market. 'We handle anything that our clients can produce, including TV, radio and theatre'. Not interested in 'books that authors have written in lieu of going to a psychotherapist . . . we wish to hear from people who can write (at least a letter, to start with)'. They avoid on principle mss entitled 'Battle of the River Plate', 'Battle of the Bulge', 'My Battle', or anything else including 'My' in the title. Prospective clients should approach the agency with a shortish letter plus synopsis and sample chapter (double spaced) in the first instance. *Commission* Home 10%; US 15–20%; Translation 20%. *Overseas associates* **Writers House** (Al Zuckermann), New York, plus agents throughout Europe.

Douglas Rae Ltd

28 Charing Cross Road, London WC2H 0DB
☎01–836 3903

Contact *Douglas Rae, Jenne Casarotto*

FOUNDED 1975. Novels, biographies, screenplays, theatre and TV plays. No short stories or poetry. Good reputation for both film and television rights, the main work of the company. Not so happy with books. *Special interests* novels with film and television potential. Unsolicited mss not welcome. Write, enclosing s.a.e. However, 'Not taking on new clients at present.' No reading fee. CLIENTS include John Briley, Derek Marlowe, David Yallop *Commission* Home 10%; US 15%; Translation 20%.

Margaret Ramsay Ltd

14a Goodwins Court, St Martins Lane, London WC2N 4LL
☎01–240 0691/836 7403

Contact *Margaret Ramsay, Tom Erhardt* (foreign rights), *Stephanie Tanner* (television)

Established in the 1960s. The grand dame of the agency business Margaret (Peggy) Ramsay has been immortalised in book, play and film as Joe Orton's business brain. In the spring of 1987, the following plays on in London or touring had come out of the Margaret Ramsay agency: *Les Liaisons Dangereuses*; *Coming in to Land*; *Woman in Mind*; *A Piece of my Mind*; *A Chorus of Disapproval*. Also handles scripts for TV, radio and film. Writers should approach by letter or phone in the first instance. No reading fee. CLIENTS include David Wood, Samuel Beckett. *Commission* Home 10%; US 10%; Translation 10%. *Overseas associates* South America, France, Germany, Holland, Israel, Italy, Japan and Scandinavia.

Rogers, Coleridge & White Ltd

20 Powys Mews, London W11 1JN
☎01–221 3717   Telex 25930 DEBROG G

Contact *Deborah Rogers, Gill Coleridge, Patricia White, Ann Warnford Davis* (Foreign rights)

FOUNDED 1979. Recent change of name from **Deborah Rogers Ltd**. The fashionable literary agent of the 1970s. According to *The Times*, 'some of the highest talents in the land bloomed under her care'. CLIENTS include Ian McEwan, Angela Carter, Ronald Blythe, Stephen Pile, Timothy Mo. Fiction and nonfiction. No poetry, plays or technical books. *Commission* Home 10%; US 15%. *Overseas associates* ICM, New York.

Rostrum Literary Agency Limited

Suite 477, Royal Exchange, Manchester M2 7DD
☎061–456 8035

Directors *Eric Falk, Marj Falk, Lynn Peters*

FOUNDED 1986. Full length fiction and non-fiction; biography and autobiography (ghostwriting facilities available); film, TV, radio and theatre scripts. No poetry, short stories. No unsolicited mss. Preliminary letter with s.a.e. in the first instance. CLIENTS include Christopher Beddows, Shirley Goode, Madeleine Keeffe, Molly Lillis, Joe Cooper. *Commission* Home 10%; US 19%.

Herta Ryder

c/o Toby Eady Associates Ltd,
7 Gledhow Gardens, London SW5 0BL
☎01–948 1010/370 6292

Contact *Herta Ryder*

FOUNDED 1984. Fiction; non-fiction (except technical/textbooks); children's (particularly for older children); popular music (i.e. 'lives' rather than specialist); military history; German books of quality (London representative of Liepman AG, Literary Agency, Zurich). No scripts, poetry, individual short stories/ articles. Reliable and conscientious. *Special interests* children's and books from Canada (London agent for Macmillan of Canada). Unsolicited mss considered but explanatory letter first preferred. CLIENTS include Gwyneth Jones (Ann Halam), Jean Morris, Farley Mowat, Judy Blume.
Commission Home 10%; US 15%; Translation 20%. *Overseas associates* Harold Ober Associates, New York, plus associates in most other countries.

Sheri Safran Literary Agency

8 Pembridge Studios, 27a Pembridge Villas, London W11 3EP
☎01–221 3355   Telex 262284

Contact *Sheri Safran*

FOUNDED 1976. Health books for, by, and about women only. No scripts, no other subjects. No unsolicited mss. Letter essential in first instance.   CLIENTS include Janet Horwood (*Comfort*), Shere Hite (*Hite Report*), Julie Orbach (*Understanding Women*).
Commission Home 15%; US 20%; Translation 20%.

Tessa Sayle Agency

11 Jubilee Place, London SW3 3TE
☎01–352 4311 (books);
01–352 2182 (drama)

Contact *Tessa Sayle* (books),
Penny Tackaberry (drama)

FOUNDED 1976 (under present ownership; previously traded as *Hope, Leresche & Sayle*).

Fiction: literary, upmarket novels, rather than category fiction. Non-fiction: current affairs, social issues, biographies, historical. Also scripts handled for all media. No children's, poetry or textbooks. Quick to catch on to new talent. No unsolicited mss. Preliminary letter essential, including a brief biographical note and a synopsis. No reading fee. CLIENTS include Thomas Keneally, David Pallister, William Styron, Phillip Knightley (books); Shelagh Delaney, Robert David McDonald, Geoff McQueen (film/TV plays).
Commission Home 10%; US 20%; Translation 20%. *Overseas associates* in USA, Japan and throughout Europe.

Linda Seifert Associates

18 Ladbroke Terrace, London W11 3PG
☎01–229 5163/221 0692   Fax 01–439 1355
Telex Linda London 21879 G

Contact *Linda Seifert, Elizabeth Dench, Nicky Hart*

FOUNDED 1972. Scripts for television, radio and film only. Unsolicited mss will be read, but a letter with sample of work and c.v. (plus s.a.e.) is better.   CLIENTS include Stephen Volk *Gothic*, Chris Menges *A World Apart*, Michael Radford *White Mischief*.
Commission Home 10%. *Overseas associates* Leading Artists, Triad (both Los Angeles).

James Sharkey Associates Ltd

3rd Floor, 15 Golden Square, London W1R 3AG
☎01–434 3801   Telex 295251 JSALON G

Contact *Sebastian Born*

FOUNDED 1983. Actors' and literary agency. *Special interest* all dramatic scripts: film/TV/ theatre/radio. Some books. Preliminary letter preferred. No reading fee.
Commission 10% across the board.

Vincent Shaw Associates

20 Jays Mews, Kensington Gore,
London SW7 2EP
☎01–581 8215

Contact *Vincent Shaw, Cherry Palfrey*

FOUNDED 1954. TV, radio and theatre scripts only. Unsolicited mss welcome; approach in writing (no phone calls) enclosing s.a.e. No reading fee.
Commission Home 10%; US and Translation by negotiation. *Overseas associates* Herman Chessid, New York.

Anthony Sheil Associates Ltd

43 Doughty Street, London WC1N 2LF
☎01–405 9351/2/3/4/5/6
Telex 946240   Fax 01–831 2127

Contact *Anthony Sheil, Giles Gordon, Mic Cheetham, Jane Shilling* (books), *Janet Fillingham, Tessa Ross* (film drama)

FOUNDED 1962. Full length fiction and non-fiction. Theatre, film, radio and TV scripts. Unsolicited mss welcome. Preliminary letter and return postage essential. No reading fee. CLIENTS include John Fowles, Peter Ackroyd, Sue Townsend, Catherine Cookson.
Commission Home 10%; US 20%; Translation 20%. *Overseas offices* Wallace & Sheil Inc., 177 East 70th Street, New York, NY 10021, USA.

Caroline Sheldon Literary Agency

23 Cumberland Street, London SW1V 4LS
☎01–821 8051

Contact *Caroline Sheldon*

FOUNDED 1985. Adult fiction, and in particular women's, both commercial sagas and literary novels. Full length children's fiction. No scripts unless the writer also does books. Unsolicited mss welcome. Send letter with all relevant details of ambitions and four chapters of proposed book (and large s.a.e.). No reading fee.
Commission Home 10%; US 20%; Translation 20% (Translation handled by *Jennifer Luithlen*, The Rowans, 88 Holmfield Road, Leicester).

Jeffrey Simmons

10 Lowndes Square, London SW1X 9HA
☎01–235 8852

Contact *Jeffrey Simmons*

FOUNDED 1978. Biography and autobiography, cinema and theatre, fiction (both quality and commercial), history, law and crime, politics and world affairs, parapsychology, sports and travel (but not exclusively). No children's books, cookery, crafts and hobbies, gardening. Scripts handled only if by book-writing clients. *Special interests* personality books of all sorts and fiction from young writers (i.e. under 40) with a future. Writers become clients by personal introduction or by letter, enclosing a synopsis if possible, a brief biography of the author, a note of any previously published books, plus a list of any publishers/agents who have already seen the mss. CLIENTS include Michael Bentine, Fenton Bresler, Doris Collins, Adrienne Corri, Daniel Easterman, John Feltwell, Tim Fitzgeorge-Parker, Greenpeace Books, Fred Lawrence Guiles, Rosie Swale.
Commission Home 10–15%; US 15–20%; Translation 20%.

Richard Scott Simon Ltd

32 College Cross, London N1 1PR
☎01–607 8533

Contact *Richard Simon, Vivien Green*

FOUNDED 1971. General non-fiction and fiction, biography, travel, cookery, humour. No scripts, romantic novels, poetry, academic, scientific, educational, children's. Prior letter with s.a.e. essential. CLIENTS include Rabbi Lionel Blue, William Boyd, Hunter Davies, Duff Hart-Davis, Tom Sharpe, Carolyn Slaughter, Rose Tremain. Recent titles: *Rich*, Melvyn Bragg and Sally Burton; *Blood Orange*, Sam Llewellyn; *Yes, Mama*, Helen Forrester; *Zest for Life*, Barbara Griggs; *Cotswolds*, Susan Hill; *Three Cities*, Stephen Brook.
Commission Home 10%; US 15%; Translation 20%. *Overseas associates* **Georges Borchardt Inc.**

Carol Smith Literary Agency

25 Hornton Court, Kensington High Street, London W8 7RT
☎01–937 4874

Contact *Carol Smith*

FOUNDED 1976. Ex-**A. P. Watt**. Fiction and general non-fiction. Scripts for TV/film only rarely. Absolutely no children's or technical. General fiction of all sorts. Reputed to be good on encouraging talented young novelists. Unsolicited mss welcome with return postage. Introductory letter preferred. No reading fee. CLIENTS include Sarah Harrison, Katie Stewart, Mike Wilks, Alexander Frater.
Commission Home 10%; US 15%; Translation 20%.

Solo Syndication & Literary Agency Ltd

8 Bouverie Street, London EC4Y 8BB
☎01–583 9372
Telex 925235 SOLO G   Fax 01–353 1292

Contact *Don Short* (Chairman), *John Appleton* (Senior Executive & Accounts), *Trevor York* (Syndication Manager)

FOUNDED 1978. Non-fiction. *Specialises* in celebrity autobiographies, unauthorised biographies, outback & adventure stories, wildlife, nature & ecology, crime, fashion, beauty & health. Fiction from established authors only. No unsolicited mss. Preliminary letter essential. CLIENTS include Fred Perry, Mike Gatting, Britt Ekland, James Oram, Sir James Mancham.
Commission Home 15%; US 20%; Translation 20–30%.

Also specialises in worldwide newspaper syndication of photos, features, cartoons. Professional contributors only. CLIENTS include *Daily Mail, Mail on Sunday, YOU Magazine, The Evening Standard,* **Guinness Books,** *Guinness Book of Records,* News Limited of Australia and others. Also fifty Fleet Street and international freelance journalists. Syndication commission terms: 50/50%.

Elaine Steel

25/27 Oxford Street, London W1R 1RF
☎01–437 1097
Telex 8954713 ALFA G   Fax 01–434 1726

Contact *Elaine Steel*

FOUNDED 1986. Fiction and non-fiction. Scripts. No technical or academic. Prefer initial phone call or letter. CLIENTS include Troy Kennedy Martin, G. F. Newman, Les Blair, Karl Francis.
Commission Home 10%; US 20%; Translation 20%. *Overseas associates* Susan Burgholz, New York; Geoffrey Sandford, Los Angeles.

Abner Stein

10 Roland Gardens, London SW7 3PH
☎01–373 0456/370 7859

Contact *Abner Stein*

FOUNDED 1971. Full length fiction and non-fiction. General non-fiction only; no scientific, technical, etc. No scripts. Letter and outline preferred to unsolicited mss.
Commission Home 10%; US 15%; Translation 20%.

Peter Tauber Press Agency

94 East End Road, London N3 2SX
☎01–346 4165

Contact *Peter Tauber, Robert Tauber* (directors)

FOUNDED 1950. Celebrity biographies/autobiographies, popular medical (by experts only), quality full-length fiction, literature, and well researched historical fiction. No poetry, short stories, scripts, plays or children's. Preliminary letter with synopsis, author's c.v. and s.a.e. essential. No reading fee.
Commission Home 20%; US 20%; Translation 20%.

J. M. Thurley

213 Linen Hall, 156–170 Regent Street, London W1R 5TA
☎01–437 9545/6

Contact *Jon Thurley, Mary Alderman*

FOUNDED 1976. All types of fiction, non-fiction, coffee table books, etc. Also scripts for TV/radio/theatre. No short stories or children's illustrated books. No unsolicited mss; approach by letter in first instance. No reading fee.
Commission Home 10%; US 15%; Translation 15%.

Harvey Unna & Stephen Durbridge Ltd

24–32 Pottery Lane, London W11 4LZ
☎01–727 1346
Telex 27618 Author G   Fax 01–727 9037

Directors *Stephen Durbridge, Wendy Gresser, Girsha Reid*

Theatrical literary agency, specialising in theatre/TV/film/radio scripts. No books. No unsolicited mss; preliminary letter and outline essential. No reading fee.
Commission Home 10%; US and Translation varies. *Overseas associates* worldwide.

Ed Victor Ltd

162 Wardour Street, London W1V 3AT
☎01–734 4795   Telex 263361

Contact *Ed Victor, Maggie Phillips*

FOUNDED 1976. A broad range, from Iris Murdoch to Irving Wallace, Paula Yates to Stephen Spender, tending towards the more commercial ends of the fiction and non-fiction spectrums. No scripts, or heavily academic. Preliminary letter essential, setting out very concisely and clearly what the book aims to do. No unsolicited mss. 'Takes on very few new writers'. After trying book publishing and literary magazines, Ed Victor, an ebullient American, found his true vocation. Now he is the leading contender for the 'Trendiest Agent in London' title. Strong opinions, very pushy and works hard for those whose intelligence he respects. Loves nothing more than a good title auction. CLIENTS include Iris Murdoch, Erich Segal, Irving Wallace, Douglas Adams, Stephen Spender.

Commission Home 15%; US 15%; Translation 20%.

S. Walker Literary Agency

96 Church Lane, Goldington,
Bedford, MK41 0AS
☎0234 216229

Contact *A. Oldfield, C.-L. Oldfield, E. K. Walker*

FOUNDED 1939. Full length fiction, some non-fiction, children's stories. No poetry, short topical articles. No unsolicited mss. Preliminary letter enclosing synopsis and return postage required.
Commission Home 10%; US 20%; Translation 20%. *Overseas associates* Works in conjunction with agencies in most European countries and also negotiates directly with foreign publishers.

Cecily Ware Literary Agency

19c John Spencer Square, Canonbury, London N1 2LZ
☎01–359 3787

Contact *Cecily Ware* (film/television), *Gilly Schuster* (film/television),
Elizabeth Comstock-Smith (books, theatre, radio)

FOUNDED 1972. Primarily a script agency, with particular interest in television material. But also handles film and TV tie-ins (*Rockliffe's Babies, Howard's Way*); children's books (Stanley Bagshaw books by Bob Wilson) and fiction, both popular and literary. Also non-fiction which relates to film, theatre etc. No poetry, autobiography, sport, joke books or technical. Books that have a strong potential as television series, single plays or even films, with a strong storyline and good characterisation, are particularly sought after. No unsolicited mss, or phone calls, and no synopses; approach in writing only. No reading fee. CLIENTS include Charles Humphries, Gerry Huxham (*Eastenders*), Bob Wilson, Helen Wykham, James Andrew Hall (who did the adaptation

of *David Copperfield* for the BBC), Jenny McDade (script writer for *Supergran*).
Commission Home 10%; US 10%; Translation 10%.

Watson Little Ltd

Suite 8, 26 Charing Cross Road,
London WC2H 0DG
☎01–836 5880

Contact *Sheila Watson, Amanda Little*

Very catholic range of subjects. *Specialist interests* military, gardening and business books. No scripts. Would not be interested in an author who wishes purely to be an academic writer. Always write a preliminary ('intelligent') letter rather than send unsolicited synopsis. £10 reading fee.
Commission Home 10%; US 19%; Translation 19%. *Overseas associates*: MacIntosh & Otis, New York; Mohrbooks, Zurich; La Nouvelle Agence, Paris; Agenzia Lettaria Internazionale, Milan; Rombach & Partners, Netherlands; Suzanne Palme, Scandinavia; Carmene Balcells, Spanish & Portuguese (world-wide); Tuttle Mori, Japan.

A. P. Watt

20 John Street, London WC1 2DR
☎01–405 6774   Telex 297903 APWATT G

Contact *Hilary Rubinstein, Caradoc King, Rod Hall* (plays), *Pamela Todd* (children's books)

FOUNDED 1875. Oldest established literary agency in the world. All full length typescripts, including children's books, screenplays for film and TV, and plays. No poetry, academic or specialist works. Unsolicited mss and outlines welcome, preferably preceded by introductory letter, and return postage included. No reading fee.   CLIENTS include Alison Lurie, Nadine Gordimer, Michael Holroyd (for whom Hilary Rubinstein achieved the record advance of £625,000 for Shaw's biography), Graham Swift, Garrison Keillor, Lucy Irvine, Jan Morris, Bill Tidy, Frank Muir, Yeats and Kipling estates.
Commission Home 10%; US 20%; Translation 20%. *Overseas associates* Ellen Levine, Inc. (USA).

Whose Right to Copy?

For writers, the new Copyright Act is less a revision of the law than a restatement – a cleaning up operation designed to simplify the rules and make them easier to implement.

To start with what is actually new in the Bill, authors have at last been given the 'moral rights' which colleagues elsewhere in Europe have long enjoyed. A writer can now insist on being identified as the creator of a particular work and he can resist 'unjustified modification' of his words.

But these rights are not absolute. In certain circumstances they can and, no doubt, should be waived. The most obvious examples are in journalism where staff and freelancers invariably consign copyright as part of their terms of employment or commission. With news items, destined to perish with the next edition, the concession is hardly worth bothering about. It takes on a greater significance with features, maybe extending to a thousand words or more, which qualify for numerous reprints at home and abroad.

At issue here is not simply the right to be identified and to be consulted on changes but the entitlement to supplementary fees. No wonder the National Union of Journalists urges freelancers to hang on to their copyright for dear life; or to give it up only in return for a payment substantial enough to compensate for lost royalties.

That the sums involved can be worth pursuing is made clear by the efforts of less scrupulous employers to bamboozle writers into signing away their copyright. Handing out agreements with critical clauses in minute print is a common trick; so too is the payment cheque which can only be cashed after the recipient has countersigned over a promise to grant rights to the issuing company. The golden rule is, never sign anything unless you understand and accept the obligations; and never act hastily. It is so easy to respond generously to a publisher who shows interest, even when he makes the cheekiest demands. Winners of competitions are frequent victims. Promoters of literary jamborees are all too ready to demand copyright in return for some miserable prize or a derisory pay off.

In a recent issue of *The Author*, a correspondent quotes the invitation he had received to allow his work to appear in the TV-am Poetry Book:

'You will recall that some time ago you entered the above poem(s) in our poetry competition. We are pleased to advise you that your poem(s) has been selected to be included in a TV-am poetry book ... In order to proceed with the publishing of this book, TV-am now wish to acquire all copyright and any other rights in your poem(s) in all media world wide for the full period of copyright and any extensions and renewals thereof . . . In consideration of you assigning to TV-am all the above rights, TV-am shall pay to you the sum of £10.'

Every writer is grateful for recognition but, surely, not at the risk of humiliation.

Corporate Television

As far as it is possible to tell, script writing for non-commercial videos such as company training courses or advertising features almost always requires the surrender of copyright to the client. As this is a fast expanding source of income, it is likely that the writers' organisations will have more to say about it in the years ahead. But to be fair, a writer who is working to order, that is, using material provided and turning it into presentable shape has a slender claim to copyright.

The same argument applies to sponsored books where the client, usually a company, pays directly for a document of record, a volume celebrating an important anniversary, for example. The writer may think it essential to stick by the principle of retaining copyright come what may, but there is no question that this may exclude him from a prosperous sector of the market.

The Basis of Copyright

Copyright extends to books, plays, films and records. In most books a copyright notice appears on one of the front pages. In its simplest form this is the symbol © followed by the name of the copyright owner and the year of first publication. The assertion of copyright may be emphasised by the phrase 'All rights reserved', and in case there are any lingering doubts the reader may be warned that 'No part of this publication may be reproduced or transmitted in any form or by any means without permission'.

But this is to overstate the case. It is perfectly legitimate for a writer to quote from someone else's work for 'purposes of criticism or review' as long as 'sufficient acknowledgement' is given. What he must not do is to lift 'a substantial part' of a copyright work without permission. Unfortunately, there is little agreement on what constitutes 'a substantial part', since the Copyright Act does not define the term. Legal precedents suggest that the quality of the 'part' and its value to the user must be taken into account as well as its length in determining whether it is 'substantial'. This explains how, in one case, four lines from a thirty-two line poem were held to amount to 'a substantial part'. On the other hand, even a 'substantial' quotation from a copyright work may be acceptable if a reviewer or critic is engaged in 'fair dealing' with his subject. But no-one should be surprised to hear that 'fair dealing' is another of those terms which is open to legal interpretation.

What Does Copyright Cover?

In Britain, copyright protection lasts for fifty years from the end of the year in which the author dies. For a published work of joint authorship, protection runs from the end of the year of the death of the author who dies last. The fifty year rule applies to all written work including letters.

US Copyright

These terms of copyright apply to all the member countries of the Berne Union. But the

United States, which is outside the Berne Union, goes further. The US Copyright Act of 1909 provided for two separate terms of copyright, a period of twenty-eight years from publication followed by a renewal period of a further twenty-eight years. A new copyright act, which came into force in January 1978, made changes in the duration of copyright protection and set out rules for the transition of existing works.

Copyrights registered before 1950 and renewed before 1978 were automatically extended by the new act until December of the seventy-fifth year of the original date of registration. This meant that all copyrights in their second term were extended for nineteen years. But copyrights registered after 1950 and before December 1977 had to be renewed. The repercussions continue to this day since a work published in 1960 must be renewed before 31 December 1988 (1960 + 28) in order to obtain protection for the full seventy-five year period. Renewal forms can be obtained from the Register of Copyrights, Library of Congress, Washington DC 20559.

Works created after the new law came into force are automatically protected for the author's lifetime, and for an additional fifty years after the author's death.

Copyright on Ideas

In radio and television, in particular, writers have the problem of trying to sell ideas for which it is almost impossible to stake an exclusive claim. The law will be of no help at all if, for example, having revealed to a television producer an outline for a series tied to the exploits of a one-legged mountaineer, you subsequently find the idea cropping up in the schedules over someone else's name.

It is not that broadcasters are a naturally devious crowd (though there may be some disagreement on that). Rather, so much unsolicited material comes the way of the script departments, the duplication of ideas is inevitable.

Frequent complaints of plagiarism have led major production companies to point out the risks whenever they acknowledge an unsolicited synopsis or script. For example, **Thames Television** warns correspondents, 'it is often the case that we are currently considering or have already considered ideas that may be similar to your own'. The standard letter goes on:

> 'The fact that we are prepared to consider your material implies no obligation on our part to use your work. Equally, it does not mean that you are under any obligation to Thames: you are free to submit your material to any other parties you wish. We cannot undertake to consider your work on any basis of confidentiality. We must be free to discuss your work openly in the course of our consideration . . .'

If these conditions are not acceptable, the letter concludes, 'we will not be able to consider your material'.

It is a fair warning though probably of little comfort to those who have suffered the attention of unscrupulous rivals. In a highly competitive, fast-moving business, manuscripts can end up in the wrong hands. If there are worries on this score, a useful precaution is to copy a manuscript, send it to yourself by registered post, then deposit the package and dated receipt at a bank or other safe place. At least then no one can fault your memory on essential detail.

Copyright on Characters

Even when a script is accepted for broadcasting, problems of copyright can still occur. A frequent source of dispute is the lifting of characters from one series to another when there are two or more writers involved. Kenneth Royce had this experience when his detective, George Bulman was transferred from *The XYY Man*, a TV adaptation of four Royce books, to a new series, *Strangers*, and later to yet another series called *Bulman*. By then Kenneth Royce's involvement was limited to 'one begrudging credit on the last episode of every series'.

A more complex and, one might guess, a more costly wrangle is centred on the use of characters invented by Wilfred Greatorex for the Yorkshire TV series *Airline*. It came as a shock to him when he saw the same characters, played by the same actors appearing in an advertisement for the British Airports Authority. The saga of Wilfred Greatorex's efforts to gain compensation was reported in *The Guardian* (20.7.87). At that time, after several months of claim and counter-claim there was still no prospect of a settlement.

Disputes of this sort will doubtless continue under the new Copyright Act. 'TV people like to believe that the character becomes their own', writes Kenneth Royce, 'forgetting that without the author's original, there would be no such character'. As a minimum precaution he urges a writer approaching a TV deal 'to resist strongly any attempt to change the names of his characters'. Why make stealing easier than it already is?

Copyright in Titles

If copyright over characters is difficult to establish, it is near impossible with titles. Only when a title is distinctive and clearly identified with the work of a particular author is there any chance of gaining an injunction against its use, or something very close to it, by another writer.

The question is, how close is close? Of recently published titles, Sally Beauman's blockbuster novel *Destiny* was thought by one critic to imply a link with the television soap opera, *Dynasty*. But to this extent, most popular literature is imitative and no reader is likely to be deceived into thinking that the two creations are the same. But if you are planning to write the fictional diaries of a pimply teenager, a title like *The Secret Diaries of Adrian Pole* will almost certainly get you into trouble with Sue Townsend.

The new Copyright Act does make a half-hearted attempt to come to terms with the new technology. An author's right to compensation when his work is photocopied or rented out on sound tape or video is accepted in principle though, at the time of writing, it is not clear how fees will be collected and redistributed. Something on the lines of Public Lending Right is anticipated but without government funding.

The big disappointment is the absence of any attempt to make reparation to authors for home taping. The loss of income caused by the domestic use of sound and video recorders runs into millions. And with the advance of technology the problem is bound to worsen. Yet the proposal of the **Writers' Guild** and others to compensate copyright holders by a levy on blank tapes has been unexpectedly rejected by the government. Why this should be so is not clear. The blank tape levy is administered elsewhere in Europe without difficulty and is widely accepted as the only practical solution to a glaring abuse of copyright. Eventually the government will be forced to think again. Writers must hope that it will be sooner rather than later.

All the News That's Fit to Print – A Quick Guide for Freelancers in Search of a Story

Hard news belongs to televison. It is rare nowadays for newspapers to take their readers by surprise on any matter of national importance. The morning headlines are simply confirmation of what has been seen on screen the evening before, which may explain why, in readership surveys, a high proportion of those questioned seem to skip the front pages altogether.

This may seem obvious enough. But newspaper owners and editors, schooled in the bullish tradition of Fleet Street, are reluctant to accept what they see as a secondary role. As part of their counter-attack they have changed the rules to accommodate a wider definition of news. For example, news may be any of the following.

News = Speculation

A student newspaper once doubled its circulation (for one week only) with the headline, 'Queen not to get divorce' and a page of denials of a rumour which had started in the union bar. The national press is not so audacious (is it?) but much political hearsay (Maggie decides against Election) and social gossip comes within this category.

News = A Stunt

This is where the public relations industry moves in. An otherwise unremarkable event can achieve wide coverage when it is matched with a gimmick – especially one that makes a good picture. Thus, while 'Mayor opens fête' is for the back page of the local free sheet, 'Mayor lands by parachute to open fête,' will make at least one of the nationals.

All the newspapers, not just the tabloids, go for the unusual, not to say the downright cranky. Witness the coverage for Eddy the Eagle, the ski jumper whose fame rests on an indomitable capacity for coming last.

News = A Strong Opinion

But only if it is in line with editorial policy. Over forty years ago the columnist Hannen Swaffer defined press freedom as a licence to write 'of such of the proprietor's prejudices as the advertisers don't object to'.

News = A Personality

Usually one who is already famous for being in the news. It is no matter that the interview will be largely a rehash of earlier interviews. In modern journalism, familiarity breeds contentment.

News = A Self-publicist with a Taste for Adventure

The prize goes to Richard Branson. His balloon crossing of the Atlantic set him back £750,000 but the publicity he attracted for his company was worth many millions.

News = A Survey

Whatever two out of three people think about anything is news, but they have to talk to an opinion pollster before their views can be taken into account.

News = An Excuse to Sell Advertising

Business supplements are popular for this reason. So, too, are articles about countries which spend a lot of money on propaganda.

News = Follow My Leader

Journalists spend much time mugging up on the work of other journalists. Their aim is to beat the competition at its own game. So, if one paper comes out with a story on, say, killer dogs, the other paper will follow with yet more horrific reports on the same theme.

News = The Same as Last Year

Some news items and features turn up year after year. Come mid-August, for example, expect reports on the declining fortunes of British seaside resorts. (They have been declining for over forty years.)

News = An Anniversary

In 1986, not a single editor wanted to know 'Whither India?' In 1987, they were all asking the question and giving the answer at enormous length. The only difference in timing was between thirty-nine years after Independence and forty years after Independence. Forty, like ten, twenty-five, fifty and one hundred are magic anniversary dates. 1988 produced a bumper crop of anniversaries: the Spanish Armada (1588), the Glorious Revolution (1688), Byron's birth and the arrival of the first Australian settlers (1788), the Ripper murders (1888), the Anschluss (1938), the communist takeover of Czechoslovakia (1948) and the Czech uprising against the Soviets (1968). Australia's bicentennial alone released a deluge of travel supplements.

News = Where the Broadcasters Cannot Reach

It is here that the press is genuinely informative – explaining issues which television covers superficially, stimulating debate when the broadcasters are held back by their vow of neutrality, and investigating matters of concern which might otherwise go unreported.

This is the smallest section of any newspaper. Would that it was the largest.

Practical Freelancing

The economics of newspaper and magazine publishing have helped to promote the freelancer. It makes sense for editors to keep a news team on the payroll, but no sense at all to take on board occasional contributors who can just as easily work from home. Quite a few of the top freelancers are journalists who previously held full-time jobs. Though income is variable and the demands heavy, none of them would willingly go back to regular employment.

For the newcomer, *The Writer's Handbook* listings of press and periodicals identifies receptive editors and advises on how best to make an approach. But there is no substitute for a careful study of the publication in which you hope to see your byline. It is not simply a matter of getting the subject matter right; there is also the style and length of an article to consider. What will attract one publication will repel another.

The aim of the freelancer who wants to make all or a regular part of his income from writing should be to move quickly from speculative work – where it is up to the editor to accept or reject whatever is sent in – to commissioned articles where the journalist can claim certain rights. Wherever possible, before accepting a commission, extract some sort of agreement in writing. True, a verbal commitment is binding, but if disaster strikes, like a paper folding or the editor changing his job, it is often difficult to prove that the commission was ever made.

The other advantage of a written agreement is that it compels both sides to think carefully about what is involved. What level of expenses is required? Do you want part of the fee up front? (The answer here must always be 'Yes'.) What happens if the material submitted does not fulfil the terms of the commission or is suitable but not published for other reasons? In the first case, a reject fee, not less than half the original figure, should be paid. In the second case, the full fee should be paid.

Beware of talking too freely about great ideas for articles before you have a piece of paper acknowledging that you are the writer who will transform them into copy. In the chaos of the typical newspaper or magazine office, it is common for ideas to be lifted, unintentionally.

A freelancer who contributes regularly to a single publication has the right to ask for a contract, renewable say every year or six months. One of the many virtues of a contract is that it offers an element of security in an otherwise highly insecure business. At the very least, it can be waved at the bank manager when asking for an extension of the overdraft.

Both the **National Union of Journalists** and the **Institute of Journalists** have freelance sections which offer constructive advice to members and give welcome backing in disputes where a journalist who speaks for himself is liable to be shouted down. Two years ago, the NUJ adopted a code of practice for the treatment of freelancers. It decrees that conditions and rates of pay should be established clearly when work is accepted or commissioned, that freelancers should be paid for providing background information and research material, and that work commissioned or accepted should be paid for at a date agreed which should normally be no more than a month after delivery. Other clauses relate to expenses (to be paid on the same basis as for permanent staff), copyright (to remain with the freelancer unless there is a signed agreement to transfer) and the responsibility of staff journalists to watch over the interests of their freelance colleagues.

The rewards of freelancing vary wildly and though where possible we have shown the minimum rates on offer from papers and journals, it must be emphasised that all publications are prepared to pay over the odds for contributors and articles they really want. Not that they will meekly concede special rates. Hard bargaining may be called for, not least with editors of national papers who will not blink at paying their in-house feature writers £30,000 or more a year.

Invited by *The Spectator* to describe the pleasures and perils of freelancing (for which he was paid £90), Chaim Bermant berated *The Times* for giving 'the impression that anyone privileged enough to appear in its pages should, if paid at all, be content with a token fee'.

As for *The Guardian* and *The Observer*, 'both have a social conscience, and perhaps they keep their fees low to give their contributors first-hand experience of the poverty and hardship on which they dwell at such length'.

As a general guide there are the comprehensive freelance agreements negotiated by the NUJ with leading publishers. For magazines, the highest band is £250 per thousand words for features and £25 a hundred words for news. This applies to magazines like *Reader's Digest, Woman's Own* and *Radio Times*. On the lowest band (*Film Review, Everywoman*) rates fall to £80 per thousand words for features and £8 per hundred words for news. Many journals, including some of the most prestigious, pay below these rates. When it is clear that a publication is run on a shoestring, you may feel justified in giving it support by contributing on derisory terms. But as a principle, writers should not expect, or be expected, to provide a charity service for their readers. On the national press, news reports start at £15–£20 for up to a hundred words, features at £175 per thousand words (£188 for Sundays) and colour supplement features £250 per thousand words.

The regional and local press is more of a gamble. The NUJ minimum for weekly papers is £6.80 up to one hundred words and £6.40 a hundred thereafter. The rate for dailies is a straight £8.74 per hundred words. But if our research shows anything it is that in the provinces, all deals are possible. Newspaper editors who plead poverty are seldom to be taken seriously.

National Newspapers

Daily Express

121 Fleet Street, London EC4P 4JT

☎01–353 8000　　　　　　Telex 21841

Owner *United Newspapers plc*
Editor *Nicholas Lloyd*
Circulation 1.69 million

Unsolicited mss generally welcome, though the weekly total is 'too numerous to count'. The general rule of thumb is to approach in writing with an idea; all departments are prepared to look at mss without commitment. *Payment* depends on the nature of the article accepted.

News Editor *Michael Parry*

Diary Editor *Ross Benson*
Features Editor *Christopher Williams*
Literary Editor *Peter Grosvenor*
Sports Editor *David Emery*
Women's Page *Cathy Galvin*

The *Daily Express* magazine is *dx* **Editor** *Chris Williams*. A monthly colour magazine distributed in the south of England. (See also **Magazines** section p. 226–7.)

Daily Mail

Northcliffe House, Tudor Street, London EC4Y 0JA

☎01–353 6000　　　　　　Telex 28301

Owner *Lord Rothermere*
Editor *Sir David English*
Circulation 1.81 million

In-house feature writers and regular columnists provide much of the material. Photo-stories and crusading features often appear; it's essential to hit the right note to be a successful Mail writer, so close scrutiny of the paper is strongly advised. Not a good bet for the unseasoned.

News Editor *Tim Miles*

Diary Editor *Nigel Dempster*
Features Editor *Susan Douglas*
Literary Editor *Gordon McKenzie*
Showbiz *Baz Bamigboye*
Sports Editor *Peter Lea*
Women's Page (Femail) *Diana Hutchinson*

Daily Mirror

Holborn Circus, London EC1P 1DQ

☎01–353 0246　　　　　　Telex 27286

Owner *Robert Maxwell*
Editor *Richard Stott*
Circulation 3.1 million

No freelance opportunities for the inexperienced. Strong writers who understand what the tabloid market demands are, however, always needed.

News Editor *Tom Hendry*

Diary Editor *Garth Gibbs*
Features Editor *John Penrose*
Literary Editor *George Thaw*
Sports Editor *Keith Fisher*
Women's Page *Christena Appleyard*

The Daily Telegraph

South Quay Plaza, Marsh Wall, Isle of Dogs, London E14 8NX

☎01–353 4242
Telex 22874 Telenews London

Owner *Daily Telegraph plc*
Editor *Max Hastings*
Circulation 1.2 million

Unsolicited mss not generally welcome – 'all are carefully read and considered, but only about one in a thousand is accepted for publication'. As they receive about 20 weekly, this means about one a year. Contenders should approach the paper in writing making clear their authority for writing on that subject. No fiction.

News Editor *James Allan* Tip-offs or news reports from *bona fide* journalists. Must phone the news desk in first instance. *Words* initial 200. *Payment* minimum £10 (tip)

Arts Editor *Miriam Gross*
Business Editor *Roland Gribben*
Diary Editor *Peter Birkett* Diary pieces always interesting, contact *Peterborough* (Diary column).
Features Editor *Veronica Wadley* By commission from established contributors. However, new writers are tried out by arrangement with the features editor. Approach in writing. *Words* 1500. *Payment* Between £60–£450 and by special arrangement.
Literary Editor *Nicholas Shakespeare*
Sports Editor *Radford Barrett* Occasional opportunities for specialised items.

Evening Standard
PO Box 136, 118 Fleet Street,
London EC4P 4DD
☎01–353 8000   Telex 21909

Owner *Lord Rothermere*
Editor *John Lees*
Circulation 503,811

Long-established and staunchly conservative evening paper serving Londoners with news and feature material. Genuine opportunities for general but particularly London-based features, which abound particularly at the weekend.

News Editor *Philip Evans*

Arts Editor *Michael Owen*

Literary Editor *John Walsh*
London Life *Maggie Alderson*
Londoner's Diary *Richard Addis*
Metro (Thursday, Arts) *John Walsh*
Sports Editor *Michael Hurd*
Weekend *Anne de Courcy*

The *Evening Standard* magazine is *ES*. **Associate Editor** *Jayne Gould*. This monthly magazine is issued with the *Evening Standard*. (See also **Magazines** section, p. 229.)

Financial Times
Bracken House, 10 Cannon Street,
London EC4P 4BY
☎01–248 8000   Telex 8954871

Owner *Pearson plc*
Editor *Geoffrey Owen*
Circulation 307,000

FOUNDED 1888. Business and finance oriented certainly, but by no means as 'featureless' as some suppose. All feature ideas must be discussed with the department's editor in advance, but the FT isn't presently snowed under with unsolicited contributions – they get only about one a week, the lowest of any national newspaper. Approach in writing in the first instance.

News Editor *David Walker*

Arts Editor *J. D. F. Jones*
City/Financial Editor *Barry Riley*
Features Editor *Ian Hargreaves*
Literary Editor *Anthony Curtis*
Sports Editor *Michael Thompson-Noel*
Women's Page *Lucia van der Post*

The Guardian
119 Farringdon Road, London EC1R 3ER
☎01–278 2332   Telex 8811746

Owner *Guardian Trust*
Editor *Peter Preston*
Circulation 460,000

Still settling in after a radical revamp. Probably the greatest opportunities for freelance writers of all the nationals, if only because it has the greatest number of specialised pages which use freelance work. But mss should be directed at a specific slot.

News Editor *Paul Johnson* No opportunities except in those regions where there is presently no local contact for news stories.

'Computer Guardian' Editor *Jack Schofield* A major part of Thursday's paper, almost all written by freelancers. Expertise essential – but not a trade page, written for 'the interested man in the street', and from the user's point of view. Prefer delivery of mss by disk or electronic mail.
Diary *Andrew Moncur*
Education Editor *John Fairhall* Expert pieces on modern education (covers many pages of Tuesday's paper).
Features Editor *Richard Gott* Receive up to 30 unsolicited mss a day; these are passed on to relevant page editors.
'Grassroots' Editor *John Course* Manchester based 'forum' page dealing with a wide variety of subjects: 'the only rule of thumb is, nothing to do with London', and ordinarily not by London writers. However, the page is heavily oversubscribed; probably only 1% of contributions are successful.
'Guardian Tomorrow' Editor *Ann Shearer* Social welfare, psychology and theology, both academic and popular. Experts who write well rather than journalists. Forward looking, offbeat. Maximum of twelve pieces weekly.
Media Editor *Peter Fiddick* Approximately 4 pieces a week plus diary. Outside contributions are considered. All aspects of modern media, advertising, PR, consumer trends in arts/entertainments. Background insight important. Best approach: note followed by phone call.
People *Stuart Wavell* Contributions should be 'offbeat, humorous, topical'. Phone first.
Women *Brenda Polan* After the revamp now has 'Women's Page' every day. This includes 'Guardian Style', 'First Person', 'Third Person', 'Choices'. Unsolicited mss used if they show an appreciation of the page in question.

The Independent
40 City Road, London EC1Y 2DB
☎01–253 1222   Telex 9419611

Owner *Newspapers Publishing plc*
Editor *Andreas Whittam Smith*
Circulation 361,000

FOUNDED October 1986, the first new quality national in over 130 years, and the first newspaper to be very precisely targeted and researched before its launch. Aimed at a professional/office working readership, better educated and more affluent than their parents, the label 'the first yuppie newspaper' is not without justification. The content is geared towards those who only have time to dip into a paper at odd times during the day. Particularly strong on its arts/media coverage. The paper has a high proportion of feature material, and theoretically opportunities for freelancers are good. However, unsolicited mss are not welcome; most pieces originate in-house or from known and trusted outsiders. Ideas should be submitted in writing.

News Editor *Jonathan Fenby*

Arts Editor *Thomas Sutcliffe*
Business Editor *Sarah Hogg*
Diary Editor *Francis Wheen*
Features Editor *John Morrison*
Literary Editor *Sebastian Faulks*
Sports Editor *Charles Burgess*

The Mail on Sunday
Northcliffe House, Tudor Street
London EC4Y 0JA
☎01–353 6000   Telex 28372

Owner *Lord Rothermere*
Editor *Stewart Steven*
Circulation 1.9 million

Sunday paper with a high proportion of newsy features and articles. Experience and judgement required to break into its band of regular feature writers.

News Editor *John Ryan*

Arts Editor *John Butterworth*

Diary *Nigel Dempster*
Features Editor *Sue Reid*
Literary Editor *Paula Johnson*
Sports Editor *Ken Haskell*

The colour supplement is *You Magazine*. **Editor** *Nicholas Gordon*. Many feature articles are supplied entirely by freelance writers. (See also **Magazines** section, p. 285–6.)

Morning Star

75 Farringdon Road, London EC1M 3JX
☎01–405 9242   Telex 916463

Editor *Tony Chater*
Circulation 28,749

Not to be confused with *The Star* (formerly the *Daily Star*), the *Morning Star* is our farthest left national daily. Those with a penchant for a Marxist reading of events and ideas can try their luck, though feature space is as competitive here as in the other nationals.

News Editor *Roger Bagley*

Arts Editor *John Blevin*
Features Editor *John Blevin*
Literary Editor *Helen Bennett*
Sports Editor *Tony Braisby*
Women's Page *Helen Bennett*

The News of the World

1 Virginia Street, London E1 9XR
☎01–481 4100   Telex 262136

Owner *News International – Rupert Murdoch*
Editor *Wendy Henry*
Circulation 5.1 million

Highest circulation paper. Wendy Henry, who is just thirty-four, is the first female national newspaper editor. She is said to be tough, dynamic and unshockable.

News Editor *Robert Warren*

Diary *Paul Connew*
Entertainments *Ivan Waterman*
Features Editor *Paul Connew*
Literary Editor *Roy Stockdill*
Sports Editor *Bill Bateson*

Women's Page *Unity Hall*

The News of the World magazine is *Sunday*. **Editor** *Colin Jenkins* FOUNDED 1981, this weekly colour supplement magazine welcomes freelance writers' ideas and material. (See also **Magazines** section, p. 271.)

The Observer

Chelsea Bridge House, Queenstown Road, London SW8 4NN
☎01–627 0700   Telex 772532

Owner *Lonhro plc*
Editor *Donald Trelford*
Circulation 764.000

FOUNDED 1791. WEEKLY. Occupies the middle ground of Sunday newspaper politics. Unsolicited mss are not generally welcome, 'except from distinguished, established writers'. Receives too many unsolicited offerings. No news, fiction, or 'special pages' opportunities. However, Features concede that 'occasional opportunities' arise.

News Editor *Robin Lustig*

Arts/Features Editor *Nicholas Wapshott*
Business Editor *Melvyn Marckus*
Diary Editor *Tim Walker*
Literary Editor *Blake Morrison*
Sports Editor *Robert Low*
Women's Page *Anne Barr*

The Observer magazine is *M* **Editor** *Angela Gordon*. Freelance writers are used extensively, but an experienced and comprehensive pool of writers. (See also **Magazines** section, p. 247.)

The Star

121 Fleet Street, London EC4P 4JT
☎01–353 8000   Telex 21841

Owner *United Newspapers plc*
Editor *Brian Hitchen*
Circulation 1,278,058

Recently in competition with *The Sun* for 'most flesh and least hard news' title. Now returning to family fare to halt slide in circulation. Freelance opportunities almost non-existent. Few features and both these and news coverage supplied in-house or from regular outsiders.

News Editor *David Mertens*

Diary *Peter Tory*
Entertainments *Patt Codd*
Features Editor *Jill Guyte*
Sports Editor *J. Pyke*
Women's Page *Alix Palmer*

The Sun

1 Pennington Street, London E1 9BD
☎01–481 4100   Telex 267827

Owner *News International – Rupert Murdoch*
Editor *Kelvin Mackenzie*
Circulation 4,049,991

Highest circulation daily newspaper. Right wing populist outlook; very keen on gossip, pop stars, tv soap, scandals and exposés of all kinds. Not much room for feature writers; 'investigative journalism' of a certain hue is always in demand, however. Top of Press Councils Complaints League for 1987.

News Editor *Tom Petrie*

Entertainments *Nick Ferrari*
Features Editor *Gerry Holmberg*
Sports Editor *David Balmforth*
Women's Page *Martin Dunn*

Sunday Express

121 Fleet Street, London EC4P 4JT
☎01–353 8000   Telex 21841

Owner *United Newspapers plc*
Editor *Robin Esser*
Circulation 2.2 million

FOUNDED 1918. Unsolicited mss are generally welcome. Prefer to be approached in writing with an idea. One of that rare breed, a newspaper which still uses fiction. *Payment* by arrangement.

News Editor *Henry Macrory* Occasional news features by experienced journalists only. All submissions must be preceded by ideas. *Words* 750.

Diary Editor *Lady Olga Maitland*
Features Editor *Max Davidson* General features *Words* 1000. Profiles of personalities *Words* 900. Showbiz features *Words* 1000–1500.
Fiction Editor *Max Davidson* Short stories of around 1800 words.
Literary Editor *Graham Lord*
Women's Page *Veronica Papworth*

The weekly *Sunday Express Magazine* **Editor** *Dee Nolan*, does not welcome unsolicited mss. (See also **Magazines** section, p. 271.)

Sunday Mirror

Mirror Group Newspapers, 33 Holborn, London EC1P 1DQ
☎01–353 0246   Telex 27286

Owner *Robert Maxwell*
Editor *Eve Pollard*
Circulation 2.9 million

Eve Pollard's husband, Nick Lloyd, is editor of *The Daily Express*.

The *Sunday Mirror* receives anything up to 90 unsolicited mss weekly. In general terms, these are welcome, though the paper patiently points out it has 'more time for contributors who have taken the trouble to study the market'. Initial contact in writing preferred, unless 'a live news situation'. No fiction.

News Editor *Wensley Clarkson* The news desk is very much in the market for tip-offs and inside information. Contributors would be expected to work with staff writers on news stories.

Arts Editor *Madeleine Harmsworth*
Features Editor *Robert Wilson* 'Anyone who has obviously studied the market will be dealt with constructively and courteously.' Cherishes its record as a breeding ground for new talent.
Literary and Diary Editor *Peter Miller*
Sports Editor *Anthony Smith*
Women's Page *Frankie McGowan*

The Sunday People

Orbit House, New Fetter Lane,
London EC4A 1AR
☎01–353 0246   Telex 888963

Owner *Robert Maxwell*
Editor *Ernest Burrington*
Circulation 2.9 million

Slightly up-market version of *The News of the World*. Keen on exposés and big name gossip.

News Editor *P. J. Wilson*

Arts Editor *Maurice Krais*
Diary *Frank Jeffery*
Features Editor *John Smith*
Sports Editor *N. Holtham*
Women's Page *John Smith*

Sunday Sport

50 Eagle Wharf Road, London N1 7ED
☎01–251 2544   Telex 269277 SSPORTG

Owner *David Sullivan*
Editor *John Bull*
Circulation 400,000

FOUNDED 1986. Sunday tabloid catering for a particular sector of the male 18–35 readership. As concerned with 'glamour' (for which, read page 3) as with human interest, news features and sport. Unsolicited mss are welcome; they apparently receive about 90 a week. Approach should be made by phone in the case of news and sports items, by letter for features. No fiction. *Payment* is negotiable, agreed in advance and made on publication.

News Editor *Rab Anderson* Offbeat news, human interest, preferably with photographs.

Features Editor *Sue Blackhall* Regular items: 'Glamour', Showbiz and television, as well as general interest.
Sports Editor *Tony Flood* Hardhitting sports stories on major soccer clubs and their personalities, and leading clubs and people in other sports. Strong quotations to back up the news angle essential.

Sunday Telegraph

Peterborough Court, South Quay,
181 Marsh Wall, London E14 9SR
☎01–538 5000

Owner *Conrad Black*
Editor *Peregrine Worsthorne*
Circulation 739,000

Right of centre quality Sunday paper (meaning it has the least tendency to bend its ear to the scandals of the hour). Traditionally starchy and correct, it is in the process of trying to pep up its image and attract a younger readership.

News Editor *Graham Paterson*

Arts Editor *Derwent May*
Diary *Kenneth Rose*
Features Editor *Denis Pilgrim*
Literary Editor *Derwent May*
Sports Editor *David Grice*

The weekly magazine supplement is the *Telegraph Sunday Magazine*. (See also **Magazines** section, p. 272.)

The Sunday Times

1 Pennington Street,
Wapping, London E1 9BD
☎01–481 4100   Telex 262139

Owner *News International – Rupert Murdoch*
Editor *Andrew Neil*
Circulation 1.3 million

FOUNDED 1820. Generally right of centre with a strong crusading, investigative tradition. Unsolicited mss are always welcome, especially on the features pages, which are, by virtue of the sheer size of the newspaper, more extensive than other papers. Approach the relevant editor with an idea in writing. Close scrutiny of the style of each section of the paper is strongly advised before sending mss. No fiction. All fees by negotiation.

News Editor *Andrew Hogg* Opportunities are very rare.

Arts Editor *John Whitley*
Business Editor *Roger Eglin*

Atticus (Political Diary) *Michael Jones*
Entertainments Editor *Patrick Stoddart*
Features Editor *Robin Morgan* Submissions
are always welcome, but the paper commis-
sions its own, uses staff writers or works
with literary agents, by and large. The fea-
tures sections where most opportunities
exist are 'Screen', 'Look', 'Leisure' and
'Spectrum'.
Literary Editor *Penny Perrick*
Look Editor (includes Women's/Beauty/
Fashion) *Liz Jobey*
Review Editor *David Sinclair*

Distributed with *The Sunday Times* is the
weekly colour supplement *The Sunday Times
Magazine.* Editor *Philip Clarke.* (See also
Magazines section, p. 271.)

The Times

1 Pennington Street, London E1 9BD
☎01−481 4100   Telex 262141

Owner *News International − Rupert Murdoch*
Editor *Charles Wilson*
Circulation 447,000

Generally right (though columns/features
can range in tone from diehard to libertar-
ian). *The Times* receives a great many unsolicited offerings. Writers with feature ideas
should approach by letter in the first instance. No fiction.

Arts Editor *John Higgins*
Business Editor *Kenneth Fleet*
Diary Editor *Rosemary Unsworth*
Features Editor *Nicholas Brett*
Home News Editor *John Jinks* Approach by
phone.
Literary Editor *Philip Howard*
Sports Editor *Tom Clarke*

Today

Allen House, 70 Vauxhall Bridge Road,
Pimlico, London SW1V 2RP
☎01−630 1300   Telex 919925

Owner *News UK Ltd*
Editor *David Montgomery*
Circulation 339,000

The first of the new technology papers. Originally middle-of-the-road but now under
Rupert Murdoch, turning sharply to the
right. Feature opportunities look to be declining fast.

News Editor *Colin Myler*

Business Editor *Jonathan Hunt*
Entertainments Editor *Paul Donovan*
Features Editor *Sue Ryan*
Sports Editor *Colin Mafham*
Weekend Editor *Bill Hagerty*
Women's Page *Sue Ryan*

Regional Newspapers

Regional newspapers are listed in alphabetical order by town or county. Thus the *Daily Record* appears under 'G' for Glasgow.

Aberdeen

Evening Express

PO Box 43, Lang Stracht,
Mastrick, Aberdeen AB9 8AF
☎0224 690222

Owner *Thomson Regional Newspapers*
Editor *Richard J. Williamson*
Circulation 80,000

Unsolicited mss welcome 'but if possible on a controlled basis'. Receive up to four a week.

News Editor *David Smith* Freelance news contributors welcome.

Features Editor *Moreen Simpson* Women, Fashion, Showbiz, Health, Hobbies, Property – anything will be considered on its merits. *Payment* £30–40.

The Press & Journal

PO Box 43, Lang Stracht,
Mastrick, Aberdeen AB9 8AF
☎0224 690222   Telex 73133

Owner *Thomson Regional Newspapers*
Editor *Harry Roulston*
Circulation 110,000

A well-established regional daily (approaching its 240th year) which receives more unsolicited mss a week than the *Sunday Mirror* – about 120 on average. Unsolicited mss are nevertheless welcome; approach should be made in writing. No fiction.

News Editor *Eric Stevenson* Wide variety of hard or offbeat news items, relating to 'the northern half of Scotland'. *Words* 500. *Payment* by arrangement.

Features Editor *Norman Harper* Tightly written topical pieces, preferably with a Scottish flavour. *Words* 1000. *Payment* by arrangement.

Basildon

Evening Echo

Newspaper House, Chester Hall Lane,
Basildon, Essex SS1 3BL
☎0268 22792

Owner *Westminster Press*
Editor *J. J. Worsdale*
Circulation 60,000

Rely almost entirely on staff/regular writers' contributions, but will consider material sent on spec. Approach the editor in writing.

Bath

Bath & West Evening Chronicle

33 Westgate Street,
Bath, Avon BA1 1EZ
☎0225 63051

Owner *Wessex Newspapers*
Editor *David Flintham*
Circulation 27,188

News Editor *Simon Whitby*

Diary Editor *Simon Toft*
Features Editor *David Hamlett*
Women's Page *Tina Currie*

Belfast

Belfast Telegraph

Royal Avenue, Belfast BT1 1EB
☎0232 321242

Owner *Thomson Regional Newspapers*
Editor *Roy Lilley*
Circulation 150,000

News Editor *Norman Jenkinson*

Features Editor *Tom Carson*
Women's Page *Lindy McDowell* Plus colour
supplement 4 times yearly.

The Irish News
Donegall Street, Belfast BT1 2GE
☎0232 242614

Editor *Jim Fitzpatrick*
Circulation 42,439

News Editor *Noel Russell*

Features Editor *Dave Culbert*
Women's Page *Anne Donegan*

News Letter
Donegall Street, Belfast BT1 2GB
☎0232 244441

Owner *Century Newspapers Ltd*
Editor *Sam Butler*
Circulation 44,483

News Editor *Harry Robinson*

Arts Editor *Theo Snoddy*
Features Editor *Harry Robinson*
Women's Page *Niki Hill* Also 6 issues a year
of supplement *Accent*.

Birmingham
Birmingham Daily News
78 Francis Road, Edgbaston,
Birmingham B16 8SP
☎021–454 8800

Owner *Reed International*
Editor *Malcolm Ward*
Circulation 341,000

FOUNDED 1984. Britain's first free daily newspaper. Unsolicited mss generally welcome.
Approach the editor in writing in the first
instance.

News Editor *Claire Wolfe*

Birmingham Evening Mail
28 Colmore Circus, Queensway,
Birmingham B4 6AX
☎021–236 3366

Owner *The Birmingham Post & Mail Ltd*
Editor *Ian Dowell*
Circulation 287,554

Features Editor *Dan Mason*
Women's Page *Barbara Henderson*
Freelance contributions are welcome, particularly topics of interest to the West Midlands and Women's Page pieces offering
original and lively comment.

The Birmingham Post
28 Colmore Circus, Queensway,
Birmingham B4 6AX
☎021–236 3366

Owner *The Birmingham Post & Mail Ltd*
Editor *Peter Saunders*
Circulation 28,500

One of the leading regional newspapers.
Freelance contributions are welcome.

News Editor *Nigel Pipkin*

Features Editor *Jonathan Daumler-Ford*
Women's Page Editor *Barbara Henderson*
Particularly welcomes topics of interest to
the West Midlands and Women's Page pieces
offering original and lively comment.

Sunday Mercury
Colmore Circus, Birmingham B4 6AZ
☎021–236 3366

Editor *John Bradbury*
Circulation 168,024

News Editor *Bob Haywood*

Features Editor *Peter Whitehouse*

Blackburn
Lancashire Evening Telegraph
New Telegraph House, High Street,
Blackburn, Lancs BB1 1HT
☎0254 63588

Owner *Thomson Regional Newspapers*
Editor *Peter R. Butterfield*
Circulation 54,951

Both news stories and feature material with an East Lancashire flavour welcome. Approach in writing with an idea in the first instance. No fiction.

News Editor *David Allin*

Features Editor *Neil Preston* Either a local angle or written by a local person.

Blackpool

West Lancashire Evening Gazette
PO Box 20, Preston New Road,
Blackpool, Lancs FY4 4VA
☎ 0253 66136

Owner *United Newspapers*
Editor *Brian Hargreaves*
Circulation 53,500

In theory unsolicited mss are welcome. Approach the editor in writing with an idea.

Bolton

Bolton Evening News
Newspaper House, Churchgate, Bolton,
Greater Manchester BL1 1HU
☎ 0204 22345

Owner *Northern Counties Newspapers*
Editor *Chris Walder*
Circulation 54,578

News Editor *Melvyn Horrocks*

Features Editor *Derrick Grocock*
Women's Page *Angela Kelly*

Bournemouth

Evening Echo
Richmond Hill, Bournemouth BH2 6HH
☎ 0202 24601

Owner *Southern Newspapers plc*
Editor *W. M. Hill*
Circulation 58,000

FOUNDED 1900. DAILY. Unsolicited mss welcome, but the needs of the paper are special-ised and the rejection rate is high. Receive and use a large number of features from established agencies. Ideas in writing, rather than by phone. Prefer to see finished copy, or well thought out suggestions backed up by evidence of writing ability.

News Editor *Ray Horsfield* Few opportunities.

Features Editor *Allan Bannister*
Fiction Opportunities rare; fiction may be considered if topical.

Bradford

Telegraph & Argus
Hall Ings, Bradford BD1 1JR
☎ 0274 729511

Owner *Westminster Press*
Editor *Terry Quinn*
Circulation 83,000

Unsolicited mss not welcome. Approach in writing with samples of work. No fiction.

News Editor/Features Editor *Neil Benson* Local features and general interest. Showbiz pieces. *Words* 600–1000, max. 1500. *Payment* NUJ rates for members; negotiable for others.

Brighton

Evening Argus
89 North Road, Brighton, Sussex BN1 4AU
☎ 0273 606799

Owner *Westminster Press*
Editor *Terry Page*
Circulation 99,275

News Editor *Chris Oswick*

Deputy Editor (features) *Chris Fowler*

Bristol

Bristol Evening Post
Bristol United Press, Temple Way,
Old Market, Bristol BS99 7HD
☎ 0272 20080

Owner *Bristol United Press*
Editor *Brian Jones*
Circulation 113,304

Unsolicited mss welcome; they get around a dozen a week. Approach in writing with ideas.

Western Daily Press
Temple Way, Bristol BS99 7HD
☎0272 20080

Owner *Bristol United Press*
Editor *Ian Beales*
Circulation 70,000

News Editor *Peter Gibbs*

Features Editor *Derek Whitfield*

Burton upon Trent
Burton Mail
65–68 High Street,
Burton upon Trent, Staffs DE14 1LE
☎0283 512345

Editor *Brian Vertigen*
Circulation 22,000

Cambridge
Cambridge Evening News
51 Newmarket Road, Cambridge CB5 8EJ
☎0223 358877

Owner *Cambridge Newspapers Ltd*
Editor *Robert Satchwell*
Circulation 47,003

News Editor *Peter Wells*

Features Editor *Rodney Tibbs*

Cardiff
South Wales Echo
Thomson House, Cardiff CF1 1WR
☎0222 223333

Owner *Thomson Regional Newspapers*
Editor *Geoffrey Rich*
Circulation 100,704

News Editor *Stuart Minton*

Features Editor *Alan Gathergood*
Women's Page *Jenny Longhurst*

Western Mail
Thomson House, Cardiff CF1 1WR
☎0222 223333

Owner *Thomson Regional Newspapers*
Editor *John Humphries*
Circulation 78,500

Mss welcome if of a topical nature, and preferably of Welsh interest. No short stories or travel. Approach in writing to the features editor, who receives between 5 and 10 mss daily.

News Editor *Denis Gane*

Features Editor *Gareth Jenkins* 'Usual subjects already well covered, e.g. motoring, travel, books, gardening. We look for the unusual.' Maximum 1000 words. *Payment* dependent on quality and importance. Also opportunities on **Femail** women's page, and **That's Entertainment** television previews and interviews.

Carlisle
Evening News & Star
Newspaper House, Dalston Road,
Carlisle CA2 5UA
☎0228 23488

Owner *Cumbrian Newspapers Group Ltd*
Editor *J. Vernon Addison*

News Editor *Steve Johnston*

Features Editor *Keith Richardson*

Colchester
Evening Gazette
43–44 North Hill, Colchester, Essex CO1 1TZ
☎0206 761212

Owner *Essex County Newspapers*
Editor *Ken Runicles*
Circulation 32,500

Unsolicited mss not generally used, as 'we rely on regular contributors' and don't receive very many.

News Editor *Dick Lumsden*

Features Editor *Kelvin Brown*

Coventry

Coventry Evening Telegraph

Corporation Street, Coventry CV1 1FP
☎0203 633633

Owner *Coventry Newspapers Ltd*
Editor *Geoffrey Elliott*
Circulation 95,000

Recently bought by Ralph Ingersoll, American press baron. Unsolicited mss are read, but few are published. Approach in writing with an idea. No fiction. **Features** maximum 600 words. *Payment* £25–30. All unsolicited material should be addressed to the editor.

Darlington

The Northern Echo

Priestgate, Darlington,
Co. Durham DL1 1NF
☎0325 381313

Owner *North of England Newspapers*
Editor *Allan Prosser*
Circulation 90,000

FOUNDED 1870. DAILY. Freelance pieces welcome if arranged by telephone first.

News Editor *Rachel Compey* Reports involving the North–East or North Yorkshire. Preferably phoned in. *Words* and *payment* by negotiation.

Celebrity interviews *S. Pratt*
Features Editor *Trevor Willis* Background pieces to topical news stories relevant to the area. Must be arranged with the features editor before submission of any material. *Words* and *payment* by negotiation. **Fiction** Serialisation of best-sellers only. **Holiday Pages/ Supplements** *D. Kelly* **Local industrial reports** *Terry Murden* **Special Pages** *Words* and *payment* by arrangement. **Sports Features** *M. Howey*

Derby

Derby Evening Telegraph

Northcliffe House, Derby DE1 2DW
☎0332 291111

Owner *Northcliffe Newspapers*
Editor *Neil Fowler*

News Editor *Stan Szecowka*

Features Editor *Chris Ward*

Devon

Herald Express

Harmsworth House, Barton Hill Road,
Torquay TQ1 1BD
☎0803 213213

Owner *Western Times Co Ltd*
Editor *J. C. Mitchell*
Circulation 30,000

Unsolicited mss generally not welcome. Receive about 2 dozen a year. Approach the editor in writing.

Doncaster

Doncaster Star

40 Duke Street, Doncaster DN1 3EA
☎0302 344001

Editor *Adrian Taylor*

Dorset

Dorset Evening Echo

57 St Thomas Street,
Weymouth, Dorset DT4 8EQ
☎0305 784804

Owner *Southern Newspapers plc*
Editor *Michael Woods*
Circulation 23,459

News Editor *Paul Thomas*

Dundee

Dundee Courier and Advertiser

7 Bank Street, Dundee DD1 9HU
☎0382 23131

Editor *Iain Stewart*

Features Editor *Eddy McLaren*
News Editor *Irene Rowe*
Women's Page *Sandra Young*
Welcome features on a wide variety of subjects, not only of local/Scottish interest. Two pages devoted to features each weekend, supplied by freelancers and in-house. Also Women's Page/Thursday Pop Page. Only rule of thumb: keep it short. *Words* 500 max. Very occasionally publish fiction.

Evening Telegraph & Post
7 Bank Street, Dundee DD1 9HU
☎0382 23131

Editor *Harold Pirie*
Circulation 48,395

News Editor *Alan Proctor* All material should be addressed to the editor.

East Anglia

East Anglian Daily Times
See under *Ipswich*

Eastern Daily Press
See under *Norwich*

Eastern Evening News
See under *Norwich*

Edinburgh

Evening News
20 North Bridge, Edinburgh EH1 1YT
☎031–225 2468   Telex 72255/727600

Owner *Thomson Regional Newspapers*
Editor *Ian A. Nimmo*
Circulation 123,000

FOUNDED 1873. DAILY. Unsolicited feature material welcome. Approach by telephone call to appropriate department head.

News Editor *Douglas Middleton* NUJ only.

Features Editor *Bill Clapperton* Features for 'Weekender' magazine supplement of broad

general interest/historical interest. Occasionally run 'Platform' pieces (i.e. sounding off, topical or opinion pieces). *Words* 1000. *Payment* NUJ/House rates.

The Scotsman
20 North Bridge, Edinburgh EH1 1YT
☎031–225 2468

Editor *Magnus Linklater*
Circulation 98,863

Despite its smallish circulation, a national Scottish newspaper of quality. Conservative in outlook, it vies with the *Glasgow Herald* for the top dog position in the Scottish press. Many unsolicited mss come in, and stand a good chance of being read, although a small army of regulars supply much of the feature material not written in-house.

News Editor *James Seaton*

Senior Assistant Editor (features) *Ruth Wishart* The features page carries a great variety of articles. The 6-page *Weekend* section ditto, including book reviews and travel articles.
Lifestyle Editor *Melanie Reid* Lifestyle replaces the Women's Page. Once weekly (features welcome).

The Scotsman Magazine is a monthly magazine that is issued with the newspaper. **Editor** *Richard Wilson* (See also **Magazines** section, p. 264.)

Exeter

Express & Echo
160 Sidwell Street, Exeter, Devon EX4 6SB
☎0392 73051

Editor *John Budworth*
Circulation 36,210

News Editor *Mike Byrne*

Glasgow

Daily Record
Anderston Quay, Glasgow G3 8DA
☎041–248 7000

Owner *Mirror Group Newspapers*
Editor *Bernard Vickers*
Circulation 763,866

Mass market Scottish tabloid.

News Editor *M. B. Speed*

Features Editor *R. Steel*
Women's Page *Fidelma Cook*

Evening Times
195 Albion Street, Glasgow G1 1QP
☎041–552 6255

Owner *George Outram & Co Ltd*
Editor *George McKechnie*
Circulation 191,910

News Editor *Robbie Wallace*

Features Editor *Ron Clark*
Women's Page *Rosemary Long*

Glasgow Herald
195 Albion Street, Glasgow G1 1QP
☎041–552 6255

Owner *George Outram & Co. Ltd*
Editor *Arnold Kemp*
Circulation 127,636

Lively quality Scottish daily whose readership spreads beyond the city of Glasgow.

Arts Editor *John Fowler*
Business Editor *R. E. Dundas*
Diary *T. Shields*
Features Editor *Raymond Gardner*
Sports *E. Rodger*
Women's Page *Anne Simpson*

Sunday Mail
Anderston Quay, Glasgow G3 8DA
☎041–248 7000

Owner *Scottish Daily Record*
Editor *Endell J. Laird*
Circulation 839,166

Downmarket Scottish Sunday paper.

Features Editor *Archibald McKay*

Sunday Post
144 Port Dundas Road,
Glasgow G4 0HZ
☎041–332 9933

Owner *D. C. Thomson & Co Ltd*
Editor *William Anderson*
Circulation 1,481,640

All material should be sent to the editor.

Features Editor *Brian Wilson*

Gloucester
The Citizen
St John's Lane, Gloucester GL1 2AT
☎0452 424442

Owner *Northcliffe Newspapers*
Editor *Colin Walker*
Circulation 39,685

News Editor *R. Gardiner*

Gloucestershire Echo
1 Clarence Parade,
Cheltenham, Glos. GL50 3NY
☎0242 526261

Owner *Cheltenham Newspaper Co. Ltd*
Editor *Adrian Faber*
Circulation 29,512

News Editor *Tony Shaw*

Greenock
Greenock Telegraph
2 Crawford Street, Greenock PA15 1LH
☎0475 26511

Owner *Orr Pollock & Co Ltd*
Editor *Kenneth Thomson*
Circulation 22,500

Unsolicited mss are considered 'if they relate to the newspaper's general interests'. Don't receive too many. Approach by letter. No fiction.

News Editor *David Carnduff* Regional material only. *Words* 600. *Payment* lineage: 12p per line.

Features Editor *James Hunter* Locally slanted material wanted. *Words* 1500. *Payment* lineage: 12p per line.

Grimsby

Grimsby Evening Telegraph
80 Cleethorpe Road,
Grimsby, South Humberside DN31 3EH
☎ 0472 59232

Owner *Northcliffe Newspapers*
Editor *Peter Moore*
Circulation 75,000*

*Combined with sister paper, *Scunthorpe Evening Telegraph*

In general the *Telegraph* welcomes unsolicited mss. Receives 'not too many'. Approach in writing. No fiction.

News Editor *J. V. McDonagh* Hard news stories welcome. Approach in haste by telephone. No fiction.

Guernsey

Guernsey Evening Press & Star
Braye Road, Vale, Guernsey CI
☎ 0481 45866

Editor *Dave Prigent*
Circulation 16,160

Arts Editor *Peter Witterick*
Features Editor *Peter Witterick*
Women's Page *Jill Chadwick*

Halifax

Evening Courier
PO Box 19, Halifax, West Yorkshire HX1 2SF
☎ 0422 65711

Editor *Edward Riley*
Circulation 37,873

News Editor *Jack Shaw*

Features Editor *William Marshall*

Hartlepool

Hartlepool Mail
Clarence Road, Hartlepool,
County Cleveland TS24 8BX
☎ 0429 274441

Owner *Portsmouth & Sunderland Newspapers Ltd*
Editor *Andrew C. Smith*
Circulation 29,365

Huddersfield

Huddersfield Daily Examiner
Ramsden Street,
Huddersfield, West Yorkshire HD1 2TD
☎ 0484 537444

Editor *Ivan M. Lee*
Circulation 44,118

News Editor *P. D. Hinchcliffe*

Features Editor *Malcolm Cruise*

Hull

Daily Mail
PO Box 34, 84 Jameson Street, Hull HU1 3LF
☎ 0482 27111

Owner *Northcliffe Newspaper Group*
Editor *Michael Wood*
Circulation 107,113

News Editor *Mark Acheson*

Features Editor *Roy Woodcock*
Women's Page *Heather Dixon*

Ipswich

East Anglian Daily Times
30 Lower Brook Street,
Ipswich, Suffolk IP4 1AN
☎ 0473 230023

Owner *East Anglian Daily Times Co Ltd*
Editor *Ken R. Rice*
Circulation 50,000

FOUNDED 1874. DAILY. Unsolicited mss generally unwelcome; 3 or 4 received a week, almost none are used. Prefer to be approached in writing in the first instance. No fiction.

News Editor *David Henshall* Hard news stories involving East Anglia (Suffolk, Essex particularly) or individuals resident in the area are always of interest. *Words* vary. *Payment* NUJ rates.

Features Editor *Cathy Brown* Mostly in-house, but will occasionally buy in when the subject is of strong Suffolk/East Anglian interest. Photo-features preferred (extra payment). *Words* 1000. *Payment* £15. **Special Features pages** *Carmen Moyes* Special advertisement features are regularly run, in for instance 'Home Improvements', 'Holidays', 'Properties of Distinction'. Arranged in liaison with Carmen Moyes. *Words* 1000. *Payment* £20.

Evening Star

30 Lower Brook Street,
Ipswich, Suffolk 1P4 1AN
☎0473 230023

Owner *East Anglian Daily Times Co Ltd*
Editor *Crawford Gillan*
Circulation 36,664

News Editor *David Henshall*

Features Editor *Carol Carver*
Women's Page *Judy Rimmer*

Ireland

The Irish News
See under *Belfast*

Jersey

Jersey Evening Post
Five Oaks, St Saviour, Jersey CI
☎0534 73333

Editor *M. Rumfitt*
Circulation 24,128

News Editor *Philip Jeune*

Features Editor *P. Stuckey*
Women's Page *Elaine Hanning*

Kent

Kent Evening Post
395 High Street, Chatham, Kent ME4 4PG
☎0634 830600

Owner *South Eastern Newspapers Ltd*
Editor *David Jones*
Circulation 26,936

News Editor *John Hammond*

Features Editor *John Nurden*

Kent & Sussex Courier
Longfield Road,
Tunbridge Wells, Kent TN2 3HL
☎0892 26262

Owner *Courier Printing & Publishing Co Ltd*
Editor *William Stengel*

Kent Messenger
Messenger House, New Hythe Lane,
Larkfield, Maidstone, Kent ME20 6SG
☎0622 77880

Owner *Kent Messenger Group*
Editor *John Evans*
Circulation 50,000

Lancashire

Lancashire Evening Post
See under *Preston*

Lancashire Evening Telegraph
See under *Blackburn*

West Lancashire Evening Gazette
See under *Blackpool*

Leamington Spa

Leamington & District Morning News
PO Box 45, Tachbrook Road,
Leamington Spa CV31 3EP
☎0926 21122

Owner *Heart of England Newspaper Group*
Editor *Bruce Harrison*
Circulation 10,950

News Editor *Nikki Lennox*

Leeds

Yorkshire Evening Post
Wellington Street,
Leeds, West Yorkshire LS1 1RF
☎0532 432701

Owner *Yorkshire Post Newspapers Ltd*
Editor *M. G. Barker*
Circulation 150,000

News Editor *Fred Willis*

Diary *Derek Naylor*
Features Editor *Howard Corry*
Women's Page *Anne Patch*

Evening sister of the *Yorkshire Post*.

Yorkshire Post
Wellington Street,
Leeds, West Yorkshire LS1 1RF
☎0532 432701   Telex 55425

Owner *Yorkshire Post Newspapers Ltd*
Editor *John Edwards*
Circulation 92,000

A serious-minded, quality regional daily
with a generally conservative outlook. 3 or 4
unsolicited mss arrive a day; all will be considered. Initial approach in writing preferred. All submissions should be addressed to
the editor. No fiction. **Features** open to suggestions in all fields (though ordinarily commission from specialist writers).

Leicester

Leicester Mercury
St Georges Street, Leicester LE1 9FQ
☎0533 512512

Owner *Northcliffe Newspaper Group*
Editor *Alex Leys*
Circulation 150,000

News Editor *Anita Syuret*

Lincoln

Lincolnshire Echo
Brayford Wharf East, Lincoln LN5 7AY
☎0522 25252

Owner *Northcliffe Newspaper Group*
Editor *Cliff Smith*
Circulation 34,513

News Editor *Alan Whitt*

Liverpool

Daily Post
PO Box 48, Old Hall Street,
Liverpool L69 3EB
☎051-227 2000   Telex 629396

Owner *Liverpool Daily Post & Echo Ltd*
Editor *John Griffith*
Circulation 75,000

Unsolicited mss welcome. Receive about six a
day. Approach in writing with an idea. No
fiction.

News Editor *Neil Maxwell*

Features Editor *Peter Surridge* Local,
national and international news, current
affairs, profiles – with pictures. *Words* 800–
1000. *Payment* £30–50.

Liverpool Echo
PO Box 48, Old Hall Street,
Liverpool L69 3EB
☎051-227 2000   Telex 629396

Owner *Liverpool Daily Post & Echo Ltd*
Editor *Chris Oakley*
Circulation 207,489

One of the major regional dailies. Unsolicited
mss welcome; they receive on average 20 a
week. Prefer to be approached in writing
first.

News Editor *Joe Holmes*

Features Editor *Carolyn Taylor*. *Words* 1000.

London

Evening Standard
See **National Newspapers**, p. 177.

Manchester

Manchester Evening News

164 Deansgate, Manchester M60 2RD
☎061–832 7200   Telex 668920

Owner *Manchester Evening News Ltd*
Editor *Michael Unger*
Circulation 313,000

One of the major regional dailies. Unsolicited mss are welcome. Initial approach in writing preferred. No news or fiction opportunities.

Features Editor *Ken Wood* Personality pieces and showbiz profiles particularly welcome. *Words* 1000. *Payment* by negotiation.

Middlesbrough

Evening Gazette

Borough Road, Middlesbrough,
Cleveland TS1 3AZ
☎0642 245401

Owner *Thomson Regional Newspapers*
Editor *David James*
Circulation 78,733

News Editor *Graham Marples*

Features Editor *David Whinyates*
Women's Page *Christine Lane*

Newcastle upon Tyne

Evening Chronicle

Thomson House, Groat Market,
Newcastle upon Tyne,
Tyne and Wear NE1 1ED
☎091–232 7500

Owner *Thomson Regional Newspapers*
Editor *Graeme Stanton*
Circulation 142,479

The *Evening Chronicle* receive 'an awful lot' of unsolicited material, much of which they can't use. Approach initially in writing.

News Editor *John Ritson*

Features Editor *Ian Wilson* Limited opportunities due to full-time feature staff. Maximum 1000 words.
Sports Editor *John Gibson*

The Journal

Thomson House, Groat Market,
Newcastle upon Tyne NE1 1ED
☎091–232 7500

Owner *Thomson Regional Newspapers*
Editor *Christopher Cox*
Circulation 66,106

News Editor *Tom Patterson*

Features Editor *Norman Davison*
Women's Page *Avril Deane*

Sunday Sun

Thomson House, Groat Market,
Newcastle upon Tyne NE1 1ED
☎091–232 7500

Owner *Thomson Regional Newspapers*
Editor *Jim Buglass*
Circulation 125,058

News Editor *Alistair Baker* All material should be sent to him.

Newport

South Wales Argus

Cardiff Road, Maesglas,
Newport, Gwent NP9 1QW
☎0633 810000

Editor *Steve Hoselitz*
Circulation 42,385

News Editor *Peter John*

Features Editor *Gerry Thurston*
Women's Page *Josephine Type*

The North of England

The Northern Echo

See under *Darlington*

Northampton

Chronicle and Echo

Upper Mounts, Northampton NN1 3HR
☎0604 231122

Owner *Northampton Mercury*
Editor *Philip Green*
Circulation 42,000

Unsolicited mss are 'not necessarily unwelcome but opportunities to use them are rare'. Some 3 or 4 arrive weekly. Approach in writing with an idea. No fiction.

News Editor *Mrs J. Oldfield*

Features Editor *Chris Hilsden*

Northamptonshire Evening Telegraph
Northfield Avenue,
Kettering, Northants NN16 9JN
☎0536 81111

Owner *EMAP*
Editor *Paul Deal*
Circulation 42,804

News Editor *Ian Donaldson*

Arts Editor *Anne Bratley*
Features Editor *Lester Cowling*
Women's Page *Fiona Fitzgibbon*

Northcliffe Newspapers Group Ltd
Editorial Department, 31–32 John Street,
London WC1N 2QB
☎01–242 7070

Editor *Bill Sneyd*

Central editorial office of the regional papers belonging to the group: *The Citizen* (Gloucester); *Daily Mail* (Hull); *Derby Evening Telegraph*; *Evening Herald* (Plymouth); *Evening Sentinel* (Stoke); *Express & Echo* (Exeter); *Glos. Echo* (Cheltenham); *Grimsby Evening Telegraph*; *Herald Express* (Devon); *Leicester Mercury*; *Lincolnshire Echo*; *Scunthorpe Evening Telegraph*; *South Wales Evening Post* and *Kent & Sussex Courier*. See separate listings for details.

Norwich

Eastern Daily Press
Prospect House, Rouen Road,
Norwich NR1 1RE
☎0603 628311   Telex 975276

Owner *Eastern Counties Newspapers*
Editor *L. Sear*
Circulation 92,000

Unsolicited mss welcome. Approach in writing. News if relevant to Norfolk. Features up to 900 words. Other pieces by commission. Submissions and suggestions to the editor.

Eastern Evening News
Prospect House, Rouen Road,
Norwich, Norfolk NR1 1RE
☎0603 628311

Owner *Eastern Counties Newspapers*
Editor *Peter Ware*
Circulation 51,857

News Editor *Paul Durrant*

Features Editor *James Ruddy*

Nottingham

Nottingham Evening Post
Forman Street, Nottingham NG1 4AB
☎0602 482000   Telex 377884

Owner *T. Bailey Forman Ltd*
Editor *Barrie Williams*
Circulation 136,000

Unsolicited mss welcome. Send ideas in writing.

Features Editor *Tony Moss* Good local interest only. Maximum 800 words. No fiction.
Special Pages *Tony Moss*

Nuneaton

Evening Tribune
Watling House, Whitacre Road,
Nuneaton, Warwicks CV11 6BJ
☎0203 382251

Owner *Watling Publications Ltd*
Editor *Roger Jeffrey*
Circulation 13,500

All material to be addressed to the editor.

Oldham

Oldham Evening Chronicle

172 Union Street,
Oldham, Lancs OL1 1EQ
☎061–633 2121

Owner *Hirst Kidd & Rennie Ltd*
Editor *Gordon Maxwell*
Circulation 42,000

'We welcome the good but not the bad'. Receive two or three mss weekly.

News Editor *Jim Williams*

Features Editor *Robert Morton* Humour, travel, local history and the unusual. Maximum 1500 words. *Payment* £15–20.

Oswestry

Evening Leader

Caxton Press, Oswald Road,
Oswestry, Salop SY11 1RB
☎0691 655321

Owner *North Wales Newspapers*
Editor *Reg Herbert*

News Editor *Steven Rogers*

Features Editor *Jeremy Smith*
Women's Page *Gail Cooper*

Oxford

Oxford Mail

Osney Mead, Oxford OX2 0EJ
☎0865 244988

Owner *Oxford & County Newspapers*
Editor *Edward Duller*
Circulation 39,970

Unsolicited mss are considered; a great many unsuitable offerings are received. Approach in writing with an idea rather than phoning. No fiction. All fees negotiable.

News Editor *J. Chipperfield* Phone first.

Features Editor *Jon Hartridge* Any features of topical or historical significance. *Words* maximum 800.

Paisley

Paisley Daily Express

14 New Street,
Paisley, Scotland PA1 1XY
☎041–887 7911

Owner *Scottish & Universal Newspapers*
Editor *Murray Stevenson*
Circulation 13,000

Unsolicited mss welcome only if of genuine Paisley interest. The paper does not commission work, and will consider submitted material: 'we are more in the business of encouraging amateur writers on local topics than professionals. The budget does not extend to "scale" fees'. *Words* 1000–1500. *Payment* maximum £25. All submissions to the editor.

Peterborough

Peterborough Evening Telegraph

Telegraph House, 57 Priestgate,
Peterborough PE1 1JW
☎0733 555111

Owner *EMAP*
Editor *David Rowell*
Circulation 33,500

Unsolicited mss not welcome. Approaches should be made in writing.

Plymouth

Evening Herald

Leicester Harmsworth House,
65 New George Street,
Plymouth, Devon PL1 1RE
☎0752 266626

Owner *Western Morning News Co Ltd*
Editor *Alan Cooper*
Circulation 60,413

News Editor *Roger Clift*

All material to be addressed to the editor or news editor.

Sunday Independent

Burrington Way, Plymouth PL5 3LN
☎0752 777151

Owner *West of England Newspapers Ltd*
Editor *John Noble*

Portsmouth

The News

The News Centre, Hilsea,
Portsmouth PO2 9SX
☎0705 664488   Telex 86316

Owner *Portsmouth Printing & Publishing Ltd*
Editor *R. C. C. Poulton*
Circulation 100,000

Unsolicited mss not generally welcome. Approach by letter.

News Editor *Chris Owen*

Features Editor *Keith Ridley* General subjects of SE Hants interest. Maximum 600 words. No fiction.
Sports Editor *Chris Erskine* Sports background features. Maximum 600 words.

Preston

Lancashire Evening Post

127 Fishergate, Preston, Lancs PR1 2DN
☎0772 54841

Owner *United Newspapers plc*
Editor *Steve Kendall*
Circulation 70,000

Generally unsolicited mss are not welcome. Receive anything up to 100 a year. All ideas in writing to the editor.

Reading

Evening Post

8 Tessa Road,
Reading, Berks RG1 8NS
☎0734 575833

Owner *Thomson Regional Newspapers*
Editor *Trevor Wade*
Circulation 36,000

Unsolicited mss welcome. They get one or two every day, plus mountains of PR material. Finished copy only – no phone calls or written ideas. Fiction very rarely used.

News Editor *David Jackson*

Business Post (weekly) Topical – especially hi-tech pieces. 'Country Matters' (bimonthly) Non-technical and topical.
Features Editor *Wendy Fuller* Topical subjects, particularly of Thames Valley interest. *Words* 800–1000.

Scarborough

Scarborough Evening News

17/23 Aberdeen Walk,
Scarborough Yorks YO11 1BB
☎0723 363636

Editor *John Bird*
Circulation 18,585

News Editor *Charles Graves*

Arts Editor *Jeannie Swales*
Women's Page *Elizabeth Johnson*

Scotland

Daily Record

See under *Glasgow*

The Scotsman

See under *Edinburgh*

Sunday Mail

See under *Glasgow*

Sunday Post

See under *Glasgow*

Scunthorpe

Scunthorpe Evening Telegraph

Doncaster Road,
Scunthorpe DN15 7RG
☎0724 843421

Owner *Northcliffe Newspaper Group*
Editor *P. L. Moore*
Circulation 74,000

News Editor *Russell Ward*

All correspondence should go to the news editor.

Sheffield

The Star

York Street, Sheffield S1 1PU
☎0742 767676

Owner *United Newspapers plc*
Editor *Michael Corner*
Circulation 150,000

Unsolicited mss not welcome unless topical and local

News Editor *Martin Ross* Do accept contributions from freelance news reporters if they relate to the area.

Features Editor *Stuart Machin* Very rarely require outside features, unless on specialised subjects. *Payment* negotiable.

Shropshire

Shropshire Star

Ketley, Telford, Shropshire TF1 4HU
☎0952 44377

Owner *Shropshire Newspapers Ltd*
Editor *Robert Jones*
Circulation 93,000

Unsolicited mss not welcome. Essential to approach the editor in writing in the first instance with ideas. No news, no fiction.

Features Limited opportunities here; mostly use in-house or syndicated material. *Words* maximum 1200.

South Shields

Shields Gazette and Shipping Telegraph

Chapter Row, South Shields,
Tyne & Wear NE33 1BL
☎091–455 4661

Owner *Northern Press*
Editor *Kie Miskelly*
Circulation 28,091

Features Editor *Margaret Nicholls*
Women's Page *Janis Blower*

Southampton

Southern Evening Echo

45 Above Bar, Southampton, Hants SO9 7BA
☎0703 634134

Owner *Southern Newspapers*
Editor *Duncan Jeffery*
Circulation 90,000

Unsolicited mss are 'tolerated'. Few are received. Approach in writing with strong ideas; staff supply almost all the material. All correspondence should be addressed to the editor.

Stoke on Trent

Evening Sentinel

Sentinel House, Etruria,
Stoke on Trent, Staffs ST1 5SS
☎0782 289800

Owner *Northcliffe Newspaper Group*
Editor *Sean Dooley*
Circulation 111,676

News Editor *Michael Wood*

All material should be sent to the news editor.

Sunderland

Sunderland Echo

Pennywell Industrial Estate, Pennywell,
Sunderland, Tyne & Wear SR4 9ER
☎091–534 3011

Owner *Portsmouth and Sunderland Newspapers*
Editor *Andrew Hughes*
Circulation 66,815

News Editor *Ian Holland*

Swansea

South Wales Evening Post

Adelaide Street,
Swansea, Glamorgan SA1 1QT
☎0792 50841

Owner *Northcliffe Newspaper Group*
Editor *Nicholas Carter*
Circulation 66,445

News Editor *Kay Byrne*

Features Editor *George Edwards*
Women's Page *Betty Hughes*

Swindon

Evening Advertiser

100 Victoria Road,
Swindon, Wilts SN1 3BE
☎0793 28144

Owner *Wiltshire Newspapers*
Editor *John Mayhew*
Circulation 37,000

Unsolicited mss welcome, and many are received. Finished copy much preferred to ideas. 'All need to be strongly related to or relevant to the town of Swindon, the Borough of Thamesdown, or the county of Wiltshire, in that order of interest.' Little scope for non-staff work. Fees by the editor's valuation if by non-NUJ members.

News Editor *Alan Johnson*

Features Editor *Pauline Leighton*
Fiction *Pauline Leighton* Seldom used. Absolutely no poetry.
Special Pages numerous and various.

Thomson Regional Newspapers Ltd

3rd Floor, Pemberton House,
East Harding Street, London EC4A 3AS
☎01–353 9131

Editor *George Sivell*

London office of the group which owns the following regional daily papers: *Belfast Telegraph*; *Evening News* (Edinburgh); *Evening*

Chronicle (Newcastle); *Evening Express* (Aberdeen); *Evening Gazette* (Middlesbrough); *Evening Post* (Reading); *The Journal* (Newcastle); *Lancashire Evening Telegraph*; *The Press & Journal* (Aberdeen); *South Wales Echo* (Cardiff); *Sunday Sun* (Newcastle); *Western Mail* (Cardiff). See separate listings for details.

Wales

South Wales Argus

See under *Newport*

South Wales Echo

See under *Cardiff*

South Wales Evening Post

See under *Swansea*

Western Mail

See under *Cardiff*

The West of England

Western Daily Press

See under *Bristol*

Wolverhampton

Express & Star

Queen Street, Wolverhampton,
West Midlands WV1 3BU
☎0902 313131

Owner *Midlands News Association*
Editor *Keith Parker*
Circulation 245,872

News Editor *Derek Tucker*

Arts Editor *Barry Cox*
Features Editor *Barry Cox*
Women's Page *Sandra Parsons*

Worcester

Evening News

Berrows House, Worcester WR2 5JX
☎0905 423434

Owner *Barrow's West Midlands Ltd*
Editor *David Griffin*
Circulation 29,256

News Editor *Stephen Grocott*

Arts Editor *David Ford*
Features Editor *Chris Lloyd*
Women's Page *Mary Johns*

Yorkshire

Yorkshire Evening Post
See under *Leeds*

Yorkshire Evening Press
York & County Press,
15 Coney Street, York YO1 1YN
☎ 0904 53051

Owner *York & County Press*
Editor *Richard Wooldridge*
Circulation 55,000

Unsolicited mss not generally welcome, unless submitted by journalists of proven ability. Receive about six a week. Approach in writing only – 'phone calls always come at the wrong time, and we'd have to see the written work anyway'. No fiction.

News Editor *Bill Hearld* Accredited journalists only.

Features Editor *Terry Watson* Exceptional pieces of local relevance considered. *Words* 1000. *Payment* negotiable.

Yorkshire Post
See under *Leeds*

The Limits to Freedom – the Writer and the Law of Libel

The last edition of *The Writer's Handbook* was threatened with two libel actions: a publisher and a literary agent took exception to comments made about them. Both cases were settled by an exchange of solicitors' letters and without vast expense on either side. Still, if this genial publication can stir such emotions, what must it be like for those who enter into real controversy?

That libel is taking up an increasing proportion of lawyers' time seems highly likely; that it is becoming more expensive is undeniable. Fancy awards like the £500,000 handed out to Jeffrey Archer and the £85,000 *Private Eye* had to pay to Sir James Goldsmith, attract the punters. But they should know that the cost of bringing their grievances to a judge and jury can be horrendous. Not long ago Sir Peter Hall's action against *The Sunday Times* came to a grinding halt when he was warned that he could end up £500,000 out of pocket.

Since there is no legal aid for libel action, reflecting, as one lawyer puts it, 'an unspoken feeling that reputation matters more to those who are important or among the better off in society', the headline cases are reserved for the very rich or the very determined, while a plaintiff of modest means is generally urged to try for an out-of-court settlement. This way he will save time (a full blooded libel case can take up to three years to get to court) and hope to land a tidy tax-free sum without risking his life's savings.

Unless an author takes a perverse pleasure in litigation (and there are one or two who do) the wise and economical course is to check out the hazards before a manuscript goes to print. The litmus test for libel is to ask, 'Would the words complained of tend to lower the plaintiff in the estimation of right-thinking members of society?' This begs the question as to who is a 'right-thinking' person, but, without getting bogged down in semantics, let us assume someone who is in the conventional mould.

It may be that the defendant did not intend libel. No matter. All that the plaintiff need show is that the statement would be understood by reasonable people to refer to him. There is a clear warning here for fiction writers not to venture too close to real life. It may seem a neat idea to introduce friends and neighbours into a story – it is so much easier to describe people you know – but if one of them is cast as a villain and recognises himself, albeit in an unlikely role, then a solicitor's letter will surely follow.

Names, too, can be a trap for the unwary. If a novel features a corrupt member of parliament, a financier who fiddles his tax or a vicar with an obsessive interest in choirboys, it is as well to check that the names given to these characters do not correspond to flesh and blood people. Often, the more unlikely the name, the greater the risk. You may think you are on safe ground when you relate the dubious practices of the Reverend Harbottle Tiddles Grimston, but Sod's Law dictates that as soon as the book is in the shops, a curious coincidence will be drawn to your attention. With such an unlikely name it is difficult to argue that you have acted unwittingly. The problem is accentuated by the sure knowledge that much of what appears in novels does relate to real life, even if the writer is not immediately aware of it. It is extraordinary what can be dredged up from the subconscious. One well-known writer recalls the awful embarrassment of realising, too late, that the name of the leading protagonist in his steaming sex saga happened to be that of his fiancée. He avoided a libel action but she sent back his engagement ring.

In book publishing it is the biographers of contemporary or near-contemporary figures who tread the narrowest line. To state a known fact about an individual, that he behaved deviously or dishonestly for example, may raise questions about his friends, associates or family which they feel bound to contest. A film star who was famous for his stories of licentious adventures, usually with the wives of other film stars, was never so much as challenged by his victims. But when he died and his biographer got to work, the writs began to fly. In such cases the best hope for the writer is the plaintiff's awareness that publicity generated by his action will cause him yet more pain. As Dr Johnson reminds us, 'Few attacks either of ridicule or invective make much noise but with the help of those they provoke.'

Where a libel has been committed unintentionally or 'innocently', it is possible to alleviate the consequences by an 'offer to make amends'. This usually involves a published apology and a settlement of costs. Otherwise, unless it can be established that a statement, however defamatory, is true in substance and fact (a difficult trick to pull off), the defence against libel will probably turn on the assertion that the words complained of are fair comment on a matter of public interest. This is where the wheel turns full circle because writers, who are themselves inclined to rush to law when they feel aggrieved, often hear the 'fair comment' defence from reviewers who have savaged their work. The perimeters of 'fair comment' are wide enough to protect, in essence, the principles of free speech, so that, according to precedent, 'However wrong the opinion expressed may be in point of truth, or however prejudiced the writer, it may still be within the prescribed limit'. In other words, it is one thing to argue that a person's *views* are lunatic but quite another to assert that *he* is a lunatic.

Every writer is responsible for his own work. But this should not mean that when he makes mistakes he has to carry the can all on his own. Newspapers and broadcasting companies invariably give full backing to their contributors (in most cases they have to because they assume copyright), but traditionally book publishers are reluctant to share the risk of libel. A typical contract includes a warranty clause which entitles the publisher to be indemnified by the author against any damages and costs resulting from a libel action. It has been argued that the warranty clause is a necessary deterrent against greedy litigants who would see the chance of winning higher damages from a company than from an individual writer. But most publishers take out insurance to cover this possibility. It is surely not too much to ask that the protection should extend to authors – particularly when they are tackling controversial subjects.

At the very least, the author of a controversial work should insist that his publisher has the manuscript read for libel and he should make sure his contract does not allow for unlimited liability. In 1972 David Irving, whose book *The Destruction of Convoy PQ17* had been the subject of a successful libel action, was in turn sued by his publishers, **Cassell Ltd**, who sought to recover the libel damages and costs they had paid out. The claim was for £100,000. But fortunately for Irving he had taken the advice of the Society of Authors and amended his contract. He was liable only for breaches of his warranty that the book was free of libel unknown to the publisher. Irving argued that Cassell knew all the relevant facts before an action was brought. In the end, Cassell did not proceed with the claim.

A problem with libel insurance is that few policies extend to the US market, where claims and awards can take off like Concorde. There, a thriving libel industry has been made yet more prosperous by enterprising lawyers who assess fees as a percentage of whatever they can persuade juries to award. The consolation for defendants is that while the law of libel in the States is similar to the law here, in practical terms it is more favourable to the authors, in that the reputations of public figures are thought to be in less need of protection.

Early in 1988 a conservative-led Supreme Court allowed an appeal to overturn $200,000 damages awarded to Jerry Falwell against Larry Flynt. The peculiar fascination of the case comes from knowing the identity of the contenders. Falwell is the Reverend Jerry Falwell, founder of the Moral Majority while Flynt is the supremo of soft porn magazines. The action arose when Falwell was parodied in a cartoon which suggested that he had gained his first sexual experience with his mother. He sued for libel, invasion of privacy and emotional distress. In striking down the decision of a lower court to declare in favour of the Baptist minister, Chief Justice William Rehnquist argued that even when cartoons are 'harsh, indecent or indecorous', they are within the bounds of America's 'robust political and social satire'.

One suspects that liberalism so defined would not find favour in our courts. In the eyes of the British judiciary, reputation is very precious indeed.

Magazines

A La Carte

King's Reach Tower,
Stamford Street, London SE1 9LS
☎01–261 5615 Telex 915748 MAGDIV G

Owner *IPC Magazines Ltd*
Editor *Jeannette Arnold*
Circulation 45,000

FOUNDED 1984. TEN ISSUES PER YEAR. Specialised food, drink and gourmet travel magazine. Unsolicited contributions welcomed from food and/or wine writers of experience and authority. All mss should be sent to the editor. At present, about ten unsolicited manuscripts are received each week. Most of these are inappropriate for the magazine.

Accountancy

40 Bernard Street, London WC1N 1LD
☎01–628 7060 Fax 01–833 2085

Owner *Institute of Chartered Accountants of England and Wales*
Editor *Brian O'Kane*
Circulation 68,000

FOUNDED 1889. MONTHLY. Written ideas welcome. Approach by phone with news items.

Features *Gillian Bird* Accounting/tax/ business-related articles of high technical content aimed at professional/managerial readers. Maximum 800–3000 words. *Payment* £87 per printed page.

Main features *Gillian Bird* Major feature articles comprising part or all of cover story. Features list available. Material planned and commissioned at least six months in advance. Maximum 800–5000 words. *Payment* £87 per printed page or by negotiation.

News *Julia Irvine* News items – investigative reports related to City, EEC, industry, accounting and international accountancy in business context, maximum 500 words; Commentary – opinionated piece on any similar subject; Accounting ideas – technical based; Economic trends – up-to-date reviews or predictions. Maximum 1200 words. *Payment* by arrangement.

Accountancy Age

32–34 Broadwick Street, London W1A 2HG
☎01–439 4242 Telex 23918 VNUG

Owner *VNU*
Editor *Robert Bruce*
Circulation 77,000

FOUNDED 1969. WEEKLY. Unsolicited mss welcome, and ideas may be suggested in writing or by telephone provided they are clearly thought out.

Features Topics right across the accountancy/business/financial world. Maximum 1500 words. *Payment* at NUJ rates.

The Accountant's Magazine

27 Queen Street, Edinburgh EH2 1LA
☎031–225 5673
Telex 727530 Fax 031–225 3813

Owner *The Accountant's Publishing Co.*
Editor *Winifred Elliott*
Circulation 13,500

FOUNDED 1897. MONTHLY. New contributors are welcome, but should approach in writing in the first instance.

Features Articles welcome on topics of interest to the accountancy profession; finance, business, management etc. Must be authoritative. Maximum length 3000 words (1000–2000 preferred). *Payment* by negotiation.

ADviser

Williams Savory Ltd,
1 Winckley Street, Preston PR1 2AA
☎0772 201536

Owner *British Dietetic Association*
Editor *Neil Donnelly*
Circulation 3000

FOUNDED 1981. QUARTERLY. Unsolicited manuscripts are welcomed from dietitians, and nutritionists. Make initial approach in writing. All pieces should be appropriate to dietitians. Maximum 1200 words. *Payment* £40–50.

African Affairs

Dept. of Politics, University of Bristol,
12 Priory Road, Bristol BS8 1TU
☎0272 303200
Telex 445938   Fax 0272 732657

Owner *Royal African Society*
Editors *Richard Hodder-Williams/Peter Woodward*
Circulation 2500

FOUNDED 1901. QUARTERLY learned journal publishing articles on contemporary developments on the African continent. Unsolicited mss welcome.

Features Should be well-researched and written in a style that is immediately accessible to the intelligent lay reader. Maximum 8000 words. *Payment* for non-academics £40 per 1000 words. No payment for academics.

Alternatives

16 Ennismore Avenue, London W4 1SF
☎01–747 8292

Owner *Alternative House Ltd*
Editor *Helene Hodge*
Circulation 75,000

FOUNDED 1966. MONTHLY. Unsolicited mss and photographs welcome. Features and news on the home, work, food, travel, health, beauty, fitness, fashion, pets and organics.

Features *Lindsay Roberts*
News *Helene Hodge*

Amateur Film Maker

33 Gassiot Way, Sutton, Surrey SM1 3AZ
☎01–644 0839

Owner *Film Maker Publications*
Editor *Tony Pattison*
Circulation 3000

FOUNDED 1930. BI-MONTHLY of the Institute of Amateur Cinematographers. Reports, news and views of the Institute. Unsolicited mss welcome, but all contributions are unpaid.

Amateur Gardening

Westover House, West Quay Road,
Poole, Dorset BH15 1JG
☎0202 680586   Fax 0202 674335

Owner *IPC Magazines*
Editor *Graham Clarke*
Circulation 85,390

FOUNDED 1884. WEEKLY. New contributions are welcome provided that they have a professional approach. Of the twenty unsolicited manuscripts received each week, 90% are returned as unsuitable.

Features Topical gardening articles – to be agreed with the editor before submission. Maximum length 1100 words.

News Gardening news items are compiled and edited in-house. Maximum 200 words. ALSO One-off gardening features – to be agreed with the editor before submission. Maximum length 1100 words. *Payment* at IPC/NUJ rates.

Amateur Photographer

Prospect House, 9–13 Ewell Road,
Cheam, Surrey SM1 4QQ
☎01–661 4300

Owner *Business Press International*
Editor *Barry Monk*
Circulation 90,550

For the competent amateur with a technical interest. Freelancers are used, but writers should be aware that there is ordinarily no use for words without pictures.

Amateur Stage

83 George Street, London W1H 5PL
☎ 01–486 1732

Owner *Platform Publications Ltd*
Editor *Charles Vance*

Ambit

17 Priory Gardens, Highgate,
London N6 5QY
☎ 01–340 3566

Owner *Dr Martin Bax*
Editor *Dr Martin Bax*
Circulation 2000

FOUNDED 1959. QUARTERLY literary magazine. Publishes short stories, experimental fiction and poetry, but no features. A large number of unsolicited manuscripts received. But these are welcomed if accompanied by an s.a.e. All approaches should be made in writing, never by phone.

The American

114–115 West Street,
Farnham, Surrey GU9 7HL
☎ 0252 713366   Fax 0252 724951

Owner *British American Newspapers Ltd*
Editor *Robert Pickens*
Circulation 15,000

FOUNDED 1976. FORTNIGHTLY community newspaper for US citizens resident in the UK and as such requires a strong American angle in every story. 'We are on the lookout for items on business and commerce, diplomacy, and international relations, defence, and "people" stories.' Maximum length '5 minutes read'. *Payment* 'modest but negotiable'. First approach in writing with sample of previous work.

Angling Times

Bretton Court, Bretton, Peterborough PE 3 8DZ
☎ 0733 266222

Owner *EMAP*
Editor *Neil Pope*
Circulation 126,155

Do not send your fishing stories here: this weekly is more concerned with angling news than feature material, most of which is provided by their large staff. Occasional features from outsiders.

Features Editor *Kevin Wilmott*. *Payment* NUJ rates.

Animal World

Causeway, Horsham, West Sussex RH12 1HG
☎ 0403 64181
Telex 878484   Fax 0403 41048

Owner *RSPCA*
Editor *Elizabeth Winson*
Circulation 35,000

BI-MONTHLY RSPCA magazine. Most technical articles (pet care etc.) are written in-house. Unsolicited mss welcome.

Features and fiction Articles and stories should not contradict RSPCA policy. Illustrative photographs welcome. Maximum 1000 words. *Payment* £18 (more for illustrated articles).

Annabel

80 Kingsway East,
Dundee, Scotland DD1 9QJ
☎ 0382 44276   Fax 0382 42397

Owner *D. C. Thomson & Co. Ltd*
Editor *Sandra Monks*
Circulation 152,754

Apart from the domestic content of the magazine, material is mainly suppled by freelance writers (this is typical of a D. C. Thomson publication). Currently trying to change its image, and going for a younger, *Daily Mail*-reading audience. Need general women's interest features, interviews and topical articles. Also fiction – it doesn't have to be about marriage: 'we've also published Fay Weldon'. A maximum of 3000 words. A good bet for freelancers; although 'the slush pile' does not generally yield much in the way of ready-made features, it can provide new writers for the future. Fees negotiable.

Features Editor *Sandra Monks.*

The Antique Collector

National Magazine House,
72 Broadwick Street, London W1V 2BP
☎01–439 5000
Telex 263879 NATMAG G

Owner *National Magazine Co. Ltd*
Editor *David Coombs*
Circulation 16,500

FOUNDED 1930. MONTHLY. Opportunities for freelance features. It is best to submit ideas in writing. Feature articles have a set format: maximum length 2000 words with eight illustrations in colour and/or black and white. Their acceptance depends primarily on how authoritative and informative they are. *Payment* by negotiation.

The Antique Dealer and Collectors' Guild

Kings Reach Tower, Stamford Street,
London SE1 9LS
☎01–261 6894
Telex 915748 MAGDIV G

Owner *IPC Magazines Ltd*
Editor *Philip Bartlam*
Circulation 14,139

FOUNDED 1946. MONTHLY covering all aspects of the antiques and fine art world. Unsolicited mss are welcomed.

Features Maximum length 1500 words. Practical but readable articles welcomed on the history, design, authenticity, restoration and market aspects of antiques and fine art.

News *Philip Bartlam* Maximum length 150 words. Items welcomed on events, sales, museums, exhibitions, antiques fairs and markets. *Payment* £76 per 1000 words.

Apollo

4 Davies Street, London W1Y 1LH
☎01–629 4331

Owner *A. Cluff* and *N. Attallah*
Editor *Anna Somers Cocks*
Circulation *c.*15,000

MONTHLY. A magazine for art collectors, art historians and dealers. Articles are either art historical or critical and almost always written by experts in their fields. Unsolicited mss not welcome.

The Architectural Review

9 Queen Anne's Gate, London SW1H 9BY
☎01–222 4333
Telex 8953505   Fax 01–222 5196

Owner *The Architectural Press*
Editor *Peter Davey*

MONTHLY. Unsolicited mss welcome, but no news stories – only features.

Arena

The Old Laundry, Ossington Buildings,
London W1M 3HY
☎01–935 8232   Fax 01–935 2237

Owner *Wagadon Ltd*
Editor *Nick Logan*

New style and general interest magazine for the young and trendy man about town. Male fashion, intelligent feature articles.

Features Editor *Dylan Jones* Wide range of subject matter: film, television, politics, business, music, media, design, art, architecture, theatre – profiles and articles. Some space allocated to fiction but usually extracted from books, or commissioned from upcoming 'name' writers. *Payment* £80–90 per 1000 words.

Art Monthly

36 Great Russell Street, London WC1B 3PP
☎01–580 4168

Owner *Britannia Art Publications*
Editor *Peter Townsend, Jack Wendrer*
Circulation 4000

FOUNDED 1976. MONTHLY. News and features of relevance to those interested in modern art. Unsolicited manuscripts, of which approximately two per month are received, are welcomed.

Features Alongside exhibition reviews, which are usually 600–1000 words long and are almost invariably commissioned, articles are published on art theory (e.g. modernism, post-modernism), individual artists, art history (of the modern period) and issues affecting the arts (e.g. funding and arts education). These articles can be up to 3000 words in length. Book reviews are usually 600–1000 words but occasionally go up to 3000 words. Payments in all cases are negotiable, and all contributions should be addressed to the editors.

News Brief reports on conferences, public art etc. (250–300 words).

The Artist (Inc. Art & Artists)
Caxton House, 63–65 High Street,
Tenterden, Kent TN30 6BD
☎05806 3673

Owner *Irene Briers*
Editor *Sally Bulgin*
Circulation 17,000
FOUNDED 1931. MONTHLY.

Features *Sally Bulgin* Art journalists, artists, art tutors and writers with a good knowledge of art materials are invited to write to the editor with ideas for practical, discursive and informative features about art, materials and artists.

Arts Review
69 Faroe Road, London W14 0EL
☎01–603 7530

Editor *Graham Hughes*

A vehicle for both London and regional reviews of arts events. Opportunities for reviewers exist, depending on your specialisation, and the region you represent. They do have a large number of such people already. *Payment* currently £30 per 1000 words, but this is under review.

Artscribe International
41 North Road, London N7 9DP
☎01–609 4565   Telex 24453 OMNIBUG

Editor *Stuart Morgan*
Circulation 12,000

FOUNDED 1975. BI-MONTHLY. Unsolicited mss welcome, but freelance opportunities are limited.

Features *Stuart Morgan* Most pieces commissioned. Unlikely that freelance pieces will be used unless by established art critics. Length and payment varies.

News *Stuart Morgan/Ian Brunskill* Most news stories are written by staff, but pieces on major events in the art world considered. Contact editor in first instance.

Reviews *Ian Brunskill* Opportunities are greatest here: reviews of exhibitions more likely to be used than feature articles. Maximum 600 words. *Payment* negotiable.

Artswest
Regional Magazines, Finance House,
Barnfield Road, Exeter, Devon EX1 1QR
☎0392 216766   Fax 0392 71050

Owner *Regional Magazines*
Editor *Ian Beart-Albrecht*
Circulation 10,000

FOUNDED 1987. MONTHLY. Featured articles on the arts in the South West. Unsolicited mss welcome. Maximum 2000–2500 words. *Payment* approximately £50. First approach in writing.

Athletics Weekly
Bretton Court, Bretton,
Peterborough PE3 8DZ
☎0733 261144

Editor *Keith Nelson*
Circulation 24,827

FOUNDED 1945. WEEKLY. Features news and articles on track and field athletics, road running and cross-country. Interviews, profiles, historical articles and exclusive news. Length and payment of all articles by arrangement. Unsolicited mss welcome.

The Author
84 Drayton Gardens, London SW10 9SB
☎01–373 6642

Owner *The Society of Authors*
Editor *Derek Parker*
Circulation 5000

FOUNDED 1890. QUARTERLY. Journal of **The Society of Authors**. Unsolicited mss not welcome.

Autocar
38–42 Hampton Road,
Teddington, Middlesex TW11 0JE
☎01–977 8787
Telex 8952440 HAYMRT G Fax 01–977 0882

Owner *Haymarket Publishing*
Editor *Bob Murray*

FOUNDED 1985. WEEKLY. All news stories, features, interviews, scoops, ideas, tip-offs and photographs welcome.

Features *Michael Harvey*

News *Shaun Campbell*. *Payment* negotiable from a minimum of £100 per 1000 words.

Baby – The Magazine
21 Cross Street, Islington, London N1 2BH
☎01–359 3575
Telex 263174 MKPG   Fax 01–354 3461

Owner *Harrington Kilbridge & Partners*
Editor *Mrs J. Harrington*

QUARTERLY for mothers with children up to school age (0–5 years). Always interested in new writers who should contact Kim Sheaf for further details.

The Banker
102–108 Clerkenwell Road,
London EC1M 5SA
☎01–251 9321   Telex 23700 FINBI G

Owner *Financial Times*
Editor *Gavin Shreeve*
Circulation 13,000

FOUNDED 1926. MONTHLY. News and features on banking, finance, and the capital markets world-wide.

Basketball Monthly
'The Hollies', Hoton, Leicestershire LE12 5SF
☎0509 880208

Owner *Celebrity Group*
Editor *Richard Taylor*
Circulation 10,000

FOUNDED 1961. MONTHLY. Official journal of the English Basketball Association. Features technical, specialist, foreign and personality pieces for basketball enthusiasts. Unsolicited mss welcome.

BBC WILDLIFE Magazine
Broadcasting House, Whiteladies Road,
Bristol BS8 2LR
☎0272 732211
Telex 265781 BSA   Fax 0272 744114

Owner *BBC Enterprises Ltd* and *Wildlife Publications Ltd*
Editor *Rosamund Kidman Cox*

FOUNDED 1983. MONTHLY. Unsolicited mss not welcome.

Competition The magazine runs an annual competition for professional and amateur writers with a first prize of £1000.

Features Most features commissioned from amateur writers with expert knowledge on wildlife or conservation subjects. Unsolicited mss are usually rejected. Maximum 2000 words. *Payment* £120.

News Most news stories commissioned from known freelancers. Maximum 800 words. *Payment* £40.

Bee World

18 North Road, Cardiff CF1 3DY
☎ 0222 372409
Telex 23152 MONREF G 8390

Owner *International Bee Research Association*
Editor *Mr V. A. Cook*
Circulation 2000

FOUNDED 1919. MONTHLY. High-quality factual journal with international readership. Features on apicultural science and technology. Unsolicited mss welcome.

Bella

H. Bauer Publishing, Shirley House,
25 Camden Road, London NW1 9LL
☎ 01–284 0909

Owner *Bauer Publishing*
Editor-in-Chief *Dennis Neeld*

Latest German import into the women's weekly magazine market. A soft-centred, traditional read. FOUNDED in the UK in October 1987.

Senior Features Editor *Alison Macdonald*. Maximum length 1200–1300 words.

Senior Fiction Editor *Linda O'Byrne*. Maximum length 1500–1800 words. *Payment* varies.

Best

10th Floor, Portland House,
Stag Place, London SW1E 5AU
☎ 01–245 8847

Owner *G & J (UK)*
Editor *Iris Burton*
Circulation 993,541

FOUNDED 1987. WEEKLY women's magazine; stable-mate of *Prima*. Important for would-be contributors to study the magazine to understand the style, which differs from most women's weeklies. Multiple features, news, short stories on all topics of interest to women. First approach in writing with s.a.e.

Features Editor *Lindsay Nicholson* Maximum length 1500 words.

Fiction 'Five-minute Story', maximum 1500 words. *Payment* £100. Short Story, maximum 2500 words. *Payment* £150.

Bicycle

Northern and Shell Building,
PO Box 381, Mill Harbour, London E14 9TW
☎ 01–987 5090   Telex 24676

Owner *Cover Publications Ltd*
Editor *Steve James*
Circulation 16,000

FOUNDED 1981. MONTHLY for cyclists and cycling enthusiasts. Unsolicited mss welcome.

Features Maximum 3000 words.

Fiction Maximum 800 words (plus illustration ideas).

The Big Paper

The Design Council,
28 Haymarket, London SW1Y 4SU
☎ 01–839 8000   Fax 01–925 2130

Owner *The Design Council*
Editor *Ms Morven Mackillop*
Circulation 7,000

FOUNDED 1987. Published three times a year (for each school term). Design-related topics of interest and use to primary schools and students. The magazine gets its name from its centre pages, which fold from A3 to A2 to A1 to create a large worksheet/poster. A theme is chosen for each issue – i.e. size, shape or colour – two-page spread with A1 game or worksheet. Ideas welcome. First approach in writing with ideas of subjects covered, pictures and illustrations.

Book Reviews *Ms Morven Mackillop* 'Qualified' people can offer to review books. *Payment* £20 per review.

Features *Ms Morven Mackillop* Mostly commissioned or written in-house.

News *Ms Morven Mackillop* Maximum length 100 words. *Payment* £100 per 1000 words.

Bike Mazagine

2 St Johns Place, St Johns Square,
London EC1M 4DE
☎ 01–608 1511

Owner *EMAP Nationals Ltd*
Editor *Stewart McDiarmid*
Circulation 56,000

FOUNDED 1972. MONTHLY. News and features
on motorcycling.

Features maximum 2500 words.

News maximum 500 words. *Payment* £100
per 1000 words. Do not welcome unsolicited
mss. Receive 'too many'. First approach with
idea in writing.

Birds

The Lodge, Sandy, Bedfordshire SG19 2DL
☎ 0767 80551
Telex 82469 RSPB   Fax 0767 292365

Owner *Royal Society for the Protection of
Birds*
Editor *Annette Preece*
Circulation 351,000

QUARTERLY magazine which covers not only
wild birds, but wildlife, international and
conservation topics as well. No interest in
features on pet birds. Usually commission,
but mss or ideas welcome.

Blitz

40–42 Newman Street, London W1P 3PA
☎ 01–436 5211   Fax 01–436 5290

Owner *Cadogan Press Group*
Editor *Tim Hulse*
Circulation 60,000

Magazine covering media-related subjects
and current affairs: music, film, fashion, art,
politics and style. Aimed at an intelligent
18–35 audience. Always interested in seeing
unsolicited mss. *Payment* £70 per 1000
words.

Blue Jeans

D. C. Thomson & Co. Ltd, Albert Square,
Dundee DD1 9QJ
☎ 0382 23131   Telex 298937

Owner *D. C. Thomson*
Editor *Gayle Anderson*
Circulation 120,727

FOUNDED 1977. WEEKLY. Unsolicited mss welcome, but about 100 are received each week.
All approaches should be made in writing.

Features *Lesley Johnson* Features on popular
trivia: information on jeans, hair, romance,
etc. A lot of light-hearted information and
interesting facts. Maximum 1500 words.
Payment £40.

Fiction *Nicky Gilray* Very keen for good-
quality short stories – bearing in mind that
they are for the teenage-girl market. Maximum 1500 words. *Payment* £40.

Pop *Alison Kirker* Interviews (mainly question and answer type) with chart bands who
have a teenage appeal. Gossipy style: nothing
too technical. Maximum 1500 words. *Payment* £40.

Blueprint

26 Cramer Street, London W1M 3HE
☎ 01–486 7419   Fax 01–486 1451

Owner *Wordsearch Ltd*
Editor *Deyan Sudjic*
Circulation 10,000

FOUNDED 1983. MONTHLY. Features on fashion,
design, architecture, food and film. Maximum length 3000 words. Do not welcome unsolicited mss as 'the odds are against people
getting the tone right without talking to us
first'. Approach by phone in the first instance. *Payment* negotiable.

Boat International

58 George Street, London W1H 5RG
☎ 01–935 7207   Fax 01–486 3409

Owner *Sterling Publications*
Editor *Andrew Preece*
Circulation 35,000

FOUNDED 1983. MONTHLY. Welcome unsolicited mss.

Features Maximum length 2500 words. *Payment* £100 per 100 words.

News Maximum length 300 words. *Payment* £100 per 1000 words. First approach in writing.

Book and Magazine Collector
43–45 St Mary's Road,
Ealing, London W5 5RQ
☎01–579 1082

Owner *S. H. O'Mahony*
Editor *John Dean*
Circulation 11,900

FOUNDED 1984. MONTHLY. Welcome unsolicited feature items. First approach in writing. Maximum length 3000 words. *Payment* £25 per 1000 words.

Bookdealer
Suite 34, 26 Charing Cross Road,
London WC2H 0DH
☎01–240 5890   Fax 01–379 5770

Editor *Barry Shaw*

WEEKLY trade paper which acts almost exclusively as a platform for people wishing to buy or sell rare or out-of-print books. Six-page editorial only; occasional articles and regular book reviews done by regular freelance writers.

Booker Food Services Magazine
CPR Publishing, Northern Rock House,
20 Market Place, Guisborough,
Cleveland TS14 6HF
☎0287 3911   Fax 0287 37201

Owner *CRP Ltd*
Editor *Peter Cook*
Circulation 58,000

BI-MONTHLY. Features and news items of interest to the catering industry. Maximum length 700 words. Prefer to be approached by phone or in writing with an idea. Good colour transparencies relating to the catering industry always welcome. *Payment* negotiable.

Books
43 Museum Street, London WC1A 1LY
☎01–404 0304   Fax 01–242 0762

Editor *Matthew Bray*
Circulation 100,000

Formerly known as *Books and Bookmen*. A consumer rather than trade magazine, dealing chiefly with features on authors, reviews of books, and general aspects of the publishing business. *Payment* negotiable.

The Bookseller
12 Dyott Street, London WC1A 1DF
☎01–836 8911   Fax 01–836 2909

Owner *J. Whitaker & Sons Ltd*
Editor *Louis Baum*

Trade journal of the publishing and book trade. Essential guide to what is being done to whom. Trade news and features, including special features, company news, trends in publishing etc., are ordinarily done in-house or by commissions offered to experts within the business. Unsolicited mss rarely used. Approach in writing.

Features Editor *Helen Paddock*

News Editor *Penny Mountain*

Brides and Setting Up Home
Vogue House, Hanover Square,
London W1R 0AD
☎01–499 9080
Telex 27338 VOLON G   Fax 01–493 1349

Owner *Condé Nast Publications*
Editor *Sandra Boler*
Circulation 66,037

BI-MONTHLY. Freelance contributions are considered provided they are relevant. Much of the magazine is produced 'in-house', but a good feature on cakes, jewellery, music, flowers etc. is always welcome. Prospective contributors should telephone with an idea. Maximum length (features) 1000 words. *Payment* £120.

The British Bandsman
The Old House, 64 London End,
Beaconsfield, Bucks HP9 2JD
☎049 46 4411

Owner *Austin Catelinet*
Editor *Peter Wilson*

FOUNDED 1887. WEEKLY. News on brass bands and features on brass instruments and music. Welcome contributions but no payment.

British Birds
Fountains, Park Lane,
Blunham, Bedford MK44 3NJ
☎0767 40025

Owner *British Birds Ltd*
Editor *Dr J. T. R. Sharrock*
Circulation 10,000

FOUNDED 1907. MONTHLY ornithological magazine. Unsolicited mss welcome, but from ornithologists only.

Features Well-researched, original material relating to West Palearctic birds. Maximum 6000 words.

News *Mike Everett/Robin Prytherch* News items ranging from conservation to humorous notes. Maximum 200 words. *Payment* All contributions are unpaid.

British Judo
16 Upper Woburn Place, London WC1H 0QH
☎01–387 9304   Telex 27830 SPORTCG

Owner *British Judo Association*
Editor *Tony Reay*
Circulation 38,000

FOUNDED 1978. QUARTERLY. Issued free to all British Judo Association members and licence holders. Unsolicited mss are welcome

but all ideas must be presented to Management Committee in writing.

Features Profiles of star competitors. Items on sports injuries, sponsorship. Maximum 2000–3000 words. Humorous anecdotes 250–500 words.

Fiction Anything relevant to the sport. Maximum 2000–3000 words.

News Reports and results of judo competitions. Maximum length 500–1000 words; other sports 2000 words. *Payment* At standard rates.

British Medical Journal
BMA House, Tavistock Square,
London WC1H 9JR
☎01–387 4499

Owner *British Medical Association*
Editor *Dr Stephen Lock*

No market for freelance writers.

Broadcast
100 Avenue Road, Swiss Cottage,
London NW3 3TP
☎01–935 6611   Telex 299973 ITP LNG

Owner *International Thomson*
Editor *Marta Wohrle*
Circulation 8000

FOUNDED 1960. WEEKLY. Very few opportunities for freelance contributions, but write in the first instance to the relevant editor.

Features *Roma Felstein* Features on broadcasting issues. Maximum length 1500 words. *Payment* £100 per 1000 words.

News *Marta Wohrle* News stories on broadcasting. Maximum length 400 words. *Payment* £90 per 1000 words.

The Brownie
17–19 Buckingham Palace Road,
London SW1W 0PT
☎01–834 6242

Owner *Girl Guides Association*
Editor *Lynn Hordwell*

FOUNDED 1962. WEEKLY. Aimed at Brownies aged 7–10 years.

Articles On crafts and simple make-it-yourself items using inexpensive or scrap materials.

Features General interest. Maximum 350–400 words. *Payment* £26 per 1000 words pro rata.

Fiction Brownie content an advantage. No adventures involving children in dangerous situations – day or night – unaccompanied. Maximum 350–400 words. *Payment* £26 per 1000 words pro rata.

Building

Builder House, 1/3 Pemberton Row, Fleet Street, London EC4P 4HL
☎01–353 2300
Telex BUILDAG 25212   Fax 01–353 8319

Owner *The Builder Group Ltd*
Editor *Graham Rimmer*
Circulation 21,500

FOUNDED 1842. WEEKLY. Features articles on aspects of the modern building industry. Unsolicited mss not welcome, but freelancers with specialist knowledge of the industry are often used.

Features Focussing on the modern industry, no building history required. Maximum 1500 words. *Payment* by arrangement.

News Maximum 500 words. *Payment* by arrangement.

The Burlington Magazine

6 Bloomsbury Square, London WC1A 2LP
☎01–430 0481   Telex 291072

Owner *The Burlington Magazine Publications Ltd*
Editor *Caroline Elam*

FOUNDED 1903. MONTHLY. Unsolicited contributions are welcome provided that they are on the subject of art history and are pre-viously unpublished. All preliminary approaches should be made in writing.

Exhibition Reviews Usually commissioned, but occasionally unsolicited reviews are published if appropriate. Maximum length 1000 words. *Payment* £75 (maximum).

Main Articles Maximum length 4500 words. *Payment* £60 (maximum).

Shorter Notices Maximum length 2000 words. *Payment* £30 (maximum).

Business

234 Kings Road, London SW3 5UA
☎01–351 7351   Fax 01–351 2794
Telex 914549 INTMAG G

Owner *Business People Publications*
Editor *Stephen Fay*
Circulation 45,000

FOUNDED 1986. MONTHLY. Some opportunities for freelance feature writers, but unsolicited manuscripts are not welcomed. Prospective contributors are best advised to write in the first instance with feature ideas. Maximum length 2500 words. *Payment* £200 per 1000 words.

Business Traveller

49 Old Bond Street, London W1X 3AF
☎01–629 4688
Telex 8814624   Fax 01–629 6572

Owner *Perry Publications*
Editor *Andrew Eames*
Circulation 40,000

MONTHLY. Receive a steady flow of unsolicited contributions but they are usually 'irrelevant to our market'. It is advised that would-be contributors study the magazine first. First approach in writing. *Payment* 'variable'.

Cambridgeshire Life Magazine

Chapel House, Chapel Lane, St Ives, Huntingdon, Cambridgeshire PE17 4DX
☎0480 62844

Owner *Cambridgeshire Life Ltd*
Editor *Stuart Mayes*
Circulation 9,500

FOUNDED 1965. MONTHLY magazine featuring 'geographically relevant' articles. Maximum 1000–1500 words, plus three or four good quality photographs. Welcome unsolicited mss. First approach in writing. *Payment* varies.

Camera Weekly

38–42 Hampton Road, Teddington,
Middlesex TW11 0JE
☎01–977 8787   Fax 01–943 0986
Telex 895 2440 HAYMART G

Owner *Haymarket Publishing*
Editor *George Hughes*
Circulation 67,111

FOUNDED 1976. WEEKLY. Considerable opportunities for freelance contributors, but up to 100 unsolicited mss are received each week. There is a market here for features which detail exciting, exotic experiences within photography – plus pictures. Features should have lots of 'how-to-do-it' or factual information. No travelogues. Approach with an idea by telephone or in writing. Maximum length for articles, 1000 words. *Payment* negotiable.

Campaign

22 Lancaster Gate, London W2 3LY
☎01–402 5266

Owner *Marketing Publications*
Editor *Christine Barker*
Circulation 23,008

FOUNDED 1968. WEEKLY. Lively magazine serving the advertising and related industries. Freelance contributors are advised to write in the first instance.

Features Articles of up to 1500–2000 words. *Payment* £100 per 1000 words.

News *Jan Hawkins* Relevant news tips of up to 300 words. *Payment* between £35 and £50. Also 'City Diary', 'Close-up' and 'Media' sections.

Camping and Caravanning

11 Lower Grosvenor Place,
London SW1W 0EY
☎01–828 1012

Owner *Camping and Caravanning Club*
Editor *Peter Frost*
Circulation 88,000

FOUNDED 1901. MONTHLY. Unsolicited, relevant mss are welcomed. Out-of-London journalists are often commissioned to cover events. Local journalists with camping and caravanning knowledge should write if they wish to be on magazine's contact lists.

News/Features Items and pieces, up to a maximum of 800 words, are always welcomed, especially if illustrated.

Camping & Walking

Link House, Dingwall Avenue,
Croydon CR9 2TA
☎01–686 2599
Telex 947709   Fax 01–760 0973

Owner *Link House Magazines*
Editor *Philip Pond*

FOUNDED 1961. MONTHLY magazine with features on walking and camping for the family, especially interested in sites reports. Maximum length 1400 words. Welcome unsolicited mss.

Canal and Riverboat

Stanley House, 9 West Street,
Epsom, Surrey KT18 7RL
☎03727 41411   Fax 03727 44493
Telex 291561 VIA SOS G (AEM)

Owner *A. E. Morgan Publications Ltd*
Editor *Norman Alborough*
Circulation 14,000

Unsolicited mss are welcomed and prospective contributors are advised to make initial approach in writing.

Features *Norman Alborough* Maximum length 2000 words on all aspects of waterways and narrow boats and motor cruisers, including crusing reports, practical advice etc. Unusual ideas and personal comments are particularly welcome. *Payment* approx. £50.

Fiction Only considered when subject matter is relevant. Maximum length 1500 words. *Payment* around £35.

News *Charles Creswell* Items up to 300 words on Inland Waterways System, plus photographs if possible. *Payment* £10.

Capital Gay

38 Mount Pleasant, London WC1X 0AP
☎01−278 3764   Telex 261177

Owner *Stonewall Press Ltd*
Editor *Graham McKerrow*
Circulation 17,000

FOUNDED 1981. WEEKLY magazine with social and political news and features for London's gay community.

Arts & Entertainments *Pas Paschali* Some freelance work. Maximum 250 words. *Payment* 'low'.

Features *Graham McKerrow* Maximum 1500 words. *Payment* negotiable.

News *Graham McKerrow* Some freelance work. Maximum 400 words. *Payment* negotiable. First approach in writing.

Car

FF Publishing, 97 Earls Court Road, London W8 6QH
☎01−370 0333   Fax 01−373 7544

Owner *FF Publishing Ltd*
Editor *Gavin Green*
Circulation 130,000

FOUNDED 1962. MONTHLY. Unsolicited manuscripts of at least 1500 words are welcomed.

Features are usually commissioned from staff and known writers, but other material on new and old cars, special events and travel experiences is considered. Maximum length 3000 words.

Fiction Short stories and satire (up to 3000 words) considered. *Payment* £100−200 per 1000 words (negotiable).

News Items (up to 250 words) and photographs are always welcome, especially on new car models. *Payment* £50 (negotiable).

Cars and Car Conversions Magazine

Link House, Dingwall Avenue, Croydon, Surrey CR9 2TA
☎01−686 2599   Telex 947709 LINK HOG

Owner *Link House Magazines Ltd*
Editor *Nigel Fryatt*
Circulation 80,000

FOUNDED 1965. MONTHLY. Unsolicited mss are welcomed, but preferably after previous contact. Prospective contributors are advised to make initial contact by telephone.

Features *Nigel Fryatt* Articles of up to 2000 words on current motorsport and unusual sport-oriented roadcars are welcomed. *Payment* by negotiation.

Cat World

10 Western Road, Shoreham-by-Sea, West Sussex BN4 5WD
☎0273 462000

Owner *D. M. & J. H. Colchester*
Editor *Joan Moore*
Circulation 14,500

FOUNDED 1981. MONTHLY. Welcome unsolicited mss. Prefer to be approached in writing.

Features Lively first-hand experience features on every aspect of the cat. Breeding features and veterinary articles by acknowledged experts only. Maximum length 1000 words. *Payment* £25 per 1000 words.

News Short, concise, factual/humorous items concerning cats. Maximum length 100 words. *Payment* £5.

Poems Maximum length 50 words. *Payment* £6.

Catholic Herald
Lamb's Passage, Bunhill Row,
London EC1Y 8TQ
☎01–588 3101

Editor *Terence Sheehy*
Circulation 30,000

Feature material from freelancers is used. Interested in not only straight Catholic issues, but general humanitarian matters, Third World etc. No demand for freelance news writers, 'unless they happen to be on the spot'. *Payment* 'very little, £20 uppermost'.

Caves & Caving
342 The Green, Eccleston,
Chorley, Lancs PR7 5TP
☎0257 452763

Owner *British Cave Research Association*
Editor *Andy Hall*
Circulation 3000

FOUNDED 1970. QUARTERLY. Covers news on British and foreign caving activities, equipment reports, reviews, letters, expeditions, etc.

Features Expedition reports, new exploration in the UK, history of exploration articles. Maximum length 1500–2000 words.

News Regional items from all over the UK. Maximum length 1000 words. Welcome unsolicited mss.

Celebrity
80 East Kingsway, Dundee DD4 8SL
☎0382 44276
Telex 76380   Fax 0382 42397

Owner *D. C. Thomson & Co. Ltd*
Editor *David Burness*
Circulation 13,000

WEEKLY. Opportunities for freelance contributors, but twenty or so unsolicited manuscripts are received every week. There are no hard news pages as such, but *Celebrity* carries regular crime, royal and medical articles written in the style of 'tabloid' newspapers.

There is a six-week lead time, so forward planning is essential and features should, if possible, have a topical theme, coinciding with a new TV series, film releases etc. There is always scope for human interest articles and any offbeat or unusual stories, but no fiction.

Features Maximum length is 1000–1500 words. *Payment* £75 per 1000 words or by arrangement.

Photo-features (transparencies or black and white prints) on almost any subject will also be considered. Photos should be captioned or accompanied by a short article. *Payment* by arrangement.

Certified Accountant
Westgate House, Spital Street,
Dartford, Kent DA1 2EQ
☎0322 79131
Telex 896747   Fax 0322 20628

Editor *Leon Hopkins*
Circulation 37,000

MONTHLY. Specialist, professional readership; unsolicited mss not welcome. About 100 are received each year and prospective contributors are advised to make initial contact in writing. No news or fiction.

Features Maximum length 3000 words. All features tend to be commissioned, professional articles and accountancy analyses. *Payment* £150.

Chacom
1 Westgate, Pennylands,
Skelmersdale, Lancs WN8 8LP
☎0695 21436

Owner *Winckley Publishing*
Editor *Mrs Babs Murphy*
Circulation 3000

FOUNDED 1984. MONTHLY for commerce and industry. Unsolicited mss welcome.

Features Various topical areas of business, exports, Chamber of Commerce business, etc.

News Items on commerce and industry. Maximum 500 words. *Payment* minimal.

Challenge

Revenue Buildings, Chapel Road,
Worthing, W. Sussex BN11 1BQ
☎0903 214198

Owner *Challenge Literature Fellowship*
Editor *Donald Banks*
Circulation 10,000

FOUNDED 1958. MONTHLY Christian magazine
which welcomes unsolicited mss. Prospective contributors should send for sample
copy of writers' guidelines.

Features Commissioned only.

Fiction Short children's stories – maximum
600 words.

News Items up to 500 words (with pictures
preferably) 'showing God at work'.
'Churchy' items not wanted. *Payment* negotiable.

Channel TV Times

The TV Centre, St Helier,
Jersey, Channel Islands
☎0534 73999
Telex 4192265 CTVJYG   Fax 0534 59446

Owner *Channel Islands Communications
(Television) Ltd*
Editor *Stuart C. Guilliard*
Circulation 9585

FOUNDED 1962. WEEKLY. Mainly about the
Channel Islands. Very few unsolicited mss
are received and are not welcomed, but feature ideas on island subjects considered.

Features Maximum of 2000 words on topics
of interest to Channel Islanders. *Payment* £30
per 1000 words.

Publications Manager *Gordon J. de Ste
Croix*

Chat

195 Knightsbridge, London SW7 1RE
☎01–589 8877   Fax 01–225 2449

Owner *ITP*
Editor *Peter Genower*
Circulation 515,000

FOUNDED 1985. WEEKLY women's tabloid. No
unsolicited contributions; the magazine receives far too many of these. The features
editor may be approached by phone with an
idea.

Features Editor *Nora McGrath* Maximum
length of features 700 words.

News Editor *Peter Genower* Items usually
around 400–500 words.

Cheshire Life

The Old Custom House,
70 Watergate Street, Chester CH1 2LA
☎0244 45226   Fax 0244 48430

Owner *Oyston Group*
Editor *Jane Fickling*
Circulation 10,000

FOUNDED 1934. MONTHLY. Feature articles on
homes, gardens, personalities, business,
farming, conservation, heritage, books,
fashion, arts, science – anything which has a
Cheshire connection somewhere. Welcome
unsolicited mss. Maximum length 500–1500
words. *Payment* £50 minimum.

News 'Not a lot – small diary items only.'
Maximum length 150 words. *Payment*
£15–20. First approach in writing.

Chess

Railway Road, Sutton Coldfield,
West Midlands B73 6AZ
☎021–354 2536/7   Fax 021–355 0655

Owner *Pergamon Press*
Editor *Paul Lamford*
Circulation 20,000

FOUNDED 1935. MONTHLY magazine which
reviews the international chess scene in an
entertaining and light-hearted style. Unsolicited mss are not welcome. Query letter in the
first instance.

Chic

15 Britannia Street, London WC1X 9JP
☎01–837 3033

Owner *Channel Media Ltd*
Editor *Mary Fitzpatrick*
Circulation 40,000

FOUNDED 1984. MONTHLY glossy magazine aimed at a young black readership. Unsolicited mss are welcome, but prospective contributors are advised to write in the first instance with idea. *Payment* NUJ rates.

Child Education

Scholastic Publications, Marlborough House, Holly Walk, Leamington Spa, Warwickshire CV32 4LS
☎0926 81 3910

Owner *Scholastic Publications*
Editor *Gill Moore*
Circulation 63,000

FOUNDED 1923. MONTHLY magazine for nursery, pre-school playgroup, infant and first teachers. Articles on education of 4–7-year-olds written by teachers are welcome. Maximum length 2000 words. First approach in writing with synopsis. No unsolicited mss.

Choice

Apex House, Oudle Road, Peterborough PE2 9NP
☎0733 555123

Owner *EMAP*
Editor *Annette Brown*
Circulation 87,000

MONTHLY magazine for retirement planning. Aimed at 'better off' people approaching retiring age (i.e. 50–60). Unsolicited mss are not welcome; approach in writing only.

Deputy Editor *Neil Patrick*

Features on items, hobbies and adventure affecting 50–60-year-olds considered. Maximum length usually 800 words (occasionally 1500 words). *Payment* £80–100.

Fiction Three-part fiction considered.

Finance *Annette Brown* Features on finance/property/legal matters affecting the magazine's readership.

News All items affecting the magazine's readership: pensions, state benefits, caring for elderly relatives. Maximum 100 words. *Payment* £25.

Christian Herald

Herald House, Dominion Road, Worthing, West Sussex BN14 8JP
☎0903 821082

Owner *Herald House Ltd*
Editor *Colin Reeves*
Circulation 33,000

FOUNDED 1866. WEEKLY. Conservative evangelical Christian magazine aimed at adults with families. Most theological and spiritual articles are commissioned.

Family round up Short articles on wide range of subjects, some religious, some non-religious. Articles should appeal to whole family, especially women. Maximum 200–500 words. *Payment* at Herald House rates.

Fiction Moral, non-religious short stories, light and entertaining. Avoid Christian conversion stories. Maximum 1600 words. *Payment* £20.

General interest Various non-religious subjects. Historical subjects need light, enthusiastic touch and crisp, clear illustrations (no slides). Maximum 900–1000 words. *Payment* £20–30.

Christian Science, Monitor

Eggington House, 25–28 Buckingham Gate, London SW1E 6LD
☎01–630 8666

Owner *Christian Science Publishing Society*
Contact *British Isles Correspondent*

The London office is not an editorial one, and all unsolicited material is passed on to head office in the United States for consideration. WEEKLY in Britain, the *Monitor* has a huge circulation in America, where it is a DAILY paper. Always on the look-out for general interest feature material which appeals to an international audience.

Church News

College Gate House,
Bury St Edmunds, Suffolk IP33 1NN
☎0284 753530

Owner *Home Words & Canon Cecil Rhodes*
Editor *Canon Cecil Rhodes*
Circulation 95,000

FOUNDED 1946. MONTHLY small magazine featuring news and information on events, persons and religious subjects and debates. Unsolicited mss welcome. Maximum for articles 600 words. *Payment* by agreement.

Church of England Newspaper

Livingstone House, 11 Carteret Street,
London SW1H 9DJ
☎01–222 3464   Fax 01–222 5414

Owner *Christian Weekly Newspapers Ltd*
Editor *John K. Martin*
Circulation 12,500

FOUNDED 1828. WEEKLY. Almost all material is commissioned, but unsolicited mss considered.

Features *Polly Hudson* Unless commissioned, preliminary enquiry in writing is essential. 1700 words maximum. *Payment* NUJ/IOJ rates

News *Colin Blakely* News items must be sent promptly and have a church/Christian relevance. 250 words maximum. *Payment* NUJ/IOJ rates.

Church Times

7 Portugal Street, London WC2A 2HP
☎01–405 0844   Fax 01–405 5071

Owner *G. J. Palmer & Sons Ltd*
Editor *Bernard H. Palmer*
Circulation 44,797

FOUNDED 1863. WEEKLY. Unsolicited mss considered.

Features *Bernard Palmer* Articles on religious or social topics. Length 700–1500 words. *Payment* £25 per 1000 words minimum.

News *Susan Young* Occasional reports on out-of-London events, but only when commissioned. Length and *Payment* by arrangement.

City Limits

8–15 Aylesbury Street, London EC1R 0LR
☎01–250 1299

Owner *London Voice Ltd*
Editor *Cynthia Rose*
Circulation 30,000

FOUNDED 1981. WEEKLY independent, co-operatively-owned London publication with news, reviews and features. Recommend first approach by telephone. 'We have a lead period of six weeks so we advise would-be contributors to contact us well in advance.'

Features Maximum length 1500–2000 words. *Payment* £60 per 1000 words.

Reviews Maximum length 250 words. *Payment* £15 per review.

News Maximum length 250 words. Welcome unsolicited material.

Classical Guitar

Ashley Mark Publishing Company,
Unit 23D, Airport Industrial Estate,
Newcastle-upon-Tyne NE3 2JW
☎091–214 0001   Fax 091–286 3220

Owner *Ashley Mark Publishing Company*
Editor *Colin Cooper*

FOUNDED 1982. MONTHLY.

Concert reviews *Chris Kilvington* Maximum length 250 words. *Payment* by arrangement.

Features *Colin Cooper* Usually use staff writers. Maximum length 1500 words. *Payment* by arrangement.

News *Colin Cooper* Small paragraphs and festival/concert reports welcome. Maximum length 100 words. *Payment* none. First approach in writing.

Classical Music

241 Shaftesbury Avenue,
London WC2H 8EH
☎01–836 2383
Telex 264675 GILDED G   Fax 01–240 0897

Owner *Rhinegold Publishing Ltd*
Editor *Graeme Kay*

FOUNDED 1976. FORTNIGHTLY. A specialist magazine using precisely targeted news and feature articles, so unsolicited manuscripts are not welcome. Prospective contributors may approach in writing with an idea, but should familiarise themselves beforehand with the style and market of the magazine. *Payment* £50 per 1000 words.

Climber

Ravenseft House, 302–304 St Vincent Street,
Glasgow G2 5NL
☎041–221 7000

Owner *Holmes McDougal Ltd*
Editor *Cameron McNeish*
Circulation 20,000

FOUNDED 1962. MONTHLY. Unsolicited mss welcome (they receive about 10 a day). Finished features only – no ideas. No fiction.

Features Freelance features (maximum 2000 words) are accepted on climbing, mountaineering and hill-walking in UK and abroad. The standard of writing must be extremely high.

News No freelance opportunities – all in-house. *Payment* negotiable.

Club International

2 Archer Street, London W1V 7HE
☎01–734 9191   Telex 22638

Owner *Paul Raymond*
Editor *Stephen Bleach*
Circulation 180,000

FOUNDED 1972. MONTHLY. Features, fiction and short, humorous items 'in the style of *Viz, Private Eye, Punch* etc.'

Features and **Fiction** Maximum 2500 words. *Payment* £100 per 1000 words.

Shorts Maximum 200–750 words. *Payment* negotiable.

Coarse Fisherman/Big Fish

61 Main Street, Long Lawford,
Rugby, Warwickshire CV23 4AZ
☎0788 68458

Owner *W. M. Print Ltd*
Editor *Dave Phillips*
Circulation 22,500

Coarse Fisherman – MONTHLY. *Big Fish* – BI-MONTHLY. Unsolicited mss welcomed but prospective contributors should first study magazines for content and style. Up to 20 mss arrive each month.

Features Material 'must be top rate to be accepted'.

Fiction Fiction on the subject of angling is welcome – but it must be *funny* and satire should not be clichéd. Maximum length 1500 words.

News Particularly keen to hear from writers with an understanding of angling who can relate it to environmental and current affairs. Maximum length 2000 words. *Payment* negotiable.

Coarse Fishing Handbook

Bretton Court, Bretton,
Peterborough PE3 8DZ
☎0733 264666   Telex 32157

Owner *EMAP*
Editor *Mike George*
Circulation 23,109

FOUNDED 1983. BI-MONTHLY. Unsolicited material on all coarse fishing subjects is very welcome and prospective contributors are advised to make initial contact by telephone. As the magazine is aimed at experienced anglers, submissions should be in-depth studies.

Features Maximum length 2500 words. All articles should be illustrated either with black and white photos or colour transparencies.

Fiction There is usually one piece per issue and humorous submissions are preferred. *Payment* by arrangement.

Company

National Magazine House,
72 Broadwick Street, London W1V 2BP
☎01–439 5000

Editor *Gill Hudson*
Circulation 184,668

Glossy women's MONTHLY magazine, founded, as the name suggests, to appeal to the independent and intelligent young woman. Consider themselves a good market for freelancers: 'we've got more space for them, as we have fewer staff feature writers'. 1500–2000 words. Keen to encourage bright new young talent, but uncommissioned material rarely accepted. Feature outlines preferred plus evidence of writing ability – especially cuttings.

Computer Weekly

Quadrant House, The Quadrant,
Sutton, Surrey SM2 5AS
☎01–661 3122

Owner *Reed Business Publishing*
Editor *Dave Madden*
Circulation 113,000

FOUNDED 1966. Unsolicited material generally not welcome unless an outline has been discussed and agreed. Unsolicited items (up to 700 words) are welcomed for the 'Platform' section, but there is no fee. No fiction.

Features *David Barrett* Always looking for new, good writers with specialised industry knowledge. Maximum length 1200 words. Special Show Features for industry events (e.g. Previews) up to 1200 words welcomed.

News *Charles Arthur* Maximum length 300 words. Some possibilities for regional or foreign news items only. *Payment* £120 per 1000 words.

Computing

32–34 Broadwick Street, London W1A 2HG
☎01–439 4242   Telex 23918 VNU G

Owner *VNU*
Editor *Sarah Underwood*
Circulation 116,000

WEEKLY. New contributors are welcome, and are advised to write in the first instance with ideas.

Connections

Sea Containers House, 20 Upper Ground,
London SE1 9PF

Editor *Alison Booth*
Circulation over 2 million

The THRICE-YEARLY magazine of Sealink Ferries, distributed to those travelling with the company. Carry around 3 articles per issue, mostly connected with places en route. Unsolicited material not generally welcome, nor ideas; happy with their current contributors, and commission when necessary.

Contemporary Review

61 Carey Street, London WC2A 2JG
☎0252 713883

Owner *Contemporary Review Co. Ltd*
Editor *Rosalind Wade, OBE*

FOUNDED 1866. MONTHLY. One of the first periodicals to devote considerable space to the arts. Today it remains liberal without any specific political affiliations. A wide spectrum of interests includes home affairs and politics, literature and the arts, history, travel and religion. There is also a monthly book section, quarterly fiction and film reviews. Unsolicited mss welcome: maximum 3000 words. No fiction.

Cosmopolitan

National Magazine House,
72 Broadwick Street, London W1V 2BP
☎01–439 7144

Editor *Linda Kelsey*
Circulation 404,234

Popular mix of articles, emotional advice and strong fiction designed to appeal to a late-teen/early-twenties modern-minded female. Known to have a policy of not considering unsolicited mss, but does nevertheless sometimes look at those it receives. This is because it is always on the look-out for new writers. 'The thing to do is to ring the features desk with an idea; if they are interested they will ask to see something.'

Features Editor (and long-standing humour writer for the magazine) *Marcelle D'Argy Smith.*

Cotswold Life
Alma House, 73 Rodney Road,
Cheltenham, Gloucestershire GL50 1HT
☎0242 577775

Owner *Roy Faiers*
Editor *Christopher Mole*
Circulation 5,000

FOUNDED 1968. MONTHLY. News and features on life in the Cotswolds. Most news written in-house but welcome contributions for features on interesting places, and people; reminiscences of Cotswold life in years gone by; historical features on any aspect of Cotswold life. First approach in writing. Maximum 1500–2000 words for features. *Payment* by negotiation after publication.

Country Homes and Interiors
Carlton House, 25 Newman Street,
London W1P 3HA
☎01–631 3939

Owner *Carlton Magazines Ltd*
Editor *Vanessa Berridge*
Circulation 90,131

FOUNDED 1986. MONTHLY. The best approach for prospective contributors is with an idea in writing as unsolicited manuscripts not welcomed.

Features *Vanessa Berridge* and *Julia Watson* There are two main features per month, one a personality interview, the other an examination of a topic of interest to an intelligent, affluent readership (both women and men) aged 25–44. Maximum length 1500–2000 words. *Payment* negotiable.

Travel *Julia Watson* Pieces of 1200 words. Also hotel reviews, leisure pursuits, weekending pieces in England and abroad – 750 words. *Payment* negotiable.

Country Life
King's Reach Tower, Stamford Street,
London SE1 9LS
☎01–261 7070   Fax 01–261 5139

Owner *IPC Magazines*
Editor *Jenny Greene*
Circulation 51,600

Part of this social fabric of English rural life, the magazine has recently come under the wing of a new editor determined to widen the readership and generally blow the dust off. Features which relate to the countryside, wildlife, rural events, sports and pursuits welcome. Strong, informed material rather than amateur enthusiasm. *Payment* £106 per 1000 words minimum, more if exceptional.

Country Living
National Magazine House,
72 Broadwick Street, London W1V 2BP
☎01–439 7144   Fax 01–437 6886

Editor *Deirdre McSharry*
Circulation 139,000

Regards itself as a women's magazine, but has a strong male readership as well. Upmarket, takes living in the country seriously (generally in a soft-focus middle-class way) and tends to be people-oriented. Welcomes features on people, conservation, wildlife, houses, gardens, animals, country businesses etc. Suggestions welcome. Pays good fees as very keen to be literate and well researched; often uses 'name writers'. Articles are mostly commissioned; writers new to the magazine should send a synopsis and examples of published work. *Payment* negotiable, but never less than £150 per 1000 words, often more.

Country Sports
59 Kennington Road, London SW1 7PZ
☎01–928 4742

Owner *British Field Sports Society*
Editor *Derek Bingham*
Circulation 50,000

FOUNDED 1983. THRICE-YEARLY. No unsolicited mss.

The Country Times (formerly Out of Town)

Evro Publishing Ltd, Thames House,
5–6 Church Street, Twickenham,
Middlesex TW1 3NJ
☎01–891 6070
Telex 01–895 2440   Fax 01–891 4373

Owner *Haymarket*
Editor *Simon Courtauld*

Out of Town FOUNDED 1983, relaunched as *The Country Times* May 1988. MONTHLY. Unsolicited mss not used 'very often' but welcome contributions. First approach in writing.

The Countryman

Sheep Street, Burford OX8 4LH
☎099 382 2258

Owner *The Countryman Ltd*
Editor *Christopher Hall*
Circulation 80,000

FOUNDED 1927. QUARTERLY. Unsolicited mss with s.a.e. are welcome; about 75 are received each week. Prospective contributors are advised to make initial approach in writing having read a few issues of the magazine to understand its character.

Creative Camera

Battersea Arts Centre, Old Town Hall,
Lavender Hill, London SW11 5TF
☎01–924 3017

Owner *Registered Charity*
Editor *Peter Turner*
Circulation *c.*6000

FOUNDED 1968. MONTHLY. Most of the magazine's content is commissioned, but new contributors are welcome and are best advised to approach in writing.

Features Reviews of photographic books and exhibitions. Maximum length 750 words. *Payment* £50.

Creative Review

50 Poland Street, London W1V 4AX
☎01–439 4222

Editor *Lewis Blackwell*

The trade magazine of advertising and related industries, including film, design and illustration. Expert contributors only. Send in samples of work, whether published or not; feature needs are organised on a commission basis, and writers of talent may be taken up.

The Cricketer International

29 Cavendish Road,
Redhill, Surrey RH1 4AH
☎0737 772221   Fax 0737 771720

Owner *Ben G. Brocklehurst*
Editorial Director *Christopher Martin-Jenkins*
Executive Editor *Peter Perchard*
Circulation 42,000

FOUNDED 1921. MONTHLY. Unsolicited mss welcome.

Cue World

Cavalier House, 202 Hagley Road,
Edgbaston, Birmingham B16 9PQ
☎021–455 6230

Owner *Snooker Publications Ltd*
Editor *John Dee*
Circulation 24,000

FOUNDED 1976. MONTHLY for snooker enthusiasts. Unsolicited mss not welcome. All approaches should be made in writing.

The Dalesman

Dalesman Publishing Company Ltd,
Clapham, Lancaster LA2 8EB
☎04685 225

Owner *Dalesman Publishing Company Ltd*
Editor *David Joy*
Circulation 56,000

FOUNDED 1939. MONTHLY magazine with articles of specific Yorkshire interest. Welcome unsolicited mss and receive approximately 10 per day. First approach in writing. Maximum 2000 words. *Payment* negotiable.

Dance & Dancers

248 High Street, Croydon, Surrey CR0 1NF
☎01–681 7817

Owner *Plusloop Ltd*
Editor *John Percival*

FOUNDED 1950. MONTHLY magazine covering ballet, modern dance and related arts throughout the world.

Features *John Percival* 'There is opportunity for writers of good quality with special preference for knowledge of ballet as performer.'

News *Nadine Meisner* Almost all information is written in-house. Preliminary discussion is always advisable. *Payment* is 'low'.

Dance Theatre Journal

Laban Centre for Movement and Dance, Laurie Grove, London SE14 6NH
☎01–692 4070 ext 38

Owner *Laban Centre for Movement and Dance*
Editors *Chris de Marigny and Alastair Macaulay*

FOUNDED 1983. QUARTERLY. Interested in features on every aspect of the contemporary dance scene. Unsolicited mss welcome. Specially interested in articles concerning issues such as the funding policy for dance as well as critical assessments of choreographers' work and latest developments in various schools of contemporary dance. Maximum 3700 words. *Payment* £15 per 1000 words.

The Dancing Times

Clerkenwell House,
45–47 Clerkenwell Green, London EC1R 0BE
☎01–250 3006

Owner *Private company*
Editor *Mary Clarke*

FOUNDED 1910. MONTHLY. Approaches in writing should be made by specialist dance writers and photographers only.

Darts World

2 Park Lane, Croydon, Surrey CR9 1HA
☎01–681 2837

Owner *World Magazines Ltd*
Editor *A. J. Wood*
Circulation 24,500

Features Single articles or series on technique and instruction welcomed. Maximum length 1200 words.

Fiction Short stories with darts theme of no more than 1000 words.

News Maximum length 800 words. Tournament reports, general and personality news required. *Payment* negotiable.

David Hall's Match Fishing Magazine

51–53 Albert Street,
Rugby, Warwickshire CB21 2SG
☎0788 535218

Owner *Chrisreel Ltd*
Editor *David Hall*
Circulation 19,000

FOUNDED 1987. BI-MONTHLY. Dealing with all aspects of match fishing. News and features on pollution, fishing matches, events and general fishing topics. Unsolicited mss welcome. Maximum 2000 words. *Payment* £40.

Decanter

St John's Chambers, 2–10 St John's Road, London SW11 1PN_
☎01–350 1551
Telex 946240 CWEASY Ref 19010760

Editor *Paul Dymond*
Circulation 25,000

FOUNDED 1975. Glossy wines and spirits magazine. Unsolicited material welcomed. No fiction.

News and **Features** All items and articles should concern wines and spirits and related subjects.

Departures

6 Haymarket, London SW1Y 4BS
☎ 01–930 4411
Telex 8950931   Fax 01–930 4842

Owner *American Express*
Editor *Lucretia Stewart*
Circulation 300,000

FOUNDED 1984. BI-MONTHLY. A literary travel magazine, specialising in high-quality travel writing and glossy colour photography. Prospective contributors are best advised to approach with an idea in writing only.

Descent

Wych Cottage, Langport Road,
Somerton, Somerset TA11 6HX
☎ 0458 73238

Owner *Ambit Publications*
Editor *Bruce Bedford*

FOUNDED 1969. BI-MONTHLY for cavers. Plenty of opportunities for freelance contributors who can write accurately and knowledgeably on aspects of caving.

Features Maximum 3000 words. *Payment* varies.

Design

28 Haymarket, London SW1Y 4SU
☎ 01–839 8000   Fax 01–925 2130

Owner *Design Council*
Editor *Marion Hancock*
Circulation 15,000

FOUNDED 1948. MONTHLY. Unsolicited mss not welcome; approach by phone or in writing.

Book Reviews Various lengths *Payment* approximately £100 per 1000 words.

Features On most design-related areas, particularly product and consumer goods design. Interviews with designers, managers and consultancies. Maximum length 1500 words. *Payment* £100–140 per 1000 words.

Designing

The Design Council, 28 Haymarket,
London SW1Y 4SU
☎ 01–839 8000   Fax 01–925 2130

Owner *The Design Council*
Editor *Ms Morven Mackillop*
Circulation 7,000

Published three times per year (for each school term). A thirty-two-page paper with news, features, book reviews and special supplements. Design-related subjects on a wide range and on work going on in schools. Welcome unsolicited mss. 'We do not receive enough.' First approach in writing with ideas of subjects covered, ideas of pictures and illustrations. Primary and secondary schools and student readership.

Book Reviews *Ms Morven Mackillop* 'Qualified' people can offer to review books. *Payment* £20 per review.

Features *Ms Morven Mackillop* Science, engineering, textiles, graphics, cookery, work being done in secondary schools. Maximum length 800–1200 words. *Payment* £100 per 1000 words.

News *Ms Morven Mackillop* Short paragraphs on relevant events. Maximum length 100–300 words. *Payment* £100 per 1000 words. Also special supplements in designing – eight pages per topic. 'Much of the material is written in-house, but we may look around for authors.' Maximum length 8–12 eight-hundred-word pages. *Payment* £100 per 1000 words.

Devon Life

Regional Magazines, Finance House,
Barnfield Road, Exeter, Devon EX1 1QR
☎ 0392 216766   Fax 0392 71050

Owner *Regional Magazines*
Editor *Ian Beart-Albrecht*
Circulation 9,000

FOUNDED 1965. MONTHLY. Featured articles on any aspect of life in Devon. Unsolicited mss welcome. Maximum 2000–2500 words. *Payment* approximately £50. First approach in writing.

Director

10 Belgrave Square, London SW1X 8PH
☎01–235 9122

Editor *George Bickerstaffe*
Circulation 36,000

Published by the Institute of Directors for its members. Wide range of features from design to employment to general interest articles; plus book reviews, technology, health. Use regulars, but unsolicited mss will be considered. *Payment* negotiable.

Dog and Country

Corry's Farm, Roestock Lane,
Colney Heath, St Albans, Herts AL4 0QW
☎0727 22614

Owner *Gilbertson & Page Limited*
Editor *Edward Askwith*

QUARTERLY magazine regularly featuring gundog training, veterinary, countryside matters and gardening. Unsolicited mss welcome.

Features Articles, maximum 1200 words, based on actual experience or expert knowledge, of household, gun and working dogs, natural history, game, coarse and sea angling and conservation are particularly welcomed. *Payment* £7.50 per A5 page. Most articles occupy two pages or more.

Dorset Life

Market Street,
Crewkerne, Somerset TA18 7JU
☎0460 73076

Owner *Smart Print Publications Ltd*
Editor *Jack Rayfield*
Circulation 8,500

FOUNDED 1977. MONTHLY magazine with features on any subject of interest (e.g. historical, geographical, arts, crafts) to people living in Dorset. Maximum length 1000–1500 words. Welcome unsolicited mss. Receive 'dozens!' First approach in writing. *Payment* negotiable.

Dorset Tatler

St Lawrence House, Broad Street,
Bristol BS1 2EX
☎0272 291069   Fax 0272 225633

Owner *Regional Magazines Ltd*
Editor *Heidi Best*
Circulation 8,000

FOUNDED 1988. MONTHLY.

Features 'We use a fair percentage of freelance contributors'. Welcome ideas. First approach in writing. Maximum length 1600 words. *Payment* by arrangement.

News Only small items which will still be newsworthy eight weeks after submission. Maximum length 200 words. *Payment* by arrangement.

Drama

British Theatre Association,
Regent's College, Inner Circle, Regent's Park,
London NW1 4NW
☎01–935 2571

Owner *British Theatre Association*
Editor *Christopher Edwards*
Circulation 7000

FOUNDED 1919. QUARTERLY theatre review. Unsolicited manuscripts are rarely used, due to a shortage of space, but prospective contributors are advised to approach by phone or in writing (with samples of their work). All enquiries should be directed to the **Assistant Editor** *Jane Yettran* Feature articles on current theatrical scene (bearing in mind that *Drama* is a quarterly), interviews and profiles. Maximum length *c.*3000 words. *Payment* £30–40 per printed page. Also book reviews; maximum length *c.*1500 words. *Payment* £15–30.

dx (Daily Express magazine)

121 Fleet Street, London EC4P 4JT
☎01–353 8000   Telex 21841

Owner *United Newspapers plc*
Editor *Nicholas Lloyd*
Circulation 1.69 million

MONTHLY colour magazine distributed in the south of England. (Plans to issue weekly with nationwide distribution being discussed.) Features on homes, fashion and beauty, shopping, entertainment, travel, politics, property. Interested in considering ideas from freelance writers. Write with idea in the first instance. Thanks to its large format, plenty of scope for big pictures. Maximum length 1500 words. *Payment* negotiable.

Early Days

16 Trinity Churchyard,
Guildford, Surrey GU1 3RR
☎0483 577533

Owner *Bond Clarkson Russell*
Editor *Fiona Macpherson*
Circulation 400,000

FOUNDED 1984. Three issues a year dealing with all aspects of the first few months of a baby's life. Unsolicited mss not welcome as all features are commissioned. Readers' letters on relevant issues and experiences are considered for publication. No fees.

Early Times

PO Box 119, Cobham, Surrey KT11 2HD
☎0273 675375

Owner *Garth Publications Ltd*
Editor *Nicky Smith*
Circulation 50,000

WEEKLY quality newspaper aimed at bright, enquiring children. First issue in January 1988 sold out on the day of issue. Originally conceived for the 8–14 age group but now attracting a wider age range. Plans to lower the price to 38p should result in a large increase in circulation. News and features on national and international issues. Mainly use a pool of freelance writers but welcome items of 300 words maximum. *Payment* £100 per 1000 words.

The Economist

25 James's Street, London SW1A 1HG
☎01–839 7000
Telex 24344   Fax 01–839 2968

Owner *50% Financial Times, 50% individual shareholders*
Editor *Rupert Pennant-Rea*
Circulation 300,885

FOUNDED 1843. WEEKLY. Prospective contributors should approach the editor in writing. Unsolicited contributions are not welcomed.

Edinburgh Review

48 Pleasance, Edinburgh EH8 9TJ
☎031–558 1117/8

Owner *Polygon Books*
Editor *Peter Kravitz*
Circulation 1500

FOUNDED 1969. QUARTERLY. Articles and fiction on Scottish and international literary, cultural and philosophical themes. Unsolicited contributions are welcomed (1600 received each year) but prospective contributors are strongly advised to study the magazine first. Maximum length for fiction should be 6000 words, and translations from little-known world writers are particularly welcomed. Feature articles do not have to be tied in to a recent anniversary, and interest will be shown in accessible articles on philosophy and its relationship to literature. In addition, each issue now contains an Encyclopaedia Supplement, consisting of approximately twenty pages of short items on matters of cultural and political importance which aims to show knowledge and ideas to be 'the collective property of humankind'. Entries for this supplement may vary from a few words to a maximum of 1000 words.

Education

21–27 Lamb's Conduit Street,
London WC1N 3NJ
☎01–242 2548

Owner *Longman Group*
Editor *George Low*
Circulation 10,000

WEEKLY journal read by educational administrators and professionals; articles which appeal to these groups only. Practical administration, and 'how schools are run', plus comment on the state of administration at the present time. Freelancers tend to be a regular network of writers. *Payment* NUJ rates.

Education and Training

62 Toller Lane, Bradford,
West Yorkshire BD8 9BY
☎0274 499821   Telex 51317 MCBUNI G

Owner *MCB University Press Ltd*
Editor *Derek Bradley*
Circulation 3000

FOUNDED 1959. BI-MONTHLY. Unsolicited mss are welcomed provided they are practically orientated and not purely academic. No fees are paid for contributions.

Elle

Rex House, 4–12 Lower Regent Street,
London SW1Y 4PE
☎01–930 9050

Owner *News International/Hachette Ltd*
Editor *Sally Brampton*
Circulation 250,000

FOUNDED 1985. MONTHLY glossy. Unsolicited contributions, of which 20 are received each week, are welcomed only if written specifically for *Elle*. Prospective contributors are best advised to approach the relevant editor in writing.

Features *Louise Chunn, Elissa van Poznak* Maximum length 2000 words.

News (Insight) *Lisa Armstrong* Short articles on current/cultural events with emphasis on national and not just London-based readership. Maximum length 500 words. *Payment* for all pieces £150 per 1000 words.

Embroidery

PO Box 42B, East Molesley, Surrey KT8 9BB
☎01–943 1229

Owner *Embroiders Guild*
Editor *Valerie Campbell-Harding*
Circulation 12,100

FOUNDED 1933. QUARTERLY. Features articles on embroidery techniques with illustrations. Unsolicited mss welcome. Maximum 2000 words. *Payment* £15–100.

Encounter

44 Great Windmill Street,
London W1V 7PA
☎01–434 3063

Owner *Daily Telegraph*
Editors *Melvin J. Lasky, Richard Mayne*
Circulation 20,000

FOUNDED 1953. 10 ISSUES PER YEAR. Hit by falling dollar (half the circulation is in US). Might have closed but for rescue by Conrad Black, proprietor of the *Telegraph*. Publishes reportage and articles of a political and philosophical interest together with one short story per issue and a maximum of six poems. Intending contributors are strongly advised to study the magazine in advance. Unsolicited manuscripts generally welcomed but thousands are received each year and, due to lack of space, very few accepted. Short stories should be 5000 words maximum. *Payment* £10 per 1000 words, and should be sent to the literary editor. *Payment* for poetry varies. An s.a.e. is essential if unsuitable work is to be returned.

The Engineer

30 Calderwood Street, London SE18 6QH
☎01–855 7777
Telex 896238 MORGAN G   Fax 01–855 7571

Owner *Morgan-Grampian*
Editor *John Pullin*
Circulation 40,000

FOUNDED 1856. WEEKLY specialist magazine for engineers.

Features *Martin Ince* Most outside contributions are specially commissioned, but good ideas are always welcome. Maximum 2000 words. *Payment* by arrangement.

News *Peter Eustace* Some scope for specialist regional freelancers and for tip-offs. Maximum 500 words. *Payment* by arrangement.

Techscan *Colin MacIlwain* Technology news. Freelance opportunities as for **News**. Maximum 500 words. *Payment* by arrangement.

Engineering

28 Haymarket, London SW1Y 4SU
☎01–839 8000   Fax 01–925 2130

Owner *Design Council*
Editor *Richard Wood*
Circulation 22,000

FOUNDED 1866. MONTHLY. Unsolicited manuscripts not welcome, but prospective contributors may approach by telephone with an idea, which should be followed up with a written synopsis.

Features *Andrew Beevers* Developments in technology, product design, marketing and trade. Maximum 1800 words. *Payment* £200.

News *Andrew Beevers* Little opportunity for freelancers here, but 'outstanding new developments in technology' always considered. Maximum 350 words. *Payment* £40. Also, applications of advanced plastic composite materials are of great interest – good stories in this area always required. Maximum 1800 words. *Payment* £200.

Environment Now

Ravenseft House, 302–304 St Vincent Street, Glasgow G2 5NL
☎041–221 7000   Fax 041–221 3981

Owner *Holmes McDougall Ltd*
Editor *Roger Smith*
Circulation 32,000

FOUNDED 1987. BI-MONTHLY. **Features** on all aspects of the environment from energy through waste management and pollution, to habitat and species protection, and including the urban environment, will be considered. Good photographic coverage essential – can be arranged by magazine if required.

News items done in-house. Welcome unsolicited mss but receive 'far more than we can use'. Prefer to be approached in writing.

ES (Evening Standard magazine)

PO Box 136, 118 Fleet Street,
London EC4P 4DD
☎01–353 8000   Telex 21909

Owner *Lord Rothermere*

MONTHLY magazine issued with the *London Evening Standard*.

Associate Editor *Jayne Gould*, to whom all unsolicited mss should be addressed. Potential contributors should study the magazine for its style and content. *Payment* by negotiation.

Everywoman

34 Islington Green, London N1 8DU
☎01–359 5496

Editor *Barbara Rogers*
Circulation 15,000

Magazine which provides general news and features angled towards women's current affairs interest, employment and money, relationships, rather than being a traditional 'for women' glossy. Regular slots on health, etc. Some areas are not open to freelance contributions, including arts – no reviewers please. Keen on getting more humour in the magazine, and to get away from a London bias. It is essential to read the magazine first because 'our style, humour and general approach is different'.

Excel Magazine

Lex House, 3–6 Alfred Place,
London WC1 2EB
☎01–323 3232
Telex 9419132 LEX BSL G   Fax 01–631 0035

Owner *White Line Publishing Co. Ltd*
Editor *Rod Fountain*
Circulation 70,000

FOUNDED 1986. MONTHLY. Magazine with news and features on the business and financial world. Receives 100 unsolicited mss per month. Prefer to see a synopsis or brief outline for features in the first instance.

Features *Rod Fountain, Paul Palmer* Offbeat, witty, business-related generic stories or profiles of young men and women in the City.

News *Rod Fountain, Paul Palmer*

Odds *Jane Simon* Quirky short items on unusual business matters, success or failure.

Payment by arrangement but not less than £100 per 1000 words.

Executive Post
2–4 Fitzwilliam Gate, Sheffield S1 4JH
☎0742 704603   Fax 0742 755200/755208

Editor *Alison Bird*
Circulation 130,000

Mailed to jobseekers registered with Professional and Executive Recruitment (PER). Will consider any aspect of executive-level employment or jobhunting as a feature. No news opportunities. *Payment* Rates negotiated.

Executive Retirement (with Fifty Plus)
Aldwych Publishing plc,
17–19 Redcross Way, London SE1 1TB
☎01–407 7541

Owner *Aldwych Publishing plc*
Editor *Aidan Reynolds*
Circulation 20,000

FOUNDED 1985. BI-MONTHLY. Welcome unsolicited news, features, and fiction (though only 6 stories published each year).

Features Well illustrated (colour and black and white, good quality transparencies) items on travel, serious skills, crafts and hobbies. Interviews with prominent or exceptionally interesting people. Maximum length 2000 words. *Payment* £50 per 1000 words.

Fiction Maximum length 2000 words. *Payment* £50 per 1000 words.

News Maximum length 1000 words. *Payment* £50 per 1000 words. First approach in writing with s.a.e. ('NB Higher fees may be paid for commissioned work or work submitted by professional and experienced writers.')

Executive Travel
242 Vauxhall Bridge Road,
London SW1V 1AU
☎01–821 1155   Fax 01–630 1000
Telex 924015 TRANEW G

Editor *Mike Toynbee*
Circulation 49,738

FOUNDED 1979. MONTHLY for business travellers. Unsolicited mss welcome.

The Expatriate
25 Brighton Road,
South Croydon, Surrey CR2 6EA
☎01–681 5545   Telex 295112 NHG G

Owner *Expatriate Publications Ltd*
Editor *Jack Walder*
Circulation *c.*500

FOUNDED 1977. MONTHLY serving the British expatriate community. Unsolicited mss are welcome.

Features Special features on working in particular countries. Psychological problems for spouses, education difficulties, pensions, investment and taxation features, health matters. Maximum 1200 words.

News Information on facilities for expatriates, e.g. mail-order presents, financial services, relocation agents, etc. Maximum 1000 words. *Payment* negotiable.

Expatxtra!
PO Box 300, Jersey, Channel Islands
☎0534 36241

Owner *Expatxtra Ltd*
Editor *Catherine Richmond*
Circulation 15,000

FOUNDED 1982. MONTHLY aimed at working or retired UK expatriates. The magazine is dominated by its laid-back style. It is therefore important to look at a copy before sending mss. No news or fiction.

Features *Vikki Clair* Up to a maximum of 1500 words on travel, fashion, education, etc. *Articles on all financial matters* are popular, e.g. taxation, investment, banking, life assurance, etc. *Payment* £100 per 1000 words.

Expression

20–26 Brunswick Place, London N1 6DJ
☎01–490 1444

Editor *Geoffrey Aquilina-Ross*
Circulation 570,000

Upmarket glossy mailed to American Express cardholders. Upmarket glossy features always welcome, on travel, food, wine, and general consumer matters – anything of genuine interest to the discerning with a disposable income. Some features are produced in-house, others by regular freelancers, but they occasionally find unsolicited articles which hit the right note. *Payment* £150 per printed page (generally between 800 and 1000 words).

Extra Special

63 Shrewsbury Lane, Shooters Hill,
London SE18 3JJ
☎01–854 7309

Owner *Impex Fashions Ltd*
Consultant Editor *Dennis Winston*
Circulation 50,000+

FOUNDED 1986. BI-MONTHLY colour magazine for the larger woman (size 16+) of all ages.

Features Upbeat articles on fashion, psychology, medicine, beauty, business, show business, success stories about larger people, fitness, humour. No pieces on how to lose weight or diet required. Contributors must show appreciation of everyday and long-term problems of the fit larger woman and her need for understanding and practical support. Most articles are commissioned from known writers, but approaches should

be made in writing. Maximum 1500 words. *Payment* by negotiation.

The Face

The Old Laundry, Ossington Buildings,
London W1M 3HY
☎01–935 8232   Fax 01–935 2237

Owner *Wagadon Ltd*
Editor *Nick Logan*
Circulation 95,000

FOUNDED 1980. Perhaps the ultimate magazine of the Style Generation, concerned with who's what and what's cool. Profiles, interviews and stories. No fiction. Acquaintance with the 'voice' of *The Face* is essential before sending mss on spec.

Features 3000 words. *Payment* £80 per 1000 words. New contributors should telephone with their ideas and speak to **Features Editor** *Kimberley Leston*. Also **Intro** (diary) pages, with photo-based short pieces (350 words). *Payment* as for **Features**.

Diary Editor *Kate Flett* No news stories.

Family Circle

38 Hans Crescent, London SW1X 0LZ
☎01–589 2000
Telex 21746   Fax 01–225 2761

Owner *International Thomson Publishing Ltd*
Editor *Jill Churchill*
Circulation 625,290

FOUNDED 1964. 13 ISSUES PER YEAR. Most of the magazine's material is produced in-house, and there is very little scope for freelancers. Unsolicited material is never used, although 15 such manuscripts are received each week. Prospective contributors are best advised to send written ideas to the relevant editor.

Beauty *Helen Speed*

Cookery *Gilly Cubitt*

Fashion *Janine Steggles*

Features *Carrie Taylor* Very little outside work commissioned. Maximum length for features 2500–3000 words.

Fiction *Gill Adams* Maximum length for serial fiction 6000 words.

Home *Caroline Rodriguez*

News ('Full Circle') *Vivien Donald*   *Payment* for all contributions not less than £100 per 1000 words.

Family Wealth

57–61 Mortimer Street, London W1N 7TD
☎01–637 4383
Telex 8956007   Fax 01–631 3214

Owner *Stonehart Magazines*
Editor *Andrew Etchells*
Circulation 64,244

FOUNDED 1987. MONTHLY. Welcome unsolicited mss, with s.a.e. First approach in writing. *Payment* from £100 per 1000 words.

Farming News

Morgan Grampian House,
30 Calderwood Street, London SE18 6QH
☎01–855 7777

Owner *Morgan Grampian Ltd*
Editor *Marcus Oliver*
Circulation 105,773

Occasionally use freelance writers.

Farmers Weekly

Carew House, Railway Approach,
Wallington, Surrey SM6 0DX
☎01–661 4867

Owner *Reed Business Publishing*
Editor *Ted Fellows*
Circulation 104,000

Wide-ranging feature material relating to practising farmers' problems and interests, plus news stories. Farm life, whether practical or general interest, also specific sections on arable, livestock farming, etc. Unsolicited mss considered. *Payment* negotiable.

Fast Lane

Prospect House, 9–13 Ewell Road,
Cheam, Surrey SM1 4QQ
☎01–661 4384   Telex 892084 BISPRS G

Owner *Prospect Magazines*
Editor *Peter Dron*
Circulation 55,400

FOUNDED 1984. Monthly car magazine. Many unsolicited mss are received but they are rarely used. Prospective contributors are advised to make initial approach in writing.

Fiction

Pioneer House, 44–48 Clerkenwell Road,
London EC1M 5PX
☎01–250 1504   Fax 01–251 0798

Editor *Chris Maillard*

Short stories published up to 7000 words, although shorter ones (up to 5000) will be more likely to find acceptance. Style and genre are entirely up to the author – the magazine encourages variety and originality. Poetry is by no means ruled out, though not featured as prominently as fiction. Reviews and interviews are usually commissioned by the editor. *Payment* £100 per story used, paid approximately six weeks after publication.

The Field

Carmelite House, Carmelite Street,
London EC4Y 0JA
☎01–353 6000

Owner *Mail Newspapers Ltd*
Editor *J. A. Spencer*
Circulation 30,925

FOUNDED 1853. MONTHLY magazine for those serious about the British countryside and its pleasures. Unsolicited mss welcome; preliminary approach should be made in writing.

Features Exceptional work on any subject concerning the countryside, mainly commissioned. *Payment* varies according to material.

Film Review

Spotlight Publications Ltd,
Greater London House, Hampstead Road,
London NW1 7QZ
☎01–387 6611   Telex 299485 MUSIC G

Owner *Spotlight Publications Ltd*
Editor *David Aldridge*
Circulation 50,000

MONTHLY. Profiles, interviews and special reports on films. Maximum length 1500 words. Prefer to be approached by telephone.

Financial Weekly

14 Greville Street, London EC1N 8SB
☎01–405 2622   Fax 01–831 2625

Owner *Staff and other investors*
Editor *Tom Lloyd*
Circulation 15,000

FOUNDED 1979. WEEKLY. There are few opportunities for freelancers here, as most of the stories and features are produced in-house. Unsolicited manuscripts not encouraged.

Features *Edward Russell-Walling* An occasional 'perspective' feature, well written, well researched and accompanied by appropriate artwork might be bought. Maximum length 1500 words.

News *John Manley* An exclusive news story, supported by evidence and analysis, may be bought very occasionally. Maximum length 800 words. *Payment* £100 per 1000 words.

First Choice

Home & Law Publishing,
Greater London House, Hampstead Road,
London NW1 7QQ
☎01–388 3171
Telex 269470   Fax 01–387 9518

Owner *The Ladbroke Group*
Editor *Catherine Rendall*
Circulation 3.5 million

Published THRICE YEARLY. Recipes, humour, items of women's and family interest. Will consider unsolicited mss if they 'tie in with planned editorial'. First approach by phone.

First Down

Spendlove Centre,
Charlbury, Oxon OX7 3PQ
☎0608 811266
Telex 837883 SPEND G   Fax 0608 811380

Owner *Mediawatch*
Editor *Alan Lees*
Circulation 45,000

FOUNDED 1986. Unsolicited mss welcome.

Features *Alan Lees* Ideas for commission are welcome.

News *Stephen Anglesey* Tip-offs and news items, maximum 300 words, relating to American football in the UK are welcome. *Payment* by negotiation.

Fitness

Deltamere Ltd, 40 Bowling Green Lane,
London EC1R 0NE
☎01–278 0333   Telex 267247

Editor *Claire Gillman*
Circulation 75,000

FOUNDED 1983. MONTHLY. Freelance contributions are welcome; it is advisable to write with ideas in the first instance.

Focus

108 Twyford House, Chisley Road,
London N15 6PB
☎01–809 1406

Owner *British Science Fiction Association*
Editor *Liz Holliday*
Circulation 1100

FOUNDED 1979. TRIENNIAL. The writers' magazine of the BSFA, containing articles of interest to science fiction writers at all stages of their careers. Unsolicited mss and proposals welcome. Maximum length usually 4000 words.

Focus also has a workshop section, in which fiction is published and criticised.

Promising authors are welcome to submit but only on the understanding that their mss, if accepted, will be workshopped. Maximum length usually 2500 words. *No payment.*

Folk Roots

PO Box 73, Farnham, Surrey GU9 7UN
☎0252 724638

Owner *Southern Rag Ltd*
Editor *Ian A. Anderson*
Circulation 12,000

FOUNDED 1979. MONTHLY. Unsolicited mss welcome, but a large number are received and an initial phone call is preferred.

Features Features on folk and roots music and musicians. Maximum 3000 words. *Payment c.£20 per 1000 words.*

Football Monthly

28 Croydon Road, Reigate, Surrey RH2 0PG
☎07372 21158   Fax 07372 23047

Owner *Proud Print Ltd*
Editor *Tony Pullein*
Circulation 30,000

FOUNDED 1951. MONTHLY.

Features 'All contributions are considered. Prefer interviews with current players/ managers.' Maximum length 1600 words. *Payment* from £30, depending upon topicality, etc. Historical items compiled by team of regular contributors.

Frills

8th Floor, Albany House,
Hurst Street, Birmingham B5 4BD
☎021–622 2899   Fax 021–622 2308

Owner *Second City Advertising & Publishing Ltd*
Editor *Adrienne Hall*
Circulation 120,000

FOUNDED 1987. MONTHLY. Welcome feature articles on items of women's interest (not family, kitchen). Maximum length 1000 words. *Payment* £50. Welcome ideas for quizzes.

Maximum length 800 words. *Payment* negotiable.

Garden Answers

Bushfield House, Orton Centre,
Peterborough PE2 0UW
☎0733 237111   Telex 32157

Owner *EMAP*
Editor *Ray Edwards*
Circulation 67,565

FOUNDED 1982. MONTHLY. 'It is unlikely that unsolicited manuscripts will be used, as writers rarely consider the style and format of the magazine before writing'. Prospective contributors should approach the editor in writing.

Garden News

Bushfield House, Orton Centre,
Peterborough PE2 0UW
☎0733 237111   Telex 32157

Owner *East Midland Allied Press*
Editor *Pam Deschamps*
Circulation 129,716

FOUNDED 1958. WEEKLY news and features on gardening topics. Most material is written in-house, but there are opportunities for news items or offbeat articles. All approaches should be made in writing.

Gay Life Magazine

Medlock Publishing, 1–3 Stevenson Square,
Manchester M1 1DN
☎061–236 6026

Editors *Jan Huyton* and *Nick Delves*

FOUNDED 1986. MONTHLY. News on northern gay topics; features and fiction of a gay/ feminist relevance. Articles on 'Lifestyles'; reviews, clubbing. Welcome unsolicited mss. First approach in writing. Receive approximately 20 mss per month.

Features *Jan Huyton* and *Nick Delves* Maximum length 2000 words.

Fiction *Jan Huyton* Maximum length 900 words.

News *Jan Huyton* and *Nick Delves* Length 50 or 800 words.

Reviews *Nick Delves* Maximum length 250 words, telephone in the first instance. *Payment* No fees paid but pay expenses for all sections.

Gay Times inc. Gay News
283 Camden High Street, London NW1 7BX
☎01–482 2576

Owner *Millivres Ltd*
Editor *John Marshall*

Publish a wide range of feature articles on all aspects of gay life, and general interest likely to appeal to the gay community. Includes arts reviews and news section. Use regular freelance writers and also consider unsolicited contributions. Also publish fiction.

Features Editor *Peter Burton*. *Payment* negotiable.

Gibbons Stamp Monthly
Stanley Gibbons Ltd, Parkside,
Ringwood, Hants BH24 3SH
☎04254 2363
Telex 41271   Fax 0425 470247

Owner *Stanley Gibbons Magazines Ltd*
Editor *Hugh Jefferies*
Circulation 22,000

FOUNDED 1890. MONTHLY. News and features. Welcome unsolicited mss, particularly feature items of a specialised nature. First approach in writing.

Features *Hugh Jefferies* Maximum length 2000 words. *Payment* £17–25. 'Open to suggestions' for other pages of special interest.

News *Michael Briggs* Maximum length 500 words. No *Payment*.

Girl
Commonwealth House,
1–19 New Oxford Street, London WC1A 1NG
☎01–404 0700

Owner *IPC Magazines*
Editor *June Smith*
Circulation 134,244

Teen magazine for girls. Photostories only (i.e. strips done in storyboard-with-words fashion). Always on the look-out for new writers with strong photostory plotlines. Send ideas to the editor.

Girl About Town
141–143 Drury Lane, London WC2B 5TS
☎01–836 4433   Fax 01–836 3156

Owner *Girl About Town Magazine Ltd*
Editor *Louisa Saunders*
Circulation 125,000

FOUNDED 1972. WEEKLY free distribution magazine for women. Some news – 'but they'd have to beat us to it'. Some features, but standards are 'exacting' and would not commission from unknown writer. No fiction. Unsolicited mss 'have occasionally proved useful'. Receives 5–10 weekly. Maximum length for news 200 words. *Payment* £29. Maximum length for features 1600 words. *Payment* £100 per 1000 words.

Giroscope
c/o Girobank plc,
Bootle, Merseyside G1R 0AA
Telex 628021   Fax 051–523 6078

Editor *Ned Halley*
Circulation 1.5 million

Girobank's magazine for customers, published BI-MONTHLY, carries Girobank financial information and around four general interest features in each issue. Articles are welcome on housing, personal finance, holidays and leisure, and similar consumer-interest topics.

Gloss
Baltic Chambers, 50 Wellington Street,
Glasgow G2 6HJ
☎041–248 7799/041–221 2658

Owner *Loraine Chassels*
Editor *Loraine Chassels*
Circulation 50,000

FOUNDED JULY 1985. MONTHLY Glasgow/ Edinburgh women's glossy. Unsolicited mss welcome; any approach in writing should include a telephone number.

Features *Carlo Tedescht* Maximum 3000 words. *Payment* £15–50.

Golden Age

111–17 Victoria Street, Bristol BS1 6AX
☎0272 299521

Owner *Tony Davies*
Editor *Marion Webb*
Circulation South West edition: 200,000/ National edition: 300,000

FOUNDED 1982. MONTHLY. Unsolicited mss welcome but first approach by brief letter recommended.

Features Informative features on pre-retirement/retirement issues – financial, property, travels, welfare rights, health care, leisure. Maximum length 1250 words. *Payment* negotiable.

Fiction 'With a mature perspective'. *Payment* negotiable.

News Hard news relevant to the retired or those about to retire. Maximum length 500 words. *Payment* negotiable.

Golf World

Advance House, 37 Mill Harbour,
Isle of Dogs, London E14 9TX
☎01–538 1031   Fax 01–538 4106

Owner *New York Times*
Editor *Peter Haslam*
Circulation 91,511

FOUNDED 1962. MONTHLY. Unsolicited mss not welcome, but prospective contributors should approach with ideas in writing.

Good Food Retailing

161–5 Greenwich High Road, London
SE10 8JA
☎01–853 5444

Owner *Dewberry Publications*
Editor *Nicola Graimes*
Circulation 10,203 (controlled)

FOUNDED 1980. MONTHLY. Serves the food retailing industry. Unsolicited mss are welcome.

Good Health

13 Park House, 140 Battersea Park Road, London SW11 4NB
☎01–720 2108

Owner *Hawker Publications*
Editor *D. Hawkins*
Circulation 30,000

FOUNDED 1986. BI-MONTHLY. Freelance material welcome; approach in writing in first instance.

Features Health-related topics. Maximum length 700 words. *Payment* £100 per 1000 words.

Good Housekeeping

National Magazine House,
72 Broadwick Street, London W1V 2BP
☎01–439 7144   Telex 366580

Owner *National Magazine Co. Ltd*
Editor *Noelle Walsh*
Circulation 346,000

FOUNDED 1922. MONTHLY glossy. Freelance contributors are advised to write in the first instance to the appropriate editor. Unsolicited manuscripts are always read, but are not encouraged.

Features *Gillian Fairchild* Most features are specially commissioned, but there is room for freelance contributions of approximately 900 words to the 'Comment' page. *Payment* £120.

Fiction *Shirley Heron* Most fiction is received from agents or publishers, though unsolicited manuscripts will be read.

News *Noelle Walsh* 'Newslines', four pages of short news stories on subjects from food and travel to film stars and money. Maximum 350 words. *Payment* £120 per 1000 words. New ideas for writing about food are always welcome.

Good Ski Guide

1/2 Dawes Court, 93 High Street,
Esher, Surrey KT10 9QD
☎0372 69799   Telex 8951417

Owner *John Hill*
Editor *John Hill*
Circulation 200,000

FOUNDED 1976. QUARTERLY. Unsolicited mss
are welcomed from writers with a knowledge
of skiing and ski resorts. Up to 2000 manuscripts are solicited through the magazine.
Prospective contributors should make contact in writing only as ideas and work need to
be seen before any discussion can take place.
Payment 'better than NUJ'.

ASSOCIATE TITLES *A—Z Resorts Guide* and *A—Z*
Fashion and Equipment Guide.

Gramophone

177—9 Kenton Road, Harrow, HA3 0HA
☎01—907 4476

Editor *Christopher Pollard*
Circulation 64,682

Classical music magazine which is 95% reviews. At any one time they are using around
50 regular freelance writers, who provide
classical music reviews, and on occasion, features or interviews. Reviewing is the starting
place on the magazine, however. Submit
samples of work, whether published or not,
to the editor.

Granta

Bill Buford, 44a Hobson Street,
Cambridge CB1 1NL
☎0223 315290

Editor *Bill Buford*

Magazine of literature and politics published
in book form in association with **Penguin**.
Highbrow, diverse, contemporary, it works
in a thematic way. Presently QUARTERLY, this
may increase to six times yearly in 1988. Do
consider unsolicited mss and fiction, and do a
lot of commissioning. Important to read the
magazine first to appreciate its very particu-

lar fusion of cultural and political interests.
No reviews. *Payment* depends on length, but
not less than £100 per 1000 words.

The Great Outdoors

Ravenseft House, 302—4 St Vincent Street,
Glasgow G2 5NL
☎041—221 7000

Owner *Holmes McDougall Ltd*
Editor *Peter Evans*
Circulation 27,000

FOUNDED 1970. MONTHLY. Deals with walking,
backpacking and countryside topics. Unsolicited mss are welcome.

Features *Roger Smith* Well-written and illustrated items on relevant topics. Maximum
2000 words. *Payment* £60—80.

News *Peter Evans* Short topical items or
photographs. Maximum 300 words. *Payment*
£10—20.

Greenscene

Parkdale, Dunham Road, Altrincham,
Chesthire WA14 4OG
☎061—928 0793

Owner *Vegetarian Society UK Ltd*
Editor *Juliet Gellatley*
Circulation 5000

First issue March 1988. Aimed at 13—18 age
group. Welcome non-fiction stories with
vegetarian angle. Particularly interested in
animal rights issues. Short stories. Unsolicited contributions welcome. *Payment* negotiable (small).

Guitarist

Alexander House, 1 Milton Road,
Cambridge CB1 1UY
☎0223 313722   Fax 0223 323399

Owner *Music Maker Publications (Holdings)*
Group
Editor *Neville Marten*
Circulation 30,000

FOUNDED 1984. MONTHLY. Welcome unsolicited mss. First approach by phone or in
writing.

Hair Now!

Spotlight Publications,
Greater London House, Hampstead Road,
London NW1 7QZ
☎01–387 6611
Telex 299485 MUSIC G   Fax 01–388 5010

Owner *Spotlight Publications*
Editor *Pat Roberts*
Circulation 54,000

FOUNDED 1986. QUARTERLY. Welcome unsolicited mss, if acompanied by s.a.e. First approach in writing.

Hairflair

20–26 Brunswick Place, London N1 6DJ
☎01–490 1444

Owner *Redwood Publishing*
Editor *Katrina Goldstone*
Circulation 50,000

FOUNDED 1982. MONTHLY featuring original, interesting hair-related ideas written in a young, lively style to appeal to readership aged 16–24 years. Unsolicited mss not welcome, but ideas in writing are considered.

Features Maximum 1000 words. *Payment* £75 per 1000 words.

Handgunner

39 High Street, Brightlingsea, Essex CO7 0AQ
☎0206 305204

Owner *J. A. Stevenson*
Editor *J. A. Stevenson*
Circulation 28,000

FOUNDED 1980. BI-MONTHLY. Unsolicited mss are welcome, but material should be incisive and in-depth. Make initial contact by telephone.

Features Really top quality material can be used, related to firearms in economic, political, industrial, police, military and technical fields. Length is dictated by subject matter. *Payment* about £20 per page.

Harpers & Queen

72 Broadwick Street, London W1V 2BP
☎01–439 7144

Owner *National Magazines*
Editor *Nicholas Coleridge*
Circulation 100,000

MONTHLY. Up-market glossy that combines the Sloaney and the streetwise. Receive 1000 unsolicited mss a year and publish 4 or 5 of these. Approach in writing (not phone) with ideas.

Features *Meredith Smith* Ideas only in the first instance.

Fiction *Selina Hastings* Fiction welcome. Maximum 6000 words.

News *Nicholas Coleridge* Snippets welcome if very original. *Payment* negotiable.

Health Express

Victory House, Leicester Square, London WC2H 7NB
☎01–494 3431

Owner *Argus Health Publications*
Editor *Lelsey Keen*
Circulation 500,000

Free health magazine distributed at Holland & Barrett healthfood shops. Do use freelance writers occasionally, usually for specific projects, but also 'names' like vegetarian-cookery writer Rose Elliott. Features on health and health-related topics, including products sold at the stores, and alternative medicine. Write with ideas. *Payment* negotiable.

Health Now

Seymour House, South Street,
Godalming, Surrey GU7 1BZ
☎0483 426064
Telex 859511   Fax 0483 426005

Editor *Alice Peet*
Circulation 400,000

FOUNDED 1977. BI-MONTHLY. Unsolicited mss welcome only if related to the specialised interests of the magazine. Prospective contributors are advised to make their first approach in writing.

Here's Health

Argus Health Publications, Victory House, 14 Leicester Place, Leicester Square, London WC2H 7NB

☎01–494 3431   Fax 09323 49040

Owner *Argus Health Publications*
Editor *Sarah Bounds*
Circulation 65,000

FOUNDED 1956. MONTHLY dealing with health and related subjects. Unsolicited mss welcome.

Features Maximum 1500 words. *Payment* £100 per 1000 words.

Hi-Fi News and Record Review

Link House, Dingwall Avenue, Croydon, Surrey, CR9 2TA

☎01–686 2599

Owner *Link House*
Editor *Steve Harris*
Circulation 39,000

FOUNDED 1956. MONTHLY. Write in the first instance with suggestions based on knowledge of the magazine's style and subject. All articles must be written from an informed technical or enthusiast viewpoint. *Payment* Rates are negotiable, according to technical content of the item concerned.

High Life

47 Whitcomb Street, London WC2H 7DX

☎01–930 8691

Owner *Headway Publications*
Editor *William Davis*
Circulation 215,000

MONTHLY glossy. British Airways in flight magazine. Almost all the content is commissioned, so there are few opportunities for freelancers and unsolicited manuscripts are not welcome. Approach with ideas in writing only.

Him (formerly known as National Gay)

28 Camden High Street, London NW1 7BX

☎01–482 2576

Owner *Out Publications Ltd*
Editor *Bryan Derbyshire*

MONTHLY gay magazine with listings (entertainment, gay pubs and clubs), news and features.

News Editor *David Smith*

Holiday Which?

2 Marylebone Road, London NW1 4DX

☎01–486 5544

Telex 918197   Fax 01–935 1606

Owner *Consumers Association*
Editor *Jonathan Shephard*
Circulation 170,000

QUARTERLY. All research and writing is by permanent staff or by occasional special commission. No real opportunities for freelancers. Unsolicited mss not considered.

Home and Country

39 Eccleston Street, Victoria, London SW1W 9NT

☎01–730 0307

Owner *National Federation of Women's Institutes*
Editor *Penny Kitchen*
Circulation 101,200

FOUNDED 1919. MONTHLY official journal of the Federation of Women's Institutes. General interest articles of interest to women considered. Unsolicited mss welcome. *Payment* by arrangement.

Home & Freezer Digest

Glenthorne House, Hammersmith Grove, London W6 0LG

☎01–846 9922

Telex 919001   Fax 01–741 7762

Owner *British European Associated Publishers*
Acting Editor *Shirley Shelton*
Circulation 200,000

FOUNDED 1974. MONTHLY for freezer owners. Unsolicited mss welcome, but most features are commissioned so freelance opportunities are scarce.

Home Farm

Broad Leys Publishing Co., Buriton House, Station Road, Newport, Saffron Walden, Essex CB11 3PL
☎0799 40922   Fax 0799 41367

Owner *D. & K. Thear*
Editor *Katie Thear*
Circulation 14,000

FOUNDED 1975. BI-MONTHLY journal of the Small Farmers' Association. Unsolicited mss welcome, and around 30 are received every week. Articles should be detailed and practical, based on first-hand knowledge, about aspects of small farming and country living. 'We do not welcome twee urban nostalgia about the countryside.' 'Poetry Corner' publishes verse which 'reflects some aspect of country living today'.

Home Mover

First Avenue Publishing, The Coach House, 90 Alma Road, Windsor, Berkshire SL4 3ET
☎0753 830130   Fax 0753 867262

Owner *First Avenue Publishing*
Editor *Hugh Johnstone*
Circulation 150,000

FOUNDED 1987. MONTHLY. News and features on buying a home, moving house and home improvements. All news written in-house. Welcome ideas for features, humorous articles, etc. Maximum length 2000 words. *Payment* negotiable. First approach by phone or letter.

Homebrew Today

30 Station Approach, West Byfleet, Surrey KT15 6NF
☎09323 49123

Owner *Argus Publications*
Editor *Evelyn Barrett*
Circulation 250,000

FOUNDED 1986. QUARTERLY featuring articles on all aspects of home brewing and the use of homemade wine in cooking, etc. Unsolicited mss welcome.

Homes and Gardens

King's Reach Tower, Stamford Street, London SE1 9LS
☎01–261 5000   Telex 915748 MAGDIV G

Owner *IPC Magazines/Reed Publishing*
Editor *Amanda Evans*
Circulation 200,000+

FOUNDED 1919. MONTHLY. Almost all published articles have been specially commissioned. No fiction or poetry. Best to approach in writing with an idea.

Homes Overseas

387 City Road, London EC1V 1NA
☎01–278 9232   Fax 01–833 2892

Owner *Cresta Holdings plc*
Editor *Michael Furnell*
Circulation 17,000

FOUNDED 1965. MONTHLY of interest to those buying or owning property abroad, particularly those areas popular for tourism: south of Spain, Algarve, France, Italy, Cyprus, Malta.

Features maximum length 1000 words. *Payment* by arrangement.

News up-to-date information on new housing developments for holidays or retirement. Maximum length 750 words. *Payment* £30 or by arrangement.

Horse and Hound

King's Reach Tower, Stamford Street, London SE1 9LS
☎01–261 6315   Telex 915748 MAGDIV G

Owner *IPC Magazines*
Editor *Michael Clayton*
Circulation 72,000

WEEKLY. The magazine has been re-launched with modern make-up, and sharpened-up news and features sections. Contains regular veterinary advice and instructional articles, as well as authoritative news and comment on international showjumping, horse trials, dressage, driving and cross-country riding – plus weekly racing and point-to-points, breeding reports and articles. The magazine nowadays includes a weekly junior and young rider section. Regular books and art reviews, and humorous articles and cartoons are frequently published. Plenty of opportunities for freelancers. Welcome unsolicited contributions. *Payment* NUJ rates.

Horse & Pony

Bretton Court, Bretton,
Peterborough PE3 8DZ
☎0733 264666   Fax 0733 265515

Owner *EMAP*
Editor *Sarah Haw*
Circulation 50,130

Magazine for owners and addicts of the horse, generally aged between 12 and 16. Features include horse-care articles, pony club news, celebrities in the horse world. Not really interested in freelancers: most feature material is produced in-house by staff writers.

Horse and Rider

104 Ash Road, Sutton, Surrey SM3 9LD
☎01–641 4911

Owner *D. J. Murphy (Publishers) Ltd*
Editor *Kate O'Sullivan*
Circulation 30,000

FOUNDED 1949. MONTHLY. Unsolicited mss welcome, and should be addressed to the editor. Adult readership, largely horse-owning. Fiction especially welcome. General interest features welcome. News and instruc-

tional features, which make up the bulk of the magazine, are almost all commissioned. Approach in writing with ideas.

House & Garden

Vogue House, Hanover Square,
London W1R 0AD
☎01–499 9080
Telex 27338 VOLON G   Fax 01–493 1345

Owner *Condé Nast*
Editor *Robert Harling*
Circulation 140,000

Much of their feature material is produced in-house, but do use a small proportion of freelancers, particularly in the wine and food sections. These are mostly commissioned or from known writers, but ideas and mss will be considered. *Payment* Rates vary according to subject, length, rights, etc., particularly in the food section where recipes are involved.

House Buyer

137 George Lane, South Woodford,
London E18 1AJ
☎01–530 7555

Owner *Brittain Publications*
Editor *Con Crowley*
Circulation 25,000

MONTHLY magazine with features and articles for house buyers. Unsolicited mss welcome.

Ice Hockey World and Skating Review

9 Victoria Road, Mundesley-on-Sea,
Norfolk NR11 8JG
☎0263 720038

Editor *Phil Drackett*
Circulation 5000

FOUNDED 1935. MONTHLY during the season. Submissions welcome if preceded by letter/phone. All mss to be addressed to the editor.

Features always welcome. Maximum 1000 words. *Payment* maximum £20.

Fiction rarely, but interested in occasional good short story. Maximum 1000 words. *Payment* by negotiation.

News from local stringers – occasional vacancies.

I D Magazine
27–29 Macklin Street, London WC2E 5LX
☎01–430 0871

Owner *Levelprint*
Editor *Caryn Franklin*
Circulation 50,000

Fashion and style magazine for both sexes age 16–24. Very hip. 'We have opportunities for freelance writers but can't offer fees for non-commissioned work.' Tend to use known writers. A different theme each issue – past themes included the green politics issue, taste, and film – means it is advisable to discuss feature ideas in the first instance.

Ideal Home
King's Reach Tower, Stamford Street,
London SE1 9LS
☎01–261 6505

Owner *IPC Magazines*
Editor *Terence Whelan*
Circulation 3,267,003

FOUNDED 1920. MONTHLY glossy. Unsolicited feature articles are welcomed when appropriate to the magazine (one or two are received each week). Prospective contributors wishing to submit ideas should do so in writing to the Editor only. Home interest features: length of article and *Payment* negotiable. Features should be on furnishings and decoration of houses, kitchens or bathrooms; interior design, soft furnishings; furniture; home improvements, etc. No fiction.

News Editor *Linda Gray* Suggestions/press releases etc. *Payment* negotiable.

The Illustrated London News
20 Upper Ground, London SE1 9PF
☎01–928 6969   Telex 8955803

Owner *James Sherwood*
Editor *Henry Porter*
Circulation 53,000

FOUNDED 1842. MONTHLY. There are few opportunities for freelancers but all unsolicited manuscripts are read – on average, ten a week. The best approach is with an idea in writing.

In Britain
Thames Tower, Black's Road,
London W6 9EL
☎01–846 9000   Telex 21231 BTAADM G

Owner *BTA*
Editor *Bryn Frank*
Circulation 100,000

Magazine of the British Tourist Authority, about things to do and places to visit. Unsolicited mss not encouraged.

Inform
Home & Law Publishing,
Greater London House, Hampstead Road,
London NW1 7QQ
☎01–388 3171
Telex 269470   Fax 01–387 9518

Owner *The Ladbroke Group*
Editor *Debbi Scholes*
Circulation 300,000

BI-ANNUAL magazine with articles on health education and general interest items for teenagers. 'Occasionally' welcome unsolicited mss. First approach by phone.

Intercity
Redwood Publishing,
20–26 Brunswick Place, London N1 6DJ
☎01–490 1444   Fax 01–490 0494
Telex 265871 Ref 81: RED001

Owner *Redwood Publishing, sponsored by British Rail*
Editor *Peter Crookston*
Circulation 250,000

FOUNDED 1985. 10 ISSUES PER YEAR. Complimentary business magazine distributed to passengers on Intercity rail routes. Receive two unsolicited mss weekly, but prefer to be approached by phone with idea initially, followed up by a letter with cuttings if the writer's work is unknown to the editor.

Deputy Features Editor *Beth Richards*

Interior Design

Audit House, Field End Road, Eastcote, Ruislip, Middx HA4 9LT
☎01–868 4499

Owner *AGB Business Publications Ltd*
Editor *Katherine Tickle*
Circulation 10,000

The trade magazine of the commercial interior design industry (no domestic interior design interest). Freelance opportunities are limited, as much of the material is produced in-house or by commission. Informed contributions, case studies etc. are always considered. (Also do *Lighting Design* supplement, for which informed contributions are welcome.) *Payment* £100 per 1000 words.

Interzone

124 Osborne Road, Brighton, East Sussex BN1 6LU
☎0273 504710

Owners *David Pringle, Simon Ounsley*
Editors *David Pringle, Simon Ounsley*
Circulation 4000

FOUNDED 1982. BI-MONTHLY magazine of science fiction and fantasy fiction. Unsolicited mss are welcome from writers who have a knowledge of the magazine and its contents.

Features Science fiction and fantasy book reviews, film reviews, interviews with writers and occasional short articles. Length and *Payment* by arrangement.

Fiction Science fiction and fantasy stories. Maximum length 8000 words. *Payment* £30 per 1000 words.

Investors Chronicle

Greystoke Place, Fetter Lane, London EC4A 1ND
☎01–405 6969   Telex 883694 IC LON G

Owner *Financial Times*
Associate Editor *David Webster*
Circulation 70,000

FOUNDED 1861. WEEKLY. Opportunities for freelance contributors in the survey section only. All approaches should be made in writing. About thirty surveys are published each year on a wide variety of subjects mainly with a financial, business or investment emphasis. Copies of survey list and synopses of individual surveys are obtainable from the Associate Editor. Maximum length 1000 words. *Payment* from £100.

Irish Post

Lex House, 77 South Road, Southall, Middlesex UB1 1SQ
☎01–574 2058/3916

Owner *Irish Post Ltd*
Editor *Donal Mooney*
Circulation 78,000

FOUNDED 1970. WEEKLY. News and features relating to the Irish community in Britain. Welcome unsolicited mss. First approach by telephone.

Jackie

D. C. Thomson, Albert Square, Dundee DD1 9QJ
☎0382 23131   Fax 0382 22214

Owner *D. C. Thomson & Co. Ltd*
Editor *Anne Rendall*
Circulation 250,000

FOUNDED 1964. WEEKLY. Scope for freelance contributors; write in the first instance to the relevant editor.

Features *Catherine Haughney* Emotional/fun features dealing with boys, school, friends, parents and growing up. Maximum length 1500 words.

Fiction *Moira Gee, Steve le Comber* Romantic/humorous text stories and serials. Also photostories. Maximum length 1500 words. *Payment* for all contributions £45 + .

Jazz Journal International

35 Great Russell Street,
London WC1B 3PP
☎01–580 7244

Owner *Jazz Journal Ltd*
Editor-in-Chief *Eddie Cook*
Circulation 11,500

FOUNDED 1949. MONTHLY. A specialised jazz magazine using only expert contributors whose work is known to the editor. Unsolicited mss not welcome, with the exception of news material (for which no *Payment* is made).

Jewish Chronicle

25 Furnival Street, London EC4A 1JT
☎01–405 9252

Owner *Kessler Foundation*
Editor *Geoffrey D. Paul*
Circulation 50,000

Unsolicited mss welcome if 'the specific interests of our readership are borne in mind by writers'. Approach in writing unless it's urgent current news. No fiction. In all cases, maximum 2000 words. *Payment* negotiable. This also applies to the *Jewish Chronicle Colour Magazine*.

News Editor (home) *Hyam Corney;* (foreign) *J. Finklestone*

Colour Magazine/Supplements *Gerald Jacobs*

Features Editor *Meir Persoff*

Women's Page *Jan Shure*

The Journalist

NUJ, Acorn House,
314–320 Gray's Inn Road,
London WC1X 8DP
☎01–278 7916   Telex 892384

Owner *NUJ*
Editor *Tim Gopsill*
Circulation 35,000

MONTHLY journal of the NUJ. Pieces of interest to journalists or relevant to the industry welcome, though most material is produced in-house and outside contributions are not usually paid for.

Just Seventeen

52–55 Carnaby Street, London W1V 1PF
☎01–437 8050

Owner *EMAP Metro*
Editor *Bev Hillier*
Circulation 268,370

FOUNDED 1983. WEEKLY. Top of the mid-teen market. News, articles and fiction of interest to girls aged 12–20. Ideas are sought in all areas. Prospective contributors should send ideas to the relevant editorial department, then follow up with phone call.

Beauty *Fiona Gibson*

Features *Jenny Tucker*

Fiction *Jacqui Deevoi* No more than 2000 words.

News Editor *Tim Nicholson. Payment* £90 per 1000 words.

Keep Fit Magazine

8th Floor, Albany House,
Hurst Street, Birmingham B5 4BD
☎021–622 2899

Owner *Second City Advertising & Publishing*
Editor *Ms Helen White*
Circulation 75,000

FOUNDED 1985. BI-MONTHLY for keep-fit enthusiasts. *Payment* and length of articles by negotiation. Unsolicited mss welcome.

Kennel Gazette

Kennel Club, Clarges Street,
Piccadilly, London W1Y 8AB
☎01–493 6651

Owner *Kennel Club*
Editor *Charles Colborn*
Circulation 10,000

FOUNDED 1873. MONTHLY concerning dogs and their breeding. Unsolicited mss welcome.

Features Maximum 2500 words.

Fiction Maximum 1500 words.

News Maximum 500 words. *Payment* £30 per 1000 words.

Keyboard Player
18 Tileyard Road, Off York Way,
London N7 9AN
☎01–609 5781/2

Owner *Mr S. Miller & Mr I. Seymour*
Editor *Ms J. Haynes*
Circulation 14,000

FOUNDED 1979. Unsolicited mss welcome. Prospective contributors should make initial contact in writing to the Editor who is particularly interested in hearing from writers with a technical/playing knowledge of any keyboard instrument.

Knit and Stitch
PO Box 553, Iver, Bucks SL0 0PD
☎0753 656221   Telex 847505 PINEWD G

Owner *Ingrid Publishing Ltd*
Editor *Sheila Berriff*
Circulation 30,000

FOUNDED 1985. MONTHLY. Mostly patterns, with occasional features. Unsolicited mss not welcome; approach in writing only.

The Lady
39–40 Bedford Street, Strand,
London WC2E 9ER
☎01–836 8705

Owner *T. G. A. Bowles*
Editor *Joan L. Grahame*
Circulation 64,332

FOUNDED 1885. WEEKLY. Unsolicited manuscripts are welcome: they get about 5000

every year. Nothing is accepted on politics, religion or medicine, or on topics covered by staff writers, i.e. fashion and beauty, household, gardening, finance and shopping.

Features Pieces on British and foreign travel are particularly welcomed, and on all other topics except those already mentioned. Maximum length 1500 words. All material to the Editor. *Payment* £38 per 1000 words.

Leisure Express
Newspaper House, 22 Vineyard Road,
Wellington, Shropshire TF1 1DJ
☎0952 51100

Owner *Leisure Newspapers Ltd*
Editor *Ron Newell Evans*
Circulation 400,000

MONTHLY railway magazine (British Rail) which welcomes unsolicited manuscripts. Prospective contributors may make initial contact either in writing or by telephone.

Lincolnshire Life
10 Dudley Street, Grimsby,
South Humberside DN31 2AX
☎0472 356094

Owner   *Lincolnshire Standard Group*
Editor *David N. Robinson*
Circulation 8000

FOUNDED 1961. MONTHLY 'The magazine is based on unsolicited contributions' and they receive a great deal. First approach in writing with s.a.e.

The Listener
199 Old Marylebone Road,
London NW1 5QS
☎01–258 3581

Owner *BBC and ITV*
Editor *Alan Coren*
Circulation 30,000

WEEKLY The magazine of broadcasting. International in scope, stylishly literate in approach and presentation, committed not only to all aspects of television and radio, but also to broad coverage of politics, business, design, technology, books, music, sport, arts and entertainment. *The Listener* is happy to discuss and commission work from the best freelance writers and cartoonists. Suggestions and outlines must be submitted in writing only. *Payment* by negotiation.

Literary Review
51 Beak Street, London W1R 3LF
☎01–437 9392   Telex 919034

Owner *Namara Group*
Editor *Auberon Waugh*
Circulation 15,000

FOUNDED 1979. MONTHLY. Publishes book reviews (commissioned), features and articles on literary subjects, plus short fiction. Prospective contributors are best advised to contact the editor in writing. Unsolicited manuscripts not welcomed (over 500 a month are currently received). *Payment* Book reviews: £25 for 800 words. Literary features: £25–40. Maximum length 1000 words. Short stories: £50 for stories up to 1500 words.

Living
38 Hans Crescent, London SW1X 0LZ
☎01–589 2000

Owner *International Thomson*
Editor *Dena Vane*
Circulation 354,423

Women's and family interest glossy magazine sold at supermarket check-outs. Most features are commissioned from outside freelance writers, but **Associate** and **Features Editor** *Barbara Baker* is keen to encourage new talent and will look at unsolicited mss – or write with ideas in the first instance. Wide-ranging feature needs include family, education, medical issues, 'successful women in small businesses'-type one-offs, and major issues (divorce, drugs, etc.). *Payment* by arrangement.

London Magazine
30 Thurloe Place, London SW7
☎01–589 0618

Owner *Alan Ross*
Editor *Alan Ross*
Circulation 4000–5000

FOUNDED 1954. MONTHLY. Art, memoirs, travel, poetry, criticism, theatre, music, cinema, book reviews, photographs. According to *The Times*, '*London Magazine* is far and away the most readable and level-headed, not to mention best value for money, of the literary magazines.' Receives 150–200 unsolicited mss weekly. Prefers to be approached in writing.

Fiction Maximum length 5000 words. *Payment* £100 maximum. Unsolicited mss welcome; s.a.e. essential.

London Review of Books
Tavistock House South, Tavistock Square, London WC1H 9JZ
☎01–388 6751

Owner *LRB Ltd*
Editor *Karl Miller*
Circulation 15,000

FOUNDED 1980. FORTNIGHTLY. Fiction, news, poems and short stories plus reviews, essays and articles on political, literary, cultural and scientific subjects. Unsolicited contributions welcomed (approximately 35 received each week) and it is best to contact the editor in writing. There is one editorial department covering all aspects of the magazine. *Payment* £50 per 1000 words for prose; £30 per poem.

Look Now
25 Newman Street, London W1P 3HA
☎01–631 3939   Fax 01–631 3649

Owner *Carlton Magazines*
Editor *Deborah Bibby*
Circulation 115,261

FOUNDED 1972. MONTHLY. Freelance contributions are welcomed, but five are received a day and many are unsuitable for the magazine. Prospective contributors are advised to read the magazine thoroughly to pick up on its style. It is best to send ideas in writing to the relevant editor.

Features *Nikki Groocock*

Fiction *Nikki Groocock*

News *Stephanie Crean* Material should be suitable for the 18–24 age range and can be short fiction, serious topical features or light-hearted 'fun' pieces. Maximum length for contributions 1000–2500 words. *Payment* £120 per 1000 words.

Look-in

195 Knightsbridge, London SW7 1RS
☎01–589 8877   Telex 27813

Owner *ITV Publications Ltd*
Editor *Colin Shelbourn*
Circulation 204,000

FOUNDED 1971. WEEKLY children's TV magazine featuring ITV programmes and personalities. Unsolicited mss not generally welcome; prospective contributors are advised to make initial approach in writing.

Features TV, pop, sport, general interest, quizzes, etc. – all aimed at children aged 7–12. *Payment* by negotiation.

Looks

42 Great Portland Street, London W1N 5AH
☎01–437 5430
Telex 32157   Fax 01–631 0781

Owner *EMAP*
Editor *Ramune Burns*
Circulation 153,000

MONTHLY magazine for young women aged 15–20, which concentrates on fashion, beauty and hair matters, as well as general interest features, including celebrity news and interviews, fiction, quizzes, etc. Freelance writers are used in all areas of the magazine. Contact the editor with ideas. *Payment* varies.

Loving

King's Reach Tower, Stamford Street, London SE1 9LS
☎01–261 5000

Owner *IPC Magazines*
Editor *Ms Gerry Fallon*
Circulation 80,000

WEEKLY. Downmarket romantic. About 50–75 unsolicited manuscripts are received each week, but many are unsuitable for the magazine. No features.

Fiction *Lorna Read* New writers are encouraged but are best advised to send an s.a.e. for 'Authors Guidelines' and to read at least three copies of the magazine before attempting to write their stories. All must be in the first person in a young, breezy, slangy style and conversational tone. 'Plots and characters should be rooted in everyday working-class experience and situations; stories which sound middle-class, with well-educated characters, are automatically rejected.'

M (Observer magazine)

Chelsea Bridge House, Queenstown Road, London SW8 4NN
☎01–627 0700   Fax 01–627 5572

Editor *Angela Gordon*
Contact *Angela Mason/Gaythorne Silvester*

First colour supplement to be bound with a spine. Freelance writers used extensively, but an experienced and competitive pool of writers; only very strong ideas and demonstrable talent will succeed here.

Machine Knitting Monthly

Weir House, 62 King Street, Maidenhead, Berks SL6 1EQ
☎0628 770033
Telex 846366   Fax 0628 770658

Owner *Anne Smith*
Editor *Anne Smith*
Circulation 50,000–55,000

FOUNDED 1986. MONTHLY. Will consider unsolicited mss as long as they are applicable to this specialist publication. 'We have our own regular contributors each month but I'm always willing to look at new ideas from other writers.' First approach in writing.

Magazine Week

224–249 Temple Chambers, Temple Avenue, London EC4Y 0DT
☎01–583 6463

Owner *Bouverie Publishing Ltd*
Editor *Tony Loynes*
Circulation 12,000

FOUNDED MARCH 1988. WEEKLY magazine of features and news for everyone who works in the magazine industry.

Features Maximum length 1200 words.

News Maximum length 400 words. No unsolicited mss. Query phone call in the first instance; generally only use material written by professional journalists. *Payment* NUJ rates.

Management Today

30 Lancaster Gate, London W2 3LP
☎01–402 4200

Owner *Management Publications Ltd*
Editor *Lance Knobel*
Circulation 103,000

General business topics and features. A brief synopsis to the editor. *Payment* negotiable.

Marketing Week

St Giles House, 50 Poland Street, London W1V 4AX
☎01–439 4222

Owner *Centaur Communications*
Editor *Howard Sharman*
Circulation 37,095

Trade magazine of the marketing industry. Features on all aspects of the business written in a newsy and up-to-the-minute style from expert commentators always welcome. Ideas first, to **Features Editor** *Stuart Smith*. *Payment* negotiable.

Match

Stirling House, Bretton Court, Bretton, Peterborough PE3 8DJ
☎0733 260333
Telex 32157   Fax 0733 265515

Owner *EMAP*
Editor *Melvyn Bagnall*
Circulation 98,472

FOUNDED 1979. WEEKLY football magazine aimed at 10–18 year olds. Consult the editor or the news editor before making any submission. Contact may be made either by telephone or in writing. Most material is generated in-house by a strong news and features team.

Features/News *Paul Stratton* Good and original material is always welcome. Maximum length: 600 words.

Gossip column Humorous, off-beat snippets for this regular column. Quality Scottish material will also be considered. *Payment* negotiable.

Maternity and Mothercraft

Greater London House (ground floor), Hampstead Road, London NW1 7QQ
☎01–388 3171

Owner *The Newbourne Group*
Editor *Catherine Fleischmann*
Circulation 130,000

FOUNDED 1965. BI-MONTHLY. Unsolicited mss are not welcomed but any prospective contributor should make initial contact by telephone.

Features There is a features list and there are occasional opportunities for writers with relevant experience. (Being a mother of young children is an added advantage.) Maximum length: 600–700 words.

Matrix

114 Guildhall Street, Folkestone, Kent CT20 1ES
☎0303 52939 (evenings)

Owner *British Science Fiction Association*
Editor *Maureen Porter*
Circulation 1000

FOUNDED 1965. BI-MONTHLY newsletter of the BSFA giving all Science Fiction-oriented news, gossip, pre-publication details of new SF books, details of SF societies, magazines, media, etc. Initial approach in writing preferred. No fiction. No literary criticism or author interviews. No *Payment*.

The Mayfair Times

47 Upper Grosvenor Street,
Mayfair, London W1X 9PG
☎01–493 6935
Telex 296472 Fundin G   Fax 01–629 9303

Owner *P. A. R. Wetherel*
Editor *Peter I. Wright*
Circulation 20,000

FOUNDED 1985. MONTHLY. Features on Mayfair of interest to both residential and commercial readers. Welcome unsolicited mss.

Melody Maker

1st floor, Berkshire House,
168–173 High Holborn, London WC1V 7AA
☎01–379 3581

Owner *IPC Magazines*
Editor *Allan Jones*
Circulation 69,313

Freelance contributors are used on this tabloid magazine competitor to *NME* and *Sounds*, but opportunities exist in reviewing rather than features.

Features Editor *Steve Sutherland* A large in-house team plus around six regulars produce the feature material. Send in sample reviews, whether published or not, on pop, rock, soul, funk, etc. to **Reviews Editor** *Ted Mico*. *Payment* NUJ rates in all cases.

Mensa Magazine

British Mensa Ltd, Bond House,
St John's Square, Wolverhampton WV2 4AH
☎0902 772771/2/3

Owner *British Mensa Ltd*
Editor *Simon Clark*
Circulation 18,000

MONTHLY. Unsolicited mss welcome (about ten per month are received). Priority is given to members of the Society, but contributions from non-members are also considered.

Features *Simon Clark* Any general interest topic (e.g. science, travel, education, astrology, etc.) maximum 2500 words. Pieces should be entertaining, informative and concise. Other short articles (500–1200 words) which offer the writer's own opinions on controversial issues are welcome.

Mind Your Own Business

106 Church Road, London SE19 2UB
☎01–771 3614   Fax 01–771 4592

Owner *B. Gledhill/M. Brown*
Editor *Bill Gledhill*
Circulation 61,000

FOUNDED 1978. MONTHLY. Unsolicited material with management appeal is welcomed. About 12 articles are received each week, of which one or two may be of interest.

Features *Bill Gledhill* Should appeal to management.

Fiction *Sarah Pritchard* Light-hearted, humorous articles with a moral to the story and management-oriented. *Payment* £80–120 per 1000 words approx. Minimum NUJ rates, final fee assessed on quality of finished material.

Mizz

Commonwealth House,
1–19 New Oxford Street,
London W1A 1NG
☎01–404 0700

Owner *IPC Magazines*
Editor *Maureen Rice*
Circulation 104,472

FORTNIGHTLY magazine for the 15–19 year-old girl: 'a useful rule of thumb is to write for a 16 year-old'. A wide range of freelance articles welcome, from emotional issues to careers to beauty features. Also fiction – short stories published every issue. Send samples with a letter, or an idea with synopsis in the case of features; the finished mss in the case of fiction, to Maureen Rice.

Money Week
Abbot's Court, 34 Farringdon Lane,
London EC1R 3AU
☎01–490 0888   Fax 01–253 6707

Owner *EMAP*
Editor *Bryan Hubbard*
Circulation 50,000

Enthusiastic about freelance writers and use them in all areas of this personal finance magazine. As *Money Week* is aimed at the personal finance industry itself, writers tend to be specialised, or experienced financial journalists. Major part of the magazine is given to features of around 800 words on all aspects of the business.

News Editor *Ian Harper. Payment* £150 per 1000 words.

Moneycare
Athene House, 66–73 Shoe Lane,
London EC4P 4AB
☎01–377 4633   Telex 922488 Bureau G

Owner *Headway Publications*
Editor *Michael Imeson*
Circulation 1,000,000

The National Westminster Bank Magazine. FOUNDED 1983. BI-MONTHLY on money management. Most articles are commissioned so unsolicited mss are rarely used.

More!
42 Great Portland Street, London W1N 5AH
☎01–436 5430

Owner *EMAP Metro*
Editor *Wendy Bristow*
Circulation 225,000

First edition April 1988. FORTNIGHTLY women's magazine aimed at the working woman aged 18–30. News and features plus a lot of 'how-to' articles. Fairly short, snappy style. Maximum length 1700 words. Will consider unsolicited items but highly recommend that the magazine should be studied for style of writing.

Features Editor *Gillian Carter. Payment* £150 per 1000 words.

The Mortgage Magazine
12 Sutton Row, London W1V 5FH
☎01–734 5716

Owner *Brass Tacks Publishing*
Editor *Stephen Quirke*
Circulation 30,000

FOUNDED 1986. MONTHLY magazine covering finance and property. Unsolicited mss welcome. Make initial approach by telephone to discuss idea, and follow up in writing.

Features Ideas concerning finance and building are always welcome. More peripheral subjects such as interior design, legal matters and housing politics will also be considered. *Payment* £100 per 1000 words.

Mother
12–18 Paul Street, London EC2A 4JS
☎01–247 8233
Telex 8951167   Fax 01–377 9709

Owner *Argus Consumer Publications Ltd*
Editor *Sarah Touquet*
Circulation 73,029

FOUNDED 1936. MONTHLY. New contributors are welcome, but should study the specific style of the magazine in advance. The best approach is in writing with an idea.

Features Bright, lively features on being a mother and on aspects of babies and children. No fiction. Maximum length 1500 words. *Payment* varies.

News Very little opportunity for freelancers, as there is just one page of news per issue. Maximum length 200 words. *Payment* varies.

Mother and Baby

12–18 Paul Street, London EC2A 4JS
☎01–247 8233
Telex 8951167 Fax 01–377 9709

Owner *Argus Consumer Publications*
Editor *Eileen Fielding*
Circulation 110,000

FOUNDED 1956. MONTHLY. No unsolicited mss, except personal 'birth stories' and 'Viewpoint' pieces. Approaches may be made by telephone or in writing.

Motor Boat & Yachting

Quadrant House, The Quadrant,
Sutton, Surrey SM2 5AS
☎01–661 3298
Telex 892084 REED BP G Fax 01–661 3263

Owner *Reed Business Publishing*
Editor *Tom Willis*
Circulation 37,000

FOUNDED 1904. MONTHLY for those interested in motor cruising.

Features *Alan Harper* Cruising features, practical features especially welcome. Illustrations (mostly colour) as important as the text. Maximum 3000 words. *Payment* £75 per 1000 words or by arrangement.

News *Alan Harper* Factual pieces only, without comment. Maximum 200 words. *Payment* up to £25 per item.

Motor Cycle News

PO Box 11, Huxloe Place, High Street,
Kettering NN16 8SS
☎0536 81651

Owner *EMAP*
Editor *Malcolm Gough*
Circulation 143,364

Use freelancers, but mostly an established network of contributors. As a WEEKLY, the magazine is news-oriented: particularly keen on motor racing, rallying and events reportage. Feature material is mostly produced in-house. Ideas to **Deputy Editor** *Simon Arron*.

Motorway Express

Newspaper House, 22 Vineyard Road,
Wellington, Shropshire TF1 1DJ
☎0952 51100

Owner *Leisure Newspapers Ltd*
Editor *Ron Newell Evans*
Circulation 250,000

MONTHLY magazine which welcomes unsolicited manuscripts. Prospective contributors may make initial contact either in writing or by telephone.

Mountain Bike UK

Woodstock House, Luton Road,
Faversham, Kent ME13 8HQ
☎0795 538903

Owner *Pacificon Ltd*
Editor *Tyn Manley*
Circulation 30,000

FOUNDED MAY 1988. Unsolicited mss are welcomed if informative articles on mountain biking. Maximum length 2500 words. Prospective contributors are advised to make initial approach in writing. *Payment* negotiable.

The Musical Times

8 Lower James Street, London W1R 4DN
☎01–734 8080 Telex 27937

Owner *Novello & Co. Ltd*
Editors *Andrew Clements and Alison Latham*

Serious-minded journal with a scholarly approach to its subject. *Payment* negotiable.

My Guy

Commonwealth House,
1–19 New Oxford Street, London WC1
☎01–829 7770

Owner *IPC*
Editor *Lesley Robb*

FOUNDED 1977. WEEKLY teen magazine for girls. Unsolicited mss welcomed, provided they suit the magazine's style. Best approach by telephone with idea.

Features *Lesley Robb* One 1000-word story published each week.

My Story

PO Box 94, London W4 2ER
☎01–995 0590

Owner *Atlantic Publishing Co.*
Editor *Geoff Kemp*
Circulation 38,000

FOUNDED 1956. Downbeat romantic story MONTHLY. Fiction only, provided it is in keeping with the usual style publishing. Best to study previous issues before sending anything in. *My Story* receives around 250 mss a week. *Payment* £14 per 1000 words.

My Weekly

80 East Kingsway, Dundee DD4 8SL
☎0382 44276

Owner *D. C. Thomson & Co. Ltd*
Editor *S. D. Brown*
Circulation 696,279

A traditional women's WEEKLY which, like others in the D. C. Thomson stable, is currently trying to attract a younger readership, and compete for the young working woman's attention in the marketplace (while not alienating its traditional, loyal readership). Particularly interested in humour and human interest pieces which by their very nature appeal to all age groups: 1000–2500 words; and fiction. Three stories a week range from the emotional to the offbeat and unexpected: 2000–4000 words. Also serials. D. C. Thomson has long had a philosophy of consultation and help for writers of promise. *Payment* negotiable.

Nature

4 Little Essex Street, London WC2R 3LF
☎01–836 6633

Owner *Macmillan Magazines Ltd*
Editor *John Maddox*
Circulation 33,530

Covers all fields of science. Very little use for freelance writers or unsolicited mss; approach specialists when appropriate. No features – articles and news on science policy only.

Netball

Francis House, Francis Street,
London SW1P 1DE
☎01–828 2176

Owner *All England Netball Association Ltd*
Editor *Sylvia Eastley*
Circulation 5000

FOUNDED 1940. QUARTERLY. No freelance or unsolicited mss are accepted.

New Democrat

9 Poland Street, London W1V 3DG
☎01–434 1059

Owner *Letterhurst Ltd*
Editor *Harry Cowie*
Circulation 8000

FOUNDED 1982, published FIVE TIMES YEARLY. Unsolicited mss welcome. Submissions should be in writing.

Features Profiles, or features on policies and events of interest to Alliance (Liberal/SDP) supporters. Maximum length 1500 words. No *Payment*.

New Home Economics

Forbes Publications Ltd,
120 Bayswater Road, Queensway,
London W2 3JH
☎01–229 9322

Owner *Forbes Publications Ltd*
Editor *Dilys Wells*
Circulation 5100

TEN ISSUES YEARLY. Contributors should bear in mind that all readers are fully qualified home economists or students of the subject.

Features Articles up to 1200 words welcomed on the topics listed below.

News Items welcomed on food and nutrition, textile studies, childcare and development, health education, money topics and consumerism. Maximum length 500 words. *Payment* by negotiation.

New Humanist

88 Islington High Street, London N1 8EW
☎01–226 7251

Owner *Rationalist Press Association*
Editor *Jim Herrick*
Circulation 3000

FOUNDED 1885. QUARTERLY. Unsolicited mss welcome.

Features Articles with a humanist perspective are welcomed in the following fields: religion (critical), humanism, human rights, philosophy, current events, literature, history and science. Usual length 2000–4000 words. *Payment* negotiable, but 'minimal'. No fiction.

Book reviews by arrangement with the editor. Usually between 750 and 1000 words.

New Internationalist

42 Hyth Bridge Street, Oxford OX1 2EP
☎0865 728181

Owner *New Internationalist Publications Ltd*
Editor *Chris Brazier*
Circulation 60,000 worldwide

Concerned with world poverty and global issues of peace and politics, with the emphasis on the Third World: radical, and broadly leftist in approach, though unaligned. Difficult to use unsolicited material, as they work to a theme each month, and the editor commissions features on that basis. The way in is to send examples of published or unpublished work; writers of interest are taken up.

New Left Review

6 Meard Street, London W1V 3HR
☎01–734 8839

Editor *Robin Blackburn*
Circulation 35,000

Magazine of theoretical politics, history and related issues, plus (to a lesser degree) a Marxist reading of the arts and humanities. Generally provided by academics and expert commentators in the field rather than journalists. No *Payment*.

New Musical Express

4th Floor, Commonwealth House,
1–19 New Oxford Street,
London WC1A 1NJ
☎01–404 0700

Owner *IPC Magazines Ltd*
Editor *Alan Lewis*
Circulation 99,000

Britain's best selling musical WEEKLY. *NME* does use freelancers, but always for reviews in the first instance. Specialisation in areas of music (or film, which is also covered) is a help.

Review editors: Books *Sean O'Hagan*

Film *Gavin Mead*

LPs *Alan Jackson*

Live *Helen Mead* Send in examples of work, whether published or specially written samples.

New Socialist

150 Walworth Road, London SE17 1JT
☎01–703 0833

Owner *Labour Party*
Editor *Nigel Williamson*
Circulation 16,000

FOUNDED 1981. BI-MONTHLY. Unsolicited mss (with s.a.e.) welcome.

Features Articles on socialist themes. Maximum 2000–3000 words.

News 'Frontline' section – short news items. 500 words.

Reviews *Nigel Williamson* Short reviews of film, theatre, music, television, books, etc. 500 words.

New Statesman and Society

Foundation House, Perseverance Works,
38 Kingsland Road, London E2 8BA
☎01–739 3211
Telex 28449 NSTAT   Fax 01-739 9307

Owner *New Statesman and Nation Publishing Co.*
Editor *Stuart Weir*
Circulation 29,000

WEEKLY magazine of the political left which is the result of a merger in May 1988 of *New Statesman* and *New Society*. Unsolicited contributions welcomed. New contributors are best advised to contact **Deputy Editor** *Mike Poole.*

Literary Editor *Tony Gould*
Music Editor *Stuart Cosgrove*
Political Editor *Sarah Benton*

19 (incorporating Honey)

King's Reach Tower, Stamford Street,
London SE1 9LS
☎01–261 6360

Owner *IPC Magazines*
Editor *Deirdre Vine*
Circulation 147,000

MONTHLY magazine aimed at the 17–20 year-old girl. A little different to the usual teen magazine mix: *19* are now aiming for a 50/50 balance between the fashion/lifestyle aspects and meatier, newsier material on *Young Guardian* lines, e.g. articles on women in prison, and life in East Berlin. Also 'Speak for Yourself', a platform page for ordinary readers rather than professional journalists to speak out on any subject. 40% of the magazine's feature material is commissioned, ordinarily from established freelancers. 'But we're always keen to see original bold vigorous writing from people just starting out...' Letter with ideas first, to **Deputy Editor** *Jane Dowdeswell.*

Northamptonshire and Bedfordshire Life

Chapel House, Chapel Lane, St Ives,
Huntingdon, Cambridgeshire PE17 4DX
☎0480 62844

Owner *Cambridgeshire Life Ltd*
Editor *Stuart Mayes*
Circulation 9,500

FOUNDED 1972. MONTHLY magazine featuring articles which are 'geographically relevant'. Maximum 1000–1500 words, plus three or four good quality photographs. Welcome unsolicited mss. First approach in writing. *Payment* varies.

Nursing Times

4 Little Essex Street, London WC2R 3LF
☎01–379 0970

Owner *Macmillan Magazines Ltd*

A large proportion of *Nursing Times* feature content is from unsolicited contributions sent on spec., although they also commission articles. Pieces on all aspects of nursing and health care, both practical and theoretical, written in a lively and contemporary way, are welcomed. *Payment* varies; NUJ rates of £100 per 1000 words for commissioned work.

Office Secretary

Streatfield House, Carterton,
Oxford OX8 3XZ
☎0993 845484   Fax 0993 845882

Owner *Trade Media Ltd*
Editor *Penny Commerford*
Circulation 160,000

FOUNDED 1986. QUARTERLY. Features articles of interest to female office staff aged 25–50. Unsolicited mss welcome.

Features Chatty but informative pieces on current affairs, health, office-related topics. Maximum 2500 words. *Payment* £100 per 1000 words or by negotiation.

On The Move

South Bank Business Centre,
13 Park House, 140 Battersea Park Road,
London SW11 4NB
☎01–622 4185

Owner *Travel & Leisure Services*
Editor *Clive Lewis*
Circulation 18,000

FOUNDED 1985. TEN ISSUES YEARLY. Travel and leisure opportunities in the UK and into Europe for discriminating travellers. Prospective contributors are advised to make initial contact by telephone.

Features *Derek Cox* Maximum 1200 words. Items, in the main, specifically commissioned. Views and opinions on travel and public transport (up to a maximum of 1000 words) are welcomed.

News *Clive Lewis* All pieces are specifically commissioned. Maximum 600 words. *Payment* negotiable.

Onboard Windsurfing Magazine
Andrew House, 2a Granville Road,
Sidcup, Kent DA14 4BN
☎01–302 6069

Owner *Stone Independent Publications Ltd*

FOUNDED 1970. MONTHLY. Official magazine for the UK Boardsailing Association and the Scottish and Irish Associations.

Features and **News** Short items about local/regional teams, etc. Maximum length 1500–2000 words. *Payment* £35 with picture.

Opera
1A Mountgrove Road, London N5 2LU
☎01–359 1037   Fax 01–354 2700

Owner *Opera Magazine Ltd*
Editor *Rodney Milnes*
Circulation 15,500

FOUNDED 1950. MONTHLY review of the current opera scene. Almost all articles are commissioned and unsolicited mss are not welcome. All approaches should be made in writing.

Options
25 Newman Street, London W1P 3HA
☎01–631 3939

Owner *Carlton Magazines Ltd*
Editor *Jo Foley*
Circulation 226,380

Options aims to entertain the modern renaissance woman, worker, mother and wife; more for the woman who has arrived than the *Cosmopolitan* emotional/sexual issues market. Almost all written by freelancers, these tend to be a regular bunch, but new writers are encouraged, and 'commissioned non-commissioned pieces' are requested from new feature writers of promise. The full page 'Speak Out' column is a platform for even the most amateur writer with something to say.

Out Of Town
Standard House, Epworth Street,
London EC2A 4DL
☎01–628 4741

Owner *Narod Press Ltd*
Editor *Richard Cavendish*
Circulation 15,000

FOUNDED 1983. MONTHLY. Unsolicited mss are welcomed and prospective contributors are advised to make initial contact in writing.

Features up to a maximum of 2000 words on heritage, countryside matters and places to visit are welcome. *Payment* from £50 per 1000 words.

Over 21 Magazine
Greater London House, Hampstead Road,
London NW1 7QZ
☎01–837 6611   Fax 01–388 5010

Owner *United Magazines Ltd*
Editor *Pat Roberts* (Managing Editor)
Circulation 92,000

FOUNDED 1972. MONTHLY. When a writer is new to them, they prefer ideas in writing, together with examples of the writer's published work, details of experience etc. They do not accept unsolicited manuscripts, of which they receive approximately 30 per week, but mss accompanied by an s.a.e. will be returned.

Features Feature ideas appropriate to the magazine should be submitted in writing. Not generally interested in 'round robin' lists of ideas circulated to other publications.

Fiction For the past three years *Over 21* has been running an extremely successful Short Story Competition and publishing the winners and runners-up. A fourth competition is planned for 1988. They are therefore not currently in the market for fiction.

News The 'News and Views' pages at the beginning of the magazine occasionally use freelance contributors who should contact *Guy Pierce*, editor of the 'Now' Section.

Paperback Inferno

1 The Flaxyard, Woodfall Lane, Little Neston, South Wirral L64 4BT
☎051 336 3355

Owner *British Science Fiction Association*
Editor *Andy Sawyer*
Circulation 1000

FOUNDED 1977. BI-MONTHLY. Publishes reviews of Science Fiction paperbacks and professional SF magazines. Unsolicited material not welcome as all reviews are commissioned.

Parents

Victory House, Leicester Place, London WC2H 7NB
☎01–437 9011   Telex 266400

Owner *Gemini Magazines Ltd*
Editor *Jackie Highe*
Circulation 94,940

FOUNDED 1976. MONTHLY. Specialist writers and professional freelancers are requested to write with suggestions for consideration.

Patches

Albert Square, Dundee DD6 8JB
☎0382 23131   Fax 0382 22214

Owner *D. C. Thomson & Co. Ltd*
Editor *Mrs Moira Chisholm*

Magazine for the 12–16 year-old girl. A mixture of photostories, short stories and features, which should be teen-oriented and deal with the emotional and practical issues affecting girls of this age. Unsolicited pieces sent in on spec. will be considered. *Payment* for features starts at around £40.

Penthouse

Northern & Shell Building, PO Box 381, Mill Harbour, London E14 9TW
☎01–987 5090   Telex 24676 NORSHL G

Owner *Richard Desmond*
Editor *Linzi Drew*
Managing Editor *Isabel Koprowski*
Circulation 100,000 +

FOUNDED 1965. 13 ISSUES YEARLY.

Features *Isabel Koprowski* Maximum length 3500 words. *Payment* negotiable 'but generally pretty good'. Unsolicited mss welcome, 'but most of those we do receive are unsuitable because the authors haven't looked at the magazine'. First approach by phone or in writing with ideas.

News *Sandy Robertson* Limited opportunities for unsolicited material. Must have a fairly long-term appeal.

People's Friend

80 Kingsway East, Dundee DD4 8SL
☎0382 44276

Owner *D. C. Thomson & Co. Ltd*
Editor *Douglas Neilson*
Circulation 572,000

Traditional WEEKLY magazine which caters for a family audience. Mostly fiction: short stories should be suitable for family reading: 'the normal problems of the normal family next door'. Any length from 1000–3000 words. Not much of a market for non-fiction, but short filler articles of 500–2000 words are welcome. *Payment* negotiable.

Performance Tuning

538 Ipswich Road, Slough SL1 4EQ
☎0753 820161   Fax 0753 22691

Owner *C. W. Editorial Ltd*
Editor *Ian Ward*
Circulation 35,000

Formerly entitled *Sports Car Monthly*. Relaunched as *Performance Tuning* January 1988. Features on tuned or modified cars, both sports and saloon. Maximum length 2500 words. No unsolicited mss. First approach in writing. *Payment* negotiable.

Period Homes
Apex House, Vincent Walk, South Street, Dorking, Surrey RH4 2HA
☎0306 887676   Fax 0306 881970

Owner *Noble Weston Hays Publishing Ltd*
Editor *Gary Noble*
Circulation 20,000

FOUNDED 1980. MONTHLY magazine devoted to renovation and restoration of period houses. Interested in receiving histories of restoration work, case studies, historical development and profiles of period and listed houses. Also craft and other 'heritage' articles. Prefer to be approached by telephone in the first instance.

Personnel Management
.1 Hills Place, London W1R 1AG
☎01-734 1773   Telex 51714 PRINTN G

Owner *Personnel Publications Ltd*
Editor *Susanne Lawrence*
Circulation 40,000

FOUNDED 1969. MONTHLY specialist magazine for personnel managers. Unsolicited mss welcome, from specialists in the personnel field only.

Features *Susanne Lawrence* Only interested in material written by specialists in their field. Occasional scope for articles by those with experience or knowledge of employment, industrial relations, training, pay areas. Maximum 3000 words. *Payment* NUJ rates. ·

News *David Turner* Sometimes interested in reports of events where staff member was not present. Length varies. *Payment* NUJ rates.

Photoplay
1 Golden Square, London W1R 3AB
☎01-437 0626

Owner *Argus Specialist Publications Ltd*
Editor *Ken Ferguson*

Features on the film, video and TV scene. s.a.e. essential for return of unsolicited material. *Payment* by arrangement.

Plays and Players
248 High Street, Croydon, Surrey CR0 1NF
☎01-681 7817

Owner *Plus Publications*
Editor *Robert Gore-Langton*
Circulation 8000

Theatre MONTHLY, which publishes a mixture of reviews, features on aspects of the theatre, festival reports etc. Rarely use unsolicited material, but writers of talent are taken up. Almost all material is commissioned. *Payment* under review, but small.

Plays International
55 Hatton Garden, London EC1N 8HP
☎01-720 1950

Owner *Chancery Publications*
Editor *Peter Roberts*

Freelance writers are used, but are a well-established team of regulars, and unsolicited material cannot be considered. *Plays International* is a mixture of interviews, reviews and a complete play text every month. One-off pieces are only rarely commissioned.

Poetry Review
21 Earls Court Square, London SW5 9DE
☎01-373 7861

Owner *The Poetry Society*
Editor *Peter Forbes*
Circulation 3500

FOUNDED 1909. QUARTERLY poetry magazine. Approximately 5000 unsolicited manuscripts received each year (mostly poetry) and these are welcome, but the odds should be taken into account by prospective contributors. Almost all prose is commissioned. A preliminary letter is advisable before submitting reviews or features.

Pony

104 Ash Road, Sutton, Surrey SM3 9LD
☎01–641 4911

Owner *Marion O'Sullivan*
Editor *Julia Goodwin*
Circulation 36,000

FOUNDED 1948. Lively MONTHLY aimed at 10–18 year olds. News, instruction on riding, stable management, veterinary care, interviews. Features welcomed. Not more than 1500 words. *Payment* £50 per 1000 words. News written in-house. Welcome photographs and illustrations (serious and cartoon). *Payment* negotiable. Regular short story of not more than 1800 words. *Payment* £50 per 1000 words. Prefer to be approached in writing.

Powerboat International

The Poplars, New Road,
Armitage, Staffordshire WS15 4BJ
☎0543 491818
Telex 335622   Fax 0543 490515

Owner *Pat Ainge*
Editor *Pat Ainge*
Circulation 8000

FOUNDED 1983. MONTHLY. This is a specialised powerboat racing magazine whose policy is to welcome outside contributions, especially from overseas. Length and *Payment* negotiable. At present only one or two unsolicited contributions are received a month.

Practical Computing

Reed Business Publishing Ltd,
Quadrant House, The Quadrant,
Sutton, Surrey SM2 5AS
☎01–661 3633
Telex 892084/REEDBP G   Fax 01–661 3948

Owner *Reed Business Publishing Ltd*
Editor *Glyn Moody*
Circulation 37,000

FOUNDED 1977. MONTHLY. Unsolicited mss not welcome; prospective contributors must send an outline in writing before sending mss. *Payment* negotiable.

Practical Gardening.

Bushfield House, Orton Centre,
Peterborough, Cambs PE2 0UW
☎0733 237111
Telex 32157   Fax 0733 231137

Owner *EMAP*
Editor *Mike Wyatt*
Circulation 90,382

FOUNDED 1960. MONTHLY. Unsolicited mss welcome, but there are few acceptances out of 150 offered each year. Submit ideas in writing.

Features Occasionally features/photos on gardens (*not* famous gardens or stately homes) are required if they suit the *Practical Gardening* style. Maximum length 1200 words. *Payment* from £60 per 1000 words.

Practical Health & Slimming

4 Bloomsbury Square, London WC1A 2RL
☎01–404 0188

Owner *International Thomson Publishing Ltd*
Editor *Michele Simmons*
Circulation 180,000–200,000

BI-MONTHLY. No unsolicited mss. Query letter in the first instance with samples of style.

Practical Motorist

Unit 8, Forest Close,
Ebblake Industrial Estate, Verwood,
Wimborne, Dorset BH21 6DQ
☎0202 823581

Owner *Practical Motorist Ltd (A member of the Mayfair Publishing Group)*
Editor *Denis Rea*
Circulation 40,000

FOUNDED 1934. MONTHLY. Welcome unsolicited mss. All approaches should be made to the editor. Maximum length 1500 words. *Payment* 'on merit'. 'Ours is a very specialised field and not many can hope to match our established contributors.'

Practical Photography
Bushfield House, Orton Centre, Peterborough, Cambs PE2 0UW
☎0733 237111
Telex 32157   Fax 0733 231137

Owner *EMAP*
Editor *Richard Hopkins*
Circulation 100,000

MONTHLY. Unsolicited mss welcome if relevant to the magazine and its readers. Preliminary approach may be made by telephone. Always interested in new ideas.

Features Anything relevant to the readership – but not 'the sort of feature produced by staff writers'. Bear in mind that there is a three-month lead-in time. Maximum 2000 words. *Payment* varies.

News Only 'hot' news applicable to a monthly magazine. Maximum 800 words. *Payment* varies.

Prediction
Link House, Dingwall Avenue, Croydon CR9 2TA
☎01–686 2599
Telex 947709 LINKHO G   Fax 01–760 0973

Owner *Link House Magazines*
Editor *Jo Logan*
Circulation 35,000

FOUNDED 1936. MONTHLY. The magazine covers astrology and topics with an occult slant and unsolicited material in these areas is welcomed. 200–300 mss are received every year.

Astrology Pieces ranging from 800–2000 words should be practical as well as of general interest. Charts and astro data should accompany them, especially if profiles. *Payment* £25–75.

Features *Jo Logan* Articles on earth mysteries, alternative medicine and psychical/occult experiences and phenomena are considered. Maximum length 2000 words.

News *Jon Taylor* News items of interest to readership welcomed. Maximum length 300 words. No *Payment*.

Prima
Portland House, Stag Place, London SW1E 5AU
☎01–245 8700

Owner *G & J*
Editor *Sue James*
Circulation 1,000,000

FOUNDED 1986. Top selling women's MONTHLY. A German import.

Features *Lesley Dobson* Features are mostly practical and written by specialists or commissioned from known freelancers. Unsolicited mss not welcome.

Private Eye
6 Carlisle Street, London W1V 5RG
☎01–437 4017

Owner *Pressdram*
Editor *Ian Hislop*
Circulation 240,000

FOUNDED 1961. FORTNIGHTLY humour and satire magazine. A great number of unsolicited contributions are received and these are welcomed if they are stories or cartoons, but no jokes are required. Prospective contributors are best advised to approach the editor in writing. News stories and feature ideas are always welcomed. *Payment* in all cases is 'not great', and length of piece varies as appropriate.

Property Mail
90–92 King Street, Maidstone, Kent ME14 1BH
☎0622 670246

Owner *Property Mail Ltd*
Editor *Allan Bishop*
Circulation 551,000 (8 editions)

FOUNDED 1983. WEEKLY. Unsolicited manuscripts are welcome, but prospective contributors are welcome to make a preliminary approach by telephone.

Psychic News

20 Earlham Street, London WC2H 9LW
☎01–240 3032/3/4   Fax 01–379 0620

Owner *Psychic Press Ltd*
Editor *Tony Ortzen*

FOUNDED 1932, *Psychic News* is the world's only WEEKLY Spiritualist newspaper. It covers such subjects as psychic research, hauntings, ghosts, poltergeists, spiritual healing, survival after death and paranormal gifts. Never use unsolicited mss (although receive enormous amounts).

Punch

23–27 Tudor Street, London EC4Y 0HR
☎01–583 9199   Telex LDN 265863

Owner *United Newspapers*
Editor *David Taylor*
Circulation 65,000

FOUNDED 1841. WEEKLY humorous magazine. New image is taking it a long way from dentists' waiting rooms. Unsolicited contributions 'are tolerated', but prospective contributors should note that *Punch* receives 50 to 60 unsolicited manuscripts per week. Only finished pieces are accepted and these should be around 1200 words, typed and accompanied by an s.a.e.

Q

42 Great Portland Street,
London W1N 5AH
☎01–637 9181

Owner *EMAP Metro*
Editor *Mark Ellen*
Circulation 60,000

FOUNDED 1986. MONTHLY. Glossy aimed at educated rock music enthusiasts in their thirties. Very few opportunities for freelance writers, and unsolicited mss are strongly discouraged. Prospective contributors should approach in writing only.

RA

Friends of the Royal Academy of Arts,
Royal Academy of Arts,
Burlington House, Piccadilly,
London W1V 0DS
☎01–734 9052   Fax 01–434 0837

Owner *Friends of the Royal Academy*
Editor *Nick Tite*
Circulation 40,000

FOUNDED 1983. QUARTERLY magazine with a controlled circulation. Articles relating to or about the Royal Academy, its members and exhibitions. Unsolicited mss considered but no unsolicited material has yet been published. Important to make initial contact in writing. Features should be no longer than 1500 words. *Payment* £100.

The Racing Pigeon

19 Doughty Street, London WC1N 2PT
☎01–242 0565   Fax 01–831 0056

Owner *The R. P. Publishing Co. Ltd*
Editor *Colin Osman*
Circulation 33,000

FOUNDED 1898. WEEKLY news magazine for racing pigeon enthusiasts. Only specialist writers considered. Maximum 1000 words. Unsolicited mss welcome.

Radio Times

35 Marylebone High Street,
London W1M 4AA
☎01–580 5577

Owner *BBC Publications*
Editor *Nicholas Brett*
Circulation 3,224,038

WEEKLY. Best selling house magazine. Christmas issue tops 11 million. Detailed BBC television and radio listings in this magazine are accompanied by interviews and feature material relevant to the week's output. 95% of this is provided by freelance writers, but, obviously, the topicality of the pieces needed means close consultation with editors. Unlikely to use the unsolicited material they receive, but do take up writers of interest to work on future projects.

Features Editor *Veronica Hitchcock*

The Railway Magazine

Prospect House, 9–13 Ewell Road,
Cheam, Surrey SM1 4QQ
☎01–661 4480/1/2   Telex 892084

Owner *Reed Business Publishing*
Editor *John Slater*
Circulation 38,000

FOUNDED 1897. MONTHLY. Welcome unsolicited mss for features. Maximum 2000 words. *Payment* negotiable.

Rambler

1–5 Wandsworth Road, London SW8 2XX
☎01–586 6826

Owner *Ramblers' Association*
Editor *Frances Rowe/Alan Mattingly*
Circulation 53,500

BI-MONTHLY. Unsolicited material welcome.

Features Freelance features are invited on walking in Britain and abroad, the natural world and conservation. Transparencies should accompany when possible and pieces should be 1500–2000 words long. *Payment* around £50 per 1000 words.

The Reader's Digest

25 Berkeley Square, London W1X 6AB
☎01–629 8144

Owner *Reader's Digest Association Ltd*
Editor *Russell Twisk*
Circulation 1.5 million

In theory, a good market for general interest features of around 2500 words. However, 'a tiny proportion' comes from freelance writers. Opportunities for short humorous contributions to regular features – 'Life's Like That', 'Humour in Uniform' – for which the fee is £100.

Record Collector

43 St Mary's Road, Ealing,
London W5 5RQ
☎01–579 1082

Owner *Johnny Dean*
Editor *Peter Doggett*

FOUNDED 1979. MONTHLY. Features detailed, well-researched articles on any aspect of record collecting or any collectable artiste in the field of popular music (1950s–1980s) with complete discographies where appropriate. Unsolicited mss welcome. *Payment* by negotiation.

Record Mirror (RM)

Greater London House, Hampstead Road,
London NW1 7QZ
☎01–387 6611   Telex 299485 MUSIC G

Owner *Spotlight Publications*
Editor *Betty Page*
Circulation 52,000

FOUNDED 1954. WEEKLY. Unsolicited manuscripts are not welcome except as examples of a writer's work not intended for publication. Prospective contributors are advised to make initial contact by telephone.

Features *Eleanor Levy* Opportunities for young, new writers with specific feature ideas.

News *Robin Smith* News tips used occasionally.

Review Pages (Lives) *Tim Nicholson* Opportunities for young writers nationwide wanting to review young new bands. *Payment* at current NUJ rates.

Resident Abroad

108 Clerkenwell Road, London EC1M 5SA
☎01–251 9321
Telex 23700 FINBI G   Fax 01–251 4686

Owner *Financial Times*
Editor *William Essex*
Circulation 17,514

FOUNDED 1979 MONTHLY magazine aimed at British expatriates. Unsolicited mss welcome.

Features of up to 2000 words on finance, employment opportunities and other topics likely to appeal to readership, such as living conditions in 'likely countries'.

Fiction rarely published, but exceptional, relevant stories (no longer than 2000 words) might be considered. *Payment* on acceptance £100 per 1000 words.

RIBA Interiors
66 Portland Place, London W1N 4AD
☎01–580 5533

Owner *RIBA Magazines Ltd*
Editor *Richard Wilcock*
Circulation 21,000

BI-MONTHLY sister journal to *The RIBA Journal*.

Features Interiors by architects and other relevant subjects treated in specialist manner. Maximum 1200 words. *Payment* £100 per 1000 words.

The RIBA Journal
66 Portland Place, London W1N 4AD
☎01–580 5533

Owner *RIBA Magazines Ltd*
Editor *Richard Wilcock*
Circulation 27,500

MONTHLY journal of Royal Institute of British Architects.

Features Specialist articles on architecture and matters of practice. Maximum 1200 words. *Payment* £100 per 1000 words.

Riding
Corner House, Foston,
Grantham NG16 2JU
☎0400 82032

Owner *Scott Publications Ltd*
Editor *Helen Scott*
Circulation 34,000 approx.

Most of the writers on *Riding* are freelancers. It's aimed at a mostly adult, horse-owning audience: the 'serious leisure rider'. Feature opportunities are limited, as regular columnists take up much of the magazine. However, new and authoritative writers always welcome. *Payment* negotiable.

Rugby World and Post
Weir Bank, Bray-on-Thames,
Maidenhead SL6 2ED
☎0628 770011
Telex 847591   Fax 0628 39519

Owner *Rugby Publishing*
Editor *Nigel Starmer-Smith*
Circulation 30,000

MONTHLY. Features of special rugby interest. Unsolicited contributions welcome but prior approach by phone or in writing preferred.

Running Magazine
57–61 Mortimer Street,
London W1N 7TD
☎01–637 4383

Owner *Stonehart Magazines Ltd*
Editor *David Calderwood*
Circulation 60,331

Freelancers are used, but are mostly a team of regular contributors. Specialist knowledge is needed to have features accepted – 'we would never take a feature from someone new'. However, they do accept and publish personal accounts from readers – personal experience running stories are welcome.

RYA News
Royal Yachting Association, RYA House,
Romsey Road, Eastleigh,
Hampshire SO5 4YA
☎0703 629962
Telex 47393 BOATIN G   Fax 0703 629924

Owner *Royal Yachting Association*
Editor *Vicki Davies*
Circulation 65,000

FOUNDED 1975. QUARTERLY. Unsolicited mss welcome if they concern general cruising matters with a RYA slant. Prospective contributors are advised to make their first approach in writing.

Features Maximum length 1500 words. *Payment* negotiable but small.

Saga Magazine

The Saga Building, Bouverie Square, Folkestone, Kent CT20 5SL
☎0303 47523
Telex 966331   Fax 0303 48622

Owner *Saga Publishing Ltd*
Editor *Paul Bach*
Circulation 650,000

FOUNDED 1984 from *Saga News*. TEN ISSUES PER YEAR. '*Saga Magazine* sets out to celebrate the role of older people in society. It reflects their achievements, promotes their skills, protects their interests, campaigns on their behalf. A warm personal approach, addressing the readership in an upbeat and positive manner.' It has a hard core of celebrated commentators/writers (e.g. Brian Redhead) as regular contributors but there is scope for well-written features. Subjects include achievement, hobbies, finance, food, wine, social comment, motoring, fitness, diet, etc. Maximum length 1600 words (preferred length 1000–1200). *Payment* 'Very competitive'.

Sailplane and Gliding

281 Queen Edith's Way, Cambridge CB1 4NH
☎0223 247725

Owner *British Gliding Association*
Editor *Gillian Bryce-Smith*
Circulation 7500

FOUNDED 1930. BI-MONTHLY for gliding enthusiasts. A specialised magazine with very few opportunities for freelancers *Payment* No fees for contributions.

Sales Direction

2 St John's Place, London EC1M 4DE
☎01–253 2427   Fax 01–608 0865

Owner *Sales Direction Magazine Ltd*
Editor *Nick de Cent*
Circulation 25,000

FOUNDED 1986. MONTHLY. Unsolicited mss are welcomed as long as they are relevant to sales management/business readership. It is strongly advised that initial contact (either by telephone or in writing) is made with an idea before full submission is made.

Features Lifestyle features up to 1000 words and interesting sports pursuits relevant to business people.

Interviews with top sales directors and business people in the public eye. Prior discussion essential. Between 1500 and 2000 words.

News No longer than 300 words. *Payment* £100 per 1000 words.

Sales and Marketing Management

ISE Publications Ltd, 13 Vaughan Road, Harpenden, Herts AL5 4HU
☎05827 62038/63810   Fax 0582 453640

Owner *David Waller*
Editor *Jayne Bridges*
Circulation 18,682

ELEVEN ISSUES YEARLY. A great many unsolicited mss are received. These are welcome if on topics relevant to sales and marketing management. Prospective contributors are advised to make initial contact in writing and to present other published work where possible.

Features up to 2000 words dealing with sales techniques, motivation, modern management practice, etc, are welcomed. No fiction. *Payment* negotiable.

Sanity

22–24 Underwood Street, London N1 7JG
☎01–250 4010

_er CND Publications Ltd
_itor Caroline Williamson
Circulation 40,000

FOUNDED 1961. MONTHLY CND magazine. Unsolicited mss are welcomed. About 100 mss come in each month, most not suitable for publication.

Features Mostly written by people involved in the peace movement or with specialist political/scientific knowledge. Maximum length 3000 words.

News Most news is commissioned on arms race, international and domestic news. Maximum length 500 words. *Payment* NUJ rates.

Scan

The Old Village Hall, Church Street, Paddock, Huddersfield HD1 4UB
☎0484 542205

Owner *Live Publishing*
Editor *Stuart Price*
Circulation 75,000

MONTHLY magazine with news and features on travel, homes, gardens, health, arts, plus a 'What's on' section. Welcome unsolicited material, particularly items of local interest. *Payment* by negotiation.

Scotland's Runner

62 Kelvingrove Street, Glasgow G3 7SA
☎041–332 5738

Owner *Scotrun Publications*
Editor *Alan Campbell*
Circulation 10,000

FOUNDED 1986. MONTHLY with features on athletics, fitness, nutrition and health. Welcome unsolicited mss. First approach in writing.

The Scots Magazine

D. C. Thomson & Co. Ltd,
7–25 Bank Street, Dundee DD1 9HU
☎0382 23131
Telex 76380   Fax 0382 27159

Owner *D. C. Thomson & Co. Ltd*
Editor *Maurice Fleming*
Circulation 82,000

FOUNDED 1739. MONTHLY. 'It has to be stressed that this is a magazine produced in Scotland for people who know the country. It's not an "outside" view of Scotland. Besides a core of regular writers, we do consider any good freelance work which comes our way for any category in the magazine. A study of the magazine is advised.'

Features Maximum 4000 words. *Payment* 'according to quality and length'.

Fiction 'Must depict Scottish life and character – not sordid or depressing; good plot essential.' *Payment* as for features.

News Brief stories of interest. *Payment* by arrangement. Photographic features (colour transparencies), and also series which are open to freelancers.

The Scotsman Magazine

20 North Bridge, Edinburgh EH1 1YT
☎031–225 2468
Telex 72255/727600   Fax 031–225 7302

Owner *Thompson Regional Newspapers*
Editor *Richard Wilson*
Circulation 180,000

MONTHLY magazine issued with *The Scotsman* newspaper. Features of general interest, preferably with Scottish emphasis. Good pictures particularly important. 'Novelty appreciated, but straightforward, serious approach expected'. Only occasional fiction – 'Tale End' feature on Scottish themes. Receive four or five items per week. Welcome unsolicited mss but prefer to be approached by phone in the first instance.

Features Maximum 2000 words. *Payment* £110 per 1000 words.

Fiction Maximum 1200 words. *Payment* £125.

Scottish Field

302 St Vincent Street, Glasgow G2 5NL
☎041–221 7000

Owner *Holmes McDougall Ltd*
Editor *Joe Stirling*
Circulation 20,000

FOUNDED 1903. MONTHLY.

Features *Joe Stirling* Articles of breadth and authority with a Scottish dimension and good visual impact. Maximum length 1200 words. *Payment* 'above average'.

Fiction *Joe Stirling* One short story monthly by Scottish author or on well-defined Scottish subject. Maximum length 1400 words. *Payment* 'above average'. Welcome unsolicited mss but writers should study the market.

Scottish Football Today

c/o Forth Sports Marketing Ltd,
3 Marchfield Grove, Edinburgh EH4 5BN
☎031–336 2374

Owner *Forth Sports Marketing Ltd*
Editor *Norman Sutherland*
Circulation 20,000+

FOUNDED 1985. MONTHLY. Unsolicited mss are welcome. Receive approximately ten per month. First approach in writing.

Screen

29 Old Compton Street, London W1V 5PL
☎01–734 5455

Owner *Society for Education in Film & Television*
Editor *Mandy Merck*
Circulation 2,500

QUARTERLY academic journal of film and television studies for a readership ranging from undergraduates to media professionals. There are no specific departments but articles – based on a knowledge of the magazine and its markets – are welcomed from freelancers. The best approach is with an idea in writing.

Screen International

6–7 Great Chapel Street, London W1V 4BR
☎01–734 9452

Owner *King Publications Ltd*
Editor *Nick Roddick*

Trade paper of the film, video and television industries. No unsolicited mss, though expert freelance writers are occasionally used in all areas.

Sea Breezes

202 Cotton Exchange Building,
Old Hall Street, Liverpool L3 9LA
☎051–236 3935

Owner *Jocast Ltd*
Editor *Mr C. H. Milsom*
Circulation 18,500

FOUNDED 1919. MONTHLY. The magazine covers virtually everything relating to ships and shipping of a non-technical nature. Unsolicited mss welcome; they should be thoroughly researched and accompanied by relevant photographs. Articles about nautical history, shipping company histories, epic voyages etc. should be up to 5000 words. *Payment* £5 per 1000 words.

She Magazine

National Magazine House,
72 Broadwick Street, London W1V 2BP
☎01–439 5000   Fax 01–437 6886

Owner *National Magazine Co. Ltd*
Editor *Joyce Hopkirk*
Circulation 232,000

MONTHLY. Women's glossy with less gloss and much more general interest reading than comparable monthlies. Feature material can include social issues, health, spiritual matters, unusual subjects of any kind, as well as traditionally 'female' concerns. Articles should be of around 1200 words. Fiction is used from time to time: again, general rather than 'women's' reading. Regular freelancers used, but open to new talent. *Payment* NUJ rates.

Shoot Magazine

King's Reach Tower, Stamford Street,
London SE1 9LS
☎ 01–261 5000
Telex 915748   Fax 01–829 7707

Owner *IPC Magazines*
Editor *Peter Stewart*
Circulation 163,000

FOUNDED 1969. WEEKLY football magazine. Present ideas for news, features or colour photo-features to the editor in writing. No unsolicited mss.

Features Hard-hitting, topical and off beat. 450–1500 words.

News Items welcome, especially exclusive gossip and transfer speculation. Maximum length 150 words. *Payment* £36–75.

Shooting and Conservation

Marford Mill, Rossett,
Wrexham, Clwyd LL11 0HL
☎ 0244 570881   Fax 0244 571678

Owner *BASC*
Editor *James McKay*
Circulation 74,285

QUARTERLY. Unsolicited mss are welcomed. In both **Features** and **Fiction** sections, good articles, stories on shooting, conservation and related areas, up to 2000 words, are always sought. *Payment* negotiable.

Shooting News

Unit 21, Plymouth Road Ind. Est,
Tavistock, Devon PL19 9QN
☎ 0822 616460

Owner *V. Gardner*
Editor *C. Binmore*
Circulation 13,050

FOUNDED 1982. WEEKLY. Unsolicited material is welcome, six or seven submissions are received each week, and a list of special editions and subjects covered by the magazine is available on request.

Features Should be on any fieldsport topic and no longer than 1500 words.

News Items considered. No fiction. *Payment* Rates available on request.

Shooting Times & Country

10 Sheet Street, Windsor, Berkshire SL4 1BG
☎ 0753 856061   Fax 0753 859652

Owner *Associated Newspapers Holdings plc*
Editor *Jonathan Young*
Circulation 44,000

FOUNDED 1882. WEEKLY. Articles on shooting, fishing and related countryside topics. Unsolicited mss considered. Maximum length 950 words. *Payment* by negotiation.

The Sign

St Thomas House, Becket Street,
Oxford OX1 1SJ
☎ 0865 242507

Owner *Mowbray Publishing*
Editor *Dr A. L. Moore*
Circulation 256,000

FOUNDED 1907. MONTHLY inset for Church of England parish magazines. Unsolicited mss welcome.

News, Features and **Fiction** all considered. Maximum 400 words. *Payment* negotiable.

Signature

7–11 St John's Hill, London SW11 1TN
☎ 01–228 3344

Owner *Reed Publishing Services*
Editor *Mary Ratcliffe*
Circulation 50,000

RELAUNCHED 1986. The magazine for Diners Club Cardholders, issued TEN TIMES YEARLY. Unsolicited mss rarely used, but written suggestions welcome.

Features Most of the main features are commissioned from regular writers. Most articles are based on travel or food. Maximum 2000 words. *Payment* negotiable.

Special One special section each month on subjects such as health, sport, gardening and fashion. Maximum 1000 words. *Payment* negotiable.

Singles Magazine
23 Abingdon Road, London W8 6AH
☎01–938 1011

Owner *John Patterson*
Editor *Lorraine Furneaux*
Circulation 23,000

FOUNDED 1976. MONTHLY magazine for single people. Unsolicited mss welcome; ideas in writing only.

Features Anything of interest to, or directly concerning, single people. Maximum 2500 words. *Payment* from £35–45 per 1000 words.

News All news items required at least six weeks ahead. Maximum length 2500 words. *Payment* from £35–45 per 1000 words.

Ski Survey
118 Eaton Square, London SW1W 9AF
☎01–245 1033   Telex 291608

Owner *Ski Club of Great Britain*
Editor *Elisabeth Hussey*
Circulation 24,000

FOUNDED 1903. FIVE ISSUES YEARLY. All articles are commissioned.

The Skier
1 Grimsdells Corner, Sycamore Road,
Amersham, Bucks HP6 5EL
☎02403 28967
Telex 838791 JMC   Fax 02403 22626

Owner *Charles Hallifax*
Editor *Charles Hallifax*
Circulation 25,000

MONTHLY from September to January. Unsolicited manuscripts welcome. Approximately 15 are received each season.

Features of 1000–3000 words on any topic involving 'action' such as skiing, climbing,

white-water rafting, etc. Articles of 1000–3000 words, written in a light, humorous style are particularly welcome.

News Items of varying length are always welcome. *Payment* negotiable.

Skiing UK Ltd
22 King Street, Glasgow G1 5QP
☎041–552 4067/0957   Telex 94011565

Owner *Skiing UK Ltd*
Editor *Ian McMillan*
Circulation 12,500

FOUNDED 1985. FIVE ISSUES YEARLY. Unsolicited mss are welcome on all skiing topics. Approach either in writing or by telephone. No fiction.

Features Should be no longer than 1200 words. *Payment* £70 per 1000 words.

News Items should be no longer than 300 words. *Payment* £50 per 100 words.

Slimmer
Tolland, Lydard St Lawrence,
Taunton, Somerset TA4 3PS
☎0984 23014

Owner *Slimmer Publications Ltd*
Editor *Judith Wills*
Circulation 140,058

FOUNDED 1976. BI-MONTHLY. Freelance contributors should write with synopsis and c.v., or with cuttings of previously published work. Ideas for features are preferred to completed manuscripts.

Features First-person slimming stories and features on nutrition, research etc. Must be in a chatty style. Maximum length 1500 words. *Payment* £10 per 100 words.

News Titbits – serious or amusing – on slimming and fitness. Maximum length 200 words. *Payment*, on publication, £10 per 100 words.

Slimming
Victory House, 14 Leicester Place,
London WC2H 7QP
☎01–437 9011

Owner *Argus Press*
Editor *Patience Bulkeley*
Circulation 250,000

FOUNDED 1969. BI-MONTHLY. Basically a scientific magazine with most of its material written by staff, so the opportunities for freelance contributors are very few indeed. There is some scope for first-person experiences of weight control/loss, but only a small number of those received prove suitable. It is best to approach with an idea in writing. *Payment* by negotiation.

Smash Hits

52–55 Carnaby Street, London W1V 1PF
☎01–437 8050   Fax 01–437 2738

Owner *EMAP Metro*
Editor *Barry McIlhengy*
Circulation 533,930

FOUNDED 1979. FORTNIGHTLY. Top of the mid-teen market. Unsolicited manuscripts are not accepted, but prospective contributors may approach in writing.

Snooker Scene

Cavalier House, 202 Hagley Road,
Edgbaston, Birmingham B16 9PQ
☎021–454 2931

Owner *Everton's News Agency*
Editor *Clive Everton*
Circulation 18,000

FOUNDED 1971. MONTHLY. Unsolicited material is not welcome; any approach should be in writing with an idea.

Social and Liberal Democrat News

4 Cowley Street, London SW1P 3NB
☎01–222 7999

Owner *Social and Liberal Democrats Party*
Editor *Paul Sample*

FOUNDED MARCH 1988. WEEKLY. As with the political parties, a merger of the two publications, *Liberal News* and *The Social Democrat*. Political and social topics of interest to party members and supporters. Unsolicited contributions welcome.

Features Maximum length 500 words.

News Maximum length 350 words. *Payment* All contributions are unpaid.

Somerset & Avon Life

St Lawrence House, Broad Street,
Bristol BS1 2EX
☎0272 291069   Fax 0272 225633

Owner *Regional Magazines Ltd*
Editor *Heidi Best*
Circulation 9,500

FOUNDED 1976. MONTHLY.

Features 'We use a fair percentage of freelance contributors'. Welcome ideas. First approach in writing. Maximum length 1600 words. *Payment* by arrangement.

News Only small items which will still be newsworthy eight weeks after submission. Maximum length 200 words. *Payment* by arrangement.

Sounds

Greater London House,
Hampstead Road, London NW1 7QZ
☎01–387 6611
Telex 299485 MUSIC G   Fax 01–388 5010

Owner *Spotlight Publications Ltd*
Editor *Tony Stewart*
Circulation 60,770

Popular music WEEKLY tabloid. 99% of their material is provided by freelancers. Send trial reviews in to be considered for work; reviews writers of talent can go on to feature-writing.

Reviews Editor *Robbi Millar*

Features Editor *Tony Stewart*. *Payment* £82.40 per 1000 words.

South Magazine

New Zealand House, 13th Floor,
Haymarket, London SW1Y 4TS
☎01–930 8411
Telex 8814201   Fax 01–930 0980 (Group 3)

Publisher *Humayun Gauhar*
Editor *Andrew Graham-Yooll*
Circulation 86,000

FOUNDED 1980. MONTHLY magazine of the Third World. Unsolicited mss considered, but it's better to make initial contact in writing so that editors can consider the subject and discuss it with writer. Many articles are received from all over the world.

Arts & Leisure Of interest to the Third World.

Business & Finance *Melvyn Westlake*

Features *Raana Gauhar* and *Judith Vidal Hall* Any Third World topic is considered, as long as it carries a strong business and financial interest.

Fiction Rarely published.

Science and Technology *Maria Elena Hurtado* Innovations in the field – all pieces must consider the problems of the Third World. *Payment* Finance and political features £140 per 1000 words; Arts & Leisure £100 per 1000 words.

The Spectator
56 Doughty Street, London WC1N 2LL
☎01–405 1706
Telex 27124   Fax 01–242 0603

Owner *The Spectator (1828) Ltd*
Editor *Charles Moore*
Circulation 37,000

FOUNDED 1828. WEEKLY political and literary magazine. Taken over April 1988 by the Telegraph Newspaper Group. Maximum length for all contributions is 1500 words, and prospective contributors should write in the first instance to the relevant editor. Unsolicited manuscripts welcomed, but over 20 received every week.

Arts *Jenny Naipaul*

Books *Mark Amory*

Features *Charles Moore, Dominic Lawson*

News *Charles Moore. Payment* in all cases is 'small'.

Sport & Fitness
75 South Western Road, Twickenham, Middlesex TW1 1LG
☎01–891 6885   Fax 01–892 0975

Owner *Edward Hankey*
Editor *Edward Hankey*
Circulation 27,000

FOUNDED 1984. MONTHLY magazine with articles on weight training, nutrition, and bodybuilding. Welcome unsolicited mss. Receive approximately 8 per month. Maximum length 2500 words. *Payment* £35 per 1000 words.

The Sporting Life
Alexander House, 81–89 Farringdon Road, London EC1M 3HJ
☎01–831 2102

Owner *Odhams Newspapers Ltd*
Editor *Monty Court*
Circulation 84,984

DAILY magazine-newspaper of the horse-racing world. Always on the look-out for specialised racing writers – not necessarily established sports writers, but certainly well-informed. No unsolicited mss – phone or write with an idea. The talented will be taken up and used again.

Contact *Alistair Down* (Features Editor).

Sporting Life Weekender
Alexander House, 81–89 Farringdon Road, London EC1M 3HJ
☎01–831 1808   Telex 263403

Owner *Odhams Newspapers Ltd*
Editor *Neil Cook*
Circulation 40,000

FOUNDED 1983. WEEKLY. Prospective contributors should write with ideas in first instance as no articles are published before discussion. *Payment* NUJ rates.

Sportswoman International (1), Sportsworld International (2)

25 Prentis Road, London SW16 1QB
☎01–769 0753/01–749 0262

Owner *Lyn Guest de Swarte*
Editor *Lyn Guest de Swarte*
Circulation (1) 20,000 (2) 30,000

Many unsolicited mss are received, and are welcome. A crisp, non-sexist style is preferred. No fiction.

Features *Lyn Guest de Swarte* Particularly human interest and 'inside' sports stories as well as articles on health-related topics. Maximum length 1500 words.

News *Cathy Gibb* Interesting snippets up to a maximum of 300 words needed. *Payment* NUJ rates.

Squash Player International

Stanley House, 9 West Street,
Epsom, Surrey KT18 7RL
☎03727 41411   Fax 03727 44493
Telex 291 561 VIA SOS G (AEM)

Owner *A. E. Morgan Publications Ltd*
Editor *I. R. McKenzie*
Circulation 10,000

MONTHLY. Mss welcome; sample material and synopsis preferred.

Features Instructive club and commercial news.

News Tournament reports.

Squash World

Chiltern House, 184 High Street,
Berkhamsted, Hertfordshire HP4 3AP
☎04427 74947   Fax 04427 3152

Owner *Dennis Fairey Publishing Ltd*
Editor *Larry Halpin*
Circulation 10,000

FOUNDED 1986. MONTHLY. Unsolicited mss welcome; approach by telephone with ideas. Resident experts generally cover topics of health, diet, fitness and coaching, but material of 1200–1500 words from other experts would be considered.

Features *Larry Halpin* Phone with ideas for articles of 1200–1500 words.

News *Larry Halpin* Stories of a maximum of 500 words on tournaments, new clubs, sponsorship, etc., always welcome. *Payment* by negotiation.

The Stage and Television Today

47 Bermondsey Street, London SE1 3XT
☎01–403 1818

Owner *Carson and Comerford Ltd*
Editor *Peter Hepple*
Circulation 43,422

FOUNDED 1880. WEEKLY. Unsolicited manuscripts are not welcome; prospective contributors should write with ideas in the first instance.

Features Occasional feature suggestions are considered. Preference is given to material with a business or financial orientation rather than personal pieces or interviews. Maximum length 1200 words. *Payment* £100 per 1000 words.

News News stories from ouside London are always welcome. Maximum length 300 words. *Payment* £10 + .

Status UK

108 New Bond Street, London W1
☎01–372 6745

Owner *A. B. International Ltd*
Editor *Michael Hornett*
Circulation 60,000

FOUNDED 1985. Published FIVE TIMES YEARLY. A broadbased luxury magazine for men and women distributed in London, New York, Japan, Paris and Milan. Topics relating and appealing to luxury lifestyle are of interest, 'especially well written'. *Payment* £65–75 per 1000 words.

The Strad

8 Lower James Street, London W1R 4DB
☎01–734 8080   Telex 27937.

Owner *Novello & Co.*
Editor *Eric Wen*
Circulation 10,000

FOUNDED 1889 MONTHLY for classical string musicians and enthusiasts. Unsolicited mss welcome.

Features Profiles of string players and musical instruments. Maximum 3000 words. *Payment* £150.

Sunday

PO Box 7, 2nd Floor, 214 Gray's Inn Road, London WC1X 8EZ
☎01–481 4100
Telex 297918 KRM G   Fax 01–833 7373

Owner *Murdoch Magazines (UK) Ltd*
Editor *Colin Jenkins*
Circulation 5,200,000

FOUNDED 1981. WEEKLY colour supplement magazine published with *The News of the World*. Freelance writers' ideas and material are always welcomed. Showbiz interviews and strong human-interest features make up most of the content, but there are no strict rules about what is 'interesting'.

Features *Nick Ferrari* Length and *Payment* subject to negotiation.

Sunday Express Magazine

Newspaper House, 8–16 Great New Street, London EC4A 3AJ
☎01–353 8000   Telex 21841

Owner *United Newspapers plc*
Editor *Dee Nolan*
Circulation 2,206,494

WEEKLY. Unsolicited mss are not welcome or considered, as features on all topics are commissioned from freelance writers. Any ideas, however, should be offered in writing.

The Sunday Times Magazine

214 Gray's Inn Road, London WC1X 8EZ
☎01–481 4100

Owner *News International*
Editor *Philip Clarke*
Circulation 1,300,000

FOUNDED 1962. WEEKLY colour supplement distributed with *The Sunday Times*. Almost all features are specially commissioned, prospective contributors should write in the first instance with ideas. No unsolicited mss are accepted.

Supercar Classics

FF Publishing, 97 Earls Court Road, London W8 6QH
☎01–370 0333   Fax 01–373 7544

Owner *FF Publishing Ltd*
Editor *Mark Gillies*
Circulation 40,000

FOUNDED 1983. MONTHLY. Unsolicited mss of at least 1500 words are welcomed: make initial contact either by phone or in writing.

Features are usually commissioned from staff and known writers, but other reports of classic older cars, no longer in production, would be welcomed. Maximum length 3000 words.

Fiction Short stories and satire (up to 2000 words) are considered. *Payment* £100–200 per 1000 words (negotiable).

Survival Weaponry & Techniques

89 East Hill, Colchester, Essex CO1 2QN
☎0206 861130

Owner *Aceville Ltd*
Editor *Greg Payne*

MONTHLY publication on outdoor survival techniques. The only unsolicited material welcomed are specialist articles from experienced survival writers. Articles are paid for on publication. *Payment* £14 per 1000 words.

Swimming Times

Harold Fern House, Derby Square,
Loughborough LE11 0AL
☎0509 234433

Owner *Amateur Swimming Association*
Editor *R. H. Brown*
Circulation 15,600

FOUNDED 1923. MONTHLY about competitive swimming and associated subjects. Unsolicited mss welcome.

Features Technical articles on swimming, diving or synchronised swimming. Length and *Payment* negotiable.

The Tablet

48 Great Peter Street, London SW1P 2HB
☎01–222 7462

Owner *The Tablet Publishing Co. Ltd.*
Editor *John Wilkins*
Circulation 13,494

FOUNDED 1840. WEEKLY (50 p.a.). Quality magazine featuring articles of interest to Roman Catholic laity and clergy. On average, five unsolicited manuscripts are received daily, but these are only accepted when relevant. The usual article length is 1500 words. *Payment* is approximately £30 upwards. All approaches should be made in writing.

Taste

58 Old Crompton Street, London W1V 5PA
☎01–846 9922

Owner *BEAP Ltd*
Editor *Marie-Pierre Moine*

A small staff means articles are mostly by freelance writers, and usually commissioned. Always on the look-out for 'new regulars' though. Food, travel, cookery, wine/drink, kitchen, and general interest features with a foodie angle, e.g. the growth of nouvelle cuisine. Glossy and upmarket, 'but not as upmarket as *A La Carte*'. New writers should approach the editor with ideas and samples of written work, whether published or not.

The Tatler

Vogue House, Hanover Square,
London W1R 0ED
☎01–499 9080

Owner *Condé Nast*
Editor *Emma Soames*
Circulation 49,124

Upmarket glossy from the *Vogue* stable. New writers should send in copies of either published work or unpublished material; writers of promise will be taken up. The magazine works largely on a commission basis: they are unlikely to publish unsolicited features, but will ask writers to work to specific projects.

Features Editor *Rebecca Fraser*

Telegraph Sunday Magazine

Peterborough Court, Southquay,
181 Marsh Wall, London E14 9SR
☎01–538 5000

Editor *Felicity Lawrence*
Circulation 700,000

WEEKLY magazine supplement to the *Sunday Telegraph*. Well-written articles on subjects of national interest with a human angle. Must have very good picture potential. Interested contributors should write in first instance. *Payment* negotiable. Maximum length 1500 words.

Tennis World

Chiltern House, 184 High Street,
Berkhamsted, Herts HP4 3AP
☎04427 74947/8   Fax 04427 3055

Owner *Dennis Fairey Publishing Ltd*
Editor *Alastair McIver*
Circulation 15,000

FOUNDED 1969. MONTHLY. Unsolicited mss welcome.

Features Any ideas on tennis features or tennis personalities are welcome. Maximum 1000 words. *Payment* £75.

Texas Homecare Magazine

Home & Law Publishing,
Greater London House, Hampstead Road,
London NW1 7QQ
☎01–388 3171
Telex 269470   Fax 01–387 9518

Owner *The Ladbroke Group*
Editor *Catherine Rendall*
Circulation 3.5 million

THRICE YEARLY with features on DIY and gardening. Will consider unsolicited mss if they 'fit the planned editorial'. First approach by phone.

This England

PO Box 52, Cheltenham, Glos GL50 1YQ
☎0242 577775

Owner *Pickwick Press Ltd*
Editor *Roy Faiers*
Circulation 175,000

Published FOUR TIMES YEARLY, and with a strong overseas readership. Celebration of England and all things English: famous people, natural beauty, towns and villages, history, traditions, customs and legends, crafts etc. Generally a rural basis. The 'Forgetmenots' section publishes readers' recollections and nostalgia. They receive up to 100 unsolicited pieces a week. 250–2000 word articles will be considered. *Payment* negotiable.

Time

Time & Life Building, New Bond Street,
London W1Y 0AA
☎01–499 4080   Telex 22557

Owner *Time Inc.*
Editor *Christopher Ogden* (London Bureau Chief)
Circulation 509,000,000 (worldwide)

FOUNDED 1923. WEEKLY current affairs and news magazine. There are no opportunities for freelancers on *Time* as almost all the magazine's content is written by staff members from the various bureaux around the world. Unsolicited manuscripts are not read.

Time Out

Tower House, Southampton Street,
London WC2E 7HD
☎01–836 4411   Fax 01–836 7118

Owner *Tony Elliott*
Editor *Don Atyeo*
Circulation 80,000

FOUNDED 1968. WEEKLY magazine of news and entertainment in London.

Features *John Gill* and *Simon Garfield* 'Usually written by staff writers or commissioned, but it's always worth submitting an idea if particularly apt to the magazine.' Maximum length 2500 words.

Fiction *Don Atyeo* and *John Gill* Creative writing competitions at Christmas. Maximum length 2500 words.

News *Andy Bell* Despite having a permanent team of staff news writers, always willing to accept contributions from new journalists, 'should their material be relevant to the issue'. Maximum length Sidelines: 250 words, Features: 1000 words. Other sections occasionally take on freelance writers. Submit pieces to section heads (see masthead of current issue).

Times Educational Supplement

Priory House, St John's Lane,
London EC1M 4BX
☎01–253 3000   Telex 24460 TTSUPP

Owner *News International*
Editor *Stuart MacLure CBE*
Circulation 109,000

FOUNDED 1910. WEEKLY. New contributors are welcome, and should phone with ideas for news or features, write for reviews.

Arts and Books *Heather Neill* Unsolicited reviews are not accepted. Anyone wanting to review should write, sending examples of their work and full details of their academic and professional background to either the literary editor or the media and resources editor. Maximum length 1200 words.

Features *Bob Doe* 'Platform': A weekly slot for a well-informed, cogently-argued viewpoint – maximum length 1500 words; 'Second Opinion': A shorter comment on an issue of the day by somebody well placed to write on the subject – maximum length 570 words; 'Features': These are longer articles on contemporary practical subjects of general interest to the *TES* reader. Longer or multi-part features are rarely accepted – maximum length 1000–1500 words. *Payment* varies. 'Extra' *Pamela Cooley* Subjects covered include: science, travel, music, modern languages, home economics, school visits, primary education, history, geography, mathematics, health, life skills, environmental education, CDT, special needs. Articles should relate to current educational practice. Age range covered is primary to sixth form. Maximum length 1000–1300 words. *Payment* £65 per 1000 words.

Media and Resources Editor *Gillie Macdonald*

Times Educational Supplement Scotland

37 George Street, Edinburgh EH2 2HN
☎031–220 1100   Fax 031–220 1616

Owner *Times Newspapers Ltd*
Editor *Willis Pickard*
Circulation 6500

FOUNDED 1965. WEEKLY. Unsolicited mss welcome, but many more are received than can be used.

Features Articles on education in Scotland. Maximum 1500 words. *Payment* NUJ rates for NUJ members.

News News items on education in Scotland. Maximum 600 words.

The Times Higher Education Supplement

Priory House, St John's Lane,
London EC1M 4BX
☎01–253 3000
Telex 24460   Fax 01–608 1599

Owner *Times Newspapers*
Editor *Peter Scott*
Circulation 15,367

FOUNDED 1971. WEEKLY. Unsolicited mss are welcome but most articles and *all* book reviews are commissioned.

Books *Brian Morton*

Features *Peter Aspden* Most articles are commissioned from academics in higher education.

News *David Jobbins* Very occasional freelance opportunities.

Science *Jon Turney*

Science Books *Robbie Vickers* 'In most cases it is better to write, but in the case of news stories it is all right to phone.' *Payment* NUJ rates.

The Times Literary Supplement

Priory House, St John's Lane,
London EC1M 4BX
☎01–253 3000
Telex 24460 TTSUPP   Fax 01–608 1599

Owner *News International*
Editor *Jeremy Treglown*
Circulation 30,000

FOUNDED 1902. WEEKLY review of literature. Contributors should approach in writing and be familiar with the general level of writing in the *TLS*.

Libraries Articles considered on libraries and archives, both famous and out of the way, in which the author has spent some time engaged on a particular subject. Potential contributors are advised to consult back issues, and write briefly to the editor proposing their subject.

News *Isabel Fonseca* News stories and general articles concerned with literature, publishing and new intellectual developments anywhere in the world. Length by agreement. *Payment* at NUJ rates.

Titbits

Northcliffe House, London EC4Y 0JA
☎01–583 0350   Fax 01–583 2133

Owner *Mail Newspapers plc*
Editor *Brian Lee*
Circulation 160,000

FOUNDED 1881. MONTHLY. There are opportunities for freelance contributors with features on show business, television, pop music, medical topics, women's interests, animals and pets, royalty and the supernatural. Unsolicited manuscripts are welcomed, but ten are received every day so write with ideas in first instance. Articles with pictures (or picture references) stand the best chance.

Features Maximum length 1500 words. *Payment* £80–120. No news stories or fiction required, but there is a call for 100–300-word 'fillers'. *Payment* for these is £8.

Today's Guide

17–19 Buckingham Palace Road,
London SW1W 0PT
☎01–834 6242

Owner *Girl Guides Association*
Editor *Mrs J. V. Rush*
Circulation 25,000

FOUNDED 1962. MONTHLY aimed at Girl Guides aged 10–14 years. Unsolicited mss welcome.

Features and Fiction General interest with a Guiding background. Maximum 750–1000 words. *Payment* £26 per 1000 words pro rata.

Today's Runner

Bretton Court, Bretton,
Peterborough PE3 8DZ
☎0733 264666
Telex 32157   Fax 0733 265515

Owner *EMAP Pursuit*
Editor *Paul Richardson*
Circulation 40,000

FOUNDED 1985. MONTHLY. Instructional articles on running and fitness, plus running-related activities and health.

Features Specialist knowledge an advantage. Good pictures 'hold the key'.

News 'Lots of opportunities, especially if backed by photographs.'

'Tried & Tested' and **Women's Pages** *Fionn Lawlor* Limited opportunities unless writers approach with ideas. *Payment* negotiable.

Tracks

5 Pemberton Row, London EC4 3BA
☎01–353 0369   Fax 01–583 1415

Owner *Trevor Wells*
Editor *Deanne Pearson*
Circulation 500,000

FOUNDED 1985. MONTHLY aimed at singles and albums buyers, mainly of chart music but also country, retro and film soundtracks. The magazine also covers films, video and books. Unsolicited manuscripts are not welcome: telephone with idea in the first instance and follow up with brief synopsis in writing.

Features Should be tied in with monthly albums/singles releases. Also major film/video releases, books and compact discs. There is also a new band section focusing predominantly on signed bands. Freelance suggestions welcome in this area, particularly exclusive access to big-name artists. Maximum length 2000 words. *Payment* £70 per 1000 words.

News Not much opportunity for freelance contributions, but inside information, not available from usual PR sources, is welcome. Maximum length 200 words. *Payment* £70 per 1000 words (£10 minimum).

Reviews Subjects as for **Features**. 350 words maximum. *Payment* £70 per 1000 words (£10 minimum).

Traditional Homes

BCP Schweppes House, Grosvenor Road,
St Albans, Herts AL1 3TN
☎0727 59166   Fax 0727 64218

Owner *Benn Consumer Publications*
Circulation 25,000

FOUNDED 1984. MONTHLY magazine covering conservation, architecture, antiques and interior design. Unsolicited mss are welcome. *Payment* £100 per 1000 words.

Traditional Interior Decoration
BCP Schweppes House, Grosvenor Road, St Albans, Herts AL1 3TN

☎0727 59166

Owner *Benn Consumer Publications*
Editor *Jo Newson*
Circulation 40,000

FOUNDED 1986. BI-MONTHLY. Unsolicited mss welcome but it's preferable to submit a full proposal in writing. They receive around six per issue.

Features of up to 2500 words considered on houses with impressive interiors; design and designers; fabrics and wallpaper; crafts.

News Under 'Carousel' section, short write-ups of a maximum of 500 words are welcomed on conservation, interiors, events, exhibitions in art and antiques world. Other sections include 'Bazaar' which covers new products and companies including crafts and design, and 'Under the Hammer' which covers auctions. Maximum length 2500 words. *Payment* varies.

Trailfinder Magazine
42–48 Earls Court Road, London W8 6EJ
☎01–937 9631
Telex 919670   Fax 01–937 9294

Owner *Trailfinders Ltd*
Editors *David Thompson/Linda Zeff*
Circulation 175,000

FOUNDED 1970. THREE ISSUES YEARLY (March, July & December) of this travel magazine. Unsolicited mss are welcome and prospective contributors should make initial contact in writing. No fiction.

Features *Linda Zeff* Lightweight, anecdotal travel features, specialising in Asia, Australasia, Far East, North and South America and Africa are welcomed. Maximum length 1000 words. *Payment* £50 (plus £15 for accompanying colour transparency; £10 B & W).

Travel Europe
3 New Burlington Street, London W1X 1FE
☎01–439 2431

Owner *Centurion Press*
Editor *Lyn Thompson*
Circulation 100,000

FOUNDED 1985. QUARTERLY. A travel information magazine, covering Europe. Unsolicited mss are not welcome: prefer to discuss material with the writer before it is submitted.

Features On places of interest to a traveller. Maximum length 1000 words.

News Should be brief. *Payment* £80.

Traveller
45 Brompton Road, London SW3 1DE
☎01–581 4130
Telex 297155 WEXAS G   Fax 01–589 8418

Owner *Dr I. M. Wilson/Wexas*
Editor *Caroline Sanders*
Circulation 33,000

FOUNDED 1970. THREE ISSUES YEARLY. Unsolicited mss welcome, but a preliminary letter is preferred.

Features Four colour features per issue – authors should supply pictures. Contributors' guidelines available with s.a.e., but all articles should be off-beat, independent, travel-based. Maximum 2000 words. *Payment* £50 per 1000 words.

Travelling on Business
St George's House, 44 Hatton Garden, London EC1N 8ER
☎01–242 7744

Owner *Ravenshead Press Ltd*
Editor *Peter D. Smith*
Circulation 21,000

FOUNDED 1982. QUARTERLY. Most articles, which are about business travel and of general management interest, are commissioned. Any approach should be in writing.

Features Maximum length 1500 words. *Payment* negotiable.

Tribune

308 Gray's Inn Road, London WC1X 8DY
☎01–278 0911

Owner *Tribune Publications Ltd*
Editor *Phil Kelly*
Circulation 10,000

'We have plenty of opportunities for freelancers, though unfortunately we can't pay them anything.' Opportunities in features – current affairs with the emphasis on left politics; reviewing, and newswriting. Either send mss in on spec. or ring to discuss an idea.

Features Editor *Paul Anderson*

Trout Fisherman

Bretton Court, Bretton,
Peterborough PE3 8DZ
☎0733 264666   Fax 0733 265515

Owner *EMAP Pursuit Publications*
Editor *Chris Dawn*
Circulation 36,000

FOUNDED 1977. MONTHLY instructive magazine on trout fishing. Most of the articles are commissioned, but unsolicited mss welcome.

Features *Steve Windsor* Maximum 1500 words. *Payment* varies.

True Romances

12–18 Paul Street, London EC2A 4JS
☎01–247 8233
Telex 8951167   Fax 01–377 9709

Owner *Argus Consumer Publications Ltd*
Managing Editor *Veronica Dunn*
Circulation 74,187

FOUNDED 1934. MONTHLY. Romantic fiction aimed at the teen and twenties market.

Group Story Editor *Gill Pilcher* Occasionally use unsolicited mss, though receive 'too many'. Subjects: teenage/young love/young marrieds, written in first-person. More off-beat than others in this market. 'Lovemaking takes place only within long-term faithful relationships.' 1000–6000 words. *Payment* negotiable on acceptance. *News/Features* all written in-house.

The Truth

1 Leighton Road, London NW5 2QD
☎01–485 9290

Owner *Stranger than Fiction Ltd*
Editor *Stephen Caplin*

FOUNDED 1987. MONTHLY magazine rivalling *Private Eye*. News, features and fiction. Most material supplied by staff writers but welcome contributions if 'very funny'. Features which would support good visual ideas particularly welcome. Maximum length 200 words. First approach in writing but allow at least a month for a reply as they are 'snowed under' with unsolicited material.

TV Times

247 Tottenham Court Road,
London W1P 0AU
☎01–323 3222
Telex 24643   Fax 01–580 3986

Owner *ITP Ltd*
Editor *Richard Barber*
Circulation 3,003,017

FOUNDED 1968. WEEKLY magazine of listings and features serving the viewers of Independent Television. Almost no freelance contributions used, except where the writer is known and trusted by the magazine. No unsolicited contributions.

The Universe

33–39 Bowling Green Lane,
London EC1R 0AB
☎01–278 7321   Fax 01–278 7320

Owner *Universe Publications Ltd*
Editor *Tom Murphy*
Circulation 160,902

Occasional use of new writers, though a substantial network of regular contributors exists. Interested in a very wide range of material, all subjects which might bear on Christian life, from politics to occasional fiction. *Payment* negotiable.

Update

Update Press Ltd, 350 Fulham Road,
London SW10 9UH
☎01–376 5517
Telex 8950511 Ref: 38528001
                    Fax 01–351 0170 or 01–449 5986

Owner *John Lee-Graham*
Editor *Peter Day*
Circulation 45,000

FOUNDED 1987. SIX ISSUES YEARLY. Fashion magazine with a heavy slant on the modelling business. Only interested in model-related themes (fashion and photographic models). Also items on make-up and photography.

Consultant Editor *Marcel C. Mueller* First approach by telephone. *Payment* negotiable.

Vector

23 Oakfield Road, Croydon,
Surrey CR0 2UD
☎01–688 6081

Owner *British Science Fiction Association*
Editor *David V. Barrett*
Circulation 1300

FOUNDED 1957. BI-MONTHLY. The critical journal of the BSFA, containing articles mainly about science fiction and its writers. Unsolicited mss welcome, especially if authoritative and well-written, but most contributors are either professional science fiction authors or BSFA members. No fiction.

Book Reviews *Paul Kincaid* Most are submitted by BSFA members. Should be no longer than 500 words.

Features Articles up to 4000 words are welcome. Interviews with SF authors, editors, publishers etc. are welcome. Maximum length 4000 words. No *Payment*.

The Vegan

33–35 George Street, Oxford OX1 2AY
☎0865 722166

Owner *Vegan Society*
Editor *Barry Kew*
Circulation 10,000

FOUNDED 1944. QUARTERLY. Features articles on the ethical, health, ecological and other aspects of veganism. Unsolicited mss welcome. Maximum 1500 words. *Payment* negotiable.

The Vegetarian

Parkdale, Dunham Road,
Altrincham, Cheshire WA14 4OG
☎061–928 0793

Owner *Vegetarian Society UK Ltd*
Editor *Bronwen Humphreys*
Circulation 20,000

FOUNDED 1848. BI-MONTHLY. Unsolicited mss welcome, but no cookery or herb growing, please.

Consumer News *Rosie Billings* All products must be vegetarian.

Features Animal rights issues, world food problem with vegetarian angle, vegetarian sports people or celebrities, plus anything vegetarian with an unusual slant, organic gardening, etc. Maximum 1000 words plus photo or illustration. *Payment* negotiable (small).

Veteran Car

Glaspant Farmhouse, Glaspant Manor,
Cael Iwan, Newcastle Emlyn,
Dyfed SA38 9LS
☎0559 370928

Owner *The Veteran Car Club of Great Britain*
Editor *Michael Worthington-Williams*
Circulation 2000

FOUNDED 1938. BI-MONTHLY magazine which exists primarily for the benefit of members of The Veteran Car Club of Great Britain, although it is available on subscription to non-members. It is concerned with all aspects of the old vehicle hobby – events, restoration, history, current world news, legislation, etc. All contributions are from professional writers, but 'no budget for paid contributions'. Approach in writing in the first instance.

Video – The Magazine

8 Dorset Square, London NW1 6PU
☎01–723 8823

Owner *Alan Walsh*
Editor *Martin Coxhead*
Circulation 24,000

FOUNDED 1983. MONTHLY. Few opportunities for freelancers, but ideas for original topics within the video field may be considered if submitted in writing.

Video World Magazine

The Northern & Shell Building,
PO Box 381, Mill Harbour,
London E14 9TW
☎01–987 5090   Telex 24676 (NORSHL G)
Fax ITT 3520 01–987 2160

Owner *Richard Desmond*
Editor *Steven Shields*
Circulation 29,000

FOUNDED 1984. MONTHLY. Features on anything relevant to film and video. Welcome unsolicited contributions.

Vogue

Vogue House, Hanover Square,
London W1R 0AD
☎01–499 9080
Telex 27338 VOLON G   Fax 01–493 1345

Owner *Condé Nast*
Editor *Liz Tilbens*
Circulation 177,187

Features are upmarket general interest rather than 'women's', with a good proportion of highbrow art and literary articles, as well as travel features, gardens, food, home interest, reviews. Typically of Condé Nast magazines, tend to use known writers and commission what's needed, rather than using unsolicited mss. Contacts are useful. No fiction.

Features Editor *Liz Jobey*

Voyager

24 Beauval Road, Dulwich,
London SE22 8UG
☎01–693 6463

Owner *Reed Publishing Services*
Editor *Roger St Pierre*

FOUNDED 1986. MONTHLY. Welcome ideas for feature articles although at present a team of regular writers is used. 'Planned expansion could change this.' Maximum length 1500 words. *Payment* £100.

Waterways World

Kottingham House, Dale Street,
Burton-on-Trent, Staffs DE14 3TD
☎0283 42721   Telex 342260 Zilec G

Owner *Waterway Productions Ltd*
Editor *Hugh Potter*
Circulation 18,905

FOUNDED 1972. MONTHLY magazine for inland waterway enthusiasts. Unsolicited mss welcome, provided the writer has a good knowledge of the subject. No fiction.

Features *Hugh Potter* Articles (preferably illustrated) are published on all aspects of inland waterways in Britain and abroad including recreational and commercial boating on rivers and canals.

News *Euan Corrie* Maximum length 500 words. *Payment* £25 per 1000 words.

Wedding and Home

Greater London House,
Hampstead Road, London NW1 7QQ
☎01–388 3171

Owner *Home and Law Publishing Ltd*
Editor *Maggi Taylor*
Circulation 40,000

BI-MONTHLY for women planning their wedding, honeymoon and first home. Most features are written in-house or commissioned from known freelancers. Unsolicited mss are not welcome, but approaches may be made in writing.

Weekend

New Carmelite House, Carmelite Street,
London EC4Y 0JA
☎01–353 6000

Owner *Mail Newspapers plc*
Editor *Graham Love*
Circulation 280,000

FOUNDED 1953. WEEKLY. Freelance contributions are welcome, should be 800 words maximum, and sent to the features editor. Preferred subjects are showbiz features, especially British and American 'soaps', royalty, fashion and beauty, general human interest and true-life dramas.

Features *Grant Lockhart Payment* £100 for 800 words.

Weekly News

Albert Square, Dundee DD1 9QJ
☎0382 23131

Owner *D. C. Thomson & Co. Ltd*
Editor *W. Kelly*
Circulation 715,737

Newsy, family-oriented and quaintly old-fashioned magazine designed to appeal to the busy housewife. 'We get a lot of unsolicited stuff and there is great loss of life among them'. Usually commission, but writers of promise will be taken up. Series include showbiz, royals, television. No fiction. *Payment* negotiable.

Weight Watchers Magazine

141–143 Drury Lane, London WC2B 5TS
☎01–836 4433   Fax 01–836 3156/2610

Owner *GAT Publishing*
Editor *Harriet Cross*
Circulation 107,000

BI-MONTHLY. For slimmers and the health-conscious. Unsolicited mss not normally accepted, but approaches may be made in writing.

Features are usually commissioned by editor or features editor – length and *Payment* vary depending on subject.

What Car?

38–42 Hampton Road, Teddington,
Middlesex TW11 0JE
☎01–977 8787   Fax 01–977 9792

Owner *Haymarket Publishing Ltd*
Editor *Sam Brown*
Circulation 136,019

Reports on cars, and consumer-based articles to do with motoring generally. Freelancers are used for both, but testing is only offered to the few, and general articles on aspects of driving must be by writers known and trusted by the magazine, as some of the conclusions they come to can be controversial, and need to be scrupulously researched. Not interested in receiving unsolicited mss. *Payment* NUJ rates.

What Diet & Lifestyle

AIM Publications Ltd, Silver House,
31–35 Beak Street, London W1R 3LD
☎01–437 0796   Fax 01–437 8787

Owner *D. C. Thomson & Co. Ltd*
Editor *Helen Williams*
Circulation 45,000

FOUNDED 1983. BI-MONTHLY. Unsolicited mss not welcome as all news and feature articles are written by in-house or regular commissioned freelance writers.

What Investment

Ground Floor, Boundary House,
91–93 Charterhouse Street,
London EC1M 6HR
☎01–250 0646   Fax 01–250 0637

Owner *Publishing Holdings*
Editor *Mike Beacher*
Circulation 25,530

FOUNDED 1983. MONTHLY. Features articles on
a variety of savings and investment matters.
Unsolicited mss not welcome. All approaches
should be made in writing.

Features Maximum 2000 words (usually
less). *Payment* NUJ rates.

What Mortgage

Boundary House, 91–93 Charterhouse Street,
London EC1M 6HR
☎01–250 0646   Fax 01–250 0637

Owner *Publishing Holdings*
Editor *Valerie Bayes*
Circulation 20,000

FOUNDED 1983. MONTHLY magazine on property purchase, choice and finance. Unsolicited mss welcome; prospective contributors
may make initial contact either by telephone
or in writing.

Features Up to 1500 words on related topics
are considered. Particularly welcome are new
angles, new ideas or specialities. *Payment*
£100 per 1000 words.

What Video

Third Floor, 72–80 Leather Lane,
London EC1N 7TR
☎01–831 6731

Owner *W. V. Publications*
Editor *Colin Goode*
Circulation 35,000

FOUNDED 1980. MONTHLY. Features on video
equipment and user features on video – TVs,
VCRs, camcorders, accessories. Welcome
unsolicited mss. Particularly interested in
application features – 'outside broadcast'

video movies, novel trips with video. Maximum 1000 words. *Payment* £70 minimum
plus illustrations.

What's New in Building

Morgan-Grampian House,
30 Calderwood Street, Woolwich,
London SE18 6QH
☎01–855 7777   Telex 896238

Owner *Morgan-Grampian*
Editor *Derrick Jolley*
Circulation 35,500

MONTHLY. Specialist magazine covering new
products for building; unsolicited manuscripts not generally welcome. The only freelance work is rewriting press-release
material. This is offered on a monthly basis of
25–50 items of about 150 words each. *Payment* £4.35 per item.

What's New in Farming

Morgan-Grampian House,
30 Calderwood Street,
Woolwich, London SE18 6QH
☎01–855 7777 (ext. 3420)   Telex 896238

Owner *United Newspapers*
Editor *Jonathan Theobald*
Circulation 75,000

FOUNDED 1977. MONTHLY. The magazine is primarily a guide to new agricultural products,
with little feature space. Most copy is written
in-house, and unsolicited mss are not
welcome.

Features *Debbie Sly/Jonathan Theobald*
Articles on relevant agricultural topics.
Maximum length 2000 words. *Payment* nego-
tiable.

What's New in Interiors

Morgan-Grampian House,
30 Calderwood Street, Woolwich,
London SE18 6QH
☎01–885 7777
Telex 896238 Morgan G   Fax 01–855 2342

Owner *Morgan-Grampian Ltd*
Editor *Anthea Bain*
Circulation 13,519

FOUNDED 1981. TEN ISSUES YEARLY. Aimed at interior designers, architects and specifiers. Unsolicited manuscripts welcome if they are exclusive, well-researched and aimed at readership. Make initial contact in writing.

Features Good, technical journalists who know the contract interiors market are always sought. Maximum length: 1500 words. Opportunity for writers of interiors application stories and specialised profiles. *Payment* £100 per 1000 words.

What's On In London

182 Pentonville Road, London N1 9LB
☎01–278 4393   Fax 01–837 5838

Owner *E. G. Shaw*
Editor *David Parkes-Bristow*
Circulation 38,000

FOUNDED 1932. WEEKLY information magazine. News, features and reviews. Special 'Health & Fitness' pages. Like to receive well-thought out and professionally presented mss. Feature items must have London/Home Counties connection, except during tourist season when they can be 'Historic England'. Prefer first approach by telephone. *Payment* by arrangement.

Cinema *Michael Darvell*

Classical Music *Marshall Julius*

Pop Music *Jon Homer*

Theatre *Lydia Conway*

Windsurfers Magazine

Woodstock House, Luton Road,
Faversham, Kent ME13 8HQ
☎0795 538903

Owner *Pacificon Limited*
Editor *Tym Manley*
Circulation 25,000

FOUNDED 1984. NINE ISSUES YEARLY. Unsolicited manuscripts are welcomed, if informative articles on windsurfing (maximum 2500 words). Prospective contributors are advised to make initial approach in writing. *Payment* £30 per 1000 words.

Wine

Thames House, 5–6 Church Street,
Twickenham, Middlesex TW1 3NJ
☎01–891 6070   Fax 01–891 4373

Owner *The Euro Publishing Co.*
Editor *Margaret Rand*
Circulation 40,000

FOUNDED 1983. MONTHLY. Unsolicited mss not welcome.

News and **Features** Wine, food and travel stories. Prospective contributors should approach in writing.

Wisden Cricket Monthly

6 Beech Lane, Guildford, Surrey GU2 5ES
☎0483 32573

Owner *Wisden Cricket Magazines Ltd*
Editor *David Frith*
Circulation *c.*42,000

FOUNDED 1979. MONTHLY. Very few uncommissioned articles are used, but would-be contributors are 'not discouraged': approach in writing. *Payment* rates vary.

Woman

King's Reach Tower, Stamford Street,
London SE1 9LS
☎01–261 5000
Telex 915748   Fax 01–261 5997

Owner *IPC Magazines*
Editor *David Durman*
Circulation 1.5 million

Celebrating its 50th anniversary in 1988.

Features Editor *Mary Frances* Maximum length 1000–3000 words.

Fiction Editor *Rosie Burston* Maximum length 1500–3000 words. *Payment* negotiable.

Woman and Home

King's Reach Tower, Stamford Street,
London SE1 9LS
☎01–241 5423   Telex 915748 MAGDIV G

Owner *IPC Magazines*
Editor *Sue Dobson*
Circulation 611,803

FOUNDED 1926. MONTHLY Unsolicited contributions – of which 200 are received each month – are not welcome; prospective contributors are advised to write with ideas, plus photocopies of other published work or details of magazines to which they have contributed. Most freelance work is specially commissioned.

Features *Jean Williams*

Fiction *Kati Nichol* Short stories are usually submitted by agents, serials are always submitted by agents or publishers.

OTHER DEPARTMENTS
Fashion, home knitting, beauty, cookery and travel, all covered by staff writers and specially commissioned freelancers. No poetry is published. An s.a.e. is required for return of mss. *Payment* c.£90 per 1000 words.

Woman's Journal

IPC Magazines, King's Reach Tower,
Stamford Street, London SE1 9LS
☎01–261 6220
Telex 915748 MAGDIV G   Fax 01–261 6023

Owner *IPC Magazines*
Editor *Laurie Purden* MBE

MONTHLY. Unsolicited non-fiction mss welcome.

Features *Victor Olliver* Maximum length 2500 words. Major features are generally commissioned but new ideas on all subjects welcome.

Fiction *Christie Hickman* Maximum length 4000 words. Unsolicited material is not accepted; stories are mainly bought from agents and publishers direct. Also **Design**

and Homes *Jane Graining* Fashion *Alex Parnell* Food *Katie Stewart* Health and Beauty *Vicci Bentley*. *Payment* negotiable.

Woman's Own

King's Reach Tower, Stamford Street,
London SE1 9LS
☎01–261 5474   Telex 915748 MAGDIV

Owner *IPC Magazines*
Editor *Bridget Rowe*
Circulation 1,065,367

WEEKLY. Prospective contributors should contact the features editor in writing in the first instance before making a submission.

Features *Sarah Crompton*

Fiction *Susan Oudot* Unsolicited fiction mss are not accepted, but there is an annual short story competition, for which the first prize in 1987 was £5000. Maximum length for fiction is 3500 words.

Woman's Realm

King's Reach Tower, Stamford Street,
London SE1 9LS
☎01–261 5708

Owner *IPC Magazines Ltd*
Editor *Ann Wallace*
Circulation 608,034

FOUNDED 1958. WEEKLY. Scope here for freelancers who should write in the first instance to the appropriate editor.

Features *Christine Evans* Interested in one-page human interest pieces or emotional features. 1200–2000 words. *Payment* at NUJ rates. Best vehicle for new freelancers is the half-page humorous slot, described as 'wry looks at family life', c.700 words. *Payment* £100.

Fiction *Sally Bowden* One short story and a serial instalment used every week. Aimed at an intelligent, family-minded woman aged 23 upwards. Very wide range; not much romance. A high standard of writing is essential. Serials are usually bought from agents or publishers but ideas for serials (with sample chapter) welcomed. 1000–4000 words. *Payment* £150 and upwards.

Woman's Story

12–18 Paul Street, London EC2A 4JS
☎01–247 8233
Telex 8951167   Fax 01–377 9709

Owner *Argus Consumer Publications Ltd*
Managing Editor *Veronica Dunn*
Circulation 57,754

MONTHLY sister magazine to *True Story* and *True Romances*.

Fiction Welcome; finished mss, not ideas, should be addressed to the editor. No serials. Receive 80–100 mss weekly. Subjects: romantic, domestic crises, marriage and job problems. An older, slightly more sophisticated market than its sister magazines. No explicit sex. Written in first- or third-person, possibly from a man's viewpoint. Twists of plot, uncertain endings are frequent features. 1500–5000 words. *Payment* on acceptance.

Woman's Weekly

King's Reach Tower, Stamford Street,
London SE1 9LS
☎01–261 6131

Owner *IPC Magazines*
Editor *Judith Hall*
Circulation 1,268,665

Mass market women's WEEKLY, now competing with *Woman* and *Woman's Own*, and like them concerned with strong human interest, film and television personalities, as well as a more traditional, homemaking angle. Occasionally use freelancers, but at this level tend to be experienced magazine journalists.

Fiction Editor *Gaynor Davies* Short Stories 2500–4500 words; serials of 45,000–55,000 words. Their guidelines for fiction writers – 'a strong romantic emotional sensual theme...with a conflict not resolved until the end' (serials); short stories are more varied. They get around 500 unsolicited stories a month.

Woman's World

25 Newman Street, London W1P 3HA
☎01–631 3939

Owner *Carlton Publishing*
Editor *Kerry MacKenzie*
Circulation 208,000

FOUNDED 1977. MONTHLY. There are opportunities for freelancers but it is best to write with ideas and samples of published work in the first instance. Approximately 150 unsolicited mss are received every week.

Work-Out Magazine

City House, 72–80 Leather Lane,
London EC1N 7TR
☎01–831 6219   Fax 01–831 3097

Owner *W. V. Publications Ltd*
Editor *Julie Milton*
Circulation 42,000

Title bought in 1985. MONTHLY. Health and exercise magazine. Unsolicited mss welcome; however a number of freelance contributors are regularly used.

Features on topics covered by magazine, often with human interest involvement. Maximum length 1000 words.

News In-house only. *Payment* approximately £60–75.

Workbox

40 Silver Street, Wiveliscombe,
Somerset TA4 2NY
☎0984 24033

Owner *Audrey Babington*
Editor *Audrey Babington*
Circulation 35,000

FOUNDED 1984. BI-ANNUAL. The magazine caters for the enthusiast and professional in all branches of needlecrafts.

Features covers a *very* wide range of needlecrafts but no 'how-to-make' items.

News Any items welcomed especially about new products, processes, etc., and events. s.a.e. essential. *Payment* by arrangement.

World of Knitting

1–2 East Market Street,
Newport, Gwent NP9 2AY
☎ 0633 58216

Owner *Sandra Williams*
Editor *Sandra Williams*
Circulation 29,114

FOUNDED 1983. Unsolicited mss welcome on knitting and related crafts. Prospective contributors are advised to make initial contact in writing, outlining proposal and accompanied by illustration where appropriate. No fiction.

Features up to 1000 words on yarns, knitwear fashions as well as 'how-to-make' pieces. Special features, e.g. picture knitting, Fair Isle patterns, etc., are particularly sought after.

News Reports up to 1000 words on knitting-related subjects. *Payment* around £50 per 1000 words.

Writers' Monthly

The Writer Ltd, 18–20 High Road,
London N22 6DN
☎ 01–888 1242

Owner *The Writer Ltd*
Contributing Editor *Alison Gibbs*
Circulation 9000

FOUNDED 1984. MONTHLY magazine (incorporating *The Writer*) aimed at freelance writers, both beginners and professionals. News and features of interest to writers.

Features Maximum length 2000 words. 'Always on the look-out for new writers'.

News compiled in-house; very little scope for outside contributors. Monthly short story competition open to subscribers. First prize of £100; 2nd prize of £50; two runners-up prizes of £25 each. The winning story is published in future editions of the magazine, subject to available space. Query letter with synopsis in the first instance. 'The main reason for material being rejected is usually because writers have not studied the magazine. Articles must be clear and concise.'

Yachting Monthly

Room 2209, King's Reach Tower,
Stamford Street, London SE1 9LS
☎ 01–261 6040   Telex 915748 MAGDIV G

Owner *IPC Magazines*
Editor *Andrew Bray*
Circulation 46,023

FOUNDED 1906. MONTHLY magazine for yachting enthusiasts. Unsolicited mss are welcome, but between 50 and 80 are received each month. Prospective contributors should make initial contact in writing.

Features *Howard Cheedle* A wide range of features concerned with maritime subjects and cruising under sail; well-researched and innovative material always welcome, especially if accompanied by colour transparencies. Maximum length 3000 words. *Payment* maximum £76 per 1000 words.

News *Andrew Bray* News items (up to a maximum of 500 words) are received from a series of correspondents 'Around the Coast'. *Payment* £5.03 per 100 words.

You and Your Barclaycard

Advertising Department, Barclaycard,
Northampton NN1 1SG
☎ 0604 234234   Fax 0604 253153

Owner *Barclaycard*
Editor *E. A. Hackett*
Circulation 4–5 million

FOUNDED 1983. BI-MONTHLY. Practical product-oriented features, e.g. lighting, furniture, fashion, etc. Do not welcome unsolicited mss but will consider suggestions for future topics. Approach in writing in the first instance.

You Magazine (Mail on Sunday)

New Carmelite House, Carmelite Street,
London EC4Y 0JA
☎ 01–353 6000   Fax 01–353 2602

Editor *Nicholas Gordon*

Lively, substantial colour supplement whose many feature articles are supplied entirely by freelance writers. These tend to be established magazine journalists: 'as far as we know there hasn't yet been a single case of an unsolicited feature ending in publication'. In such a competitive market there is a glut of talent anyway. On the other hand, always hoping to find new writers who understand their needs. Articles, whether general interest or issue based, are always people oriented, and interview based. This is the only general guideline in writing for the magazine; otherwise, it's a strong idea that counts. Send these to the **Commissioning Editor** *John Koski*. Other contacts on the Commissioning Desk are *Laurie Sharples, Tim Willis, Hugh St Clair* and *Gordon McKenzie*.

Young Mother
The Schoolhouse Workshop,
51 Calthorpe Street, London WC1X 0HH

Owner *Family Publications Ltd*
Editorial Director *David Peck*
Circulation 67,500

FOUNDED 1986. BI-MONTHLY. Features information and articles of interest to those caring for young children aged 0–5 years. Unsolicited mss welcome, but ideas in writing are preferred.

Features Maximum 2500 words. *Payment* by negotiation.

Your Future
89 East Hill, Colchester, Essex CO1 2QN
☎0206 870786   Fax 0206 860824

Owner *Aceville Publications Ltd*
Editor *Lin Wieland*

Formerly *Exploring the Supernatural*, relaunched with its new title in September 1987. MONTHLY publication which covers topics such as divination, astrology, alternative therapies. Freelance contributions welcomed. 'No guarantee is offered for the safety or return of mss.' Articles are paid for on publication. *Payment* £17.50 per 1000 words.

Your Horse
Bretton Court, Bretton,
Peterborough, Cambs PE3 8DZ
☎0733 264666   Fax 0733 265515

Owner *EMAP*
Editor *Liz Benwell*
Circulation 39,765

A magazine for all ages which deals with practical horsecare: the skills and problems involved in keeping or riding horses. They get a lot of unsolicited offerings from knowledgeable readers, some of which are used. But it's best to send ideas in the first instance, to the editor. *Payment* by negotiation.

Your Money
361A Upper Richmond Road West,
London SW14 8QN
☎01–392 1378   Fax 01–878 0341

Owner *Fredericks Place Holdings plc*
Editor *Quentin van Marle*
Circulation 50,000

FOUNDED 1987. BI-MONTHLY. News and features on the financial world. No unsolicited mss. Willing to discuss ideas. Contact either by phone or in writing.

Yours Newspaper
Apex House, Oundle Road,
Peterborough PE2 9NP
☎0733 555123   Fax 0733 312025

Owner *Help the Aged*
Editor *Peter Kelly*
Circulation 130,417

FOUNDED 1973. MONTHLY. Readership is in the age group of 55 plus and unsolicited mss are welcome.

Features Maximum length 1000 words, and genuinely appealing to readership, would be considered.

Fiction – as for features.

News Short newsy items (300 to 500 words) of interest to readership are welcomed. *Payment* negotiable.

Sound and Screen

Welcome to the revolution. The sound of gunfire (snipers mostly) can be heard throughout broadcasting and though so far there has been little bloodshed, except in the senior ranks of the BBC, heavy casualties are expected.

The end of tranquillity in broadcasting was signalled in 1986 by the Peacock Report, the first serious attempt to come to grips with the new technology and the opportunities for wider consumer choice. Since then we have had a breakthrough in satellite television with the promise of a rash of at least a dozen channels in 1989, a revival in the fortunes of cable television, a government commitment to break the BBC monopoly of national radio and to diversify local services, and an advance in the fortunes of independent producers who are now the most fertile source of programme ideas.

Two satellite services are due to be launched in 1989. Astra, a medium power European satellite with a sixteen-channel potential is based in Luxembourg. It is largely owned by financial institutions but with **Thames Television**, **Ulster Television** and **TSW** among its investors. Their aim is to give viewers a 24-hour mix of news, music, sport, culture, children's programmes and feature films beamed simultaneously to several countries and in several languages.

The rival to Astra is British Satellite Broadcasting (BSB), a UK-only operation, supported by, among others, **Granada**, **Anglia TV**, Pearson, Virgin and Reed International. Its three channels will carry *Now*, a 24-hour news and sports service; *Galaxy* for **downmarket entertainment**; and, sharing their third channel, *Zig Zag*, for children, and *Screen*, the peak evening hours slot for feature films.

Both satellites will generate revenue from a mix of advertising and viewers' subscriptions. But they are not alone in their efforts to woo customers and viewers. After a quiet start, it looks as if cable television will soon be competing for attention, at least in the cities. Birmingham is leading the way with a planned service capable of supplying up to half a million homes. Central London is set to follow.

It must be said that some professionals are still dubious about cable. One senior television executive recently described it as 'a technology whose time has gone'. With two of the first eleven pilot franchises awarded in 1983 – Merseyside and Ulster – still to get going and a third, Guildford, only starting last summer, scepticism would seem to be in order. But supporters point to the enormous success of cable in West Germany where it is now available to nine million homes (34 per cent of the total) and in the United States where networks are changing hands at more than $2000 a subscriber in billion dollar deals. The rapid advance of cable in the US accounts for the eagerness of financial institutions like Prudential–Bache and Paine–Webber to help finance the London and Birmingham projects.

Meanwhile, the government is looking to the probability of launching one or more channels using conventional transmitters. By the early 1990s viewers could be spoiled for choice.

Likewise radio listeners. The government wants three new national commercial stations, each providing 'a diverse and varied programme service', and several hundred new local and community stations. No sooner was the announcement made – in early 1988 – than bidders for the first national franchise, including Carlton Communications and Virgin, stepped smartly forward. At the same time the BBC made known its interest in two more national services – one on events network (including coverage of Parliament and state occasions), the other based on the World Service and the Open University.

On the face of it, the broadcasting revolution should favour writers – not to mention producers, directors and the army of technicians who must come together to fill the empty hours. But it is hard to assess the impact when so little is revealed of programme planning. We know, for example, that BSB is in the market for 380 movies a year and that ITN has been contracted to produce eight hours daily of news magazines but, at the time of writing, tenders for the other services have yet to be submitted.

For its output, Astra looks to be passing the buck to existing suppliers such as Rupert Murdoch's Sky Channel, the ITV companies' Super Channel, and the W.H. Smith's children's channel.

What this will mean in terms of writing opportunities is, presently, anyone's guess. The cynics argue that even if all the new channels survive (by no means a certainty) they will make little difference to programme makers here because satellite and cable output will consist predominantly of American imports.

This must be taken as the accountant's option – buying in programmes is at least two-thirds cheaper than origination. But viewers may not be ready to cooperate. Audience research suggests that indigenously produced programmes of high quality are far more popular than the drop-offs from the Hollywood conveyor belt.

A deluge of inferior product, from home or overseas, will have an adverse effect on advertising revenue which in turn will force the programme makers to mend their ways. This is what happened when the BBC and ITV began to share the screen in the mid 1950s. Viewers were thrown a lot of rubbish early on but over a period standards did improve. Does anyone argue that television today on four channels is not infinitely better than the television of thirty years ago when it was dominated by a single public service channel?

The same applies to radio though here the real danger for writers is that music will be allowed to overwhelm the spoken word.

'If', asks *The Times*, 'the three franchises for the national channels are to be offered to the highest bidder, does that mean that less lucrative but more imaginative proposals will be squeezed out? Will the **Channel 4**-style service, commissioning programmes for minorities from independent producers, which was proposed by London's Institute of Contemporary Arts, get a look in?'

Only time will tell. But it is encouraging that the BBC, faced with the certainty of radio deregulation, is sharpening up its act in terms of channel content and presentation. It promises well for the quality of public service broadcasting that those responsible for the more mundane areas of programming are being jolted out of their sinecures.

The government, meanwhile, is holding fast to a basic tenet of public service broadcasting – that those who control the airwaves have a duty to inform as well as to entertain.

Radio Drama

Whatever happens on the commercial side, BBC radio is likely to remain the biggest single market for writers. In addition to special reports, story readings and talks, Radios 3 and 4 transmit some five hundred new plays every year – fifty times more than the **National Theatre** and the **Royal Shakespeare Company** put together. This output amounts to an annual 96 hours on Radio 3 (1.5 per cent of the total) and 852 hours on Radio 4 (11 per cent). No other country does so many radio plays.

The main slots on Radio 4 are:

The Monday Play (repeated Saturday afternoons)
75 or 90 minutes or sometimes longer.
Opportunities for original writing on complex themes.
Also a showcase for classic stage plays and occasional dramatisation of novels.
Saturday Night Theatre (repeated Monday afternoons)
75 or 90 minutes.
Family entertainment with a strong narrative line.
The Afternoon Play (Wednesday and Thursday)
45 to 55 minutes.
A balanced diet of original entertainment and demanding plays.
Thirty Minute Play (Tuesday afternoon)
Drama equivalent of the short story.

At least seventy new writers achieve production each year. But competition is stiff. Richard Imison, chief script editor and deputy head of radio drama, receives up to 10,000 scripts a year, of which only 5 per cent make the grade.

The consolation is that all submissions are paid the compliment of serious and often valuably constructive criticism.

The BBC claims that less attention is given to the subject matter of a play than to its suitability for sound treatment – in other words, the writer has freedom to venture into contentious areas. But while it is true that Radio 3 has attempted some brave experiments and that Radio 4 has long since lost its aura of gentility, ('Bath-chair theatre', as Richard Imison calls country house thrillers and sickly romances, is now a rarity) the impression remains that caution will usually prevail over controversy.

A close study of the *Radio Times* soon reveals the guidelines writers would be wise to follow. Radio 4, for example, has regular programmes for antique collectors, farmers, businessmen and financiers but none for trade unionists, blacks, gays or the unemployed. And none too, it must be added, for far out right-wing causes.

'Imagine', writes the media columnist Paul Johnson, 'a play putting, say, the ordinary white South African in a good light. It might be written with the skill of Shakespeare but it would not get on the BBC.'

Departures from the norm must be judged in perspective. In a month in which Radio 3 was earning well deserved praise for the John Arden and Margaretta D'Arcy 9-part history of Christianity (said Michael Billington, 'They have fashioned a drama which only an enlightened public service would commission'), Radio 1 cancelled a Michael Wall play when he refused to agree to changes and **Radio 4** cancelled a repeat of Ken

Blakeson's *Excess Baggage* because 'it contained too much bad language for an afternoon audience'.

The BBC is enormously helpful in advising writers how to structure and present their work. Various publications are available from any of seven production centres (see BBC TV listings) and occasional seminars for aspiring playwrights are run by the Script Unit.

This year the BBC launched a Young Playwrights Festival with two weeks of radio drama placings set aside for writers aged between 15 and 30. It is too early to predict the future of the project but there is strong support for making it an annual event.

For every newcomer the critical pointer to success is an understanding of the potential and limitations of sound. Even established writers fall into the error of including too many characters (confusing the listener particularly if they talk over each other) or of failing to ring the changes in pace and location. The longer the sequence the more difficult it is to sustain interest.

Probably the best advice to newcomers is encompassed in the list of questions script readers must consider before recommending a play.

- Is it basically a good story?
- If it is, are the characters and dialogue equally good?
- If they are, will it make good *radio*?
- If it will, to which spot is it best suited?
- If the script is viable on all the counts listed above, is it the right length?
  If not, can it be cut or expanded without artistic loss?
  If so, where?
- Even if the script is still viable, how might it be improved?
  Is the beginning sufficiently compelling?
  Is the cast too big?
  Does it maintain dramatic tension?
  Is everything that should be conveyed sufficiently well planted in the *dialogue*?
- If it's a good story, well told in radio terms, are there any special problems?
  (e.g. controversial themes liable to misunderstanding by the audience; foreign settings calling for difficult or expensive casting; technical backgrounds likely to attract expert criticism; etc.)
- If the play passes on all these counts, it's obviously a strong possibility for broadcast.
  How could the author make it *better*?

To start on the right side of the script reader is to follow certain basic rules of presentation – rules which apply with equal force to any form of script writing.

- Use a typewriter or word processor. Handwritten scripts are hardly ever considered.
- Type on one side of the paper only. (A4 size preferably.)
- Make sure all the pages are firmly fastened and numbered consecutively.
- Use plenty of spacing.
- Put your name and address on the title page.

- Give names of characters in full throughout the script and clearly separate them from speech.
- Clearly distinguish technical information such as location changes and sound effects from speech.
- Attach a synopsis of the play to the completed script together with a full cast list and notes on the main characters.

With at least a thousand submissions under consideration at any one time, nobody should expect a quick response. A two or three months wait is common even for a straight rejection. A further wait suggests that the writer has become part of the BBC's internal politics. Somebody for some reason is nervous of saying 'yes' but reluctant to say 'no'. Early in his career when Alan Bennett sent a play to the BBC (television in this case) they took so long to think about it that when an acceptance did come through the play had been on in the West End for six months.

Radio Features and Comedy

Beyond drama, to talks and features, there is another crowd of writers jostling for attention. But they have more of a problem in identifying the best person to contact with a proposal. Most of the production centres have features editors and in London, the heads of departments or their minions will pass on an idea to whatever producer they think might be interested.

But long-established programmes like *Woman's Hour* or *You and Yours* have their own pecking order of contributors. The editors do not seem to spend much time assessing material from unknown outsiders. Much depends on sheer good fortune – catching the right producer with the right idea at the right time. It also helps to boast expert knowledge. The views of everyman are little appreciated except on *Any Answers*.

Comedy programmes like *Week Ending* and *The News Huddlines* are in the market for short sketches. Success here can be an entrée to the world of comedy series where, for once, there is a dearth of good material. But if demand is high so is the failure rate. Perhaps the broadcasters are their own worst enemies in calling for more and yet more situation comedies – a patch of humour which has been so heavily cultivated as to be close to exhaustion. Iconoclastic humour in the tradition of *The Goons* is now a rarity though when it is tried, as in the marvellous *Radio Active* series, the BBC achieves its declared objective of reaching a younger audience.

Morning Story is a great radio institution which relies exclusively on outside contributors. With a quarter hour slot, anything of more than two and a half thousand words is overwritten. A strong plot stands a better chance with the editor than impressive writing. Steer clear of controversial topics.

Specialist journalists who are not career broadcasters can often find themselves a comfortable niche within the BBC, in sports, say, or current affairs where they are not so much reporters as professional interviewers. The call for expertise also attracts certain voluble academics.

Educational broadcasting is thick with specialists but is ever hungry for more. Despite having to stick with a narrow curriculum and to work on pathetic budgets, programmes for schools and colleges are a good training ground for writers and pre-senters.

So too is local radio, though if anything, funds are tighter than in education. The recent cuts imposed by the BBC – up to ten per cent over the next five years – will leave many local stations floundering. Independent radio is in not much better shape with many stations running at a loss or barely breaking even. Still, they do attract enthusiastic and hard-working staff who are open to ideas and willing to take chances.

Television

In television, the stakes (in terms of rating, reputation and reward) are higher than in radio but the odds on winning are much longer. Take drama. Notwithstanding *Screen Two, The Play on One* from **BBC Scotland**, and *Film on Four*, the chances of finding a slot for a one-off original play are slight indeed. Long gone are the days of *Armchair Theatre* and *The Wednesday Play*, the forcing ground for writers like Alan Plater, David Mercer, Jack Rosenthal, Peter Nichols and Dennis Potter. The demand now is for serial drama which can build up audience loyalty to a point when viewers switch on as a matter of routine.

So, where to start?

The soaps want new ideas (please!) but at the serious end of the market there is a clear preference for second-hand product. Alan Plater, once a prolific dramatist and now a prolific adapter (*Fortunes of War* is his latest), laments the decline of television drama. 'Television, like the movie industry, seems increasingly distrustful of original work.' Yet more disturbing is Plater's assertion that producers are unwilling to consider any ideas but their own.

> '. . . every dramatisation I have written during the past twenty years was initiated by a producer or production company. They ring me, generally when they have acquired the rights and done an advantageous co-production deal or two. For a decade or so I have tried to persuade producers that Gwyn Thomas's brilliant autobiography, *A Few Selected Exits*, would make a wonderful film . . . . Everybody tells me it can't be done. I tell everybody it can be done. There are no absolute Rights and Wrongs in such matters, but this time I know I'm right.'

He is. But will anyone listen?

Possibly one of the growing number of independent production companies might show an interest. Here, if anywhere, are the mould breakers of television. Given their first impetus by the creation of **Channel 4** seven years ago, the independents have responded to another friendly push by the government with its instructions to BBC and ITV to take 25 per cent of their programmes from outsiders by 1990.

The showcase for the independent is *Film on Four*, a commissioning slot for the best original drama on television and source of quality low budget movies for the British cinema. That such films as *Wish You Were Here*, *My Beautiful Laundrette*, *A Room With a View* and *Mona Lisa* reached the screen at all is thanks entirely to financial backing from **Channel 4** (often short of 100 per cent but enough to start the ball rolling) and the readiness of the independent producers to take risks.

For the newcomer, the independents can be easier to penetrate than the BBC and ITV establishment. Nobody is going to offer a full blown screenplay to an unknown, though some like Hanif Kureishi (*My Beautiful Laundrette*) have made their break with slight experience. But there is always the prospect of starting on modest bread-and-butter productions.

The biggest market is for training and promotional videos, directly commissioned by industry. Budgets are tight and there is little opportunity for imaginative writing (business clients are notoriously conservative). But new writers are welcome and a few corporate videos can do wonders for a beginner's reputation.

The problems for writers involved in corporate television is the absence of any guidelines on payment. No doubt the **Writers' Guild** and other professional associations will soon have something to say about this. Meanwhile, the writer must fend for himself. Since he is working to a tight brief, usually with material supplied by the client, he is expected to surrender copyright. There is therefore no question of repeat fees or royalties. But if the production company is honest and the client is sensible enough to want a professional writer, the rewards can be up to the level of network television and far beyond that of radio.

A guess at standard rate would be £2000 plus for an hour-long programme. Some writers prefer to value their time on a daily rate and this too is generally acceptable.

If a writer and production company have not previously worked together it is as well to ask for an advance on payment to show goodwill. Some production companies with respectable client lists are nonetheless run on a shoestring. They are not above telling their accounts departments that when it comes to payments, writers are last in the pecking order.

The next step from corporate television might be into drama documentaries (though here the writer who is his own director has the best chance of success) or light entertainment.

The demand for television comedy is apparently insatiable. Extravagant rewards are promised to those who can come up with a winning formula. Unfortunately, there is little agreement on what is likely to make people laugh. The more obvious pitfalls can be avoided by studying the advice and information leaflets put out by the BBC. Here, for example, are the guiding principles for writing situation comedy:

'The laughs should arise naturally and logically from the interactions of character and plot, not from a string of gags and funny lines fired off into the blue. Where so many beginners go wrong is that they provide no situation: the characters are not at grips with each other over some matter that is important to them, in which something crucial is at stake. Famous comedy series like *Dad's Army*, *The Good Life*, *Porridge* and *Sorry* were very different, but they all had one thing in common: fundamentally they were about the serious matter of sheer survival in the teeth of perilous circumstances. This is what made them funny. Do not be seduced into following in the steps of somebody like, say, Roy Clarke since it needs great experience and tremendous skill to pull off something like *The Last of the Summer Wine*.'

But is is difficult not to conclude that pot luck has a big part to play in any comedy success. The call is out for writers to come up with ideas that are original and off-beat but few seem to make it to the screen. That comedy is expensive to produce (£70,000 to £100,000 an hour) deters budget controllers from taking chances. For the same reason they are liable to chop series which are not immediately popular. It is a sobering thought that *Black Adder* and *A Very Peculiar Practice*, now awash with praise, almost did not make it to their second seasons.

To catch the interest of a producer, a pilot episode with a few brief story lines is the most that is needed. The temptation to try to break into an existing series ('I can do better than that') should be resisted as an almost certain waste of time. Writers will have been hired and programmes stockpiled well before the opening transmission.

The prospects of success are improved enormously if the writer is in an alliance with an agent who specialises in TV (see Agents listing). But agents who stay in business are very choosy about their clients. Not one of them will move a step on behalf of a dubious or untried talent.

The way forward for comedy writers could be eased considerably if there were more opportunities to try out ideas and to test viewer reaction. This valuable function used to be performed by *Comedy Playhouse*, a weekly slot for pilot episodes, which the BBC unaccountably axed some years ago. First timers should campaign for its revival. And every writer must wish for an end to the tyranny of the thirty-minute rule. That situation comedy is in such a poor way is surely not entirely unrelated to the problem of having to squeeze every story line into a half hour. At the moment, the schedules are as rigid as a school timetable and every bit as stultifying.

To end on a safe generalisation, the best training ground for television writers is the soap opera, where the demand for words is inexhaustible. This is certainly the view of Susanna Capon, head of the BBC's script unit.

> 'Whether they like it or not, writers starting out in television have to be prepared to work on things like *EastEnders* because producers are loath to take a chance on a one-off play with a writer whose work they do not know.'

This may not say much for producers' critical faculties, but there it is.

A final word of encouragement: every writer is entitled to a collection of rejection slips. They should be chalked up to experience, and valuable experience at that. Moreover, scripts that wing back to the sender should be treated with respect. Their day might come. Ted Whitehead tells how his play *Alpha Beta* was dismissed by the BBC as 'a pointless drama about a couple quarrelling'. It went on to make his name with a successful run in the West End.

Basic Pay – Radio, Television and Film

The **Writers' Guild, The Society of Authors** and the **National Union of Journalists** have led the way in negotiating minimum fees for writers of radio and television scripts. Full details of their agreement with the broadcasting authorities can be obtained from these bodies (see **Professional Associations** p. 417–30 for addresses) but the following is a guideline to the offers that writers might expect from the BBC and ITV.

Radio

- A beginner in radio drama should receive at least £915 for a sixty-minute script. For an established writer – one who has three or more plays to his credit – the minimum rate goes up to £1386.
- Fees for dramatisations range from 60 to 85 per cent of the full drama rate depending on the degree of original material and dialogue.
- An attendance payment of £23.10 per production is paid to established writers.
- For talks, the level of fees starts at £9.15 per minute for script only and £12.45 per minute for script and read.
- Features and documentaries begin at £16.50 per minute with a minimum fee of £115.50.
- Higher fees are limited to writers' experience and to 'the particular circumstances of the engagement'.
- Fees for short stories start at a beginner's rate of £82.00 for 15 minutes rising to £107.50 for writers who have contributed six or more stories.
- Repeat fees are nearly always part of an agreement but terms vary according to the type of production.
- Basic rates for news reporting are covered by an NUJ agreement with the BBC and the Association of Independent Radio Contractors.
- For the BBC, news reports start at £25.10 for up to two minutes plus £5.68 for each extra minute on network radio. Local radio is £12.85 for up to two minutes plus £4.62 for each extra minute.
- In the commercial sector news reports make £13.50 for the first two minutes and £4.50 a minute thereafter.
- There are special day rates and separately negotiated fees for specialist reporting such as sports coverage.

Television

The following are examples of minimum rates negotiated by the **Writers' Guild** with the BBC and ITV. The BBC is currently negotiating new rates.

For a sixty-minute teleplay the BBC will pay an established writer at least £4212 and a beginner £2673. The corresponding figures for ITV are £5824 for the established writer, £4139 for a writer new to television, but with a solid reputation in books, film, radio or theatre, and £3967 for other writers.

- The day rates for attendance at read-throughs and rehearsals is £35 for the BBC and £44 for ITV.
- The NUJ agreement on news reporting guarantees a BBC rate to freelancers of £30.94 for up to two minutes and £7.68 for each extra minute. The ITV rate is tied to a minimum of £32.61

Feature Films

An agreement between the **Writers' Guild, The British Film and Television Pro-ducers' Association** and **The Independent Programme Producers' Association** allows for a minimum writer's fee of £20,000 on a high budget feature film (in excess of £1½ million) and £12,000 on a lower budget movie. Writers can also expect additional TV fees to cover transmission at home and abroad.

The contrast with Hollywood rates is instructive. This is from David Thomson, a member of the **Writers' Guild of America:**

> 'Last year, I did a script on just a diagram and twenty minutes of talk. The business believes in excitement, energy and conviction. If an idea needs thinking over or explanation, it won't be done: doubt isn't movie-like. That's why screenwriters work on those single, arresting sentences.
>
> The writer gets a development deal: money to write a first draft and a set of revisions. Considerable money. The Minimum Basic Agreement is set at $35,000 for that task, with three times that if the picture is made. And that's the *minimum*. Established writers will get six-figure sums as up-front guarantees. Screenwriters can earn more than $1 million, depending on their track record, the agent's bravado, the studio's need and that hoary phantom "being hot".'

No wonder there's a brain drain!

National and Regional Television

The BBC

BBC Television

Television Centre, London W12 7RJ
☎ 01–743 8000

Editor, Television News *Chris Cramer*
Editor, Current Affairs *Tony Hall*
Head of Drama *Peter Goodchild*
Features & Documentaries *Will Wyatt*
Light Entertainment *James Moir*
Comedy *Gareth Gwenlan*
Music & Arts *Leslie Megahey*
Religious Programmes *John Whale*
Children's Programmes *Anna Home*
Series & Serials *Colin Rogers*
Community Programmes *Tony Laryea*

BBC Breakfast Time

Lime Grove, London W12 8QT
☎ 01–576 7502

Editor *David Stanford*
Contact *Forward Planning*

BBC TV Documentary Features

Kensington House, Richmond Way,
London W14 0AX
☎ 01–743 1272

Contact *Angela Holdsworth*

BBC TV Midlands

Broadcasting Centre, Pebble Mill Road,
Birmingham B5 7QQ
☎ 021–414 8888

Home of the Pebble Mill Studio

Head of Drama *Michael Wearing* OUTPUT *Run For the Lifeboat; Lovebirds; Air Base; Rainbow.*

News and Current Affairs *Richard Thompson*

Also makers of one-offs like *Cool It* with Phil Cool, *Ebony*, the black magazine series, *Top Gear* and *Farming*. *Farming's* Editor Mike Fitzgerald will seriously consider unsolicited material if well reseached.

BBC TV North East (Leeds)

Broadcasting Centre, Woodhouse Lane,
Leeds LS2 9PX
☎ 0532 441188

Since the reorganisation of the BBC television regions in 1987, Leeds is now the head of the North East region. Though presently its major production is the nightly news magazine programme *Look North*, there are plans to expand the repertoire. No drama department.

Features Editor *Mark Roland*

News Editor John Lingham

BBC TV North East (Newcastle upon Tyne)

Broadcasting House, 54 New Bridge Street,
Newcastle upon Tyne NE99 2NE
☎ 091–232 1313

Although Leeds is now the headquarters of the North East region, Newcastle continues to make its own programmes.

Features Editor *John Mapplebeck* Features, documentaries and drama come under this department. Very little drama is made, but there is a strong feature-making unit, particularly for programmes of direct local relevance. They make forty 30-minute programmes a year, some of which are nationally broadcast.

News and Current Affairs *John Bird*

BBC TV North West

New Broadcasting House, Oxford Road, Manchester M60 1SJ
☎061–236 8444

Network production in Manchester breaks down into 4 departments: features, children's, sports and entertainments.

Features (General Programmes) *Brass Tacks* **Editor** *Colin Cameron.*
Open Air **Editor** To be appointed

Children's Editor *Edward Pugh* No childrens' drama – light entertainment for kids, like *It's Wicked*, and *The Saturday Picture Show.*

Sports Editor *Ian Edwards. A Question of Sport.*
Entertainments in a fragmented state at the moment. *No Limits* and *Fax* current programmes.

Executive Producer, Independent Productions *Peter Ridsdale Scott* Deals with proposals from independent producers (which the BBC is increasingly using), though not direct from writers alone.

BBC Northern Ireland

Broadcasting House, 25–27 Ormeau Avenue, Belfast BT2 8HQ
☎0232 244400

Current Affairs *Andy Colman*
Drama *Robert Cooper. The Rockingham Shoot.*
General Programmes *Ultan Guilfoyle. A Taste of Ireland* (food series)
Religious Programmes *Father Jim Skelly.*

Series: *Spotlight* **Editor** *Andy Colman*
Children's Programmes *Tony McAuley*
Sport *Joy Williams.*

BBC TV Nottingham (BBC Midlands)

Wilson House, Derby Road, Nottingham N91 5HX
☎0602 472395

An opt-out station from BBC TV Midlands Birmingham office, and served by the programmes made in Birmingham. Nottingham makes local news only.

BBC TV Plymouth (South West)

Broadcasting House, Seymour Road, Plymouth PL3 5BD
☎0752 229201

Programmes for the South West region are made in the regional network centre in Bristol. Plymouth makes one 'opt-out' programme for its own region a week. Direct mss to the Bristol office.

BBC Scotland

Broadcasting House, Queen Margaret Drive, Glasgow G12 8DG
☎041–330 2345

Head of Drama *Bill Bryden* 'A strong commitment to drama production.' Productions include, in the *Play on One* slot, *Down Where the Buffalo Go; The Dumroamin' Rising; The Dark Room.* Also, the award winning serial, *Tutti Frutti.*

Head of Features *David Martin* Encompasses the old Light Entertainment department, plus documentaries, *Animal Roadshow*, and the schools' quiz show, *First Class.*

Special Projects *Desmond Wilcox. The Visit.* No children's programmes except those made in the Gaelic department.

Head of Gaelic *Ken McQuarrie.*

BBC Scotland (Aberdeen)

Beechgrove Terrace, Aberdeen,
Scotland AB9 2ZT
☎0224 635233   Telex 739622

Editor *Dennis Dick*

No real market. BBC Aberdeen make features, but these are nearly always commissioned.

BBC Scotland (Dundee)

12/13 Dock Street, Dundee DD1 4BT
☎0382 25025

News only.

BBC Scotland (Edinburgh)

Broadcasting House, 5 Queen Street,
Edinburgh EH2 1JF
☎031–225 3131

All programmes made in Glasgow.

BBC South and East

BBC Elstree Centre, Clarendon Road,
Borehamwood, Herts WD6 1JF
☎01–953 6100

Home of the history and archaeology unit, *Global Report* and the general programmes unit which makes leisure and one-off programmes. No drama production.

History & Archaeology *Bruce Norman* *Timewatch* and *The Great Journeys* series.

Global Report *Barry Dixon* Documentary programmes on, for example, Third World issues. Usually devised and made in-house.

General Programmes Unit *Mastermind, Masterteam*, chess and bridge programmes, and *Lifeline*.

BBC TV South and East (Norwich)

St Catherine's Close, All Saints Green,
Norwich NR1 3ND
☎0603 619331

The second centre (after Elstree) of the BBC TV South and East region. They occasionally make network programmes; Norwich is more than a regional opt-out station simply making its own local news programmes. Very locally oriented scripts should be sent to their small features unit.

Television Features *R. Bufton*.

BBC TV South West

Broadcasting House, Whiteladies Road,
Clifton, Bristol BS8 2LR
☎0272 732211

Bristol no longer has a drama department, but does have a strong features department, and houses the BBC's much praised natural history unit.

Features *Jon Shearer* Output has included *Antiques Roadshow, Scott Free, Whicker's World, Probation, Under Sail, Mountain Men* and *The Healing Arts*.

Natural History *Dr John Sparks* Programmes have included *Kingdom of the Ice Bear, The Living Planet, The Living Isles* and *Wildlife on One*. Specialist writers only.

BBC TV Southampton (South West)

South Western House, Canute Road,
Southampton SO9 1PF
☎0703 226201

Programmes for the South West region are made in Bristol, to whom all mss and programme ideas should be sent. Southampton makes one weekly local opt-out programme only.

BBC Wales

Broadcasting House, Llantrisant Road,
Llandaff, Cardiff CF5 2YQ
☎0222 564888

News and Current Affairs *David Morris Jones*

Drama *John Hefin* OUTPUT *Going Home; Heaven on Earth; Babylon By-passed*.

General Programmes *Huw Brian Williams*

Children's Programmes *Dyfed Glynn Jones.* BBC Wales also make programmes for S4C in Welsh.

BBC Wales (Bangor)

Broadcasting House, Meirion Road, Bangor LL57 2BY
☎0248 362214

News only.

Independent Television

Anglia Television

Anglia House, Norwich NR1 3JG
☎0603 615151
Telex 97424   Fax 0603 631032

Head of Drama *John Rosenberg* Anglia has a strong tradition of drama production for the ITV network. Current productions include *Menace Unseen*, P.D. James' *A Taste for Death*, and *Tales of the Unexpected*. The Natural History Unit produces the *Survival* wildlife documentaries. Regional programmes include *About Anglia* (daily news magazine), *Anglia Reports* (weekly current affairs series), *Cross Question* (political debate), *Folio* (arts magazine) and *Farming Diary*. Network entertainment: *Lucky Ladders* (word game), *Anything Goes* (leisure & travel magazine), *Knightmare* (computer game show), *Heirloom* (antiques series), *Stocks and Shares Show* (Channel 4 investment game show).

Controller News Programmes *Jim Wilson*

Political Editor *Malcolm Allsop*

Border Television

Television Centre, Durranhill, Carlisle, Cumbria CA1 3NT
☎0228 25101   Telex 64122

Contact *Paul Corley* (Programme Controller)

News Editor *Lis Howell*

Documentaries etc. *Paul Corley* Most scripts are provided in-house but are occasionally commissioned. Writers should not submit written work apart from notes before their ideas have been fully discussed. In last couple of years, Border has greatly increased its programme production, including children's television – features and documentaries rather than drama. Also contributes programmes to **Channel 4**: *The Drove*, *Sheer Genius*, *The Writing on the Wall*, *The Hills Are Alive*.

Central Independent Television

East Midlands Television Centre, Lenton Lane, Nottingham NG7 2NA
☎0602 863322   Telex 377696

Contact *Christopher Walker* (Head of Scripts)

'Although some television companies ask to see a synopsis first, the Script Unit always prefers to read scripts from new writers. However, it is rare for a finished script to be purchased – writers are normally assessed for possible future commissions.' A few single plays are made by the company, but the bulk of the Drama output takes the form of series and serials. The Light Entertainment department makes situation comedy series, and other shows which need sketches and one liners. Young People's Programmes include single plays for the 'Dramarama' slot, serials and light entertainment. The Script Unit welcomes scripts and tries to read everything which comes in. 'However, this process does take time, so writers should not expect an instant response.'

Channel 4

60 Charlotte Street, London W1P 2AX
☎01–631 4444

Launched in November 1982, Channel 4 broadcasts 80 hours of programmes a week, all of them made by independent producers or other independent television companies. Channel 4 does not make any of its great diversity of programmes, except for the weekly *Right to Reply*. The role of its commissioning editors is to sift through proposals for programmes and see interesting projects through to broadcast.

Deputy Controller of Programmes *Liz Forgan*
Commissioning Editors
Entertainment *Mike Bolland*
Fiction *David Rose*
Education *Naomi Sargeant*
Drama Series *Peter Ansorge*
Young People *Stephen Garrett*
Multi Cultural *Farrukh Dhondy*
Single Documentaries *Nick Hart-Williams*
Arts *Michael Kustow*
Current Affairs *David Lloyd*
Documentary Series *Thomasz Malinowski*

Channel Television

The Television Centre, St Helier, Jersey, Channel Isles
☎0534 73999

Chairman *John Riley*

News, current affairs and documentaries provide the bulk of programmes although 1988 sees the first venture into drama with *Midnight Clear*. Make programmes for the network. Ideas are assessed but only commissioned after sale is made to the network.

Programme Controller *John Henwood* OUTPUT Regular weekday magazine programme *Channel Report*; monthly religious magazine programme *Link Up*; series for **Channel 4** on islands throughout Great Britain, *Great British Isles*.

Grampian Television

Queen's Cross, Aberdeen AB9 2XJ
☎0224 646464

Grampian Television serves an area stretching from Fife to Shetland.

Head of Documentaries *Edward Brocklebank* OUTPUT *The Blood Is Strong* – a trilogy of hour long programmes for **Channel 4** on the Gaelic Scots and their fortunes at home and abroad.

Head of News and Current Affais *Alistair Gracie*

Other areas of production, light entertainment, schools, children's and religious programmes, come under **Head of Production** *John Hughes*. These tend to be for regional broadcast only. Light entertainment is usually of the chat show/quiz show sort, and children's programmes are both light entertainment and educational.

Granada Television

Granada TV Centre, Manchester M60 9EA
☎061-832 7211

Director of Programmes *Steve Morrison*

Drama *Michael Cox, Steve Hawes* Drama series, film production. OUTPUT *Small World*; *Game, Set and Match* (13-part film); *After the War*; *The Return of Sherlock Holmes*; *The Magic Toyshop*. Opportunities for freelance writers have decreased of late but will consider mss from professional writers. All mss to Gerald Hagan, Head of Scripts.

Features, Arts & Education *David Boulton, Rod Caird* OUTPUT *All Our Yesterdays*; *Socially Unacceptable*; *Disappearing World*.

Light Entertainment *David Liddiment* OUTPUT *The Krypton Factor*; *Busman's Holiday*. Unlikely to be opportunities for the freelance writer.

News & Current Affairs *Ray Fitzwalter, Andrew McLaughlin*.

Sport *Paul Doherty*.

HTV Wales

TV Centre, Cardiff CF5 6XJ
☎0222 590590

Productions sought with an authentic Welsh dimension.
News *Bob Symonds*.
Features *Cenwyn Edwards*
Drama/Fiction *Graham Jones*
Light Entertainment *Peter Elias Jones*
Documentaries *Huw Davies*

Recent productions: Drama *Wall of Tyranny*; *Ballroom*; *Better Days*. Documentaries *To Ride a Wild Horse*; *The Pity of War*. Light Entertainment *Tom Jones, Born To Be Me*. Health Series *Stress*.

HTV West

Television Centre, Bath Road,
Bristol BS4 3HG
☎0272 778366

Head of News and Current Affairs *Steve Matthews*

There are no heads of departments as such (unlike its sister company **HTV Wales**). For **Drama**, contact *Patrick Drongoole* (Senior Producer).
Director of Programmes *Ron Evans* and **Programme Controller** *Derek Clarke* make programme-planning decisions in other areas. Strong local programme making in all departments has included feature programmes like *Along the Cotswold Way* and *The Royal Forest of Dean*.

London Weekend Television

South Bank Television Centre, Kent House,
Upper Ground, London SE1 9LT
☎01–261 3434   Telex 91823

Head of Light Entertainment *Marcus Plantin*
Controller of Drama and Arts *Nick Elliot*
Head of Arts *Melvyn Bragg*
Deputy Controller of Drama *Linda Agran*
Controller of Features and Current Affairs *Jane Hewland*.

Makers of weekend entertainment: *You Bet, Surprise Surprise, Me and My Girl, Hot Metal*. Drama series such as *London's Burning, Wish Me Luck*; also *The South Bank Show* and *Aspel & Company*. LWT provides a large proportion of the network's drama and light entertainment, and is a major supplier to **Channel 4**.

Scottish Television

Cowcaddens, Glasgow G2 3PR
☎041–332 9999

Controller of News and Current Affairs *David Scott*
Sport and Features *Russell Galbraith*
Controller of Drama *Robert Love*
Controller of Entertainment *Sandy Ross*

'Encouragingly, an increasing number of STV programmes are networked, and seen nationally. The detective series *Taggart*, the popular series *Take the High Road*. A new network series *Bookie*, a new series of *The Campbells* (a co-production with Canadian television) and a series of children's plays which are part of the *Dramarama* series.

Sianel Pedwar Cymru (Welsh 4th Channel)

Clos Sophia, Cardiff CF1 9XY
☎0222 43421   Telex 497146 Pedwar G

Deputy Programme Controller
Deryk Williams

S4C commissions some $4\frac{1}{2}$ hours of programmes from independent producers each week, to be produced in the Welsh language. There is a demand for drama scripts, comedy and documentary programmes.

Thames Television

Thames Television House, 306 Euston Road,
London NW1 3BB
☎01–387 9494

Head of Documentaries *Ian Martin*
Controller Drama *Lloyd Shirley*
Controller Features *Catherine Freeman*
Head of Comedy *James Gilbert*
Head of Variety *John Fisher*
Controller of Light Entertainment *John Howard Davies*
Head of News and Current Affairs *Barrie Sales*.

Perhaps the strongest of drama production departments: *Minder, London Embassy, The Fear, Rumpole of the Bailey, The Bill, Hannay*. Light Entertainment output includes *The Benny Hill Show, The Des O'Connor Show, Give Us a Clue, After Henry, All at No. 20, Home James, Strike It Lucky*. Documentaries and features have included *Unknown Chaplin, A Source of Innocent Merriment, The Mikado, Take 6 Cooks, Mavis on 4, Catherine*. Children's programmes: *Rainbow, Sooty, Splash, Creepie Crawlies, The Gemini Factor*.

TSW – Television South West

Derry's Cross, Plymouth PL1 2SP
☎ 0752 663322   Telex 45566

Head of News and Documentaries *David Atkins*
Features/Drama/Light Entertainment *Paul Stewart Laing*

Programmes made for the network have included the adult educational series, *Food: Fad or Fact?*; *Three Score Years and Then?*, and a five-part series on architectural oddities and follies entitled *Bats in the Belfry*. Other documentaries include *Surcouf – Diving to Disaster*; *A Head of Time* and *Affairs of the Hart*, an hour-long documentary on stag hunting. TV's only canine quiz show called *That's My Dog*. For **Channel 4** a drama entitled *Someday Man*. Young people's programmes: *Look and See*, and *Gus Honeybun's Magic Birthdays*.

TVS Television

Television Centre, Northam,
Southampton, SO9 5HZ
☎ 0703 634211   Telex 477217

Controller Entertainment *John Kaye Cooper*
Head of Features *John Miller*
Children's Programmes *Nigel Pickard*
Head of Religious Programmes *Andrew Baur*
Local Documentaries *Anthony Howard*
Science & Industry *Philip Geddes*
Youth Programming *John Dale*
Head of News & Sport *Mark Sharman*

Full range of regional and network ITV programmes from drama to documentary, children's programmes and light entertainment. Recent output has included *A Guilty Thing Surprised* and *Shake Hands Forever* both by Ruth Rendell; *Gentlemen and Players* (drama series for ITV); *Mandela* (**Channel 4** film); *That's Love* (situation comedy); *Tahiti Witness* and *Inside the Bank of England* (networked documentaries); *Mr Majeika* (children's series); *Americas Cup* (sailing series for **Channel 4**); *Frocks on the Box* (networked fashion series).

Tyne Tees Television Limited

The Television Centre, City Road,
Newcastle upon Tyne NE1 2AL
☎ 091–261 0181   Telex 53279

Drama *Geraint Davies*
Entertainment, Children's and Music Programmes *Trish Kinane*
Factual Programmes *Jim Manson*
News and Sport *Clive Page*
Religious Programmes *Paul Black*
Programme output includes *Northern Life* (news magazine); *Extra Time* (sport); *Commercial Break* (business); *Crosswits* (quiz); *Kellyvision* (children's); *Morning Worship* (religious).

Ulster Television

Havelock House, Ormeau Road,
Belfast BT7 1EB
☎ 0232 328122   Telex 74654

Current affairs *Hugh Owens*
News Editor *Colm McWilliams*
Sports Editor *Terry Smyth*

General programme planning comes under the office of **Assistant Controllers** *Michael Beattie* and *Andrew Crockart*. *Michael Beattie* is particularly responsible for current affairs; *Andrew Crockart* for documentary features. Drama, light entertainment, children's and religious programme ideas can be addressed to either. Recent credits include *Shadow in a Landscape*, a dramatised documentary on the life and work of Irish impressionist painter Roderic O'Connor. *After the Gold*, a profile of the Belfast-born pianist, Barry Douglas. *Celtic Church in Ireland*. The networked series *Sing Out*. A new series of book programmes, *The Write Stuff*. *No Poor Parish*, a new series of documentaries.

Yorkshire Television

Television Centre, Leeds LS3 1JS
☎ 0532 438283   Telex 557232

Editor *Richard Gregory*

Drama *Carol Williams* Drama series, film productions, studio plays and long-running series like *Emmerdale Farm*. Always looking for strong writing in these areas, and make great use of agents to find it. Around 20 unsolicited mss received weekly. Unknowns should submit at least the first act, ideally the first episode if submitting a series, and synopsis.

Documentaries *John Willis* Opportunities are rare here, as scripts are usually provided by producers. However, adaptations of published work put to the department as a documentary subject are considered. Output includes *First Tuesday*.

Light Entertainment *Vernon Lawrence* Comedy series like *Home to Roost* and *Singles*. Opportunities for writers of series/episodes in theory, but in reality there is a well-established circle of professionals in this area which it is difficult to infiltrate. Best approach is through a good agent.

Regional Features *David Lowen* Documentaries and special features. No scripts, ideas only. Recent output has included *Calendar Commentary*, *Calendar Lunchtime Live*, *You and E.Y.E.*, *Enterprize '88*.

National Radio

BBC Radio (News and current affairs)
Broadcasting House, London W1A 1AA
☎ 01–580 4468

News and Current Affairs Editor
Jenny Abramsky
RADIO 4 EDITORS **Kaleidoscope** *Richard Bannerman* **Today** *Phil Harding* **The World at One/The World This Weekend** *Martin Cox* **PM** *Roger Mosey* **Woman's Hour** *Clare Selerie-Grey* **The World Tonight** *Blair Thomson* **Motoring Unit** *Irene Mallis* **Week Ending** *contact the producer* **You and Yours** *contact the editor*. See also **BBC Radio 4** (fiction and drama opportunities).
RADIO 3 **Contact** *Ann Winder* at Room 8053, Broadcasting House. Features, Arts and Education department welcomes either finished mss or written ideas for 20- or 40-minute talks and documentaries for broadcast on the BBC's 'classical music station'.
RADIO 2 There are no general opportunities for original work, but welcomes and uses contributions from outside writers to existing series. These, naturally, change with the seasons, but presently include **The News Huddlines** *Mark Robson* (Producer)

BBC Radio (fiction and drama opportunities)
Broadcasting House, London W1A 1AA
☎ 01–580 4468

Contacts *Sheila Fox* (Morning Story), *Enyd Williams* (evening drama R4), *Penny Gold* (Afternoon Play), *Richard Imison* (Fear on Four and R3)

Contributions to 'Morning Story' (see **Sound and Screen** article) should be sent to *Sheila Fox*, 'Morning Story', Room 7074, at the above address. The evening drama slots on Radio 4 are: 'Classical Serial' (for obvious reasons not a good bet for new writing); 'Thirty-Minute Series and Serials' (open to new plays); 'Saturday Night Theatre' (open to new writing of either 75 or 90 minutes length). Scripts should be sent to *Enyd Williams* at Room 6087, although it should be noted that currently they are fully scheduled for the next two years and any incoming mss have to have 'stunning potential', 'Fear on Four' (open to new plays) scripts to *Richard Imison* (**Deputy Head Radio Drama**). Probably the best bet for new plays on Radio 4 is 'Afternoon Play'. Its producers are too numerous to list here; scripts should be sent to **Senior Script Editor** *Penny Gold*.

BBC External Services
Central Talks and Features Department, Bush House, Strand, London WC2B 4PH
☎ 01–240 3456

Contact *Alan Jones*

Provide scripts in English for translation and broadcast by the 36 foreign language services that make up the **BBC External Services**. Cover the following areas: (a) analysis of international current affairs; (b) cultural, social and economic affairs in Britain; (c) science, technology and export promotion. Contributors should bear in mind that the target audience cannot be taken to have a ready familiarity with life in this country or with British institutions. Translation skills are not necessary, as this is done exclusively by their own professionals.

BBC Northern Ireland

Broadcasting House, 25–7 Ormeau Avenue,
Belfast BT2 8HQ
☎0232 244400

Contact *Arwel Ellis Owen*
(Programme Controller)

For BBC Northern Ireland radio see also
Radio Foyle (Local Radio section)

BBC Radio Scotland

Queen Margaret Drive, Glasgow G12 8DG
and 5 Queen Street, Edinburgh EH2 1JF
☎041–330 2345 (G); 031–225 3131 (E)

News Editor *Jack Regan* (G) **Features Editor**
John Arnott (E) **Fiction/Drama Producer**
Stewart Conn (E) **Comedy** *Colin Gilbert* (G)
Talks and Features *John Arnott* (E)

Produces a full range of news and current
affairs programmes, comedy; documentaries;
drama; short stories; talks and features. The
emphasis is on speech-based programmes
(rather than music etc.) and programmes reflecting Scottish culture.

Scottish BBC Radio has two aspects: a
national radio service contributed to by
programme-making in Glasgow, Edinburgh,
Aberdeen and Dundee; and the local community stations, which take the national programmes and splice this with local material.
These stations are **BBC Highland**, nan Gaid-
heal, Orkney, Shetland, **Solway** and **Tweed**.

BBC Radio Scotland (Aberdeen)

Beechgrove Terrace,
Aberdeen AB9 2ZT
☎0224 625233   Telex 739622

Editor *Chris Lowell*

No real market. Only involved in features
(don't make any drama) and these are virtually all commissioned. **News**, local only.

BBC Radio Scotland (Dundee)

12–13 Dock Street, Dundee DD1 4BT
☎0382 25025

Small office producing news coverage only.
No openings.

BBC Radio Wales

Broadcasting House, Llantrisant Road,
Llandaff, Cardiff CF5 2YQ
☎0222 564888

Contact *Meirion Edwards* (Head of Radio)

As with **BBC Radio Scotland**, there are two
aspects to the working of the Welsh network.
There are three centres of programme-
making, in Cardiff, Bangor and Swansea, for
the national Welsh BBC network, but in addition two community stations which provide
local material for local audiences. These,
Radio Clwyd and **Radio Gwent**, are listed
under **Local Radio**.

BBC Radio Wales (Bangor)

Broadcasting House, Meirion Road,
Bangor LL57 2BY
☎0248 362214

Contact *Elwyn Jones* (Senior Producer)

BBC Radio Wales (Swansea)

32 Alexandra Road, Swansea SA1 5DZ
☎0792 54986

Contact *Lyn Jones (Mr)*
(Programme Controller)

Independent Radio News

Communications House, Gough Square,
London EC4P 4LP
☎01–353 1010

News Editor *John Perkins*

IRN supplies national and international news
coverage to all independent local radio stations throughout Britain.

Local Radio

BBC Local Radio

BBC Radio Bedfordshire
PO Box 476, Hastings Street,
Luton, Beds LU1 5BA
☎0582 459111   Telex 825979 RADBED G

Station Manager *Mike Gibbons*
Contact *Jim Latham* (Programme Organiser)

No news opportunities, and few in drama
and light entertainment. Locally written contributions about Bedfordshire, north and
west Hertfordshire and north Buck-
inghamshire are encouraged. Particularly
interested in historical topics (five minutes
maximum). Also encourage freelance contributions from the community across a wide
range of radio output, including interview
and feature material.

BBC Radio Cambridgeshire
104 Hills Road, Cambridge CB2 1LD
☎0223 315970

Contact *Margaret Hyde* (Station Manager),
Mike Robinson (Programme Organiser)

BBC Radio Cleveland
Broadcasting House, PO Box 1548,
Middlesbrough, Cleveland TS1 5DG
☎0642 225211

Contact *Mick Wormald*
(Programme Organiser)

Material used is almost exclusively local to
Cleveland, County Durham and North Yorkshire, or written by local writers.

BBC Radio Clwyd
The Old School House, Glanrafon Road,
Mold CH7 1PA
☎0352 59111

Contact Senior Producer

BBC Radio Cornwall
Phoenix Wharf, Truro, Cornwall TR1 1UA
☎0872 75421

Contact *Andy Joynson*
(Programme Organiser)

BBC Radio Cumbria
Hilltop Heights, London Road,
Carlisle CA1 2NA
☎0228 31661

Contact *Kath Worrell* (Programme Organiser)

BBC Radio Derby
PO Box 269, Derby DE1 3HL
☎0332 361111

Contact *Bryan Harris* (Station Manager)

BBC Radio Devon
PO Box 100, Exeter EX4 4DB
☎0392 215651   Telex 42440

Manager *Roy Corlett*
Contact *John Lilley*

Special projects mounted annually have
included a short story competition (1985), a
play-writing competition (1986), and the
Armada Playwrighting competition (1988).

BBC Essex

198 New London Road, Chelmsford CM2 9XB
☎0245 262393

Station Manager *Richard Lucas*
Contact *Martin Ward*
News Editor *Jane Peel*
Drama/Documentaries/Features/Fiction
Keith Roberts

BBC Radio Foyle

PO Box 927, Londonderry BT48 7NE
☎0504 262244/5/6

Contact *Joe Mahon*

Radio Foyle broadcasts both its own programmes and those made in Belfast for
national transmission. Occasionally programmes made by Radio Foyle will be taken
up by the national network.

BBC Radio Furness

Hartington Street, Barrow-in-Furness,
Cumbria LA14 5FH
☎0229 36767

Contact *Keith Daniels* (Senior Producer)

A **Radio Cumbria** community sub-station.

BBC Radio Gwent

Powys House, Cwmbran, Gwent NP44 1YF
☎06333 72727

Contact *Adrian Hearn* (Senior Producer)

BBC Highland

Broadcasting House, 7 Culduthel Road,
Inverness IV2 4AD
☎0463 221711

Contact *Allan Campbell* (Station Manager)

BBC Highland radio is a community station.

BBC Radio Humberside

63 Jameson Street, Hull,
North Humberside HU1 3NU
☎0482 23232   Telex 597031

Programme Organiser *Barry Stockdale*
Contact *Margaret Garbett*

Broadcast a daily short story each afternoon
at 2.35 pm. 75% of the material is provided
by local writers.

BBC Radio Kent

Sun Pier, Chatham, Kent ME4 4EZ
☎0634 830505   Telex 965011

Contact *Michael Marsh* (Manager)

Opportunities exist for writers on the afternoon magazine programme plus the specialist
arts programme *Scene and Heard*. Features
need to be of strong local interest, as does
drama/fiction, for which there are few openings. Occasional commissions are made for
local interest documentaries and other
one-off programmes.

BBC Radio Lancashire

King Street, Blackburn BB2 2EA
☎0254 62411

Manager *Michael Chapman*
Contact *Programme Organiser*

Not very many opportunities for writers.
Some use of local features about Lancashire
life, past and present. Generally no interest
in material from outside the county.

BBC Radio Leeds

Broadcasting House, Woodhouse Lane,
Leeds LS2 9PN
☎0532 442131

Contact *Stuart Campbell*
(Programme Organiser)

BBC Radio Leicester

Epic House, Charles Street,
Leicester LE1 3SH
☎0533 27113

Station Manager *Jeremy Robinson*

BBC Radio Lincolnshire

PO Box 219, Newport, Lincoln LN1 3XY
☎0522 40011   Telex 56186

Manager *David Wilkinson*
Contact *Chris Olney*

Unsolicited material only considered if locally relevant. Maximum 1000 words; straight narrative preferred, ideally with a topical content.

BBC Radio London

PO Box 4LG, 35a Marylebone High Street, London W1A 4LG
☎01–486 7611

Contact *Tony Freeman*

BBC Radio Manchester

New Broadcasting House, PO Box 90, Oxford Road, Manchester M60 1SJ
☎061–228 3434

Programme Organiser *John McManus*

Very few opportunities, apart from a planned playwrighting competition for local writers.

Features *Richard Hemmingway* (Senior Producer)

BBC Radio Newcastle

Broadcasting Centre, PO Box Newcastle upon Tyne NE99 1RN
☎091–232 4141

Manager *Tony Fish*

Opportunities for freelance writers are extremely rare.

BBC Radio Norfolk

Norfolk Tower, Surrey Street, Norwich NR1 3PA
☎0603 617411   Telex 975515

Contact *Keith Salmon* (Station Manager)

Features/Documentaries *Keith Salmon* Good local material welcome, but must relate directly to Norfolk/North Suffolk. **News Editor** *Jill Bennet* 'Minimal' opportunities.

BBC Radio Northampton

PO Box 1107, Abington Street, Northampton NN1 2BE
☎0604 239100

Contact *Penny Young*

Features rarely used; judged on merit plus local relevance. No drama or fiction, no news opportunities. **Light Entertainment** rarely used, perhaps one series a year.

BBC Radio Nottingham

York House, Mansfield Road, Nottingham NG1 3JB
☎0602 415161

Contact *Nick Brunger* (Programme Organiser)

BBC Radio Oxford

242–54 Banbury Road, Oxford OX2 7DW
☎0865 53411

Contact *David Freeman*

Limited opportunities: short stories are used from time to time.

BBC Radio Sheffield

60 Westbourne Road, Sheffield S10 2QU
☎0742 686185

Contact *Frank Mansfield* (Programme Organiser)

'Radio Sheffield is keen to develop local writing talent through the radio station. We broadcast short stories from local writers on merit.' Plays are broadcast 'very occasionally'. Poetry workshops held twice a week. Also involved, with **Sheffield City Libraries**, in a scheme called 'Write Back', and hope to broadcast material coming out of this in the near future.

BBC Radio Shropshire

PO Box 397, Shrewsbury, Shropshire SY1 3TT
☎0743 248484   Telex 35187

Station Manager *Lawrie Bloomfield*

Opportunities exist in the afternoon programme (2.00–3.30 pm) for Shropshire writers. Stories or prose pieces of around 1000 words, or poetry 'if it is easily understood'. Because the programme is not an arts slot as such, the work should be of general interest. Aims to be an outlet for local creative talent. *Payment* not usually.

BBC Radio Solent

South Western House, Canute Road, Southampton SO9 4PJ
☎0703 631311   Telex 47420

Station Manager *Steve Panton*

Occasional short story competitions.

BBC Radio Sussex

Marlborough Place, Brighton, Sussex BN1 1TU
☎0273 680231

Contact *David Arscott* (Programme Organiser)

BBC Radio Tweed

Municipal Buildings, High Street, Selkirk TD7 4BU
☎0750 21884

Contact *Colin Wight* (Senior Producer)

BBC Radio WM

PO Box 206, Birmingham B5 7SD
☎021–414 8484

Contact *Tony Inchley* (Editor)

Interested in short stories, plays, documentaries, preferably but not necessarily local interest.

BBC Radio York

20 Bootham Row, York YO3 7BR
☎0904 641351   Telex 57444

Station Manager *John Jefferson*
Programme Organiser *Chris Choi*

'A limited outlet for short stories and features provided they are either set locally or have some other local relevance.'

Independent Local Radio

Beacon Radio

PO Box 303, 267 Tettenhall Road, Wolverhampton WV6 0DQ
☎0902 757211   Telex 336919

Contact *Pete Wagstaff* (Programme Controller)

BRMB

PO Box 555, Radio House, Aston Road North, Birmingham B6 4BX
☎021–359 4481   Telex 339707

Programme Controller *Mike Owen*
Contact *Brian Savin*

Occasionally use drama; hold an annual short story competition; have some demand for comedy material; and there are opportunities for writers in the various feature series the station puts out.

Light Entertainment *Brian Valk*
News *Brian Sheppard*

Capital Radio

PO Box 958, Euston Tower, London NW1 3DR
☎01–388 1288

Contact *Matthew Bannister*

Britain's largest commercial radio station. Recently acquired a package of minority stakes in thirteen independent local radio stations. Also has a 60% holding in Monte Carlo-based Riviera Radio. Matthew Bannister covers current affairs, features, news and talks. Opportunities exist on the daily (weekdays) 7 pm programme *The Way It Is*. Also opportunities for comedy writing.

Chiltern Radio

Chiltern Road, Dunstable, Beds LU6 1HQ
☎ 0582 666001   Telex 825175

Radio scripts contact *Phil Fothergill*
News Editor *Katrina Balmforth*

Opportunities existing for radio drama only, and these are rare. However, if a script of exceptional local interest is offered, Chiltern Radio will consider it.

County Sound

The Friary, Guildford, Surrey GU1 4YX
☎ 0483 505566

Contact *Paul Owens* (Deputy Programme Controller)

Devonair Radio

35–7 St David's Hill, Exeter EX4 4DA
☎ 0392 30703   Telex 42496

Now owned by **Capital Radio**. No opportunities for freelance writers.

Downtown Radio

Newtownards, Co. Down,
Northern Ireland BT23 4ES
☎ 0247 815555   Telex 747570

Programme Head *J. Rosborough*

Essex Radio

Radio House, Cliftown Road,
Southend on Sea, Essex SS1 1SX *and* Radio House, 53 Duke Street,
Chelmsford CM1 1SX
☎ 0702 333711/0245 51141
Telex 995480 (Southend)

Editor *Bob Smith*
Contact *Keith Rogers*

No real opportunities for writers' work as such, but will often interview local authors of published books.

GWR Radio

PO Box 2000, Swindon SN4 7EX or
PO Box 2000, Watershed, Cannon's Road,
Bristol BS9 7EN
☎ 0793 853222 or 0272 279900
Telex 44450 (Swindon)

Contact *Simon Cooper*
(Programme Organiser)

Very few opportunities. Almost all material originates in-house.

Hereward Radio

PO Box 225, Queensgate Centre,
Peterborough PE1 1XJ
☎ 0733 46225   Telex 32738

Contact *Andy Gillies* (Editor)

Not usually any openings offered to writers as all material is compiled and presented by in-house staff.

Invicta Radio

15 Station Road East, Canterbury,
Kent CT1 2RB
☎ 0227 67661   Telex 965360

Contact *Roger Day* (Programme Manager)

LBC

Communications House, Gough Square,
London EC4P 4LP
☎ 01–353 1010

Contact *Peter Thornton*
(Programme Controller)

Leicester Sound

Granville House, Granville Road,
Leicester LE1 7RW
☎ 0533 551616   Telex 341953

Contact *Chris Hughes*
(Programme Controller)

Marcher Sound

The Studios, Mold Road, Gwersyllt,
Wrexham LL11 4AF
☎ 0978 752202   Telex 63140

Contact *Paul Mewies* (Programme Controller)

Mercia Sound

Hertford Place, Coventry,
West Midlands CV1 3TT
☎0203 633933   Telex 31413

News Editor *Colin Palmer*
Contact *Stuart Linnell*

Metro Radio

Newcastle upon Tyne NE99 1BB
☎091–488 3131   Telex 537428

Contact *Steve Martin* (Features Editor)

Very few opportunities for writers.

Moray Firth Radio

PO Box 271, Scourgurie Place,
Inverness IV3 6SF
☎0463 224433   Telex 75643

Contact *Brian Anderson*
(Programme Controller)

Northants 96

71b Abington Street,
Northampton NN1 2HW
☎0604 29811

Senior Programmer *C. Wilsher*

NorthSound

45 King's Gate, Aberdeen AB2 6BL
☎0224 632234   Telex 739883

Contact *Edith Stark* (Senior Producer)

Ocean Sound Ltd

Whittle Avenue, Segensworth West,
Fareham, Hants PO15 5PA
☎04895 89911   Telex 47474

Contact *Michael Betton* (Programme Controller)

For economic reasons, Ocean Sound rarely considers commissioning an external writer to produce drama/short stories for the station. All submissions are, however, considered, but only those with a special local connection are likely to be taken further.

News *Chris Rider*

Pennine Radio

PO Box 235, Pennine House, Forster Square,
Bradford BD1 5NP
☎0274 731521

Contact *Colin Slade* (Programme Controller)

Piccadilly Radio

127–31 The Piazza, Piccadilly Plaza,
Manchester M1 4AW
☎061–236 9913   Telex 667203

Contact *Michael Briscoe* (Editor)

Documentaries submit draft plans for discussion. **Drama** if of a 'pop' nature, especially short comedies or soaps. No light entertainment. **Features** only if local interest. **News** qualified journalists only.

Plymouth Sound

Earl's Acre, Alma Road, Plymouth PL3 4HX
☎0752 227272

Contact *Louise Churchill*
(Head of Programmes)

Radio Aire

PO Box 362, Leeds LS3 1LR
☎0532 452299

Contact *Christa Ackroyd*

Radio Broadland

St Georges Plain, 47–9 Colegate,
Norwich NR3 1DB
☎0603 630621   Telex 975186

Contact *Mike Stuart* (Programme Controller)

Radio City (Sound of Merseyside)

PO Box 194, Liverpool L69 1LD
☎051–227 5100   Telex 628277

Contact *Brian Harvey*

Opportunities for writers are very few and far between.

Radio Clyde

Clydebank Business Park,
Clydebank G81 2RX Scotland
☎041–941 1111   Telex 779537

Contacts *Hamish Wilson* (Drama),
Alex Dickson (Other)

Radio Clyde has few opportunities for outside writers, as programmes usually originate
in-house or by commission. Good local news
items always considered. Feature openings
rare. Few opportunities for dramatists,
beyond the work of Scottish writers. 'A set-
in-Glasgow very funny comedy script/series
is always considered'. All documentary material is made in-house.

Radio Forth

Forth House, Forth Street,
Edinburgh EH1 3LF
☎031–556 9255   Telex 727374

Contact *Tom Steele* (Editor)

Features *Colin Somerville* Opportunities in
the 2-minute feature series *The story of* . . .
Light Entertainment *Tom Steele* 60-minute
Radio Cartoons. **News** *David Johnston* News
stories welcome from freelancers.

Radio Hallam

PO Box 194, Hartshead, Sheffield S1 1GP
☎0742 766766
Telex 547338   Fax 0742 738909

Contact *Dean Pepall*
(Presentation Co-ordinator)

Radio Luxembourg (London) Ltd

38 Hertford Street, London W1Y 8BA
☎01–493 5961   Telex 263912

Contact *Rodney Collins* (Editor)

Some freelance opportunities in news only.

Radio Mercury

Broadfield House, Brighton Road,
Crawley, West Sussex RH11 9TT
☎0293 519161   Telex 87503

Programme Controller *J. Wellington*

No fiction or features opportunities. The
newsroom occasionally take freelance news
stories, though most of these come from
established contacts.

Radio Merseyside

55 Paradise Street, Liverpool L1 3BP
☎051–708 5500

Contact *Caroline Adams, First Heard*
News Editor *Liam Fogarty*

No opportunities in news. Very rarely in
light entertainment, drama or fiction. However, *First Heard* broadcasts previously unpublished work by local writers, gives
information about workshops and competitions, and features interviews with successful authors. *First Heard* goes out
fortnightly, with every fourth edition devoted to poetry and poets.

Radio Orwell

Electric House, Lloyds Avenue, Ipswich,
Suffolk IP1 3HZ
☎0473 216971   Telex 98548

Contact *Simon Cornes* (Editor)

Features Editor *Sally Gordon* Few openings
here; 'even fewer' in drama and light entertainment.

Radio Solway Dumfries

Loves Walk, Dumfries DG1 1NZ
☎0387 68008

Editor *Iain McConnell*

Radio Stoke

Cheapside, Hanley, Stoke on Trent ST1 1JJ
☎0782 208080   Telex 36104

Programme Organiser *Mervyn Gamage*
Contact *Arthur Wood*

The station has long had a policy of encouraging material suitable for a Radio Stoke
audience, whether this be short or longer essays, short stories, original research and writ-

ing on local history, or other subjects of local interest. The station is particularly keen on receiving these from locally-based authors. Very occasionally use scripts of great local relevance. (All scripts lacking local links are rejected.)

Radio Tay

PO Box 123, Dundee DD1 9UF
☎0382 200800   Telex 76412

Contact *Tom Steele* (Programme Controller)
See also **Radio Forth**.

Radio Tees

74 Dovecot Street,
Stockton on Tees TS18 1HB
☎0642 615111   Telex 587232

Programme Controller *Brian Lister*
Features *Andy Hollins*

Limited opportunities at present – 'however, we are always willing to consider new ideas'.

Radio Trent

29–31 Castlegate, Nottingham NG1 7AP
☎0602 581731
Telex Rad Trent Nottm 37463

Contact *Chris Hughes*
(Programme Controller)

Few opportunities, although a short story series is run from time to time. **Documentaries** 'perhaps if locally orientated and discussed up-front'. **Features** *John Shaw* Rarely used. **Light Entertainment** Christmas material only.

Radio 210

PO Box 210, Reading RG3 5RZ
☎0734 413131   Telex 848503

Contact *Terry Mann* (Programme Controller)

Radio Wyvern

PO Box 22, 5–6 Barbourne Terrace,
Worcester WR1 3JS
☎0905 612212   Telex 335292

Contact *Norman Bilton* (Managing Director)

One of the smallest of the regional radio stations; has little money for contributors. Very occasionally, a local writer may be commissioned to produce something of interest to the Wyvern audience.

Red Dragon Radio

Radio House, West Canal Wharf,
Cardiff CF1 5XJ
☎0222 384041

Contact *Mike Henfield*
(Programme Controller)

See also **Red Rose Radio** based in Preston.

Red Rose Radio

PO Box 301, St Paul's Square, Preston,
Lancs PR1 1YE
☎0772 556301   Telex 677610

Contact *Mike Henfield* (Head of Programmes)

See also **Red Dragon Radio.** Just opened a new station, Blackpool Rock FM; all-day rock music.

Saxon Radio

Long Brackland,
Bury St Edmunds, Suffolk IP33 1JY
☎0284 701511   Telex 98548

Contact *Sally Gordon* (Programme Controller)

Severn Sound

PO Box 388, 67 Southgate Street,
Gloucester GL1 2DQ
☎0452 423791   Telex 0437271

Contact *Eddie Vickers*
(Programme Controller)

Signal Radio

Studio 257, Stoke Road, Shelton,
Stoke on Trent ST4 2SR
☎0782 417111   Telex 367444

Contact *John Evington*
(Head of Presentations)

Southern Sound Radio

Radio House, Franklin Road, Portslade,
Brighton, Sussex BN4 2SS
☎0273 422288　　　　　Telex 878246

Contact *Andy Ivy* (Features) *Vince Geddes*
(Programme Controller)

Swansea Sound

Victoria Road, Gowerton, Swansea SA4 3AB
☎0792 893751　　　　　Telex 48594

Contact *David Thomas* (Programme Controller)

**Features, Drama/Fiction and Light
Entertainment** *David Thomas*
News *Hugh Turnbull*

Two Counties Radio

5 Southcote Road, Bournemouth BH1 3LR
☎0202 294881　　　　　Telex 418362

Contact *Rosemary Mundy*

Documentaries *Stan Horobin*
**Features, Drama/Fiction and Light
Entertainment** *Rosemary Mundy*

Viking Radio

Commercial Road, Hull HU1 2SG
☎0482 25141　　　　　Telex 597572

Contact *Alma Cooper* (News Editor)

Features *Steve King*

West Sound

Radio House, 54 Holmston Road,
Ayr KA7 3BE
☎0292 283662　　　　　Telex 776235

Contact *John McCauley*
(Programme Controller)

Film, TV and Video Production Companies

A & M Sound Pictures
136 New Kings Road, London SW6 4LZ
☎01–736 3311   Telex 916342

Contact *Steven Lavers*

Not currently acting as producers; commission other production companies when required.

A.C.T. Films Ltd
111 Wardour Street, London W1A 4AY
☎01–437 8506   Fax 01–437 8268

Contact *Richard Gates*

Low budget features, television documentary. Unsolicited mss welcome. 'We are pleased to read anything and are prepared to try and help writers revise scripts to make them acceptable.'

Abbey Video Ltd
Five Lamps Studio, West Avenue,
Derby DE1 3HR
☎0332 40693

Contact *Richard Faulkner*

Makers of corporate video for a variety of industrial clients.

Acme Arts Ltd
12 Vauxhall Grove, London SW8 1SY
☎01–735 9099

Contact *Jim Field*

Horticultural and educational films for television and video.

Action Time
22 Woodstock Street, London W1R 1HF
☎01–409 3421   Telex 262187

Contact *Jeremy Fox*

Makers of television programmes: 'format shows' like *Game For A Laugh*, *Odd One Out* and *The Krypton Factor*, both for the UK and America.

Advent Video Productions
Ely House, 37 Dover Street,
London W1X 4AH
☎01–409 1343

Contact *Dominic Roncoroni*

Documentary, educational and corporate video; also commercials.

After Image Ltd
32 Acre Lane, London SW2 5SG
☎01–737 7300

Contact *Jane Thorburn*

Makers of television, with a particular interest in the arts and unusual people and events. OUTPUT *Alter Image*, the alternative arts magazine, with no presenter; *Pookiesnackenburger* (musical series); *Map of Dreams* (arts video, dance and effects). After Image concentrate on the visual aspects of television; interested to read new writing, and to work with author towards new pieces, specifically for television.

Agender Films
25 Denmark Street, London WC2H 8NJ
☎01–379 5304/5346

Contact *Sarah Boston, Rachel Trezise*

Documentaries. OUTPUT (most recent) *Just Sex*, which they made as 51% Productions; *Merely Mortal* for **Channel 4**.

Aisling Films Ltd
17–21 Bruce Street, Belfast BT2 7JD
☎0232 327434   Fax 0232 327820

Contact *Bill Miskelly, Marie Jackson*

Film and television drama and documentary. No unsolicited mss. Interested in all new work, but 'don't have the time to comment on unsolicited scripts'. OUTPUT *The End of the World Man* (children's feature film); *The Schooner* (TV drama).

The Britt Allcroft Group Limited
61 Devonshire Road, Southampton SO1 2GR
☎0703 331661
Telex 47408 BALAHA G   Fax 0703 332206

Contact *Britt Allcroft, Angus Wright*

Television programmes – notably specialising in family and children's, led by *Thomas the Tank Engine and Friends*.

Allied Stars
17 Waterloo Place, London SW1 4SR
☎01–839 5285

Contact *Luke Randolph*

Feature films. OUTPUT *Chariots of Fire; Breaking Glass; F/X Murder by Illusion; Government Issue; Rocket*. Unsolicited mss welcome: 'we read everything'.

Alligator Productions Ltd
68–70 Wardour Street, London W1V 4JA
☎01–734 0101   Telex 25554 PECLDN

Contact *Catherine Skinner*

A collection of freelance directors and other professionals who make commericals and promo films for video and television, and also act as a useful bridge between scripts and potential directors.

Amber Films
5 side (rear), Newcastle upon Tyne NE1 3JE
☎091–232 2000

Contact *Peter Roberts*

Television programmes, cinema and animation. OUTPUT has included *Keeping Time, Byker, Seacoal* and *T. Dan Smith*.

Antelope Films Ltd
3 Fitzroy Square, London W1P 5AH
☎01–387 4454
Telex 266205 AFL G   Fax 01–388 9935

Contact *Clive Syddall*

Makers of drama and television documentaries. Welcome unsolicited mss. OUTPUT has included *The Triple Crown: The Paradox of the Papacy, The Spirit of the Alcazar: 50 Years in a Spanish City, Vidal in Venice, Heart of the Dragon* (12 part series on China for **Channel 4**) and *Portrait of Russia* (7-part series for Turner Broadcasting); *Testament* (7-part series for **Channel 4**).

Antonine Productions/Black Cat Studios
830 Springfield Road, Glasgow G31 4HG
☎041–554 4667

Contact *Paddy Higson*

Films for television, feature films (particularly thrillers and road movies). OUTPUT *The Girl in the Picture* (1985) *Brond* (**Channel 4**, 1987). Scripts accepted from both writers and agents: 'delighted to see new work'.

Arbor Productions Ltd
10 Museum Street, London WC1A 1LE
☎01–379 5847

Contact *Mary Jane Walsh*

Makers of television programmes, cinema, corporate and educational video. Specialises in arts, documentary and drama and music. OUTPUT has included *Body Styles for* **Channel 4**.

Aspect Film & Television Production Ltd

36 Percy Street, London W1P 9FG
☎01–636 5303

Contact *Marian Lacey*

Drama, documentary and corporate television. OUTPUT has included *On the Piste*, a documentary about skiing, and *Stirring Stuff*, about tea drinking.

Aspen Spafax Television Ltd

Aspen House, 1 Gayford Road,
London W12 9BY
☎01–743 8618   Fax 01–740 9333

Contact *Mike Raggett*

Commercials and corporate film and video production for corporate communications, company and product promotion. OUTPUT has included training films for accountants Peat, Harwick, McLintock, promotional videos for the Leeds Building Society, Tie Rack, ICI, Glaxo, and British Gas.

Associated Video Productions

29a Eccleston Road, London W13 0RA
☎01–840 4222

Contact *Jon Sinigaglia*

Corporate production for big-name commercial clients; also arts, documentary and music for television.

Astramead Ltd

38 Gloucester Mews, London W2 3HE
☎01–723 4678

Contact *Mark Shivas*

Television programmes, cinema and drama on film and video. OUTPUT has included the television series *Telford's Change*; *Can You Hear Me at the Back?*, and *The Price* for **Channel 4** and *Late Starter* for the **BBC**.

Athos Film Productions Ltd

65 High Street, Hampton Hill,
Middx TW12 1NH
☎01–783 0533   Telex 28905 ref: 325

Contacts *Mr. P.G.A. Bucknall* (Director) and *Mr R. Orr-Ewing* (Director)

Films and videos. No unsolicited mss. Interested in seeing CVs.

Aurora Productions

Weavers House, Mountergate,
Norwich NR1 1PY
☎0603 630097

Contacts *Steve Bloomfield, Trevor Machin*

Video marketing and training programmes; radio drama and radio commercials. Only undertake commissioned work (except for radio drama) and only interested in seeing unsolicited mss as examples of work.

Robert Austen Communications Ltd

The Chequers, 2 Church Street,
High Wycombe, Bucks HP11 2DE
☎0494 44377   Fax 0494 464353
Telex 265871 MONREF G TCC/097

Contacts *Bob Austen, Charlene Hamlin*

Film/video/TV/drama/documentaries/commercials. Do most of their own writing but will consider unsolicited mss.

AVC Group

Walters Farm Road, Tonbridge,
Kent TN9 1QT
☎0732 365107   Fax 0732 362600

Contact *Alistair McGawn Lees*

A specialist business communication company who work as consultants for corporate clients in the field of conferences, corporate and financial communications, PR events and award ceremonies, safety, sales and marketing, and training.

AVL

1 Rectory Road, Wokingham,
Berks RG11 5AS
☎0734 790500

Contact *Gerry Clarke*

Video production and corporate communications for commercial and industrial clients; documentary, current affairs and training films.

Michael Barratt Ltd

5–7 Forlease Road, Maidenhead,
Berks SL6 1RP
☎0628 770800   Fax 0628 770144

Contact *Michael Barratt*

Corporate and educational video, also television programmes – but these are mostly about the Royal Family, for international television.

Peter Batty Productions

Claremont House, Renfrew Road,
Kingston, Surrey KT2 7NT
☎01–942 6304
Telex 261507 MONREF 2685

Contact *Peter Batty*

Television programmes and commercials. Primarily broadcast documentaries. OUTPUT has included *The Divided Union* (on the American Civil War) and *The Perfect Partnership* (about Nureyev and Fonteyn, a one-off for **Channel 4**).

Beat Ltd/The Media Show Ltd

4th Floor, 24 Scala Street, London W1P 1LU
☎01–323 3270

Contact *Michael Jackson*

Documentary series/features. OUTPUT *The Sixties*, for RSO; *Open the Box*, for **Channel 4**; *The Media Show*, also for **Channel 4**. Material is produced in-house, or by commission direct to writers. Rarely use agents. Happy to consider new documentary ideas: write in the first instance with outline. Of **The Media Show Ltd**, intended expansion means 'there should be more opportunities for writers here'.

Behr Cinematography

22 Redington Road, London NW3 7RG
☎01–794 2535

Contact *Arnold Behr, Betty Burghes*

Documentary, educational, corporate film and video on subjects ranging from care of the terminally ill, through sport for the handicapped, to custom building of motor cars. No unsolicited mss.

Stuart Bell & Partners Ltd

40 Frith Street, London W1V 5TF
☎01–439 2700

Contact *Stuart Bell*

Video and film – commercials, corporate training, broadcast documentaries. Welcome unsolicited mss. 'Can help new writers meet production companies.'

Bentorm Ltd

26B Thorney Crescent, London SW11 3TR
☎01–585 1592

Contact *David Deutsch*

Television and cinema producers, particularly in drama and arts fields. OUTPUT has included *Shakespeare Lives* and *Reflections*, both for **Channel 4**, and the feature film *The Chain* (script by Jack Rosenthal).

Paul Berriff Productions Ltd

The Chestnuts, Woodfield Lane, Hessle,
North Humberside HU13 0EW
☎0482 641158

Contact *Paul Berriff*

Television, documentary features. OUTPUT has included *Lakeland Rock* for **Channel 4** *Lifeboat* series for BBC 1, *Fire* for **BBC '40 Minutes'**, *Animal Squad* for BBC 1 and *Dianne's Children* for BBC2

Bevanfield Films

22 Soho Square, London W1V 5FJ
☎01–734 1051

Contact *Mary Swindale*

Television programmes, cinema and animation, including an animation series for **Channel 4** and *Bill the Minder* for **Central**.

Black Cat Studios
See **Antonine Productions**

Blackrod Ltd
Threeways House, 40–44 Clipstone Street, London W1P 7EA
☎01–637 9376
Telex 269859   Fax 01–580 9143

Contact *Clive Moffat*

Television film and video services to commercial and industrial clients. One of the biggest corporate video makers, they have won a fistful of awards for excellence in the field.

Blackwell Videotec Ltd
7 John Street, London WC1N 2ES
☎01–430 0044

Contact *Jo-Anne Winston*

Subsidiary of **Blackwell Scientific Publications** (see **Publishers**). Corporate, educational, medical, promotional and scientific programmes. OUTPUT has included *Risk*, looking at the risks in medical practice, which won the gold award in the 1985 New York film and television festival.

Matt Boney Associates
'Woodside', Holdfast Lane, Grayswood, Haslemere, Surrey GU27 2EU
☎0428 56178

Contact *Matt Boney*

Video, television – commercials, documentary, sport and travel. No unsolicited mss.

Braham Hill Ltd
14 King Street, Covent Garden, London WC2E 8HN
☎01–240 6941

Contact *Michael Braham, Liz Beaumont*

Factual/current affairs/business programmes and corporate video. **Television** *The Business Programme*. **Corporate Work** training, customer care, safety at work, and financial matters such as pensions. 'All material has a tendency towards the financial sector, where most of our clients come from'. No unsolicited mss.

Britannic Film & TV Ltd
Pinewood Studios, Iver, Bucks SL0 0NH
☎0753 651700   Telex 847505

Contact *Peter R.E. Snell* (Chief Executive)

Film production. OUTPUT *Turtle Diary*; *Lady Jane*; *A Prayer for the Dying*. No unsolicited mss.

Broadside Ltd
74 Moss Lane, Pinner, Middx HA5 3AU
☎01–866 5271

Contact *Angela Spindler-Brown*

An all-woman independent production company. OUTPUT has included a current affairs series for **Channel 4**. *Thinking About Conflict, Female Focus* and *Five Women Photographers*, also for **Channel 4**.

Broadwick Productions
26 Charlotte Street, London W1P 1HJ
☎01–580 1923

Contacts *Sarah Wickham, Simon Lethbridge*

Wide range of corporate productions including documentary, educational, financial, point of sale programme-making, production of pop promos and training. Unsolicited mss welcome. 'Always attempt to use at least two new writers each year for corporate production. Opportunity varies according to quantity and quality of incoming work.'

Brook Productions
103–9 Wardour Street, London W1V 3TD
☎01–439 9871

Contact *Anne Lapping*

Makers of arts, current affairs, documentary and music television. OUTPUT has included *A Week in Politics* for **Channel 4**, *Shape of the World*, *Voices*, *The Writing on the Wall* and *David Low*.

Burbank Film & Video Ltd

Ebury Rooms, Bury Lane, Rickmansworth, Herts WD3 1DT
☎0923 771222

Contact *Rae Evans*

Film and video documentaries. Commercial, industrial, medical and scientific films, video programmes and children's television; programmes for industry, commerce and television. Will consider unsolicited mss, but 'as our output is so specialised, we feel it may be a wasted effort by writers'. Mostly use staff writers.

Burrill Productions

51 Lansdowne Road, London W11 2LG
☎01–208 0866   Fax 01–450 1544

Contact *Timothy Burrill*

Feature film production company. OUTPUT *Alpha Beta* for **BBC**; *Tess* Roman Polanski; *Pirates of Penzance*; *Supergirl*; *The Fourth Protocol*. No unsolicited mss. Policy of encouragement for new screenwriters.

The Callender Company

4th floor, 82 Wardour Street,
London W1V 3LF
☎01–240 8644   Fax 01–240 8647

Contact *Andi Wright*

Major drama series and feature films. OUTPUT *The Belly of an Architect* by Peter Greenaway; *The Bretts*, co-produced with **Central TV** for Mobil Masterpiece Theatre. Mss are considered only if they come by way of established literary agents.

Camden Productions

20 Jeffreys Street, London NW1 9PR
☎01–482 0527

Contact *Theresa FitzGerald, Philip Kemp*

Camden Productions consists of two writers and develops their work exclusively. No unsolicited mss.

Caravel Film Techniques Limited

The Great Barn Studios, Cippenham Lane, Slough, Berks SL1 5AU
☎0753 821218

Contact *Nick See*

Film, video, television – documentary and commercials. No unsolicited mss. 'We keep a file on writers' details and always welcome any new information'.

Pearl Catlin Associates

16a Carlisle Mansions, Carlisle Place, London SW1P 1HX
☎01–834 1660

Contacts *Pearl Catlin, Philip Bond*

Commercials, promotional, corporate – film and video. No unsolicited mss but interested in creative ideas.

Celador Productions Limited

39 Long Acre, London WC2E 9JT
☎01–240 8101
Telex 2654593 COMCEL G Fax 01–836 1117

Contact *Bob Louis*

Film and television: documentary, light entertainment, drama for both British and international television markets. OUTPUT *Spellbound* (series co-produced with **Ulster Television**); *Celebrating St Patrick* (ITV co-production with **Ulster Television**); *Delorean* (four-hour mini-series for international television).

Chameleon Television Ltd

The Magistretti Building, 1 Harcourt Place, West Street, Leeds LS1 4RB
☎0532 438536

Contact *Chris Lister*

Television has included documentaries for **Channel 4**, ITV and **BBC**, and PR videos for corporate clients.

Charisma Films
Russell Chambers, Covent Garden,
London WC2E 8AA
☎01–379 4267

Contact *David Gideon Thomson*

Contrary to popular belief, don't make music promos (the company grew out of Charisma Records). Theatrical and drama television producers. OUTPUT has included *The Best of British*, a compilation of old Rank film clips for the **BBC**, and *Sir Henry at Rawlinson End*, a feature film broadcast on **Channel 4** in 1987.

Chatsworth Television Ltd
97–9 Dean Street, London W1V 5RA
☎01–734 4302   Telex 28604

Contact *Malcolm Heyworth*

Drama and light entertainment television makers of 16 years' experience.

Cheerleader Productions
Limehouse Studios, Canary Wharf,
West India Docks, London E4 9SJ
☎01–987 2090
Telex 27782 TRIDIS G   Fax 01– 538 4750

Sports programme makers. Have produced American football, tennis and golf programmes for **Channel 4**. Also corporate video makers.

CHG Communications
108 Clarendon Road, London W11 2HR
☎01–727 4269   Fax 01–727 3918

Contact *Jeremy Hamp*

Film and video business communications. Commissioned work only. No unsolicited mss, although always keen to meet scriptwriters.

Cinexsa Film Productions Limited
209 Manygate Lane, Shepperton,
Middx TW17 9ER
☎0932 225950   Telex 266389 KINLON G

Contact *Jimmy Wright*

Film, video and TV –documentary and commercials. No unsolicited mss but 'new writing is welcomed'.

City Photographic and Video Services
14 Milton Terrace, Mount Pleasant,
Swansea SA1 6XP
☎0792 467688

Contact *R.H. Kneath*, LMPA

Film, video and TV – commercials and documentary. Welcome unsolicited mss. 'Willing to look into any ideas.'

Peter Claridge Pictures Ltd
Post 59, Lee International Studios,
Studios Road, Shepperton,
Middx TW17 0QD
☎ 0932 562611
Telex MOVIES G 929416   Fax 0932 568989

Contacts *Peter Claridge, Geraldine Morgan*

Film and TV production – commercials, corporate communication, promos, special projects and titles. Welcome unsolicited mss.

Cleveland Productions
5 Rainbow Court, Oxhey, Herts WD1 4RP
☎Tel 0923 54000

Contact *Michael Gosling*

Film and video – documentary and commercials.

Colchester Filmmakers
74 High Street, Colchester CO1 1UE
☎0206 560255

Contact *Carol Comley*

Promotion and documentary work for the voluntary and arts sectors. New writing welcome.

Collier Marsland Films

44 Berwick Street, London W1V 3RE
☎01–437 6684

Contact *Kevin Marsland*

Documentary, light entertainment, children's television programmes, but the main emphasis recently has been corporate video for architects (Lloyds building, Hong Kong Bank etc.). Work proceeding on a documentary for television, and *Ali Bongo* for video sale.

Colstar Communications Entertainment Ltd

1 Wardour Mews, D'Arblay Street,
London W1V 3FF
☎01–437 5725   Telex 8951859 Basil G

Contact *Robert Angell*

Make sponsored, corporate, training and promotion films, plus documentary films for an international market. OUTPUT has included *The Poacher, The Hunter, The Gamekeeper* and *Roots of Tomorrow*.

Communications Concept Ltd (trading as Concept)

Five Lamps Studio, West Avenue,
Derby DE1 3HR
☎0332 3833322   Fax 0332 291268

Contacts *Mollie Kirkland, David Regan*

Industrial video, conferences and audio visual. Total in-house facilities, including writing. No unsolicited mss.

Compact Television

13 Imperial Studios, 7 Imperial Road,
Fulham, London SW6 2AG
☎01–731 6151   Telex 237333 CROSS K

Contact *Kent Walwin*

Drama and light entertainment for television and cinema.

Compass Film Produc...

Third Floor, 18–19 Warwick Str...
London W1R 5RB
☎01–439 6456

Contact *Simon Heaven*

Specialists since 1974 in documentary, educational and promotional programmes for television and corporate clients. 1987/8 OUTPUT includes *Another Way of Life* (on mental handicap) for **Channel 4** and *Music of the Outsiders* for **Channel 4**.

Component Television Productions Ltd

1 Newman Passage, London W1P 3PP
☎01–631 4400   Fax 01–323 1184

Contact *Gaby Bedford*

Corporate videos, documentary, drama, retail videos, TV. Welcome unsolicited mss, 'of documentary style only'.

Consolidated Productions Ltd

5 Jubilee Place, London SW3 3TD
☎01–376 5151   Telex 946449

Contact *Annette Kiely*

World-wide television. OUTPUT *Deceptions*, mini-series co-produced with Columbia and **BBC**; *Gathering of Old Men*, 2-hour feature film; *Where Do I Come From?*, animated cartoon.

Cosmos Productions

42–4 Hanway Street, London W1P 9DE
☎01–631 3041

Contact *Ronis Varlaam*

Television makers. OUTPUT includes *Enthusiasts*, six half-hour documentaries for **Channel 4**, plus *Well You Didn't Expect Us To Sit Around Doing Nothing Did You?* (on unemployment, also for **Channel 4**.

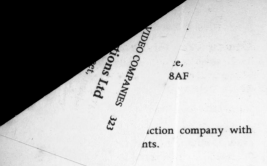

...e,
8AF

...iction company with
...nts.

Cristo Films and Television

New Tythe Street, Long Eaton,
Nottingham NG10 2DC
☎0602 727160

Contact *D. Barton*

Children's, current affairs, documentary and
light entertainment television.

Cromdale Films Limited

12 St Paul's Road, London N1 2QN
☎01–226 0178

Contact *Ian Lloyd*

Film, video and TV – drama and documentary. OUTPUT *The Face of Darkness* (feature
film); *Drift to Dawn* (rock music drama); *The
Overdue Treatment* (documentary).

Crystalvision Productions Ltd

Communications House, Blue Riband Estate.
Roman Way, Croydon CR9 3RA
☎01–681 7171
Telex 881 4079   Fax 01–681 2340

Contact *Fraser Ashford* (Executive Producer)

Film, video, TV and cable/satellite programming – children's, documentary, drama,
music, sports. OUTPUT *Shady Tales* (13-part
drama co-production for **Thames TV**); *The
History of Cricket*; *The Other China*; *World
Invitation Club Basketball Championships*;
Nicky & the Newsgang (children's). Welcome
unsolicited material which should have
treatment/outline page. 'Each project is
studied on merit; if the story/idea is good we
would work with new writers.'

CTR Productions

31 Lismore Crescent, Broadfield, Crawley,
West Sussex RH11 9DA
☎0293 548475

Contact *Ian Cunningham*

Arts, corporate, documentary, educational
and music video producers. Specialise in promotional work/documentaries for churches,
schools, education authorities and voluntary
organisations. OUTPUT includes *Sex Matters*
for **Channel 4** and *Christians and Trade
Unions*.

Cwmni'r Castell Cyf

1 Coed Pella Road, Colwyn Bay,
Clwyd LL29 7AT
☎0492 533148

Contact *Elwyn Vaughan Williams*

Television programmes. OUTPUT has included
The Scouts Holiday, a mute comedy film for
S4C, and light entertainment programmes
containing comedy sketches.

Dareks Production House

58 Wickham Road, Beckenham,
Kent BR3 2RQ
☎01–658 2012

Contact *David Crossman*

Independent producers of broadcast television. Situation comedies, children's factual
and fictional programmes for ITV and **Channel 4**. OUTPUT *The Cannon & Ball Show*; *Metal
Mickey*; *The Pocket Money Programme*.
Unsolicited mss welcome: 'we are looking for
original minds, and have an interest in tragic
situations in modern contexts.'

Dateline Productions Ltd

79 Dean Street, London W1V 5HA
☎01–437 4510/1834

Contact *Miranda Watts*

Film and video – documentary and corporate. Welcome unsolicited mss. 'We are

always interested in widening our list of possible writers.'

DBA Television

21 Ormeau Avenue, Belfast BT2 8HD
☎0232 231197   Telex 747001

Contact *David Barker*

Makers of documentary, news and current affairs television and also corporate video. OUTPUT includes *McCrea Goes to Nashville* and *Someone's Always Leaving*; also contributed to **Channel 4**'s *Irish Angle*, its *Poets* series, plus *The Other Emerald Isle*.

DBI Communication

21 Congreve Close, Warwick,
Warwickshire CV34 5RQ
☎0926 497695

Contact *David B. Impey*

Video – corporate, promotion, safety, training and sales. Do not welcome unsolicited mss as programmes are 'customised'. OUTPUT *Play Safe*, with Keith Chegwin (about the dangers of children entering quarries), shown in schools nationwide.

Debonair Production Co. Ltd

38 Canfield Gardens, London NW6 3LA
☎01–624 5571

Contact *Maggie Coates*

Drama and documentary television. OUTPUT has included *Common Interest*, *Politics of Health*, *People of the Islands* and *Backstage at the Kirov*.

Deptford Beach Productions Ltd

79 Wardour Street, London W1V 3TH
☎01–734 8508

Contact *Tony Kirkhope*

FOUNDED 1985 to make independent productions for **Channel 4**. OUTPUT includes documentary about Jean-Luc Godard, directed and written by him.

Dibgate Productions Ltd

Studio 4, Parkstead Lodge, 31 Upper Park Road, London NW3 2UL
☎01–722 5634

Contact *Nicholas Parsons*

Make documentary and travel films for television and, increasingly in recent years, shorts for cinema audiences. OUTPUT has included *A Fair Way to Play*, *Mad Dogs and Cricketers*, *Relatively Greek*, *Viva Menorca* and *Terribly British*.

Diverse Productions Ltd

6 Gorleston Street, London W14 8XS
☎01–603 4567   Telex 28363 DIVERS G

Contact *Graham Walker*

News and current affairs programmes for **Channel 4**, all produced in-house. OUTPUT has included *Diverse Reports*, *The Aids Brief* and *Election Brief*; plus films for NUPE and the TGWU.

Drake A-V Video Ltd

89 St Fagans Road,
Fairwater, Cardiff CF5 3AE
☎0222 560333   Fax 0222 554909
Telex 497618 TYPES G DRAKED

Contact *Ian Lewis*

Corporate A-V film and video – mostly documentary and promotional. No unsolicited mss. Query letter and brief synopsis in the first instance.

Dumbarton Films

Dumbarton House, 68 Oxford Street,
London W1N 9LA
☎01–631 4926

Contact *Jane Lighting*

Makers of television and cinema, plus educational and home videos. Specialises in developing and producing feature films. OUTPUT has included *No Surrender*, Alan Bleasdale; *Loyalties*, Sharon Riis and *Birdsville*, a Carl Schultz film.

Edifex Limited

The Boundary House, Old Warwick Road, Lapworth, Warwickshire B94 6LU
☎05643 3958/0836 261186

Contact *John Pluck* (Senior Producer)

Produce broadcast television documentaries and feature series on film and video for ITV and **BBC TV**. Will be increasingly looking towards cable, satellite and home video to broaden output. Welcome ideas for television documentaries. Send a treatment in the first instance, particularly if the subject is 'outside our area of current interest'. OUTPUT television programmes on heritage and antiques. Also on industry. Projects on heritage and sports for the home video front.

The Elstree (Production) Co. Ltd

Cannon Elstree Studios, Shenley Road, Borehamwood, Herts WD6 1JG
☎01–953 1600   Telex 922436 E FILMS G

Contact *Lynne Donovan*
(Development Executive)

Produces feature films and television drama/situation comedy. OUTPUT *Prospects* for **Euston Films/Channel 4**; *Rude Health* for **Channel 4**. Two feature films currently in development with Australian partners, and another twelve projects on the boil; 'we are actively looking for more, across the whole range of television and films'. Unsolicited mss welcome. Elstree has a positive policy towards new writers, and is proud to have brought some of them to the point of having their material produced.

Emitel

65 Beak Street, Soho, London W1R 3LF
☎01–439 9882

Contact *Malcolm Craddock*

Shorts for the cinema, corporate video, training and educational films, sponsored films. Multi-award-winning company.

Enigma Productions Ltd

11–15 Queen's Gate Place Mews, London SW7 5BG
☎01–581 8248   Fax 01–225 2230

Enlightenment AV & Video

The Studio, Warrens Lane, Botesdale, Diss, Norfolk IP22 1BW

☎0379 898434   Fax 0379 898987

Contact *Adrian Tayler*

Video productions for training and industrial marketing. All scripts currently produced in-house, or commissioned by a client for a specific project, but will consider unsolicited mss if appropriate to their market, e.g. technical subjects such as insurance, animal health or computers.

Equal Time

Heath Lodge, Heathside, London NW3 1BL
☎01–431 1927

Contact *Martin Minns*

Documentaries on music, the arts and current affairs. No opportunities as all material is produced in-house.

Eurofilm Productions Ltd

47 Ossington Street, London W2 4LY
☎01–243 1613

Contact *Andrzej Swoboda*

OUTPUT includes *Modern Polish Composers* for **Channel 4** and *King Size*, a short science fiction comedy feature.

Euston Films

365 Euston Road, London NW1 3AR
☎01–387 0911

Contact *Jenny Goodman*

Television programmes and films for cinema. Euston is the film-making arm of **Thames Television**: their most recent credit is the mini-series *The Fear*. OUTPUT also includes *A*

Month in the Country and *Bellman and True*; and the feature film *Consuming Passions*, released in 1988.

F.M. Television Limited

92 Water Lane,
Wilmslow, Cheshire SK9 5BB
☎0625 533580
Telex 667028 Wilsec G   Fax 0625 531992

Contact *Ms Hilary Pinnock*

Sports programmes for international broadcasters; corporate videos for industry. OUTPUT *Budweiser Grand Prix* series for powerboats, world dragster car racing. No unsolicited mss.

Fairwater Films

389 Newport Road, Cardiff CF2 1RP
☎0222 460302
Telex 497492 CHACOM G   Fax 0222 489785

Contact *Naomi Jones*

Makers of animated films for **BBC Wales**, **HTV Wales**, and other outlets. OUTPUT includes a cartoon series for S4C, *Hanner Dwsin*.

Fidelity Films Ltd

34–6 Oak End Way, Gerrards Cross,
Bucks SL9 8BR
☎0753 884646
Telex 846723 AUDVIS G   Fax 0753 887163

Contacts *John Fewlass, Graham Harris*

Corporate, training, sales and exhibition videos. Welcome unsolicited mss; 'always willing to try new scriptwriters'.

Filmessence Limited

302 Clive Court, Maida Vale,
London W9 1SF
☎01–289 5850

Contact *Don Morrison*

Film and video – drama, documentary and commercials. Unsolicited mss welcome.

Filmfair Ltd

Jacobs Well Mews, London W1H 5PD
☎01–935 1596   Telex 28170

Contact *Barrie Edwards*

FOUNDED 1966. Makers of children's and educational television, cable and video. OUTPUT *The Wombles*; *Paddington Bear*; *Portland Bill*; *The Perishers*; *The Blunders*; *Bangers and Mash*. 'If unsolicited mss come in, they are read.'

Flamingo Pictures

47 Lonsdale Square, London N1 1EW
☎01–607 9958

Contact *Christine Oestreicher*

Television programmes and cinema films. Mostly cinema and mostly fiction. OUTPUT has included *Every Picture Tells a Story* for **Channel 4**, *Loser Takes All*, Graham Greene, for cinema release in 1988 and *Dibs*, also for cinema release.

Flickering Picture Productions Ltd

Rosemount Studios, Pyrford Road,
West Byfleet, Weybridge, Surrey KT14 6LD
☎09323 53757   Fax 09323 49008

Contacts *Paul Gawith, David Haggas*

Film and video – medical, educational and corporate documentary. No unsolicited mss but looking for writers who understand scriptwriting for television.

Flickers Productions

Dumbarton House, 68 Oxford Street,
London W1N 9LA
☎01–580 0044   Telex 269578 FLICKS G

Contacts *Neil Zeiger, Baz Taylor*

Intelligent feature films and comedies. OUTPUT *Lamb* Bernard MacLaverty. Developing nine screenplays at present. Very interested in young writers with strong scripts. Writers for Flickers have included Howard Brenton, P.G. Duggan, Anthony Garner, Ron Hutchinson.

Forever Films

82D Warwick Avenue, London W9 2PU
☎01–286 1948

Contact *Clare Downs*

Describe their intended audience as 'specialised to crossover feature film audience'. OUTPUT *The Dress* (short romantic fantasy, BAFTA award winner); *High Season* (serious comedy feature); *Buster's Bedroom* (absurdist drama). No unsolicited mss. Very interested in writing which has energy and wit, with a serious undertone.

Formula Communications

19A Marlowes,
Hemel Hempstead, Herts HP1 1LA
☎0442 50247

Contacts *Colleen Bending, Steve Arnold*

Business presentations, conferences, A-V, video, films, commercials, radio. No unsolicited mss.

Mark Forstater Productions Ltd

42a Devonshire Close, London W1N 1LL
☎01–631 0611   Fax 01–580 2248
Telex 8954665 VBSTLX G Ref MFP

Contact *Nicola Lund*

Active in the selection, development and production of material for film, television and theatre. OUTPUT *Monty Python and the Holy Grail; The Odd Job; The Grass is Singing; Xtro; Forbidden; The Fantasist.* Unsolicited mss considered, but prefer writers to send synopses in the first instance.

Freeway Films

31 Albany Street, Edinburgh EH1 3QN
☎031–557 0882   Fax 031–558 3137

Contacts *John McGrath, Susie Brown*

Film outlet for John McGrath's work. OUTPUT has included *Blood Red Roses* and *There is a Happy Land* for **Channel 4**, *The Dressmaker*, from the novel by Beryl Bainbridge, scripted by John McGrath, for *Film on 4* International

and British Screen. New projects: *Border Warfare*, a three-part series on Anglo-Scots relations, and *The Long Roads*, a feature film.

Frontroom Productions Ltd

79 Wardour Street, London W1
☎01–734 4603

Contact *Angela Topping*

Television and cinema, both shorts and full-length features. OUTPUT has included *Acceptable Levels, Ursula Glenys, Intimate Strangers* and *The Love Child*.

John Gau Productions

Burstow House, 1 Burstow Road, Putney, London SW15
☎01–788 8811   Fax 01–789 0903

Contact *John Gau*

Documentaries and series for television, plus corporate video. OUTPUT has included *Assignment Adventure, Money Spinners* and *Sputniks, Bleeps and Mr Perry* for **Channel 4** and the *Korea* series for BBC 1.

Gibb Rose Organisation Ltd

Pinewood Studios, Iver, Bucks SLO ONH
☎0753 651700
Telex 847505 PINEW G   Fax 0753 656935

Contacts *Sydney Rose* (Managing Director), *Keith Belcher* (Creative Director)

Film, video and TV. Corporate and sales videos through to independent productions for ITV (music, film, documentary) to full feature film. Unsolicited mss not welcome unless at full screenplay level. 'We will examine ideas and scripts after initial discussion with the author.'

Bob Godfrey Films

55 Neal Street, London WC2
☎01–240 1793/1889

Contact *Mike Hayes, Sue Alcock*

Animated films, children's TV series, adult political work, plus shorts for cinema and television. Unsolicited mss welcome provided they are suitable for animation. Bob Godfrey is one of the judges in the **Ryman's Short Story/Essay Writing Competition** for children.

Goldcrest Films and Television Ltd

Waverley House, 7–12 Noel Street,
London W1V 3PB
☎01–437 8696
Telex 267458 Goldcr   Fax 01–437 4448

Once stood for all that was best in the British film industry. 1987, bought by Masterman, a company jointly owned by the producer-entrepreneur Brent Walker and the Merchant Newy Offices Pension Fund. Modest productions promised. Developing material for feature films but only scripts through agents with directors attached.

Grandplay Ltd

Orchard House, Adam and Eve Mews,
169 Kensington High Street,
London W8 6SH
☎01–938 4766
Telex 917293   Fax 01–938 4992

Contacts *Yves Pasquier, Katri Skala*

Television and feature film drama. Welcome unsolicited mss only if relevant to policy of the company, i.e. international co-productions with special emphasis on France, Germany and Italy. OUTPUT *Hemingway*, **Channel 4** series starring Stacey Keach.

Grasshopper Productions Ltd

50 Peel Street, London W8 7PD
☎01–229 1181

Contact *Joy Whitby*

Children's programmes and adult drama. FOUNDED 1970 by Joy Whitby, who has no use for outside writing as this is her own area of expertise. No unsolicited mss.

Greenpark Productions Ltd

St Wilfreds, 101 Honor Oak Park,
London SE23 3LB
☎01–699 7234   Telex 25247 GPK

Contact *David Morphet*

Makers of specialised and business-sponsored films, television (general) who welcome unsolicited mss.

Greenpoint Films

5a Noel Street, London W1V 3RB
☎01–437 6492

Contact *Ann Scott, Patrick Cassavetti*

A small company whose members act as individual producers and directors. No facilities for reading or using unsolicited mss.

Colin Gregg Films Ltd

Floor 2, 1–6 Falconberg Court,
London W1V 5SG
☎01–439 0257

Contact *Colin Gregg*

Feature films for **Channel 4** and BBC2. OUTPUT *Remembrance*; *To The Lighthouse*; *Lamb*; *Hard Travelling*. Unsolicited mss are welcome. Original scripts are preferred to adapted material.

Griffin Productions Ltd

3 Fitzroy Square, London W1P 5AH
☎01–388 5811
Telex 8813271 GECOMS G Fax 01–388 9830

Contact *Adam Clapham*

Arts, current affairs, documentary and drama television. OUTPUT has included *Painting With Light*, with Tom Keating, for **Channel 4**, *The Bombay Hotel* for 'Forty Minutes', BBC 2, *Odyssey*, the monthly magazine for **Channel 4** and *Maharajas* for BBC2.

Nick Hague Productions Ltd

Filmhouse, 142 Wardour Street,
London W1V 3AU
☎01–637 4904/01–734 1600
Telex 24865 SVCLTD G   Fax 01–437 1854

Contacts *Nick Hague, Michael Algar, Rosalind Allen*

Film, video and TV – commercials, corporate, drama, documentary. No unsolicited mss.

David Hall Productions
30–38 Dock Street, Leeds LS10 1JF
☎0532 422584/465757

Contact *David Hall*

Makers of television drama and documentaries, film, corporate video. Welcomes unsolicited mss. Encourages and supports new writing but 'unfortunately, I do not have the financial resources to provide development funding for speculative projects'. OUTPUT *Maggie's Children* and *All of You Out There* (both documentaries for **Channel 4**); *Silver Shadows* (feature film in development).

Hamilton Film and Television Ltd
Lee International Studios, Shepperton, Middx TW17 OQD
☎0932 562611
Telex 929416 MOVIES G   Fax 0932 68989

Contact *Christopher Hamilton*

International co-productions, film and TV – drama and commercials.

Hamilton Perry
Carnaby House, 27–9 Beak Street, London W1R 3LB
☎01–434 3041
Telex 894039   Fax 01–437 1586

Contacts *Kenneth Moon, Angie Laycock*

Video production. Corporate videos for a wide range of clients in the UK and Europe. Scripts written in-house. No unsolicited mss.

Handmade Films
26 Cadogan Square, London SW1X 0JP
☎01–581 1265
Telex 8951338 EURODO   Fax 01–584 7338

Contact *Margot Gavan Duffy*

OUTPUT *Mona Lisa; Shanghai Surprise; A Private Function; Privates on Parade; The Missionary; Time Bandits* and, more recently, *Withnail and I; Five Corners; Bellman and True; Track 29; The Lonely Passion of Judith Hearne*. Company policy is not to accept unsolicited mss direct from writers, though they do consider submissions from literary agents, publishers and producers.

John Hemson BSc
The Bakehouse, Media Resource Centre, Bedford Road, Aspley Guise, Milton Keynes MK17 8DH
☎0908 583062

Contact *John Hemson*

Film and television – training, sales, documentary. Wishes to encourage new writing. Unsolicited mss welcome.

Hines Video Ltd
Britannic Building, Hargreaves Street, Burnley, Lancs BB11 1DU
☎0282 52521   Fax 0282 30297

Contacts *David E. Hines, Peter Hunt, Lawrence Windley*

Video – corporate, exhibition and documentary. Welcome unsolicited mss if on related areas of work.

Holmes Associates
10–16 Rathbone Street, London W1P 1AH
☎01–637 8251   Fax 01–637 9024

Contact *Andrew Holmes*

Prolific originators, producers and packagers of children's, comedy, documentary, drama and music television. OUTPUT includes *Piece of Cake*, a new £4 million drama mini-series for **LWT**, *Who Dares Wins* and the *Well Being* series for **Channel 4**, *Video and Chips* for **HTV** and *Chish and Fips* for **Central**.

ICM International

ICM House, 53–5 Frith Street,
London W1V 5TE
☎01–434 0929

Contact *Linda Lucas*

Prominent makers of corporate video for major commercial and industrial clients.

ICP – Innovative and Creative Productions

Studio Centre, Ackhurst Road,
Chorley, Lancs PR7 1ND
☎02572 66411/4   Fax 02572 68490

Contact *Michael Mulvihill*

Multi-media production for a great variety of clients.

The Ideas Factory

(formerly at 4th Floor, Central Buildings, Peter Street, Manchester M2 5QR) At the time of going to press new address is not known but telephone number is:
☎061–834 4557

Contact *Martin Duffy*

Film, video and TV. OUTPUT has included ICI recruitment video and *Aids Ahead* (teaching about AIDS to deaf people, **BBC**). Unsolicited mss welcome.

Illuminations

16 Newman Passage, London W1P 3PE
☎01–580 7877   Telex 23152 Monret G

Contact *Linda Zuck*

Primarily a documentary production company, making cultural programmes for a **Channel 4** audience. OUTPUT *State of the Art* (six-part documentary series); *Ghosts in the Machine* (six-part video compilation series); plus other documentaries about art and television. No unsolicited mss.

Imagicians

5 Newburgh Street, London W1V 1LH
☎01–439 2244
Telex 299200 MOLI G   Fax 01–734 6813

Contact *Alan Scales*

Diverse productions, from television documentary features to in-flight videos. OUTPUT includes *The Great Palace – the Story of Parliament*.

In-House Corporate Video

The Boundary House, Old Warwick Road,
Lapworth, Warwickshire B94 6LU
☎05643 3958

Contact *John Pluck* (Senior Producer)

Corporate films and videos for training, marketing and public relations. No unsolicited mss, but interested in hearing from writers with corporate experience, with a sample of writing in this area.

Inca Video & Film Productions

Park House Studios, PO Box 111,
London SE26 5DB
☎01–778 8318

Contact *Peter Ashton*

Video and film – travel, commercials, promotional, and sales. No unsolicited mss.

Independent Film Production Associates

87 Dean Street, London W1V 5AA
☎01–734 3847   Fax 01–734 0776
Telex 265871 Ref: MMU441

Contact *Aileen McCracken*

Makers of documentary and entertainment television, plus corporate video. Unsolicited mss are 'sometimes welcome . . . if it's good we go with it.'

Infovision Ltd

Bradley Close, White Lion Street,
London N1 9PN
☎01–837 0012

Contact *John Mayhew* (Managing Director)

Corporate video makers in the areas of training, marketing, and internal communications. Household-name clients.

Insight Productions Ltd

Sortridge Manor, Horrabridge, Yelverton,
Devon PL20 7UA
☎0822 853100

Contact *Brian Skilton*

TV and film – drama, documentary and light entertainment. OUTPUT *Streets Ahead* (contemporary dance series, **Channel 4**); *Playing Away* (feature film – *Film on 4 International*); *Dartmoor the Threatened Wilderness* (**Channel 4** series). No unsolicited mss. 'We welcome new ideas or scripts for films for cinema or TV but prefer to discuss the subject before accepting a script to read or comment upon.'

Iona Productions

22 Woodstock Street, London W1R 1HF
☎01–493 8623   Telex 262187 ACTION G

Contact *Alan Wright*

Television documentary and drama. OUTPUT has included *Beyond Belief* (**Channel 4**), *Route 66* (**Central**), *Land* (**BBC**) and *Headstart* (**UTV**). Welcome unsolicited mss provided 'the writers are prepared to be patient'. Keen to encourage new writing for British television.

Peter Isaac Limited

94 High Street, Bildeston, Suffolk IP7 7EB
☎0449 741248

Contact *Peter Isaac*

Film, video and TV – documentary and commercials. Special interest in medical and animal husbandry. Open to new writing but no unsolicited mss. OUTPUT *Cats* (RSPCA Corporate); *Understanding Chemotherapy*; *Early Detection of Breast Cancer*; *Understanding Cystic Fibrosis*.

Isolde Films Ltd

4 Kensington Park Gardens,
London W11 3HB
☎01–727 3541
Telex 267409 Isolde G   Fax 01–727 3632

Contact *Maureen Murray*

Film and television – drama and documentary. OUTPUT *Mozart in Japan* (TV film); *Maria Callas* (TV film); *Testimony* (film). No unsolicited mss.

Paul Joyce Productions

5 Townley Road, Dulwich, London SE22
☎01–693 6006

Contact *Paul Joyce*

Development and production of arts, adventure, current affairs, documentary, drama and music, television and cinema. OUTPUT has included *Nothing as it Seems* (the films of Nicolas Roeg), *The Man Who Left His Soul on Film*, *Summer Lightning* for 'Film on 4', *Out of the Blue and Into the Black* (about Dennis Hopper) and *Tickets for the Titanic: Everyone a Winner*, with Jonathan Pryce and Anna Carteret. Publication in autumn 1988: *Hockney on Photography: Interviews with Paul Joyce* (**Jonathan Cape**).

Kay Communications Limited

Gauntley Court Studios, Gauntley Court,
Nottingham NG7 5HD
☎0602 781333   Fax 0602 783734

Contacts *John Alexander, Gary Hope*

Makers of industrial video programmes and training programmes. Scripts written in-house. No unsolicited mss.

Knaves Acre Productions

The Crest, Hoe Lane, Abinger Hammer,
Dorking, Surrey RH5 6RL
☎0306 731007

Contact *Bryan Izzard*

Makers of broadcast television principally for **Channel 4** and ITV. Unusual biographies of unusual composers, comedy (particularly sit-com), popular drama (live soaps). OUTPUT *The Middle of the Road* (with **HTV**, 1987); *The Garden of Evelyn*, (**Channel 4**, 1987); *Video Alice* (90-minute special for **Channel 4**, 1986). Unsolicited mss welcome.

Landseer Film and Television Productions

100 St Martin's Lane, London WC2N 4AZ
☎01–240 3161   Fax 01–240 8975

Arts, adventure, children's, current affairs, documentary, drama and music television. Principally arts documentaries (and videos of performances), but also television drama. OUTPUT has included *Mr Pye* with Derek Jacobi and *A Penny for Your Dreams*, a co-production with **BBC Wales** and S4C.

Limehouse Productions

Limehouse Studios, Canary Wharf, West India Docks, London E14 9SJ
☎01–987 2090   Telex 296149 LIMHSE G

Contacts *Janet Walker, Terence Pritchard*

Dramatic adaptations made for television and video (mostly video). OUTPUT *But What if it's Raining*; *Rocket to the Moon*; *To Have and To Hold*. 'Not besieged' by unsolicited scripts, which are welcome direct from writers.

Little Bird Limited

91 Regent Street, London W1R 7TA
☎01–434 1131   Fax 01–434 1803

Contact *James Mitchell*

Makers of film and television programmes. OUTPUT recently includes *The Irish R.M.*, *Troubles* and *Joyriders*.

London Film Productions Ltd

44a Floral Street, London WC2E 9DA
☎01–379 3366
Telex 896805   Fax 01–240 7065

Contact *Rose Baring*

Makers of a wide range of international television and film. OUTPUT *The Scarlet Pimpernel*; *Kim*; *Country Girls*; *Poldark*; *I Claudius*. No unsolicited mss; a brief synopsis/outline is essential. Work by new writers is considered, and a strong speculatively written script would be taken up; however, the commissioning of a new writer to complete a script is a rare event.

Loose Alliance

80 Appley Lane North, Appley Bridge, Wigan WN6 9AQ
☎02575 4825

Contacts *Alan Marsden, Janice Davinson*

Film, video and TV – drama, documentary, commercials. Camera services, including steadicam on 130 episodes of *Brookside*. Unsolicited mss very welcome. Particularly interested in work from northern writers keen to foster low-budget broadcast drama.

Magda Films Ltd

The Old Vicarage, Cragg Vale, Hebden Bridge, West Yorks HX7 5TB
☎0422 882755

Contact *Lorne Magory*

Film, video and TV – corporate, documentary, children's drama. Encourage and welcome new writers/unsolicited mss.

Magic Hour Productions Ltd

143 Chatsworth Road, Willesden Green, London NW2 5QT
☎01–459 3074

Contact *Ms D.J. Robinson*

Makers of television and films for a serious adult audience. Documentaries, drama series, serials, shorts, and television and feature films. Unsolicited mss welcome, provided an s.a.e. is provided for their return.

Malone Gill Productions Ltd

16 Newman Passage, London W1P 3PE
☎01–580 6594
Telex 8951182   Fax 01–255 1473

Contact *Georgina Denison*

Mainly documentary, but also some drama productions. OUTPUT *Gauguin*; *Vintage: The Story of Wine* (by Hugh Johnson); *No Man Hath Seen God*; *Matisse in Nice*; *Space Craft*; *Pride of Place: Building the American Dream*; *Treasure Houses of Britain*. Prefer an outline proposal with letter in the first instance.

'Always interested in seeing new writing of quality.'

Marking Inc Productions

5 Mercer Street, Covent Garden,
London WC2H 9QP
☎01–240 2345

Contact *Stacy Marking*

Film and TV – drama and documentary. OUTPUT **Channel 4** *Guide to Genius* series. Query letter in the first instance.

MediaLab Ltd

Chelsea Wharf, 15 Lots Road,
London SW10 0QH
☎01–351 5814   Telex 296426 NIGHT G

Contact *John Gaydon* (Chairman)

FOUNDED1982. Film and video production. Pop promos, TV documentaries, video, and a feature film with Godley & Creme. Interested in ideas for pop promos and investigative journalistic documentaries.

The Media Show Ltd
See Beat Ltd

Medical & Scientific Productions

PO Box 493, Cookham, Maidenhead,
Berks SL6 9TD
☎06285 31148
Telex 849462   Fax 0628 810029

Contact *Peter Fogarty*

Corporate – medical programmes for health care professionals. Welcome health care ideas. No unsolicited mss.

Meditel Productions Ltd

Bedford Chambers, The Piazza, Covent Garden, London WC2 8HA
☎01–836 9216/9364
Telex 262284 Ref no 3348
Fax 01–831 9489 & 01–405 1656

Contacts *Joan Shenton, Jad Adams*

Intelligent documentaries, afternoon programmes factually-based with an element of fun, evening programmes with hard story lines (no fun required). OUTPUT *Who Cares* (series of four health-care documentaries); *Kill or Cure?* (two series on the international drugs industry); *10 Million* (two consumer series for the over-sixties); many single documentaries. No unsolicited mss; writers should submit programme ideas on factual subjects including drama/documentary ideas with strong story lines. Either previous experience is essential, or new writers will work closely with a producer appointed by the company.

Bill Melendez Productions Ltd

32–4 Great Marlborough Street,
London W1V 1HA
☎01–439 4411/01–734 0691
Fax 01–439 6808

Contact *Steven Melendez, Graeme Spurway*

Animated films aimed mainly at a family audience, produced largely for the American market, and prime-time network broadcasting. Also develops and produces feature films (six thus far). OUTPUT *Peanuts* (half-hour TV specials); *The Lion, The Witch and The Wardrobe*; *Babar the Elephant* (TV specials); *Dick Deadeye or Duty Done*, a rock musical based on Gilbert & Sullivan operettas. Generally produces own projects or work in collaboration with other producers/TV companies; 'however, three of the above walked in through the door'. Always interested in seeing new scripts and ideas.

Merchant Ivory Productions

46 Lexington Street, London W1P 3LH
☎01–437 1200

Contact *Ismail Merchant, James Ivory*

Makers of quality, literate cinema for an international market. OUTPUT includes *Shakespeare Wallah*, *Heat and Dust*, *The Bostonians*, *Quartet*, *Room With A View* and

Maurice. A tradition of adaptation rather than original work seems by 1988 to have become entrenched.

The Mersey Television Company Ltd

18 Rodney Street, Liverpool L1 2TQ
☎051–708 7846

Contact *Andrew Corrie*

Makers of television programmes – drama and fiction serials for popular consumption only. OUTPUT includes *Brookside* and *What Now?* for **Channel 4**.

Metcalf & Mills Ltd

34–8 Westbourne Grove, London W2 5SH
☎01–221 4077

Contact *Charlotte Metcalf*

Commercials, concert films, documentary, pop promos, television. Welcome unsolicited mss. 'Being such a small, young company, we are open to anything'. OUTPUT *Vivat Regina*, a documentary for **Channel 4**; *Anthrax Live* (at Hammersmith Odeon); *Julian Cope Live* (at Westminster Hall, *Old Grey Whistle Test*); TV commercials for *Atlantic Soul Classics* and *Tango in the Night*.

Metropolis Pictures Limited

147 Crouch Hill, London N8 9QH
☎01–340 4649

Contact *Nick Dubrule*

A small independent film production company producing commissioned works for television. Its thirteen-year track record has been in quality documentaries/drama documentaries, though there are plans to produce low-budget fictional projects in the future. OUTPUT *Before Hindsight*, (documentary feature on 1930s newsreels); *Of Muppets and Men* (documentary for Henson Associates); *10 Years in An Open Necked Shirt*, featuring John Cooper Clarke; *The Rupert Bear Story*, directed by Terry Jones; *My Mama Done Told Me (A Torch Song)*, a TV special on the theme

of obsessive love, featuring Lynn Seymour, for **Channel 4**. Very interested in working with new writers; but are presently too small a company to cope with unsolicited mss.

Midnight Films Ltd

26 Soho Square, London W1V 5FJ
☎01–434 0011
Telex 268157 OJK G   Fax 01–434 9625

Contact *Michael Hamlyn*

FOUNDED 1976. Became active in 1981 when Julien Temple and Michael Hamlyn formed a partnership to produce *The Secret Policeman's Other Ball*. Developed *Absolute Beginners* until Julien Temple left to set up his own company. Produced *White City* (1985), a music feature starring Pete Townshend. Recently the emphasis has been on pop promos, in which the directors usually bring in their own writers. OUTPUT *Come Dancing* (Kink's promo). Currently producing a full-length feature film for U2, part-concert film, part-cinema vérité documentary.

John Mills Video Productions

11 Hope Streeet, Liverpool L1 9BJ
☎051–709 9822

Contact *Andrew Mills*

Corporate and training videos. No unsolicited mss.

Mirus Productions

9 Carnaby Street, London W1V 1PG
☎01–439 7113

Contact *Mike Wallington*

Documentary, music and arts television. OUTPUT many programmes for **Channel 4**, most recently *This Joint is Jumping* and *Colonial Madness* (1987), and projects on *One Love* and *Art Tatum* for 1988.

MJW Productions

13 Carlisle Road, London NW6 6TL
☎01–968 6542

Maggie Williams

of television programmes, cinema,
and educational video. OUTPUT has
included a series for the Design Council and a
Channel 13 film (New York) about the compo-
ser Steve Reich.

MNV

2 Lyston House, Clifton Road, Wimbledon,
London SW19 4QY
☎01–946 1306

Contact *Michael Norman*

Video – corporate, training, communications. Video publishing – special interest. No
unsolicited mss but interested in new
writers.

Moving Direction

Ground Floor, 97 Strawberry Vale,
Twickenham, Middx TW15 4SJ
☎01–891 2604

Contact *Shaun Gale* (Director/Producer)

Makers of documentary and fictional productions on video and film. Welcome unsolicited mss, 'providing they do not require
enormous budgets'. Open to new ideas and
prefer writing in screenplay form. OUTPUT
Truckers Delight; *Dick Head*, a gangster spoof
privately funded for children's television.

Moving Picture Company

25 Noel Street, London W1V 3RD
☎01–434 3100   Fax 01–437 3951

Contact *David Jeffers*

Drama and documentary for television, corporate video and commercials. OUTPUT
includes *In the Shadow of Fujisan* for the **BBC**;
Heinz Superchamps (children's programme
for **Channel 4**); *The Stars*, sequel to *The
Planets*, plus the features *The Assam Garden*
and *Stormy Monday*.

Multiple Image Productions Ltd

Milton Road Baths & Health Hydro,
Milton Road, Swindon SN1 5JA
☎0793 611741

Contact *Tim Langford*

TV drama and documentary. Corporate and
educational training and promotional films.
Welcome unsolicited mss. Interested in
exploring co-production possibilities and
nurturing new talent. OUTPUT *We're Not Mad
. . . We're Angry*; *Looking Back*; *Right to be
Understood*.

Network 5

11 Ospringe Road, London NW5 2JA
☎01–267 9492

Contact *Kathy O'Neil*

TV documentary/drama documentary/drama
corporate video. New company with outlets
in **Channel 4**, **BBC** and ITV. Unsolicited mss
welcome. 'Need new writers. Keen and
enthusiastic for joint projects.'

Normandy Film Productions

49 Observatory Road, East Sheen,
London SW14 7QB
☎01–878 2646

Contact *David Turnbull*

Broadcast TV. Documentary and drama. Welcome unsolicited mss. 'Wish to encourage
new writing'. OUTPUT *The Song & The Story*
(Prix Jeunesse winner – Munich 1982,
BAFTA nominated).

Ocean Pictures Ltd

25 Melody Road, London SW18 2QW
☎01–870 5345

Contact *Roger Brown, Lucinda Sturgis*

Particularly interested in drama and docu–
drama for film and TV.

Original Image Ltd

3 Grosvenor Gardens, London SW1 0BD
☎01–630 7552
Telex 8956658 TPSH   Fax 01–630 5893

Contacts *Edward Riseman, Nick Scott*

Makers of drama and documentary programmes. OUTPUT *Lichfield on Photography*;

Daley Thompson's Bodyshop (**Channel 4**). Welcome unsolicited mss. Wish to encourage new writing.

Orion Picture Corporation
31–2 Soho Square, London W1V 3FF

London office of an American giant.

Oxford Film & Video Makers
The Stables, North Place, Headington, Oxford OX3 9HY
☎0865 60074

Contact *Anne Marie Sweeney*

Makers of film and video for community, educational, trade union audiences. OUTPUT *Aids: Myth and Reality*; *Road or Reservation*. Unsolicited mss not welcome; 'we have enough work on already'. Though all their productions involve new writing, most of it is done in-house on a low budget.

Oxford Scientific Films
Lower Road, Long Hanborough, Oxford OX7 2LD
☎0933 881881

Contact *Ian Moar*

Commercials, corporate and documentary film production.

Pace Productions Limited
12 The Green, Newport Pagnell, Bucks MK16 0JW
☎0908 618767   Fax 0908 617641

Contacts *Geoff Ide, Jean Reid, Chris Pettit*

Film, video and TV – drama, documentary and commercials.

Pacesetter Productions Ltd
New Barn House, Leith Hill Lane, Ockley, Surrey RH5 5PH
☎0306 70433   Fax 0306 881021

Contact *Adele Spencer*

Corporate and educational material, feature and documentary films and television. No unsolicited mss; all material is produced in-house.

Palace Productions
16–17 Wardour Mews, London W1V 3FF
☎01–734 7060

Contact *Stephen Wooley, Nik Powell*

OUTPUT *Company of Wolves*; *Letter to Brezhnev*; co-produced *Absolute Beginners*; *Mona Lisa*. Unsolicited mss not welcome. As a small company, they aim to encourage new writing but can only do so 'on a limited basis'.

Parallax Pictures Ltd
7 Denmark Street, London WC2H 8LS

Contact *Sally Hibbin*

Documentaries and commercials. Some **Channel 4** projects.

Paramount Pictures (UK) Ltd
162–70 Wardour Street, London W1V 4AB
☎01–437 7700   Telex 263361 PARAUK G

'It is Paramount's policy not to accept unsolicited scripts'.

Peak Viewing Film and Video Productions Limited
130 Canalot Production Studios, 222 Kensal Road, London W10 5BN
☎01–969 7139

Contact *Wendy Smith*

Film and video non-broadcast programmes for commercial business and voluntary organisations. Contributions to broadcast documentaries. No unsolicited mss at present though 'moving towards developing new work for cinema in the future'.

Pelicula Films

7 Queen Margaret Road, Glasgow G20 6DP
☎041–945 3333

Contact *Mike Alexander*

Television producers. Makers of drama documentaries for **Channel 4**, including *Gramsci, Down Home* and *Scapa Flow – 1919*.

Picture Palace Productions Ltd

1 Beak Street Studios, 65–9 Beak Street, London W1R 3LF
☎01–439 9882

Contact *Malcolm Craddock, Tim O'Mara*

Television and cinema film and drama. OUTPUT *Tandoori Nights* series; *Ping Pong* (for Film on 4 International); *Four Minutes* for **Channel 4**; *Eurocops*; *Hunting The Squirrel*. Unsolicited mss welcome for feature-length films and TV drama, and also for *Four Minutes*, which uses only writers new to television. 'Always interested in new writers'.

Picture Partnership Productions Ltd

73 Newman Street, London W1R 3LS
☎01–637 8056

Contact *Brian Eastman*

FOUNDED 1978. Picture Partnership makes feature films and popular entertainment television, with the emphasis on comedy. OUTPUT *Father's Day* (**Channel 4**); *Blott on the Landscape* (**BBC**); *Whoops Apocalypse*; *Porterhouse Blue*. Unsolicited mss welcome if relevant to their particular field. In general terms encourage new writing.

Polygram Movies

30 Berkeley Square, London W1X 5DB
☎01–493 8800

Contact *Michael Kuhn*

Music-related visual programming, suspense/thriller movies with psychological depth and integrated commercial musical score.

Portman Entertainment

Tennyson House, 159–65 Great Portland Street, London W1N 6NR
☎01–637 4041

Contact *Victor Glynn*

A new company which amalgamates Portman Productions and the TV distribution company, Global TV. Feature films and miniseries for television. OUTPUT *Praying Mantis*; *Letters to an Unknown Lover*; *Tusitala*; *A Woman of Substance*; *Hold the Dream* (Bradford-Portman co-production). They receive a great many unsolicited scripts, all of them thus far unsuitable for production. Letters with treatments/outlines are read in hope: send these before submitting a finished script.

Poseidon Productions Ltd

113–17 Wardour Street, London W1V 3TD
☎01–734 4441/5140
Telex 22347 POSFILM

Contact *Frixos Constantine*

Television and film makers/distributors, for an adult, educated art-loving film audience. OUTPUT *Pavlova* (drama); television series for **Channel 4** on the Greek philosophers. No unsolicited mss.

Primetime Television Limited

Seymour Mews House, Seymour Mews, Wigmore Street, London W1H 9PE
☎01–935 9000
Telex 22872 TV Film G   Fax 01–487 3975

Contacts *Madeleine Warburg, Deirdre Simms*

Children's programmes, family drama, nature programmes and series (political, thrillers). OUTPUT has included *Gunfighters, Waltz Through the Hills, Fortunes of War* (**BBC**), *Durrell in Russia* (**Channel 4**) and *Return to Treasure Island*. Welcome unsolicited mss. Wish to extend a wide range and original writing.

The Production Pool Ltd

52 Tottenham Street, London W1P 9PG
☎01–323 0691   Fax 01–436 6287

Contact *Ann Wingate*

Film and television drama. 'Always interested to read new scripts'. OUTPUT *Making Waves*, short film for British screen and **Channel 4**. Three drama projects in development.

Quad Production Co.

Studio One, 2 Downshire Hill, Hampstead, London NW3 1NR
☎01–435 6953   Fax 01–435 6954

Contacts *Andy Dean, Graham Grimshaw*

Promotional and training programmes for commerce and industry. Radio commercials. Specialising in property, financial services and engineering. Welcome unsolicited mss.

Quanta Ltd

44 Newman Street, London W1P 3PA
☎01–580 7222/7223

Contact *Nicholas Jones*

Documentary makers, with science programming a speciality. Also produce interactive corporate video. OUTPUT *Horizon*, (BBC 2); *Equinox* (**Channel 4**). A relatively young company (FOUNDED 1982), Quanta currently write all their own material in-house. No unsolicited mss.

Ragdoll Productions

34 Harborne Road, Edgbaston, Birmingham B15 3AA
☎021–454 5453/4344

Contact *Anne Wood*

Makers of children's television programmes. OUTPUT has included *Pob's Programme* and *Pob's Playtime* for **Channel 4** and *Playbox* for **Central Television**.

Alvin Rakoff Productions Ltd

1 The Orchard, Chiswick, London W4 1JZ
☎01–994 1269

Contact *Alvin Rakoff*

TV and film. Welcome unsolicited mss. OUTPUT *Paradise Postponed* (TV mini-series); *A Voyage Round my Father*; *The First Olympics – 1896*; *Dirty Tricks* (film).

Red Rooster Films

11–13 Macklin Street, London WC2B 5NH
☎01–405 8147
Telex 291829 TLX G   Fax 01–831 0679

Contacts *Linda James, Christian Routh*

An independent film and television production company, whose productions range from drama series and feature films to documentaries, all destined for international distribution. A speciality in the past has been quality drama for children. OUTPUT *Joni Jones* (five-part drama series about a 1940s Welsh childhood); *The Flea and the Giants* (three-part documentary series on the technological revolution); *Coming Up Roses* (feature film for S4C); *The Falcon's Malteser* (comedy feature film for **Twentieth Century Fox** and King's Road Entertainment). Although unsolicited mss are not encouraged, treatments or outlines are welcome, and much more likely to receive a prompt response.

Riverfront Pictures Limited

Dock Cottages, Peartree Lane, Glamis Road, Wapping, London E1 9SR
☎01–481 2939

Contact *Jeff Perks* (Producer/Director), *Tony Freeth* (Producer/Director)

Arts, comedy, documentary, drama, music, and young people's programmes. Production of broadcast programmes, specialising in cultural subjects, with an emphasis on music programmes. OUTPUT *Our Lives*; *A Wee Bit Cheeky*; *Everyone a Special Kind of Artist*; *Breaking Through*; *The New Eastenders*; *Cola Cowboys*; *Raag Rung*; *Chorus Theatre of Mani-*

pur, all for **Channel 4**, and *Night Moves* for the **BBC**.

Sandfire Productions

Pinewood Studios, Iver, Bucks SL10 0NH
☎0753 651700   Telex 847505 PINEWD G

Contact *Anthony Williams*

Feature films. Unsolicited mss welcome; 'interested to see new stories or completed screenplays but unlikely to commission'.

Schonfield Productions International

BCM-Summer, London WC1N 3XX
☎01–435 1007

Contact *Victor Schonfield*

Arts, natural history, current affairs documentary programmes for television. OUTPUT has included *Shattered Dreams* for **Central**; *The Animals Film* and *Like Other Children, to Live in the Same World*, plus contributions to **Channel 4**'s *Years Ahead* and *The Friday Alternative*.

Scimitar Films Ltd

6–8 Sackville Street, London W1X 1DD
☎01–734 8385

Contact *Michael Winner* (Chairman)

Feature films for the international market. OUTPUT *The Sentinel*; *The Big Sleep* (1977); *Death Wish I, II & III*; *The Wicked Lady*; *Appointment with Death*; *Chorus of Disapproval*. No unsolicited mss. Scimitar has employed many first-time scriptwriters in the past, however, including Dick Clement and Ian La Frenais, Peter Draper, Gerald Wilson and Michael Hastings.

Siren Film & Video Co-op

Customs House, St Hilda's, Middlesbrough, Cleveland TS2 1EA
☎0642 221298

Contact *Peter Woodhouse*

Local distribution to community groups, etc., plus work for **Channel 4**.

Siriol Animation Ltd

3 Mount Stuart Square, Butetown,
Cardiff CF1 6RW
☎0222 488400
Telex 497244   Fax 0222 732211

Contact *Robin Lyons*

Animated films aimed at a family audience. OUTPUT TV specials: *A Winter Story*; *Space Baby*; serials: *SuperTed*; *Wil Cwac Cwac*; also *The Easter Egg*; *The Princess and The Goblin*. Ideas and scripts for animated programmes are welcome (though no unsolicited ms has thus far been produced). Shorts and full-length films. Presently most of the writing is done by Robin Lyons, but new blood will be needed in the future.

Skippon Video Associates Ltd

43 Drury Lane, London WC2B 5RT
☎01–240 8777   Telex 25247 SKP

Have their own team of script writers and do not welcome unsolicited material from outside.

Skyline Productions Ltd

1st Floor, 24 Scala Street, London W1P 1LU
☎01–631 4649   Fax 01–436 6209

Contact *Steve Clark-Hall*
also at 4 Picardy Place, Edinburgh EH1 3JT
☎031–557 4580   Fax 031–558 1555

Contact *Trevor Davis*

A major supplier of programmes to **Channel 4**, Skyline also make health, educational and corporate films. OUTPUT includes *Years Ahead*, *Radicals*, *98 Not Out*, *Roy and Bob* and *International Volleyball*, all for **Channel 4**.

Spectacle Films Ltd

16 Chelmsford Road, London E11 1BS
☎01–539 2306

Contacts *Roger Ashton-Griffiths,*
Richard Coverley

Film, non-broadcast and broadcast video.
OUTPUT includes business television projects
and a feature film under development. Spec-
tacle Films is largely self-contained and
rarely has use for unsolicited mss.

Spectel Productions Limited

744–6 Warwick Road, Tyseley,
Birmingham B11 2HG
☎021–708 0931

Contact *David Webster*

Film and video – documentary, corporate
and video publishing. Welcome unsolicited
mss. Wish to encourage new writing.

Tom Steel Productions

56 Sutherland Square, London SE17 3EL
☎01–701 6695

Contact *Tom·or Jackie Steel*

Documentary television. The company write
and develop their own material (though not
necessarily always). OUTPUT has included
Touch and Go – the Battle for Crete and *Scotland's Story* (twenty four half-hour episodes
for **Channel 4**).

Swanlind TV

The Production Centre, Stafford Road,
Fordhouses, Wolverhampton
☎0902 784848/789212
Telex 338490 Swanlind Chacom G
Fax 0902 788840

Contact *Tom Coyne*

Film, video and TV – commercials, corporate
and drama. OUTPUT *Hidden Attractions* (1987
award-winning drama); *It's No Big Deal*
(1988 award-winning drama); *Great Western
Experience* (TV and video release about the
Great Western Railway). 'Looking for new
writers in corporate field.' Synopses of
broadcast ideas welcome.

The Television Co-operative

7 Strath Terrace, London SW11 1RF
☎01–223 4951

Contact *John Underwood*

A production co-operative specialising in the
media, arts, politics, making documentary
television. OUTPUT has included *Ireland the
Silent Voices* for **Channel 4**, *A Beauty Awakes*
for the National Trust and *Between Object and
Image* for the **British Council**.

Teliesyn

3 Mount Stuart Square, The Docks,
Cardiff CF1 6EE
☎0222 480911   Fax 0222 481552

Contacts *Mary Simmonds, Richard Staniforth*

Film and video – broadcast TV drama, documentary music and sport. Will consider
unsolicited mss only if accompanied by
synopsis. Will encourage new writing wherever possible, often with a script editor on
hand. Involved in the Celtic Film Festival and
Cyfle (Welsh Language Film Training
course). OUTPUT *Will Six* (1920s period
drama); *Paris–Dakar Motor Rally*; *Dihirod
Dyfed* (West Wales murder drama series); *In
Two Minds* (feature film); *Cracking Up* (documentary series for **Channel 4**).

Third Eye Productions Ltd

Phillip House, 20 Chancellors Street,
Hammersmith, London W6 9RL
☎01–741 8691
Telex 8951182 GECOMS G Fax 01–318 1439

Contact *Margaret Young*

Makers of television programmes. OUTPUT
Talking Shop for **Channel 4**; *All in a Day's
Life* and *Bert Hardy's World*, also for **Channel 4**. Although a major supplier of documentary programmes to **Channel 4**, this
exclusivity isn't by design.

TPS Productions

111A Wardour Street, London W1V 3TD
☎01–437 9428

Contact *Neil Davies*

Television and video programmes. Corporate videos. Always interested in new writing; welcome unsolicited mss.

Tripod Films Limited
111A Wardour Street, London W1V 3TD
☎01−439 0729   Fax 01−437 0304
Telex 8950051 (ONE ONE G) Ref 13643001

Contact *Evan Morgans*

Film and video − TV documentary, corporate, commercials. No unsolicited mss. Most scripts commissioned or written in-house.

Twentieth Century Fox Productions Ltd
Twentieth Century House, 31−2 Soho Square, London W1V 6AP
☎01−437 7766   Telex 27869

Contact *Company Secretary*

London office of the American giant. Unsolicited mss will be considered.

Ty Gwyn Films Ltd
Y Ty Gwyn, Llanllyfni, Caernarfon, Gwynned LL54 6DG
☎0286 881235

Contact *Gareth Wynn Jones*

Situation comedy, contemporary gritty Welsh subjects, spy thrillers (spies are the current vogue). Bilingual productions. New writing welcome, in English as well as Welsh. Their primary role is to provide output for the Welsh fourth channel, S4C.

Tyburn Productions
Pinewood Studios, Iver Heath, Bucks SL0 0NH
☎0753 651700   Telex 847505

Contact *Kevin Francis*

Television producers, specialising in popular drama. OUTPUT has included TV movies *The Masks of Death*, *Murder Elite*, *Courier* and *The Abbot's Cry*.

UBA (Developments) plc (United British Artists)
Russell Chambers, Covent Garden, London WC2E 8AA
☎01−240 9891   Telex 269141 STRAT G

Contact *Christina Robert*
(Creative Affairs Executive)

Quality feature films and television for an international market. OUTPUT *The Lonely Passion of Judith Hearne*; *Taffin*; *Castaway*; *Turtle Diary*. In development: *Batavia*; *Rebel Magic*; *One Last Glimpse*; *Duke and Duchess of Beverly Hills*; *Sketchlife*; *Carolina Madness*; *Windprints*; *Tale Told by an Idiot*; *Happy Feet*; *Kerry Babies*; *My Old Sweetheart*; and *Rosa*, as well as several television projects. Prepared to commission new writing whether adapted from another medium or based on a short outline/treatment. Concerned with the quality of the script (*Turtle Diary* was written by Harold Pinter) and breadth of appeal; they do not welcome 'exploitation material'.

Umbrella Films
31 Percy Street, London W1P 9FG
☎01−631 0625
Telex 296538   Fax 01−436 9442

Contact *Marc Samuelson, Stacy Bell*

OUTPUT British feature films: *Nineteen Eighty Four*; *Another Time Another Place*; *Loose Connections*; *Hotel du Paradis*; *Nanou*; *White Mischief*. No scripts, treatments only.

Verronmead Ltd
257 Liverpool Road, London N1 1LX
☎01−607 8405

Contact *Maureen Harter, David Wood*

Children's programmes, documentaries, dramas and women's programmes, mostly for **Channel 4**. Unsolicited mss and new writing welcome.

Video Arts Television
17−19 Foley Street, London W1P 7LB
☎01−636 9421   Telex 924557 VATV

Contact *Jane Lighting*

A division of **Dumbarton Films** which specialises in the production of major series for an international market. OUTPUT has included *Fairly Secret Army* for **Channel 4**, *From the Face of the Earth*, *Free to Choose*, *The Search for Alexander the Great* and *Start Here – Adventures into Science*. Distribution company representing **Channel 4** and other independent production companies for world-wide TV sales.

Video at Work

10 King Street Lane, Winnersh,
Berks RG11 5AS
☎0734 790500   Fax 0734 776345

Contact *Gerry Clarke*

Corporate video production: sales and training. OUTPUT has included staff training videos for British Airways and Midland Bank. Unsolicited mss welcome.

Videotel Productions/Living Tape Productions

Ramillies House, 1–2 Ramillies Street,
London W1V 1DF
☎01–439 6301   Telex 298596

Contact *Nick Freethy*

Film, video, TV, mainly but not exclusively, of a broadly educational nature. Welcome unsolicited mss in the education and training field only. 'We would like to support new writers who can put up with the ego-bashing they are likely to get from industrial and commercial sponsors'. OUTPUT *Catering with Care* (Open College and **Channel 4**); *Tourism: The Welcome Business* (Open College and **Channel 4**); *Dead Ahead – AIDS advice for Seafarers* (Royal Navy).

Vidox Video Productions Ltd

Milton House, Roper Close, Canterbury,
Kent CT2 7EP
☎0227 763888

Contact *Robin Ochs*

Makers of corporate and training videos and TV commercials. Welcome unsolicited mss.

Virgin Films and Video

328 Kensal Road, London NW10 5XJ
☎01–968 8888   Telex 892890

Contact *Mike Watts*

Television programmes, cinema, educational and animated films. In 1987, made Ken Russell's *Gothic*. Also made *Absolute Beginners* (co-producers) and *Captive*. No television at present, but will be exploring this avenue in the future. Likely to bid for one of Britain's new national commercial radio stations.

The Visual Connection (TVC) Ltd

1 Rostrevor Mews, London SW6 5AZ
☎01–731 6300
Telex 995801 Ref V1   Fax 01–736 9462

Contact *Hugh Price*

Corporate film and video; conference and audiovisual production. Unsolicited mss welcome.

VPS Limited

22 Brighton Square, Brighton,
Sussex BN1 1HD
☎0273 728686/821567

Contacts *Alan Holden* (Production Director), *Tracy Garrett* (Production Manager)

Film and video – corporate training, medical, interactive video production.

Vulgar Productions

3–5 St Johns Street, London EC1M 4AE
☎01–608 2131

Contact *Sue Hayes*

Makers of television programmes. Recent credits include *Arthur & Phil* series for **Channel 4**.

The Walnut Production Partnership

Crown House, Armley Road,
Leeds LS12 2EJ
☎0532 456913   Telex 265871 MONREF G
Quoting 72:MAG31593

Contact *Geoff Penn*

Corporate videos mainly, plus some film. Welcome script examples from corporate productions to broaden pool of available writers. Also welcome unsolicited mss for independent production with a northern regional slant.

Warner Sisters

21 Russell Street, London WC2B 5HP
☎01–836 0134   Fax 01–836 6559

Contacts *Lavinia Warner, Jane Wellesley*

Television and film drama, documentaries. OUTPUT *Tenko*; *Lizzie – An Amazon Adventure*; *GI Brides*; *Wish Me Luck*. Now expanding in other directions. Several series are in development, including one based on the Hitler Diaries scandal and a feature film. New scripts will always be considered.

White City Films

29 Sutton Court Road, Chiswick,
London W4 3EQ
☎01–994 6795/4856   Fax 01–995 9379
Telex 265871 Quoting REF: 84WCR001

Contact *Aubrey Singer*

Films. No unsolicited mss. OUTPUT *The Restoration of the Sistine Chapel* (NTV); *The Witness of the Long March* (**Channel 4**).

Maurice Winnick Associates Ltd/ Philip Hindin Ltd

33 Albert Street, London NW1 7LU
☎01–380 0375

Contact *Vera Marsh, Philip Hindin*

Makers of TV panel and quiz game shows and light entertainment. No unsolicited mss.

Working Title Films Limited

10 Livonia Street, London W1V 3PH
☎01–439 2424
Telex 914106 WORKIN G   Fax 01–437 9964

Contact *Tim Bevan, Sarah Radclyffe, Alison Jackson*

Feature films and television programmes, drama and documentary subjects. OUTPUT has included *My Beautiful Laundrette, Personal Services, Caravaggio, Wish You Were Here, Sammy and Rosie Get Laid* and *Echoes* (for **Channel 4**).

WSTV Productions Ltd

4th Floor, Tennyson House,
159–63 Portland Street, London W1N 5FD
☎01–580 5896

Contacts *Bill Stewart, Rex Berry, Sian Coombes*

Corporate video, commercials, TV programmes. No unsolicited mss.

Yo-Yo Films

108 Grove Park, London SE5 8LE
☎01–733 1806

Television commercials, documentaries, drama, features. Welcome unsolicited mss.

Zenith Productions Ltd

8 Great Titchfield Street, London W1P 7AA
☎01–637 7941   Telex 23348

Contact *Scott Meek* (Head of Development), *Archie Tait* (Head of Scripts)

Feature films and television. Formerly the feature arm of **Central TV**, now owned by Carlton Communications, one of the leading independents. OUTPUT Films: *The Hit; The Dead; Insignificance; Wetherby; Personal Services; Prick Up Your Ears; Slam Dance; Wish You Were Here.* Television: *Heart of the Country; Finnegan Begin Again; Fields of Fire; Escape from Sobibor; Inspector Morse.* Unsolicited mss are acceptable.

Zooid Pictures

52 Crouch Hill, London N4 4AA

☎01–272 9115

Contact *Richard Philpott, Jasmine Nicholas*

Zooid aim to combine their experimental, multi-media interests with commercial viability. OUTPUT *Road Movie* and *The Spirit of Albion*, both for **Channel 4**. Writing has been entirely in-house so far, but if mss which understand their work are submitted they will always be considered.

Playing to the Gallery

It came as a surprise when Alan Ayckbourn was not listed by *Money Magazine* as one of the two hundred richest people in Britain. After all, Andrew Lloyd Webber, Jack Higgins and Catherine Cookson were there and it is a fair assumption that their revenue generating power is no greater than Mr Ayckbourn's. And he is every bit as popular. To ask the man in the street to name the two best-known English playwrights is to invite a stock response – Shakespeare and Ayckbourn. Or, maybe, Ayckbourn and Shakespeare.

If Alan Ayckbourn is the shining example of a playwright who has hit the jackpot, there are others who have achieved enviable financial success. Willy Russell, Harold Pinter, John Osborne and Tom Stoppard spring to mind. It seems that Tom Stoppard had early prescience of his good fortune. When, in 1967, he attended **The National Theatre**'s opening night of *Rosencrantz and Guildenstern Are Dead*, the play which was to make his name, someone asked him what it was about. He replied, 'It's about to make me very rich.'

Twenty years on, the playwright whose work is well received at **The National** can feel equally confident. On a deal guaranteeing 10% of box office receipts, a production in one of the main houses playing to 70% capacity at an average ticket price of £10 will bring the writer an income (albeit temporary) in the order of £700 a night.

Then there is the enticing prospect of a West End transfer followed by regional and overseas productions and possibly a film or TV adaptation; not to mention the royalties from publishing. *Rosencrantz and Guildenstern Are Dead*, now a school examiners' favourite, regularly sells 20,000 copies a year.

Margaret Ramsay, the doyenne of play agents who set Joe Orton on his way, reckons that fifteen of her clients earn at least £100,000 a year.

The other side of the picture is presented by the **Theatre Writers' Union**. A 1986 survey of over 300 writers reveals just 8% who earn more than £20,000 a year, while 69% make under £5000

It is a sad fact of the modern theatre that playwrights of known talent but unknown names have difficulty in finding any outlets for their work, let alone a place in the West End. Over the five years up to 1986 the proportion of new plays put on by the grant-aided sector was never higher than 22% and in one year fell to under 16%. The average turns out to be just over 100 new plays a year. And these are by no means all new plays by new writers. **The National** and the **Royal Shakespeare Company**, for example, tend to favour the latest offerings from established writers – Shaffer, Ayckbourn, Nichols, Hampton or Hare.

The repertory theatres including the 'Big Seven' (**Birmingham Rep**, **Bristol Old Vic**, **Leicester Haymarket**, **Liverpool Playhouse**, Manchester **Royal Exchange**, **Nottingham Playhouse**, and Sheffield **Crucible**) have a better record for putting on the work of lesser-known writers, though most of their new plays are presented in the studio theatres rather than in the main houses.

Then there are the small theatres, mostly in London, which declare a strong commitment to new writing. The **Bush**, **Hampstead**, the **Tricycle**, the **Half Moon**, the **Soho Poly** and **Hull Truck** are in this category. In a class of its own is the **Royal Court**, which from 1981 to 1986 presented nearly nine new plays a year, over three-quarters of its total.

With the notable exception of London, says the **Theatre Writers' Union**, the best new play producers are concentrated in the Midlands and the North. The main houses in the South take the prize for narrow conservatism.

Identifying a theatre or producer with an active interest in new writing (see listings) is the start of a long and often frustrating haul towards fulfilment. Leading companies like **The National** and the **Royal Court** receive up to 1000 unsolicited manuscripts a year. Of these, a tiny proportion are judged to be worthy of further consideration.

In a recent interview, Michael Attenborough who, until July 1988, was artistic director of **Hampstead Theatre**, spoke of the pressure of having seven slots a year to fill with new plays. 'I know it upsets unperformed writers out there but the bulk of what comes in is quite awful. There's a clear sense in which many people are attempting to have their wildest personal fantasies staged in front of a few hundred onlookers.'

Whatever their personal convictions, all producers are restrained in their choice of new work by what they believe their audiences – or their paymasters – will accept. Early in the year, the much admired Alan Strachan, director of **Greenwich Theatre**, was sacked by his board apparently for being too adventurous with the repertoire.

The comfort for the aspiring playwright is in knowing that the decision to reject a manuscript is seldom taken lightly. The **Royal Court** employs no less than three literary managers and eighteen readers. A new play which is judged to be at all interesting is seen by at least three readers before it enters what is known as *The Grid*. This means it is available to be read by directors, designers and anyone else working within the theatre who might have a point of view. Luck enters here in a big way because much depends on the play attracting the interest of a particular director who might then act as a patron, encouraging the writer to make necessary changes while at the same time promoting his cause to influential colleagues.

Rejection is not death. Every playwright has his collection of producers' put-downs. When Peter Terson (*Zigger Zagger*, *Strippers* and *Good Lads at Heart*) made his first approach to **The National**, he wrote to the then literary editor, Kenneth Tynan, declaring, with all the arrogance of youth, 'This is probably my finest work. I should like to give you the opportunity of being the first to produce it.' Tynan replied, 'I'm glad you admire your own talent. I wish I could share your enthusiasm.'

Two decades later, Terson made another assault on **The National**. This time the literary editor was more positive. He told the writer that while his play was not quite right for them, he should persevere. Terson might reasonably have thought that twenty years was long enough for anyone to stick at it but he took the advice and soon afterwards made his breakthrough. He still has not worked for **The National** but he does have a commission from the **RSC**.

However dispiriting, a reader's report is worth careful study. Writers who are prepared to accept constructive criticism and are willing to look for ways to improve their skills are often those who eventually secure commissions to submit new work.

At the **Soho Poly**, a tiny venue with a proud record for nurturing talent, writers of promise are invited to workshop sessions in which they gather with actors and directors to explore how best to develop their work. Similar schemes are run by **The National** at its Studio Theatre, where plays selected by the literary department are given the chance of a reading by professional actors, and by the Riverside Studios where scripts can be promoted from a private to a public reading.

Other projects designed to help new playwrights are mentioned in our listing of production companies. Information on one-off events is readily available from the regional arts associations (list on p. 000).

Of particular interest to the latest generation of writers is the Young Playwrights Festival held at the **Theatre Royal Stratford East** in March. Six days of workshops, seminars and lectures cover every aspect of writing for the theatre. Submitted scripts can either be performed or discussed in depth at a private script surgery.

Writers who have proved their ability but feel the need for the stimulation that comes with an everyday association with the theatre should aim for one of the coveted places for writers-in-residence. Of the special grants available, the **Thames Television** bursaries (worth £4000 a year) are well established (Alan Bleasdale, Mike Stott and Mary O'Malley are among the early beneficiaries), but there are many theatres which operate their own scheme and can boast some imaginative appointments.

Heidi Thomas, former winner of the Texaco National Youth Theatre Award for the Most Promising Playwright, is writer-in-residence at the **Liverpool Playhouse**. At 24 she is also the youngest writer ever to have a full production at the **RSC**.

Jacqueline Holborough, ex-*Crossroads* star and ex-prisoner, founded the Clean Break Theatre Company to portray the experience of women in prison before becoming a writer-in-residence at the **Bush**.

At the **RSC** their first writer-in-residence, supported by an award from the Richard Burton Trust, lives on a council estate in Derby. Lucy Gannon started writing when she was unemployed. 'I enjoyed the plays on Radio 4 and I tried to write an hour-long play. I always felt words were the only way I was going to make anything of myself.' Her first play won the Richard Burton prize, her second was given a brief airing by the **RSC**, her third was staged by **Derby Playhouse** and her fourth by the **Bush**.

One of the great virtues of the writer-in-residence experience is that it teaches the budding playwright that the theatre is a collaborative enterprise. This is not to everyone's taste. Writers who are averse to having their words changed about, often so dramatically that their end product is unrecognisable against the original draft, find the theatre sheer agony.

Another form of disappointment can come to those who pitch their expectations too high. 'Theatre is beset by trendiness,' argues Tony Marchant who, at 28, has a string of radical plays to his name. 'By promoting writers as flavour of the month, you can encourage unrealistic expectations. Theatres pick up writers and then discard them. Writers are not professional athletes – they need to be able to turn their talent into craft.'

Those who succeed in turning talent into craft might reasonably expect to find a niche in the West End. But while producers loudly proclaim their enthusiasm for new writing, it has to be said that very little of it gets to Shaftesbury Avenue – unless it is supported by instantly recognisable names. Michael Codron is one of the few big commercial producers to have made his reputation by adopting writers at the outset of their careers. But even he has become conservative, trusting to the output of his star attractions, like Tom Stoppard. Part of the reason is the escalation in costs. 'In the early sixties I could put on a play for anything between £8000 and £10,000. Now that same play would cost between £150,000 and £200,000.

Musicals and revivals are also expensive, but, as matters stand, they have a better chance of making money.

It is interesting that Michael Attenborough, who in his time at Hampstead has promoted several plays which have transferred to the West End, has joined the Turnstyle Group, a project aimed at attracting new writing to the West End and Broadway. Perhaps a change of fashion is on the way.

Meanwhile, most playwrights must seek a living outside mainstream commercial theatre. This fact of life underlines the achievement of the **Theatre Writers' Union**, the **Writers' Guild** and the **Scottish Society of Playwrights** in securing a minimum terms agreement with the Theatre Management Association, the governing body for the reps and their studios, fringe venues and touring groups.

In the old days, all playwrights, whatever their standing, were paid either by a straight box office royalty or, more rarely, by a commission set against royalty earnings. This simple formula was undermined by the emergence of the subsidised theatre and its law of diminishing returns. The smaller the theatre, the higher the proportion of subsidy per seat and the more unrealistic the box office takings on which the playwright's earnings were calculated. The writer's sense of injustice was accentuated by the knowledge that the salaries of directors, actors and managers were not subject to the same degree of risk.

Enter the white knight in the shape of **The Arts Council**. A strategy was devised whereby theatres were supposed to offer an outright commission fee backed by guaranteed minimum royalties. In reality commissions were few and far between and royalty supplements were last in line for payment.

A new technique was tried. **The Arts Council** specified a proportion of each of its theatre grants to be set aside for new writing. But when the playwrights' unions began negotiations on a minimum terms agreement it soon became clear that theatre managers were bending the rules to divert writers' money into their general budgets. **The Arts Council** duly tightened its rules by threatening to claw back funds that were misdirected away from theatre writing. The response was immediate. Most theatres affected by the change responded by spending more on writing than was actually expected of them.

Meanwhile, the Theatre Management Association accepted the need for setting out minimum terms for writers. The current agreement allows for four grades of commission related to size of venue. The fees are £2000, £1600, £1400 and £1300. In Grade One, £500 is set against royalties; in the other grades, £400. In addition, theatres must pay £250 for exclusive rights to perform a play in a given period, guarantee a royalty of £1000 (Grade One) or £600 (Grades Two to Four) and pay for 12 days' rehearsal time (£296.04, £259.08, £238.20 and £220.00). When these figures are put together, the minimum payment to writers in the four grades adds up to: £3296.04, £2509.08, £2228.20 and £2172.00. The royalties under the TMA agreement are 7.5% rising to 10% above the guarantee point.

A second agreement embraces **The National Theatre**, the **RSC** and the **Royal Court**. Currently up for renegotiation, the deal at the moment is for **The National** and **RSC** to pay £3500 as a commission or option fee with £1750 up front (against royalties in the main houses but not in the Cottesloe, Other Place and The Pit) and £25 a day for rehearsals.

The corresponding figures for the **Royal Court** are £3250 and £1500 for the main house (75% against royalties) and £1200 and £600 for the **Theatre Upstairs**. Rehearsal payments are set at a minimum of £600 (downstairs) and £500 (upstairs). Other parts of the agreement cover West End and overseas options.

This leaves the fringe, represented by the **Independent Theatre Council**. In the absence of a national agreement, payments vary enormously from one part of the country to another. In London fees are generally in line with **TMA** guidelines but in Yorkshire and the West Midlands, for example, companies have been known to pay writers very badly or not at all. The unions' strategy is to work towards a guaranteed payment equal to an actor's salary for 26 weeks (the **Equity** minimum is £137.50) for a non-commissioned play and 13 weeks plus fee for a commissioned play. The **Writers' Guild** and the **Theatre Writers' Union** are also fighting hard for the right of consultation on casting and the appointment of directors and designers.

In a recent report (*Playwrights: A Species Still Endangered?*) the **Theatre Writers' Union** sets a modestly optimistic tone. New work continues to be presented though new writers find it hard to break in. The Union wants specific help for first-timers from **The Arts Council** and the **Regional Arts Associations**. A source of finance is suggested – a Dead Writer Levy – in effect, a royalty to be collected on the production of out of copyright plays. It is a neat idea but one that is unlikely to find favour with the theatrical establishment which is wedded to the classics or with playgoers who are ever quick to react against increases in seat prices.

Theatre Producers

Aba Daba

30 Upper Park Road, London NW3 2UT
☎ 01–722 5395

Plays and satirical pantomimes performed at venues like the Water Rats and the Canal Café in London. The company write all their material themselves. They would be happy to consider some of the great piles of unsolicited mss they receive, were it not for the fact that there is absolutely no money available for outsiders.

Actors Touring Company

Alford House, Aveline Street,
London SE11 5DQ
☎ 01–735 8311

Contact *Mark Brickman* (Artistic Director – until December 1988)

ATC are well known for producing lively new versions of classic works. They take plays by Shakespeare, Molière, Ibsen and others, and work with writers in adapting them for ATC use. Unsolicited mss with classic/epic features or intentions are welcome. Intend to work more with writers in the future.

Akela Ltd

14 Talbot House, 98 St Martin's Lane,
London WC2N 4AX
☎ 01–379 0123

Contact *Colin Brough*

A new company which aims to continue the policy and West End profile of Colin Brough's former outfit, The Lupton Theatre Company. Lupton produced *Rose*, Andrew Davies; *When the Wind Blows*, Raymond Briggs; *Big in Brazil*, Bamber Gascoigne; *Phaedra*, translated from Racine by Robert David MacDonald, among other West End and touring shows. Akela hope to produce a high proportion of new work. No unsolicited mss – they aren't read. Scripts preferred through agents; if approaching direct, write in the first instance.

Albemarle of London

74 Mortimer Street, London W1N 7DF
☎ 01–631 0135

Pantomimes only, and Albemarle write their own scripts.

Aldersgate Productions

12 Palace Street, London SW1E 5JF
☎ 01–828 6591

Contact *Ronald Mann* (Artistic Director)

Produce plays of a broadly Christian nature, for children, family groups and church groups. Productions have included *Ride Ride*, a musical about John Wesley; *Sentenced to Life*, a play about euthanasia; *Song of the Lion*, a one man show about C.S. Lewis and *The Lion, The Witch and The Wardrobe*. Most scripts are original; many by new writers.

Almeida Theatre

Almeida Street, Islington, London N1 1TA
☎ 01–226 7432

Contact *Nigel Hinds* (Programme Co-ordinator)

FOUNDED 1980. The Almeida now has an outstanding reputation in the field of contemporary arts in Britain and throughout the world. It presents a mixture of theatre, dance, mime and music, and one of its main annual events is its internationally acclaimed contemporary music festival. Productions have included *The Saxon Shore*, David Rudkin, and *The Tourist Guide*, Botho Strauss. Do not welcome unsolicited mss; 'our producing programme is very limited and linked to individual directors and producers'.

Alternative Theatre Company Limited
(trading as the Bush Theatre)
Bush Theatre, Shepherds Bush Green, London W12 8QD
☎01–602 3703

Contact *Matthew Lloyd*

FOUNDED 1972. Produce about six new plays a year (principally British, some foreign) and invite in up to three visiting companies also producing new work – 'we are a writer's theatre'. Scripts are read by a team of associates and then discussed with the management, a process which takes between two and three months. The theatre offers commissions, recommissions to ensure further drafts on promising plays and a guarantee against royalties so writers are not financially penalised even though the plays are produced in a small house. New plays at the Bush have included: *The Fosdyke Saga*, Alan Plater and Bill Tidy; *The Tax Exile*, Jonathan Gems; *Amabel, Unsuitable for Adults*, Terry Johnson; *Duet for One*, Tom Kempinski; *Commitments*, Dusty Hughes; *The Miss Firecracker Contest, Crimes of the Heart*, Beth Henley; *Hard Feelings, Progress*, Doug Lucie; *Writer's Cramp, Candy Kisses*, John Byrne; *When I Was a Girl, I Used to Scream and Shout. . .* , Sharman Macdonald; *Kiss of the Spiderwoman, Mystery of the Rose Bouquet*, Manuel Puig; *Soul of the White Ant, More Light*, Snoo Wilson; *Raping the Gold*, Lucy Gannon.

Yvonne Arnaud Theatre
Millbrook, Guildford, Surrey GU1 3UX
☎0483 64571

Contact *Val May* (Director)

New work always considered. Credits include *Melon*, Simon Gray; *Mr & Mrs Nobody*, Keith Waterhouse; *Breaking the Code*, Hugh Whitemore; *Holiday Snaps*, Michael Pertwee and John Chapman; *Cuckoo*, Emlyn Williams; *Sweet William*, Bernard Slade; *Groucho*, Arthur Marx and Robert Fisher.

Arts Management
Redroofs, Littlewick Green, Maidenhead, Berks.
☎0628 822982

Contact *June Rose* (Artistic Director)

Only interested in full-scale children's musicals based on classic titles, and potted versions of Shakespeare for schools. Mss are welcome if they meet these exact requirements. Recent productions have included *Charlie and the Chocolate Factory*; *The Lion, The Witch and The Wardrobe* (musical); and *Once Upon a Time*.

Belgrade Theatre, Coventry
Belgrade Square, Coventry CV1 1GS
☎0203 56431

Contact *Robert Hamlin* (Director)

The Belgrade Theatre regularly presents new work in both main house and studio. In the main house, it was the world première of Julian Garner's *Guardian Angels* in Autumn 1987, and Rob Bettinson's *Bare Necessities* in June 1988. Most of the productions in the studio theatre are dedicated to new writing, either first or second productions. Some plays are commissioned and the theatre reads a large number of submitted scripts.

Birmingham Repertory Theatre
Broad Street, Birmingham B1 2EP
☎021–236 6771

Contact *John Adams* (Artistic Director)

John Adams, who took over from longstanding Artistic Director Clive Perry in 1987, is looking for new plays for the main house, though probably no more than one or two a year in the next four years. Such new plays will need to fill the Rep's enormous stage (with its 60-foot proscenium) and its large auditorium (900 seats), Any Studio Theatre new plays in the coming year will be aimed at specific audiences – especially 15–25-year-olds, or Birmingham's ethnic minority groups.

Borderline Theatre Company
Darlington New Church,
North Harbour Street, Ayr KA8 8AA
☎0292 281010

Contact *Morag Fullarton* (Artistic Director)

FOUNDED 1974. A touring company taking shows to main house theatres in city centres and small venues in outlying districts, plus the Edinburgh Festival, Mayfest and, occasionally, London. Mainly new and contemporary work, plus revivals: *Trumpets and Raspberries*, Dario Fo; *A Night in the Ukraine*, Voxburgh and Laxarus; *Four in a Million*, Les Blair; *Shanghied*, Liz Lochhead; plus pantomime and children's plays. Synopsis with cast size preferred in the first instance. Borderline try to include one new work every season. 'We are looking for writing which is stimulating, relevant and, above all, entertaining, which will lend itself to dynamic physical presentation.'

Bristol Express Theatre Company
20 Mocatta House, Brady Street,
Whitechapel, London E1 5DL
☎01–247 4156/7965

Contact *Michael Quinn* (Literary Manager)

Bristol Express, a non-funded professional middle-scale national touring company, has a continuing commitment to the discovery, development and encouragement of new writers and new writing, principally through a research and development programme – consisting of public and private staged and rehearsed readings, skill workshop productions and full productions – called *The Play's The Thing!* 'We look for plays that are soc-

ially/emotionally/theatrically/politically significant, analytical and challenging. The company is concerned to produce work which attempts to mix genres (and create new ones!), is eloquent and honest, while remaining accessible and entertaining.... It's unusual for a play sent to (or commissioned by) the company to be accepted on its receipt.' Past productions have included *Child's Play*, Jonathan Wolfman; *Winter Darkness*, Allan Cubitt; *Wide-Eyes Kingdom*, Nick Fisher.

Bristol Old Vic Company
Theatre Royal, King Street, Bristol BS1 4ED
☎0272 277466

Contact *Paul Unwin* (Artistic Director)

A producing theatre with a script reading committee which meets regularly to consider all new work submitted. New work is produced – both in the main house and the New Vic Studio – and 'we are constantly looking for dynamic, innovative and exciting texts'.

Bush Theatre
See **Alternative Theatre Company**

Cambridge Theatre Company
8 Market Passage, Cambridge CB2 3PE
☎0223 357134

Contact *Bill Pryde* (Artistic Director)

Cambridge Theatre Company have no script facilities, and rarely produce new work. They admit that unsolicited mss are seldom read, though letters and synopses are welcome.

Caricature Puppet Centre
Perch Buildings, 9 Mount Stuart Square,
Bute Town, Cardiff CF1 6EE
☎0222 497918

Contact *Jane Phillips*

Formerly a specialist children's theatre company working with masks and puppets, Caricature no longer functions, as a company. It is expecting to get an Arts Council grant to set up a feasibility study for an international puppet centre in Cardiff's docklands.

Channel Theatre Trust Ltd

Granville Theatre, Victoria Parade,
Ramsgate, Kent CT11 8DG
☎0843 588280

Contact *Philip Dart*

Based at the Granville Theatre, the company divides its productions between a commercial summer season there and Arts Council tours to smaller venues, arts centres, etc. It also has an attached Theatre-in-Education and Community Theatre Company. Productions have included *The Normal Heart*, the play about AIDS; *Dracula: A Pain in the Neck*; a new version of *The Canterbury Tales*; *What the Butler Saw*. Interested in new writing, particularly Theatre-in-Education and small-scale work of quality. Of the unsolicited mss received none has yet come to anything 'but that's only because we haven't had a good script thus far'.

Jean Charles Productions

4A Jointon Road, Folkestone, Kent CT20 2RF
☎0303 52413

Contact *Jean Charles*

Jean Charles produces variety, panto and summer shows much of which is scripted elsewhere. However, she is always on the look-out for good new comedy material – sketches and jokes particularly. Write a letter first.

Churchill Theatre

High Street, Bromley, Kent BR1 1HA
☎01—464 7131

Contact *Nick Salmon*

The Churchill produces a broad variety of popular plays, both new and revivals. Recent productions have included *Dangerous Obsession*, N.J. Crisp; *Kindly Keep It Covered*, Dave Freeman; *Dangerous Corner*, J.B.

Priestley; *King's Rhapsody*, Ivor Novello; and *Oklahoma*. Most productions go on to either tour or into the West End. New scripts welcome.

City Theatre Productions

11A Friern Mount Drive, London N20 9DP
☎01—445 7961

Contact *Jon Rumney*

The company is currently dormant, but if a good script came along, would awake to produce it. Enjoyed great success at the Edinburgh Festival in the past, with international plays and new work. 'We're after topical interest, humour, a very small cast and strong actors' parts. . . .'

Alan Clements Productions

Mill House, St Ives Cross,
Sutton St James, Spalding, South Lincs.
☎094 585466

Contact *Alan Clements*

Small-scale operation, producing pantomimes and only one or two plays a year. Of these, very little is new – *Sweeney Todd* being a recent exception. There is generally little hope for new writers here: 'Because we're a commercial, non-subsidised company, everything we do has to be a fairly safe bet.'

Ron Coburn International

Vaudevilla, Elliot Road, Dundee DD2 1SY
☎0382 69025

Contact *Ron Coburn*

Ron Coburn writes and produces internationally touring musical variety shows like *A Breath of Scotland* and *The Waggle o' the Kilt*. Venues range from Carnegie Hall to Mablethorpe and Skegness. As the material needs to travel to North America and is usually of a topical nature, it's not feasible to use outside writers.

Michael Codron Ltd

Aldwych Theatre Offices,
Aldwych, London WC2B 4DF
☎01–240 8291

Contact *Joe Scott Parkinson*
(General Manager)

Michael Codron Ltd manage the Aldwych and Adelphi theatres, and own the Vaudeville Theatre in London's West End. The plays they produce don't necessarily go into these theatres, but always tend to be big-time West End fare like *Woman in Mind* with Julia Mackenzie. There is no particular rule of thumb on subject matter or treatment, the acid test being 'whether something appeals to Michael'. 'The reason we haven't done much in the last six months is that nothing has appealed sufficiently.' Straight plays rather than musicals. Generally enthusiastic about new work and resolve to read everything which is submitted.

The Coliseum, Oldham

Fairbotton Street, Oldham OL1 3SW
☎061–624 1731

Contact *Paul Kerryson* (Artistic Director)

Considered a good bet for new playwrights, The Coliseum is besieged by more scripts than it can read. However, they do put on new work: 'We like to do new writing that's popular and relevant to our audience . . . it's got to be popular.' Do not welcome unsolicited scripts. First approach with letter and synopsis. Recent plays have included *A Night on the Tiles*, Frank Vickery; *Girlfriends*, Howard Goodall; *Stage Fright*, Peter Fieldson; *The Steamie*, Tony Roper; *Clowns on a School Outing*, Ken Campbell. Two further new plays scheduled for Autumn 1988 season. Often plays come by way of contacts or commissions, but good unsolicited scripts still stand a chance. Just don't expect a swift decision.

Communicado Theatre Company

Royal Lyceum Theatre, Grindlay Street,
Edinburgh EH3 9AX
☎031–229 7404

Contact *Gerard Mulgrew* (Artistic Director)

FOUNDED 1982. Small-scale touring company which 'aims to entertain the widest range of audience'. Want to encourage new writing, especially Scottish. Welcome unsolicited mss. Recent productions include: *Carmen*, Stephen Jeffreys; *The Hunchback of Notre Dame*, Andrew Dallmeyer; *Mary Queen of Scots Got Her Head Chopped Off*, Liz Lochhead; *Tales of the Arabian Nights*, Gerard Mulgrew.

Compass Theatre Company

13 Shorts Gardens, London WC2H 9AT
☎ 01–379 7501

Contact *Edward Kemp* (Assistant Director)

Sir Anthony Quayle founded this company in 1984 to produce revivals and large-cast classics; it has a particular interest in touring. Productions have included *The Government Inspector*; *King Lear*, *Dandy Dick*; *The Tempest*; *St Joan*; *The Clandestine Marriage*; *After the Ball is Over*. To date, not much demand for new writing, though current developments in policy should enable productions of new plays to be considered, especially those of a large-scale or epic nature.

Condor Productions

101A St Martin's Lane, London WC2N 4AZ
☎01–379 5327

Contact *Robert Cogo-Fawcett* (Managing Director)

FOUNDED 1987. Produce both new plays and classics. No musicals. Welcome unsolicited mss.

Mervyn Conn Organisation

MC House, 14 Orange Street,
London WC2H 7ED
☎01–930 7502

The *Annie* tour is the first theatre Mervyn Conn have produced (ordinarily they produce one-offs like the Silk Cut Country & Western Festival). No facilities for reading mss, and no interest in new work.

Contact Theatre Company

Oxford Road, Manchester M15 6JA

☎061–274 3434

Contact *Anthony Clark* (Artistic Director)

FOUNDED 1966. Play predominantly to a young audience (15–35) with a particular interest in new work, especially from the north-west. Up to 5 plays a year are commissioned. In 1987/88 new plays included *Dreams with Teeth*, Cindy Artiste; *My Mother Said I Never Should*, Charlotte Keatley; *The Little Prince*, Exupery/Clark; *McAlpine's Fusilier*, Kevin Fegan.

Crucible Theatre

55 Norfolk Street, Sheffield S1 1DA

☎0742 760621

Contact *Director's secretary*

Under the artistic direction of Clare Venables, the Crucible has developed a strong policy on new writing and tries to do one new main house show a year, with plenty of others appearing in the Studio. All premières over recent years have resulted from commissions from established writers or from new writers of promise. Unsolicited scripts are seen by a reader and a small number may go on to a rehearsal reading/workshop. Full devising and commissioning TIE company working in Sheffield and South Yorkshire schools; usually 'concept' based to reflect school's needs and curriculum, eg racism, sexuality. New plays have included *A Passion in 6 Days*, Howard Barker; *It's A Bit Lively Outside*, Joyce Holliday; *Here We Go*, Andy de la Tour; *Plague of Innocence*, Noel Greig. The Crucible was, incidentally, the producer to commission Chris Martin's *Who Killed Hilda Murrell?* Finished scripts are always preferred to synopses or ideas.

Bernard Delfont Organisation Ltd

Prince of Wales Theatre,
Coventry Street, London SW1

☎01–930 9901

No longer acting as theatre producers.

Charles Dickens Theatre Company

Sunrise House, Gibraltar Road,
Otley, Ipswich IP6 9LL

☎047385 672

Contact *Charles Peter Mugleston*

A new company which will consider plays of all kinds. New writing considered; s.a.e. in all cases.

Dramatis Personae Ltd

122 Kennington Road, London SE11 6RE

☎01–735 0831

Contact *Nathan Silver*

Run by Nathan Silver and Maria Aitken, the company turns its hand to a variety of projects (and is currently co-producing with the BBC on arts documentary subjects). Interested to read new plays, which most often come by way of contacts in the business, but can occasionally be taken up from unknowns who send scripts on spec. Good plays are put into provincial rep and brought to London if successful. Letters and synopses asked in the first instance.

E & B Productions Ltd

Suite 1, Waldorf Chambers,
11 Aldwych, London WC2B 4DA

☎01–836 2795

Contact *Paul Elliott, Brian Hewitt-Jones*

Theoretically, at least, interested in seeing new scripts, although the schedule for the last half of 1987 was taken up with touring shows like *Run for Your Wife* and *Double Double*, plus the preparation of 14 pantomimes for the winter. Previous productions included *Crown Matrimonial*, *Gaslight* and *Crystal Clear*, as well as the new play *The Secret Life of Cartoons* by Clive Barker.

Field Day Theatre Company

Orchard Gallery, Orchard Street,
Derry BT48 6BG

☎0504 360196

Contact *Maureen Loughran* (Administrator)

A touring company which usually commissions its plays from Irish writers. Past productions have included *Pentecost*, Stewart Parker. No scripts or ideas as all work is commissioned.

Foco Novo

1/2 Alfred Place, London WC1E 7EB
☎ 01–580 4722/3

Contact *Roland Rees* (Artistic Director)

Foco Novo is one of Britain's foremost touring theatre companies. It exists to produce new work and commissions many of these. They were the first company to produce *The Elephant Man*. Other recent productions have included *Bloody Poety*, Howard Brenton; *Deathwatch*, Jean Genet; a new version of Gorki's *Lower Depths* by Tunde Ikoli; *The Cape Orchard*, Michael Picardie; and the first English production of Marguerite Duras's *Savannah Bay*. Unsolicited mss welcome but synopsis with introductory letter preferred.

Vanessa Ford Productions Ltd

62 Uverdale Road, London SW10 0SS
☎ 01–352 1948/351 9293
Telex 8950511 ONEONE 6

Contact *Vanessa Ford*

Recent work has included *Winnie the Pooh*; *The Voyage of the Dawn Treader*; *The Lion, The Witch and The Wardrobe*, touring and West End, as well as classical seasons touring and in London. Often do their own writing and adaptation in-house but also keen to see new plays of all kinds, whether finished scripts, ideas or synopses.

Clare Fox & Brian Kirk Ltd

Suite 17, 26 Charing Cross Road,
London WC2H 0DG
☎ 01–379 4985/4676   Fax 01–379 5898

Contact *Clare Fox*

Producers and general managers from the commercial West End. Past involvement

include *Bent*, Martin Sherman; *Mr & Mrs Nobody*; *Breaking the Code, Pack of Lies, Best of Friends*, Hugh Whitemore; *Of Mice and Men*, John Steinbeck; *The Amen Corner*, James Baldwin. Unsolicited mss are welcome, 'but they take a long time to process'. Very interested in new writing.

Robert Fox Limited

6 Beauchamp Place, London SW3 1NG
☎ 01–584 6855/6
Telex 936221   Fax 01–225 1638

Contact *Robert Fox*

In 1987, co-producers of *Chess* in London's West End, Peter Shaffer's *Lettice and Lovage* and Ronald Harwood's new play *J.J. Farr*. Scripts, while usually by established playwrights, are always read. Bear in mind, however, that the company is usually concerned with work suitable for West End production.

Freeshooter Productions Ltd

10 Clorane Gardens, London NW3 7PR
☎ 01–794 0414

Contact *Andrew Empson*

Past productions have included *The Petition*, Wyndhams Theatre; *Siegfried Sassoon*, Apollo Theatre; *Kipling*, Mermaid Theatre; *St Mark's Gospel*, on tour; *March of the Falsettos*, Manchester and the Albery Theatre, London and *Godspell* on national tour. Unsolicited scripts welcome.

Mark Furness Ltd

10 Garrick Street, London WC2E 9BH
☎ 01–836 7373

Contact *Mark Furness*

Recent productions have included two West End productions: *Peter Pan* (the musical) at the Cambridge Theatre and *Dangerous Obsession* at the Fortune Theatre. In 1987 their summer seasons included tours of *Run for Your Wife* and *The Mating Game*, *'Allo 'Allo* in the West End, and a new play by Donald Churchill, *Mixed Feelings*. Unsolicited mss welcome but bear in mind that they need to be suitable for touring. Not necessarily comedy – also produce thrillers such as *A Murder is Announced*.

John Gale
Strand Theatre,
Aldwych, London WC2B 5LD
☎01–240 1656

Contact *John Gale*

John Gale is also director of Chichester Festival Theatre (scripts can also be sent to him there: Festival Theatre Productions Co. Ltd, Oaklands Park, Chichester, Sussex, tel. 0243 784437). In London, *No Sex Please We're British*; other recent plays have included *Jane Eyre* and *Miranda* with Penelope Keith. The general pattern is, typically, classic revivals in the main house, new plays in the studio (unless very saleable). But both London and Chichester are interested in seeing new work of quality.

Gallery Productions Ltd
The Old Fire Station, Station Road,
Merstham, Surrey RH1 3EE
☎073 744833

Contact *Robert Kennedy, Lee Dean*

A touring company founded in 1985, with seven productions in 1987, and increasingly interested in new work. Past productions have included *Widow's Weeds*, Anthony Shaffer; *Rough Crossing*, Tom Stoppard; *The Haunting*, Shirley Jackson. No 'avant-garde' work; prefer contemporary subjects traditionally written. Synopses in the first instance; scripts by invitation.

Glasgow Citizens Theatre
Gorbals, Glasgow G5 9DS
☎041–429 5561

Contact *Paul Bassett*

The Cits have no formal policy on new writing; although interested in seeing new work, in practice they haven't produced any in the last couple of years. Productions tend to be classic revivals, or else adaptations/translations done by the resident dramaturge Robert David MacDonald. There isn't generally the money to put on new plays which might not be popular.

Globe Players Theatre Company
36 St James Avenue, Hampton Hill,
Middlesex TW12 1HN
☎01–979 5497

Shakespeare and fairy stories only, for touring to schools in the London area. All fairy stories originate in-house, for financial reasons. Not interested in receiving mss or synopses.

Derek Glynne (London) Pty Ltd
25 Haymarket, London SW1Y 4EN
☎01–930 1981   Fax 01–935 6638
Telex 919150

Contact *Mrs Denise Parker*

Derek Glynne (who also trades at the same address as The London Company Ltd) is in partnership with American and Australian producers. There are two aspects of the company's work – taking companies like the **Royal Shakespeare Company** abroad and producing plays largely for Australian and American audiences. Most of these originate abroad, so in general there is little hope for playwrights here. However, they are about to do a new play which was commissioned by them, and unsolicited mss/ideas of promise are passed on for consideration. In addition, they are often consulted or asked to co-produce.

Great Eastern Stage
Steinkirk Block, Dunkirk Road,
Lincoln LN1 3UJ
☎0522 34924

Contact *Ian McKeand* (Artistic Director)

Active in local (and some national) touring. Welcome plays with a local theme particularly; planning to do more locally-based plays in the near future.

Greenwich Theatre

Crooms Hill, London SE10 8ES
☎01–858 44447

At the time of going to press, Alan Strachan, the artistic director, had recently been sacked by his board for being too adventurous in his choice of plays. His replacement is to be Sue Dunderdale, formerly of the **Soho Poly**. Future policy on new writing was not available. Under Alan Strachan there was a policy of reading all submitted scripts. Always had a big backlog of scripts and an approach with an idea in the first instance was recommended.

Raymond Gubbay Ltd

163 High Street, Barnet, Herts.
☎01–441 8940

Although Raymond Gubbay does from time to time act as a theatrical producer, these are mostly one-offs and rarely straight plays. For the moment, he is concentrating on music and is active as a concert promoter. Has also begun to develop exhibition promotion. With Caroline Penman he presented The City of London Antiques Fair at the Barbican in November 1987, and the City of London Antiques and Fine Arts Fair will run concurrently at the Barbican in November 1988.

Half Moon Theatre

213 Mile End Road, London E1 4AA
☎01–791 1141

Contact *Chris Bond* (Artistic Director)

The Half Moon produce six shows a year and are very interested in new writing, but 'we're not a writers' theatre for the sake of it, and aren't prepared to produce new work unless it's of a high standard'. A third to a half of their output meets these exacting requirements. Occasionally commissions to complete further drafts of promising work will be offered. Productions have included *Moll Flanders*, Clare Luckham; *Sink the Belgrano*, Steven Berkoff; *Elizabeth*, Dario Fo (first English translation); and the first English production of the Jamaican pantomime *Trash*, by Barbara Gloudon.

Hampstead Theatre

Swiss Cottage Centre, London NW3 3EX
☎01–722 9224

Contact *Alan Drury*

A new writing theatre, with 85 per cent of plays produced new to Britain. Looking for a distinctive quality in the writing rather than a worthy attempt at a responsible subject. Recent past productions have included *Spookhouse*, Harvey Fierstein; *That Summer*, David Edgar; *Curtains*, Stephen Bill; *Separation*, Tom Kempinski; *The Film Society*, Jon Robin Baitz; *Danger: Memory!*, Arthur Miller. Runs a workshop scheme jointly with the **Tricycle Theatre**.

Hazemead Ltd

1st Floor, 235–41 Regent Street,
London W1R 5DD
☎01–629 4817

Contact *Anne Chudleigh*

Producers of summer seasons and pantomimes all over the country. Interested in plays, sitcoms and sketches. New writers and scripts come to them principally through recommendation, but unsolicited mss and letters are always welcome.

Hiss & Boo Ltd

The Strand Theatre,
Aldwych, London WC2B 5LD
☎01–379 0453   Fax 01–240 2056

Contact *Ian Liston*

Productions have included *Novello, Benefactors, Cluedo, Mr Men Musical, Mr Men's Magical Island, Mr Men and the Space Pirates, Nunsense, Corpse!, Groucho: A Life in Revue, See How They Run, The Rivals*. Keen to see and read as much new work as possible, provided a synopsis and introductory letter is offered in the first instance. Unsolicited mss not welcome.

Horseshoe Theatre Company Ltd

The Shrubbery, Cliddesden Road,
Basingstoke, Hants RG21 3ER
☎0256 55844

Contact *Ian Mullins* (Artistic Director)

Productions this season have included *Having A Ball*, Alan Bleasdale; *As You Like It*; an entirely new musical, *Castaway* based on the story of Robinson Crusoe by Ian Reeves, music by Ian MacPherson; *Master Harold and the Boys*, Athol Fugard; *Busman's Honeymoon*, Dorothy L. Sayers. Still to come, *Who Killed Hilda Murrell?*, Chris Martin; *Intimate Exchanges*, Alan Ayckbourn; *The Real Thing*, Tom Stoppard. New plays are more likely to be commissioned than taken up from unsolicited scripts, and the theatre can't afford to do as much new work as it would like. The commissioned play, *Pluck'd Off in a Far Off Land* by Paul Doust, planned for the 1988 season, 'had to be cancelled'.

Hull Truck Theatre Company
Spring Street, Hull HU2 8RW
☎ 0482 224800

Contact *Barry Nettleton* (Administrator)

John Godber, the Artistic Director of this high-profile northern company since 1984, dominates the scene with his own successful plays. However, a change of direction is in the offing. Although the company will be doing at least one of John's plays a year, there is a new emphasis on outside writers. (Already this has produced plays like Phil Woods' *The Dock* and Jane Thornton's *Cut and Dried*.) Most of the new plays have been commissioned, and the company admits it doesn't always get around to reading unsolicited mss. Synopses and letters are preferred. Bear in mind the artistic policy of Hull Truck, which is 'accessibility and popularity'. In general they are not interested in musicals, or in plays with many more than 5 characters.

Richard Jackson
59 Knightsbridge, London SW1
☎ 01–235 3671

Independent-minded producer who does 'strong plays which appeal to me'. Besieged by mss and tends to go out for what he wants (particularly European material). Currently working in smaller-scale London fringe theatre, like the Offstage Downstairs, where he can take risks the West End can no longer afford. Credits include bringing *Quentin Crisp* to a theatre audience, *A Day in Hollywood, A Night in the Ukraine*; *The Singular Life of Albert Nobbs*. More recently *Latin*, Stephen Fry; *Swimming Pools at War*, Yves Navarre; *Matthew, Mark, Luke and Charlie*, Robert Gillespie; *Pasolini*, Michael Azama; *I Ought to Be in Pictures*, Neil Simon; *Starting in the Middle*, Sally-Jane Heit's one-woman show (1987).

Stephen Joseph Theatre
Valley Bridge Parade, Scarborough YO11 2PL
☎ 0723 370540

Contact *Alan Ayckbourn* (Artistic Director)

A small theatre-in-the-round seating 307 people, with positive policy on new work. For obvious reasons, Alan Ayckbourn's work is featured heavily in the repertoire, but plays from other sources are encouraged. Recently, productions of *Touch Wood and Whistle*, Stephen Mallatratt; *Calling*, Paul Copley. Up to 80% première productions in each season. This current year sees *State of the Union*, new work from Peter Tinniswood; *The Parasol*, Frank Dunai; *The Ballroom*, Peter King; and two new plays from Alan Ayckbourn.

Bill Kenwright Productions
55–59 Shaftesbury Avenue,
London W1V 7AA
☎ 01–439 4466

Contact *Bill Kenwright*

Both revivals and new shows for West End and touring theatres. New work tends to be by established playwrights: *The Business of Murder*, Richard Harris; *A Fighting Chance*, Norman Crisp; *Up On The Roof*, Jane Prowse and Simon Moore. For children, *James and the Giant Peach*, Herbert Chappell (adapted from Roald Dahl). 'We have no particular system established for the reading of unsolicited mss': send a letter with synopsis and a few sample pages in the first instance.

King's Head Theatre Club

115 Upper Street, London N1 1QN
☎01–226 8561

Contact *Dan Crawford* (Administrator)

New scripts are welcome and are farmed out to consultants for reading and evaluation. An unpretentious little café theatre, the King's Head nevertheless produces some strong work, notably in 1987 *Diary of a Somebody* by John Lahr, about the life and death of Joe Orton. Other productions have included *Heyday*, Herbert Appleman; *The Secret Garden* adapted by Diana Morgan; *This Savage Parade*, Anthony Shaffer; *The Fling*, Asher; and Noel Coward's *Easy Virtue*, which transferred to the West End.

David Kirk Productions

12 Panmuir Road, London SW20 0PZ
☎01–947 0130

Contact *David Kirk*

Commercial management touring post-London revivals and some new plays to provincial and suburban theatres. Productions usually have two or three TV names in them, but David Kirk is very interested in scripts strong enough not to need these. Not interested in verse plays, rock musicals or 'scripts more suited to the fringe'. No unsolicited mss without preliminary letter and return postage. Productions have included the post-London tours of *Middle Age Spread*; Alan Ayckbourn's *Taking Steps*; David Pownall's *Master Class*; Peter Terson's *Strippers*; Bob Larbey's *A Month of Sundays*; John Lahr's *Diary of a Somebody*. New plays have included *Murder Sails at Midnight*, Ngaio Marsh; *The Golf Umbrella*, William Douglas Home; *Local Murder*, Peter Whalley; *Mr Fothergill's Murder*, Peter O'Donnell; *Agenda for Murder*, Denis Cleary and Joseph Boyer.

Knightsbridge Theatrical Productions

15 Fetter Lane, London EC4A 1JJ
☎01– 583 2266

Contact *Joan Robinson*

Straight plays suitable for production in the West End only. No musicals. Occasionally plays are then taken on tour. New writing is welcome; unsolicited mss will always be considered

Leeds Playhouse

Calverley Street, Leeds LS2 3AJ
☎0532 442141

Contact *John Harrison* (Artistic Director)

'Always on the look-out for new plays, but good ones are hard to find.' Of 10 or 11 plays a season, at least one is likely to be a première. Recently *Torpedoes in the Jacuzzi*, Phil Young, which came out of improvisation, and Barry Hillman's *The Amazing Dancing Bear*. Have recently commissioned a play from Leeds-based writer, Kay Mellor. Also do 'regional premières', i.e. plays new to Leeds, though not new as such.

Leicester Haymarket Theatre

Belgrave Gate, Leicester LE1 3YQ
☎0533 530021

Contact *Peter Lichtenfels*

Peter Lichtenfels, the artistic director since mid-1987, brings from his old job at the **Traverse Theatre** in Edinburgh a desire to put on more new work in Leicester, both in the studio and main house. He plans to do at least 6 new plays a year. Recent output has included *Fat Pig*, a musical by Henry Kreiger and Mark Bramble, and *The Traveller* by Jean Claude van Itallie. Scripts preferred to outlines or ideas.

Liverpool Playhouse

Williamson Square, Liverpool L1 1EL
☎051–709 8478

Contact *Kate Rowland* (Associate Director)

Regional theatre very active in promoting new writing, with an impressive record on first plays: *Leave Taking*, Winsome Pinnock; *Changing Gear*, Jim Morris; *Watching*, Jim

Hitchmough, which transferred to the **Bush Theatre** in London; *Shamrocks and Crocodiles*, Heidi Thomas; and Anne Devlin's *Ourselves Alone* were all first plays premièred at the Liverpool Playhouse. Finished scripts preferred to synopses and ideas. Committed to developing new work in both its auditoria. Young Writers Award to be held for a second year.

Logan Theatres Ltd

112 Hamilton Avenue,
Pollokshields, Glasgow G41 4EX
☎041–427 6743

Contact *Jimmy Logan*

Productions vary, but mostly star Jimmy Logan. Laughter and comedy appealing to a genuine family audience. Past productions include *Run for Your Wife*, *A Bedful of Foreigners*, *Not Now Darling* and *Lauder*. Prepared to consider new writing if it is funny and doesn't rely on extraneous four-letter words for laughs.

The Lyric Theatre, Hammersmith

King Street, London W6 0QL
☎01–741 0824

Contact *Peter James* (Artistic Director)

Theatre with a long tradition of putting on new work, and always keen to receive scripts, which are read by a permanent team of three. Currently the main house is concentrating on modern European drama, rather than new plays by British playwrights, but the studio is always on the look-out for good new scripts. Productions have included *Scout's Honour*, Christopher Douglas; *Massage*, Michael Wilcox; *Your Obedient Servant*, Kay Eldridge; *Public Enemy*, Kenneth Branagh; *Mumbo Jumbo*, Robin Glendinning (Mobil Prizewinner); *Atonement*, Barry Collins. Finished scripts only – they take at least 6 weeks to process, but a report is made on every ms received.

Cameron Mackintosh

1 Bedford Square, London WC1B 3RA

Producer of *Cats, Les Miserables, Phantom of the Opera, Little Shop of Horrors* and *Follies*, Cameron Mackintosh is one of the most important producers in London's West End. Unsolicited scripts are read and considered (there is no literary manager, however) but chances of success are slim. This is because they only produce musicals, and never more than one a year – which is likely to come by way of contacts. Fixed up for the whole of 1988 by June 1987. There is a strong possibility that after the next production, *Miss Saigon*, production of new musicals will close for several years.

Marianne McNaghten

c/o 8 Redwoods, Alton Road,
London SW15 4NL
☎02657 31215

Contact *Marianne McNaghten*

One of the army of freelance directors who also act as producers. Consulted by other producers so often able to pass on good ideas. Handles many revivals/classic works, but also interested in new writing: 'I don't see nearly enough', whether straight plays, musicals or good children's plays. Both scripts and synopses are welcome.

Marcellus Productions Ltd

11 Chelverton Road, London SW15 1RN
☎01–788 5663

Contact *Jimmy Thompson*

Jimmy Thompson acts more as a director than producer, but is always on the look-out for new plays. Recent productions have included *Don't Misunderstand Me* (Patrick Cargill); *The Quiz Kid* (which was written by the Thompsons); *Wind in the Willows* (Vaudeville Theatre); and *My Giddy Aunt* (tour with Mollie Sugden). Regularly produce a revue for the West End, *The Englishman Amused*. Not really in the market for avant-garde or social plays, but will consider revue, farce and romantic comedy.

Lee Menzies Limited

20 Rupert Street, London W1V 7FN

☎01–437 0127   Fax 01–439 0297

Contact *Lee Menzies*

Interested in new commercial plays. Currently producing Jeffrey Archer's *Beyond Reasonable Doubt*. Later this year presenting *Dry Rot* in which Sir Brian Rix will make his long-awaited return to the West End.

Merseyside Everyman Theatre Company

5–9 Hope Street, Liverpool L1 9BH

☎051–708 0338

Contact *Glen Walford* (Artistic Director)

FOUNDED 1964. Of five shows a year, two to three are usually new plays. The theatre tend to produce new versions of old classics, idiosyncratic Shakespeares, Willy Russell, Brecht, rock-and-roll panto – a very catholic repertoire. The common ingredient is an upfront bold style; productions are designed to appeal to non-traditional audiences. 'But no working-class angst plays please. If you spend all day in a tower block, you don't want to go out and see a play about it.' Recent productions have included *Comedians* (written for an all-female cast); *Cabaret*; *Aladdin Liverpool*; *Hamlet*; *Entertaining Mr Sloane*; *Three Sisters*. 'In theory we welcome unsolicited mss, but in practice we find we don't have the staff to do a proper reading job on them.'

Midland Arts Centre

Cannon Hill Park, Birmingham B12 9QH

☎021–440 4221

Contact *Robert Petty*

Home of Cannon Hill Puppet Theatre, Central Junior Television Workshop, City of Birmingham Touring Opera, etc., and base for Readers and Writers, an annual festival held in the last two weeks of November.

Barry J. Mishon Associates

159 Great Portland Street, London W1N 5FD

☎01–637 7548

Contact *Barry Mishon*

Not in the market for straight plays by either new or established writers. Devise and produce one-offs, events such as *The Night of 100 Stars*.

Kenneth More Theatre

Oakfield Road, Ilford, Essex IG1 1BT

☎01–553 4464

Contact *Vivyan Ellacott*

Productions range from rock musicals to grand opera, gay theatre to Shakespeare, for an audience of both local senior citizens and young, upwardly mobile East-Enders. Unsolicited mss are not welcome, as there aren't the resources to cope with them; studio plays around 30 minutes long are welcome, however, as there is a great demand for these.

Norman Murray & Anne Chudleigh Ltd

1st floor, 235/241 Regent Street, London W1

☎01–629 4871

Contact *Anne Chudleigh*

Present pantomimes, but in general act more as agents than producers, handling light entertainment performers as well as comedy writers. 'We are always looking for new ideas in respect of comedy material, situation comedy and plays.'

The National Theatre

South Bank, London SE1 9PX

☎01–928 2033   Telex 297306

Contact *Nicholas Wright*

Unsolicited mss are read, but the majority of The National's new plays come about as a result of a direct commission. There is no quota for new work, though so far more than a third of plays presented have been the work of living playwrights. Writers new to the theatre would need to be of exceptional talent to be successful with a script here, though the NT Studio acts as a bridge between the theatre and a limited number of playwrights through readings, workshops and discussion. In some cases a new play is presented as a Studio Night in the Cottesloe Theatre. NT Platforms, 45-minute plays with the minimum of décor, are a further outlet for original work.

Newgate Theatre Company

13 Dafford Street, Larkhall,
Bath, Avon BS1 6BW
☎0225 318335

Contact *Jo Anderson*

'We need more that a script; we need a concept.' Newgate might be termed 'theatre packagers'; formed as a loose ensemble of actors and directors, they write their own material and respond to specific projects (often on a commission basis) for festivals, the BBC and fringe theatres such as the **Bush**, **Half Moon** and **Theatre Royal Stratford East**. London production and tour of *Solstice*, Jo Anderson, co-produced by Bristol Express in 1988. Tour by **Orchard Theatre** company of *Hitler's Whistle* in 1989. New concepts always welcome. At the same address: *Air Play* – a newly formed co-operative designed to 'bridge the ever increasing divide that lies between the lonely writer and the man at the top production desk'. Consists of an experienced major radio drama director, mainstream actors and access to a well-equipped stereo recording facility. Cassettes of plays are made for writers to promote their work. Cover stage plays, radio plays and, in the case of screen and teleplays, incorporate an exposition of visuals. Author's copyright is protected and the cost lies 'somewhere between that for mss typing and vanity publishing'.

Newpalm Productions

26 Cavendish Avenue,
Finchley, London N3 3QN
☎01–349 0802

Contact *Phil Compton*

Don't often produce new plays: *As Is* by William M. Hoffman, which came from Broadway to the **Half Moon Theatre** in August 1986 was an exception to this. National tours of *Noises Off*, *Seven Brides for Seven Brothers* and *Rebecca* at regional repertory theatres are examples of their more usual shows. However, unsolicited mss, whether plays or musicals are welcome; scripts are always preferable to synopses.

North Bank Productions

103B Victoria Road, London NW6 6TD
☎01–328 8563

Contacts *Jon Bromwich, Chris Hayes*

An established production company interested in both revivals and new plays. New writing often comes to them through writers they know and have used in the past, like Colin Bennet, who did *Hancock's Finest Hour* for them at the Boulevard Theatre, London. Other productions have included *The Anastasia File*, Royce Ryton (now published by **French**); *Supergran*, Phil Woods; *Educating Rita*, Willy Russell; *Funny Peculiar*, Mike Stott. All incoming scripts will be read – allow six weeks for their return.

Northcott Theatre

Stocker Road, Exeter, Devon EX4 4QB
☎0392 56182

Contact *George Roman*

A self-producing regional theatre keen to present new writing of quality. However, much of the material which comes in is uninspiring and the theatre often find they need to go out and find new work. Commissions and contacts are generally the order of the day and in 1988 two new plays will be produced which they got by these means. Productions have included a new musical, *Katerina*; *Peter's Passion*, Martin Harvey; and *The Cape Orchard*, Michael Picardie (a co-production with **Foco Novo**).

Norwich Puppet Theatre

St James, Whitefriars,
Norwich, Norfolk NR3 1TN
☎0603 615564

Contact *Pat Holtom*

Mostly a young audience (ages 4–16), although on occasions shows are put on for an adult audience interested in puppetry. Christmas and summer season shows, plus school tours. Unsolicited mss welcome if relevant.

Nottingham Playhouse

Nottingham Theatre Trust,
Wellington Circus, Nottingham NG1 5AF
☎0602 474361

Contact *Les Smith* (Director of Writing)

They expect to do around two new plays a season, though no quota exists. Plays must, however, have popular appeal – they have to fill a 700-seat main house. No formal studio space exists though a small room which can seat forty people is used for rehearsed readings (including the Writing '87 Festival, which presented four plays chosen from a submitted 130). Les Smith gets around 300 scripts a year and tries to criticise constructively all of these, though only 5% or so show genuine promise. Past productions include *Y'Shunta Joined*, Barry Heath; *Queer Folk*, Rosie Logan; *Too Good for This World*, John Ward; *A Tossed Coin*, Will Coburn. Unsolicited mss welcome.

Nuffield Theatre

University Road, Southampton SO9 5NH
☎0703 671871
Fax 0703 671778 (must be marked 'Nuffield Theatre')

Contact *Patrick Sandford* (Artistic Director)

Well known as a good bet for new playwrights, the Nuffield gets an awful lot of scripts. They tend to do a couple of new plays every season, often by established playwrights, though not as a matter of policy. Recent productions have included *The Hired Man*, Goodall and Bragg; *A Month of Sundays*, Bob Larbey; *A Piece of My Mind*, Peter Nichols; *The Fit Up*, John Constable. In April 1988 premièred *The Little Heroine*, Nell Dunn's first play since *Steaming*. They are open-minded about subject and style, and produce musicals as well as straight plays. Scripts preferred to synopses in the case of writers new to theatre. All will, eventually, be read.

Open Air Theatre

Regent's Park, London NW1 4NP
☎01–935 5884

Contact *Ian Talbot* (Artistic Director)

Shakespeare and revivals only, except for summer lunchtime children's theatre (which in 1988 has been specially commissioned).

Orange Tree Theatre

45 Kew Road, Richmond, Surrey TW9 2NQ
☎01–940 3633

Contact *Sam Walters* (Artistic Director)

One of those just-out-of-London fringe theatre venues good for new writing, both full productions and rehearsed readings. New plays have included *Four Attempted Acts* (winner of the Giles Cooper Award), *A Variety of Death Defying Acts* and *Definitely the Bahamas*, all by Martin Crimp; *Revisiting the Alchemist*, Charles Jennings; *Brotherhood*, Don Taylor; *A Smile on the End of the Line*, Michael Vinaver, translated by Peter Meyer; *The Hole in the Top of the World*, Fay Weldon. Prospective playwrights should bear in mind, however, that unsolicited mss are read in one great blitz every spring. Those submitting scripts in the early autumn could be in for a long wait.

Orchard Theatre

108 Newport Road,
Barnstaple, Devon EX32 9BA
☎0271 71475

Contact *Nigel Bryant* (Artistic Director)

FOUNDED 1969. Plays appealing to a wide age range, which tour some 60 or 70 cities, towns and villages through Devon, Cornwall, Dorset, Somerset, Avon and Gloucestershire. Programme includes classics, new adaptations, outstanding modern work, musicals and newly commissioned plays on West Country themes: *The Cuckoo* and *The Lie of the Land*, Jane Beeson; *Sedgemoor* and *The Death of Arthur*, John Fletcher. 'A large proportion of our work is concerned with the history, literary traditions and present-day life of the region. Unsolicited mss are read, but are usually unsuccessful simply because the theatre is committed to several commissioned new plays at any one time.'

Oxford Stage Company

Beaumont Street, Oxford OX1 2LW
☎0865 723238

Contact *Richard Williams*

A touring company generally playing to a middle-class audience, with plays like *Travesties*, *Hamlet*, *Dr Faustus*, new works like *Airbase* and adaptations like *Tristram Shandy*. Unsolicited mss welcome. Produce at least one new play or new adaptation a year.

Paines Plough – the writers' company

121–122 Tottenham Court Road,
London W1P 9HN
☎01–380 1188

Contact *Robin Hooper* (Literary Manager)

Produce nothing but new writing. Recent plays have included *Berlin Day, Hollywood Nights*, Nigel Gearing; *The Way to go Home*, Rona Munro. They receive around six unsolicited scripts a week and reports are made on all plays received.

Palace Theatre, Watford

Clarendon Road, Watford WD1 1JZ
☎0923 35455

Contact *Lou Stein* (Artistic Director)

Try to get a new play or adaptation into each season's schedule. Recently these have included Edna O'Brien's *Madame Bovary* and Jacqui Shapiro's *Winter in the Morning*. In the previous year they premièred Michael Frayn's new adaptation of *The Seagull*.

Pentameters

Three Horseshoes, 28 Heath Street,
London NW3
☎01–435 6757

Contact *Leonie Scott-Matthews*

Occasional plays and poetry readings. Very interested in new plays ('we've been a new writing theatre since 1968') but no resources to deal with an influx of scripts, so send letters and synopses first. Broad-minded in terms of subject matter and style: 'It's not just Soho Poly working-class angst . . . we've even put on farce, which isn't supposed to work in fringe venues, but it does.'

Permutt–Hadley Productions Ltd

6 Denmark Street, London WC2H 8LP
☎01–836 3317

Contact *P. Permutt*

Touring and West End musicals and plays. Unsolicited mss not welcome.

James Perry Productions Ltd

1F Morpeth Terrace, Westminster,
London SW1P 1EW
☎01–828 2203

Contact *Jimmy Perry*

FOUNDED 1956. James Perry Productions is a small company which exists solely to handle the work of Jimmy Perry.

Plantagenet Productions

Westridge Open Centre, Highclere,
nr Newbury, Berks. RG15 9PJ
☎0635 253322

Contact *Dorothy Rose Gribble*

Recorded library of the spoken word (classical, no unsolicited mss). Short list of drawing-room recitals based at Westridge Open Centre, a showcase for visiting recitals, mainly of music, small seminars, healing studies and holidays.

Players' Theatre

Villiers Street, Strand, London WC2N 6NG
☎01–839 3256

Contact *Dennis Martin* (Director)

Present Victorian music hall entertainment, researched largely from sources like the **British Library**. No market for playwrights here.

Playfare Productions

1 Hogarth Terrace, London W4
☎01–995 0065

Produce plays for children, both classics and fairy tales, for ages 4–14, which are written by a regular team, who know Playfare's needs. No interest in new scripts from other sources.

Polka Children's Theatre

240 The Broadway, London SW19 1SB
☎01– 542 4258

This Wimbledon theatre is interested in receiving scripts suitable for children of all ages, but principally 3–5, 5–7 and 8–11. 'Our overall writing policy is to present excellent theatre for children which is both educational and entertaining'. Looking for 'scripts that don't talk down to them'. Varied subjects and styles – often use plays based on existing stories, folk tales or novels. Main house productions include original plays connected to school project work; Christmas plays; summer musical-plays; adaptations of classic stories, novels and folk tales; and puppet plays. Plays that need a cast of no more than five to seven people particularly welcome.

Q20 Theatre Company

Ivy Lea, Fyfe Lane, Baildon,
Shipley, West Yorks. BD17 6DP
☎0274 581316

Contact *John Lambert*

Produce shows mainly for school and community venues. Particularly interested in plays for children. Q20 write a lot of their own material, and haven't the resources to pay professional contributors. Write initially with ideas.

Quill Theatre Productions

247 Norwood Road, London SE24 9AG
☎01–674 1050

Contact *Ann Parnell McGarry*
(Artistic Director)

Quill exist to produce new work and suffer enormous gaps in their production schedule when, as is often the case, decent new work can't be found. Writing can be set in any period, as long as it offers fresh insights, and relationships are strongly and authentically represented. 'Originality of approach is the most important thing.' In the market for serious work, fast witty comedies, musicals and children's plays. Finished scripts are preferred to synopses, unless someone wants to try out 'a truly brilliant idea which we can develop together. We have no preconceptions on size of cast.'

Really Useful Theatre Company

Palace Theatre, Shaftesbury Avenue,
London W1V 8AY
☎01–734 0762

Contact *Bridget Hayward* (Administrator)

Commercial/West End theatre producers whose output has included *Cats, Phantom of the Opera, Starlight Express, Daisy Pulls It Off, Lend Me a Tenor, Arturo Ui.* Have a positive policy towards new writing and welcome unsolicited mss.

Michael Redington

10 Maunsel Street, London SW1P 2QL
☎01–834 5119

Contact *Michael Redington*

Recent West End productions have included *Breaking the Code* and *The Best of Friends*, Hugh Whitemore; *Mr & Mrs Nobody*, Keith Waterhouse. Interested in new work but unsolicited mss not welcome; new plays generally come to him by way of contacts in the business: 'I am only interested in new work and working with people whose work I know.'

Royal Court Theatre (English Stage Company Ltd)

Sloane Square, London SW1W 8AS
☎01–730 5174

Contacts *Kate Harwood* (Literary Manager), *Michael Hastings* (Senior Script Associate)

The English Stage Company was founded by George Devine in 1956 to put on new plays. John Osborne, John Arden and Arnold Wesker, Edward Bond and Caryl Churchill, Howard Barker and Michael Hastings are among the writers this theatre has discovered. Other writers (Christopher Hampton, David Hare) have worked in the literary department. The Royal Court always seeks topical plays on radical subjects and it remains the principal venue for new writing in England. This year's writer-in-residence is Harwant Bains.

Royal Exchange Theatre Company

St Ann's Square, Manchester M2 7DH
☎061–833 9333

Contact *Michael Fox* (Literary Manager)

FOUNDED 1976. The Royal Exchange has developed a New Writing Policy, which they find is attracting a younger audience to the theatre. They produce English and foreign classics, modern classics, adaptations, as well as new musicals and plays by young dramatists like Jeff Noon and Iain Heggie. The Royal Exchange receives up to 500 scripts a year, which are read by Michael Fox with a team of readers. Only a tiny percentage is suitable, but opportunities also exist for rehearsed readings, workshops and consultation on new work of promise. Currently there is one writer-in-residence, and a number of plays are commissioned each year. At the time of going to press there is some doubt over the future of the **Mobil Playwriting Competition.**

Royal Shakespeare Company

Barbican Centre, London EC2Y 8DS
☎01–628 3351   Fax 01–628 6247

Contact *Colin Chambers* (Literary Manager)

The literary department at the RSC, headed by Colin Chambers, receives around 500 unsolicited mss a year of which 98 per cent are totally unsuitable. But the RSC is interested in new work. The Pit in London and The Other Place in Stratford are new writing venues and roughly a quarter of the company's total output is new work. This, however, is generally commissioned and unsolicited offerings from unknowns are rarely successful. Bear in mind that they are *not* interested in straightforwardly biographical plays (they get an awful lot of Lives of Elizabeth I) or singlemindedly topical writing and have no use for reworkings of Shakespeare. They don't generally welcome musicals and particularly not rewritings of *Kiss Me Kate* or *Les Misérables* (these have arrived by the sackful of late). There is, they find, a tendency among playwrights to assume that because the RSC have done a play once, they're in the market for more of the same. Usually the reverse is true, and it's wise to check whether a subject has been covered previously before submitting mss. The RSC doesn't generally hold rehearsed readings and workshops – their 'Early Stages' series (held early in 1987) is unlikely to become a regular event.

7:84 Theatre Company, Scotland

31 Albany Street, Edinburgh EH1 3QN
☎031–557 2442

Contact *John Haswell* (Associate Artistic Director)

Interested in scripts 'that show an awareness of reality in the 1980s, with particular reference to working-class life in Scotland, and the varied culture that this implies'. Past productions have included *Men Should Weep*, Ena Lamont Stewart; *There Is a Happy Land*, John McGrath; *The Incredible Brechin Beetle Bug*, Mat McGinn; *The Albannach*, adapted by John McGrath. At the time of going to press it was announced that the company had lost its Arts Council grant.

Stanley Sher Enterprises Ltd

28 Oakhampton Court, Park Avenue,
Roundhay, Leeds LS8 2JK
☎0532 731348

Contact *Stanley Sher*

FOUNDED 1962. Produce plays for a family audience: pantomime and popular theatre, plus children's productions. Unsolicited mss welcome.

Soho Poly Theatre

16 Ridinghouse Street, London W1P 7PB
☎01–580 6982

Contact *Tony Craze* (Script Consultant)

A new writing theatre, which presented its first revival for some years in 1987. The system for dealing with unsolicited mss is as follows: scripts go out to a team of readers; those they find interesting are passed on to Tony Craze, who invites writers of promise to his Writers' Workshops. An expansion of the workshop programme is under way. In addition, there is an annual three-week-long workshop especially for young writers (Blue Prints, held in the spring). This is designed to help young and inexperienced writers to develop their ideas in the professional environment. Those interested (aged between 16–25) should send a one-page proposal for a play and a few details about themselves. The Soho Poly produces around six shows a year. Output has included *Releevo*,

David Spencer (winner of the Verity Bargate Award 1986); *The Last Waltz*, Gillian Richmond.

SRO Productions Ltd

c/o Freedman Panter Associates, 2nd Floor,
Russell Chambers, The Piazza,
Covent Garden, London WC2E 8AA
☎01–240 9891

Contact *A. Stirling*

Produce theatre aimed at Everyman: past productions include *Once a Catholic, Candida, A Nightingale Sang, The Streets of London, Born in the Gardens, Beecham, Are You Now Or Have You Ever Been?* Unsolicited mss welcome. 'Delighted to read new or experienced authors; particularly the former, who must write the play as they wish to express themselves, not in the way which they think will be most acceptable to budget-conscious producers – we can always tailor the cloth later!'

Barrie Stacey Productions/Santa Fe Productions Ltd

Flat 8, 132 Charing Cross Road,
London WC2H 0LA
☎01–836 6220/4128

Contact *Barrie Stacey*

The company is now setting up tours of various subjects, some Barrie Stacey's, some other writers'. Also always interested in two- or three-handers for production. Also film synopses.

Stoll Moss Theatres Ltd

Cranbourn Mansions,
Cranbourn Street, London WC2H 7AG
☎01–437 2274
Telex 296882   Fax 01–434 1217

Contact *Louis Benjamin*

One of the most influential theatrical empires, with 12 theatres including the Globe, Lyric, Apollo and Queens in Shaftesbury Avenue. These tend to be the theatres which host straight plays, whereas Her Majesty's and the Palladium tend to be musical venues. Recent plays have included *Up on the Roof*, and *The House of Bernarda Alba*. Less recently, *Singin' in the Rain*. *Barnum* and *La Cage Aux Folles*. Louis Benjamin comments that after some years as theatre managers, in which other producers brought their own shows into Stoll Moss theatres, the group is now about to move into a new phase. This will mean a return to production, and a policy, still in the planning stage, of considering all kinds of subjects and treatments: 'The size of our operation means we are likely to have a slot for anything which interests us.' The policy will be to read everything, and to reply thoughtfully 'rather than sending a bland rejection note'. Well-constructed synopses and letters are more likely to be considered than finished mss: 'we are looking into the possibility of commissioning plays where we consider the talent merits it'. Though letters/scripts should be addressed to Louis Benjamin, they are passed on to one of his staff for consideration.

Swan Theatre

The Moors, Worcester WR1 3EF
☎0905 726969

Contact *Pat Trueman* (Artistic Director)

Pat Trueman took over from John Ginman as artistic director in May 1988 and at the time of going to press her policy on new writing was unknown, although the theatre tries to produce one new play each season in the main house (the Studio Theatre is currently not in use). Euan Smith was writer-in-residence for part of 1988 but it is not known if this is to be a regular appointment. Local writers' workshops will continue to be run by the director.

Swansea Little Theatre Ltd

Dylan Thomas Theatre, Maritime Quarter, 7 Gloucester Place, Swansea SA1 1TY
☎0792 473238

Contact *Mrs F. Davies* (Secretary)

Produce Anglo-Welsh plays. Repertoire ranges from Shakespeare to family comedies. Include one new play each season as a matter of policy. A panel of reader/producers considers new scripts.

Bob Swash Ltd

44 Lonsdale Square, London N1 1EW
☎01–607 8291

Contact *Bob Swash*

In 1987, output included *One for the Road* and *Shirley Valentine*, both by Willy Russell; and *Evita* on tour. New plays welcome – finished scripts only. 'We've found commissioning doesn't work . . . interesting novelists rarely produce workable plays.'

Talbot Hay Productions Ltd

14 Langley Street, London WC2H 9JH
☎01–379 4322

Contact *Philip Talbot, Pamela Hay*

West End and touring shows. Current production: *The Fifteen Streets*, Catherine Cookson. Unsolicited mss welcome, 'typed and bound please!'

H.M. Tennent Ltd

Globe Theatre, Shaftesbury Avenue, London W1V 7HD
☎01–437 3647

Contact *Anne Rawsthorne* (General Manager)

London's oldest established theatre production company, and among the most prolific. Recent productions have included *A Month of Sundays*, Bob Larbey; *Number One*, adapted by Michael Frayn; and *Ducking Out*, adapted by Mile Stott. Haven't produced work by new writers for some time, but do try out new plays and hope to encourage playwrights of promise. Very interested to read new work of all kinds.

Theatr Clwyd

County Civic Centre, Mold, Clwyd CH7 1YA
☎0352 56331

Contact *Toby Robertson* (Artistic Director)

Lively theatre company with a policy of genuine encouragement as far as new writing is concerned. All scripts are passed on to an in-house reader – scripts are preferred to synopses and ideas. Open-minded on subjects – musicals and children's are considered. New work has included *Barnaby and the Old Boys*, Keith Baxter; *Self Portrait*, Sheila Yeger.

Theatre Foundry

The Drama Centre, Slater Street, Darlaston, West Midlands WS10 8EE
☎021–526 6947

Contact *Jeremy Bell* (Artistic Director)

FOUNDED 1982. Small-scale touring company which plays to community audiences in boroughs of Walsall and Dudley, with increasing emphasis on working-class audiences and neighbourhood groups. 'Our policy is to encourage and advance new writing whenever possible – especially on material about, or from, writers based in the Black Country.' Welcome unsolicited mss. Recent productions include *Trafford Tanzi*, Clare Luckham; *Red Devils*, Debbie Horsfield; *Mother Courage* and *The Good Person of Setzuan*, Brecht; *How I Got to Spain*, *ABC* and *Drink the Mercury*, David Holman; *Some Kind of Hero* and *It's Bobby's Job*, Les Smith; *Crossing the Line*, Stephen Bill.

Theatre of Comedy Company

219 Shaftesbury Avenue, London WC2H 8EL
☎01–925 2608

Contact *Leslie Lawton* (Artistic Co-ordinator)

FOUNDED 1983 to produce new work, and regard themselves as a good bet for new plays, though since then most of the new work has been by Ray Cooney, one of the most prolific and successful of West End comedy writers. Interested in strong comedy in the widest sense – Chekov comes under the definition. No unsolicited mss (there's a serious backlog of scripts) but letters and synopses are considered.

Theatre Projects Associates Ltd

14 Langley Street, London WC2H 9JH
☎01–240 5411   Telex 27522

Contact *Pamela Hay*

West End and touring shows. Past productions have included *Edward II*, *Richard II*, *She Stoops to Conquer*, *I'm Not Rappaport*, *Cabaret*, *Fiddler on the Roof*, *A Little Night Music*. Unsolicited mss welcome, provided they are 'well written and interesting'.

Theatre Royal Stratford East

Gerry Raffles Square, London E15 1BN
☎01–534 7374

Contact *Jeff Teare* (Associate Director)

Lively east London theatre catering for a very mixed audience, both local and London-wide. A good bet for new work – unsolicited mss are welcome 'and we read them – eventually!' Produce new plays, musicals, classics, youth theatre, plus local community plays/events. Hosts to the London Playwrights Festival and its workshop.

Tigerwise Theatrical Management

71 St Georges Square, London SW1V 3QN
☎01–828 3349

Contact *Anthony Smee*

Perhaps best known as concert and dance promoters (they handle the touring drumming groups Kodo, Samul Nori, and The Netherlands Dance Theatre). Although they admit to also acting as producers, they are not keen to specify of what. 'We will consider anything, including straight theatre, musicals and children's. . . .' No unsolicited mss; letters and synopses in the first instance.

Traverse Theatre

112 West Bow, Grassmarket,
Edinburgh EH1 2HH
☎031–226 2633

Contact *Jane Ellis*

The Traverse is the most well-known theatre in Scotland for new writing; indeed it has a policy of putting on nothing but new work, by new writers. They also have a strong international programme of work in translation and visiting companies. Recent productions include *Man to Man*, Manfred Karge; *Kathie & the Hippopotamus*, Mario Vargas Losa; *Losing Venice, Lucy's Play* and *Playing with Fire*, all by John Clifford. Jane Ellis heads a reading panel who read and comment upon every script received. Unsolicited mss welcome.

Andrew Treagus Associates Ltd

18/19 Warwick Street, London W1V 5RB
☎01–734 4274
Telex 263899   Fax 01–434 4478

Contact *Andrew Treagus*

Produce shows for a London and provincial audience 'used mainly to commercial fare', from large-scale musicals to small-scale straight plays. Unsolicited mss are welcome. Policy of encouraging new writing with possible play readings, or fringe productions of their work.

Trends Management

54 Lisson Street, London NW1 6ST
☎01–723 8001

Theatre production is just one facet of their work (also act as an agency and have an extensive wardrobe department for the designing, making and hiring of costumes). Product on the light entertainment side – particularly revues and pantomime. Provide most material for these themselves; shows like *Sweet Charity* and *Palm Beach Revue*. No unsolicited mss.

Tricycle Theatre

269 Kilburn High Road, London NW6 7JR
☎01–372 6611

Contact *Kerry Crabbe*

FOUNDED 1980. Destroyed by fire in 1987. Re-opening at the beginning of 1989. Audiences culturally very mixed, both ethnically and in class. Encourage new writing from ethnic minorities. Look for a strong narrative drive with popular appeal. Not 'studio' plays. Run workshops for writers. Recent productions include *Playboy of the West Indies, Great White Hope, The Hostage, Trinidad Sisters*.

Triumph Theatre Productions

Suite 4, Waldorf Chambers,
11 Aldwych, London WC2B 4DA
☎01–836 0187

Contacts *Duncan Weldon, Peter Wilkins*

A major producer of West End and touring shows, mostly revivals but with a regular output of new work. Recent productions have included co-producing *Kiss Me Kate* at the Old Vic; *Caught in the Act; You Never Can Tell; The Deep Blue Sea*; and *A Touch of the Poet*; but also new work like *Melon*, Simon Gray; *A Piece of My Mind*, Peter Nichols. New work tends to be by established playwrights, but the company are always on the look-out for talented newcomers. They receive a great many unsolicited mss 'and we read them all'. Letters and synopses preferred in the first instance.

Tyne Theatre Company

Tyne Theatre and Opera House, Westgate Road, Newcastle upon Tyne NE1 4AG
☎091–232 3366

Contact *Andrew McKinnon* (Artistic Director and Chief Executive)

The Tyne Theatre Company is a newly formed production company based in the Tyne Theatre, a large Victorian lyric theatre in the heart of the city. New writing strategies are still in the process of formulation, but scripts will continue to be read. There is as yet no literary manager, though it is hoped that an appointment can be made by the beginning of 1989. The reading of scripts is therefore likely to be a fairly lengthy process. The company plans to involve itself in the production of new work, including co-productions with other local companies. Writers' workshops are likely to be arranged and these will be announced separately.

Umbrella Theatre

46a Compton Avenue,
Brighton, East Sussex BN1 3PS
☎0273 775354

Contact *David Lavender*

Theatre for 'a discerning, intelligent, and adventurous' audience. Particularly interested in new writing from abroad and welcome translations as well as scripts in their original language. Past productions include *Komiker Kaberett*, based on the work of Karl Valentin (Germany); *Angel Knife*, Jean Sigrid (Belgium); *Joseph and Mary*, Peter Turrini (Austria); *On the Ruins of Carthage*, René Kalisky (Belgium); *Cabaret Camique*, based on the writings of French humourist Pierre-Henri Cami; *The World of Café Waiters*, and *Boum! Voila!*, two shows based on original writings for the early French cabaret. Unsolicited mss welcome.

Charles Vance

83 George Street, London W1H 5PL
☎01–486 1732

Contact *Charles Vance*

In the market for small-scale touring productions and summer season plays, although they haven't done much lately, as Charles Vance has been busy editing *Amateur Stage*. In 1985, tours of *Jane Eyre* and *Mr Cinders*, 4 pantomimes in 1986, and summer season and pantomimes in 1987. They don't commission plays, and don't often do new work, though writing of promise stands a good chance of being passed on to someone who does.

W & J Theatrical Enterprises Ltd

51a Oakwood Road, London NW11 6RJ
☎01–458 1608

Contact *W.D. Roberton*

Represent actors and comedians as theatrical agents, direct farces, and write and direct pantomimes. Unsolicited mss are welcome.

John Wallbank Associates Ltd

St Martin's Theatre, West Street,
London WC2N 3NH
☎01–379 5665

Contact *John Wallbank*

Plays and musicals suitable for West End production and occasionally touring. New writing is welcome.

The Warehouse Theatre Croydon

Dingwall Road, Croydon CR0 2NF
☎01–681 1257

Contact *Kevin Hood* (Literary Manager)

A new writing theatre on a small scale, seating around 120, producing six new plays a year. Recent productions have included *Upside Down at the Bottom of the World*, David Allen; *Children of the Dust*, Anne Aylor; *Sinners and Saints*, James Mundy (co-production with **Soho Poly**). Hold a playwriting festival each autumn (South London Playwriting Festival) and aim in general to be the new writing theatre of South London. Receive between two and five unsolicited scripts a day. It can take a long time for promising mss to come to anything because the theatre is committed so far in advance – nine months, in some cases.

Watermill Theatre

Bagnor, Newbury, Berks. RG16 8AE
☎0635 45834

Contact *Jill Fraser*

The Watermill occasionally put on new work. Recent new plays include *The Killing Time* by Euan Smith (who has written for them before) and, in 1985, Fay Weldon's *Woodworm*, as well as regular new Christmas shows for young children aged between 5 and 12 and their families. In 1987, *The Quest for the Rose and the Ring*, a musical adventure story by Euan Smith and Peter Murray. Plans for 1988 include a new farce by Christopher Lillicrap and Jonathan Izard entitled *My Wife Whatsername*.

Westminster Productions Ltd

Westminster Theatre, Palace Street,
London SW1E 5JB
☎01–834 7882

Contact *Hugh Steadman Williams* (Artistic Director)

FOUNDED 1961. Encourages new writing 'which explores fundamental spiritual and moral values in a contemporary and relevant context'. Have produced 28 West End productions/co-productions, five feature films and three video dramas, plus school productions. Plays range from children's/family shows like *The Lion, The Witch and The Wardrobe* to classics like *An Inspector Calls*, plus good new plays. An outline or synopsis in the first instance is essential.

Whirligig Theatre

14 Belvedere Drive,
Wimbledon, London SW19 7BY
☎01–947 1732

Contact *David Wood*

Produce one play a year, which tends to be a musical play for children, for primary school audiences and weekend family groups. All new mss should exploit the theatrical nature of children's tastes. Previous productions have included: *The Plotters of Cabbage Patch Corner; The Ideal Gnome Expedition; The Gingerbread Man; The Old Man of Lochnagar*. David Wood may offer a writing course in the near future, in conjunction with the **British Theatre Association**.

Michael White

13 Duke Street St James's,
London SW1Y 6DB
☎01–839 3971   Fax 01–839 3836

Contact *Michael White*

Contributions are passed by Michael White to a script reader for consideration. Recent productions by this high-output company have included *On Your Toes, Chorus Line*.

Winged Horse Touring Productions

6 The Old Schoolhouse,
1 Dean Path, Edinburgh EH4 3BG
☎031–226 3520

Contact *John Carnegie* (Artistic Director)

FOUNDED 1979. Touring company which plays to a wide variety of diverse audiences in urban and rural venues throughout Scotland and northern England. New plays are the core of their output and are by Scottish-based writers (both established and new) and narrative-based. No unsolicited mss. Receive 'piles' of scripts but tend to seek out authors to commission. However, will consider synopsis with sample dialogue. Recent productions include *Hecuba*, Stewart Conn; *Tales of an Island People*, Robin Munro; *Blood and Ice*, Liz Lochhead.

York Theatre Royal

St Leonard's Place, York YO1 2HD
☎0904 651862

Contact *Jonathan Petherbridge* (Artistic Director)

Recent productions have included *Charley's Aunt; The American Clock; Pride and Prejudice; Taking Steps; Groping for Words; As You Like It; The Country Wife; The Island of Doctor Moreau; Peter Pan*. Jonathan Petherbridge, formerly at the Duke's Playhouse, Lancaster, took over from Andrew McKinnon as Artistic Director in the spring of 1988. He is planning to set up a reader network but stresses that writers who sent mss to him at Lancaster should not now send them to York. He has an 'energetic' policy on new writing. Unsolicited mss welcome.

US Publishers

Abingdon Press

201 Eighth Avenue S, Box 801,
Nashville, TN 37202
☎0101 615 749 6301

Contact *Michael E. Lawrence* (Trade Books),
Davis Perkins (Reference/Academic Books),
Etta Wilson (Children's Books)

Publishes fiction (children's books only);
non-fiction; religious (lay and professional);
children's religious books; and academic
texts. Average 100 titles a year. Approach in
writing with synopsis only.

Harry N. Abrams Inc.

100 Fifth Avenue, New York, NY 10011
☎0101 212 206 7715
Telex 23–4772   Cable ABRAMBOOK

Editor-in-chief *Paul Gottlieb*

Subsidiary of Times Mirror Co. *Publishes* art,
nature, science, outdoor recreation; no fiction. Average 65 titles a year. Submit completed mss (no dot matrix).

Academic Press Inc.

1250 Sixth Avenue, San Diego, CA 92101
☎0101 619 231 6616

Part of **Harcourt Brace Jovanovich** *Publishes* scientific books and journals.

Addison-Wesley Publishing Co. Inc.

General Books Division, Jacob Way,
Reading MA 01867
☎0101 617 944 3700
Telex 94–9416   Cable ADIWES

Publisher *David Miller*

Publishes biography, business/economics,
health, how-to, photography, politics, psychology and science: also 'tools for living'
books on finance, health, education and
parenting 'by people well known and respec-
ted in their field.' No fiction. Average 50
titles a year. Approach in writing or phone
call in first instance, then submit synopsis
and one sample chapter.

University of Alabama Press

Box 2877, University, AL 35468

Director *Malcolm MacDonald*

Publishes academic books only. 40 titles a
year.

Amacom

135 West 50th Street, New York, NY 10020
☎0101 212 586 8100

Contact *Weldon P. Rackley*

Publishing division of American Management Associations
Publishes management books.

Arbor House

235 E. 45th Street, New York, NY 10017
☎0101 212 599 3131/687 9855
Cable ARBORPUB

Editor-in-chief *Ann Harris*

Publishes fiction, romance, science fiction,
fantasy, adventure, suspense. Non-fiction —
autobiography, cookery books, how-to, self-
help; including Americana, art, business,

economics, health, history, politics, psychology, recreation. Non-fiction, approach editors in writing in first instance. Fiction, write or submit synopsis and sample chapters.

University of Arizona Press

1615 E. Speedway, Tucson, AZ 85719
☎0101 602 621 1441

Director *Stephen Cox*
Editor-in-chief *Gregory McNamee*

FOUNDED 1959. Academic non-fiction only, particularly with a regional-cultural link. Average 40 titles a year.

Associated Book Publishers Inc./ Methuen Inc.

Box 657, Scottsdale AZ, 85261–5657
☎0101 602 837 9388

Editor *Ivan Kapetanovic*

Publishes wide range of school textbooks and bibliographies, including non-fiction translations. Average three to four titles a year. No length requirement for mss, but artwork/photos should be submitted as part of package.

Atheneum Publishers

115 Fifth Avenue, New York, NY 10003
☎0101 212 614 1300

Editor-in-Chief *Thomas A. Stewart*

Publishes general trade material – politics, history, cookery, sports and general non-fiction. (Not less than 40,000 words.) No fiction. Write or submit synopsis and sample chapter.

Atlantic Monthly Press

19 Union Square West, New York, NY 10003
☎0101 212 645 4462

Editor-in-Chief *Gary Fisketjon*

Publishes fiction: general; poetry; non-fiction: general. Average 60 titles a year. Approach in writing, submitting sample chapter (especially fiction).

TITLES *Tupelo Nights*, John Ed Bradley; *Coming First*, Paul Bryers; *How to Keep the Children You Love Off Drugs*, Ken Barun and Philip Bashe; *The Singing*, Theron Raines; *The Ginger Man*, J.P. Donleavy; *Our Hollywood*, David Strick.

Avon Books

105 Madison Avenue, New York, NY 10016
☎0101 212 481 5606

Editor-in-chief *Susanne Jaffee*

Publishes general fiction and general non-fiction, including children's books, no textbooks. Average 300 titles a year. Submit synopsis and first three chapters (fiction).

Ballantine/DelRey/Fawcett Books

201 E. 50th Street, New York, NY 10022
☎0101 212 751 2600

Executive Editor (science fiction/fantasy) *Owen Locke* Trade Books *Joelle Delbourgo* Senior Editor, Ballantine *Ann La-Farge* Senior Editor, Fawcett *Barbara Dicks*

Publishes fiction – general fiction, science fiction and fantasy. No poetry. Non-fiction – general. (Mss not less than 50,000 words.) Average 700 titles a year.

Bantam Books Inc.

666 Fifth Avenue, New York, NY 10103
☎0101 212 765 6500
Cable BANTAMBOOK NY

President/Publisher/Editor-in-Chief *Linda Grey*
Vice-President/Editor-in-Chief *(adult fiction and non-fiction) Steve Rubin*

A division of the Bantam Doubleday Dell Publishing Group Inc. *Publishes* general fiction and children's books. Category books: mysteries, westerns, romance, war books, science fiction. No poetry or general non-fiction. No queries or unsolicited mss.

IMPRINTS
Spectra (science fiction), **New Age**, **Bantam New Fiction** (original fiction in trade paperback).

Beacon Press

Beacon Street, Boston, MA 02108
☎0101 617 742 2110   Cable BEAPRESS

Director *Wendy J. Strothman*

Publishes general non-fiction. No fiction or poetry. Average 50 titles a year. Approach in writing or submit synopsis and sample chapters with International Reply Coupons to **Editorial Assistant** *Amy Ellis*.

Beaufort Books Inc.

9 E. 40th Street, New York, NY 10016
☎0101 212 685 8588

Editor-in-Chief *Susan Suffes*

Publishes fiction – mystery, thriller, contemporary and literary novels, including translations from French (no science fiction or first novels). General non-fiction. Average 40–50 titles a year. Write or submit complete mss (fiction). Write or submit synopsis and three sample chapters or completed mss (non-fiction).

Berkley Publishing Group

200 Madison Avenue, New York, NY 10016
☎0101 212 686 9820

Editor-in-Chief *Ed Breslin*

IMPRINTS
Publishers of **Berkley, Berkley Trade Paperbacks, Jove, Charter, Second Chance at Love, Pacer** and **Ace Science Fiction.**

Publishes general fiction, including young adult; non-fiction: 'how to', inspirational, family life, philosophy and nutrition. Average 900 titles a year. Submit synopsis and first three chapters (for **Ace Science Fiction** only). No unsolicited mss.

University of California Press

2120 Berkeley Way, Berkeley, CA 94720

Director *James H. Clark*

Publishes non-fiction, generally by academics. Also fiction and poetry, but only in translation. Average 225 titles in 1987. Preliminary letter with outline preferred.

Carolrhoda Books Inc.

241 First Avenue North,
Minneapolis, MN 55401
☎0101 612 332 3345

Publishes children's books. Picture books, nature, biographies, history, beginning readers, world cultures, photo essays.

University of Chicago Press

5801 South Ellis Avenue, Chicago, IL 60637
☎0101 312 702 7748

Publishes academic non-fiction only.

Chronicle Books

275 Fifth Street, San Francisco, CA 94103
☎0101 415 777 7240

Editor *Jay Schaefer* **Children's Book Editor** *Victoria Rock*

Publishes non-fiction and fiction, visual books, children's books. Averages 60 titles a year. Query or submit synopsis and sample chapters. Must enclose International Reply Coupon and envelope for response.

Citadel Press

120 Enterprise Avenue, Secaucus, NJ 07094
☎0101 212 736 0007

Editorial Director *Allan J. Wilson*

Publishes limited fiction. Biography, film, psychology, humour and history. No poetry, religion or politics. Write initially, before submitting synopsis and three sample chapters.

Contemporary Books

180 North Michigan Avenue,
Chicago, IL 60601
☎0101 312 782 9181

Editors *Nancy Crossman, Shari Lesser Wenk, Ilyce Glink, Susan Bontrock, Stacy Prince, Bernie Shir-Cliff*

Publishes broad range of general non-fiction, professional and school test preparation, adult education books and sports.

Coward McCann Inc.

200 Madison Avenue, New York, NY 10016
☎0101 212 576 8900

Publisher *Phyllis Grann*
Editor-in-chief (children's) *Refra Wilkin*

Part of the Putnams Publishing Group.

Publishes general books, children's, religious, biography, mystery, history. Major fiction publisher.

Crown Publishers Inc.

225 Park Avenue South,
New York, NY 10003
☎0101 212 254 1600

IMPRINTS
Include **Clarkson Potter, Arlington House, Harmony** and **Julian Press.**

Publishes non-fiction only: Americana, animals, art, biography, children's, cookery, health, history, hobbies, how-to, humour, music, nature, philosophy, photography, politics, psychology, recreation, reference, science, self-help and sport. Average 250 titles a year. Preliminary letter essential.

Jonathan David Publishers

68–22 Eliot Avenue,
Middle Village, NY 11379
☎0101 718 456 8611

Editor-in-chief *Alfred J. Kolatch*

Publishes general adult non-fiction, including cookery, self-help and sport. Average 25–30 titles a year. Approach in writing in first instance.

Dell Publishing

666 Fifth Avenue, New York, NY 10103
☎0101 212 832 7300
Telex 23–8781 DELL   Cables DELL PUB

A division of Bantam Doubleday Dell Publishing Group, Inc.

IMPRINTS
Include **Dell, Delacorte Press, Delta Books, Dell Trade Paperbacks, Laurel Delacorte Press** books for young readers, **Yearling** and **Laurel Leaf.**

Publishes (Make sure query is directed to right department.) Fiction: **Delacorte** – topnotch commercial fiction; **Dell** – mass market paperbacks, rarely original fiction, sagas, romance, adventure, suspense, horror and war: **Delta** – interested in original fiction. **Dell Trade** interested in non-fiction and regional cookbooks. **Yearling** and **Laurel Leaf** – children and young adults. Average of 500 titles a year. Unsolicited mss: do not send mss, sample chapters or art work; do not register, certify or insure your letter; send only a four-page synopsis with covering letter stating previous work published or relevant experience.

Dodd, Mead & Co.

79 Fifth Avenue, New York, NY 10003
☎0101 212 627 8444   Cable DODD NY

Managing Editor *Chris Fortunato*
Director of Children's books *Jo Ann Daly*

Publishes fiction – literary novels, mysteries, romantic suspense; non-fiction – biography, popular science, sports, music. Very rarely poetry, children's books. Average 200 titles a year. Write for permission before submitting mss to editorial department (60,000–100,000 words for adult books, 1500–75,000 for children's books).

Doubleday

666 Fifth Avenue, New York, NY 10103
☎0101 212 765 6500

A division of Bantam Doubleday Dell Group, Inc. Can only consider fiction for mystery/suspense, science fiction and romance. Send complete mss (60,000–80,000 words) to **Crime Club Editor, Foundation Editor** for science fiction, or **Loveswept Romance Editor.**

Dow Jones Irwin

1818 Ridge Road, Homewood, IL 60430
☎0101 312 798 6000

Editor-in-Chief *Richard J. Staron*

Publishes non-fiction only, on business and financial subjects. Write with outline. Average 100 titles a year; latest include Stan Weinstein's *Secrets For Profiting in Bull & Bear Markets* and *Street Smart Real Estate Investing*.

Farrar, Straus & Giroux Inc.

19 Union Square West, New York, NY 10003
☎0101 212 741 6900

Children's Editors *Stephen Roxburgh, Margaret Ferguson*

Publishes fiction, picture books and novels for children and young adults. Limited number of non-fiction titles. Approximately 100 titles each year.

TITLES *The Bonfire of the Vanities*, Tom Wolfe; *Presumed Innocent*, Scott Thurow. Submit synopsis and sample chapters (artwork/photographs as part of package).

David R. Godine

Horticultural Hall,
300 Massachusetts Avenue,
Boston, MA 02115
☎0101 617 536 0761
Telex 3794227 GODIN

Publishes fiction and non-fiction. Photography, art, history, natural history, children's, poetry, typography and graphic art. 47 titles in 1987. 380 titles in print.

Lists published under Godine imprint: **Nonpareil Books** paperbacks licensed for trade paperback line; **Godine Storytellers** children's books issued in paperback format.

Greenwood Press

Box 5007, Westport, CT 06881
☎0101 203 226 3571

Publishes non-fiction reference books, professional books in business and law, scholarly books (the **Praeger** imprint). Average 600 titles a year. Preliminary letter essential, with synopsis and sample chapter.

Grove Press Inc.

920 Broadway, New York, NY 10010
☎0101 212 529 3600

Contact *Fred Jordan*

Publishes general fiction and non-fiction.

Harcourt Brace Jovanovich

Orlando, Florida 32887
☎0101 305 345 2760

Takeover bid by Robert Maxwell repelled summer 1987 – but the predator has not lost his appetite.

Publishes fiction and non-fiction. Non-fiction: educational, textbooks, biography, travel, children's, science travel, current affairs, history. Also poetry.

Harper & Row Publishers Inc.

East Washington Square,
Philadelphia, PA 19105
☎0101 215 238 4400

Chief Executive *George Craig*

Jointly owned by Collins and News International. *Publishes* general fiction and non-fiction. Average 300 titles a year. No unsolicited mss or queries.

Harvard University Press

79 Garden Street, Cambridge, MA 02138
☎0101 617 495 2600   Telex 92–1484

Editor-in-chief *Maud Wilcox*

Publishes Scholarly non-fiction only. Average 120 titles a year. Free book catalogue and mss guidelines.

D. C. Heath & Co.

125 Spring Street, Lexington, MA 02173
☎0101 617 862 6650

Editors-in-chief (College division) *Barbara Piercecchi*, (Lexington books) *Robert Bovenschule*, (School division) *Roger Rogalin*

Publishes textbooks, professional, scholarly, and software. Textbooks at college level in all subjects. Average 300 titles a year. Preliminary letter essential.

Hippocrene Books Inc.
171 Madison Avenue, New York, NY 10016
☎0101 212 685 4371

Publishes general non-fiction, and reference books, particularly strong on maps and travel guides. No fiction.

Holiday House Inc.
18 E. 53rd Street, New York, NY 10022
☎0101 212 688 0085

Vice-President and Editor-in-Chief *Margery Cuyler*

Publishes children's general fiction and non-fiction (pre-school to secondary school). Average 35–40 titles a year. Submit synopsis and three sample chapters or complete ms, without art work.

Houghton Mifflin Co.
2 Park Street, Boston, MA 02108
☎0101 617 725 5000
Telex 94–0959   Cables HOUGHTON

Director *Joseph Kanon*

Publishes general fiction including poetry; general non-fiction including 'how to' and self help. Average 110 titles a year. Approach in writing in the first instance.

University of Illinois Press
54 E. Gregory, Champaign, IL 61820
☎0101 217 333 0950

Editorial Director *Richard L. Wentworth*

Publishes both fiction and non-fiction. Fiction: ethnic, experimental, mainstream, short story collections only, no novels. Non-fiction: scholarly and reference books – particularly in the humanities, and Americana. Average 90 titles a year. Letter first.

Indiana University Press
10th & Morton Streets,
Bloomington, IN 47405
☎0101 812 337 4203

Director *John Gallman*

Publishes scholarly non-fiction. Especially interested in non-fiction works in women's studies, Soviet and East European studies, music, African studies, and Jewish studies. Average 125 titles a year. Approach in writing or submit synopsis and sample chapters.

Alfred A. Knopf Inc.
201 E. 50th Street, New York, NY 10022
☎0101 212 751 2600

Senior Editor *Ashbel Green* **Children's Book Editor** *Ms Frances Foster*

Publishes fiction (of literary merit); non-fiction: including books of scholarly merit. Published 204 titles in 1986. Submit complete ms (fiction 30,000–150,000 words). Write in first instance for non-fiction (ms should be 40,000–150,000 words).

Lerner Publications Co.
241 First Avenue North,
Minneapolis, MN 55401
☎0101 612 332 3345

Publishes books for children and young adults. Geography, social issues, biographies, history, economics, ethnic studies, science, nature, activities, hi-lo, sports, some fiction. The *Visual Geography Series* is a new addition.

Little, Brown & Co. Inc.
34 Beacon Street, Boston, MA 02108
☎0101 617 227 0730   Telex 94–0928

Contact *Editorial Department* (Trade Division)

Publishes contemporary popular fiction as well as literary fiction; limited poetry list usually by recognised poets. Non-fiction: how-to, distinctive cookbooks, biographies, history, science and sports. Average 100 + titles a year. Mss accepted only from published authors. Write or submit synopsis and sample chapters for both fiction and non-fiction – including artwork in the non-fiction package.

May soon follow **Simon & Schuster** in opening a UK subsidiary.

Longman Inc.
95 Church Street, White Plains, NY 10601
☎0101 914 993 5000

Publishes primary, secondary, tertiary and professional textbooks. No trade, art or children's books. Average 200 titles a year.

Louisiana State University Press
Baton Rouge, LA 70803
☎0101 504 388 6618

Associate Director and Executive Editor *Beverly Jarrett*

Publishes Fiction: 2 novels, 2 short story collections and 6 volumes of poetry a year. Non-fiction: southern history, French history, southern literary criticism, American literary criticism, political philosophy, and some Latin American studies. Average 60 titles a year. Send International Reply Coupons for ms guidelines.

Lyle Stuart Inc.
120 Enterprise Avenue, Secaucus, NJ 07094
☎0101 201 866 0490/212 736 1141

Editor-in-Chief *Mario Sartori*

Publishes both fiction and non-fiction: biography, books of gay and lesbian interest, how-to books, illustrated and self help. Average 100 titles a year. Unsolicited mss not

considered – write in first instance. Strong, even controversial ideas welcome.

McGraw-Hill Book Co.
College Division,
1221 Avenue of the Americas,
New York, NY 10020
☎0101 212 512 2000

Editor-in-Chief (Social Sciences & Humanities) *Phillip A. Butcher* (Science, Mathematics & Nursing) *Anne Duffy* (Business, Economics & Data Processing) *S. Kaye Pace* (Engineering & Computer Science) *Eric Muson*

Publishes no fiction. Non-fiction: college textbooks (social, business and physical sciences, and engineering).

David McKay Co. Inc.
2 Park Avenue, New York, NY 10016
☎0101 212 340 9800

Publisher *Richard T. Scott*

Average five titles a year. No unsolicited mss or proposals considered or acknowledged.

Macmillan Publishing Company
Children's Book Department,
866 Third Avenue, New York, NY 10022
☎0101 212 702 2000

Publishes children's fiction and non-fiction. Average 60 titles a year.

Merrill Publishing Co.
1300 Alum Creek Drive,
Columbus, OH 43216
☎0101 614 890 1111

Editor-in-Chief *Steve Clapp* (education) *Franklin Lewis (college)*

Parent company Bell & Howell.
Education Division *publishes* texts, workbooks and software in science, language, arts, mathematics and social studies for school level. College Division publishes higher level books and materials in hum-

anities, business, mathematics, science and technology. Average 400 titles a year. Synopsis and three sample chapters.

University of Missouri Press
200 Lewis Hall, Columbia, MO 65211
☎0101 314 882 7641

Director *Edward King*

Fiction and academic non-fiction. Fiction, drama and poetry only considered in February and March of odd-numbered years through Breakthrough Contest. Letter essential. Average 40 titles a year.

MIT Press
28 Carleton Street, Cambridge, MA 02142
☎0101 617 253 1693

Acquisitions Co-ordinator *Christina Sanmartin*

Publishes no fiction. Non-fiction: technologically sophisticated books including computers, sciences, engineering, economics, architecture, linguistics and philosophy. Average 100 titles a year. Submit synopsis, academic resumé and sample chapters.

William Morrow and Co.
105 Madison Avenue, New York, NY 10016
☎0101 212 889 3050

Editor (Greenwillow Books – children's) *Susan Hirschman* **Editor (Lothrop, Lee and Shephard** – children's) *Dorothy Briley* **Editor (Morrow Junior Books)** *David Reuther* **Managing Editor (Quill** – Trade Paperback) *Allison Brown-Cerier*

Publishes fiction, including poetry. General non-fiction. Approach only in writing. No unsolicited mss or proposals, which should only be submitted through a literary agent (50,000–100,000 words).

New American Library
1633 Broadway, New York, NY 10019
☎0101 212 397 8000

Editor-in-Chief *Maureen Baron*

Publishes New work and reprints. Average 350 titles a year. Approach in writing only.

University of New Mexico Press
Journalism 220, Albuquerque, NM 87131
☎0101 505 277 2346

Director *Elizabeth C. Hadas*

Publishes scholarly and regional non-fiction only. No fiction. Average 60 titles a year.

University of North Carolina Press
Box 2288, Chapel Hill, NC 27515–2288
☎0101 919 966 3561

Editor-in-Chief *Iris Tillman Hill*

Publishes scholarly and regional trade books. No fiction. Particularly interested in American history and Southern studies. Average 60 titles a year.

North Point Press
850 Talbot Avenue, Berkeley, CA 94706
☎0101 415 527 6260

Contact *Kathleen Moses*

Hardcover and trade paperback originals; non-fiction and fiction. 30 titles in 1987.

TITLES *West with the Night*, Beryl Markham; *Ghost Dance*, Carole Maso. Mss must be accompanied by International Reply Coupons.

W. W. Norton & Company
500 Fifth Avenue, New York, NY 10110
☎0101 212 354 5500   Telex 12-7634

Managing Editor *Liz Malcolm*

Publishes general adult fiction and general non-fiction. No occult, paranormal, religious, cookbooks, arts and crafts, genre fiction (formula romances, science fiction or westerns), children's books or young adult. Average 213 titles a year. Submit synopsis and two or three sample chapters, for both fiction and non-fiction.

Ohio University Press

Scott Quad, Ohio University,
Athens, OH 45701
☎0101 614 593 1155

Director *Duane Schneider*

Publishes no fiction. General scholarly non-fiction with emphasis on nineteenth-century literature and culture, and African studies. Average 25–30 titles a year. Approach in writing in first instance.

University of Oklahoma Press

1005 Asp Avenue, Norman, OK 73019
☎0101 405 325 5111

Editor-in-Chief *John Drayton*

Publishes non-fiction only: American Indian studies, Western American history, classical studies, literary theory and criticism, women's studies. Average 50 titles a year.

Open Court Publishing Co.

Box 599, LaSalle, IL 61301
☎0101 815 223 2520

Director *Dr Andre Carus* (General Books)

Publishes no fiction: Non-fiction: scholarly books, mainly philosophy, psychology, religion, economics and science; also German and French non-fiction translations. Average 30 titles a year. Write or submit synopsis and 2–3 sample chapters and artwork/photos as part of package.

Pantheon Books

201 E. 50th Street, New York, NY 10022
☎0101 212 751 2600

Contact *Adult Editorial Department* (28th Fl.)/*Children's Department* (6th Fl.).

Publishes fiction: less than five novels a year. Some foreign fiction in translation. Non-fiction: political and social subject, emphasis on Asia, medicine, how-to books. Some children's books. Average 90 titles a year. Write in first instance concerning non-fiction, no mss accepted. No fiction queries accepted at all.

Pelican Publishing Company

1101 Monroe Street, Box 189,
Gretna, LA 70053
☎0101 504 368 1175

Assistant Editor *Dean M. Shapiro*

Publishes fiction: very limited requirement (including children's books); non-fiction: general non-fiction (especially cookbooks, travel, art, architecture, and inspirational). Average 30–40 titles a year. Write and submit mss and artwork (non-fiction); submit synopsis and sample chapters (fiction), but query preferred in the first instance. No multiple submissions. Include International Reply Coupons with all inquiries.

Persea Books Inc.

60 Madison Avenue, New York, NY 10010
☎0101 212 779 7668

Editorial *Karen Braziller*

Publishes literature, poetry, fiction, belles lettres, and women's studies.

Plenum Publishing

233 Spring Street, New York, NY 10013
☎0101 212 620 8000

Senior Editor (trade books) *Linda Greenspan Regan*

Publishes quality non-fiction for the intelligent layman and the professional. Areas include the sciences, the social sciences and the humanities.

Pocket Books

123 Avenue of the Americas,
New York, NY 10020
☎0101 212 698 7000

Publishes fiction: adult, mystery, science fiction, romance, westerns. Non-fiction: history, biography, reference and general books.

IMPRINTS
Washington Square Press – high quality mass market; **Poseidon Press** – hardcover

fiction and non-fiction. No unsolicited mss; write in the first instance.

Prentice Hall Inc. Business and Professional Books Division

Gulf & Western, Sylvan Avenue, Eaglewood Cliffs, NJ 07632

☎0101 212 592 2000

Publishes 'how to', reference, self-help, and technical non-fiction, on business, economics, sport, law, accountancy, computing and education. Average 150 titles a year. Particularly interested in high level books which will sell well by direct mail marketing.

Princeton University Press

41 William Street, Princeton, NJ 08540

☎0101 609 452 4900

Editor-in-Chief *Sanford G. Thatcher*

Publishes art history, literary criticism, history, philosophy, religion, political science, economics, anthropology, sociology and science. Also poetry, which is judged solely in competition (mss to *Robert Brown*). Average 150 titles a year.

Putnam Publishing Group

200 Madison Avenue, New York, NY 10016

☎0101 212 576 8900

Editorial *Gene Brissie, Bernadette Ford, Patty Gauch, Neil Nyrer*

Publishes general fiction and non-fiction, including children's books. Particularly strong on history, literature, economics, political science, natural science. Major fiction publisher.

Quartet Books Inc.

Suite 2005, 2155 Park Avenue, New York, NY 10003

☎0101 212 254 2277

Editor *Catherine Norden.*

Part of the Namara Group. *Publishes* animal, biography, business, history, jazz, philos-

ophy, photography, politics, psychology, sociology, and middle Eastern subjects. Particularly interested in coffee table and illustrated books. Fiction: literary, adventure, crime and feminist. Books must appeal to both US and UK markets. Outline and sample chapters for non-fiction books.

Raintree Publishers Inc.

310 W. Wisconsin Avenue, Milwaukee, WI 53202

☎0101 414 273 0873

Editor-in-Chief *Russell Bennet*

Publishes fiction and non-fiction – usually on an 'outright purchase' basis. Non-fiction: children's and reference books on animals, health, history, nature, photography, and reference. Books for schools. Fiction: adventure, historical and science fiction. Synopsis and sample chapters in first instance.

Rand McNally & Co.

PO Box 7600, Chicago, IL 60680

☎0101 312 673 9100

Editor *Jon Leverenz*

Publishes world atlases and maps; road atlases of North America and Europe; city and state maps of the United States and Canada; marketing guides and banking directories; educational wall maps; atlases and globes.

Random House Inc.

201 E. 50th Street, New York, NY 10022

☎0101 212 751 2600

Publishes general fiction and non-fiction, plays, reference books, children's.

IMPRINTS
Include **Reader's Digest** and **IBM Computer Books.**

The Rosen Publishing Group, Inc.

29 East 21st Street, New York, NY 10010

☎0101 212 777 3017

Publishes non-fiction books for a young adult audience, on careers, personal and guidance subjects; also art, theatre, music and health. Average 45 titles a year. Write with outline and sample chapters.

IMPRINT
Pelion Press Classical music and opera subjects.

St Martin's Press, Inc.
175 Fifth Avenue, New York, NY 10010
Tel 0101 212 674 5151

Editorial Director *Tom McCormack*

FOUNDED 1952. Publishes over 1000 new titles a year. The company is particularly noted for its fiction and mystery publishing programmes. General trade books, college textbooks, scholarly and reference. Will consider unsolicited mss but recommend enquiry letter in the first instance.

Schocken Books Inc.
201 East 50th Street, New York, NY 10022
☏0101 212 751 2600

Publishes general non-fiction (including reprints), Jewish studies, women's studies, cookbooks, history, and social science.

Scholastic Inc.
730 Broadway, New York, NY 10003
☏0101 212 505 3000

Editor *Ann Reit*

Publishes teen fiction for girls: romance, historical romance, 40,000–45,000 words. Average 36 titles a year. Send International Reply Coupons for guidelines essential before submitting mss.

Charles Scribner's Sons
Children's books department,
866 Third Avenue, New York, NY 10022
☏0101 212 702 7879

Editorial Director *Clare Costello* (children's books)

Publishes fiction and non-fiction. Fiction includes adventure, fantasy, historical, humour, mystery, science fiction and suspense. Send synopsis and sample. Non-fiction on animals, art, biography, health, hobbies, humour, nature, photography, recreation, science and sports. Write in first instance. Average 25 titles a year.

Simon & Schuster
Trade Books Division,
1230 Avenue of the Americas,
New York, NY 10020
☏0101 212 698 7000

Unsolicited mss returned unread. Fiction and non-fiction, through agents only. *Publishes* general adult fiction and non-fiction. No textbooks, specialised, poetry or plays.

Stanford University Press
Stanford, CA 94305
☏0101 415 723 9434

Editor *William W. Carver*

Publishes non-fiction only. Scholarly works in all areas of the humanities, social sciences and natural sciences, plus more general interest, middle-brow academic books. Average 65 titles a year. Write in first instance.

Sterling Publishing
2 Park Avenue, New York, NY 10016
☏0101 212 532 7160

Contact *Sheila Anne Barry*

Publishes non-fiction only: 'alternative lifestyle', games/puzzles, how-to books, health, home medical, business, cookery, hobbies, children's humour, occult, pets, photography, recreation, self-help, sports, collecting, wines, woodworking, and reference. Average 80 titles a year. Write in first instance enclosing sample chapter list, synopsis and two sample chapters.

Taplinger Publishing Co

132 W. 22nd Street, New York, NY 10011
☎0101 212 741 0801

Editors *Ms Bobs Pinkerton, Roy Thomas*

Fiction and non-fiction hardbacks. No children's. Fiction: serious and contemporary. Non-fiction: art, biography, calligraphy, history, theatre, general trade books. Write in first instance. Average 75 titles a year.

IMPRINT
Crescendo music books.

Temple University Press

Broad and Oxford Streets,
Philadelphia, PA 19122
☎0101 215 787 8787

Editor-in-Chief *Michael Ames*

Publishes scholarly non-fiction only. American history, sociology, women's studies, health care, philosophy, public policy, labour studies, urban studies, photography, and black studies. Average 60 titles a year. Authors generally academics. Write in first instance.

Time-Life Books Inc.

777 Duke Street, Alexandria, VA 22314
☎0101 703 838 7000

Editor *George Constable*

Publishes non-fiction general interest books only; usually heavily illustrated and originating in-house. Rarely consider unsolicited mss. Average 40 titles a year.

Times Books Inc.

201 East 50th Street, New York, NY 10022
☎0101 212 872 8110

Editorial Director *Jonathan B. Segal*

Publishes non-fiction only: business, economics, science and medical, biography, history, women's issues, cookery, current affairs, language and sports. Unsolicited mss not considered. Letter essential. Average 45 titles a year.

Universe Books

381 Park Avenue South,
New York, NY 10016
☎0101 212 685 7400

Editorial Director *Louis Barron*

Publishes non-fiction only, on animals, art, architecture and design, ballet, crafts, economics, history, linguistics, music, nature, performing arts, politics, reference, and social sciences. Also some biography and 'how to'. Monographs on specialist subjects in arts and natural history.

TITLES *The Puppet Emperor*, Brian Power; *Locomotive* Raymond Loewy; *Sculpture Since 1945*, Edward Lucie-Smith. Averages 45 titles a year. Synopsis with two to three sample chapters.

Van Nostrand Reinhold Co. Inc.

115 5th Avenue, New York, NY 10003
☎0101 212 254 3232

Publishes technical and scientific, business, medical, arts, crafts, design, aeronautical, marine, energy, photography, reference, encyclopaedias and handbooks.

Vanguard Press Inc.

424 Madison Avenue, New York, NY 10017
☎0101 212 753 3906

Editor-in-Chief *Bernice S. Woll*

Publishes fiction and non-fiction. Fiction: adventure stories, experimental fiction, humorous, mystery, and literary. Non-fiction: all general and popular areas. No coffee table books, reference or technical. Average 20 titles a year.

Viking Books

40 West 23rd Street, New York, NY 10001
☎0101 212 337 5200

Senior Editor *Nan Graham*

Publishes hardcover and paperbound books: art, classical literature, fiction, history, politics, biography and autobiography. All unsolicited mss returned unopened. Proposals through agents only.

Walker & Co
720 Fifth Avenue, New York, NY 10019
☎0101 212 265 3632

Contact *Submissions Editor*

Publishes fiction and non-fiction. Fiction: adventure, mystery, romantic suspense, regency romance, historical romance, spy/thriller, westerns, science fiction and fantasy. Non-fiction: Americana, art, biography, business, histories, how-to books, children's, science, history, medical, psychiatric, music, nature, sports, parenting, psychology, recreation, reference, popular science, self-help. Average 150 titles a year.

Warner Publishing Co.
666 5th Avenue, New York, NY 10103
☎0101 212 484 2900

Editor *Nancy Neiman*

Publishes fiction and non-fiction, both hardcover and mass market paperbacks.

University of Wisconsin Press
114 North Murray Street,
Madison, WI 53715
☎0101 608 262 5379

Acquisitions Editor *Barbara Hanrahan*

Publishes academic non-fiction only. Complete mss only.

Yale University Press
302 Temple Street, New Haven, CT 06520
☎0101 203 432 0960

Publishes academic books.

US Agents

International Reply Coupons

Most agents ask correspondents to pay for any return postage. This can be done by International Reply Coupon which for an ordinary letter costs 55 pence, but when mss are involved it is essential to check the cost with the Post Office.

Carol Abel Literary Agency
160 West 87th Street, New York, NY 10024
☎0101 212 724 1168

FOUNDED 1979. Contemporary women's fiction, thrillers, health and medical, history, and self-help. No science fiction. No scripts. Will consider unsolicited mss but prefer proposal and sample chapters. No reading fee. CLIENTS include Freda Bright (*Infidelities*); William P. Kennedy (*The Masakado Lesson*); Janice Cauwels (*Bulimia*); John Willis (*Churchill's Few*); K. Ketcham (*Recovering: How to Get and Stay Sober*); Justine Valenti. *Commission* Home 15%; Dramatic 15%; Foreign 20%. *UK associates* **David Grossman Literary Agency.**

Dominick Abel Literary Agency, Inc.
Suite 12C, 498 West End Avenue, New York, NY 10024
☎0101 212 877 0710

Contact *Dominick Abel* (President)

FOUNDED 1975. Non-fiction and novels. No scripts. Prefers to work with established/published writers. No unsolicited mss. First approach with query letter and International Reply Coupons. No reading fee. *Commission* Home 10%; Dramatic 15%; Foreign 20%. *UK associates* **David Grossman Literary Agency.**

Edward J. Acton, Inc.
928 Broadway, New York, NY 10010
☎0101 212 675 5400

Contact *Inge Hanson*

FOUNDED 1975. Specialises in politics, celebrities, sports and historical romances. Nonfiction and novels. No reading fee. CLIENTS include Tip O'Neill, Peter Rose, Jason Miller. *Commission* Home 15%; Dramatic 15%; Foreign 19%.

James Allen Literary Agent (In association with Virginia Kidd Literary Agents)
Box 278, Milford, PA 18337

Contact *James Allen*

FOUNDED 1974. Prefers to work with established/published authors. Specialises in mysteries, occult, horror, science fiction, contemporary and historical romance, fantasy, young adult novels and mainstream novels. No juveniles or westerns. No unsolicited mss. No reading fee for outlines. CLIENTS include Elsie Lee, Dixie McKeone, Chet Williamson. *Commission* Home 10%; Dramatic 20%; Foreign 20%.

Marcia Amsterdam Agency
Suite 9A, 41 West 82nd Street, New York, NY 10024
☎0101 212 873 4945

Contact *Marcia Amsterdam*

FOUNDED 1969. Specialises in mainstream fiction, horror, suspense, humour, young adult, TV and film scripts. No poetry, 8-10 age group, 'how-to' books. No unsolicited mss. First approach by letter only and International Reply Coupons. No reading fee for outlines and synopses. CLIENTS include Christopher Hinz, Ruby Jean Jensen, Joyce Sweeney, Kristopher Franklin, William Lovejoy.
Commission Home 15%; Dramatic 15%; Foreign 15%.

Applegate Byford and Associates Talent Agency

Suite 214, 6305 Yucca Street, Hollywood, CA 90028
☎0101 213 461 2726

Contact *Arthur Dreifuss*

FOUNDED 1986. Film and TV scripts. No reading fee.
Commission Home 10%.

The Axelrod Agency, Inc.

126 Fifth Avenue, New York, NY 10011
☎0101 212 929 1704

Contact *Steven Axelrod* (President)

FOUNDED 1983. Specialises in mainstream and genre fiction and non-fiction. No reading fee for outlines and synopses. CLIENTS include Sydney Biddle and William Novak, La Vyrle Spencer.
Commission Home 10%; Dramatic 10%; Foreign 20%.

The Balkin Agency

850 West 176th Street, New York, NY 10033
☎0101 212 781 4198

Contact *Richard Balkin*

FOUNDED 1973. Specialises in adult non-fiction only. No reading fee for outlines and synopses.
Commission Home 15%; Foreign 20%.

Virginia Barber Literary Agency, Inc.

353 West 21st Street, New York, NY 10011
☎0101 212 255 6515

Contact *Virginia Barber*

FOUNDED 1974. Non-fiction and novels. No reading fee for outlines and synopses.
Commission Home 10%; Dramatic 10%; Foreign 20%.

Maximilian Becker

115 East 82nd Street, New York, NY 10028
☎0101 212 988 3887

Contact *Maximilian Becker* (President)

FOUNDED 1950. Non-fiction, novels and stage plays. No reading fee. CLIENTS include David Irving, Clara Rising.
Commission Home 15%; Foreign 20%.

Bill Berger Associates, Inc.

444 East 58th Street, New York, NY 10022
☎0101 212 486 9588–9

Contact *William P. Berger* (President), *Henriette E. Neatrour*

FOUNDED 1960. Full length and short fiction. Thrillers and historical novels. No science fiction. No scripts. No unsolicited mss. First approach with query letter. No reading fee.
Commission Home 10%; Dramatic 10%; Foreign 20%.

Lois Berman

The Little Theatre Building,
240 West 44th Street, New York, NY 10036
☎0101 212 575 5114

Contact *Lois Berman*

FOUNDED 1972. Dramatic writing only (and only by recommendation).

The Blake Group Literary Agency

Suite 105, 4300 North Central Expressway, Dallas, TX 75206
☎0101 214 828 2160

Contact *Miss Ledd B. Halff*

FOUNDED 1979. Prefers to work with established/published authors. Magazine fiction, non-fiction books, novels, textbooks, juvenile books, film, radio, TV and stage scripts, poetry. No reading fee.
Commission Home 10%; Dramatic 15%; Foreign 20%.

Blassingame–Spectrum Corp.
432 Park Avenue South, Suite 1205,
New York, NY 10016
☎0101 212 532 7377

Contact *Eleanor Wood*

FOUNDED 1978. Preliminary letter and International Reply Coupon essential. No unsolicited mss.
Commission Home 10%; Foreign 20%.

Bloom, Levy, Shorr and Associates
Suite 9, 800 South Robertson Blvd,
Los Angeles, CA 90035
☎0101 213 659 6160

Film and TV scripts. No reading fee.
Commission Home 10%.

The Book Peddlers
18326 Minnetonka Boulevard,
Deephaven, MN 55391
☎0101 612 475 3527

Contact *Vicki Lansky*

FOUNDED 1984. Non-fiction, novels, syndicated material. Specialise in parenting/child care books. No scripts. Will consider unsolicited mss but prefer approach by query letter with International Reply Coupons. No reading fee but once a client's material is accepted a charge of $5 per publisher submission is made. If the mss sells this fee is taken out of the advance; if not the client is billed. CLIENTS include Evelina Chao (*Gates of Grace*); Tim Rumsey (*Pictures from a Trip*); Pat Dorff (*File – Don't Pile*); Eileen Yoder (*Allergy-Free Cook-*

ing); Robert McHatton (*Telemarketing*); Diane Mason (*No More Tantrums*).
Commission Home 15%; Foreign 20%.

Georges Borchardt Inc.
136 East 57th Street, New York, NY 10022
☎0101 212 753 5785

Contact *Georges Borchardt* (President)

FOUNDED 1967. Prefers to work with established/published authors. Specialises in fiction, biography and general non-fiction of unusual interest. Does not read mss. CLIENTS include James Atlas, Edmund Morris, Robert Alter.
Commission Home 10%; Dramatic 10%; Foreign 20%.

The Bradley-Goldstein Agency
Suite 6E, 7 Lexington Avenue,
New York, NY 10010
☎0101 718 672 7924

Contact *Paul Bradley* (President),
Martha Goldstein (Director)

FOUNDED 1985. Specialises in non-fiction: biographies, politics, science, social science, business, current affairs and the arts. No unsolicited mss. Query by letter with International Reply Coupons. No reading fee for outlines and synopses. CLIENTS include A. Manley, M.M. Mangum, Klaus Goetze, Christopher Reaske, Maxine Fisher.
Commission Home 15%; Foreign 25%.

Brandt & Brandt Literary Agents, Inc.
1501 Broadway, New York, NY 10036
☎0101 212 840 5760

FOUNDED 1914. Non-fiction books and novels. No poetry or children's books. No unsolicited mss. First approach by letter 'describing background and ambitions'. No reading fee.
Commission Home 10%; Dramatic 10%; Foreign 20%. *UK associates* **A.M. Heath & Co. Ltd.**

Pema Browne Ltd

185 East 85th Street, New York, NY 10028
☎0101 212 369 1925

Contact *Perry J. Browne*

FOUNDED 1966. Specialises in men's adventure, thrillers, mainstream historical, regencies and contemporary romances, young adult, children's, reference, 'how-to' and other types of non-fiction. No reading fee. CLIENTS include Joseph R. Rosenberger, Joanne Goodman, Charlotte St John. *Commission* Home 15%; Dramatic 10%; Foreign 10%.

Shirley Burke Agency

Suite B-704, 370 East 76th Street,
New York, NY 10021

Contact *Shirley Burke* (President)

FOUNDED 1948. Non-fiction books and novels. No reading fee for outlines and synopses. *Commission* Home 10%; Foreign 20%.

Ruth Cantor, Literary Agent

Room 1133, 156 Fifth Avenue,
New York, NY 10010
☎0101 212 243 3246

Contact *Ruth Cantor*

FOUNDED 1952. Prefers to work with established/published authors. Non-fiction books, novels and juvenile books. No reading fee for outlines and synopses. *Commission* Home 10%; Dramatic 10%; Foreign 20%.

The Carpenter Co.

1516 West Redwood Street,
San Diego, CA 92101
☎0101 619 542 0951

Contact *Lee Carpenter*

FOUNDED 1981. Prefers to work with established/published authors. Specialises in fantasy, science fiction, adventure and period (historical) books, TV and film scripts. Does not read unsolicited mss. *Commission* Home 15%.

Maria Carvainis Agency, Inc.

235 West End Avenue, New York, NY 10023
☎0101 212 580 1559

Contact *Maria Carvainis* (President)

FOUNDED 1978. Specialises in mainstream fiction, historicals, category romance, regencies, westerns, mysteries, suspense, young adult fiction, business and finance, women's issues, political biography, medicine, psychology and popular and social science. No reading fee for outlines and synopses. *Commission* Home 15%; Dramatic 10%; Foreign 20%.

Terry Chiz Agency

Suite E, 5761 Whitnall Highway, North Hollywood, CA 91601
☎0101 818 506 0994

Contact *Terry Chiz* (President)

FOUNDED 1984. Prefers to work with established/published authors. Specialises in film and TV. Novels. No romance or historical. No reading fee for outlines and synopses.

Connie Clausen Associates

Suite 16H, 250 East 87th Street,
New York, NY 10128
☎0101 212 427 6135

Contact *Connie Clausen, Guy Kettelhack*

FOUNDED 1976. Prefers to work with established/published authors. Specialises in trade non-fiction of all kinds and some fiction. Does not read unsolicited mss. CLIENTS include Quentin Crisp, Robert Haas. TITLES *Are You Lonesome Tonight?*, Lucy de Barbin & Dary Matera; *Caught in the Crossfire*, Jan Goodwin; *Death of a Jewish American Princess*, Shirley Frondorf; *Streetsmart Investing*, K. Sokoloff & G. Claremont; *Palm-Aire Spa 7-Day Plan*, Eleanor Berman.

Commission Home 15%; Dramatic 15%; Foreign 20%. *UK associates* **David Grossman Literary Agency**.

Hy Cohen Literary Agency

111 West 57th Street, New York, NY 10019
☎0101 212 757 5237

Contact *Hy Cohen* (President)

FOUNDED 1975. Novels and non-fiction. No scripts. Welcome unsolicited mss but prefer synopsis and 100 pages. International Reply Coupons essential. No reading fee. CLIENTS and TITLES *Serious Living*, Tom Lorenz; *Jenny's Mountain*, Elaine Long; *In Search of the Black Box*, Alport; *Commonsense ESP*, Robert Ferguson; *Terror in the Skies*, David Grayson; *The Wit and Wisdom of Mark Twain*, Alex Ayres; *Let's Go Kill a Neighbour*, David Goodnough.
Commission Home 10%; Dramatic 10% Foreign 10%. *UK associates* **Albert Stein**.

Ruth Cohen, Inc.

Box 7626, Menlo Park, CA 94025
☎0101 415 854 2054

Contact *Ruth Cohen* (President)

FOUNDED 1982. Prefers to work with established/published authors. Specialises in juvenile, young adult, adult non-fiction and genre books: historical romance, mystery and western. No reading fee for outlines and synopses; International Reply Coupons essential.
Commission Home 15%; Dramatic 15%; Foreign 20%.

Collier Associates

Suite 1003, 875 Avenue of the Americas, New York, NY 10001
☎0101 212 563 4065

Contact *Oscar Collier* (Manager)

FOUNDED 1976. Specialises in fiction trade books (war, crime and historical novels) and non-fiction trade books on business and finance, biographies, popular psychology, ma-

thematics for general readership, puzzles and games, politics, exposés, medicine, nature and outdoors, history, cookbooks by highly qualified experts, nutrition and sports. CLIENTS include Christopher Britton, James E. Wavada, Margot Arnold.
Commission Home 10%; Dramatic 10%; Foreign 20%.

Columbia Literary Associates, Inc.

7902 Nottingham Way, Ellicott City, MD 21043
☎0101 301 465 1595

Contact *Linda Hayes, Kathryn Jensen*

FOUNDED 1980. Specialises in mass market, mainstream fiction and non-fiction, contemporary romance (category and single title), suspense, intrigue, cookbooks, general popular non-fiction and book series. No reading fee for outlines and synopses. Return postage required.
Commission Home 12–15%; Dramatic 20%; Foreign 20%.

Connor Literary Agency

640 West 153rd Street, New York, NY 10031
☎0101 212 491 5233

Contact *Marlene Connor*

FOUNDED 1985 Specialises in commercial fiction, particularly thrillers, romantic suspense, current affairs, horror. Illustrated, 'how-to' and reference books. No reading fee for outlines. CLIENTS include Charles Gatewood, Harry Rinker.
Commission Home 15%; Foreign 25%.

Bill Cooper Associates Inc.

Suite 411, 224 West 49th Street, New York, NY 10019
☎0101 212 307 1100

Contact *Nancy Frank, William Cooper*

FOUNDED 1964. Prefers to work with established/published authors. Specialises in contemporary fiction. No reading fee.
Commission Home 15%; Dramatic 15%; Foreign 20%.

Richard Curtis Associates, Inc.

Suite 1, 164 East 64th Street,
New York, NY 10021
☎0101 212 371 9481

Contact *Richard Curtis* (President), *Elizabeth Waxse* (Vice President)

FOUNDED 1969. Prefers to work with established/published authors. Specialises in commercial fiction of all genres, mainstream fiction and non-fiction. CLIENTS include Janet Dailey, Matthew Braun, Greg Benford, Leonard Maltin, Harlan Ellison.
Commission Home 10%; Dramatic 15%; Foreign 20%.

Liz Darhansoff Agency

1220 Park Avenue, New York, NY 10128
☎0101 212 534 2479

Contact *Abigail Thomas*

FOUNDED 1975. Specialises in literary fiction, serious non-fiction. Scripts through Lynn Pleshette, Los Angeles. No unsolicited mss. First approach by letter. No reading fee for outlines. CLIENTS include William Kennedy, Barry Hannah, Lewis Thomas, Harriet Doen, Gretel Ehrlich, Amy Hempel.
Commission Home 10%; Foreign 20%. *UK associates* **Tessa Sayle Agency**.

Joan Daves

21 West 26th Street, New York,
NY 10010–1083
☎0101 212 685 9573/9577
Fax 0101 212 685 1781

Contact *Joan Daves*

FOUNDED 1952. Tradebooks: fiction, non-fiction, juveniles. No science fiction, science, romance, textbooks. No scripts. No unsolicited mss. Query letter in the first instance. 'A detailed synopsis seems valuable only for non-fiction work. Material submitted should specify the author's background, publishing credits, and similar pertinent information.' No reading fee. CLIENTS include Elizabeth Marshall Thomas (*Reindeer Moon*); Frederick Franck (*The Zen of Seeing*); Nancy Larrick, Steven Kroll, The Estate of Martin Luther King, Jr, Professor Roger Shattuck, Henry Winterfeld.
Commission Home 10%; Dramatic 10–25%; Foreign 20%. *Overseas associates* **Maggie Noach Literary Agency**.

J. de S. Associates Inc.

Shagbark Road, South Norwalk, CT 06854
☎0101 203 838 7571/852 1396

Contact *Jacques de Spoelberch*

General fiction and non-fiction; sports books. *UK associate* **Michael Motley**.

Anita Diamant Literary Agency

310 Madison Avenue, New York, NY 10017
☎0101 212 687 1122

Contact *Robin Rue, Alex Liepa*

FOUNDED 1917. Fiction and non-fiction. No technical books. No scripts. No unsolicited mss. Approach by letter explaining project and writer's background; include International Reply Coupons. No reading fee. CLIENTS include Jean Baer (*Don't Say Yes When You Want to Say No*); U.C. Andrews (*Flowers in the Attic*); Oscar Fraley (*The Untouchables*); Mark McGarrity (*McGarr* series).
Commission Home 10–15%; Dramatic 15%; Foreign 20%. *UK associates* **A.M. Heath & Co. Ltd.**

The Jonathan Dolger Agency

Suite 9B, 49 East 96th Street,
New York, NY 10128
☎0101 212 427 1853

Contact *Jonathan Dolger* (President)

FOUNDED 1980. Prefers to work with established/published authors. Specialises in adult trade fiction and non-fiction and illustrated books. No reading fee for outlines.
Commission Home 10–15%; Dramatic 10%; Foreign 20–30%.

The Dorset Group

820 West Belmont, Chicago, IL 60657
☎0101 312 871 7126

Contact *Elizabeth Newton* (President)

FOUNDED 1983. Prefers to work with established/published authors. Non-fiction books and novels. Reading fee 'if we think there is hope for the mss'. CLIENTS include Norman Saunders, Dr Wagner and Dr Rasmussen, John Schmidt.
Commission Home 15%; Dramatic 20%; Foreign 20%.

Educational Design Services Ltd

Box 253, Wantagh, NY 11793
☎0101 718 539 4107/516 221 0995

Contact *Bertram Linder* (President)

FOUNDED 1979. Specialises in educational material, non-fiction books and textbooks. Materials for sale to school markets.
Commission Home 15%; Foreign 25%.

Peter Elek Associates

Box 223, Canal Street, Station,
New York, NY 10013
☎0101 212 431 9368

Contact *Carol Diehl*

FOUNDED 1979. Prefers to work with established/published authors. Specialises in illustrated non-fiction, current affairs, self-help, contemporary biography/autobiography, food, popular culture (all for adults); pre-school and juvenile illustrated fiction, non-fiction; contemporary adventure for adults. No reading fee for outlines. CLIENTS include Ramsay Derry, Leah Komaiko, Kathleen Perry.
Commission Home 15%; Dramatic 20%; Foreign 20%.

Ann Elmo Agency Inc.

60 East 42nd Street, New York, NY 10165
☎0101 212 661 2880/1/2/3

Contact *Lettie Lee, Mari Cronin, Ann Elmo*

FOUNDED 1940s. Literary and romantic fiction, mysteries, and mainstream; non-fiction in all subjects including biography and self-help. Juvenile (8–12-year-olds) and young adult. Scripts handled. Query letter with outline of project in the first instance. No reading fee.
Commission Home 15–20%. *UK associates* John Johnson Ltd.

John Farquharson Ltd

Suite 1007, 250 West 57th Street,
New York, NY 10107
☎0101 212 245 1993

Contact *Deborah Schneider*

FOUNDED 1919 (London) 1980 (New York). Prefers to work with established/published authors. Specialises in trade fiction and non-fiction, mysteries. No poetry, short stories or screenplays. No reading fee for outlines. CLIENTS include Carolyn Chute, Wade Davis, Oliver Sacks, Madison Smartt Bell.
Commission Home 10%; Dramatic 10%; Foreign 20%.

Farwestern Consultants Literary Agency

P.O. Box 47786,
Phoenix, Arizona 85068–7786
☎0101 602 861 3546

Contact *Elizabeth 'Libbi' Goodman* (President), *Carol Tess* (Assistant)

FOUNDED 1987. All popular fiction genres, especially women's contemporary, ethnic, mainstream literary, and popular. Short stories from established authors. Ethnic non-fiction. No category romance, juvenile, poetry. No scripts except for existing clients. Welcome unsolicited mss. (International Reply Coupons essential) but prefer query letter with synopsis. No reading fee. CLIENTS include Claire McCormick, Larry Names, Harry Paige, Roseanne Keller, Lee Damon, Serita Stevens.
Commission Home 10%; Dramatic 10%; Foreign 20%.

Florence Feiler Literary Agency

1524 Sunset Plaza Drive, Los Angeles,
CA 90069
☎0101 213 652 6920/659 0945

Contact *Florence Feiler*

FOUNDED 1967. Specialises in fiction, non-fiction, 'how-to', text books, TV and film scripts. No short stories or pornography. No unsolicited mss. First approach by letter. No reading fee. CLIENTS include literary estates of Isak Dinesen (*Out of Africa*) and Ursula Bloom.
Commission Home 10%; Foreign 20%.

Law Offices of Robert L. Fenton, PC

31800 Northwestern Highway, #390,
Farmington Hills, MI 48018
☎0101 313 855 8780

Contact *Robert L. Fenton* (President) who is also a long established entertainment attorney.

FOUNDED 1960. Specialises in non-fiction, fiction, historical romances, action and suspense. Occasionally handle film and TV scripts. (Robert Fenton is former Universal independent producer and currently producing an NBC Movie of the Week). No poetry, children's books, photographic. No unsolicited mss. First approach with preliminary letter or phone call. Reading fee. CLIENTS include Albert Lee, James W. Ellison, Maggi Brocher, Julia Grice, Hal Kantor, Douglas A. Fraser (former President of UAW), Congressman John D. Dingell.
Commission Home 15%; Dramatic 20%; Foreign 15% (subject to negotiation because of circumstances).

The Film/Publishing Group

11141 Wicks Street, Sun Valley, CA 91352
☎0101 818 767 5587

Contact *Vincent R. Ducette*

FOUNDED 1983. Prefers to work with established/published authors. Specialises in contemporary novels in the mainstream, romance novels, biographies, autobiographies, film and TV scripts, poetry collections and stage plays. No reading fee for outlines. Reading fee for mss. CLIENTS include J.L. Kullinger, John Cronis, Lee Young.
Commission Home 15%; Dramatic 15%; Foreign 20%.

Frieda Fishbein Ltd

2556 Hubbard Street, Brooklyn, NY 11235
☎0101 212 247 4398

Contact *Janice Fishbein* (President)

FOUNDED 1925. Eager to work with new/unpublished writers. Specialises in historical romance, historical adventure, male adventure, mysteries, thrillers and family sagas. Also, 'non-reporting' 'how-to' . . . and non-fiction. Books on the environment, nursing and medicine, plays & screenplays. No poetry or magazine articles or short stories. First approach with query letter. No reading fee for outlines. Reading fees of $60 for first 50,000 words, $1 per 1,000 thereafter. $75 for TV script, screenplay or play. CLIENTS include Thomas Millstead, Thomas Harris, Gary Bohlke, Herbert L. Fisher.
Commission Home 10%; Dramatic 10%; Foreign 20%

The Foley Agency

34 East 38th Street, New York, NY 10016
☎0101 212 686 6930

Contact *Joan and Joseph Foley* (Partners)

FOUNDED 1956. Prefers to work with established/published authors. Specialises in general fiction and non-fiction. No reading fee for outlines. CLIENTS include Roy Cohn, Ann Rule, John Dunning.
Commission Home 10%; Dramatic 5–10%; Foreign 10%.

Robert A. Freedman Dramatic Agency, Inc.

Suite 2310, 1501 Broadway,
New York, NY 10028
☎0101 212 840 5760

Contact *Robert A. Freedman* (President)

FOUNDED 1928 (as Brandt & Brandt Dramatic Department, Inc.), under present name since 1984. Prefers to work with established/published authors. Specialises in plays and film and TV scripts. Does not read unsolicited mss.
Commission Dramatic 10%.

Samuel French, Inc.
45 West 25th Street, New York, NY 10010
☎0101 212 206 8990

Contact *Lawrence Harbison*

FOUNDED 1830. Prefers to work with established/published authors. Specialises in plays. No unsolicited mss. First approach by letter. No reading fee. International Reply Coupon required. CLIENTS include Neil Simon, Monk Ferris, Tina Howe, August Wilson.
Commission 90% book royalties; 10% professional production royalties; 20% amateur production royalties.

Frommer Price Literary Agency Inc.
Suite 32E, 185 East 85th Street,
New York, NY 10028
☎0101 212 289 0589

Contact *Diana Price* (President)

FOUNDED 1979. Prefers to work with established/published authors. Specialises in mainstream adult fiction and adult non-fiction. No reading fee. CLIENTS include Robin Hunter, Nava Atlas.
Commission Home 15%; Dramatic 15%; Foreign 20%.

Jay Garon-Brooke Associates Inc.
415 Central Park West, 17th Floor,
New York, NY 10025
☎0101 212 866 3654

Contact *Jay Garon* (President), *Jean Free* (Vice President)

FOUNDED 1951. Fiction and non-fiction, historical & romantic historicals, suspense

thrillers, political intrigue, horror & occult, self-help. No category romance, westerns or mysteries. Occasionally handles top quality scripts. No unsolicited mss. First approach by query letter. No reading fee. CLIENTS include Burt Hirschfeld, James Leo Herlihy, Elizabeth Gage, Daoma Winston, Virginia Coffman, Patricia Matthews, Jeffrey Sacket.
Commission Home 15%; Dramatic 10–15%; Foreign 30%. *UK associates* **Abner Stein**.

Max Gartenberg, Literary Agent
15 West 44th Street, New York, NY 10036
☎0101 212 860 8451

Contact *Max Gartenberg*

FOUNDED 1954. Prefers to work with established/published authors. Specialises in non-fiction and fiction trade books. No reading fee for outlines. CLIENTS include David Roberts, Robert Minton, William Ashworth, Edwin P. Hoyt.
Commission Home 10%; Dramatic 10%; Foreign 15%.

Geddes Agency
Suite 7, 1509 North Crescent Heights,
Los Angeles, CA 90046
☎0101 213 650 4011

Contact *Eileen Orr*

FOUNDED 1964. Eager to work with new/unpublished writers. Novels, film and TV scripts. No reading fee for outlines.
Commission Home 10% (occasionally 15% for new authors); Dramatic 10%; Foreign 10%.

Lucianne S. Goldberg Literary Agents, Inc.
Suite 6A, 255 West 84th Street,
New York, NY 10024
☎0101 212 799 1260

Contact *Cyril Hildebrand*

FOUNDED 1974. Non-fiction books and novels. Reading fee of $150 for full-length mss. No reading fee for outlines. CLIENTS include

Jerry Oppenheimer, James Southwood, John Krich.
Commission Home 15%; Dramatic 25%; Foreign 25%.

Goodman Associates Literary Agents
500 West End Avenue, New York, NY 10024

Contact *Arnold or Elise Goodman*

FOUNDED 1976. Specialises in general adult trade fiction and non-fiction. No fantasy, science fiction, stories, articles or computer books. No reading fee for outlines.
Commission Home 15%; Dramatic 15%; Foreign 20%.

Irene Goodman Literary Agency
521 Fifth Avenue, 17th Floor, New York, NY 10017
☎0101 212 688 4286

Contact *Irene Goodman*

FOUNDED 1978. Specialises in women's fiction (mass market, category and historical romance), science fiction, fantasy, popular non-fiction, reference and young adult (romance and series). No reading fee for outlines. CLIENTS include Diana Gregory, Joyce Thies, Carol Katz.
Commission Home 15%; Dramatic 15%; Foreign 20%.

Graham Agency
311 West 43rd Street, New York, NY 10036
☎0101 212 489 7730

Contact *Earl Graham*

FOUNDED 1971. Prefers to work with established/published authors, but eager to work with new/unpublished writers. Specialises in full length stage plays and musicals. No reading fee.
Commission Home 10%; Dramatic 10%; Foreign 10%.

Sanford J. Greenburger Associates
55 Fifth Avenue, New York, NY 10003
☎0101 212 206 5600

Contact *Heide Lange, David Black, Diane Cleaver, Nick Ellison*

Fiction and non-fiction. No scripts. No unsolicited mss. First approach with query letter and synopsis. No reading fee.

Harold R. Greene, Inc.
8455 Beverly Boulevard, Suite 309, Los Angeles, CA 90048
☎0101 213 852 4959

Contact *Harold Greene*

FOUNDED 1985. Novels adaptable to films or TV films and film scripts. No unsolicited mss. Best approach 'through a mutual acquaintance'. No reading fee. CLIENTS include George La Fountaine, Crawford Kilian, Pamela Wallace.
Commission Home 10%; Dramatic 10%; Foreign 10%.

Thomas S. Hart Literary Enterprises
20 Kenwood Street, Boston, MA 02134
☎0101 617 288 8512

Contact *Thomas Hart* (President)

FOUNDED 1983. Prefers to work with established/published authors. Specialises in literary and mainstream fiction, sports, fitness and natural history. No reading fee. CLIENTS include Larry Pei, John Janovy Jr, Don Stop.
Commission Home 10%; Dramatic 15%; Foreign 20%.

John Hawkins & Associates, Inc (formerly Paul R. Reynolds, Inc)
71 West 23rd Street, Suite 1600, New York, NY 10010
☎0101 212 807 7040

Contact *John H. Hawkins, William Reiss*

FOUNDED 1893. General trade fiction and non-fiction. No scripts. Prefer query letter in the first instance; submit 1-page biography, 1–3-page outline and up to 50 sample pages. No reading fee.
Commission Home 10%; Dramatic 10%; Foreign 20%. *UK Associate* **Murray Pollinger**.

Heacock Literary Agency, Inc.
1523 Sixth Street, Suite #14,
Santa Monica, CA 90401
☎0101 213 393 6227/213 451 8523/4

Contact *James B. Heacock* (President), *Rosalie G. Heacock* (Vice President)

FOUNDED 1978. Works with a small number of new/unpublished authors. Specialises in non-fiction on a wide variety of subjects – diet, health, nutrition, exercise, beauty, women's studies, popular psychology, crafts, business expertise, pregnancy, parenting, alternative health concepts. Celebrity biographies. Novels (by authors who have been previously published by major houses). Film/TV scripts (only for full time professionals and members of the Writer's Guild). Do not consider unsolicited mss. Queries with International Reply Coupons only. No reading fee. CLIENTS include Don & Audrey Wood, Dr Arnold Fox & Barry Fox, Jurgen Wolff.
Commission Home 15% on first $50,000 each year & 10% thereafter; Foreign 15% if sold direct, 25% if agent used.

Heinle & Heinle Enterprises, Inc.
29 Lexington Road, Concord, MA 01742
☎0101 617 369 4858

Contact *Ms Beverly D. Heinle* (President)

FOUNDED 1973. Handles cookbooks exclusively. Not interested in any other subject. Prefers to work with established/published authors. No unsolicited mss. First approach with brief query letter. CLIENTS include Terence Janericco (*Fabulous Fruit Desserts* and *The Gourmet Galley: A Guide to Cooking on a Sailboat*); Elizabeth Reily (*The Chef's Companion: A Concise Dictionary of Culinary Terms*)
Commission Home 10%; Foreign 10%.

HHM Literary Agency
Box 1153, Rahway, NJ 07065
☎0101 201 388 8167

Contact *Haes H. Monrow*

FOUNDED 1985. Prefers to work with established/published authors. Non-fiction books, novels and juvenile books. No reading fee.
Commission Home 10%; Dramatic 15%; Foreign 20%.

Frederick Hill Associates
2237 Union Street, San Francisco, CA 94123
☎0101 415 921 2910

Contact *Fred Hill, Bonnie Nadell*

FOUNDED 1979. General fiction and non-fiction. No scripts. First approach with query letter detailing past publishing history, if any. International Reply Coupons required. CLIENTS include Randy Shilts (*And The Band Played On*); Walter Shapiro (*Eddie Black*); Eric Hansen (*Stranger in the Forest*).
Commission Home 15%; Dramatic 15%; Foreign 20%. *UK associates* **Tessa Sayle Agency**.

Alice Hilton Literary Agency
13131 Welby Way, North Hollywood,
CA 91606
☎0101 818 982 5423/982 2546

FOUNDED 1986. Eager to work with new/unpublished writers. Specialises in film and TV scripts. No reading fee.
Commission Dramatic 15%.

Hintz & Fitzgerald, Inc.
Suite 211, 207 East Buffalo Street,
Milwaukee, WI 53202
☎0101 414 273 0300

Contact *Sandy Hintz, Colleen Fitzgerald*

FOUNDED 1978. Specialises in most fiction — mysteries, westerns, science fiction, fantasy, 'how-to's, biographies, general non-fiction and juvenile fiction and non-fiction. No picture books. No reading fee for outlines. CLIENTS include Sharyn McCrumb, Gregory Vogt, Nick O'Donohoe.
Commission Home 15%.

John L. Hochmann Books

320 East 58th Street, New York, NY 10022
☎0101 212 319 0505

Contact *John L. Hochmann* (Chairman)

FOUNDED 1976. Prefers to work with established/published authors. Non-fiction books, novels and textbooks. No reading fee. CLIENTS include Donald Knox, John Canady, Noel B. Gerson.
Commission Home 15%; Foreign 10%.

International Literature and Arts Agency

50 East 10th Street, New York, NY 10003
☎0101 212 475 1999

Contact *Bonnie R. Crown* (Director)

FOUNDED 1977. Looks for works of high literary quality. Considers work by new/ unpublished authors. Specialises in translations of literary works from Asian languages, arts- and literature-related works, novels, stage plays (related to Asia or Asian Western experience) and poetry (translations of Asian classics). No reading fee for outlines. Send informative query letter for statement of policy for submissions. CLIENTS include Linda Ty-Casper, Kazuaki Tanahashi, Harold Wright, Richard John Lynn.
Commission Home 15%; Foreign 20%.

International Publisher Associates, Inc.

746 West Shore, Sparta, NJ 07871
☎0101 201 729 9321

Contact *Joe DeRogatis* (Executive Vice President)

FOUNDED 1982. Eager to work with new/ unpublished writers. Specialises in all types of non-fiction. No reading fee for outlines.
Commission Home 15%; Foreign 20%.

Janus Literary Agency

Box 107, Nahant, MA 01908
☎0101 617 593 0576

Contact *Lenny Cavallaro*

FOUNDED 1980. Non-fiction and novels. Charges reading fee of $50–200 for mss. CLIENTS include Laura Huchton, Stoker Hunt.
Commission Home 15%; Foreign 20%.

Sharon Jarvis and Co., Inc.

260 Willard Avenue, Staten Island, NY 10314
☎0101 718 273 1066

Contact *Sharon Jarvis* (President)

FOUNDED 1985. (Previously known as Jarvis, Braff Ltd). Prefers to work with established/ published authors. Does not read unsolicited mss. CLIENTS include Eric Helm, Kevin Randle, Candace Caponegro.
Commission Home 15%; Foreign 25%.

Jet Literary Associates, Inc.

124 East 84th Street, New York, NY 10028
☎0101 212 879 2578

Contact *J. Trupin* (President)

FOUNDED 1976. Prefers to work with established/published authors. Specialises in non-fiction. Will handle novels. Does not read unsolicited mss. CLIENTS include David Feldman, Jeff Roijin, Will Knott.
Commission Home 15%; Dramatic 15%; Foreign 25%.

Alex Kamaroff Associates

200 Park Avenue, Suite 303 East, New York, NY 10166
☎0101 212 557 5557

Contact *Alex Kamaroff, Paul Katz, Richard Kamsen*

FOUNDED 1985. Men's fiction, science fiction, thriller, mystery, category & historical romance, *Star Trek*. No poetry, short stories, 'how-to'. No scripts. Will consider unsolicited mss but prefer first three chapters and outline and International Reply Coupons. No reading fee for sample chapters. CLIENTS include Louis Rukeyser, Irene Kress, Diana Morgan, Joan Johnston.
Commission Home 10%; Dramatic 10%; Foreign 20%.

Kidde, Hoyt and Picard Literary Agency
333 East 51st Street, New York, NY 10022
☎0101 212 755 9461

Contact *Katharine Kidde* (Chief Associate)

FOUNDED 1981. Specialises in mainstream and literary fiction, romantic fiction (historical and contemporary), mainstream non-fiction and some young adult fiction. No reading fee for outlines. CLIENTS include Norma Seely, Jeannet Haien.
Commission Home 15%; Dramatic 15%; Foreign 15%.

Daniel P. King
5125 North Cumberland Boulevard, Whitefish Bay, WI 53217
☎0101 414 964 2903   Telex 724389

Contact *Daniel P. King* (President), *Judy Kommrusch* (Associate)

FOUNDED 1974. Mainstream fiction, crime and mystery, science fiction. Specialises in mystery and non-fiction books on crime and espionage. Scripts handled by representative office in Beverly Hills, California. No unsolicited mss. Send synopsis or sample chapter first but would prefer to see a concise 1–2 page letter describing the book. No reading fee unless an author wants a critique on his material. CLIENTS include John Bonnet, John Dunning, Cyril Joyce.
Commission Home 10%; Dramatic 10%; Foreign 20%.

Harvey Klinger, Inc.
301 West 53rd Street, New York, NY 10019
☎0101 212 581 7068

Contact *Harvey Klinger* (President)

FOUNDED 1977. Specialises in mainstream fiction (not category romance or mysteries, etc.), non-fiction in the medical, social sciences, autobiography and biography areas. No reading fee for outlines. CLIENTS include Barbara Wood, Jane Powell, C. Terry Cline, Jr.
Commission Home 15%; Dramatic 15%; Foreign 25%.

Paul Kohner, Inc.
9169 Sunset Blvd, Los Angeles, CA 90069
☎0101 213 550 1060

Contact *Gary Salt*

FOUNDED 1938. Handle a broad range of books for subsidiary rights sales to film and TV. Do not usually handle novel mss directly for placement with publishers as film and TV scripts are the major portion of the business. Specialise in true crime, biography and history. Generally prefer non-fiction to fiction in the TV markets but will handle 'whatever we feel has strong potential'. No short stories, poetry, science fiction, gothics. Unsolicited material will always be returned unread. Approach via a third-party reference or query letter with professional resume. No reading fee. CLIENTS include Donald Westlake, Alan Sharp.
Commission Home 10%; Publishing 15%; Dramatic 10%. *UK associates* **John Redway & Associates.**

Barbara S. Kouts, Literary Agent
788 Ninth Avenue, New York, NY 10019
☎0101 212 265 6003

FOUNDED 1980. Fiction, non-fiction, children's books. No romances, science fiction, scripts. No unsolicited mss. Query letter in the first instance. No reading fee. CLIENTS include Nancy Mairs, Hal Gieseking, Robert San Souci.
Commission Home 10%; Foreign 20%; *UK associates* **Murray Pollinger.**

The Lantz Office

888 Seventh Avenue, New York, NY 10106
☎0101 212 586 0200

Contact *Robert Lantz, Joy Harris*

Handles adult non-fiction and fiction. No science fiction. No unsolicited mss. Approach with query letter in the first instance. No reading fee. Film/TV scripts handled by the Los Angeles office at 9255 Sunset Boulevard, Suite 505, Los Angeles, CA 90069. CLIENTS and TITLES *Elizabeth Takes Off*, Elizabeth Taylor; *Cambodian Odyssey*, Haing S. Ngor & Roger Warner; *Many Masks – A Biography of Frank Lloyd Wright*, Brendan Gill; *Dangerous Games*, Shana Alexander; *No One Rides for Free*, Larry Beinhart; *State Scarlet*, David Aaron; *Second Son*, Robert Ferro; *Love Me Tender*, Catherine Texier.
Commission Home 10%; Dramatic 10%; Foreign 20%. *UK associates* **Abner Stein**.

Michael Larsen/Elizabeth Pomada Literary Agents

1029 Jones Street, San Francisco, CA 94109
☎0101 415 673 0939

Contact *Mike Larsen, Elizabeth Pomada*

FOUNDED 1972. Eager to work with new/ unpublished writers. Literary fiction, commercial fiction, popular psychology, finance. No scripts. No children's, poetry, westerns. No unsolicited mss. Send first 30 pages and synopsis with International Reply Coupons. No reading fee. CLIENTS include Ruth Coe Chambers, June Lune Shiplett, Marty Klein, Jay Conrad, Lia Matera.
Commission Home 15%; Dramatic 15%; Foreign 20%.

Elizabeth Lay, Literary Agent

9 Overman Place, New Rochelle, NY 10801

Contact *Elizabeth Lay* (President)

FOUNDED 1980. Specialises in fiction (women's mainstream, fantasy, mysteries, historical romances and westerns) and non-fiction (of interest to women, and health and diet). No reading fee for outlines. CLIENTS include R. Seid, S. Singer, B. Cohen.
Commission Home 15%; Dramatic 15%; Foreign 20%.

The Lee Allan Agency

P.O. Box 18617, Milwaukee, WI 53218
☎0101 414 463 7441

Contact *Andrea Knickerbocker, Lee A. Matthias*

FOUNDED 1983. Specialises in mystery, thriller, horror, western, science fiction, and fantasy. Commercial fiction, including young adult and mainstream. Some non-fiction, including self-help, cookbooks, humour, true crime, and occult. Handle feature film screenplays properly formatted to the Writer's Guild of America guidelines; no TV/stage plays/radio or joke routines. No autobiographies (except for celebrities), scholarly works, articles, short pieces, technical, and 'how-to' books. No unsolicited mss. Approach by letter, with International Reply Coupons, giving length/word count. Novels – min. 60,000 words; scripts – min. 90 pages, max. 135 pages. No reading fee. CLIENTS include Loren Estleman, Joe Lansdale, David North, John Randall, F.E. Leib.
Commission Home 10%; Dramatic 10%; Foreign 20%.

L. Harry Lee Literary Agency

Box 203, Rocky Point, NY 11778
☎0101 516 744 1188

Contact *L. Harry Lee* (President)

FOUNDED 1979. Mainly interested in screenwriters. Specialises in films, TV and contemporary novels. No reading fee for outlines. International Reply Coupon required.
Commission Home 15%; Dramatic 15% Foreign 20%.

Lenniger Literary Agency, Inc.

See **John K. Payne Literary Agency, Inc.**

Adele Leone Agency Inc.

26 Nantucket Place, Scarsdale, NY 10583
☎0101 914 961 2965

Contact *Adele Leone, Ralph Leone, Richard Monaco*

FOUNDED 1979. Prefers to work with established/published authors. Specialises in historical, gothic, regency and contemporary romance, science fiction and fantasy, westerns, horror, men's adventure, thrillers, mystery, biography and general women's and mainstream fiction; non-fiction, health, nutrition, science, New Age. No scripts. No books on photography, travel. No young adult and children's books; no poetry, Welcome unsolicited mss. Send three chapters and outline in the first instance. International Reply Coupons required. No reading fee. CLIENTS include Janelle Taylor (*Fortune's Flames*); Skipp & Spector (*The Scream*); Simon Hawke (*Time Wars* series); Eric Sauter (*Predators*).
Commission Home 15%; Dramatic 15%; Foreign 10%. *UK associates* **MBA Agency.**

Lescher & Lescher Ltd

155 East 71st Street, New York, NY 10021
☎0101 212 249 7600

Contact *Robert Lescher, Susan Lescher.*

FOUNDED 1966.
Commission Home 10–15%; Foreign 20%.

Ellen Levine, Literary Agency, Inc.

Suite 1205, 432 Park Avenue South,
New York, NY 10016
☎0101 212 899 0620

Contact *Ellen Levine* (President)

FOUNDED 1980. Handles all types of books. No scripts. No unsolicited mss. First approach by letter and proposal, synopsis or sample chapter. Send International Reply Coupons for reply and return of material submitted. No telephone calls. No reading fee.
Commission Home 10%; Dramatic 10%; Foreign 20%. *UK associates* **A.P. Watt.**

Wendy Lipkind Agency

Suite 5K, 225 East 57th Street,
New York, NY 10022
☎0101 212 935 1406

Contact *Wendy Lipkind* (President)

FOUNDED 1977. Specialises in non-fiction (social history, adventure, biography, science, sports, history) and fiction. No reading fee for outlines.
Commission Home 10%; Dramatic 10–15%; Foreign 20%.

Barbara Lowenstein Associates, Inc.

Suite 714, 250 West 57th Street, New York, NY 10107
☎0101 212 586 3825

Contact *Barbara Lowenstein* (President)

FOUNDED 1976. Specialises in non-fiction (especially science and medical-topic books for the general public) historical and contemporary romance, women's and general fiction. No reading fee for outlines.
Commission Home 15%; Dramatic 15%; Foreign 20%.

The Lund Agency

Suite 12–14, 10000 Riverside Drive, Toluca Lake, CA 91602
☎0101 818 761 0928

Contact *Cara Lund* (President)

FOUNDED 1979. Prefers to work with established/published authors. Specialises in science fiction, horror, fantasy, true accounts and action. Film and TV scripts. No reading fee for outlines.
Commission Home 10%; Dramatic 15%; Foreign 20%.

Donald MacCampbell Inc.

12 East 41st Street, New York, NY 10017
☎0101 212 683 5580

Contact *Maureen Moran*

FOUNDED 1940. Does not handle unpublished writers. Specialises in women's novels in all categories. Does not read unsolicited mss. CLIENTS include Jennifer Blake, E. Howard Hunt, Lynne Scott-Drennan. *Commission* Home 10%; Foreign 20%.

McIntosh & Otis, Inc.

310 Madison Avenue, New York, NY 10017
☎0101 212 687 7400

Contact *Julie Fallowfield* (adult books), *Dorothy Markinko* (juvenile)

FOUNDED 1928. Adult and juvenile general trade books, fiction and non-fiction. No cookbooks and textbooks. No scripts. No unsolicited mss. Approach first with a letter indicating nature of the work the writer wishes to submit plus details of writer's background. No reading fee. CLIENTS include Shirley Hazzard, Victoria Holt, Mary Higgins Clark, Harper Lee. *Commission* Home 15%; Dramatic 15%; Foreign 20%. *UK associates* A.M. Heath & Co. Ltd.

Janet Wilkens Manus Literary Agency Inc.

Suite 906, 370 Lexington Avenue, New York, NY 10017
☎0101 212 685 9558

Contact *Janet Wilkens Manus* (President)

FOUNDED 1981. Prefers to work with established/published authors. Specialises in general adult trade fiction and non-fiction. Juvenile books. No reading fee for outlines. CLIENTS include Judith Kelman, Barbar Lee and Paula M. Siegel, Diana Shaw. *Commission* Home 15%; Dramatic 15%; Foreign 20%.

Denise Marcil Literary Agency, Inc.

316 West 82nd Street, 5F, New York, NY 10024
☎0101 212 580 1071

Contact *Denise Marcil* (President)

FOUNDED 1977. Specialises in non-fiction (money, business, health, child care, parent-

ing, self-help and 'how-to's) and commercial fiction, especially women's fiction, mysteries, psychological suspense and horror. Young adult books. No reading fee for outlines. CLIENTS include Elaine Raco Chase, Douglas Forde, Elizabeth Garcia. *Commission* Home 15%; Dramatic 15%; Foreign 22½%.

Betty Marks

Suite 9F, 176 East 77th Street, New York, NY 10021
☎0101 212 535 8388

Contact *Betty Marks*

FOUNDED 1969. Prefers to work with established/published authors. Specialises in journalists' non-fiction. Novels. No reading fee for outlines. *Commission* Home 15%; Foreign 20%.

Claudia Menza Literary Agency

237 West 11th Street, New York, NY 10014
☎0101 212 889 6850

Contact *Claudia Menza* (President)

FOUNDED 1983. Specialises in unique fiction and non-fiction dealing with serious subjects (i.e. political and medical issues). No reading fee. No unsolicited mss; queries and synopses only. *Commission* Home 15%; Dramatic 15%; Foreign 20%.

Scott Meredith, Inc.

845 Third Avenue, New York, NY 10022
☎0101 212 245 5500

Contact *Jack Scovil* (Vice President)

FOUNDED 1946. Magazine articles, magazine fiction, non-fiction books, novels, textbooks, juvenile books, film, radio, TV scripts, stage plays, syndicated material and poetry. Reading fee for unpublished writers. CLIENTS include Norman Mailer, Carl Sagan, Margaret Truman. *Commission* Home 10%; Dramatic 10%; Foreign 20%. *UK associates* A.M. Heath & Co. Ltd.

The Peter Miller Agency, Inc.

Office: 220 West 19th Street,
New York, NY 10011
Package address: PO Box 760, Old Chelsea
Station, New York, NY 10011
☎0101 212 929 1222
Fax 0101 212 206 0238

Contact *Peter Miller* (President), *Jonathan Blank* (Director of Development), *Karen Loop* (Associate), *Alfred E. Guy* (Associate), *Blake Hewon* (Associate)

FOUNDED 1976. Commercial fiction and non-fiction. Specialises in true crime and Hollywood biographies. All books with film and television potential. No poetry, pornography, non-commercial academic. No unsolicited mss. Approach by letter with one page synopsis. Reading fee for unpublished authors. Fee recoupable out of first monies earned. CLIENTS include Vincent T. Bugliosi, Linda Evans, Lindsay Wagner, Christopher Cook Gilmore, Mark D. Harrell, Barry Sheinkopf, Lee Butcher.
Commission Home 15%; Dramatic 10–15%; Foreign 20–25%.

Robert P. Mills

c/o Richard Curtis Associates,
164 East 64th Street, New York, NY 10021
☎0101 212 371 9481

Contact *Richard Curtis*

Marvin Moss Inc.

601–9200 Sunset Boulevard,
Los Angeles, CA 90069
☎0101 213 274 8483

Contact *Marvin Moss* (President)

FOUNDED 1970. Prefers to work with established/published authors. Non-fiction books, film and TV scripts. No poetry, romance or children's books. Does not read unsolicited mss.
Commission Home 10%; Dramatic 10%; Foreign 20%.

Multimedia Product Development, Inc.

410 South Michigan Avenue, Suite 724,
Chicago, IL 60605
☎0101 312 922 3063

Contact *Jane Jordan Browne*

FOUNDED 1971. Biography, history, current affairs, mainstream novels, genre novels, science, psychology, social science, 'how-to'. No autobiography (except celebrities), poetry. No scripts. No unsolicited mss. Query letter with International Reply Coupons only. No reading fee. CLIENTS include Donald A. Stanwood (*The Memory of Eva Ryker* and *The Seventh Royale*); Helen Hooven Santmyer (*. . . And Ladies of the Club, Herbs & Apples, The Fierce Dispute, Ohio Town*, and *Farewell Summer*); J. Patrick Wright (*On A Clear Day you Can See General Motors*); James Kahn (*Return of the Jedi, Poltergeist One* and *Poltergeist Two*, and *The Echo Vector*).
Commission Home 15%; Dramatic 15%; Foreign 15–20%. *UK associates* **A.M. Heath & Co. Ltd.**

Charles Neighbors, Inc.

7600 Blanco Road, Suite 3607K,
San Antonio, TX 78216
☎0101 512 342 5324

Contact *Charles Neighbors, Margaret Neighbors*

FOUNDED 1966. Fiction, non-fiction (all categories). No poetry, juvenile (except young adult fiction and non-fiction). Screenplays considered. 'Happy to consider UK writers'. No reading fee for outlines, but send International Reply Coupons. CLIENTS include Bryce Webster, James Harriss, Wayne Barton.
Commission Home 15%; Dramatic 15%; Foreign 20%. *UK associates* **MBA Literary Agents** (Diana Tyler).

B.K. Nelson Literary Agency

The Steel Building, Suite 806, 149 Madison Avenue, New York, NY 10016
☎0101 212 889 0637/889 8567

Contact *Bonita K. Nelson* (President)

FOUNDED 1978. Specialises in business books. Handles New Age, 'how-to', computer state of the art and computer science; software/ game programmes – high tech and college level. Some historical romance/contemporary novels. No unsolicited mss. First approach with letter. Reading fee. CLIENTS include Herman R. Holtz, Don Beveridge, Peter Alesso, Clay Carr.
Commission Home 15%; Dramatic 15%; Foreign 20%.

New England Publishing Associates, Inc.

Box 5, Chester, CT 06412
☎0101 718 788 6641/203 345 4976

Contact *Elizabeth Frost Knappman* (President)

FOUNDED 1983. Mainly non-fiction with some fiction. Specialises in current affairs, history, science, women's studies, psychology, biography, true crime. No text books, children's, collections/anthologies. No scripts. Will consider unsolicited mss but prefer query letter or phone call. No reading fee. CLIENTS include Tom Renner, William Packard, Carl Rollyson (*Lillian Hellman: Her Legend and her Legacy*); Roger Lewin *Bones of Contention: Controversies in the Search for Human Origins*); Philip Ginsburg (*Poisoned Blood: A True Story of Murder, Passion, and an Astonishing Hoax*). *Commission* Home 15%. UK associates Scott-Ferris Agency.

New Wave

2544 North Monticello Avenue, Chicago, IL 60647
☎0101 312 342 3338

Contact *Gene Lovitz*

FOUNDED 1984. Particularly interested in historical romance novels, horror, mysteries, experimental. Reading fee charged to unpublished authors.
Commission Home 10%; Foreign 15%.

The Betsy Nolan Literary Agency

50 West 29th Street, Suite 9 West, New York, NY 10001
☎0101 212 799 0700

Contact *Betsy Nolan* (President), *Michael Powers* (Vice President)

FOUNDED 1980. Non-fiction books and novels. No reading fee for outlines.
Commission Home 15%; Foreign 20%.

Northeast Literary Agency

69 Broadway, Concord, NH 03301
☎0101 603 225 9162

Contact *Vic Levine*

FOUNDED 1973. Eager to work with new/ unpublished writers. Specialises in historical and contemporary romance, science fiction, mysteries, westerns, serious (non-genre) novels, non-fiction on remedial education, environment, women's rights, health, 'how-to', personal memoirs. No reading fee for outlines. Reading fee for mss. CLIENTS include Don Lyman, Judi Sprankle, Henry Ebel.
Commission Home 15%; Dramatic 20%; Foreign 20%.

Fifi Oscard Associates

19 West 44th Street, New York, NY 10036
☎0101 212 764 1100

Contact *Ivy Fischer-Stone*

FOUNDED 1956. Specialises in literary novels, commercial novels, mysteries, non-fiction, especially celebrity biographies and autobiographies. No reading fee for outlines. CLIENTS include Hob Broun, Mark Mathabane, Debbie Reynolds.
Commission Home 15%; Dramatic 10%; Foreign 20%.

The Otte Company

9 Goden Street, Belmont, MA 02178
☎0101 617 484 8505

Contact *Jane H. Otte*

FOUNDED 1973. Specialises in adult trade books. Non-fiction books and novels. No scripts. No unsolicited mss. Approach by letter. No reading fee for outlines. CLIENTS include Michael McDowell, Arlene E. Langseth, Cameron Foote, Robert Shaw, Nathan Aldyne.
Commission Home 15%; Dramatic 7½%; Foreign 20%. *UK associates* **Aitken & Stone Ltd.**

John K. Payne Literary Agency, Inc.
(formerly Lenniger Literary Agency, Inc.)
Suite 1101, 175 Fifth Avenue,
New York, NY 10010
☎0101 212 475 6447

President *John K. Payne*

FOUNDED 1923 (as Lenniger Literary Agency, Inc.). Specialises in popular women's fiction, historical romance, biography, sagas and Irish background, fiction/non-fiction. Reading fee. CLIENTS include Rita Clay Estrada, Diana Haviland, Elma Kelton.
Commission Home 10%; Dramatic 10%; Foreign 20%.

The Ray Peekner Literary Agency Inc.
3418 Shelton Avenue, Bethlehem, PA 18017
☎0101 215 974 9158

Contact *Barbara Puechner*

FOUNDED 1973. Prefers to work with established/published authors. Specialises in private-eye novels (hard boiled), westerns, mainstream suspense, fantasy. No romance, no scripts, no unsolicited mss. Send a query letter, but most new clients are referred by existing clients. No reading fee. CLIENTS include Loren D. Estleman, Rob Kantner, G. Clifton Wisler, Bill Crider, Thomas Sullivan, Margaret Weis and Tracy Hickman.
Commission Home 10%; Dramatic 10%; Foreign 20%. *UK associates* **Laurence Pollinger Limited.**

Sidney Porcelain
Box 1229, Milford, PA 18337
☎0101 717 296 6420

Contact *Sidney Porcelain*

FOUNDED 1952. Prefers to work with established/published authors. Specialises in fiction (novels, mysteries and suspense) and non-fiction (celebrity and exposé). First approach with letter. No reading fee. CLIENTS include Colin Stuart, Tom Cluff, Michael Avallone.
Commission Home 10%; Dramatic 10%; Foreign 10%.

Aaron M. Priest Literary Agency
Suite 812, 565 Fifth Avenue,
New York, NY 10017
☎0101 212 818 0344

Contact *Aaron Priest, Molly Freidrich*

Non-fiction books and novels. No reading fee for outlines. International Reply Coupon required. CLIENTS include Sylvia Hemlett, Elizabeth Harley, Leonard Sanders
Commission Home 10–15%.

Susan Ann Protter Literary Agent
Suite 1408, 110 West 40th Street,
New York, NY 10018
☎0101 212 840 0480

Contact *Susan Protter*

FOUNDED 1971. Fiction, fantasy, mysteries, thrillers, science fiction, non-fiction: history, auto/biography, science, health. No romantic fiction, poetry, religious, children's, sports manuals. No scripts. First approach with letter and International Reply Coupons. No reading fee. CLIENTS include Samuel Shem (*The House of God*), Terry Bisson (*Talking Man*), James Colbert (*Profit & Sheen*), Michael Weaver (*Mercedes Nights*), Rudy Rucker (*Wetware*), Robert Edwin Herzstein (*Waldheim: The Missing Years*), Myron R. Sharaf (*Fury on Earth: A Biography of Wilhelm Reich*), Ronald L. Hoffman (*The Doctor's Diet-Type Program*).
Commission Home 15%; Dramatic 15%; Foreign 25%. *UK associates* **Abner Stein.**

Raines & Raines

71 Park Avenue, New York, NY 10016
☎0101 212 684 5160

Contact *Theron Raines, Joan Raines*

FOUNDED 1961. No unsolicited mss.
Commission Home 15%; Foreign 20%.

Helen Rees Literary Agency

308 Commonwealth Avenue, Boston,
MA 02116
☎0101 617 262 2401

Contact *Catherine Mahar*

FOUNDED 1982. Specialises in books on health
and business. Biography, autobiography,
history. No scholarly, academic, technical
books. No scripts. No unsolicited mss. Prefer
query letter with International Reply Coupons. No reading fee. CLIENTS include Joan
Borysenko (*Minding the Body, Mending the
Mind*); Senator Barry Goldwater (*Goldwater
on Goldwater*); Sandra Mackey (*The Saudis*);
(*Price Waterhouse Guide to New Tax Law*).
Commission Home 15%; Foreign 20%.

Rhodes Literary Agency Inc.

140 West End Avenue, New York, NY 10023
☎0101 212 580 1300

Contact *Joan Lewis* (President)

FOUNDED 1971. Non-fiction books, novels and
juvenile books. No reading fee for outlines.
Commission Home 10%; Foreign 20%.

Eleanor Roszel Rogers, Literary Agent

1487 Generals Highway,
Crownsville, MD 21032
☎0101 301 987 8166

Contact *Eleanor Rogers*

FOUNDED 1976. Eager to work with new/
unpublished writers. Specialises in mainstream fiction and non-fiction. Juvenile
books. No reading fee.
Commission Home 10%; Foreign 20%.

Stephanie Rogers and Associates

3855 Lankershim Blvd, 218,
North Hollywood, CA 91604
☎0101 818 509 1010

Contact *Stephanie Rogers*

FOUNDED 1981. Prefers to work with
established/published authors. Specialises in
screenplays – dramas (contemporary),
action/adventure, romantic comedies and
biographies for motion picture and TV. Does
not read unsolicited mss.
Commission Home 10%; Dramatic 10%;
Foreign 10%.

Rosenstone/Wender

3 East 48th Street, 4th Floor,
New York, NY 10017
☎0101 212 832 8330

Contact *Phyllis Wender*

FOUNDED 1981. Fiction, non-fiction, children's and young adult books. Scripts for
film, TV and theatre, but not radio. Do not
welcome unsolicited mss. Prefer letter outlining the project, the writer's credits, etc. No
reading fee. CLIENTS include Jonathan Fran-
zen (*Twenty-Seventh City*); J.P. Miller (*The
Skook*); Julia Frey (*Henri de Toulouse Lautrec:
A New Biography*); Budd Hopkins (*Intruders*);
Marc Brown & Stephen Korensky (*Dinosaurs
Beware*); Hugh Whitemore, Simon Gray.
Commission Home 10%; Dramatic 10%;
Foreign 20%. *UK associates* A.P. Watt Ltd.

Jack Scagnetti Literary Agency

Suite 210, 5330 Lankershim Blvd,
North Hollywood, CA 91601
☎0101 818 762 3871

Contact *Jack Scagnetti*

FOUNDED 1974. Prefers to work with
established/published authors. Non-fiction
books, novels, film and TV scripts. No reading fee for outlines.
Commission Home 10%; Dramatic 10%;
Foreign 15%.

Schaffner Agency, Inc.

264 Fifth Avenue, New York, NY 10001
☎0101 212 689 6888

Contact *Timothy Schaffner, Patrick Delahunt.*

FOUNDED 1948. Specialises in literary fiction, science fiction, fantasy, celebrity biographies, popular self-help and general non-fiction. Query letter in first instance. No reading fee for outlines. International Reply Coupon required. CLIENTS include Maxine Hong Kingston, Lucius Shepard.
Commission Home 15%; Dramatic 15%; Foreign 20%. *UK associates* A.M. Heath & Co. Ltd.

The Susan Schulman Literary Agency, Inc.

454 West 44th Street, New York, NY 10036
☎0101 212 713 1633

Contact *Susan Schulman* (President)

FOUNDED 1978. Prefers to work with established/published authors. Because of the success of *Women Who Love Too Much*, leans towards titles in the field of psychology and sociology, trends, family issues and women's issues. No reading fee for outlines. CLIENTS include Robin Norwood, David Saperstein, Jim Arnosky.
Commission Home 10%; Dramatic 10% – (foreign) 20%; Foreign 20%. *UK associates* Seraphina Clarke.

James Seligmann Agency

Suite 1101, 175 Fifth Avenue, New York, NY 10010
☎0101 212 477 5186

Contact *James F. Seligmann*

FOUNDED 1960. Non-fiction books and novels (especially mainstream and settings from 1920s to present). No reading fee for outlines. CLIENTS include Anthony Padovano, Nona Aguilar, Frank Brady.
Commission Home 15%; Dramatic 15%; Foreign 15% plus foreign agent's commission; 20% for British sales.

Shapiro–Lichtman Talent Agency

8827 Beverly Blvd, Los Angeles, CA 90048
☎0101 213 859 8877

FOUNDED 1969. Prefers to work with established/published authors. Film and TV scripts. Does not read unsolicited mss.
Commission Home 10%; Dramatic 10%; Foreign 20%.

Bobbe Siegel, Literary Agency

41 West 83rd Street, New York, NY 10024
☎0101 212 877 4985

Contact *Bobbe Siegel, Richard Siegel*

FOUNDED 1975. Prefers to work with established/published authors. Specialises in literary fiction, detective, suspense, historical, science fiction, biography, 'how-to', women's subjects, fitness, health, beauty, sports, pop-psychology. No scripts. No cookbooks, crafts, juveniles. First approach with letter with International Reply Coupons for response. No reading fee. Will only give a critique if the writer is taken on for representation. CLIENTS include Primo Levi, Lew Dykes, Marlin Bree, Margaret Mitchell Dukore, Nina Herrmann Donnelley.
Commission Home 15%; Dramatic 20%; Foreign 20%. (Foreign & Dramatic are split with sub-agent – 10% each.) *UK associates* John Pawsey.

The Evelyn Singer Literary Agency, Inc.

P.O. Box 594, White Plains, NY 10602
☎0101 914 949 1147/212 799 5203

Contact *Evelyn Singer*

FOUNDED 1951. Prefers to work with established/published authors. Fiction and non-fiction; adult and juvenile. Adult: health, medicine, 'how-to', diet, biography, celebrity, conservation, political; serious novels, suspense, mystery. Juvenile: Educational non-fiction for all ages; fiction for the middle and teen levels. No picture books unless the author is or has an experienced book illustrator. No formula romance, poetry, sex

books, occult, textbooks, or specialised material unsuitable for trade market. No scripts. No unsolicited mss. First approach with letter giving writing background, credits, publications, including date of publication and publisher. International Reply Coupons essential. No phone calls. No reading fee. CLIENTS include William F. Hallstead, William Beechcroft, Mary Elting, Franklin Folsom, Michael Folsom.
Commission Home 15%; Dramatic 15%; Foreign 20%; *UK associates* **Laurence Pollinger Limited.**

Singer Media Corporation
3164 Tyler Avenue, Anaheim, CA 92801
☎0101 714 527 5650

Contact *Natalie Carlton*

FOUNDED 1944. Contemporary romances, non-fiction, biographies. Specialises in psychological self-help. No scripts, personal adventure novels. No unsolicited mss. Letter first. Reading fee for unpublished authors of US$200.00 for a complete critique and suggestions. Fee deducted from advance if publisher found. CLIENTS include Dr Frank S. Caprio, Dr Muriel Oberleder, W.E.D. Ross.
Commission Home 15%; Foreign 20%.

Michael Snell Literary Agency
Bridge and Castle Road, Truro, MA 02666
☎0101 617 349 3781

Contact *Michael Snell* (President), *Patti Smith* (Fiction Editor)

FOUNDED 1980. Eager to work with new/unpublished writers. Specialises in business books (from professional/reference to popular trade 'how-to'); college textbooks (in all subjects, but especially business, science and psychology); 'how-to' and self-help (on all topics, from diet and exercise to sex and personal finance); mystery and suspense fiction. Will consider unsolicited mss but prefer outline and sample chapter with International Reply Coupons. No reading fee for outlines.
Commission Home 15%; Dramatic 15%; Foreign 15%.

Elyse Sommer, Inc.
110–34 73rd Road, P.O. Box 1133, Forest Hills, NY 11375
☎0101 718 263 2668

Contact *Elyse Sommer*

FOUNDED 1950. Prefers to work with established/published authors. Non-fiction books. Some novels – strong romance novels and page turners. Good novels for juveniles. No reading fee for outlines. Some book packaging.
Commission Home 15%; Dramatic 20%; Foreign 20%.

Philip G. Spitzer Literary Agency
788 Ninth Avenue, New York, NY 10019
☎0101 212 265 6003

Contact *Philip Spitzer*

FOUNDED 1969. Prefers to work with established/published authors. Specialises in general non-fiction (politics, current events, sports, biography) and fiction, including mystery and suspense. No reading fee for outlines. CLIENTS include Robert Mayer, James Lee Burke, Thomas Allen, Norman Polmar, Andre Dubus, Sam Toperoff.
Commission Home 10%; Dramatic 10%; Foreign 20%. *UK associates* **Murray Pollinger.**

Ellen Lively Steele and Associates
Drawer 447, Organ, NM 88052
☎0101 505 382 5449

FOUNDED 1980. Writers must be referred. Novels, film and TV scripts. Does not read unsolicited mss.
Commission Home 10%; Foreign 5%.

Sterling Lord Literistic Inc.
One Madison Avenue, New York, NY 10010
☎0101 212 696 2800

Specialises in adult fiction and non-fiction in all genres. No reading fee for outlines.
Commission Home 10%; Dramatic 10%; Foreign 20%.

Gloria Stern Agency

1230 Park Avenue, New York, NY 10128
☎0101 212 289 7698

Contact *Gloria Stern*

FOUNDED 1976. 80% non-fiction; 20% serious mainstream fiction. Biography; philosophy/history. Specialises in education, women's issues, biographies, serious fiction. No scripts, 'how-to' books, poetry, short stories, first fiction of a previously unpublished author. First approach by letter stating contents of books, list of competing books, qualifications as author and including International Reply Coupons, No reading fee. CLIENTS include Hannah Arendt, Dian Dincin Buchman, Phillip Hallie, Gerald Phillips, Dr Lester Morrison.
Commission Home 10–15%; Dramatic 10%; Foreign UK 15% shared; Translation 20% shared. *UK associates* **A.M. Heath & Co. Ltd.**

Gloria Stern Agency

12535 Chandler Blvd, #3, North Hollywood, CA 91607
☎0101 818 508 6296

Contact *Gloria Stern*

FOUNDED 1984. Mainstream fiction, fantasy, film scripts. Specialises in books on relationships. No books containing gratuitous violence. Approach with a letter and synopsis. Recommendation when applicable. Reading fee charged by the hour.
Commission Home 10–15%; Dramatic 10–15%; Foreign 18%.

Stevens–Rabinowitz Agency

Suite 271, 2265 Westwood,
Los Angeles, CA 90064
☎0101 213 275 0931

Contact *Serita Stevens* (President)

FOUNDED 1979. Specialises in historical romance, romantic suspense, gothics, women's mainstream, fiction and young adult. Reading fee. CLIENTS include Laurie Grant, Judith Hagar, Serita Stevens.
Commission Home 15%; Dramatic 20%; Foreign 20%.

H.N. Swanson Inc.

8523 Sunset Blvd, Los Angeles, CA 90069
☎0101 213 652 5385

Contact *B.F. Kamsler*

FOUNDED 1934. Fiction: thrillers, adventure, non-fiction, plays – radio, audio cassettes. Specialises in science fiction. No scientific, medical, sexploitation. No unsolicited mss. Send a letter with International Reply Coupon in the first instance. No reading fee. CLIENTS include Elmore Leonard, Joseph Hayes, Arthur Hailey.
Commission Home 10%; Dramatic 10%; Foreign 20%. *UK associates* various agencies.

Patricia Teal Literary Agency

2036 Vista Del Rosa, Fullerton, CA 92631
☎0101 714 738 8333

Contact *Patricia Teal*

FOUNDED 1978. Specialises in romance (contemporary and historical). Category fiction: mysteries, men's adventure, horror, occult. Non-fiction: self-help and 'how-to' books. No religious/inspirational, autobiography, cookbooks, travel. No scripts. No unsolicited mss. First approach with letter. No reading fee. CLIENTS include Jerry Kennealy (*Polo Solo*), D.R. Meredith (*Murder by Impulse*), Laura Taylor, Jill Marie Landis (*Sunflower*).
Commission Home 10–15%; Dramatic 20%; Foreign 20%. *UK associates* Inpra, **Shelley Power.**

A Total Acting Experience

Suite 300, 6736 Laurel Canyon,
North Hollywood, CA 91606
☎0101 818 765 7244

Contact *Dan A. Bellacicco*

FOUNDED 1984. Will accept new and established writers. Specialises in romance,

science fiction, mysteries, humour, 'how-to' and self-help, juvenile books, film, TV and radio scripts and stage plays. No reading fee.
Commission Home 10%; Dramatic 10%; Foreign 10%.

Susan P. Urstadt, Inc.
Suite 2A, 125 East 84th Street,
New York, NY 10028
☎0101 212 744 6605

Contact *Susan P. Urstadt* (President), *Helen F. Pratt* (Associate)

FOUNDED 1975. Specialises in literary and commercial fiction, decorative arts and antiques, architecture, gardening, cookery, biography, performing arts, sports, current affairs, lifestyle and current living trends. First approach with letter, outline and sample chapters, and International Reply Coupons. CLIENTS include Allen Lacy, Sven Birkerts, Thomas Powers.
Commission Home 15%; Dramatic 15%; Foreign 20%.

Ralph Vicinanza Ltd
Suite 1205, 432 Park Avenue,
New York, NY 10016
☎0101 212 725 5133

Contact *Christopher Lotts*

FOUNDED 1978. Specialises in history, fantasy and thrillers. No reading fee for outlines. CLIENTS include Tim Underwood and Chuck Miller, Larry Niven and Jerry Pournelle, Robert Heinlein.
Commission Home 10% Foreign 20%.

Carlson Wade
49 Bokee Court, Room K-4,
Brooklyn, NY 11223
☎0101 718 743 6983

Contact *Carlson Wade*

FOUNDED 1949. All types of fiction and non-fiction. No poetry or textbooks. No scripts. Will consider unsolicited mss but prefer letter of description with International Reply Coupons. Reading fee of $50 for books, $10 for short script.
Commission Home 10%; Dramatic 10%; Foreign 10%.

Austin Wahl Agency Ltd
Suite 342, Monadnock Building, 53 West Jackson Boulevard, Chicago, IL 60604
☎0101 312 922 3331

FOUNDED 1935. Professional writers only. No reading fee.
Commission Home 15%; Dramatic 10%; Foreign 20%.

Mary Jack Wald Associates, Inc.
Suite 347, 70A Greenwich Avenue, New York, NY 10003
☎0101 212 254 7842

Contact *Mary Jack Wald*

FOUNDED 1985. Adult and juvenile fiction and non-fiction including screenplays and teleplays, but no episodic material for series. No unsolicited mss. Query letter in the first instance giving writing/publishing history plus synopsis. Include International Reply Coupons. No reading fee. CLIENTS include Patricia MacInnes, Jan Wahl, Christopher Bohjalian, Louis Baldwin, Marilyn MacGregor, Anthony Fragola, Neil Johnson.
Commission Home 15%; Dramatic 15%;. Foreign 15%. *UK associate* Mildred Hird.

Wallace & Sheil Agency, Inc.
177 East 70th Street, New York, NY 10021
☎0101 212 570 9090

FOUNDED 1974. No unsolicited mss.
Commission Home 10%; Dramatic 10%; Foreign 20%. *UK associates* **Anthony Sheil Associates**.

John A. Ware Literary Agency
392 Central Park West, New York, NY 10025
☎0101 212 866 4733

Contact *John Ware*

FOUNDED 1978. Specialises in biography, investigative journalism, history, health and psychology (academic credentials required). No category fiction (except mysteries). Current issues and affairs, sports, oral history, Americana and folklore. Does not read unsolicited mss. No reading fee for outlines. CLIENTS include Frank Satterthwaite PhD, William J. Rust, Armen Keteyian.
Commission Home 10%; Dramatic 10%; Foreign 20%.

Ann Waugh Agency
4731 Laurel Canyon Blvd,
North Hollywood, CA 91607
☎0101 818 980 0141

Contact *Steve Jacobson*

FOUNDED 1979. Screenplays only. 'Original ideas by authors who have studied screenwriting.' Specialises in romance, comedy, thriller and action adventure screenplays. No slasher/horror scripts. Return postage and envelope required. Also essential to send a small envelope with International Reply Coupons before sending in script to receive release form that must be signed and returned with script submission. No reading fee.
Commission Home 10%; Dramatic 10%; Foreign 10%.

Wieser & Wieser, Inc.
118 East 25th Street, New York, NY 10010
☎0101 212 260 0860

Contact *Olga B. Wieser, George J. Wieser, Anastasia M. Ashman*

FOUNDED 1976. Prefers to work with established/published authors. Specialises in literary and mainstream fiction, serious and popular historical fiction, mass market regencies, general non-fiction: business, finance, aviation, sports, photography, Americana, cookbooks, travel and popular medicine. TV and film scripts. No poetry, children's, science fiction, religious. No unsolicited mss. First approach by letter with

International Reply Coupons. No reading fee for outlines. CLIENTS include Douglas C. Jones, John Nance (*On Shaky Ground*), Joan Wolf, Steve Levenkron (*Psychotherapy for an Obsessive Age*), Dale Brown (*Flight of the Old Dog; Silver Tower*), Chet Currier.
Commission Home 15%; Dramatic 15%; Foreign 20%.

Williams/Wesley/Winant
180 East 79th Street, New York, NY 10021
☎0101 212 RE-4-0988

Contact *Jean Valentine Winant* (plays), *William A. Winant, III, William W. Winant, II*

FOUNDED 1976. Specialise in novels, short stories dealing with fantasy, mystery or mythology. Plays for the theatre (any length, any subject). Detective novels (Chandler genre). Welcome unsolicited playscripts, but for other mss a letter in the first instance is required. No reading fee.
Commission Home 10%; Dramatic 10%; Foreign 15%.

Alan Willig and Associates
Suite 409, 165 West 46th Street,
New York, NY 10036
☎0101 212 921 4460

Contact *Jack Tantleff*

FOUNDED 1985. Prefers to work with established/published authors. Specialises in plays, screenplays and television. No reading fee for outlines.
Commission Home 10%; Dramatic 10%; Foreign 10%.

Ruth Wreschner, Authors' Representative
10 West 74th Street, New York, NY 10023
☎0101 212 877 2605

Contact *Ruth Wreschner*

FOUNDED 1981. Prefers to work with established/published authors, but 'will consider very good first novels, both mainstream and genre, particularly British mystery writers'. Specialises in popular medicine, health, 'how-to' books and fiction. No screenplays or dramatic plays. First approach with query letter and International Reply Coupons. For fiction, a synopsis and first 100 pages; for non-fiction, an outline and two sample chapters. No reading fee. CLIENTS include Samuel Janus, PhD and Cynthia Janus, MD (*The American Sexual Experience*); Joseph Nowinski, PhD (*A Lifelong Love Affair*); Elayne Kahn, PhD and David Rudnitsky (*Love Codes*).

Ann Wright Representatives, Inc.
136 East 57th Street, New York, NY 10022
☎0101 212 832 0110

Contact *Dan Wright* (Head of Literary Department)

FOUNDED 1963. Prefers to work with established/published authors. Specialises in properties that will become film or television product in all categories in all countries and in all dramatic themes; i.e. thrillers, mystery, rights of passage, police, spy, relationships, etc. Also original screenplays, television films – mini-series, storylines and treatments. No non-fiction. No unsolicited mss. Prefer initial query or short outline with International Reply Coupons. No reading fee. CLIENTS include Alan Trustman, Theodore Bonnet, James Anderson, Richard Harris, Tom Dempsey, Ethan Shedley, John Peer Nugent.
Commission Home 10%; Dramatic 10%; Foreign 10%.

Writers House Inc.
21 West 26th Street, New York, NY 10010
☎0101 212 685 2400

Contact *Albert Zuckerman* (President), *Amy Berkower* (Executive Vice President), *Merrilee Heifetz* (Vice President), *Susan Cohen*, *Kathilyn Solomon*, *Sheila Callahan*.

FOUNDED 1974. Avant-garde original fiction, thrillers, science fiction, fantasy, contemporary fiction, self-help, children's and young adult books. No poetry, short story collections. No scripts. Will consider unsolicited mss but prefer letter, brief synopsis and sample chapters. No reading fee. CLIENTS include Ken Follett, Francine Pascal, Robin McKinley, F. Buck Rodgers.
Commission Home 15%; Dramatic 15%; Foreign 20%. *UK associates* Blake Friedmann Literary Agency Ltd.

Writer's Productions
Box 630, Westport, CT 06881
☎0101 203 227 8199

Contact *David L. Meth*

FOUNDED 1981. Eager to work with new/unpublished writers. Specialises in literary, quality fiction & non-fiction dealing with Asia and Asian Americans, especially Japan and Korea. Interested in important non-fiction on subjects that will have some influence on society. Book projects where video, documentary and film/TV tie-ins are possible. Expanding into video and film production but do not accept video, film or TV scripts for representation. No 'how-to', health & nutrition, medical, westerns, science fiction, cookbooks, philosophical, occult. Send a sample of thirty chapters with International Reply Coupons. No reading fee. CLIENTS include Mary Monroe, Joseph Czarneck, Ahn Junghyo, Matsumoto Seicho.
Commission Home 15%; Dramatic 20%; Foreign 20%.

Barbara W. Yedlin, Literary Agent
Pump Street, Newcastle, ME 04553
☎0101 207 563 8335

Contact *Barbara W. Yedlin*

FOUNDED 1981. Literary novels and short story collections; juvenile novels (ages 8–12); mysteries ('British type'), literary travel accounts, biography. No genre writing, with the exception of mysteries. No romance, horror, pornography, religious material of any kind. In the mystery field, no violent, sexy or

hard boiled stories. No science fiction, teenage novels, picture books. No scripts. Will consider unsolicited mss but prefer a query letter with synopsis and sample pages, with International Reply Coupons. A few sentences of background but no career resume. No reading fee.
Commission Home10%.

Susan Zeckendorf Associates

Suite 11B, 171 West 57th Street,
New York, NY 10019
☎0101 212 245 2928

Contact *Susan Zeckendorf* (President)

FOUNDED 1979. Eager to work with new/unpublished writers. Specialises in women's commercial fiction: *Riches, Scandals*; international espionage: *The Last Patriot, Endgame*; mysteries: *The Long Way to Die, Killing in Dreamland*; parenting books: *Dance-Play, Getting Ready to Read*; music: *Stormy Weather, The Story of Women in Jazz*; historical fiction: *Jermian Martin*. No category

romance, science fiction, scripts. No unsolicited mss. Send query letter describing mss. No reading fee. CLIENTS include Una Mary Parker, Robert Fowler, Jerry Patterson, James N. Frey, Diane Lynch Fraser.
Commission Home 15%; Dramatic 15%; Foreign 20%. *UK associates* **Abner Stein**.

Tom Zelasky Literary Agency

3138 Parkridge Crescent, Chamblee,
CA 30341
☎0101 404 458 0391

Contact *Tom Zelasky*

FOUNDED 1984. Prefers to work with established/published authors. Specialises in mainstream fiction or non-fiction, categorical romance, historical romance, historical fiction, westerns, action/detective mysteries, suspense, science fiction. No reading fee for outlines. International Reply Coupon required.
Commission Home 10–15%; Dramatic 10–15%; Foreign 15–25%.

American Press and Journals

The Associated Press
12 Norwich Street, London EC4A 1BT
☎01–353 1515

Chief of Bureau *Myron L. Belkind*

Baltimore Sun
14 Gough Square, London EC4A 3DE
☎01–353 3531

Chief of Bureau *Gilbert Lewthwaite*

Boston Globe
42 Jubilee Place, London SW3 3TQ
☎01–351 3692

Contact *Gordon McKibben*

Business Week
34 Dover Street, London W1X 4BR
☎01–493 1451

Bureau Manager *Richard Melcher*

The Christian Science Monitor
Eggington House, 25/28 Buckingham Gate,
London SW1E 6LD
☎01–630 8666

Contact *Julian Baum*
(British Correspondent)

Forbes Magazine
25 St James Street, London SW1A 1HG
☎01–839 7251

Contact *Richard C. Morais*
(European Correspondent)

Fortune Magazine
Time & Life Building, New Bond Street,
London W1Y 0AA
☎01–499 4080

Contact *Richard Kirkland*
(European Editor)

International Herald Tribune
Room 4/4, Bracken House, Cannon Street,
London EC4P 4BY
☎01–248 8000

Contact *John Vinocur* (Editor)

Journal of Commerce
Bailey House, Old Seacoal Lane,
London EC4M 7LR
☎01–489 1932

Contact *Janet Porter*
(European News Co-ordinator)

Life Magazine
Time & Life Building, New Bond Street,
London W1Y 0AA
☎01–499 4080

Contact *Gail Ridgwell*

Los Angeles Times
140 Sloane Street, London SW1X 9AY
☎01–730 0488

Bureau Chief *Tyler Marshall*

Miami Herald
19 Clareville Grove, London SW7 5AU
☎01–370 5532

Contact *Peter Slevin*

New York City Tribune
Room 214, Communications House,
Gough Square, London EC4
☎01–353 4805

Contact *Mark Palmer*
(London Correspondent)

The New York Times
London International Press Centre,
76 Shoe Lane, London EC4A 3JB
☎01–353 8181

Contact *Howell Raines*
(Chief Correspondent)

Newsday
119 Farringdon Road, London EC1
☎01–289 4822

Contact *Adrian Peracchio*

Newsweek
25 Upper Brook Street, London W1Y 1DP
☎01–629 8361

Contact *Gerald C. Lubenow*

People Magazine
Time & Life Building, New Bond Street,
London W1Y 0AA
☎01–499 4080

Contact *Jerene Jones*
(Special Correspondent)

Philadelphia Inquirer
14 Rodborough Road, London NW11 8RY
☎01–455 2725

Contact *Michael Leary*

Pittsburgh Post-Gazette
7 Vicarage Gate, Flat 11, London W8 4HH
☎01–937 7120

Contact *Fernand Auberjonois*
(European Correspondent)

San Francisco Examiner
53 Devonshire Road, London W5
☎01–567 9444

Contact *Dan Ehrlich*
(London Correspondent)

Sports Illustrated
Time & Life Building, New Bond Street,
London W1Y 0AA
☎01–499 4080

Contact *Lavinia Scott Elliot*
(London Correspondent)

Time Magazine
Time & Life Building, New Bond Street,
London W1Y 0AA
☎01–499 4080

Bureau Chief *Christopher Ogden*

The Toledo Blade
c/o Reuters Ltd, 85 Fleet Street,
London EC4Y 1EE
☎01–735 6905

Chief of Bureau *Fernand Auberjonois*

US News and World Report
72 New Bond Street, London W1Y 0RD
☎01–493 4643

Contact *Robin Knight*
(Senior European Editor)

Wall Street Journal
London International Press Centre,
76 Shoe Lane, London EC4A 3JB
☎01–353 0671

London Bureau Chief *Kathryn Christensen*

Washington Post
25 Upper Brook Street, London W1Y 2AB
☎01–629 8958

Contact *Karen De Young*
(London Correspondent)

Washington Times
21 Chalcot Crescent, London NW1 8YE
☎01–722 4553

Bureau Chief *James Morrison*

Professional Associations

ABSA (Association for Business Sponsorship of the Arts)
2 Chester Street, London SW1X 7RB
☎01–235 9781

A national independent organisation established by the business community, concerned with both the concept and practical details of business sponsorship of the arts, and to represent sponsors' interests. Though ABSA has not yet been involved in the commercial sponsorship of a 'purely literary work', other aspects of writing come up, and writers interested in getting involved in some way should send for *Sponsorship Manual* (£5 including p&p).

The Arts Club

40 Dover Street, London W1X 3RB
☎01–499 8581

Membership Secretary *Mrs Ridgway*
Subscription assessed individually Town, £300 maximum Country, £145 maximum

FOUNDED 1863. Some connection with the arts necessary for membership, which is only available by application with two sponsors.

The Arts Council of Great Britain

105 Piccadilly, London W1V 0AU
☎01–629 9495

Chairman *Sir William Rees-Mogg*
Secretary General *Luke Rittner*

The 1988/89 grant dispensed by the Arts Council stands at £150 million. From this fund the Arts Council supports arts organisations, artists, performers, and others: grants can also be made for particular productions, exhibitions and projects. Grants available to individuals are detailed in the free Arts Council folder *Awards & Schemes 1988/9*. The total amount set aside for literature 1988/89 is £630,000, an increase of 39 per cent.

Drama director *Ian Brown* New writing is supported through *Theatre Writing Allocations* (contact the Drama department for more details). **Literature director** *Alastair Niven* Under its new director, Dr Alastair Niven, the Literature Department has defined education, ethnic minority groups, the touring of literature and translation among its top priorities. P.D. James has been appointed as Chairperson to the Literature Advisory Panel. This year the Arts Council will be giving three grants of £5000 each to individual writers. Details available from the Literature Department from June 1988.

Arts Council of Northern Ireland

181a Stranmillis Road, Belfast BT9 5DU
☎0232 381591

Literature Officer *Michael Longley*
Drama Officer *Dennis Smith*

The Association of Authors' Agents

20 John Street, London WC1N 2DR
☎01–405 6774

Secretary *Linda Shaughnessy*
Membership fee £35 p.a.

FOUNDED 1974. Membership voluntary. The AAA maintains a code of practice, provides a forum for discussion and represents its members in issues affecting the profession.

Association of Independent Producers

17 Great Pulteney Street, London W1R 3DG
☎01–434 0181

Contact *Matthew Crampton*
Subscription £75 p.a.

FOUNDED 1976. Membership open (there are many writer members). Benefits include: an information service, a regular magazine, information packs on various aspects of production, and a free copy of the *Independent Production Handbook*. Offers information about production, how to get in touch with producers etc. The general aims of the association are to encourage film and television production and to broaden the base of finance and exhibition.

Association of Little Presses

89a Petherton Road, London N5 2QT
☎01–226 2657

Subscription £7.50 p.a.

FOUNDED 1966. Membership offered to individuals who run small presses; associate membership is available to other interested people or groups. Over 80% of all new poetry in Britain is published by little presses and magazines. ALP also publishes a magazine, *Poetry and Little Press Information* (PALP); information booklets such as *Getting Your Poetry Published* (over 32,000 copies sold since 1973) and the *Catalogue of Little Press Books in Print,* plus a regular newsletter. A full list of Little Presses (some of these, like **Bloodaxe Books**, are now sufficiently established and successful to be considered in the mainstream of the business) is available from ALP, or from the *Oriel Bookshop*, price £1.25 inc. p&p (see **Welsh Arts Council**).

Authors' Licensing and Collecting Society

7 Ridgmount Street, London WC1E 7AE
☎01–255 2034

President *Lord Willis*
Secretary General *Janet Hurrell*

Subscription £5 (+ VAT) (Free to members of **The Society of Authors, Writers' Guild**)

A non-profit making society collecting and distributing payment to writers in areas where they are unable to administer the rights themselves, such as reprography, certain lending rights, private and off-air recording and simultaneous cabling. Open to both writers and their heirs.

BAFTA (British Academy of Film and Television Arts)

195 Piccadilly, London W1V 9LG
☎01–734 0022

Director *A.J. Byrne*
Ordinary subscription £75 p.a.

FOUNDED 1947. Membership limited to 'those who have contributed creatively to the industry'. Facilities for screening, discussions; encourage research and experimentation; lobby parliament, make annual awards.

BAPLA (British Association of Picture Libraries and Agencies)

13 Woodberry Crescent, London N10 1PJ
☎01–444 7913/883 2531

Administrator *Sal Shuel*

An association of nearly 200 picture libraries and agencies who handle between them more than 100 million images, 'black and white, colour, very old, very new, pretty, terrifying, scientific, absurd, aardvarks, and Zulus and practically everything in between'. The *Directory* (obtainable from the above address) is a guide to members and subject index. Offers advice on costs, etc.

BASCA (British Academy of Songwriters, Composers and Authors)

34 Hanway Street, London W1P 9DE
☎01–240 2823

Contact *Marilyn Worsley*
Subscription from £11.50 p.a.

FOUNDED 1947. The academy offers advice and support for both established and aspiring songwriters. Issues standard contracts between publishers and writers. Benefits of membership include the quarterly magazine, assessment of beginners' work, and solicitor's advice.

Book Trust (formerly the National Book League)

Book House, 45 East Hill,
London SW18 2QZ
☎01–870 9055

Chief Executive *Keith McWilliams*
Subscription £25 p.a.

FOUNDED 1925. Benefits to members include the Book Information Service (which also provides a free service to the public) and access to the Children's Book Foundation. The Foundation acts as a bridge between those who produce books and those who read them, with a comprehensive collection of every book published in the last 24 months. Book Trust runs Children's Book Week. Other aspects of its work include organising touring exhibitions, the administering of 14 literary prizes, including the **Booker** (see *Awards, Competitions and Prizes*), and the carrying out of surveys which are then published. *Book Trust* publications include books about books, writers, prizes and education; a free list with order form is available from Book House. *Booknews*, quarterly, is free to members.

British Amateur Press Association

78 Tennyson Road, Stratford,
London E15 4DR

Subscription £4 p.a.

A non-profit making, non-sectarian society founded, in 1890, to 'promote the fellowship of writers, artists, editors, printers, publishers and other craftsmen. To encourage them to edit, print and publish, as a hobby, magazines, books and other literary works' by letterpress and other processes. Not an outlet for writing, except between other members in their private publications, but a fraternity providing contacts between amateur writers/journalists.

British American Arts Association

49 Wellington Street, London WC2E 7BN
☎01–379 7755

Director *Jennifer Williams*

Organisation addressing the problems of transatlantic cultural exchange. Offers advice and counselling in all arts disciplines, runs a conference programme, and takes on special projects. Emphasis is on the non-profit sector. BAAA is not a grant-giving organisation.

British Copyright Council

Copyright House, 29–33 Berners Street,
London W1P 4AA

Contact *Geoffrey Adams* (Secretary)

Works for the international acceptance of copyright and acts as a lobby/watchdog organisation on legal and professional matters, on behalf of the trade. An umbrella organisation, which does not deal with individual enquiries.

The British Council

10 Spring Gardens, London SW1A 2BN
☎01–930 8466 (literature)
Telex 8952201 BRICON G   Fax 01–839 6347

Contact *Press and Information Department*

The British Council's purpose is to project Britain abroad. It promotes British ideas, talents and experience in education and training, books and periodicals, the English Language, the arts, sciences and technology. It has a network of 120 offices in over 80 countries and employs 4000 staff.

British Film Institute

21 Stephen Street, London W1P 1PL
☎01–255 1444   Telex 27624 BFI LDNG

Membership £26.50 (includes Monthly
Film Bulletin)/£15.75;
Associateship £10.25 (plus concessions)

FOUNDED 1933. Committed to the development of the art and appreciation of film and television. Runs the National Film Theatre and the National Film Archive in London, and funds film theatres in the regions, as well as supporting the making of new films, video and television largely through the Regional Arts Associations, but also through direct grants.

British Guild of Travel Writers

90 Corringway, London W5 3HA
☎01–998 2223

Chairman *Peter Hughes*
Honorary Secretary *Gillian Thomas*
Subscription £25 p.a.

The professional association of travel writers, broadcasters, photographers, and editors, which aims to serve its membership's interest professionally and act as a forum for debate and discussion. Meet monthly. The guild is represented on the BTA, and its members (c.120) must earn the majority of their income from travel reporting.

British Science Fiction Association

33 Thornville Road, Hartlepool,
Cleveland TS26 8EW

Membership Secretary *Jo Raine*
Subscription £10.00 p.a.

For both writers and readers of Science Fiction and Fantasy. Publishes *Matrix* (news) *Focus* (fiction), *Vector* (criticism), *Paperback Inferno* (paperback and magazine reviews). Also offers creative writing groups, a magazine chain and an information service.

British Screen Finance

37–39 Oxford Street, London W1R 1RE
☎01–434 0291
Telex 888694 BRISCR G   Fax 01–434 9933

Contact *Adrian Hodges* (script development)

A private company aided by government grant, taking over from the NFFC in 1986. Backed by consortium including Rank, **Channel 4** and Cannon. Divided into two functions: National Film Development Fund, for script development (**Contact** *Adrian Hodges*) and production investment (**Contact** *Simon Relph*). Develop around eighteen projects per year, and have invested in twenty-six British films in the last two years.

British Theatre Association

The Darwin Infill Building, Regents College,
Inner Circle, Regents Park,
London NW1 4NW
☎01–935 2571

Director *Sally Meades*
Subscription from £15 p.a.

FOUNDED 1919. Though the British Theatre Association is a membership organisation, the Play Library, the most comprehensive in the world, is open to all. Benefits of membership include the reference and lending sections of the library, a unique theatre information service, and training courses. Publishes *Drama* magazine.

British Theatre Institute
(incorporating Drama and Theatre Education Council)

c/o NCA, Francis House, Francis Street,
London SW1

The British Theatre Institute was founded in 1971. In 1976 it called a conference of educational bodies which led to the formation of DATEC, the *Drama and Theatre Education Council*. The two joined forces in 1982. Because of this merger the BTI places particular emphasis on education and training. It also acts as a resource office and consultant on all aspects of theatre and drama education.

Subscriber members include both individuals and organisations.

Campaign for Press and Broadcasting Freedom

9 Poland Street, London W1V 3DG
☎01–437 2795

Subscription £7 p.a. (plus concessions)

Broadly based pressure group, working for more accountable and accessible media in Britain. Advises on right of reply and takes up the issue of the portrayal of minorities (incorporating CARM, the *Campaign Against Racism in the Media*). Members receive *Free Press* (bimonthly), discounts on publications and news of campaign progress.

Crime Writers' Association

PO Box 172, Tring, Herts HP23 5LP
☎044 282 8496

Secretary *Anthea Fraser*
Fees £20 for Town Members; £17 for Country Members

Full membership is limited to professional crime-writers, but publishers, literary agents, booksellers etc., who specialise in crime are eligible as Associate Members. Meetings held in Soho monthly, when informative talks are frequently given by police, Scenes of Crime officers, lawyers, etc. A weekend Conference is held annually in different parts of the country. Monthly newsheet, *Red Herrings*. Annual awards of Gold Daggers for year's best crime fiction and non-fiction. A separate award, the CWA-Cartier Diamond Dagger is presented to an author, rather than a book, for outstanding contribution to the genre. Previous winners include Eric Ambler and P.D. James.

The Critics' Circle

c/o The Stage & Television Today,
47 Bermondsey Street, London SE1 3XT
☎01–403 1818

President *David Nathan*
Honorary General Secretary *Peter Hepple*
Subscription £8 p.a.

Membership by invitation only. Aims to uphold and promote the art of criticism (and the commercial rates of pay thereof) and preserve the interests of its members, who are professionals involved in criticism of film, drama, music and ballet.

Educational Television Association

King's Manor, Exhibition Square,
York YO1 2EP
☎0904 629701

An umbrella organisation for individuals and organisations using television for education and training.

The English Association

The Vicarage, Priory Gardens,
Bedford Park, London W4 1TT
☎01–995 4236

Secretary *Ruth Fairbanks-Joseph*

FOUNDED 1906 to promote understanding and appreciation of the English language and its literature. Activities include sponsoring a number of publications and organising annual sixth-form conferences. Publications include *English*, *Year's Work in English Studies* and *Essays and Studies*.

Federation of Broadcasting Unions

c/o BETA, 181–185 Wardour Street,
London W1V 4LA
☎01–439 7585

Chairman *John Morton* (MU)
Secretary *Paddy Leech* (BETA)

Unions affiliated to the FBU are BETA, EETPU, Equity, Musicians Union, NUJ, and **The Writers' Guild**.

Federation of Film Unions
11 Wardour Street, London W1V 4AY
☎01–437 8506

Contact *Alan Sapper* (Secretary)

Represents unions involved in film production, including the **Writers' Guild of Great Britain**.

Film & Video Press Group
c/o ITVA, 102 Great Russell Street,
London WC1E 3LN

Contact *Adam Cook*

A professional association for editors, journalists, and freelance writers in the audio-visual media.

Gaelic Books Council (An Comann Leabhraichean)
Department of Celtic, University of
Glasgow, Glasgow G12 8QQ
☎041–339 8855

Chairman *Professor Derick S. Thomson*
Executive and Editorial Officer
Ian MacDonald

FOUNDED 1968. Encourages and promotes Gaelic publishing by offering publication grants, commissioning authors, organising competitions, advising readers and providing practical help for writers.

Independent Film & Video Makers Association
79 Wardour Street, London W1V 3PH
☎01–439 0460

Subscription £12 p.a.

FOUNDED 1974. Practical help and advice on script development and funding, for its writer members.

Independent Programme Producers Association
50–51 Berwick Street, London W1V 4RD
☎01–439 7034   Fax 01–494 2700

Director *Paul Styles*
Deputy Director *John Woodward*
Information Officer *Alison Selwyn*
Subscription corporate, £300 + VAT; individual, £100 + VAT

FOUNDED 1981 to protect and advance the interests of independent TV producers supplying **Channel 4**; currently pressing for access to 25% of BBC and ITV output for independent producers; membership of 550. Offers a full Industrial Relations Service, general meetings, seminars on all aspects of production, general and production advice, plus close consultation with **Channel 4** and **BBC TV**. *IPPA Bulletin* every 2 months. The association is funded by subscriptions and by a 0.5% fee levied on members' production budgets for **BBC** and **Channel 4** commissions.

Independent Publishers' Guild
147–149 Gloucester Terrace,
London W2 6DX
☎01–723 7328

Subscription £30/35 p.a.

FOUNDED 1926. Membership open to independent publishers, packagers and suppliers, i.e. professionals in allied fields. 280 members in the year 1987/88. Regular meetings, conferences, seminars, and a small publishers' group.

Independent Theatre Council
Old Loom House, Backchurch Lane,
London E1 1LU
☎01–488 1229

Contact *Philip Bernays*

The management association and representative body for small and middle scale theatres (up to around 250 seats) and touring theatre companies. They negotiate contracts and have standard agreements with Equity on behalf of all professionals working in the theatre. Currently they are negotiating with the **Theatre Writers' Union** and **Writers'**

Guild for a contractual agreement covering the rights and fee structure of playwrights writing for the 'fringe' theatres.

Institute of Journalists
2 Dock Offices, Surrey Quays Road,
London SE16 2XL
☎01–252 1187

General Secretary *John Hart* MA FIL
Subscription £45–£125 (by assessment)

FOUNDED 1884. An independent trade union and professional association for writers, broadcasters and journalists in all media. Affiliation available to part time or occasional practitioners. Employment register, freelance division, legal advice.

Institute of Translation and Interpreting
318a Finchley Road, London NW3 5HT
☎01–794 9931/435 2105

Membership is open to those who satisfy stringent admission criteria, and can provide evidence of adequate professional translation or interpreting experience. Also offer affiliation and student membership. Benefits include listing in an index which specifies the skills and languages of each member.

The Library Association
7 Ridgmount Street, London WC1E 7AE
☎01–636 7543   Fax 01–436 7218

Chief Executive *George Cunningham*

The professional body for libraries and information specialists, with 25,000 members. The library (reference only) has a good range of books relevant both to library and publishing matters; both it and the bookshop are open to all.

London Screenwriters' Workshop
37 Victoria Road, Watford, Herts WD2 5AY
(Administration)
☎0923 31342

FOUNDED 1983. A means of contact, discussion and practical help for film and television writers. Meetings, monthly seminars, script workshops. Also acts as a pressure group.

National Union of Journalists (NUJ)
Acorn House, 314 Gray's Inn Road,
London WC1X 8DP
☎01–278 1812 (freelance division)
Main office 01–278 7916   Telex 892384

General Secretary *Harry Conroy*
Subscription £104 p.a. (freelance)

Trade union. Responsible for wages and conditions agreements which apply across the industry. Advice and representation for its members, as well as administering disputes, unemployment and other benefits. Publishes *Freelance Directory* and *The Journalist*.

New Playwrights Trust
Whitechapel Library,
77 Whitechapel High Street,
London E1 7QX
☎01–377 5429

Contact *Susan Croft*
Subscriptions £9 waged; £4.50 unwaged; telephone for group rate

Organises projects and joint projects including rehearsed readings, workshops and discussions. Runs script reading service, bulletin and library service. Also Link Service between writers and theatre companies. Monthly newsletter. Membership open to would-be playwrights, also actors and directors. Recent projects include Wordplay '88 and **Bristol Express'** *The Play's the Thing*.

The Newspaper Society
Bloomsbury House, Bloomsbury Square,
74/77 Great Russell Street,
London WC1B 3DA
☎01–636 7014   Fax 01–631 5119

President *Bill Heeps* (May 1988–May 1989)
Director *Dugal Nisbet-Smith*

Organisation for the provincial morning and evening/provincial and London suburban weekly newspapers.

At the same address: **Guild of British Newspaper Editors**, **President** *Keith Parker*; **Newspaper Conference** (a Newspaper Society organisation primarily concerned with newsgathering facilities in London for the regional press); and the **Young Newspapermen's Association** for young newspaper executives **Honorary Secretary** *Paul Mee*.

Office of Arts and Libraries

Horse Guards Road, London SW1P 3AL
☎01–270 5866

Among its more routine responsibilities, the OAL funds the British Library, and is responsible for the new library project at St Pancras. It is also responsible for funding to the **Arts Council** and the *Regional Arts Associations*.

PEN

7 Dilke Street, London SW3 4JE
☎01–352 6303

General Secretary
Josephine Pullein-Thompson MBE

Subscription fees £20 (town membership); £16 (members living over 50 miles from London and overseas)

English PEN is part of International PEN, a worldwide association of writers which fights for freedom of expression and speaks out for writers imprisoned or harassed for criticising their governments or publishing other unpopular views. Founded in London in 1921, International PEN now consists of 86 centres in 60 countries. PEN originally stood for poets, essayists and novelists, but membership is now open to all writers. A programme of talks and discussion is supplemented by the publication of a twice-yearly Broadsheet.

The Penman Club

175 Pall Mall, Leigh on Sea, Essex SS9 1RE
☎0702 74438

Subscription £8.25 first year; £5.25 thereafter

FOUNDED 1950. International writers' society, offering criticism of members' work, general advice and use of writers' library.

Performing Right Society

29–33 Berners Street, London W1P 4AA
☎01–580 5544
Telex PRSLON G 892678   Fax 01–631 4138

Collects and distributes royalties arising from performances and broadcasts of its members' copyright music.

The Personal Managers' Association Ltd

1 Summer Road, East Molesey, Surrey KT8 9LX
☎01–398 9796

President *Peter Dunlop*
Secretary *Angela Adler*
Subscription £200 per annum

An association of artists' and dramatists' agents (membership not open to individuals). Monthly meetings, for exchange of information, discussion, and acts as a lobby when necessary. Applicants screened. Maintains a code of conduct. A high proportion of Play Agents are members of the PMA.

Players and Playwrights

St John's Church Hall, Hyde Park Crescent, London W2

Subscription £4 p.a.

FOUNDED 1948. A society for newcomers to play and television writing. Weekly meetings in central London. Run-throughs of members' work are staged, and a discussion follows.

Playwrights Co-operative

117 Waterloo Road, London SE1
☎01-633 9811

Contact *The Administrator*

FOUNDED 1981. Has evolved a process of script development – a sequence of readings, discussions and workshops. Also story conferences, rehearsed readings, critical and professional advice, workshops held in London venues, and help in getting the final script produced. Since its inception, an average of 34% of the scripts which have been through the Co-Op have ended in production. Only the talented are accepted for membership; the rest can become 'Playwrights Co-Op Subscribers'.

Playwrights' Workshop

22 Brown Street, Altrincham,
Cheshire WA14 2EU
☎061-928 3095

Honorary Secretary *Robert Coupland*
Subscription £2 p.a.

FOUNDED 1949. The society meets monthly in Manchester, and aims to support playwrights of all kinds interested in furthering their work. Guest speakers on all aspects of the theatre. Annual one-act play competition. Past members include Michael Dines and Harry Kershaw.

The Poetry Society

21 Earls Court Square, London SW5 9DE
☎01-373 7861

President *Danny Abse*
Chairman *Alan Brownjohn*
Director *Paul Ralph*
Membership £15 (London); £12 (Rest of Britain and Ireland); £10 (Student, senior citizens, UB40)

FOUNDED 1909 to promote poetry and is now a major arts organisation with a thriving membership. It is Britain's only major organisation dealing exclusively with poetry. Offers a wide range of services and activities including: a poetry bookshop; mail-order service supplying most contemporary poetry publications; regular poetry readings and events with leading poets; publishes *Poetry Review* quarterly; organises the Poets in Schools scheme, sponsored by W.H. Smith; provides a critical service with professional and detailed advice for aspiring poets; publishes a quarterly information bulletin giving details of new presses, writers' groups and competitions; organises poetry events and workshops for teachers and young people; arranges adult educational courses in association with the University of London; administers competitions such as the **Dylan Thomas Award**, the **Alice Hunt Bartlett Award**, and the **National Poetry Competition** (see listing). Membership gives reduced admission charges to Poetry Society events and readings.

Publishers Association

19 Bedford Square, London WC1B 3HJ
☎01-580 6321-5/580 7761/323 1548
Telex 267160 PUBASS G   Fax 01-636 5375

Chief Executive *Clive Bradley*

The national trade association (see also **The Scottish Publishers Association**) with over 500 member companies in the industry. Very much a trade body. Writers with queries are referred on to **The Society of Authors** or **Writers' Guild**. Publishes the *Directory of Publishing*, in association with **Cassell**. Also home of the Book Marketing Council, whose task it is to promote books and boost their sale, by running promotions like 'Brit Wit' on a regular basis.

The Romantic Novelists' Association

20 First Avenue, Amersham, Bucks HP7 9BJ
☎0494 727202

Secretary *Dorothy Entwistle*
Subscription fee £10 p.a.

Membership is open to published writers of romantic novels or of two or more full-length serials, and also to publishers, literary agents, booksellers and librarians. Meetings are held in London and speakers are often arranged. *RNA News* is published quarterly and issued free to members. See *Literary Prizes and Awards* for details of *Romantic Novelists' Award/Netta Muskett Award*.

The Royal Literary Fund

144 Temple Chambers, Temple Avenue, London EC4Y 0DT
☎01-353 7150

Contact *Mrs Fiona M. Clark* (Secretary)

FOUNDED 1790, the fund makes grants available to authors and their dependents in financial need on a stringently discretionary basis. (See **Bursaries** section)

Royal Society of Literature

1 Hyde Park Gardens, London W2 2LT
☎01-723 5104

President *Sir Angus Wilson*
Subscription £20 p.a.

FOUNDED 1823. Membership (limited to 300) by application to the secretary with 2 sponsors. Fellowships are conferred by the Society on the proposal of two fellows. Benefits of membership include lectures and poetry readings in the Society's rooms. Recent lecturers have included Melvyn Bragg, Helen Gardner, Francis King and Dilys Powell. Presents the **Royal Society of Literature Award**, and the **Winifred Holtby Memorial Award** (see *Literary Prizes and Awards*).

Royal Television Society

Tavistock House East, Tavistock Square, London WC1H 9HR
☎01-387 1970/1332

Subscription £25 (full UK member)

FOUNDED· 1927. Covers all disciplines involved in the television industry. Provides a forum for debate and conferences on technical, social, and cultural aspects of the medium. Presents Journalism and Programme Awards and runs a wide range of training courses.

Science Fiction Foundation

North East London Polytechnic, Longbridge Road, Dagenham, Essex RM8 2AS
☎01-590 7722 ext. 2177

Contact *Joyce Day*

A national academic body for the furtherance of science fiction studies. Publishes *Foundation* three times a year, a magazine containing academic articles about science fiction, and reviews of new fiction.

Scottish Arts Council

19 Charlotte Square, Edinburgh EH2 4DF
☎031-226 6051

Literature Director *Walter Cairns*

The council's work for Scottish-based writers (defined as those whose work can command a fee, and who have a track record of publication) includes: *Bursaries* considered twice yearly; *Travel and Research Grants* considered three times yearly; *Writing Fellowships*, posts usually advertised; *International Writing Fellowship* organised reciprocally with the Canada Council; *Writers in Schools and in Public* – a list of writers willing to participate in the schemes is published. Also publishes lists of Scottish writers' groups, awards and literary agents.

Scottish Poetry Library Association

Tweeddale Court, 14 High Street, Edinburgh EH1 1TE
☎031-557 2876

Director *Tessa Ransford*
Membership £7.50 p.a.

A comprehensive collection of work by Scottish poets in Gaelic, Scots and English, plus the work of international poets. Borrowing is free to all. A postal lending service is also offered, for which there is a small fee. Members receive a newsletter and support the Library, whose work includes exhibitions, bibliographies, information and promotion in the field of poetry.

The Scottish Publishers Association
25a South West Thistle Street Lane,
Edinburgh EH2 1EW
☎031–225 5795

Director *Lorraine Fannin*
Publicist *Alison Harley*

The Association represents over fifty Scottish publishers, from multinationals to very small presses, in a number of capacities, but primarily in the co-operative promotion and marketing of their books. The SPA also acts as an information and advice centre for both the trade and general public. It publishes seasonal catalogues, membership lists, a detailed directory of members, and provides its membership with a regular newsletter. The SPA represents its members at international bookfairs, provides opportunities for publishers' training, and carries out market research.

Scottish Society of Playwrights
Tron Theatre, 38 Parnie Street,
Glasgow G1 5HB
☎041–553 1425

Secretary *Donneil Kennedy*
Membership fee £20

FOUNDED 1973 by a group of playwrights, the society acts as a pressure group for playwrights and negotiates contracts with managements. Full membership is open to anyone who has had a play professionally produced on stage, television or radio.

Sean Dorman Manuscript Society
Union Place, Fowey, Cornwall PL23 1BY

Subscription £3.50 p.a. (after £1.50, 6 months trial period)

FOUNDED 1957. The Society trains its members in all branches of writing by co-operative methods, so avoiding the expense of writing schools. Typescripts are circulated in postal criticism folios, read, and returned with a wide range of opinions. There is also a folio, *Ideas & Markets*, where writing problems and outlets are discussed, and another, *Poetry*, solely for the work of poets and discussion thereon.

The Society of Authors
84 Drayton Gardens, London SW10 9SB
☎01–373 6642

General Secretary *Mark Le Fanu*
Annual Subscription £50 or £45 by direct debit

FOUNDED 1884. The Society of Authors is an independent trade union with some 3500 members. The Society advises on negotiations with publishers, broadcasting organisations, theatre managers and film companies; takes up complaints and pursues legal action for breach of contract, copyright infringement, etc. Along with the **Writers Guild**, the Society has played a major role in advancing the Minimum Terms Agreement for authors. Among the Society's publications are *The Author* (a quarterly journal) and *Quick Guides* to various aspects of writing. Other services include a pension fund and a group medical insurance scheme. Authors under 35, who are not yet earning a significant income from their writing, may apply for membership at a lower subscription of £32.

The Society of Indexers
16 Green Road, Birchington, Kent CT7 9JZ
☎0843 41115

Contact *Mrs H.C. Troughton* ALA (secretary)
Subscription £15 p.a.

FOUNDED 1957. Publishes *The Indexer* (bi-annually, April and October); quarterly Newsletter; *The Micro-Indexer* (bi-annually), dealing with software for computers. Issues an annual list of members and indexers available and a list of indexers and their specialist subjects. Services include 'Education in Indexing' – courses on indexing. Set rates of pay – currently £7.50 per hour.

Society of Women Writers and Journalists

2 St Lawrence Close,
Edgware, Middx HA8 6RB

Honorary Secretary *Olive McDonald*
Subscription Town £15, Country £12, Overseas £9

Lectures at monthly lunchtime meetings. Also offers advice to members, seminars, etc. Journal *The Woman Journalist* issued three times a year.

South Bank Board: Literature Office

Artistic Projects Department, Royal Festival Hall, South Bank, London SE1 8XX
☎01–921 0906
Telex 929226 SBBG   Fax 01–928 0063

Literature Officer *Maura Dooley*

A new feature of the South Bank complex is the recent appointment of Maura Dooley whose aims are to 'create a strong presence for literature on the South Bank'. Her brief covers all aspects of writing, and a venue within the Royal Festival Hall will be established for readings of fiction, poetry and plays, plus workshops, and festivals. A writer in residence may be appointed. Other plans are at the committee stage at the time of going to press. In Spring 1988, the National Poetry Library moved to the South Bank.

Television History Centre

42 Queen Square, London WC1N 3AJ
☎01–405 6627

Co-ordinators *Sharon Goulds,*
Marilyn Wheatcroft

Home of the television history workshop, the history centre 'provides a range of resources, materials, information and assistance to help people record their own history'.

Theatre Writers' Union

The Actors'Centre, 4 Chenies Street,
London WC1E 7EP
☎01–631 3619

Contact *Membership Secretary*
Annual Membership Fees (reduced rates for anyone joining part way through the year) £50, if annual income from playwriting is more than £10,000; £30, if more than £2000; £20 if less than £2000; £10 for unwaged.

Represents all writers working in the theatre, negotiates for terms and conditions, encourages new writing and presses for further funding. Anybody who has written a play is eligible to join. Activities include forums on new writing; rehearsed readings of new plays; meetings with theatre managements and regional arts associations; surveys; workshops; working parties. Services also include professional advice, support in disputes and assistance with problems. The quarterly General Meetings are the Union's decision-making body. All officers and committees must work within the policies decided at GMs. Branches in Birmingham, London, Leeds, Manchester, Nottingham, Sheffield and Wales. Any five members living in the same area can start a branch and obtain Union funds to launch the branch.

The Translators' Association

84 Drayton Gardens, London SW10 9SB
☎01–373 6642

Contact *Kate Pool*

FOUNDED 1958 as a subsidiary group within **The Society of Authors** to deal exclusively with the special problems of translators into the English language. Members are entitled to all the benefits and services of the parent Society without extra charge. The Association offers free legal and general advice and assistance on all matters relating to translators' work, including the vetting of contracts, and information on developments relating to translation including information about improvements in fees. Membership is normally confined to translators who have had their work published in volume or serial form or produced in this country for stage, television or radio. Translators of technical work for industrial firms or Government Departments are in certain cases admitted to membership if their work, though not on general sale, is published by the organisation commissioning the work.

Translators' Guild Ltd
c/o 26–27 Boswell Street,
London WC1N 3JZ

Membership is restricted to those who have passed the translator's examination in technical, scientific, commercial or social science fields. Also offers affiliation and student membership. Benefits include listing in an index which specifies the skills and languages of each member.

Welsh Arts Council
Museum Place, Cardiff CF1 3NX
☎0222 394711

Literature Director *Meic Stephens*

Funds literary magazines and book-production, Writers on Tour, competitions, a bursary scheme, the Welsh Academy and the **Welsh Books Council**, children's literature, annual Prizes and readings at the Council's bookshop, Oriel.

Drama Director *Roger Tomlinson*

Funding is 'tight', and most of the work of the department is concerned with theatres and touring companies. Of particular interest to writers is the 'Theatre Writing Scheme', with awards to commissioning theatre companies.

Welsh Books Council (Cyngor Llyfrau Cymraeg)
Castell Brychan,
Aberystwyth, Dyfed SY23 2JB
☎0970 624151

Contact *Gwerfyl Pierce Jones*

FOUNDED 1961 to stimulate interest in Welsh literature and to support authors. The Council distributes the government grant for Welsh-language publications, promotes and fosters all aspects of both Welsh and Welsh interest book production. Its four departments, Editorial, Design, Publicity and Marketing, and Wholesale Distribution Centre offer central services to publishers in Wales, and writers in Welsh and English are welcome to approach the Editorial Department for advice on how to get their manuscripts published. *Book News From Wales/Llais Llyfrau*, quarterly, includes book lists, reviews, and articles on various aspects of Welsh writing and publishing.

Women In Entertainment
7 Thorpe Close, London W10 5XL
☎01–969 2292

A pressure group for women involved in the entertainment industry.

Writers' Circles
A nationwide network of writers' circles (hundreds of them, too many to list here) exists, designed to provide an informal atmosphere of mutual help and constructive criticism for writers of all grades. Your **Regional Arts Association** (see p. 000) can usually provide a comprehensive list of those in your area.

Writers' Guild of Great Britain
430 Edgware Road, London W2 1EH
☎01–723 8074

General Secretary *Walter J. Jeffrey*
Annual subscription 1% of that part of the author's income earned in the areas in which the Guild operates, with a minimum of £50 and a maximum of £480.

FOUNDED 1959, the Writers' Guild is the writers' trade union, affiliated to the TUC, representing writers in film, radio, television, theatre and publishing. The Guild advises on all aspects of writers' agreements and leads the way in campaigns for minimum terms for writers working in film, radio and theatre. In 1979 the Guild, with the **Theatre Writers' Union**, negotiated the first ever industrial agreement for theatre writers. Along with the **Society of Authors**, the Guild has played a major role in advancing the Minimum Terms Agreement for authors. Membership is by a points system. One major piece of work (a full-length book, an hour-long television or radio play, a feature film, etc.) entitles the author to full membership; lesser work helps to accumulate enough points for full membership, while temporary membership may be enjoyed in the meantime. Temporary members can pay a minimum subscription of £30 in their first year.

Yr Academi Gymreig

3rd Floor, Mount Stuart House,
Mount Stuart Square, Cardiff CF1 6DQ
☎0222 492064

Contact *Sian Ithel* (Administrator, Welsh Language Section), *Kevin Thomas* (Administrator, English Language Section)

FOUNDED 1959 to encourage writing in Welsh. Membership by election. Publishes *Taliesin*, books on Welsh literature and an English/Welsh dictionary. English language section for Welsh writers in English, and those who write on Welsh themes. Both sections organise readings, conferences and general literary events.

Regional Arts Associations

Council of Regional Arts Associations

Litton Lodge, 13a Clifton Road,
Winchester, Hants SO22 5BP
☎0962 51063

Literature Secretary *Geoff Swallow* (at **Lincolnshire & Humberside Arts**, see entry for address and telephone number)

CoRAA is a service organisation for the corporate needs of the 13 regional arts associations of England (Scotland and Wales have their own Arts Councils, and are not regionally split in this way). 'Increasingly the RAAs are becoming development agencies for the arts in the regions, and policies develop not only in response to regional demand, but also to develop new initiatives in areas of perceived need, and these – aside from the broad objectives of all RAAs – will vary from region to region.' As well as offering advice and practical help in the form of direct funding, the associations often also initiate arts events, such as touring theatre. Associate membership is offered to individuals; rates vary regionally.

DIRECT GRANTS FOR WRITERS

While most of the RAAs designate part of their budget for allocation direct to writers, this is often a minor proportion, which new or aspiring playwrights stand little chance of receiving. Money is more readily available for the professional, though because of the emphasis on community access to the arts in many of the associations, this is often allocated to writers' appearances in schools etc, rather than to support the writer at the typewriter. It is generally accepted, too, that fun-ding is more accessible to novelists than to playwrights. Direct grants are made to writers of fiction because, usually, there is confidence that the work will be published. The grant or bursary is regarded as an investment of sorts. But for playwrights publication is rarely the end result. Funding is more likely to go into the creation of workshops and performance, to bring along a play and help shape it for public consumption: 'The present structure is as much about performance skills as writing skills,' one drama officer remarked, 'though just how the RAAs should be directing these funds has become one of the burning questions of the year.'

Buckinghamshire Arts Association

55 High Street, Aylesbury, Bucks HP20 1SA
☎0296 434704

Arts Officer *Pat Swell*

FOUNDED 1983, BAA is part of the Regional Arts Association network. It exists to encourage and develop the Arts in the county and has an active Literature policy. The Association can offer help and advice to writers, writing groups, small presses etc., and operates a 'Book the Writer' scheme offering subsidy for writers' visits and workshops with their public.

East Midlands Arts

Mountfields House, Forest Road,
Loughborough, Leics LE11 3HU
☎0509 218292   Telex 265871

Literature Officer *Lynne Hapgood*
Drama Officer *Helen Flack*

Covers Leicestershire, Nottinghamshire, Derbyshire (excluding the High Peak District) and Northamptonshire. A comprehensive information service for writers includes an extensive *Writers' Information Pack*, with details of groups and societies in the region, publishers and publishing information, a list of regional magazines which offer a market for work, advice on approaching the media, on unions, courses and grants. Also available is a directory of writers, primarily to aid people using their 'Writers' Visits Scheme', and in establishing 'Writers' Attachments'. 'Writers' Bursaries' (about 5 a year) are granted for work on a specific project – all forms of writing are eligible except for local history and biography. Writing for the theatre can come under the aegis of both Literature and Drama. A list of writers' groups is available, plus *Foreword*, the literature newsletter, and the free magazine *Steppin' Out*.

Eastern Arts

Cherry Hinton Hall, Cambridge CB1 4DW
☎0223 215355

Literature Officer (vacant) **Director of Performing Arts** *Richard Hogger*

Covers Bedfordshire, Cambridgeshire, Essex, Hertfordshire, Norfolk and Suffolk. Policy emphasises access for all in as wide an area as possible. As a self-styled arts development agency, great stress is placed upon the support of individuals, particularly in the interests of literature in the community. On the drama side, greater emphasis is placed on the creation of a structure to support the playwright – by means of adequate workshops and performance opportunities, rather than direct grants, though a small fund exists for the commissioning of work. Closely involved with the Royal Court Young People's Theatre Writing Festival. The Visiting Writers' Scheme subsidises visits by professional writers to schools and other organisations (and includes many household names). Can also supply lists of literary

groups, societies and workshops in the area, plus details of residential creative writing courses.

Greater London Arts

9 White Lion Street, London N1 9PD
☎01–837 8808

Literature Officers *Laurence Baylis,*
Vuyiswa Ngqobongwana
Drama Officer *Sue Timothy*

Awards and bursaries to individual writers are not currently offered by GLA, though this is under review. Applications are encouraged for projects which support the availability and awareness of contemporary literature, such as book and magazine distribution and representation, promotion and marketing schemes, and book fairs. Grants are also available for readings, performances and workshops involving creative writing of all kinds, as well as one-off publications and film projects. 'Writers in Schools' subsidises the cost of bringing writers into contact with students of all ages.

Lincolnshire and Humberside Arts

St Hugh's, Newport, Lincoln LN1 1RX
☎0522 533555

Literature, Film and Media Officer *Geoff Swallow*

The regional arts development agency for Lincolnshire and Humberside, developing working partnerships with regional agencies, such as local authorities, library and education services, the broadcast media and the private sector, as well as national arts funding agencies and the book trade. LHA supports the following areas of work: writers' residencies and short-term attachments; writers commissions; a programme of field worker/animateur posts in strategic centres; the development of writers' workshops through the 'Writers in Public' scheme; a programme of residential weekends for writers. LHA supports literature in performance through grants to promoters; a regular programme planning forum; and is developing a regional touring network in 1988/89. It has encouraged the live presentation of contemporary literature by British and foreign writers in major arts venues in the region as well as by independent promoters. LHA also supports independent publishers based in its region, and will consider publication grants to those based elsewhere for first publications by writers from Lincolnshire and Humberside.

Merseyside Arts

Bluecoat Chambers, School Lane,
Liverpool L1 3BX
☎051–709 0671

ADO (Drama & Literature) *Theresa Griffin*

Merseyside Arts covers Merseyside, part of Cheshire and part of West Lancashire. Presently no direct grants or bursaries are offered to individuals, writers included. Project grants, totalling £100,000 in the year 1987/88, can bring monies to writers indirectly. These go to fund existing projects and to establish new ventures Merseyside Arts feels it would like to involve itself with, and can include literature and drama projects. Similarly with fiction – grants are made towards publication, but direct to publishers, and not to writers. Residencies and the 'Writers Round Merseyside' scheme are also offered. Playwrights can find help in the form of support for rehearsed readings, commissions etc. The question of how new, and particularly young, writers should be supported is currently under review.

North West Arts

4th Floor, 12 Harter Street,
Manchester M1 6HY
☎061–228 3062

Literature Officer *Leigh Chambers*
Drama Officer *Ivor Davies*

Covers Cheshire, Greater Manchester, Lancashire (except West Lancs), and the High Peak District of Derbyshire. Gives financial assistance to a great variety of projects and schemes, including Lancaster Literature Festival and creative writing courses. A Readers' Service is offered to any writer living in the region who submits original unpublished material at a time when funds are available. Writers should send their work with s.a.e. and postcard with name etc., for filing purposes. The 'Writers in the Community' scheme subsidises writers' fees and travel expenses, when addressing societies, schools, etc. The Literature Department produces a quarterly magazine, *The Word is Out*.

Northern Arts

9–10 Osborne Terrace,
Jesmond, Newcastle upon Tyne NE2 1NZ
☎091–281 6334

Literature Officer *Jenny Attala*
Drama Officer *Sheila Harborth*

Northern Arts covers Cleveland, Cumbria, Durham, Northumberland, and Tyne and Wear, and was the first regional arts association in the country to be set up by local authorities. Supports both organisations and writers and aims to stimulate public interest in artistic events. Offers awards for published writers to release them from work or other commitments for short periods of time to enable concentration on specific literary projects. A separate scheme operates for playwrights by the Northern Playwrights Society. Northern Arts make drama awards to producers only. Also fund writers' residencies, magazines and publishing.

South East Arts

10 Mount Ephraim,
Tunbridge Wells, Kent TN4 8AS
☎0892 515210

Literature Officer *Charmian Stowell*
Drama Officer *Robert Henry*

South East Arts covers the counties of Kent, Surrey and East Sussex. The Literature panel 'aims to create a high profile for contemporary writing, and to encourage aspiring writers to develop their skills'. Information, advice and training opportunities are offered to writers. Arts centres and other organisations, independent presses and writers' groups are among the recipients of direct funding. *Writers' Information Pack* available for £1.50 from the literature department.

South West Arts

Bradninch Place, Gandy Street,
Exeter EX4 3LS
☎0392 218188

Literature Officer *Ingrid Squirrell*
Drama Officer *Moira Sutton*

SW Arts covers Avon, Cornwall, Devon, much of Dorset, Gloucestershire and Somerset. 'The central theme running through the Association's constitution is development . . . increasing, improving, encouraging, advancing and co-ordinating.' The literature policy aims to promote a healthy environment for writers of all kinds and to encourage a high standard of new writing. The programme includes residential courses, residencies, and writers in education. There is also direct investment in small presses, publishers and community groups. Literary festivals, societies and arts centres are encouraged. 'Although South West Arts cannot act as a literary agency or offer subsidy for work in progress, we do on occasion sponsor special awards, such as the **TSB Peninsula Prize**' (see *Prizes*).

Southern Arts Association

19 Southgate Street,
Winchester, Hampshire SO23 9DQ
☎0962 55099

Literature Officer (to be appointed)
Marketing and Information Officer
Keiren Phelan
Drama Officer *Fiona Ellis*

The literature panel decides on funding for fiction and poetry readings, festivals, magazines, bursaries, a literature prize, publications, residencies and attachments. A third of the budget in 1988/89 will be spent on writers in education.

West Midlands Arts

82 Granville Street, Birmingham B1 2LH
☎021–631 3121

Literature/Projects Officer *David Hart*

Covers Herefordshire, Worcestershire, Shropshire, Staffordshire, Warwickshire. 'Our policy is to contribute to the process whereby good writing, in the main by living writers, is made accessible to readers and to help provide opportunities for aspiring writers.' The 'Writers and Storytellers in the Community Scheme' pays half the fee for writers' visits. Commissions to a professional writer to produce work are also made, though publication grants are made to publishers only, never writers. The Reading Service charges £5 and reports fully on short pieces of work – such as sample chapters of a novel. Also support the local literature festival, The Birmingham Readers' and Writers' Festival. Lists of publishers of fiction and poetry in the region, national publishers of poetry magazines in the area, and contacts for writing courses, are available. List of writers' groups available. Publishes *People to People* magazine.

Yorkshire Arts

Glyde House, Bradford BD5 0BQ
☎0274 723051

Literature Officer *Jennifer Barraclough*
Drama Officer *Chrissie Poulter*

'Libraries, publishing houses and the education service all make major contributions to the support of literature. Recognising the resources these agencies command, Yorkshire Arts actively seeks ways of acting in partnership with them, whilst at the same time retaining its particular responsibility for the living writer and the promotion of activities currently outside the scope of these agencies.' There are a limited number of bursaries available for writers: other funding goes to the Arvon Foundation at Lumb Bank; the 'Live Writing' scheme, which subsidises projects involving professional writers and students at all levels; and awards to independent publishers. Also offer support for literature in performance, such as the Ilkley Literature Festival, and live poetry events.

Bursaries, Fellowships and Grants

See Subject Index for awards by category.

Aosdana Scheme

The Arts Council (An Chomhairle Ealaion),
70 Merrion Square, Dublin 2, Ireland.
☎0001 611840

Contact *Literature Officer*

Aosdana is an affiliation of creative artists engaged in literature, music and the visual arts, and consists of not more than 150 artists who have gained a reputation for achievement and distinction. Membership is achieved via competitive sponsored selection. Members are eligible to receive an annuity for a five-year term to assist them in pursuing their art full time.
Award IR£5000 (Initial annuity)

Arts Council of Great Britain Writers' Bursaries

Arts Council of Great Britain, 105 Piccadilly, London W1V 0AU
☎01–629 9495

Three awards are available to writers of outstanding literary achievement needing financial assistance for the research or writing of their next book. Open to British and non-British subjects resident in England.

The precise category of writers' eligibility is re-defined each year. Amount varies according to need.

The Authors' Foundation

The Society of Authors, 84 Drayton Gardens, London SW10 9SB
☎01–373 6642

The Authors' Foundation makes grants annually to writers whose publisher's advance is insufficient to cover the costs of research involved. At present, preference is given to non-fiction. The author should make application to the Foundation in a letter giving details, in confidence, of the advance and royalties, together with the reasons for needing additional funding. 1987 grants included: Hilary Spurling (£1500); Iain Finlayson (£1000); Alan Hayes (£500). Total of £10,000 available.

The K. Blundell Trust

The Society of Authors, 84 Drayton Gardens, London SW10 9SB
☎01–373 6642

Annual grants to writers whose publisher's advance is insufficient to cover the costs of research. Author must be under 40, has to submit copy of his/her previous book and the work must 'contribute to the greater understanding of existing social and economic organisation'. Application by letter. Final date 30 June. 1987 grants included: John Rentoul (£3000); Jenny Chapman (£1500); Nigel Lewis (£1000). Total of £10,000 available.

Bursaries in Literature

The Arts Council (An Chomhairle Ealaion),
70 Merrion Square, Dublin 2, Ireland
☎0001 611840

Contact *Literature Officer*

Annual competition awarded to creative writers (fiction, poetry, drama) to enable concentration on or completion of specific projects. Final entry: 15 April. Presentation date: August.
Award £1500–£6000

Eastern Arts Writing Fellowship

University of East Anglia, University Plain, Norwich NR4 7JT

☎0603 56161

Contact *Establishment Officer*

Awarded to a writer of established reputation in any field for the period of the Spring and Summer term. The duties of the Fellowship are discussed at an interview. It is assumed that one activity will be the pursuit of the Fellow's own writing. In addition, the Fellow will be expected to take part in some of the following activities: (a) contributing to the teaching of a formal course in creative writing or running a regular writers' workshop on an informal extra-curricular basis; (b) being available for a specified period each week to advise individual students engaged in writing; (c) giving an introductory lecture or reading at the beginning of the Fellowship; (d) organising one or two literary events involving other writers from outside the university; (e) making some contribution to the cultural and artistic life of the region (e.g. by public lecturing or reading). Applications for the Fellowship should be lodged with the Establishment Officer by 1 October each year.

Award £2000

The Economist/Richard Casement Internship

The Economist, 25 St James's Street, London SW1A 1HG

Contact *The Business Affairs Editor* (re Casement Internship)

For a journalist under 24 to spend three months in the summer writing for *The Economist* about science and technology. Applicants should write a letter of introduction along with an article of approximately 600 words suitable for inclusion in the 'Science and Technology' section.

E.C. Gregory Trust Fund

The Society of Authors, 84 Drayton Gardens, London SW10 9SB

☎01-373 6642

Annual competitive awards of varying amounts are made each year for the encouragement of young poets under the age of thirty who can show that they are likely to benefit from an opportunity to give more time to writing. Open only to British-born subjects resident in the UK. Final entry: 31 October. Presentation date: June. 1988 awards: Michael Symmons Roberts (£7000); Gwyneth Lewis (£6000); Adrian Blackledge (£5000); Simon Armitage (£4000); Robert Crawford (£3000). 1987 awards: Peter McDonald (£4250); Maura Dooley (£4000); Stephen Knight (£4000); Steve Anthony (£2750); Jill Maughan (£2500); Paul Munden (£2500).

Award £25,000 (total)

The Guardian Research Fellowship

Nuffield College, Oxford OX1 1NF

Contact *The Warden's Secretary*

Annually endowed by the Scott Trust, owner of *The Guardian*, to give someone working in the media the chance to put their experience into a new perspective, publish the outcome and give a *Guardian* lecture. Applications welcomed from journalists and management members, in newspapers, periodicals or broadcasting. Research or study proposals should be directly related to experience of working in the media. Accommodation and meals in college will be provided, and a 'modest supplementary stipend' might be arranged to ensure the Fellow does not lose from the stay.

Francis Head Awards

The Society of Authors, 84 Drayton Gardens, London SW10 9SB

☎01-373 6642

Designed to provide grants to established British authors over the age of 35 who need financial help during a period of illness or disablement.

Macaulay Fellowship

The Arts Council (An Chomhairle Ealaion),
70 Merrion Square, Dublin 2, Ireland
☎0001 611840

Contact *Literature Officer*

To further the liberal education of a young
creative artist. Candidates for this triennial
award must be under thirty years of age on
30 June, or thirty-five in exceptional circumstances.
Award £3000

Northern Arts Literary Fellowship

Northern Arts, 10 Osborne Terrace,
Jesmond, Newcastle upon Tyne NE2 1NZ
☎091–281 6334

Contact *Literature Officer*

A competitive fellowship, tenable at, and co-
sponsored by the Universities of Durham and
Newcastle upon Tyne for a period of two
academic years. £10,000 p.a.

Northern Arts Writers Awards

Northern Arts, 10 Osborne Terrace,
Jesmond, Newcastle upon Tyne NE2 1NZ
☎091–281 6334

Contact *Literature Officer*

Awards are offered to established authors
resident in the Northern Arts area on basis of
literary merit and financial need. Application: spring/summer.
Award Variable

Oppenheim John Downes Memorial Trust

36 Whitefriars Street, London EC4Y 8BH

Competitive grants to writers and artists of
all descriptions unable to pursue their
vocation by reason of their poverty.
Applicants must be British by birth and of
British parents and grandparents. Final
application date: 1 November.
Variable grant, usually between £50 and
£1500

The Margaret Rhondda Award

The Society of Authors, 84 Drayton
Gardens, London SW10 9SB
☎01–373 6642

Competitive award given to a woman writer
as a grant-in-aid towards the expenses of a
research project in journalism. Triennial,
next awarded 1990. Final entry date: 31
December. Presentation date: June. 1987
awards: Elizabeth Hilliard and Rhonda Petersen (£250 each).
Amount £500

The Royal Literary Fund

144 Temple Chambers, Temple Avenue,
London EC4Y 0DT

The Fund helps published authors and their
families when in financial need. For further
details, write for application form. (See also
Professional Associations section.)

The Scottish Arts Council Bursaries and Awards (See entry in Professional Associations)

Southern Arts Literature Bursaries

Southern Arts, 19 Southgate Street,
Winchester, Hampshire SO23 9DQ
☎0962 55099

Contact *Literature Officer*

Discretionary annual bursaries may be
awarded for periods of up to one year to
authors of published poetry or fiction resident in the Southern Arts Region. Bursaries
may be awarded to: (a) writers of literary
merit whose work might be expected to
benefit from a period of full time writing; and
(b) publishers wishing to publish work by
local writers and to small presses based in the
region.

Laurence Stern Fellowship

Laurence Stern Fellowship, Graduate Centre for Journalism, City University, 223 St John Street, London EC1V 0HB

Contact *Robert Jones*

Awarded to a young print or broadcasting journalist, it gives them a chance to work on the national desk of the *Washington Post*. Benjamin Bradlee, the *Post*'s executive editor selects from a shortlist drawn up in May.

Thames Television Playwright Scheme

Thames Television House,
306–316 Euston Road, London NW1 3BB
☎01–387 9494

Bursaries awarded to playwrights. Must be sponsored by a theatre who then submit the play for consideration by a panel. Not necessarily awarded annually – depends on quality of work submitted.
1988 winners: Harwant Bains, *The Fighting Kite*, will be attached to the **Royal Court**; Gillian Richmond, *The Last Waltz*, goes to the **Soho Poly**; Liz Lochead, *Mary Queen of Scots*, will work with the **RSC**; David Spencer, **Verity Bargate Award** winner for *Releevo*, will be with the **National Theatre**. Each award allows the playwright a twelve-month attachment.

Tom-Gallon Trust

The Society of Authors, 84 Drayton Gardens, London SW10 9SB
☎01–373 6642

A biennial award is made from this Trust Fund to fiction writers of limited means who have had at least one short story accepted. Authors wishing to enter should send a list of their already published fiction, giving the name of the publisher or periodical in each case and the approximate date of publication; one published short story; a brief statement of their financial position; an undertaking that they intend to devote a substantial

amount of time to the writing of fiction as soon as they are financially able to do so; a s.a.e. for the return of the work submitted.
1987 winner: Lawrence Scott, *The House of Funerals*.
Award £500

Travelling Scholarships

The Society of Authors, 84 Drayton Gardens, London SW10 9SB
☎01–373 6642

Annual, non-competitive awards for the benefit of British authors to enable them to travel abroad.
1988 winners: A.L. Barker, Eva Figes, Allan Massie, David Rudkin (£1100 each).
1987 winners: Shena Mackay, Vernon Scannell, Iain Crichton Smith (£1500 each).
Award £4500

West Midlands Arts Creative Writing Attachment

Brunswick Terrace, Stafford ST16 1BZ
☎0785 59231

Contact *Literature Officer*

A scheme which provides a grant for an arts, community, educational or other organisation in the West Midlands Region to establish a creative writing attachment. The grant is paid direct to the writer, who can be a practising writer of poetry, prose, journalism, etc. Payment is for a part-time six month attachment.
Award £8000 p.a. (pro rata)

Yorkshire Arts Association Literary Awards

Yorkshire Arts Association, Glyde House, Glydegate, Bradford BD5 0BQ
☎0274 723051

Contact *Literature Officer*

Due to cutbacks in subsidy, **Yorkshire Arts** will not be making awards to writers in the 'foreseeable future'.

Prizes

See Subject Index for Prizes by Category.

Joe Ackerley Prize

English Centre of International PEN,
7 Dilke Street, London SW3 4JE
☎01–352 6303

Commemorating the novelist and autobiographer, J.R. Ackerley, this Prize is awarded for a literary autobiography, written in English and published in the year preceding the award.
1988 winner: Anthony Burgess *Little Wilson and Big God*.
1987 winner: Diana Athill *After a Funeral*.
Prize £500

Alexander Prize

Royal Historical Society, University College, Gower Street, London WC1E 6BT
☎01–387 7532

Contact *Literary Director*

Awarded for an historical essay of not more than 6000 words. Competitors may choose their own subject for their essay, but must submit their choice for approval to the Literary Director of the Royal Historical Society.
Prize Medal plus £100

An Duais don bhFiliocht i nGaelige (Prize for Poetry in Irish)

The Arts Council (An Chomhairle Ealaion), 70 Merrion Square, Dublin 2, Ireland
☎0001 611840

Contact *The Literature Officer*

Awarded for the best book of poetry in the Irish language published in the preceding three years.
Prize £1000 (Triennial – next award 1989)

Hans Christian Andersen Awards

Book Trust, Book House, 45 East Hill, London SW18 2QZ
☎01–870 9055

Contact *IBBY British Section*

The only international prizes for children's literature. Two prizes are awarded to the author and illustrator whose work has made a lasting contribution to children's literature.
Award Gold medals (Biennial – even years)

Eileen Anderson/Central Television Drama Award

Central Television, Central House, Broad Street, Birmingham B1 2JP
☎021–643 9898

Contact *John Palmer*

An annual award, initiated in 1987 with money left by the late Dr Eileen Anderson, to encourage new theatre writing in the Midlands. A stage play which has been commissioned or premièred at a Midlands venue is eligible.
1987 winner: Don Hale, *Every Black Day* (commissioned by the Everyman Theatre, Cheltenham).
Prize: £500 plus a unique trophy designed each year by the local College of Education. A plaque is awarded to the theatre which commissioned the work.

Angel Literary Prize

The Angel Hotel, Angel Hill, Bury St Edmonds, Suffolk IP33 1LT
☎0284 753926

Contact *Caroline Gough*

This Award is intended to stimulate interest in, and support for, writers in East Anglia. Two prizes are given, one for a work of fiction and one for a work of non-fiction. Books must have been published between October and September and written by authors living and working in East Anglia. Entries must be in by 31 August.
1987 winners: Jan Mark, *Zero Was Here* (Cape) for fiction; George MacBeth, *A Child of War* (Cape) for non-fiction.
Prize £1000 for fiction and £500 for non-fiction.

Arvon Foundation International Poetry Competition
Kilnhurst, Kilnhurst Road,
Todmorden, Lancs OL14 6AX
☎070–681 6582

Contact *The Administrator*

FOUNDED 1980, this competition is for poems written in English and not previously broadcast or published. There are no restrictions on the number of lines, themes, age of entrants or nationality. No limit to the number of entries. Entry fee: £2.50 per poem.
1987 winner: Selima Hill, *The Notebook*.
Prize £5000 (First Prize Biennial – odd years)

Astra Prize for Medical Writing
The Society of Authors, 84 Drayton Gardens, London SW10 9SB
☎01–373 6642

Awarded for a medical textbook written and published in the United Kingdom in the year preceding the award.
1987 winner: *Textbook of Neonatology* edited by N.R.C. Roberton.
Prize £1000 (Annual)

Authors' Club First Novel Award
The Authors' Club, 40 Dover Street, London W1X 3RB
☎01–499 8581

Contact *Mrs Ridgway* (Secretary)

INSTITUTED 1954, this award is made for the most promising first novel of the year. Entries for the award are accepted from publishers, but short stories are not eligible. All books must be published in the United Kingdom.
1987 winner: Helen Harris.
Award £200 plus Silver Mounted Quill.

Verity Bargate Award
The Soho Poly Theatre Club,
16 Ridinghouse Street, London W1P 7PB
☎01–580 6982

Contact *Patrick Cox*

To commemorate the late Verity Bargate, founder and director of the **Soho Poly Theatre Club**, this award is presented annually for a new and unperformed play, suitable for performance at the Soho Poly. The Soho Poly also runs an annual young writers course to encourage young playwrights.
Previous winner: David Spencer, *Releevo*.
Award £1000 (plus publication by **Methuen**)

Alice Hunt Bartlett Award
The Poetry Society, 21 Earls Court Square, London SW5 9DE
☎01–373 7861

This award is given to the living poet the Society most wishes to honour and encourage. Special consideration is given to newly emerging poets, as merit warrants. The author must submit a volume of poetry containing no fewer than 20 poems or 400 lines. In the case of translations, the original poet must also be alive and the prize is shared equally between poet and translator.
Award £500

H.E. Bates Short Story Competition
Leisure & Recreation Department,
Northampton Borough Council, Guildhall,
Northampton
☎0604 34734

Contact *Malcolm Johnston*

Named after the late H.E. Bates, one of the masters of the short story form, this competition is for short stories of 2000 words maximum. Any writer resident in Great Britain is eligible, and there are categories for children under 11 and under 16.

Prizes £50 (First Prize)

The BBC Wildlife Awards for Nature Writing

Broadcasting House, Whiteladies Road, Bristol BS8 2LR
☎0272 732211

Contact *Rosamund Kidman Cox* (Editor of *BBC WILDLIFE Magazine*)

Annual competition for professional and amateur writers. Entries should be a single essay either on personal observations of, or thoughts about, nature – general or specific – or about reflections on human relationships with nature. Entry forms from Rosamund Kidman Cox.

Prizes £1000 for best essay by a professional or amateur writer; £400 for best essay by an amateur writer (only if a professional writer wins the top award); £200 for best essay by a young writer aged between 13 and 17; £100 for best essay by a young writer aged 12 or under.

Samuel Beckett Award

Faber & Faber, 3 Queen Square, London WC1N 3AU
☎01–278 6881

Contact *Frank Pike*

Jointly sponsored by **Channel Four**, the **Royal Court Theatre** and **Faber & Faber**, this award aims to give support and encouragement to new playwrights at a crucial stage of their careers. Two prizes are given, one for a first play for the stage and another for a first play for television. There is also the possibility of publication by **Faber**.

1987 winner: Jim Cartwright, *Road*.

Prize £1000 (each category)

Bejam Cookery Book of the Year Award

Bejam, Honeypot Lane, Stanmore, Middx HA7 1LE
☎01–951 1313

Contact *Public Relations Department*

Awarded annually for the best cookery book published in the UK between 1 September and 31 August. Particular emphasis is placed on originality of recipes, practical instructions, well-written and interesting text, health awareness and attractive presentation. Entries in by the end of August.

Previous winners include: Carol Bowen, *Versatile Vegetables*; Miriam Polunin *The New Cookbook*; Antonio Carluccio, *An Invitation to Italian Cooking*.

Award £2500 (plus commemorative gift)

David Berry Prize

Royal Historical Society, University College London, Gower Street, London WC1E 6BT
☎01–387 7532

Awarded for an unpublished essay on Scottish history within the reigns of James I to James VI, not exceeding 10,000 words. Candidates may select any subject from the relevant period, providing it has been submitted to and approved by the Council of the Royal Historical Society.

Prize £100 (Triennial – next award 1990)

Best Book of the Sea Award

1 Chesham Street, London SW1X 8NF
☎01–235 2884

Contact *Lt. Cmdr Maurice Board*

FOUNDED 1970 and sponsored by King George's Fund for Sailors, this award is given annually for a work of non-fiction which contributes most to the knowledge and/or enjoyment of those who love the sea. A second award may be given at the discretion of the judges for a work of outstanding merit.

Award £1000

Bimco-Lloyd's List Maritime Book Prize

Lloyd's of London Press Ltd, Sheepen Place,
Colchester, Essex CO3 3LP
☎0206 772277

Contact *Mrs Patricia Morris*

For the best unpublished manuscript on
operational, commercial, technical, financial
or legal aspects of any sector of maritime
industries and services.
Biennial award, next award 1989. Closing
date for entries 1 December 1988.
Prize 15,000 Swiss Francs (More than £5000)

James Tait Black Memorial Prizes

University of Edinburgh,
David Hume Tower, George Square,
Edinburgh EH8 9JX
☎031–667 1011 (ext. 6259)

Contact *Department of English Literature*

These prizes, one for biography and one for
fiction, were instituted in 1918 in memory of
a partner of the publishing firm of **A. & C.
Black Ltd**, and since 1979 they have been
supported by the Scottish Arts Council. Each
prize is awarded for a book published in
Britain in the previous twelve months.
Previous   winners   include: **Biography**,
D. Felicitas Corrigan, *Helen Waddell*; Victoria
Glendinning, *Edith Sitwell*; **Fiction**, Angela
Carter, *Nights at the Circus*; Paul Theroux *The
Mosquito Coast*; Jenny Joseph, *Persephone*.
Prize £1000 (each)

Boardman Tasker Memorial Award

56 St Michael's Avenue,
Bramhall, Stockport, Cheshire SK7 2PL
☎061–439 4624

FOUNDED 1983, this award is given for a work
of fiction, non-fiction or poetry, whose central theme is concerned with the mountain
environment and which can therefore be said
to make an outstanding contribution to
mountain literature. Authors of any nationality are eligible, but the book must have been
published or distributed in the UK for the
first time between 1 November and 31 October of the year of the prize.
1987 winners: Roger Mear and Robert
Swann, *In the Footsteps of Scott*.
Prize £1000 (May vary at Trustees' discretion)

Booker Prize for Fiction

Book Trust, Book House, 45 East Hill,
London SW18 2QZ
☎01–870 9055

The leading British literary prize. It was set
up in 1968 by Booker McConnell Ltd, with
the intention of rewarding merit, raising the
stature of the author in the eyes of the public
and increasing the sale of the books. The announcement of the winner has been televised
live since 1981, and all the books on the short-
list   experience   a   substantial   increase
in sales. Eligible novels must be written in
English by a citizen of Britain, the Commonwealth, the Republic of Ireland, Pakistan or
South Africa, and must be published in the
UK for the first time between 1 October and
30 September of the year of the prize. Entries
are submitted only by UK publishers who
may each submit not more than four novels
within   the   appropriate   scheduled   publication dates. The judges may also ask for certain other eligible novels to be submitted to
them. This has led to some controversy in
recent years with publishers accused of
'holding back' obvious favourites in order to
increase the chances of the prize going to one
of their listed authors.
Previous winners include: Penelope Lively
(1987), Kingsley Amis (1986), Salman Rushdie (1981), Paul Scott (1977), Ruth Prawer
Jhabvala (1975), John Berger (1972).
Prize £15,000 (Annual)

BP Arts Journalism Awards

Arts Council, 105 Piccadilly,
London W1V 0AU
☎01–629 9495
CoRAA, Litton Lodge, 13A Clifton Road,
Winchester, Hampshire SO22 5BP
☎0962 51063

Contact *The Press Office* (Arts Council), *CoRRA*

First presented in 1986 to recognise the contribution made by journalists throughout the UK towards understanding and appreciation of the arts. Sponsored by British Petroleum plc.

Four main categories: (a) Best news story or feature article about the arts or heritage in a newspaper or periodical. Reviews excluded. (b) Best radio programme on the arts or heritage. (c) Best television programme on the arts or heritage. (d) A picture or series of pictures published in a newspaper or periodical which best illustrates an event in the arts or heritage.
Prize £1000 first prize and £250 for runner-up in each category.

Bridport Arts Centre Creative Writing Competition

Arts Centre, South Street, Bridport, Dorset
☎0308 27183

Contact *The Administrator*

A competition for poetry and short story writing, plus sometimes a category for plays. Unpublished work only, written in English.
Prizes £1000 each; £500 & £250 for runners-up.

Katharine Briggs Folklore Award

The Folklore Society, 3 Broom Rd,
Hale, Altrincham, Cheshire WA15 9AR
☎061–928 1165

Contact *Derek Froome* (Hon. Publicity Officer)

An annual award for a book receiving its first British publication in the previous calendar year which has made the most distinguished non-fiction contribution to folklore studies. The term folklore studies is interpreted broadly to include all aspects of traditional and popular culture, narrative, belief and folklore arts.
Prize £50 plus engraved goblet.

Bristol Old Vic & HTV West Playwriting Award

Playwriting Award, PO Box 60,
Bristol BS99 7NS
☎0272 778366

INITIATED 1987, this award is open to any author, amateur or professional, over the age of eighteen and resident in the British Isles. Along with the cash prize there is a trophy and the possibility of production on the stage or television.
Award £2000

British Airways Commonwealth Poetry Prize

Commonwealth Institute,
Kensington High Street, London W8 6NQ
☎01–603 4535 ext. 269

Contact *The Arts Librarian*

An annual prize, sponsored by British Airways, for a published book of poetry by an author from a Commonwealth country including the UK. Entries in non-English officially recognised languages are accepted with a translation.
1987 winner: Philip Salom, *Sky Poems*.
Prize £6000 plus four regional awards of £1000.

British Film Institute Book Award

21 Stephen Street, London W1P 1PL
☎01–244 1444

Contact *Wayne Drew*

For a book on film or television which is both innovative and accessible with a lively approach to the media.
Previous winners include: Michel Ciment, *John Boorman*; Richard Schikel, *D.W. Griffith & the Birth of Film*.
Award £1000 (annual)

British Science Fiction Association Award

c/o The British Science Fiction Association,
7 The Thicket, Whitenap, Romsey,
Hampshire.

Contact *The Award Administrator*

Annual awards are given in four categories: Best Novel, Best Short Fiction, Best Media Presentation, Best Artist, for work first published or presented in Britain during the preceding year.
Award Trophy.

James Cameron Award

City University Graduate Centre for Journalism, Northampton Square, London EC1
☎01–253 4399

Contact *The Administrator*

Annual award for journalism. Awarded to a reporter of any nationality, writing for the British Press, whose work is judged (by a panel of journalists) to have contributed most during the year to the continuance of the Cameron tradition. Administered by the City University Graduate Centre for Journalism. 1988 winner: Michael Buerk, BBC foreign correspondent.

The Carnegie Medal

Library Association, 7 Ridgmount Street, London WC1E 7AE
☎01–636 7543

Presented for an outstanding book for children written in English and first published in the UK during the preceding year. This award is not necessarily restricted to books of an imaginative nature.
1987 winner: Berlie Doherty, *Granny was a Buffer Girl*.
Award Medal

Catullus Award

The Yeats Club, PO Box 271, Oxford OX2 6DU

FOUNDED 1986 to encourage translators of poetry. Twice yearly open competition for poetry in translation from an *ancient* language. Send s.a.e. for entry form. Complete original text must accompany translation.
Prize An original sculpture.

Cheltenham Prize

Cheltenham Festival of Literature, c/o Town Hall, Cheltenham, Glos GL50 1QA
☎0242 521621

As part of the Cheltenham Festival, an author is chosen by a leading literary reviewer from his year's reading.
Prize £500

Children's Book Award (The Federation of Children's Book Groups)

22 Beacon Brow, Bradford, West Yorks BD6 3DE
☎0274 575301

Contact *Martin G. Kromer*

FOUNDED 1980. Awarded annually for the best work of fiction (published in the UK, chosen by children for children).
Previous winner: Allan Ahlberg, *The Jolly Postman* (Heinemann).
Award Certificate

The Children's Book Circle Eleanor Farjeon Award

A. & C. Black, 35 Bedford Row, London WC1R 4JH
☎01–242 0946

Contact *Jill Coleman*, Secretary (Children's Book Circle)

This award, named in memory of the much loved children's writer, is for distinguished services to children's books either in this country or overseas, and may be given to a librarian, teacher, publisher, bookseller, author, artist, reviewer, television producer etc. at the discretion of the Children's Book Circle.
1987 winner: Valerie Bierman, Children's Organiser of the Edinburgh Book Festival.
Award £500

Cholmondeley Awards

The Society of Authors, 84 Drayton Gardens, London SW10 9SB
☎01–373 6642

In 1965, the Dowager Marchioness of Cholmondeley established these annual non-competitive awards, for which submissions are not required, for the benefit and encouragement of poets of any age, sex or nationality.

Presentation date: June.

1988 winners of £2000 each: John Heath-Stubbs, Sean O'Brien, John Whitworth.

1987 winners of £1300 each: Wendy Cope, Matthew Sweeney, George Szirtes.

Award £6000 (in total, usually divided)

Arthur C. Clarke Award for Science Fiction

Science Fiction Foundation,
North East Polytechnic, Longbridge Road,
Dagenham, Essex RM8 2AS
☎01–590 7722 ext. 2177

Contact *Joyce Day*

ESTABLISHED 1986. Annual award made by the **Science Fiction Foundation**, in conjunction with the **British Science Fiction Association** and the International Science Policy Foundation.

1987 winner: Margaret Atwood, *The Handmaid's Tale* (Cape)

Award £1000 for the best science fiction novel published in the UK.

Collins Biennial Religious Book Award

William Collins Sons & Co. Ltd,
8 Grafton Street, London W1X 3LA
☎01–493 7070

Contact *Sarah Baird-Smith*

A biennial award given for a book which has made the most distinguished contribution to the relevance of Christianity in the modern world, written by a living citizen of the Commonwealth, the Republic of Ireland or South Africa.

1987 winner: Gerard W. Hughes, *God of Surprises*.

Award £2000

Commonwealth Writers Prize

Book Trust Publicity Office, 45 East Hill,
Wandsworth, London SW18 2QZ
☎01–870 9055

Contact *Sue Bennett, Sarah Morgan*

ESTABLISHED 1987. Eligible books must be in English, written by a Commonwealth citizen. Novels, plays or collection of plays, and short stories. Administered by Book Trust.

1987 winner: Olive Senior, *Summer Lightning* (Longman)

Prizes Overall winner: £10,000. Runners-up from four regions £1000 each

The Constable Trophy

c/o Northern Arts, 10 Osborne Terrace,
Jesmond, Newcastle upon Tyne NE2 1NZ
☎091–281 6334

Contact *Literature Officer*

An annual competition supported by the five northern-based regional arts associations for fiction writers living in the North of England for a previously unpublished novel. The winning entry may be considered for publication by **Constable & Co.**, as may two runners-up.

Prize £2000 (First prize) & Trophy plus £1000 on acceptance by **Constable & Co.** in advance of royalties.

Thomas Cook Travel Book Awards

Book Trust, Book House, 45 East Hill,
London SW18 2QZ
☎01–870 9055

The annual awards are given to encourage the art of travel writing in two categories: (a) best travel book, and (b) best guide book published in the current year.

1988 winner: Colin Thubron *Behind the Wall* and Stephen Batchelor *The Tibet Guide*. Previous winners have included: Patrick Leigh Fermor, Patrick Marnham, Geoffrey Moorhouse, Tim Severin, Jonathan Raban.

Awards £2000 (a), £1000 (b)

The Duff Cooper Memorial Prize
24 Bloomfield Road, London W9 1AD
☎ 01–286 5050

Contact *The Viscount Norwich*

An annual award for a literary work in the field of biography, history, politics or poetry, published in English or French during the previous 24 months. Financed by the interest from a Trust Fund commemorating Duff Cooper, first Viscount Norwich (1890–1954), the prize has two permanent judges, the present Lord Norwich, and the Warden of New College, Oxford, as well as three others who change every five years.
Prize £250 approx.

Rose Mary Crawshay Prize
The British Academy,
20–21 Cornwall Terrace, London NW1 4QP
☎ 01–487 5966

Contact *Rachel Ollerearnshaw*

FOUNDED 1888 by Rose Mary Crawshay, this prize is given for a historical or critical work by a woman of any nationality on English literature, with particular preference for a work on Keats, Byron or Shelley. The work must have been published in the preceding 3 years.
Prize £600 (or 2 prizes of £300 each)

John Creasey Memorial Award
Crime Writers' Association, PO Box 172,
Tring, Herts HP23 5LP

Contact *The Secretary*

FOUNDED 1973 following the death of crime writer, John Creasey, who founded the **Crime Writers' Association**. This award is given annually for the best first crime novel published in the preceding year.
1987 winner: Denis Kilcommons, *The Dark Apostle.*
Award £1000 plus magnifying glass.

Crime Writers' Association Fiction Award
Crime Writers' Association, PO Box 172,
Tring, Herts HP23 5LP

Contact *The Secretary*

Prizes awarded for the best crime fiction published during the preceding year. Also Cartier Diamond Dagger awarded annually for a lifetime's achievement in the world of crime fiction.
1987 winners: Gold Dagger: Barbara Vine (Ruth Rendell); Silver Dagger: Scott Turow; Cartier Diamond Dagger: P.D. James (1987); John Le Carré 1988.
Award £1000 plus gold-plated dagger; £500 plus silver-plated dagger.

Crime Writers' Association Non-Fiction Award
Crime Writers' Association, PO Box 172,
Tring, Herts HP23 5LP

Contact *The Secretary*

An annual award for the best non-fiction crime book published during the preceding year.
1987 winners: Bernard Taylor and Stephen Knight *A Century of Unsolved Murders.*
Award £1000 plus gold-plated dagger.

Isaac Deutscher Memorial Prize
c/o Lloyds Bank, 68 Warwick Square,
London SW1V 2AS

An annual award in recognition of and as encouragement to outstanding research in the Marxist tradition of Isaac Deutscher. Made to the author of an essay or full scale work published or in manuscript. Entries should be submitted by 1 May each year. Recent winner: Professor Teodor Shanin, *Russia 1905–1907: Revolution as a Moment of Truth.*
Award £100

The George Devine Award
23 Ainger Road, London NW3

Contact *Christine Smith*

Annual award administered by the **Royal Court Theatre** to find and support a promising new playwright. Send two copies of the

script to Christine Smith by the end of March. Information leaflet available.
1987 winner: Nick Ward, *Apart from George*.
Prize £2000

Denis Devlin Award

The Arts Council (An Chomhairle Ealaion), 70 Merrion Square, Dublin 2, Ireland
☎0001 611840

Contact *Literature Officer*

Triennial award for the best book of poetry in English by an Irish poet, published in the preceding three years.
Award £1000 (next award – 1989)

DuQuesne Award

The Yeats Club, PO Box 271, Oxford OX2 6DU

FOUNDED 1986 to encourage translators of poetry. Twice yearly open competition for poetry in translation from a *modern* language. Send s.a.e. for entry form. Complete original text must accompany translation.
Prize An original sculpture.

Mary Elgin Award

Hodder & Stoughton Ltd, 47 Bedford Square, London WC1B 3DP
☎01–636 9851

To encourage gifted new writers of fiction on the **Hodder & Stoughton** publishing list. No restrictions of age, sex or nationality apply, and writers need not be first novelists. Work to have been published or submitted to **Hodder & Stoughton** during the previous 12 months.
Award £50 (Annual)

Michael Elliott Prize for the North West

See **The Mobil Playwriting Competition.**

European Prize for Translation of Poetry

European Poetry Library, Blijde Inkomstraat 9, B-3000 Leuven, Belgium

Prize offered by the European Commission in Brussels for translations of poetry, written by living poets from other Community countries. Both poems and translations must be in one of the nine official Community languages and the translations must have been published in book form in the previous four years. Submit five copies of the translation, marking envelope: 'European Prize for Translation of Poetry'.
Prize £6000

Christopher Ewart-Biggs Memorial Prize

31 Radnor Walk, London SW3

An annual award to a writer of any nationality whose work contributes most to peace and understanding in Ireland or to co-operation between members of the European community. Works must have been published in the year of presentation and written in either English or French.
1987 winner: Frank McGuinness, *Observe the Sons of Ulster Marching Towards the Somme*.
Prize £2000

Geoffrey Faber Memorial Prize

Faber & Faber Ltd, 3 Queen Square, London WC1N 3AU
☎01–278 6881

ESTABLISHED 1963 as a memorial to the founder and first chairman of **Faber & Faber**, this prize is awarded in alternate years for the volume of verse and the volume of prose fiction judged to be of greatest literary merit published in the UK in the preceding two years. Authors must be under 40 at the time of publication and citizens of the UK, Commonwealth, Republic of Ireland or South Africa.

1987 winner: Guy Vanderhaeghe, *Man Descending*.
Prize £500

Faber, *Guardian*, BBC *Jackanory* Children's Writer Competition

Faber & Faber, 3 Queen Square,
London WC1N 3AU
☎01–278 6881

Contact *Corinna Mitchell*

ESTABLISHED 1987. Competition for unpublished author of a children's novel for 7–11 year olds.
1987 winner: Billie Rosen, *Andi's War* (Faber)
Prize £2500

Prudence Farmer Award

New Statesman and Society,
Foundation House, Perseverance Works,
38 Kingsland Road, London E2 5BA
☎01–739 3211

For the best poem to have been published in the *New Statesman and Society* during the previous year (July to July).
Award £100

Fawcett Society Book Prize

46 Harleyford Road,
London SE11 5AY
☎01–587 1287

Contact *Rita Pankhurst*

An annual award to the author of a book (alternately fiction and non-fiction) which has made a substantial contribution to the understanding of women's position in society today. All works submitted for the Prize are placed in the **Fawcett Library at City of London Polytechnic**.
1988 winner: Beatrice Campbell, *The Iron Ladies: Why Do Women Vote Tory?* (Virago).
Prize £500

The Kathleen Fidler Award

c/o The Book Trust, 15A Lynedoch Street,
Glasgow G3 6EF
☎041–332 0391

For a novel for children aged 8–12, to encourage authors new to writing for this age group. The work must be the author's first attempt to write for this age range.
1988 winner: Theresa Breslin, *Simon's Challenge*
Award £1000 plus possible publication by **Blackie**.

Sir Banister Fletcher Award

The Authors' Club, 40 Dover Street,
London W1X 3RB
☎01–499 8581

Contact *Mrs Ridgway* (Secretary)

This award is financed partly by the income from a trust left by the late Sir Banister Fletcher, who was President of the Authors' Club for many years, and partly by the **Arts Council of Great Britain**. It is presented for the best book on architecture or the fine arts published in the preceding year.
1987 winner: Sir Michael Levey, *Giambattista Tiepolo: His Life and Art* (Yale).
Award £200

The John Florio Prize

The Translator's Association, 84 Drayton Gardens, London SW10 9SB
☎01–373 6642

ESTABLISHED 1963 under the auspices of the Italian Institute and the British–Italian Society, this prize is awarded biennially for the best translation into English of a Twentieth Century Italian work of literary merit and general interest and published by a British publisher in the two years preceding the prize.
Previous winner: Avril Bardoni.
Prize £700

Glenfiddich Awards

11a West Halkin Street, London SW1X 8JL

A series of awards to writers who have contributed most to the civilised appreciation of food and drink through articles or books published in the UK. Also covers radio and TV programmes.

1988 winners: Julie Sahni, *Classic Indian Vegetarian Cooking* Food Book of the Year; Hubrecht Duijker, *The Wines of Rioja* Drink Book of the Year; Michael Jackson, *The World Guide to Whisky*, Whisky Writer of the Year; Drew Smith, *The Good Food Guide* Restaurant Writer of the Year. Special Awards: Maurice Hanssen, *The New E for Additives*; Giles Macdonogh, *A Palate in Revolution*; Glenfiddich Trophy and Television Programme of the Year: *Farmhouse Kitchen*.
Award £750 plus Glenfiddich Trophy. Also category awards of £100 plus gold medal; £100 and Glenfiddich Malt Scotch Whisky.

The Kate Greenaway Medal
The Library Association,
7 Ridgmount Street, London WC1E 7AE
☎01–636 7543

First awarded in 1955. Offered annually by the **Library Association** for the most distinguished work in the illustration of children's books first published in the UK during the preceding year.
1987 winner: Fiona French, *Snow White in New York* (OUP).

Greenwich Festival Poetry Competition
25 Woolwich New Road, London SE18 6EU
☎01–317 8687

Contact *Keith Rusby*

A biennial award on even years for an unpublished poem in English of up to 50 lines by anyone over the age of sixteen.
Prize £1000 (Total prize money)

The Guardian Children's Fiction Award
24 Weymouth Street, London W1N 3FA
☎01–580 3479

Contact *Stephanie Nettell*

For an outstanding work of fiction for children by a British or Commonwealth author, first published in the UK in the preceding year, excluding picture books and previous winners.
1988 winner: Ruth Thomas, *The Runaways*.
Previous winners include: Ann Schlee, Joan Aiken, James Aldridge.
Award £500 (Annual)

The Guardian Fiction Prize
The Guardian, 119 Farringdon Road, London EC1R 3ER
☎01–278 2332

Contact *Literary Editor*

An annual award for a novel published by a British or Commonwealth writer, this is chosen by the Literary Editor in conjunction with *The Guardian*'s regular reviewers of fiction.
Previous winners include: Isabel Colegate, Peter Benson.
Prize £1000

The Hawthornden Prize
The Society of Authors, 84 Drayton Gardens, London SW10 9SB
☎01–373 6642

An annual award for a work of imaginative literature by a British subject under the age of 41 published during the previous year.
Previous winners include: Robert Shaw, V.S. Naipaul.
Prize £750

The Royal Society of Literature Award under W.H. Heinemann Bequest
Royal Society of Literature,
1 Hyde Park Gardens,
London W2 2LT
☎01–723 5104

Works of any kind of literature may be submitted by their publishers for consideration under this award, but only living authors are considered. Genuine contributions to literature originally written in English are sought, but preference will be given to publications which are unlikely to command large sales: poetry, biography, criticism, etc.

1987 winner: Richard Dawkins, *The Blind Watchmaker*.
Award Amount varies.

Historical Novel Prize in Memory of Georgette Heyer

The Bodley Head, 32 Bedford Square,
London WC1B 3EL
☎01–631 4434
or
Transworld Publishers Ltd, Century House,
61–63 Uxbridge Rd, London W5 5SA
☎01–579 2652

Contact *Jill Black* (Bodley Head)

FOUNDED 1977 in memory of the celebrated historical novelist, this is an annual prize for an outstanding previously unpublished historical novel.
Prize £5000

David Higham Prize for Fiction

Book Trust, Book House, 45 East Hill,
London SW18 2QZ
☎01–870 9055

An annual award for a first novel or book of short stories published in the UK in the year of the Award by an author who is a citizen of Britain, the Commonwealth, the Republic of Ireland, Pakistan or South Africa.
1987 winner: Adam Zameenzad, *The 13th House*.
Award £1000

Winifred Holtby Memorial Prize

Royal Society of Literature,
1 Hyde Park Gardens, London W2 2LT
☎01–723 5104

An annual award for the best regional work of fiction (or, in some cases non-fiction or poetry) written in English by a living citizen of the UK, Republic of Ireland or the Commonwealth, published in the year of the prize.
1987 winner: Maggie Hemingway, *The Bridge*.
Prize £500

Nelson Hurst & Marsh Biography Award

The Authors' Club, 40 Dover Street,
London W1X 3RB
☎01–499 8581

Contact *Mrs Ridgway* (Secretary)

A biennial award (odd years) for the most significant biography published over a two year period by a British publisher.
1987 winner: Roland Huntford.
Award £2000

Mary Vaughan Jones Award

Welsh National Centre for Children's Literature, Castell Brychan,
Aberystwyth, Dyfed SY23 2JB
☎0970 4151

Contact *The Administrator*

For distinguished services to the field of children's literature in Wales over a considerable period of time. This triennial award will next be presented in 1991.
Award £600 plus silver trophy.

The Sir Peter Kent Conservation Book Prize

The Book Trust, Book House, 45 East Hill,
London SW18 2QZ
☎01–870 9055

Established by BP Exploration Limited. A book on creative conservation of the environment. Entries from publishers in the UK.
1987 winner: Chris Baines, *The Wild Side of Town* (BBC/Elm Tree Books).
Prize £1500

The Martin Luther King Memorial Prize

National Westminster Bank Ltd,
7 Fore Street, Chard, Somerset TA20 1PJ

Contact *John Brunner*

An annual award for a literary work (including poetry, plays and TV or film scripts) reflecting the ideals to which Dr King dedicated

his life, published or performed in the UK during previous calendar year. No enquiries answered without s.a.e.
Prize £100

Kraszna-Kransz Award: Best Book on Photography
Kraszna-Kransz Foundation,
37 Gower Street, London WC1E 6HH
☎01–580 2842

Contact *John Chittock* OBE

For the book making the most original and lasting contribution to the art and practice of camera media. Details subject to annual announcement.
Prize £5000

Lakeland Book of the Year
Cumbria Tourist Board, Ashleigh,
Holly Road, Windermere LA23 2AQ
☎096 62 4444

Contact *Publicity and Information Officer*

An annual award for the best book or booklet on any aspect of Cumbria and the English Lake District published in the previous calendar year. Entries in by end of January 1989.
1987 winners: Peter Thornton, *Lakeland from the Air*; and Trevor Haywood, *Walking with a Camera in Herries' Lakeland*.
Award £100

London Newspaper Group Short Story Competition
London Newspaper Group,
Newspaper House, Winslow Road,
London W6 9SF
☎01–741 1622

Contact *The Editor*

ESTABLISHED 1985 with a total prize value of £5000. Top prize varies according to the year's sponsor – in 1987 it was the £3500 18-carat solid gold Mont Blanc fountain pen. The competition runs over a year – stories are published weekly, with a prize each month

for the 'editor's choice'. All published stories go into the final competition, which is usually judged in December.

London Tourist Board Guide Book of the Year Award
London Tourist Board,
26 Grosvenor Gardens, London SW1W 0DU
☎01–730 3450

Contact *Public Relations Manager*

An annual award for new or substantially revised guidebooks mainly on London published between 1 June and 31 May. Two categories: General Guide and Specialist.
Award Gift and certificate.

LWT Plays on Stage
LWT Plays on Stage, South Bank Television Centre, London SE1 9LT
☎01–261 3434

Contact *Michael Halifax*

A live drama competition with a total prize money of £44,000, to be divided into 1st, 2nd and 3rd prizes, to help stage three plays judged to be outstanding by a panel of 'distinguished judges'. The competition is open to producers, producing theatres and rep. companies, rather than playwrights direct.
1987 winners: 1st Cheek by Jowl, *Philoctetes* by Sophocles; 2nd **Bush Theatre**, *The Fatherland* by Murray Watts; 3rd **Wildcat Stage Productions**, *Waiting on One* by Anne Downie.
Prize 1st £15,000; 2nd £12,500; 3rd £10,000

Sir William Lyons Award
The Guild of Motoring Writers,
2 Pembroke Villas, The Green, Richmond,
Surrey TW9 1QF
☎01–940 6974

Contact *Jean Peters*

An annual competitive award to encourage young people in automotive journalism and foster interests in motoring and motor industry. Entrance by two essays and interview

with Awards Committee. Applicants must be British and resident in UK, aged 17–23. Final entry date: 1 October. Presentation date: December.
Award £500

Roger Machell Prize
The Society of Authors, 84 Drayton Gardens, London SW10 9SB
☎01–373 6642

An annual award for a non-fiction book on any of the performing arts, written in English, the work of one author and first published in the UK. This prize is sponsored by **Hamish Hamilton**.
1988 winner: Peter Conrad, *A Song of Love and Death*.
1987 winner: Kurt Ganzl, *The British Musical Theatre*.
Prize £2000

Enid McLeod Literary Prize
Franco–British Society, Room 636, Linen Hall, 162–8 Regent Street, London W1R 5TB

An annual award for a full length work of literature which contributes most to Franco–British understanding. It must be written in English by a citizen of the UK, Commonwealth, the Republic of Ireland, Pakistan or South Africa and first published in the UK.
Previous winner: Piers Paul Read, *The Free Frenchman*.
Prize £100

The Macmillan Prize for a Children's Picture Book
4 Little Essex Street, London WC2R 3LF
☎01–836 6633

Contact *Publicity Manager* (Macmillan Children's Books)

'Established in order to stimulate new work from young illustrators in art schools and to help them start their professional lives.' Fiction or non-fiction.

Prize 1st £500; 2nd £300; 3rd £100. **Macmillan Children's Books** will have the option to publish any of the prize winners.

Macmillan Silver Pen Award
The English Centre of International PEN, 7 Dilke Street, London SW3 4JE
☎01–352 6303

An annual award, from nomination by PEN Executive Committee, for an outstanding novel written in English by a British author and published in the UK in the year preceding the prize.
1988 winner: A.L. Barker, *The Gooseboy*.
1987 winner: Lewis Nkosi, *Mating Birds*.
Prize £500 plus Silver Pen.

McVitie's Prize for Scottish Writer of the Year
Michael Kelly Associates, 65 Bath Street, Glasgow G2 2BX
☎041–333 9711

Contact *Alan Clark,* McVitie's Prize

ESTABLISHED 1987. Sponsored by United Biscuits. Imaginative works in English, Scots, or Gaelic, including TV and film scripts. Eligible to writers born or now working in Scotland.
1987 winner: Davide Thomson, *Nairn in Darkness and Light* (Hutchinson).
Prize £5000

Arthur Markham Memorial Prize
University of Sheffield, Western Bank, Sheffield S10 2TN
☎0742 78555

Contact *Registrar and Secretary*

There are six categories for work specially written for this annual prize: short story, essay, poem, group of poems, prose account, first chapter of a novel on a given subject announced annually. Candidates must be manual workers at a coal mine or have been injured when so employed.
Prize £200

Emil Kurt Maschler Award
Book Trust, Book House, 45 East Hill,
London SW18 2QZ
☎01–870 9055

For 'a work of imagination in the children's field in which text and illustration are of excellence and so presented that each enhances, yet balances the other'. Books published in the current year in the UK by a British author and/or artist or someone resident for ten years are eligible.
1987 winner: Charles Keeping, *Jack the Treacle Eater.*
Award £1000

Somerset Maugham Trust Fund
The Society of Authors, 84 Drayton Gardens, London SW10 9SB
☎01–373 6642

The annual competitive awards arising from this Fund are designed to encourage young writers to travel and to acquaint themselves with the manners and customs of other countries. Candidates must be under 35 and submit a published literary work in volume form in English. They must be British subjects by birth only.
Final entry date: 31 December. Presentation date: June.
1988 winners: Jimmy Burns, Carol Ann Duffy, Matthew Kneale
1987 winners: Stephen Gregory, Jannie Howker, Andrew Motion.
Award £4000 each

Katherine Mansfield Menton Short Story Prize
The English Centre of International PEN, 7 Dilke Street, London SW3 4JE
☎01–352 6303

A triennial prize (next awarded in 1990) for a volume of short stories written in English by a British, Irish or Commonwealth writer, published in the UK in the preceding three years.
Prize 10,000 French francs.

MIND Book of the Year – The Allen Lane Award
MIND, 22 Harley Street, London W1N 2ED
☎01–637 0741

INAUGURATED 1981, this annual award in memory of Sir Allen Lane, is given to the author of the book, fiction or non-fiction, which furthers public understanding of mental illness, published in the current year.
Award £1000

Mitchell Prize for the History of Art
24 Heathfield Terrace, London W4 4JE
☎01–994 7994

Contact *The Lady Vaizey*

There are two annual prizes, one to the author of an outstanding original contribution in English to art history assessed in terms of scholarly, critical and literary merit, and the second to the most promising first book fulfilling the same criteria. Books should have been published in the 18 months preceding presentation date in USA or UK.
1987 winners: Lee Johnson, *The Paintings of Eugene Delacroix* ($10,000); Cecilia Powell, *Turner in the South* ($3000).
Prize $10,000 and $3000

The Mobil Playwriting Competition for the Royal Exchange Theatre Company
Royal Exchange Theatre, St Ann's Square, Manchester M2 7DH

Contact *The Mobil Playwriting Competition*

Awarded to an original full-length play in English. Entries should be submitted with a pseudonym and with a sealed envelope containing actual identity.
1988 winners: Michael Wall, *Amongst the Barbarians*; Rod Williams, *No Remission*; Keith Wood, *Assuming the Role*; Michele Celeste, *Hanging the President*.
NB At the time of going to press there is doubt over the future of the competition.

Also runs the **Michael Elliott Prize for the North West** for the best play with a North West setting by a North West writer. *Prizes* 1st, £10,000 with performance by **Royal Exchange Theatre Company** and publication by Oberon Books; joint 2nd prizes of £4000 each. International Prize £3000 for the best play by a foreign writer. Michael Elliott Prize for the North West, £3000.

Scott Moncrieff Prize

The Translators' Association,
84 Drayton Gardens, London SW10 9SB
☎01–373 6642

An annual award for the best translation published by a British publisher during the previous year of French Twentieth Century work of literary merit and general interest.
1987 winner: Robyn Marsack, *Le Poisson-Scorpion* by Nicolas Bouvier.
1986 winner: Barbara Wright, *Grabinoulor* by Pierre Albert-Birot.
Prize £1500

The Mother Goose Award

Books for Children, Park House,
Dollar Street, Cirencester, Glos GL7 2AN
☎0285 67081

Contact *Sally Grindley*

For the most exciting newcomer to British children's book illustration.
1988 winner: Emma Chichester Clark, *Listen to This* compiled by Laura Cecil (Bodley Head).
1987 winner: Patrick James Lynch, illustrator of *A Bag of Moonshine* by Alan Garner (Collins).
Prize £500 rising to £1000 in 1989.

Shiva Naipaul Memorial Prize

The Spectator, 56 Doughty Street,
London WC1N 2LL
☎01–405 1706

Contact *Julia Mount*

An annual competition for the writer best able to describe a visit to a foreign place or people; for the most acute and profound observation of cultures and/or scenes evidently alien to the writer. Submissions must be unpublished and no more than 4000 words.
Recent winners: Sousa Jamba and Simukai Utete.
Prize £1000 plus publication in *The Spectator*.

National Poetry Competition

The Poetry Society, 21 Earls Court Square,
London SW5 9DE
☎01–373 7861

Run in conjunction with BBC Radio 3, this is now the major annual poetry competition in Britain. The prizes are each awarded for an unpublished poem of less than 40 lines by anyone over the age of 16 who lives, works or studies in the UK or Republic of Ireland. There is an entry fee of £2 per poem, and a maximum entry of ten poems per writer. Further details and entry form available on receipt of an s.a.e.
Previous winners include: Andrew Motion, Ian Duhig.
Prizes £2000 plus an appearance on Radio 3 and publication in a special anthology produced by **The Poetry Society** (First prize); £1000 (Second prize); £500 (Third prize); plus smaller prizes.

NCR Book Award

NCR Book Award, 206 Marylebone Road,
London NW1 6LY
☎01–725 8244

Contact *The Administrator*

ESTABLISHED 1987 (first award made in 1988), the NCR Book Award is for a book written in English by a living writer from Britain or the Commonwealth and first published in the UK. Publishers only may submit titles, limited to two per imprint. The award will cover all areas of non-fiction except academic, guide books and practical listings (such as cookery books). Titles eligible for the 1989 award must be published in the 12 months between 1 April 1988 and 31 March 1989, a short-list of four books will be announced in mid-April 1989. The aim of the award is to stimulate interest in non-fiction writing and publishing in the UK.

1988 winners: £25,000 (non-fiction) David Thomson, *Nairn in Darkness and Light*; £1000 each to Claire Tomalin, *Katherine Mansfield: A Secret Life*; Max Hastings, *The Korean War*; Kathleen Tynan, *The Life of Kenneth Tynan*; Michael Ignatieff, *The Russian Album*; Nirad C. Chaudhuri, *Thy Hand, Great Anarch!*

Award £25000 (plus £1000 to each remaining short-listed book).

New Poetry

c/o English Centre of International PEN, 7 Dilke Street, London SW3 4JE
☎01-352 6303

Biennial publication, alternating with **New Stories**, produced jointly since 1952 by **PEN** and a chosen publisher. However, due to lack of funding, this is currently in abeyance until further notice.

New Stories

c/o English Centre of International PEN, 7 Dilke Street, London SW3 4JE
☎01-352 6303

Biennial publication, alternating with **New Poetry**, produced jointly since 1952 by **PEN** and a chosen publisher. However, due to lack of funding ,this is currently in abeyance until further notice.

The Odd Fellows (Manchester Unity)/Friendly Society's Social Concern Book Awards

Book Trust, Book House, 45 East Hill, London SW18 2QZ
☎01-870 9055

An annual award for the book or pamphlet of not less than 10,000 words within a specified area of social concern (varies each year). Entries must have been published in the current year in English and been written by citizens of the Commonwealth, Republic of Ireland, Pakistan or South Africa.

Award £1000

The Other Award

c/o Children's Book Bulletin,
4 Aldebert Terrace, London SW8 1BL
☎01-582 4483

Contact *The Administrator*

Children's books of literary merit that children will enjoy and which are progressive in their treatment of ethnic minorities, the sex roles and social differences are eligible for this honorary award. Books should be published in the period 1 July-30 June.

Outposts Poetry Competition

72, Burwood Road, Walton-on-Thames, Surrey KT12 4AL
☎0932 240712

Contact *Howard Sergeant*

Annual competition for an unpublished poem of not more than 40 lines.

Prize £1000 (approx.)

Catherine Pakenham Award

Evening Standard, 118 Fleet Street, London EC4P 4JT
☎01-353 8000

Contact *Managing Editor*

FOUNDED 1970 this is an annual award in memory of Lady Catherine Pakenham, and given for a published or unpublished article (of up to 2500 words) or radio or TV script (but not a short story) by women aged between 18 and 30 involved in or intending to take up a career in journalism.

1987 winner: Amanda Craig.

Previous winners include: Jaci Stephen (*Standard*); Sharon Maxwell (*Cosmopolitan*).

Award £500

Parents Magazine Best Book for Babies Award

Book Trust, Book House,
45 East Hill, London SW18 2QZ
☎01–870 9055

An annual award for the best book for the under-fours (babies and toddlers) published in Britain in the year ending 31 May.
1987 winner: Jill Murphy, *Five Minutes Peace*.
Award £1000

The Portico Prize

The Portico Library, 57 Mosley Street,
Manchester M2 3HY
☎061–236 6785

Contact *Mrs Janet Allan*

Administered by the Portico Library in Manchester. Awarded for a work of fiction or non-fiction set wholly or mainly in the North West.
1987 winner: Bill Naughton, *On The Pig's Back*.
Prize £1500

Radio Times Drama Awards

BBC Publications, PO Box 1AX,
33 Marylebone High Street,
London W1 1AX
☎01–580 5577

Contact *The Administrator*

Biennial award (even years) for an original work for either radio or television not previously performed in public. Each entry to be supported by a sponsor experienced in production. Details of awards are announced in *Radio Times* in January.
Previous winners include: Peter Ransley.
Award £5000 in each category: the winning play will be screened/broadcast.

Radio Times Radio Comedy Awards

BBC Publications, PO Box 1AX,
33 Marylebone High Street,
London W1 1AX
☎01–580 5577

Contact *The Administrator*

Biennial award (odd years) for an original 30-minute script capable of being developed into a series. Each entry to be supported by a sponsor experienced in comedy drama. Details of awards announced in *Radio Times* in January.
Award £3500

John Llewellyn Rhys Memorial Prize

Book Trust, Book House, 45 East Hill,
London SW18 2QZ
☎01–870 9055

An annual award for a memorable work of any kind by a writer who is under the age of 35 at the time of publication. Books must have been published in the UK in the year of the award, and the author must be a citizen of Britain or the Commonwealth writing in English.
1987 winner: Jeanette Winterstone, *The Passion*.
Previous winners include: Elizabeth Jane Howard, V.S. Naipaul, Shiva Naipaul, Margaret Drabble.
Prize £500

Romantic Novelists Association Major Award

2A Rye Walk, Ingatestone, Essex CM4 9AL
☎0277 352964

Contact *Mrs Eileen Huckbody*

Annual award now sponsored by Boots the Chemist for the best romantic novel of the year, open to non-members as well as members of the **Romantic Novelists Association**. Novels must be published between 1 January and 31 December of the year of entry.
1987 winner: Marie Joseph, *A Better World Than This*.
Award £5000

Romantic Novelists Association/ Netta Muskett Award

2A Rye Walk, Ingatestone, Essex CM4 9AL
☎0277 352964

Contact *Mrs Eileen Huckbody*

The award is for unpublished writers in the field of the romantic novel who must join the **Romantic Novelists Association** as Probationary Members. Mss entered for this Award must be especially written for it.

Runciman Award

Book Trust, Book House, 45 East Hill, London SW18 2QZ
☎01–870 9055

INSTITUTED 1985, an annual award by the Anglo-Hellenic League and sponsored by the Onassis Foundation, for a literary work wholly or mainly about Greece. The book may be fiction, poetry, drama or non-fiction and to be eligible must be published in its first English edition in the UK.
Award £1000

Ryman New Writers' Award

PO Box 38, Chelsea, London SW3 3NL
☎01–584 9594

Awards for previously unpublished writers in five categories: novel, short story, children's story, poetry and song lyric. Writers must be citizens of Great Britain and N. Ireland or Republic of Ireland. An entry fee is required.
Award £500 per category plus publisher's contract and minimum advance of £1000 (Annual).

The Saltire Society and Royal Bank Scottish Literary Award

The Royal Bank of Scotland plc, PO Box 31, 42 St Andrew Square, Edinburgh EH2 2YE
☎031–556 8555

An annual award for a book on or about Scotland, or for a book with Scottish connections, not necessarily written by a Scot.
1987 winner: Muriel Spark, *Collected Short Stories*.
Award £1500

Schlegel-Tieck Prize

The Translators' Association,
84 Drayton Gardens, London SW10 9SB
☎01–373 6642

An annual award for the best translation of a German Twentieth Century work of literary merit and interest published by a British publisher during the preceding year.
1987 winner: Anthea Bell, *The Stone and the Flute* by Hans Bemmen.
Prize £2000

Scottish Arts Council Book Awards

Scottish Arts Council, 19 Charlotte Square, Edinburgh EH2 4DF
☎031–226 6051

Contact *Literature Department*

A number of awards are given to authors of published books in recognition of high standards in new writing as well as work of established writers. Authors should be Scottish, resident in Scotland or writing books of Scottish interest.
1987 winners: G.F. Dutton, *Squaring the Waves*; James Kelman, *Greyhound for Breakfast*; Andro Linklater, *Compton Mackenzie: A Life*; Brian McCabe, *One Atom to Another*; Alastair Mackie, *Ingaitherins: Selected Poems*; Tom Pow, *Rough Seas*; Duncan and Linda Williamson, *A Thorn in the King's Foot*.
Award £750 each (Bi-annual)

SCSE Book Prizes

Chester College of Higher Education, Cheyney Road, Chester CH1 4BJ
☎0244 375444

Contact *L. Boucher*

Annual awards given by the Standing Conference on Studies in Education for the best book on education published during the preceding year – by nomination from members of the Standing Conference and publishers.
Prizes £500 and £300

Signal Poetry for Children Award

Thimble Press, Lockwood, Station Road,
South Woodchester, Stroud GL5 5EQ
☎045 387 2208

Contact *Nancy Chambers*

This award is given annually for particular excellence in one of the following areas: single poet collections published for children; poetry anthologies published for children; the body of work of a contemporary poet; critical or educational activity promoting poetry for children. All books for children published in Britain are eligible regardless of the original country of publication. Unpublished work is not eligible.
1988: John Mole, *Boo to a Goose*, illustrated by Mary Norman.
Award £100

André Simon Memorial Fund Book Awards

61 Church Street,
Isleworth, Middx TW7 6BE
☎01–560 6662

Contact *Tessa Hayward*

Two awards are given annually for the best book on drink and the best on food.
Award £1000

Sinclair Prize for Fiction

Book Trust, Book House, 45 East Hill,
London SW18 2QZ
☎01–870 9055

An annual award first made in 1982, this prize is sponsored by Sinclair Research Ltd and is for the best unpublished full length novel (not less than 50,000) of great literary merit and also of social or political significance. The book must be written originally in English and must be submitted by the author. Closing date for entries is 31 July. Entry form on request.
Prize £5000 plus publication by **William Heinemann Ltd.**

Smarties Prize for Children's Books

Book Trust, Book House, 45 East Hill,
London SW18 2QZ
☎01–870 9055

ESTABLISHED 1985 to encourage high standards and stimulate interest in books for children, this prize is given for a children's book written in English by a citizen of the UK or an author resident in the UK, and published in the UK in the year ending 31 October. There are three categories: 6 and under; 7–11 and innovation. An overall winner from these categories is chosen for the Grand Prix.
1987 Grand Prix winner: James Berry, *A Thief in the Village*.
Previous winners include: Ray Marshall & John Bradley (Innovation); Susanna Gretz (Under 7s); Jill Paton Walsh (Over 7s & Grand Prix).
Prizes £8000 (Grand Prix); £1000 (Other categories).

W.H. Smith Literary Award

W.H. Smith, 7 Holbein Place,
London SW1W 8NR
☎01–730 1200 ext. 5458

Contact *Public Relations*

Annual prize awarded to a Commonwealth author (including UK citizens) published in English in UK in the preceding year, for the most outstanding contribution to English literature.
1988 winner: Robert Hughes, *The Fatal Shore*.
Previous winners include: Doris Lessing, David Hughes, Philip Larkin, Elizabeth Jennings.
Prize £10,000

W.H. Smith Young Writers' Competition

W.H. Smith, 7 Holbein Place,
London SW1W 8NR
☎01–730 1200

Contact *Public Relations*

Annual awards for poems or prose by anyone in the UK under the age of 17. There are three age groups. Sixty-three individual prize-winners have their work included in a paper-back every year.

Prize £4000 (Total of range of prizes)

Southern Arts Literature Prize
Southern Arts, 19 Southgate Street,
Winchester, Hants SO23 9DQ
📞0962 55099

Contact *Literature Officer*

This prize is awarded annually to an author living in the Southern Arts Region who has made the most notable contribution to literature during the year in published fiction, poetry or collection of short stories, or non-fiction. The 1986 prize was awarded for a novel.

1987 winner: Grace Ingoldby, *Across the Water*.

Prize £1000

The Spectator & *Sunday Telegraph* Young Writer Awards
The Spectator, 56 Doughty Street,
London WC1 2LL
📞01–405 1706

An annual competition for aspiring journalists. To enter, an article of not more than 2000 words is required. This article must appeal to readers of *The Spectator* and the *Sunday Telegraph*. Use of a pen name will invalidate the entry. Entry form obtained from above address.

Prizes 1st 8 day holiday + £500; 2nd £500 + £500 credited book account; 3rd £200 + £200 credited book account; 4th £100 + £100 credited book account.

The winning article will be published in *The Spectator* and the *Sunday Telegraph* and the writer will be commissioned to compose another piece for both publications.

Stand Magazine Short Story Competition
Stand Magazine, 179 Wingrove Road,
Newcastle upon Tyne NE4 9DA
📞091–273 3280

Contact *The Administrator*

Biennial award (odd years) for a short story written in English and not published, broadcast or under consideration elsewhere.

Prize £2250 total prize money.

The Winifred Mary Stanford Prize
Hodder & Stoughton, 47 Bedford Square,
London WC1B 3DP
📞01–636 9851

This biennial award (even years) is open to any book published in the UK in English which has been in some way inspired by the Christian faith, and written by a man or woman who is under 50 years of age at the time of publication. Literary merit is a prime factor in consideration for the award, but the subject may be from a wide range including poetry, fiction, biography, autobiography, biblical exposition, religious experience and witness. Submission is invited, from publishers only, of books published in the two years prior to the award which is presented at Easter.

Prize £1000

Sunday Express Book of the Year Award

An award for a work of fiction published in the current year. Books are nominated by a panel of judges which invites entries from publishers

First winner, 1988: Brian Moore, *The Colour of Blood* (Cape).

Prize £20,000

E. Reginald Taylor Essay Competition
Journal of the British Archaeological Association, Institute of Archaeology,
36 Beaumont Street, Oxford OX1 2PG

Contact *Honorary Editor*

An annual prize, in memory of the late E. Reginald Taylor FSA, for the best unpublished essay, not exceeding 7500 words, on a subject of archaeological, art historical or antiquarian interest within the period the Roman era to AD 1830. The essay should show original research on its chosen subject, and the author may be invited to read the essay before the Association. In addition, the essay may be published in the Journal of the Association if approved by the Editorial Committee.
Prize £100

The Times/Jonathan Cape Young Writers Competition

Jonathan Cape, 32 Bedford Square, London WC1B 3EL
☎01–636 3344

This annual award is given for a first work of fiction or non-fiction written in English by an author under the age of 30.
Award £5000 plus publication by **Jonathan Cape**.

Dylan Thomas Award

The Poetry Society, 21 Earls Court Square, London SW5 9DE
☎01–373 7861

An annual award given in alternate years for poetry and short stories, established in 1983 to commemorate Dylan Thomas and encourage the two forms in which he made his outstanding contribution to literature. This is open to all published writers in the UK (all entrants must have had poetry or short stories published within two years of submission). Entries must include published work, but unpublished work may also be included.
1987 winner: Andrew Motion.
Prize £1000

Time-Life Silver PEN Award (for non-fiction)

English Centre of International PEN, 7 Dilke Street, London SW3 4JE
☎01–352 6303

An annual award, the winner being nominated by the **PEN** Executive Committee, for an outstanding work of non-fiction written in English and published in England in the year preceding the prize.
1988 winner: John Miller, *Friends and Romans: On the Run in Wartime Italy*.
1987 winner: Patrick Leigh Fermor, *Between the Woods and the Water*.
Prize £500 plus silver pen.

Times Educational Supplement Information Book Awards

Times Educational Supplement, Priory House, St John's Lane, London EC1M 4BX
☎01–253 3000

Contact *Literary Editor*

There are two annual awards made for Best Information Books, one for the age range 10–16, and another for children up to the age of 9. Books must have been published in Britain or the Commonwealth in the year preceding the award.
Award £500 (each category)

Times Educational Supplement Schoolbook Award

Book Trust, Book House, 45 East Hill, London SW18 2QZ
☎01–870 9055

An annual award for the most outstanding schoolbook in the category specified for the year, either a single book for use in class or a representative book from a series.
Award £500

The Tir Na N-Og Award

Welsh National Centre for Children's Literature, Castell Brychan, Aberystwyth, Dyfed SY23 2JB

An annual award given to the best original book published for children in the year prior to the announcement. There are two

categories: The Best Welsh book and The Best English book with an authentic Welsh background.
Award £500 (each category)

Marten Toonder Award
The Arts Council (An Chomhairle Ealaion), 70 Merrion Square, Dublin 2, Ireland.
☎0001 611840

Contact *Literature Officer*

A triennial award for creative writers.
Award £3000 (next award 1989)

The Betty Trask Awards
The Society of Authors, 84 Drayton Gardens, London SW10 9SB
☎01–373 6642

These annual awards are for authors who are under 35 and Commonwealth citizens on the strength of a first novel (published or unpublished) of a traditional or romantic (rather than experimental) nature. The awards must be used for a period or periods of foreign travel.
1988 winners: Alex Martin, Candia McWilliam (£6500 each); Georgina Andrewes, James Friel, Glenn Patterson, Susan Webster (£2000 each).
1987 winners: James Maw (£8000); Peter Benson and Helen Flint (£4500 each); Catherine Arnold, H.S. Bhabra and Lucy Pinney (£1000 each).
Award £21,000

TSB Peninsula Prize
South West Arts, Bradninch Place, Gandy Street, Exeter EX4 3LS
☎0392 218188

Contact *Literature Officer*

An annual award for unpublished works of literature submitted by anyone who is resident in or who can demonstrate strong links with the region served by South West Arts (Avon, Cornwall, Devon, Dorset – except Bournemouth, Christchurch and Poole – Gloucestershire and Somerset).
1987 winner: Roy Phillips, *The Saffron Eaters*.
Prize £1000 plus publication and £1000 advance on royalties.

Unicorn Theatre, Young Playwright's Competition
Unicorn Theatre for Children, Arts Theatre, Great Newport Street, London WC2H 7JB
☎01–379 3280

Contact *Hilary Shearing*

Annual awards to young playwrights aged between 4–12 years old for plays on a theme decided by the theatre. Entries by the end of November. Three age groups: 4–6; 7–9; 10–12. The plays are judged by a committee of writers and the winners take part in workshops on the plays with members of the Unicorn Theatre Club before performances on stage the following spring.

Ver Poets Open Competition
Haycroft, 61/63 Chiswell Green Lane, St Albans, Herts AL2 3AG
☎0727 67005

Contact *May Badman*

An annual competition for unpublished poems of no more than 30 lines written in English.
Prizes £100, £50, plus two prizes of £25.

Verbatim Essay Competition
Verbatim, PO Box 199, Aylesbury, Bucks HP20 1TQ
☎0296 27314

Contact *Hazel Hall*

Awarded for original popular articles in English of not more than 2000 words.
Prizes 1st $1000; 2nd $500 and four prizes of $250.

Wandsworth All London Competition

Town Hall, Wandsworth High Street,
London SW18 2PU
☎01–871 6364

Contact *Assistant Director of Leisure and Amenity Services* (Libraries & Arts)

An annual competition, open to all writers of 16 and over who live, work or study in the Greater London Area. There are two categories, both for previously unpublished work, in poetry and the short story.
Prize £525 (Total for each class – to be divided between the top three in each category.)

The David Watt Memorial Prize

RTZ Limited, 6 St James's Square,
London SW1Y 4LD

INITIATED 1987 to commemorate the life and work of David Watt. Eligible to writers actually engaged in writing for newspapers and journals, in the English language, on international and political affairs. The winners are judged as having made 'outstanding contributions towards the clarification of international and political issues and the promotion of a greater understanding of such issues.'
Prize £2000 (Annual)

Welsh Arts Council Prizes

Welsh Arts Council, Museum Place,
Cardiff CF1 3NX
☎0222 394711

Contact *Tony Bianchi*

Annual, non-competitive prizes are presented for works of exceptional merit by Welsh authors (by birth or residence) published in Welsh or English during the previous calendar year. There are five prizes for each language in the categories: poetry, fiction, non-

fiction, literary criticism and young writer.
Prize £1000 (each)

Whitbread Book of the Year/ Whitbread Literary Awards

The Booksellers Association of Great Britain & Ireland, 154 Buckingham Palace Road,
London SW1W 9TZ
☎01–730 8214

Contact *Andrea Livingstone*

Publishers are invited to submit books for this annual competition for writers who have been resident in Great Britain or the Republic of Ireland for five or more years. The awards are made in two stages. In the first, nominations are selected in five categories: novel, first novel, biography, children's novel and poetry. One of these is then voted by the panel of judges as Whitbread Book of the Year.
1987 Winners: Christopher Nolan, *Under the Eye of the Clock* (Biography & Book of the Year); Seamus Heaney, *The Haw Lantern* (Poetry); Geraldine McCaughrean, *A Little Lower than the Angels* (Children's); Francis Wyndham, *The Other Garden* (First novel); Ian McEwan, *The Child in Time* (Novel).
Previous winners include: *Elegies*, Douglas Dunn (Poetry & Book of the Year); *Hugh Dalton*, Ben Pimlott (Biography); *The Nature of the Beast*, Janni Howker (Children's); *Oranges are not the Only Fruit*, Jeanette Winterson (First novel); *Hawksmoor*, Peter Ackroyd (Novel).
Awards £20,000 (Book of the Year); £1000 (Remaining nominees).

Whitfield Prize

Royal Historical Society,
University College London, Gower Street,
London WC1E 6BT
☎01–387 7532

Contact *Literary Director*

An annual award for the best work on English or Welsh history by an author under

40, published in the UK in the preceding calendar year.
Prize £1000

John Whiting Award

The Drama Director, Arts Council of Great Britain, 105 Piccadilly, London W1V 0AU
☎01–629 9495

Contact *The Drama Director*

FOUNDED 1965 to commemorate the life and work of the playwright John Whiting (*The Devils, A Penny for a Song*), this award is made annually to a playwright. Any writer who has received during the previous two calendar years an award through the Arts Council's Theatre Writing Schemes or who has had a première production by a theatre company in receipt of annual subsidy is eligible to apply.
1988 winner: Nick Dear, *The Art of Success*.
Prize £3000

Mary Wilkins Memorial Poetry Competition

Birmingham & Midland Institute,
9 Margaret Street, Birmingham B3 3BS
☎021–236 3591

Contact *Mr Hunt* (The Administrator)

An annual competition for an unpublished poem not exceeding 40 lines, written in English by an author over the age of 15 and living, working or studying in the UK. The poem should not have been entered for any other poetry competition.
Prize £200 (total of four prizes)

H.H. Wingate Prize

Book Trust, Book House, 45 East Hill,
London SW18 2QZ
☎01–870 9055

An annual award of two prizes (one for fiction, one for non-fiction) for the books which best stimulate an interest in and awareness of themes of Jewish interest. Books must have been published in the UK in the year of the award and be written in English by an author resident in Britain, Commonwealth, Israel, Pakistan, Republic of Ireland or South Africa.
1987 winners: Aharon Appelfeld, *The Age of Wonders* (fiction); Dan Vittorio Segre, *Memoirs of a Fortunate Jew* (non-fiction).
Prize £2000 (each)

Wolfson Literary Awards for History and Biography

c/o Paisner & Co (Solicitors), Bouverie House, 154 Fleet Street, London EC4A 2DQ

Contact *The Wolfson Foundation*

FOUNDED 1972. Two awards totalling £15,000 made annually to authors of published historical works of outstanding scholarship and literary quality.
1987 winners: Professor R.R. Davies, *Conquest, Co-existence and Change – Wales 1063–1415* (OUP); Dr John Pemble, *The Mediterranean Passion* (OUP).

Yeats Club Awards

The Yeats Club, PO Box 271,
Oxford OX2 6DU

FOUNDED 1986. Twice yearly competition for original poetry in English. Send s.a.e. for entry form.
Prize Grand prize £250; first prize £100; 2nd prize £50; other awards at the discretion of the judges.

Yorkshire Post Art and Music Awards

Yorkshire Post, PO Box 168,
Wellington Street, Leeds LS1 1RF
☎0532 432701 ext. 512

Contact *Caroline Colmer*

Two annual awards made to authors whose work has contributed most to the understanding and appreciation of art and music. Books should have been published in the preceding year in the UK.
Award £800 each – one for book on art, one for book on music.

Yorkshire Post **Best First Work Awards**

Yorkshire Post, PO Box 168,
Wellington Street, Leeds LS1 1RF
☎0532 432701 ext. 512

Contact *Caroline Colmer*

An annual award for a work by a new author published during the preceding year.
Prize £600 plus £400 for the runner-up.

Yorkshire Post **Book of the Year Awards**

Yorkshire Post, PO Box 168,
Wellington Street, Leeds LS1 1RF
☎0532 432701 ext 512

Contact *Caroline Colmer*

There are two annual prizes, one for a work of fiction and one for a work of non-fiction published in the preceding year. The larger prize is given to the book which, in the opinion of the judges, is the better of the final two.
Prizes £800 (first prize); £600 (second prize).

Young Observer **Teenage Fiction Prize**

Young Observer, Chelsea Bridge House,
Queenstown Road, London SW8 4NN
☎01–627 0700

Contact *Sue Matthias*

An annual award for the best full-length novel written in English for teenagers. The winning author must be a citizen of British Commonwealth, Republic of Ireland, Pakistan, Bangladesh or South Africa. Books must have been published between 1 July and 30 June.
Previous winners: 1987 Margaret Mahy, *Memory*; 1986 Peter Carter, *Bury the Dead*.
Prize £600

Library Services

BBC Data Enquiry Service
Room 7, 1 Portland Place,
London W1A 1AA
☎01–927 5998   Fax 01–637 0398

Open 9.30 am to 8.00 pm Monday to Friday;
11.00 am to 3.00 pm Saturday and Sunday

Access Telephone enquiries only.

The Enquiry Service is a fee-based information broker. It was set up in 1981 to draw on the extensive information resources of the BBC and works solely for clients from outside the Corporation. The resources include press cuttings and reference libraries whose main strengths are arts and entertainment; biographical information; industrial information; political affairs; political, economic and social events; and world affairs.

British Film Institute
21 Stephen Street, London W1P 1PL
☎01–255 1444   Telex 27624 BFI LONG
Fax 01–436 7950

Open 10.30 am to 5.00 pm Monday, Tuesday, Thursday, Friday; 1.30 pm to 8.00 pm Wednesday

Open access for reference for BFI members

A vast library of books, pamphlets, newspaper clippings, scripts and other memorabilia relating to the cinema and all its aspects (including video and television).

The British Library Business Information Service
25 Southampton Buildings, Chancery Lane,
London WC2A 1AW

☎01–323 7979 (Priced Enquiry Service)
01–323 7454 (Free Service)
Telex 266959   Fax 01–323 7453
BT Gold (81) BL I 404

Priced Enquiry Service open 10.00 am to 5.00 pm Monday to Friday

Free Service open 9.30 am to 5.00 pm Monday to Friday

Library open 9.30 am to 9.00 pm Monday to Friday; 10.00 am to 1.00 pm Saturday

Open access

A resource facility for those engaged in all aspects of business, an invaluable reference source for specialist journalists.

The British Library India Office Library and Records
197 Blackfriars Road, London SE1 8NG
☎01–928 9531   Fax 01–928 9531 ext. 279

Open 9.30 am to 6.00 pm Monday to Friday; 9.30 am to 1.00 pm Saturday

Open access for reference purposes. Long term use and loans to members only.

Contains an extensive stock of printed books, prints, drawings, photographs and manuscripts related to Indological and modern South Asian studies. Large collection of manuscripts in Arabic, Persian, Sanskrit and Tibetan languages. The Records comprise the archives of the East India Company, Board of Control, India Office and Burma Office (1600–1948). A *Guide to the India Office Library* by S.C. Sutton is available to aid researchers.

The British Library Information Sciences Service (successor to The Library Association Library)

7 Ridgmount Street, London WC1E 7AE
☎01–323 7688

Open 9.00 am to 6.00 pm Monday, Wednesday, Friday; 9.00 am to 8.00 pm Tuesday and Thursday (NB From mid-July to mid-September opening hours are 9.00 am to 6.00 pm Monday to Friday)

Open access for reference (loans are to members of the Association or by British Library form)

Provides British and foreign reference material on librarianship, information science and related subjects. Has special collections of historical library annual reports and theses on librarianship. Strong on books and all stages of their production.

The British Library Manuscripts Department

Great Russell Street, London WC1B 3DG
☎01–323 7508   Fax 01–323 7039

Open 10.00 am to 4.45 pm Monday to Saturday (closed Public Holidays and second week of November)

Access to reading facilities by Reader's Pass.

A useful publication, *The British Library: Guide to the catalogues and indexes of the Department of Manuscripts* by M.A.E. Nickson is available (£1.95) to guide the researcher through this vast collection of manuscripts dating from Ancient Greece to the present day. Approximately 85,000 volumes are housed here.

The British Library Map Library

Great Russell Street, London WC1B 3DG
☎01–323 7700

Open 9.30 am to 4.30 pm Monday to Saturday

Access by British Library Reader's Pass or Map Library Pass. Application in person, with proof of identity.

A collection of 1½ million charts, globes and maps, with particular reference to the history of British cartography. Maps for all parts of the world at wide range of scales and dates. Special collections include King George III Maritime Collection and Topographical Collection, and the Crace Collection of maps and plans of London. Also satellite pictures of all areas of the world.

The British Library Music Library

Great Russell Street, London WC1B 3DG
☎01–323 7527

Open 9.30 am to 4.45 pm Monday, Friday, Saturday; 9.30 am to 8.45 pm Wednesday, Thursday

Access by British Library Reader's Pass

Special collections include the Royal Music Library (containing almost all Handel's surviving autographed scores) and the Paul Hirsch Music Library. Also a large collection (about one and a quarter million items) of printed music, British and foreign.

The British Library National Sound Archive

29 Exhibition Road, London SW7 2AS
☎01–589 6603

Open 9.30 am to 4.30 pm Monday to Friday (late opening Thursday to 9.00 pm)

Open access to library

Listening service (by appointment) 9.30 am to 4.30 pm Monday to Friday (late opening 9.00 pm Thursday).

Northern Listening Service at British Library Document Supply Centre, Boston Spa, West Yorkshire.

Open 9.15 am to 4.30 pm Monday to Friday
☎0937 843434

An archive of over half a million discs and over 45,000 hours of tape recordings including all types of music, oral history, drama, wildlife, selected BBC broadcasts and BBC Sound Archive material.

The British Library Newspaper Library

Colindale Avenue, London NW9 5HE
☎01–323 7353

Open 10.00 am to 4.45 pm Monday to Saturday. Last issue of newspapers 4.15 pm.

Access by British Library Reader's Pass or Newspaper Library Reader's Pass (available from and valid only for Colindale Avenue).

English provincial, Scottish, Irish, Commonwealth and foreign newspapers from c.1700 are housed at this library. London newspapers from 1801 and most large weekly periodicals are also in stock. (London newspapers pre-dating this period are housed in Great Russell Street.)

The British Library Official Publications and Social Sciences Service

Great Russell Street, London WC1B 3DG
☎01–323 7536

Open 9.30 am to 4.45 pm Monday, Friday and Saturday; 9.30 am to 8.45 pm Tuesday, Wednesday and Thursday

Access by British Library Reader's Pass

Provides access to current and historical official publications from all countries, plus publications of intergovernmental bodies. Also House of Commons Sessional Papers from 1715, UK legislation, current UK electoral registers and up-to-date reference books on the social sciences with special emphasis on law.

The British Library Oriental and Printed Books Department

14 Store Street, London WC1E 7DG
☎01–323 7642/7658

Open 9.30 am to 5.00 pm Monday to Friday; 9.30 am to 1.00 pm Saturday

Closed on Sundays and Public Holidays and the last complete week of October

Access to Oriental Reading Room by special pass

A comprehensive collection of printed volumes and manuscripts in the languages or related to the cultures of North Africa, the Near and Middle East and all of Asia.

The British Library Reading Room

Great Russell Street, London WC1B 3DG
☎01–636 1544 (Switchboard) 01–323 7678 (Admissions) 01–323 7676 (Bibliographical; holdings enquiries)

Open 9.00 am to 5.00 pm Monday, Friday and Saturday; 9.00 am to 9.00 pm Tuesday, Wednesday, Thursday.

Closed Sundays and Public Holidays and for the week following the last complete week in October.

Access by reader's pass. (A leaflet, *Applying for a reader's pass* is available for guidance)

A large and comprehensive stock of books and periodicals relating to the humanities and social sciences is available for reference and research which cannot easily be done elsewhere. There are also exhibitions on literary and historical figures and a permanent exhibition on the history of printing and binding. Telephone enquiries are welcome.

The British Library Science Reference and Information Service

25 Southampton Buildings, Chancery Lane, London WC2A 1AW
☎01–323 7494
Telex 266959 SCI REF G   Fax 01–323 7930

Open 9.30 am to 9.00 pm Monday to Friday; 10.00 am to 1.00 pm Saturday.

Open access

The national library for modern science and technology providing an invaluable resource facility for technical journalists. Telephone enquiries are welcome.

Central Music Library

160 Buckingham Palace Road,
London SW1W 9UD
☎01–798 2192

Open 9.30 am to 7.00 pm Monday to Friday;
9.30 am to 5.00 pm Saturday.

Open access

Extensive coverage of all aspects of music,
including books, periodicals and printed
scores.

Centre for Children's Books, Children's Reference Library

Book Trust, Book House, 45 East Hill,
London SW18 2QZ
☎01–870 9055

Open 9.00 am to 5.00 pm Monday to Friday

Open access for reference only

A comprehensive collection of children's
literature and related books and periodicals.
Houses the Linder Collection of books and
drawings by Beatrix Potter.

Commonwealth Secretariat Library

10 Carlton House Terrace, Pall Mall,
London SW1Y 5AH
☎01–839 3411 ext. 5013

Open 9.15 am to 5.15 pm Monday to Friday

Access Open for reference by prior arrangement only.

An extensive reference source concerned
with economy, development, trade, production and industry of Commonwealth countries; also a sub-library specialising in human
resources including Women, Development
and Education.

European Communities Commission Information Office

Abbey Buildings, 8 Storey's Gate,
Westminster, London SW1 3AT
☎01–222 8122

Open 2.00 pm to 5.30 pm Monday to Friday

Open access for reference

Reference works on the European Community, plus copies of all EEC publications.

Fawcett Library

City of London Polytechnic,
Old Castle Street, London E1 7NT
☎01–283 1030

Open (during term times) 10.00 am to
8.30 pm Monday and Tuesday; 10.00 am to
5.00 pm Thursday and Friday (during vaca-
tions); 10.00 am to 5.00 pm Monday to Friday

Closed Wednesday

Open access to non-Polytechnic members on
payment either of annual membership fee:
£10 (students/unwaged £5); or one-day fee:
£2 (students/unwaged £1)

The leading library for feminist studies and
research into all other aspects of women's
history with emphasis on social sciences and
the humanities. Contains extensive stocks of
books, pamphlets, photographs and archive
materials. Limited loans to members or via
British Library. (The Mary Evans Picture
Library now acts as agent for the Fawcett
Library's pictorial material.)

Fine Arts Library

Central Reference Library, St Martin's Lane,
London WC2H 7HP
☎01–798 2038

Open 10.00 am to 7.00 pm Monday to Friday;
10.00 am to 5.00 pm Saturday.

Closed access

Older books and periodicals earlier than 1970
are in storage and at least three days' notice is
required before they can be obtained.
An excellent reference source for fine arts
and crafts related subjects. Also houses the
Preston Blake Collection of works by and
about William Blake.

Foreign and Commonwealth Office Library

Cornwall House, Stamford Street,
London SE1 9NS
☎ 01–211 0117

Open 9.30 am to 5.30 pm Monday to Friday

Open access for reference purposes

An extensive stock of books, pamphlets and other reference material on all aspects of socio-economic and political subjects relating to countries covered by the Foreign and Commonwealth Office. Particularly strong on official Commonwealth publications and legislation.

The French Institute (Institut Français du Royaume-Uni)

17 Queensbury Place, London SW7 2DT
☎ 01–589 6211

Open 11.00 am to 8.00 pm Monday; 11.00 am to 6.00 pm Tuesday to Friday; 10.00 am to 1.00 pm Saturday.

Open access to reading room, but loans are to members only.

Annual membership £9.00; Students and OAPs: £6.00

A collection of over 70,000 volumes mainly centred on cultural interests with special emphasis on the French language.

HERTIS A college library network serving further and higher education and industry

Hatfield Polytechnic Library, College Lane,
Hatfield, Herts AL10 9AD
☎ 07072 79678
Telex 262413   Fax 07072 79670

Open 8.45 am to 9.30 pm Monday to Thursday; 8.45 am to 7.00 pm Friday; 10.00 am to 1.00 pm Saturday; 2.00 pm to 7.00 pm Sunday. During vacation period the library is open from 9.00 am to 5.00 pm Monday to Friday. (These times are for the Hatfield Library only, other HERTIS libraries have varying opening times.)

Access to reference material at all HERTIS libraries is open to the public.

The HERTIS group is served by Hatfield Polytechnic and twelve other colleges of further education which combine to provide a resource facility on engineering, computing, humanities (with particular reference to South East Asia), education, social and business studies as well as building, agriculture, horticulture and art and design.

Holborn Library

32–38 Theobalds Road, London WC1X 8PA
☎ 01–405 2705

Open 9.00 am to 8.00 pm Monday, Tuesday, Thursday; 9.30 am to 6.00 pm Friday; 9.30 am to 5.00 pm Saturday

Closed Wednesday and Sunday

Open access

Specialises in business, employment and law with over 35,000 items in stock.

Hulton Picture Library

35 Marylebone High Street,
London W1M 4AA
☎ 01–927 4735/4737

Open 9.00 am to 6.00 pm Monday to Friday

With more than 10 million photographs, engravings and maps, the Hulton Picture Library provides a complete visual history of twentieth century Britain. Based on the Picture Post Collection, it has been owned by the BBC since 1958 but is currently up for sale. (Robert Maxwell is among those who have shown interest in acquiring this priceless national asset.) Contained within the document of sale are provisos that the collection remains intact, is kept in this country, keeps its name, and remains commercially accessible. At present the collection is housed in three separate locations and it is anticipated that it will be rehoused after any sale.

Italian Institute of Culture

39 Belgrave Square, London SW1X 8NX
☎01–235 1461

Open 9.30 am to 5.00 pm

Open access for reference

A collection of over 20,000 volumes relating to all aspects of Italian culture. Texts are mostly in Italian, with some in English.

Liverpool City Libraries

William Brown Street, Liverpool L3 8EW
☎051–207 2147

Open 9.00 am to 9.00 pm Monday to Friday; 9.00 am to 5.00 pm Saturday

Access to all the Libraries is open to the general public

Arts and Recreations Library (ext. 33) 50,000 volumes covering all subjects in the arts and recreation.

Commercial and Social Sciences Library (ext. 29) Business and trade directories plus all UK statutes and law reports. Serves as a depository library for UNO and EEC reports.

General, Religion and Philosophy Library and Hornby Library (ext. 31) Contains stock of 68,000 volumes, 24,000 maps plus book plates, prints and autograph letters. Special collections include Walter Crane and Edward Lear illustrations.

International Library (ext. 20) Open shelf and reserve stocks on language, literature, geography and history. Special interest is the collection on British history with much on politicians and statesmen. 20,000 copies of British, American and European plays plus language tapes in twenty languages.

Music Library (ext. 49) Extensive stock relating to all aspects of music; includes 128,000 volumes and music scores, 18,500 records and over 3000 cassettes. Special collections include Carl Rosa Opera Company Collection and Earl of Sefton's early printed piano music.

Record Office and Local History Department (ext. 34) Printed and audiovisual material relating to Liverpool, Merseyside, Lancashire and Cheshire together with archive material mainly on Liverpool. Some restrictions on access, e.g. 30-year rule applies to archives.

Science and Technology Library (ext. 7) Extensive stock dealing with all aspects of science and technology including British and European standards and patents.

London Borough of Camden Information and Reference Services

Swiss Cottage Library, 88 Avenue Road, London NW3 3HA
☎01–586 5989

Open 9.30 am to 8.00 pm Monday, Tuesday and Thursday; 9.30 am to 6.00 pm Friday; 9.30 am to 5.00 pm Saturday.

Closed all day Wednesday

Open access

Over 60,000 volumes and 600 periodical titles.

London Library

14 St James's Square, London SW1Y 4LG
☎01–930 7705/6

Open 9.30 am to 5.30 pm Monday to Saturday (late opening Thursday to 7.30 pm)

Closed Sundays

Annual membership fee £75

With over a million books and 6700 members, the London Library 'is the most distinguished private library in the world; probably the largest, certainly the best loved'. Wholly independent of public funding, there are no restrictions on membership. Anybody can apply, pay the subscription and take up to ten books home immediately; fifteen if the member lives more than twenty miles from St James's Square. Particularly strong in European languages, but stock excludes science and technology, medicine and law.

Medical Library

Marylebone Library, Marylebone Road, London NW1 5PS

☎ 01–798 1039

Open 9.30 am to 7.00 pm Monday to Friday; 9.30 am to 5.00 pm Saturday

Open access for reference

Books, pamphlets and periodicals covering all aspects of medicine and the health services.

National Library of Scotland

George IV Bridge, Edinburgh EH1 1EW

☎ 031–226 4531

Open 9.30 am to 8.30 pm Monday to Friday; 9.30 am to 1.00 pm Saturday

Closed Map Room at 5.00 pm Monday to Friday; library on public holidays

Access to Reading Rooms and Map Rooms for research not easily done elsewhere via ticket

A collection of over four million volumes. The library receives all British and Irish publications. Large stock of newspapers and periodicals. Many special collections including early Scottish books, theology, polar studies, baking, phrenology and liturgies. Also large collections of maps, music and manuscripts including personal archives of notable Scottish persons.

National Library of Wales

Aberystwyth, Dyfed SY23 3BU

☎ 0970 3816

Open 9.30 am to 6.00 pm Monday to Friday; 9.30 am to 5.00 pm Saturday and general holidays.

Access to Reading Room and Map Room by reader's ticket available on application

A collection of over three million books which include large collections of period-

icals, maps and manuscripts. Particular emphasis on the humanities in foreign material, and on Wales and other Celtic areas in all collections.

National Sound Archive
See British Library National Sound Archive

Northern Listening Service
See British Library National Sound Archive

Press Association

85 Fleet Street, London EC4P 4BE

☎ 01–353 7440

Open 9.00 am to 5.00 pm

The national news agency offers public access to millions of black and white and colour photographs, and newscuttings.
Pictures personal callers welcomed, or phone ext. 3201.
Cuttings Contact News Features department, ext. 3147, or the Librarian, ext. 3160. Set scale of charges.

Sheffield City Libraries

Central Library, Surrey Street, Sheffield S1 1XZ

☎ 0742 734711   Archives 0742 734756

Open 9.30 am to 9.00 pm Monday to Friday; 9.00 am to 4.30 pm Saturday

Open access to the public, but prior arrangement should be made for consulting archive material

Stocks Fairbank collection of maps, draft plans and surveying books, together with mss collections and parochial records relating to the area.

Arts and Social Sciences Reference Library

☎ 0742 734747–9

Open 9.30 am to 9.00 pm Monday to Friday;
9.00 am to 4.00 pm Saturday

Open access to all for reference purposes

A comprehensive collection of books,
periodicals and newspapers covering all
aspects of arts and the humanities (excluding
music).

Audio Visual and Music Library
☎0742 734733

Open 9.30 am to 8.00 pm Monday to Friday;
9.30 am to 4.30 pm Saturday

Open access for reference purposes, loans
with tickets

An extensive range of books, records, scores
etc. related to music. Also a video cassette
loan service.

Business Library
☎0742 734736–8

Open 9.30 am to 5.30 pm Monday to Friday;
9.00 am to 4.30 pm Saturday

Open access for reference

A large stock of business and trade directories, plus overseas telephone directories
and reference works with business emphasis.

Local Studies Library
☎0742 734753

Open 9.30 am to 5.30 pm Monday to Friday;
9.00 am to 4.30 pm Saturday

Open access for reference use (advance
notice advisable)

Extensive material covering all aspects of
Sheffield and its population, including maps
and taped oral histories.

Science and Technology Reference Library
☎0742 734753

Open 9.30 am to 5.30 pm Monday to Friday;
9.00 am to 4.00 pm Saturday

Open access for reference

Extensive coverage of science and technology as well as commerce and commercial law.
British patents and British and European
standards with emphasis on metals. (Sheffield also houses the *World Metal Index*.)

Sheffield Information Service
☎0742 734764

Open 9.30 am to 5.30 pm Monday to Friday;
9.00 am to 4.30 pm Saturday.

Full local information service covering all
aspects of the Sheffield community.

United Nations London Information Centre
20 Buckingham Gate, London SW1E 6LB
☎01–630 1981   Telex 23737

Open 10.00 am to 1.00 pm and 2.00 pm to
5.00 pm Monday, Wednesday and Thursday

Open access for reference

A full stock of official publications and docu-
mentation from the United Nations.

Westminster History and Archives Department
Victoria Library,
160 Buckingham Palace Road,
London SW1W 9UD
☎01–798 2180

Open 9.30 am to 7.00 pm Monday to Friday;
9.30 am to 1.00 pm and 2.00 pm to 5.00 pm
Saturday

Open access for reference books

Comprehensive coverage of the history of
Westminster and selective coverage of
general London history. 18,000 books, together with a large stock of prints, photographs, and theatre programmes.

Tax and the Writer

'No man in this country is under the smallest obligation, moral or other, to arrange his affairs as to enable the Inland Revenue to put the largest possible shovel in his stores.

The Inland Revenue is not slow, and quite rightly, to take every advantage which is open to it . . . for the purpose of depleting the taxpayer's pockets. And the taxpayer is, in like manner, entitled to be astute to prevent as far as he honestly can the depletion of his means by the Inland Revenue.'

LORD CLYDE

Ayrshire Pullman v. Inland Revenue Commissioners, 1929.

Value Added Tax

Value Added Tax (VAT) is a tax currently levied at 15% on:

(a) the total value of taxable goods and services supplied to consumers.
(b) the importation of goods into the UK.
(c) certain services from abroad if a taxable person receives them in the UK for the purpose of their business.

Who is Taxable?

A writer resident in the UK whose turnover from writing and any other business, craft or art on a self-employed basis is greater than £22,100 annually, or exceeds £7,500 in one quarter, must register with HM Customs as a taxable person. Penalties will be claimed in the case of late registration. A writer whose turnover is below the quarterly and annual limits may apply for voluntary registration and this will be allowed at the discretion of Customs. A writer whose turnover is below these limits is exempt from the requirement to register for VAT, but may apply for voluntary registration.

A taxable person pays VAT on inputs, charges VAT on outputs, and remits the amount by which the latter exceeds the former. In the event that input exceeds output, the difference should be repaid by HM Customs and Excise.

Inputs

A writer's inputs are the costs of goods and services used in the course of his profession. They are taxable at the standard rate, at the zero-rate or they are exempt. A writer pays VAT on those items or services which are taxable at the full rate but not on those which are zero-rated or exempt. The writer who is registered as a taxable person will be able to offset the VAT thus paid against the VAT that should be remitted to Customs.

Outputs

A writer's outputs are taxable services supplied to publishers, broadcasting organisations, theatre managements, film companies, educational institutions, etc. A taxable writer must invoice, i.e. collect from, all the persons (either individuals or organisations) in the UK for whom supplies have been made, for fees, royalties or other considerations plus VAT. An unregistered writer cannot and must not invoice for VAT. A

Taxable at the standard rate	Taxable at the zero rate	Exempt
Advertisements in newspapers, magazines, journals and periodicals	Books	Rent
	Periodicals	Rates
	Lighting	Postage
Agent's commission (unless it relates to monies from overseas, when it is zero-rated)	Heating	Services supplied by unregistered persons
	Coach, rail and air travel	
Accountant's fees Solicitor's fees		Subscriptions to the **Society of Authors**, **PEN**,**NUJ**, etc.
Agency services (typing, copying, etc.)		Wages and salaries
Stationery and typewriters		Insurance
Artists' materials		Dividend income
Photographic equipment		Taxicab fares
Tape recorders and tapes		
Hotel accommodation		
Motor-car expenses		
Telephone		
Theatres and concerts		

NB This list is not exhaustive.

taxable writer is not obliged to collect VAT on royalties or other fees paid by publishers or others overseas for supplies.

Remit to Customs

The unregistered writer charges no VAT and therefore should have had none passed on to him from publishers, etc. The taxable writer adds up the VAT which has been paid on taxable inputs, deducts it from the VAT paid on outputs and remits the balance to Customs. If more VAT has been paid out on inputs than has been received on outputs he is entitled to claim a repayment of the difference from Customs at the end of the month in which the deficit occurred. Business with HM Customs is conducted through the local VAT Offices of HM Customs which are listed in local telephone directories, except for tax returns which are sent direct to the Customs and Excise VAT Central Unit, Alexander House, 21 Victoria Avenue, Southend-on-Sea, Essex SS99 1AA.

Accounting
A taxable writer is obliged to account to Customs at quarterly intervals. Accounts must be completed and sent to the VAT Central Unit within 28 days of the accounting date. It should be noted that only invoices are necessary to complete a VAT return, not receipts. A writer is held responsible for ensuring that the VAT that has been invoiced is, in fact, paid.

Registration
A writer will be given a VAT Registration Number which must be quoted on all VAT correspondence. It is the responsibility of the writer to inform those to whom he makes supplies, of their taxable status and Registration Number. A writer who would not normally be required to register as taxable may, on receipt of a single large payment, for example in respect of film rights or a paperback edition, find that the quarterly or annual turnover has risen above the limits and is liable to register. If the local Collector is satisfied that he will not turn over more than £22,100 in the next 12 months they may be permitted to continue unregistered. If not they must register and remain so until two complete years have passed during which the value of outputs has been below £22,100 annually. They may then de-register.

Voluntary Registration
A writer whose turnover is below the limits may apply to register. If the writer is paying a relatively large amount of VAT on taxable inputs – agent's commissions, accountant's fees, equipment, materials, or agency services, etc. – it may make a significant improvement in the net income to be able to offset the VAT on these inputs. An author who pays relatively little VAT may find it easier, and no more expensive, to remain unregistered.

Fees and Royalties
A taxable writer must notify those to whom he makes supplies of the Tax Registration Number at the first opportunity. One method of accounting for and paying VAT on fees and royalties is the use of multiple stationery for 'self-billing', one copy of the royalty statement being used by the author as the VAT invoice. A second method is for the recipient of taxable outputs to pay fees, including authors' royalties, without VAT. The taxable author then renders a tax invoice for the VAT element and a second payment, of the VAT element, will be made. This scheme is cumbersome but will involve only taxable authors. Fees and royalties from abroad will count as payments for exported services and will accordingly be zero-rated.

Agents and Accountants
A writer is responsible to HM Customs for making VAT returns and payments. Neither an agent nor an accountant nor a solicitor can take this over, although they can be helpful in preparing and keeping VAT returns and accounts. Their professional fees or commission will, except in rare cases where the adviser or agent is himself unregistered, be taxable at the standard rate and will represent some of a writer's taxable inputs. An agent's commission in respect of zero-rated fees and royalties received from abroad is not liable for VAT.

Income Tax – Schedule D

An unregistered writer can claim some of the VAT paid on taxable inputs as a business expense allowable against income tax. However, certain taxable inputs fall into categories which cannot be claimed under the income tax regulations. A taxable writer, who has already offset VAT on inputs, cannot charge it as a business expense for the purposes of income tax.

Certain Services From Abroad

A taxable author who resides in the United Kingdom and who receives certain services from abroad must account for VAT on those services at the appropriate tax rate on the sum paid for them. Examples of the type of services concerned include: services of lawyers, accountants, consultants, provisions of information and copyright permissions.

Income Tax
What is a professional writer for tax purposes?

Writers are professionals while they are writing regularly with the intention of making a profit; or while they are gathering material, researching or otherwise preparing a publication.

A professional freelance writer is taxed under Case II of Schedule D of the *Income and Corporation Taxes Act 1970*. The taxable income is the amount received, either directly, or by an agent, on his behalf, less expenses wholly and exclusively laid out for the purposes of the profession. If expenses exceed income, the loss can either be carried forward and set against future income from writing or set against other income which is subject to tax in the same year. If tax has been paid on that other income, a repayment can be obtained, or the sum can be offset against other tax liabilities. Special loss relief can apply in the opening year of the profession. Losses made in the first four years can be set against income of up to three earlier years.

Where a writer receives very occasional payments for isolated articles, it may not be possible to establish that these are profits arising from carrying on a continuing profession. In such circumstances these 'isolated transactions' may be assessed under Case VI of Schedule D of the *Income and Corporation Taxes Act 1970*. Again, expenses may be deducted in arriving at the taxable income, but, if expenses exceed income, the loss can only be set against the profits from future isolated transactions, or other income assessable under Case VI.

Expenses

A writer can normally claim the following expenses:

(a) Secretarial, typing, proofreading, research. Where payments for these are made to the author's wife or husband, they should be recorded and entered in the author's tax return, or (in the case of a married woman her husband's tax return) as earned income which is subject to the usual personal allowances.

(b) Telephone, telegrams, postage, stationery, printing, maintenance and insurance or equipment, dictation tapes, batteries, office requisites used for the profession.

(c) Periodicals, books (including presentation copies and reference books) and other publications necessary for the profession, but amounts received from the sale of books should be deducted.

(d) Hotels, fares, car running expenses (including repairs, petrol, oil, garaging, parking, cleaning, insurance, licence, road fund tax, depreciation), hire of cars or taxis in connection with

  (i) business discussions with agents, publishers, co-authors, collaborators, researchers, illustrators, etc.

  (ii) travel at home and abroad to collect background material.

(e) Publishing and advertising expenses, including costs on proof corrections, indexing, photographs, etc.

(f) Subscriptions to societies and associations, press cutting agencies, libraries, etc. incurred wholly for the purpose of the profession.

(g) Premiums to pension schemes such as the *Society of Authors Retirement Benefits Scheme*. For contributors born in 1934 and later, the maximum premium is now $17\frac{1}{2}\%$ of net earned income. Higher limits apply for those born before 1934.

(h) Rent, general rates, and water rates, etc., the proportion being determined by the ratio which the number of rooms are used exclusively for the profession bears to the total number of rooms in the residence. But see note on *Capital Gains Tax* below.

(i) Lighting, heating and cleaning. A carefully estimated figure of the business use of these costs can be claimed as a proportion of the total.

(j) Accountancy charges and legal charges incurred wholly in the course of the profession including cost of defending libel actions, damages in so far as they are not covered by insurance and libel insurance premiums. However, where in a libel case, damages are awarded to punish the author for having acted maliciously the action becomes quasi-criminal and costs and damages may not be allowed.

(k) TV and video rental (which may be apportioned for private use), and cinema or theatre tickets, if wholly for the purpose of the profession, e.g. playwriting.

(l) Capital allowances for equipment, e.g. car, TV, radio, hi-fi sets, tape and video recorders, dictaphones, typewriters, desks, bookshelves, filing cabinets, photographic equipment. Allowances vary in the Finance Acts depending upon political and economic views prevailing. At present they are set at 25%. On motor cars the allowance is 25% in the first year and 25% of the reduced balance in each successive year limited to £2000 each year. The total allowances in the case of all assets must not exceed the difference between cost and eventual sale price. Allowances will be reduced to exclude personal (non-professional) use where necessary.

(m) Lease rent. The cost of lease rent of equipment is allowable; also of cars, subject to restrictions for private use and for expensive cars.

NB It is always advisable to keep detailed records. Diary entries of appointments, notes of fares and receipted bills are much more convincing to the Inland Revenue than round figure estimates.

(n) Gifts to charitable bodies are allowed, subject to certain conditions, provided they are reasonable in amount and for a cause connected with the donor's professional activities. Tax relief is also available for three years (minimum) covenants to charities.

Capital Gains Tax

The exemption from Capital Gains Tax which applies to an individual's main residence does not apply to any part of that residence which is used exclusively for business purposes. The effect of this is that the appropriate proportion of any increase in value of the residence since 6 April 1982 can be taxed, when the residence is sold, at the maximum rate of 40% (at present).

Writers who own their houses should bear this in mind before claiming expenses for the use of a room for writing purposes. Arguments in favour of making such claims are that they afford some relief now, while Capital Gains Tax in its present form may not stay for ever. Also, where a new house is bought in place of an old one, the gain made on the sale of the first study may be set off against the cost of the study in the new house, thus postponing the tax payment until the final sale. For this relief to apply, each house must have a study, and the author must continue his profession throughout. On death there is an exemption of the total Capital Gains of the estate.

NB Writers can claim that their use is non-exclusive and restrict their claim to the cost of extra lighting, heating and cleaning so that no Capital Gains Tax liability arises.

Can a writer average-out his income over a number of years for tax purposes?

Under Section 389 of the *Income and Corporation Taxes Act 1970*, a writer may in certain circumstances spread over two or three fiscal years lump sum payments, whenever received, and royalties received during two years from the date of first publication or performance of work. Points to note are:

(a) The relief can only be claimed if the writer has been engaged in preparing and collecting material and writing the work for more than twelve months.

(b) If the period of preparing and writing the work exceeds twelve months but does not exceed twenty-four months, one-half of the advances and/or royalties will be regarded as income from the year preceding that of receipt. If the period of preparing and writing exceeds twenty-four months, one-third of the amount received would be regarded as income from each of the two years preceding that of receipt.

(c) For a writer on a very large income, who otherwise fulfils the conditions required, a claim under these sections could result in a tax saving. If his income is not large he should consider the implication, in the various fiscal years concerned, of possible loss of benefit from personal and other allowances and changes in the standard rate of income tax.

It is also possible to average out income within the terms of publishers' contracts, but professional advice should be taken before signature. Where a husband and wife collaborate as writers, advice should be taken as to whether a formal partnership agreement should be made or whether the publishing agreement should be in joint names.

Is a lump sum paid for an outright sale of the copyright or part of the copyright exempt from tax?

No. All the money received from the marketing of literary work, by whatever means, is taxable. Some writers, in spite of clear judicial decisions to the contrary, still seem to think that an outright sale of, for instance, the film rights in a book, is not subject to tax.

Is there any relief where old copyrights are sold?

Section 390 of the *Income and Corporation Taxes Act 1970* gives relief 'where not less than ten years after the first publication of the work the author of a literary, dramatic, musical or artistic work assigns the copyright therein wholly or partially, or grants any interest in the copyright by licence, and:

(a) the consideration for the assigment or grant consists wholly or partially of a lump sum payment the whole amount of which would, but for this section, be included in computing the amount of his/her profits or gains for a single year of assessment, and

(b) the copyright or interest is not assigned or granted for a period of less than two years.'

In such cases, the amount received may be spread forward in equal yearly instalments for a maximum of six years, or, where the copyright or interest is assigned or granted for a period of less than six years, for the number of whole years in that period. A 'lump sum payment' is defined to include a non-returnable advance on account of royalties.

It should be noted that a claim may not be made under this section in respect of a payment if a prior claim has been made under Section 389 of the *Income and Corporation Taxes Act 1970* (see section on spreading lump sum payments over two or three years) or vice versa.

Are royalties payable on publication of a book abroad subject to both foreign tax as well as UK tax?

Where there is a Double Taxation Agreement between the country concerned and the UK, then on the completion of certain formalities no tax is deductible at source by the foreign payer, but such income is taxable in the UK in the ordinary way. When there is no Double Taxation agreement, credit will be given against UK tax for overseas tax paid. A complete list of countries with which the UK has conventions for the avoidance of double taxation may be obtained from the Inspector of Foreign Dividends, Lynwood Road, Thames Ditton, Surrey KT7 0DP or the local tax office.

Residence Abroad

Writers residing abroad will, of course, be subject to the tax laws ruling in their country of residence, and as a general rule royalty income paid from the United Kingdom can be exempted from deduction of UK tax at source, providing the author is carrying on his profession abroad. A writer who is intending to go and live abroad should make early application for future royalties to be paid without deduction of tax to HM Inspector of Taxes, Claims Branch, Magdalen House, Stanley Precinct, Bootle, Merseyside L69 9BB. In certain circumstances writers resident in the Irish Republic are exempt from Irish Income Tax on their authorship earnings.

Are grants or prizes taxable?

The law is uncertain. Some Arts Council grants are now deemed to be taxable, whereas most prizes and awards are not, though it depends on the conditions in each case. When submitting a statement of income and expenses, such items should be excluded, but reference made to them in a covering letter to the Inspector of Taxes.

What if I disagree with a tax assessment?

Income tax law requires the Inspector of Taxes to make an assessment each year calculating the amount of income tax payable on the 'profits' of the profession. Even though accounts may have already been submitted the assessment can quite possibly be estimated and overstated.

The taxpayer has the right of appeal within 30 days of receipt of the assessment and can request that the tax payable should be reduced to the correct liability which he must estimate as accurately as possible. However, if he underestimates the amount, interest can become payable on the amount by which he underpays when the correct liability is known.

What is the item 'Class 4 N.I.C.' which appears on my tax assessment?

All taxpayers who are self-employed pay an additional national insurance contribution if their earned income exceeds a figure which is varied each year. This contribution is described as Class 4 and is calculated in the tax assessment. It is additional to the self-employed Class 2 (stamp) contribution but confers no additional benefits and is a form of levy. It applies to men aged under 65 and women under 60. Tax relief is given on half the Class 4 contributions.

Anyone wondering how best to order his affairs for tax purposes, should consult an accountant with specialised knowledge in this field. Experience shows that a good accountant is well worth his fee which, incidentally, so far as it relates to matters other than personal tax work, is an allowable expense.

The information contained in this section is adapted from **The Society of Authors** *Quick Guides to Taxation* (Nos. 4 and 7) with the kind help of A.P. Kernon, FCA.

As We Go To Press ...

Publishers

Corgi is to start a hardback children's list, headed by Philippa Dickenson.

Octopus (Paul Hamlyn) is setting up a new mass market imprint to be called **Octopus Paperbacks**. It is headed by Richard Charkin, formerly managing director of the academic division of **OUP**. The first titles are expected to appear in April 1989.

Kate Mortimer, a non-executive director of the merchant bank Rothschild, joins **Walker Books** in the newly created post of chief executive.

UK Agents

New to the list is **Superior Short Fiction**, an agency dealing in commercial short stories only. Address: 9 Mountacre Close, London SE26 6SX. Tel: 01–670 4419. **Contact** *Charles Garvie*. No unsolicited mss – telephone or enquiry letter with s.a.e. in the first instance. *Commission* 15%.

National and Regional Press

The NUJ has negotiated increases of around six per cent for freelancers working for book publishers, radio and television and national newspapers. There is no new agreement with **The Newspaper Society** representing the provincial press but the Freelance Industrial Council has agreed that a six per cent increase should be added to the Newspaper Society 1987 minimum rates.

The newspaper revolution continues with the appearance of *The Post*, a 'breezy not sleazy' down-market colour tabloid from Eddy Shah; *The Sport*, a Wednesday stablemate for *Sunday Sport*; *The Northwest Times*, a regional morning newspaper and *Scotland on Tuesday*, a weekend partner for *The Scotsman*.

The Daily Telegraph and *The Independent* launch Saturday colour magazines and the *Daily Mail* launches *Male and Female*, a fortnightly Saturday magazine.

Thirty-two regional evening newspapers are to be sold with *Plus*, a new colour magazine with a prospective circulation of 2.7 million.

The Sunday Telegraph announces a 32 page pre-print colour, tabloid second section.

Magazines

Gill Hudson takes over from Maggie Goodman as editor of *Comapny*.

Marie Claire, a popular French title is launched in Britain by European Magazines, of which IPC is part-owner. The **editor** is *Glenda Bailey*. Address: 2 Hatfields, Stamford Street, London SE1 9PG. Tel: 01–261 5508.

From the stable of *Elle* and *Sky* comes *New Woman*. Published monthly, *New Woman* is edited by *Frankie McGowan*. Address: Rex House, 4–12 Lower Regent Street, London SW1Y 4PE. Tel: 01–930 9050.

Carlton Magazines announces a glossy weekly called *Riva*. **Editor** *Sally O'Sullivan*. Address: 25 Newman Street, London W1P 3PE.

Sound and Screen

Rupert Murdoch signs a ten year deal with Astra, the Luxembourg based TV satellite, to launch four new channels under the existing Sky banner.

The **Writers' Guild** and the BBC have come to a settlement on new rates for Radio Drama. The minimum rate per minute for beginners is now £15.95 and for established writers is £24.25. Revised rates for BBC Television are likely to be agreed by the end of 1988. Details can be obtained from the **Writers' Guild** for £1. The cost of a full agreement plus new rates is £5.

Literary Prizes

Century Hutchinson and *The Observer* announce the P.G. Wodehouse Prize: £5000 plus publication and serialisation for the best unpublished comic work of fiction or non-fiction. Minimum length: 40,000 words. Further details from **Century Hutchinson**, Brookmount House, 62–5 Chandos Place, London WC2N 4NW.

Library Services

The Hulton Picture Library is sold to Brian Deutsch, chairman of Westminster Cable, who is pledged to maintain and modernise the collection.

Companies Index

The following codes have been used to classify the index entries.

Subject Index

Fiction: Agents (US) (cont)

Fiction: Bursaries/fellowships

Fiction: Film, TV and video producers

Fiction: Magazines

Fiction: Newspapers (regional)

Fiction: Packagers

Fiction: Prizes

Fiction: Publishers (UK)